New Ge

Mathematics for Sierra Leone

Junior Secondary Schools Pupils' Book 2

M F Macrae
A O Kalejaiye
Z I Chima
G U Garba
J B Channon
A McLeish Smith
H C Head

This edition prepared with advice from
Yvonne Lillian Macrae and Gabriel M Sellu

Pearson Education Limited
Edinburgh Gate
Harlow
Essex
CM20 2JE
England
and Associated Companies throughout the World

ISBN-10: 1-4058-1678-3
ISBN-13: 978-1-4058-1678-6

Printed in Malaysia (CTP - VVP)

We are indebted to Longman Zimbabwe (Pvt) Ltd for permission to reproduce an extract from 'NEW GENERAL MATHEMATICS FOR ZIMBABWE BOOK 2'. The publishers are grateful for permission to reproduce the following Escher drawing on page 34: M. C. Escher's 'Symmetry Drawing E124' © 2000 Cordon Art B. V. – Baarn – Holland. All rights reserved.

Contents

Curriculum Matching Chart v

Preliminary chapter
Review of Book 1 **1**
Number and numeration 1
Algebraic processes 3
Geometry and mensuration 5
Statistics 9

Chapter 1
Properties of numbers: Number patterns **12**
Factors, prime factors (revision) 12
Highest common factor (revision) 13
Lowest common multiple (revision) 13
Rules for divisibility 13
Number patterns 15
Squares and square roots 18

Chapter 2
Large and small numbers **20**
Large numbers 20
Writing large numbers 21
Small numbers 22
Laws of indices 23
Rounding off numbers 26
Problems with large and small numbers 27

Chapter 3
Plane shapes (2)
Quadrilaterals and patterns **29**
Parallelogram 29
Rhombus 30
Kite 31
Connections between quadrilaterals 32
Patterns with shapes 34

Chapter 4
Directed numbers (2)
Multiplication and division **36**
Adding and subtracting directed numbers (revision) 36
Multiplication of directed numbers 36
Division with directed numbers 39

Chapter 5
Inverse and identity **41**
Additive inverse 41
Multiplicative inverse 42
Inverse operations 43

Chapter 6
Angles (3)
Angles in a polygon **46**
Angles between lines (revision) 46
Angles in a triangle (revision) 47
Angles in a quadrilateral 48
Polygons 49

Chapter 7
Expansion of algebraic expressions **53**
Directed algebraic terms 53
Substitution 54
Removing brackets 54
Expanding algebraic expressions 56

Chapter 8
Everyday arithmetic (3)
Approximation and estimation **58**
Approximation 58
Estimation 60

Revision exercises and tests
Chapters 1–8 **63**

Chapter 9
Proportion, ratio, rate **69**
Fractions and percentages (revision) 69
Proportion 69
Ratio 71
Percentages 73
Rate 74

Chapter 10
Everyday arithmetic (4)
Personal, household, civic, commercial **76**
Personal arithmetic 76
Household arithmetic 78
Civic arithmetic 79
Commercial arithmetic 82

Chapter 11
Algebra: Factors, factorisation, fractions **85**
Factors of algebraic terms 85
Algebraic fractions 87

Chapter 12
The Cartesian plane and coordinates 90
The position of points on a line 90
The position of points on a plane surface 90

Chapter 13
Solving equations (2) 98
Solving equations by the balance method (revision) 98
Word problems 99
Solving equations – further examples 100
Equations with brackets 101
Equations with fractions 103

Chapter 14
Straight line graphs (1) 106
Continuous graphs 106
Discontinuous graphs 108
Choosing scales 109
Information from graphs 112

Chapter 15
Everyday arithmetic (5) Calculator skills and tables 118
Know your calculator 118
Addition and subtraction 121
Multiplication and division 122
Mixed operations, brackets 123
Squares and square root tables 124

Chapter 16
Scale drawing (1) 130
Scale 130
Scale drawing 132
Reading scale drawings 134

Revision exercises and tests Chapters 9–16 138

Chapter 17
Solving triangles (1) Pythagoras' rule 147
Pythagoras' rule 148

Chapter 18
Everyday arithmetic (6) Timetables and charts 154
Reading tabulated data 154
Timetables 155

Chapter 19
Cylinder: Area and volume 160
Circumference and area of a circle (revision) 160
The net of a cylinder (revision) 160
Surface area of a cylinder 161
Volume of a cylinder 162

Chapter 20
Angles of elevation and depression 165
Horizontal and vertical 165
Angle of elevation 166
Angle of depression 166

Chapter 21
Probability 172
Experimental probability 172
Probability as a fraction 174

Chapter 22
Inequalities (1) 178
Greater than and less than 178
Not greater than and not less than 179
Graphs of inequalities 180
Solution of inequalities 181
Word problems involving inequalities 183

Chapter 23
Bearings and distances 185
Direction 185
Surveying 190

Chapter 24
Cone: Area and volume 194
The net of a cone 194
Surface area of a cone 194
Volume of a cone 196
Estimation using mensuration formulae 198

Revision exercises and tests Chapters 17–24 201

Tables 207

Answers 213

Index 241

CURRICULUM MATCHING CHART

Chapter	Contents	Page	Curriculum Objectives	Textual Objectives	Page
1	**Properties of numbers:** **Number patterns** Factors, prime factors Highest Common Factor Lowest Common Multiple Rules for divisibility Number patterns Squares and square roots	 **12** 12 13 13 13 15 18	Number and numeration Students will be able to identify primes, factors, multiples and perfect squares	(i) Express a number as a product of its prime factor in index form (ii) Find the HCF of two or three numbers (iii) Find the LCM of two or three numbers (iv) Apply the rules of divisibility by 2, 3, 4, 5, 6, 8, 9 or 10 (v) Construct number patterns and represent them (vi) Represent number patterns in graphs (vii) Find the square root of perfect squares using the factor method (viii) Identify perfect squares (ix) Find the square roots of fractions	12 13 13 13–15 15, 16 16–18 18 18, 19 19
2	**Large and small numbers** Large numbers Writing large numbers Small numbers Laws of indices Rounding off numbers Problems with large and small numbers	**20** 20 21 22 23 26 27	Number and numeration Students will be able to conceptualise large numbers Students will be able to approximate numbers to an appropriate degree of accuracy	(i) Identify large and small numbers (ii) Express numbers in standard form (iii) Apply the basic rules for indices in writing numbers (iv) Approximate numbers to any required number of significant figures or decimal places	20–23 23 23–26 26, 27
3	**Plane shapes (2)** **Quadrilaterals and patterns** Parallelogram Rhombus Kite Connections between quadrilaterals Patterns with shapes	 **29** 29 30 31 32 34	Geometry and mensuration Students will be able to: (i) identify properties of more plane figures (ii) recognise symmetric properties of plane figures and patterns Students will be able to form patterns using plane shapes	(i) Identify the following quadrilaterals: parallelogram, rhombus and kite (ii) Identify linear, angular and symmetric properties of the above quadrilaterals and the relations between them (iii) Build patterns using basic plane shapes	29–32 32, 33 34, 35

Chapter	Contents	Page	Curriculum Objectives	Textual Objectives	Page
4	**Directed numbers (2)** **Multiplication and division** Adding and subtracting directed numbers Multiplication of directed numbers Division with directed numbers	 **36** 36 36 39	Number and numeration: Students will be able to (i) multiply; and (ii) divide directed numbers	(i) Add directed numbers (ii) Subtract directed numbers (iii) Multiply directed numbers (iv) Divide directed numbers	36 36 36–39 39, 40
5	**Inverse and identity** Additive inverse Multiplicative inverse Inverse operations	**41** 41 42 43	Number and numeration: Students will be able to find the multiplicative inverse and identity	(i) Find the additive and multiplicative inverses of numbers (ii) Solve simple equations using additive or multiplicative inverse (iii) Use inverse operations to solve problems	41–43 41–43 43–45
6	**Angles (3) Angles in a polygon** Angles between lines Angles in a triangle Angles in a quadrilateral Polygons	**46** 46 47 48 49	Geometry and mensuration: Students will be able to find the sum of the interior angles of a convex polygon	(i) Find the sum of the angles in a triangle (ii) Find the sum of the angles in a quadrilateral (iii) Find the sum of the interior angles of a polygon of *n* sides	47, 48 48, 49 49–52
7	**Expansion of algebraic expressions** Directed algebraic terms Substitution Removing brackets Expanding algebraic expressions	**53** 53 54 54 56	Algebraic processes: Students will be able to expand algebraic expressions	(i) Simplify algebraic expressions involving multiplication and division (ii) Substitute numerical values in monomial or binomial algebraic expressions (iii) Remove brackets in algebraic expressions (iv) Expand algebraic expressions	53, 54 54 54–56 56, 57
8	**Everyday arithmetic (3)** **Approximation and estimation** Approximation Estimation	 **58** 58 60	Number and numeration: Students will be able to approximate numbers to an appropriate degree of accuracy	(i) Approximate any given number to the nearest whole number (ii) Approximate any given number to a required number of decimal places or significant places (iii) Estimate numbers and quantities	58 58–60 60–62

Chapter	Contents	Page	Curriculum Objectives	Textual Objectives	Page
9	**Proportion, ratio, rate** Fractions and percentages Proportion Ratio Percentages Rate	**69** 69 69 71 73 74	Number and numeration: Students will be able to express a fraction as a ratio, decimal or percentage Students will be able to use fractions, ratio, decimals, percentages and proportion in everyday practical problems	(i) Solve problems on direct and inverse proportion using unitary method (ii) Find the ratio of two quantities in the same units (iii) Use the idea of ratio in sharing quantities (iv) Solve everyday problems involving percentages (v) Apply the idea of rate when solving word problems	69–71 71 72, 73 73, 74 74, 75
10	**Everyday arithmetic (4)** **Personal, household, civic, commercial** Personal arithmetic Household arithmetic Civic arithmetic Commercial arithmetic	**76** 76 78 79 82	Number and numeration: Students will be able to use fractions, ratio, decimals, percentages and proportion in everyday practical problems	Solve word problems involving (i) simple interest (ii) income tax (iii) discount buying (iv) instalment buying (v) Value Added Tax (VAT) (vi) electricity bills (vii) Post Office charges (viii) profit and loss (ix) commission	76, 77 77, 78 78, 79 79 79, 80 80 80–82 82, 83 83, 84
11	**Algebra: Factors, factorisation, fractions** Factors of algebraic terms Algebraic fractions	**85** 85 87	Algebraic processes: Students will be able to factorise simple algebraic expressions of not more than two terms Students will be able to simplify algebraic expressions involving fractions	(i) Obtain the factors of single algebraic terms (ii) Find the HCF of algebraic terms (iii) Factorise binomial algebraic expressions (iv) Find the LCM of binomial algebraic expressions (v) Obtain equivalent algebraic expression of an algebraic term (vi) Add two algebraic terms giving answers in the simplest form (vii) Subtract algebraic terms giving answers in the simplest form (viii) Simplify the sum and difference of algebraic fractions	85 85 85, 86 86 87 87, 88 87, 88 88, 89

Chapter	Contents	Page	Curriculum Objectives	Textual Objectives	Page
12	**The Cartesian plane and coordinates** The position of points on a line The position of points on a plane surface	**90** 90	Algebraic processes: Students will be able to plot points in the rectangular Cartesian plane	(i) Plot points on the Cartesian plane using ordered pairs of numbers	90–96
13	**Solving equations (2)** Solving equations by the balance method Word problems Solving equations – further examples Equations with brackets Equations with fractions	**98** 98 99 100 101 103	Algebraic processes: Students will be able to simplify algebraic expressions involving fractions Students will be able to solve further problems on simple equations	(i) Find the solution of simple equations involving brackets (ii) Solve word problems on simple equations involving brackets (iii) Solve simple equations involving fractions (iv) Solve word problems involving algebraic fractions	101, 102 102, 103 103, 104 104, 105
14	**Straight line graphs (1)** Continuous graphs Discontinuous graphs Choosing scales Information from graphs	**106** 106 108 109 112	Algebraic processes: Students will be able to: (i) compile tables of values; (ii) draw graphs from tables; (iii) obtain information from graphs	(i) Prepare tables of ordered pairs of values (ii) Draw graphs using the tables of values (iii) Obtain information from graphs	106–108 106–112 112–117
15	**Everyday arithmetic (5)** **Calculator skills and tables** Know your calculator Addition and subtraction Multiplication and division Mixed operations, brackets Squares and square root tables	 **118** 118 121 122 123 124	Number and numeration: The electronic age has made the construction and use of ready reckoners less significant to living. This chapter introduces students to the electronic calculator and the use of standard tables of squares and square roots	(i) Use a calculator to perform basic operations (ii) Obtain squares and square roots of numbers from four-figure tables	118–124 124–129
16	**Scale drawing (1)** Scale Scale drawing Reading scale drawings	**130** 130 132 134	Geometry and mensuration: Students will be able to draw plane objects to scale Students will be able to determine actual dimensions of plane objects from a scale drawing Students will be able to use scale drawings to: (i) locate the position of objects (ii) find distances	(i) Draw plane objects to scale (ii) Determine actual measurements of plane objects from a scale drawing	130–134 134–137

Chapter	Contents	Page	Curriculum Objectives	Textual Objectives	Page
17	**Solving triangles (1)** **Pythagoras' rule** Pythagoras' rule	 **147** 148	Geometry and mensuration: Students will be able to use Pythagoras' rule on right-angled triangles	(i) Apply Pythagoras' rule to find lengths of sides of right-angled triangles (ii) Identify pythagorean triples (iii) Use Pythagoras' rule in everyday problems	147–150 150, 151 151–153
18	**Everyday arithmetic (6)** **Timetables and charts** Reading tabulated data Timetables	 **154** 154 155	Number and numeration: Students will be able to interpret tables and schedules	(i) Read information from tables (ii) Obtain information presented in tables	154 155–159
19	**Cylinder: Area and volume** Circumference and area of a circle The net of a cylinder Surface area of a cylinder Volume of a cylinder	**160** 160 160 161 162	Geometry and mensuration: Students will be able to calculate: (i) the curved surface area; (ii) the total surface area; (iii) the volume of cylinders and cones	(i) Calculate the curved and total surface area of a cylinder (ii) Calculate the volume of a cylinder	161–162 162–164
20	**Angles of elevation and depression** Horizontal and vertical Angle of elevation Angle of depression	**165** 165 166 166	Geometry and mensuration: Students will be able to: (i) distinguish between angles of elevation and angles of depression (ii) measure angles of elevation and depression (iii) use angles of elevation and depression in calculating measurements	(i) Distinguish between angles of elevation and angles of depression (ii) Measure angles of elevation and depression (iii) Calculate measurements using angles of elevation or angles of depression	166–168 168 168–171
21	**Probability** Experimental probability Probability as a fraction	**172** 172 174	Everyday statistics: Students will be able to investigate examples which illustrate the idea of probability	(i) Perform experiments to obtain the probability of events happening (ii) Calculate theoretical probabilities	172–174 174–177
22	**Inequalities (1)** Greater than and less than Not greater than and not less than Graphs of inequalities Solution of inequalities Word problems involving inequalities	**178** 178 179 180 181 183	Algebraic processes: Students will be able to identify linear inequalities Students will be able to solve linear inequalities in one variable	(i) Use inequality signs correctly (ii) Show linear inequalities on number lines (iii) Solve linear inequalities in one variable (iv) Solve word problems involving inequalities	178–180 180, 181 181, 182 183

Chapter	Contents	Page	Curriculum Objectives	Textual Objectives	Page
23	**Bearings and distances**	**185**	Geometry and mensuration:		
	Direction	185	Students will be able to identify the bearing of an object with reference to a given point	(i) Distinguish between compass and three-figure bearings	185–188
	Surveying	190		(ii) Identify the bearing of an object in a two-dimensional plane from a given point	186–188
				(iii) Calculate bearings of points on a plane from a given point also on the plane	189–193
				(iv) Use bearings in simple surveying	190–192
24	**Cone: Area and volume**	**194**	Geometry and mensuration:		
	The net of a cone	194	Students will be able to calculate:	(i) Calculate the curved surface areas of cones	194, 195
	Surface area of a cone	194	(i) the curved surface area;	(ii) Calculate the total surface area of a cone	194–196
	Volume of a cone	196	(ii) the total surface area;		
			(iii) the volume of cylinders and cones	(iii) Calculate the volume of a cone	196–198
	Estimation using mensuration formulae	198	Students will be able to estimate numbers, dimensions, capacity, quantities, etc for a given situation	(iv) Make estimates using mensuration formulae	198–200

Preliminary chapter Review of Book 1

To make the best use of Book 2 of *New General Mathematics for Junior Secondary Schools*, readers should be familiar with the contents of Book 1. The following summary contains the key parts of Book 1 that are necessary for Book 2.

Number and numeration

a) Numbers are usually written in the decimal **place value** system (Fig. P1).

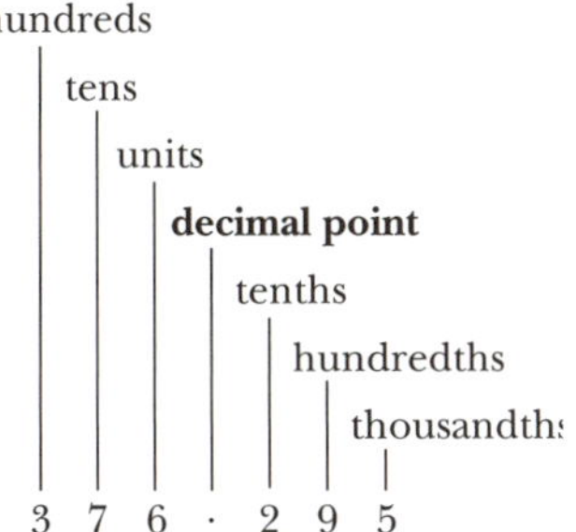

Fig. P1

The symbols 0, 1, 2, 3, 4, 5, 6, 7, 8, 9 are called **digits**.

b) $28 \div 7 = 4$. 7 is a whole number which divides exactly into another whole number, 28. 7 is a **factor** of 28. 28 is a **multiple** of 7.

c) A **prime number** has only two factors, itself and 1. 1 is *not* a prime number. 2, 3, 5, 7, 11, 13, 17, …, are prime numbers. They continue without end. The **prime factors** of a number are those factors which are prime. For example, 2 and 5 are the prime factors of 40. 40 can be written as a **product of prime factors**: either $2 \times 2 \times 2 \times 5 = 40$, or, in **index form**, $2^3 \times 5 = 40$.

d) The numbers 18, 24 and 30 all have 3 as a factor. 3 is a **common factor** of the numbers.

The **highest common factor** (HCF) is the largest of the common factors of a given set of numbers. For example, 2, 3 and 6 are the common factors of 18, 24 and 30; 6 is the HCF.

The number 48 is a multiple of 4 and a multiple of 6. 48 is a **common multiple** of 4 and 6. The **lowest common multiple** (LCM) is the smallest of the common multiples of a given set of numbers. For example, 12 is the LCM of 4 and 6.

e) A **fraction** is the number obtained when one number (the **numerator**) is divided by another number (the **denominator**). The fraction $\frac{5}{8}$ means $5 \div 8$ (Fig. P2).

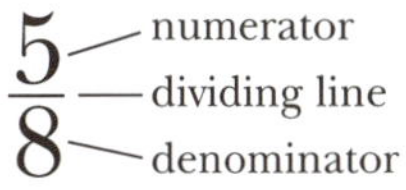

$\frac{5}{8}$ — numerator (5), dividing line, denominator (8)

Fig. P2

Fractions are used to describe parts of quantities (Fig. P3).

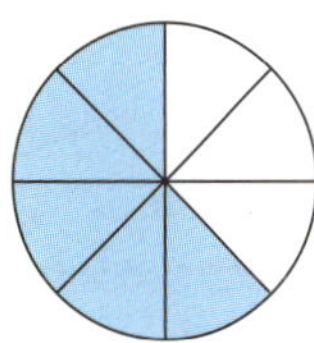

Fig. P3 $\frac{5}{8}$ of the circle is shaded

The fractions $\frac{5}{8}$, $\frac{10}{16}$, $\frac{15}{24}$ all represent the same amount; they are **equivalent fractions.** $\frac{5}{8}$ is the **simplest form** of $\frac{15}{24}$, i.e. $\frac{15}{24}$ in its **lowest terms** is $\frac{5}{8}$.

To add or subtract fractions, change them to equivalent fractions with a **common denominator**. For example:

$$\frac{5}{8} + \frac{2}{3} = \frac{15}{24} + \frac{16}{24} = \frac{15+16}{24} = \frac{31}{24} \quad (=1\tfrac{7}{24})$$

$$\frac{13}{16} - \frac{5}{8} = \frac{13}{16} - \frac{10}{16} = \frac{13-10}{16} = \frac{3}{16}$$

To multiply fractions, multiply numerator by numerator and denominator by denominator. For example:

$$\frac{5}{8} \times \frac{2}{3} = \frac{5 \times 2}{8 \times 3} = \frac{10}{24} \quad \left(= \frac{5}{12} \text{ in simplest form}\right)$$

$$12 \times \frac{5}{8} = \frac{12}{1} \times \frac{5}{8} = \frac{12 \times 5}{1 \times 8} = \frac{60}{8} \quad \left(= \frac{15}{2} = 7\frac{1}{2}\right)$$

To divide by a fraction, multiply by the **reciprocal** of the fraction. For example:

$$35 \div \frac{5}{8} = \frac{35}{1} \times \frac{8}{5} = \frac{35 \times 8}{1 \times 5} = \frac{7 \times 8}{1} = 56$$

$$\frac{5}{8} \div 3\frac{3}{4} = \frac{5}{8} \div \frac{15}{4} = \frac{5}{8} \times \frac{4}{15} = \frac{5 \times 4}{8 \times 15} = \frac{20}{120} \left(= \frac{1}{6}\right)$$

f) x % is short for $\frac{x}{100}$. 64% means $\frac{64}{100}$. To change a fraction to an equivalent **percentage**, multiply the fraction by 100. For example,

$\frac{5}{8}$ as a percentage $= \frac{5}{8} \times 100\% = \frac{125}{2}\% = 62\frac{1}{2}\%$

g) To change a fraction to a **decimal fraction**, divide the numerator by the denominator. For example:

$\frac{5}{8} = 0{\cdot}625$

```
   0·625
8)5·000
  4 8
    20
    16
     40
     40
```

When adding or subtracting decimals, write the numbers in a column with the decimal points exactly under each other. For example: *Add* 2·29, 0·084 *and* 4·3, *then subtract the result from* 11·06.

```
  2·29
  0·084      11·06
 +4·3       − 6·674
  6·674       4·386
```

To multiply decimals, first ignore the decimal points and multiply the given numbers as if they are whole numbers. Then place the decimal point so that the answer has as many digits after the point as there are in the given numbers together. For example, to multiply 0·08 × 0·3:

8 × 3 = 24

There are three digits after the decimal points in the given numbers, so, 0·08 × 0·3 = 0·024.

To divide by decimals, make an equivalent division such that the divisor is a whole number. For example, to divide 5·6 ÷ 0·07:

$$5{\cdot}6 \div 0{\cdot}07 = \frac{5{\cdot}6}{0{\cdot}07} = \frac{5{\cdot}6 \times 100}{0{\cdot}07 \times 100} = \frac{560}{7} = 80$$

h) Numbers may be positive or negative. Positive and negative numbers are called **directed numbers**. Directed numbers can be shown on a **number line** (Fig. P4).

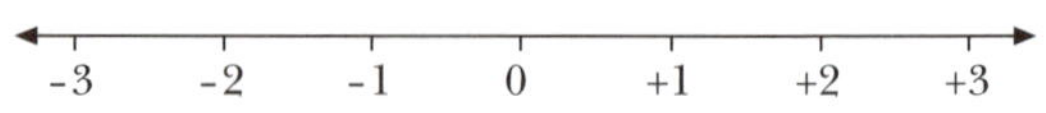

Fig. P4

The following examples show how directed numbers are added, subtracted, multiplied and divided.

addition	*subtraction*
(+8) + (+3) = +11	(+9) − (+4) = +5
(+8) + (−3) = +5	(+9) − (−4) = +13
(−8) + (+3) = −5	(−9) − (+4) = −13
(−8) + (−3) = −11	(−9) − (−4) = −5

An **integer** is any positive or negative *whole* number as shown in Fig. P4.

i) When **rounding off** numbers, the digits 1, 2, 3, 4 are rounded down and the digits 5, 6, 7, 8, 9 are rounded up. For example,

3 425 = 3 430 to 3 **significant figures**
= 3 400 to the **nearest hundred**

7·283 = 7·28 to 2 **decimal places**
= 7·3 to 1 **decimal place**
= 7 to the **nearest whole number**

Detailed coverage of number and numeration is given in Book 1, Chapters 1, 2, 4, 9, 12 and 23.

Review test 1 (Number and numeration)

Allow 20 minutes for this test. Use the answers at the back of the book to check your work. If you do not understand why some of your answers were incorrect, ask a friend or your teacher. Then try Test 2.

1 What is the value of
a) the 7 in 3·75? **b)** the 5 in 519·2?

2 Find the HCF of
a) 6, 15, 36 **b)** 84, 56, 70

3 Find the LCM of

a) 4, 5 and 10 **b)** 9, 10 and 12

4 Reduce the following fractions to their lowest terms:

a) $\frac{45}{63}$ **b)** $\frac{256}{352}$

5 Simplify:

a) $\frac{5}{12} - \frac{1}{8}$ **b)** $5\frac{3}{4} + 8\frac{3}{5}$

c) $2\frac{2}{7} \div \frac{8}{21}$ **d)** $1\frac{3}{4} \times \frac{3}{7}$

6 Express the first quantity as a percentage of the second:

a) Le2, Le5 **b)** 4 mm, 5 cm

c) 20c, Le5 **d)** 360 g, 2 kg

7 Each row of the table contains equivalent expressions. Complete the table. (The first row has been done.)

common fraction	decimal fraction	percentage
$\frac{1}{2}$	0·5	50%
$\frac{2}{5}$		
	0·75	
		60%
	0·28	
$\frac{5}{8}$		

8 Simplify

a) $-9-(-14)-3$

b) $5y - 7y - (-4y)$

c) $-40 + (-15) - (+35)$

d) $-3x + 14x - (-9x)$

9 Round off the following to the nearest (i) thousand, (ii) hundred, (iii) ten:

a) 27 536 **b)** 13 705

10 Round off the following to the nearest (i) whole number, (ii) tenth, (iii) hundredth:

a) 0·865 **b)** 7·009

Review test 2 *(Number and numeration)*

Allow 20 minutes for this test. Use the answers at the back of the book to check your work. If you do not understand why some of your answers were incorrect, ask a friend or your teacher.

1 What is the value of

a) the 3 in 0·438? **b)** the 9 in 29·7?

2 Find the HCF of

a) 44, 88 and 55 **b)** 144, 90 and 54

3 Find the LCM of

a) 3, 4 and 5 **b)** 5, 8 and 9

4 Reduce the following fractions to their lowest terms:

a) $\frac{24}{30}$ **b)** $\frac{270}{378}$

5 Simplify:

a) $\frac{8}{9} + \frac{1}{3}$ **b)** $4\frac{2}{5} - 2\frac{5}{8}$

c) $\frac{2}{5}$ of $1\frac{2}{3}$ **d)** $7\frac{1}{8} \div 4\frac{3}{4}$

6 Express the first quantity as a percentage of the second:

a) Le8, Le15 **b)** 140 m, 2 km

c) 28c, Le4 **d)** 26 g, 4 kg

7 Each row of the table contains equivalent expressions. Complete the table. (The first row has been done.)

common fraction	decimal fraction	percentage
$\frac{1}{2}$	0·5	50%
$\frac{7}{10}$		
	0·55	
		92%
$\frac{2}{3}$		
	0·525	

8 Simplify

a) $5 + (-13) - (-6)$

b) $-y - (+8y) + (-10y)$

c) $700 - (+500) - (-250)$

d) $8x - 11x - (-x)$

9 Round off the following to the nearest (i) thousand, (ii) hundred, (iii) ten:

a) 5 977 **b)** 20 066

10 Round off the following to the nearest (i) whole number, (ii) tenth, (iii) hundredth:

a) 2·388 **b)** 4·295

Algebraic processes

a) $7x - 2x + 3y$ is an example of an **algebraic expression**. The letters x and y stand for numbers. $7x$, $2x$, $3y$ are the **terms** of the expression. $3y$ is short for $3 \times y$. 3 is the **coefficient** of y.

b) Algebraic terms can be multiplied and divided as follows:

$$6a \times 5b = 6 \times a \times 5 \times b = 6 \times 5 \times a \times b = 30ab$$
$$3p \times 8p = 3 \times p \times 8 \times p = 3 \times 8 \times p \times p = 24p^2$$

$$12mn \div 3m = \frac{12 \times m \times n}{3 \times m} = \frac{12n}{3} = 4n$$

c) Simplify algebraic expressions in the following ways.

(i) **By grouping like terms**. For example:

$7x - 2x + 3y = 5x + 3y$

Notice that $7x$ and $2x$ are **like terms**; $5x$ and $3y$ are **unlike terms**.

(ii) **By removing brackets**. For example:

$$a + (2a - 7b) = a + 2a - 7b$$
$$= 3a - 7b$$

(If there is a **positive sign before the bracket**, the signs of the terms inside the bracket stay the same when the bracket is removed.)

$$5x - (x - 9y) = 5x - x + 9y$$
$$= 4x + 9y$$

(If there is a **negative sign before the bracket**, the signs of the terms inside the bracket change when the bracket is removed.)

d) $x + 8 = 3$ is an **algebraic sentence** containing an equals sign; it is an **equation in x**. x is the **unknown** of the equation. If a value is substituted for an unknown, the equation may be *true* or *false*. For example, $2y = 6$ is true when $y = 3$ and is false when $y = 5$. To **solve an equation** means to find the value of the unknown that makes the equation true. Use the **balance method** to solve simple equations. For example:

$3x - 8 = 25$

Add 8 to both sides:

$3x - 8 + 8 = 25 + 8$

i.e. $3x = 33$

Divide both sides by 3:

$3x \div 3 = 33 \div 3$

i.e. $x = 11$

In the balance method, always do the same to both sides of the equation.

In Book 1 coverage of algebraic processes appears in Chapters 5, 7, 10, 15 and 19.

Review test 3 (Algebraic processes)

Allow 20 minutes for this test. Use the answers at the back of the book to check your work. If you do not understand why some of your answers were incorrect, ask a friend or your teacher. Then try Test 4.

1 Each sentence is true. Find the number that each letter stands for.
a) $13 + 9 = p$ **b)** $q - 14 = 14$
c) $27 = r + 14$ **d)** $12 = s + s + s$

2 Find the value of the following when $x = 6$:
a) $9 + x$ **b)** $44 - x$
c) $x - 5 + x$ **d)** $7 - x + x$

3 Simplify the following:
a) $8p - 5p$
b) $8q + 3q$
c) $12r - 4 - 7r + 15$
d) $6w - y + 5z + 9z + 5y - 4w$

4 a) (i) How many weeks are there in 28 days?
(ii) How many weeks are there in d days?
b) (i) A student has five bananas. He eats one of them. How many does he have left?
(ii) Another student has b bananas. She eats two of them. How many does she have left?

5 Remove the brackets and then simplify:
a) $4 - (6a - 7)$
b) $3a - (5 - a)$
c) $(8 - 3a) - (3 - 4a)$
d) $(15x + 6y) - (8x - 7y)$

6 Solve the following equations:
a) $4a + 13 = 21$ **b)** $5b + 9 = 44$
c) $9c - 11 = 61$ **d)** $7 = 10 - 3k$

Review test 4 (Algebraic processes)

Allow 20 minutes for this test. Use the answers at the back of the book to check your work. If you do not understand why some of your answers were incorrect, ask a friend or your teacher.

1 Each sentence is true. Find the number that each letter stands for.
a) $13 - f = 8$ **b)** $24 = 15 + g$
c) $30 = m - 6$ **d)** $18 - n = n$

2 Find the value of the following when $x = 9$:
a) $x + 13$ **b)** $x - 10$
c) $x + 9 + x$ **d)** $x - 5 - x$

3 Simplify the following:

a) $7f + 7f$
b) $18g - 13g$
c) $8m - n - 5m - 3n$
d) $5x + 2y - 8 - 5x + 3$

4 a) (i) How many cm in 2 metres?
(ii) How many cm in m metres?

b) (i) In a compound there are four goats and three sheep. How many animals altogether?
(ii) In another compound there are six goats and n sheep. How many animals altogether?

5 Remove the brackets and then simplify:

a) $2a - (a + 8)$
b) $4b - (7 - b)$
c) $(7x + 2y) - (3x + y)$
d) $(5y - 3) - (4 - 3y)$

6 Solve the following equations:

a) $4a + 3 = 31$ **b)** $3b - 14 = 10$
c) $15 - 6c = 0$ **d)** $18 = 19d - 20$

Geometry and mensuration

a) Fig. P5 gives sketches and names of some **common solids**.

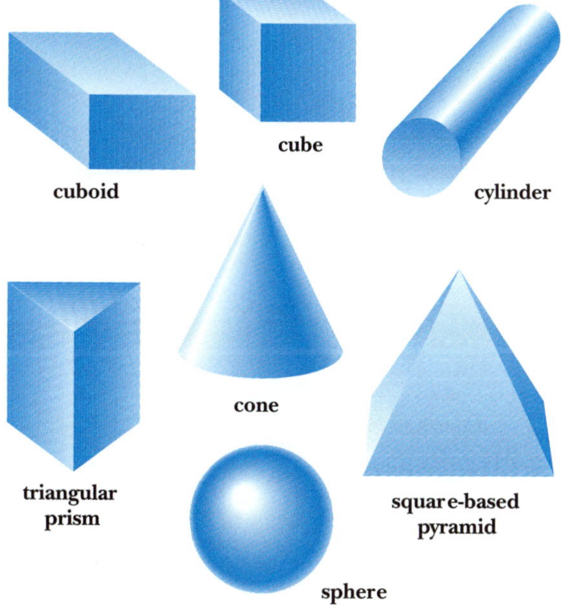

Fig. P5

All solids have **faces**; most solids have **edges** and **vertices** (Fig. P6).

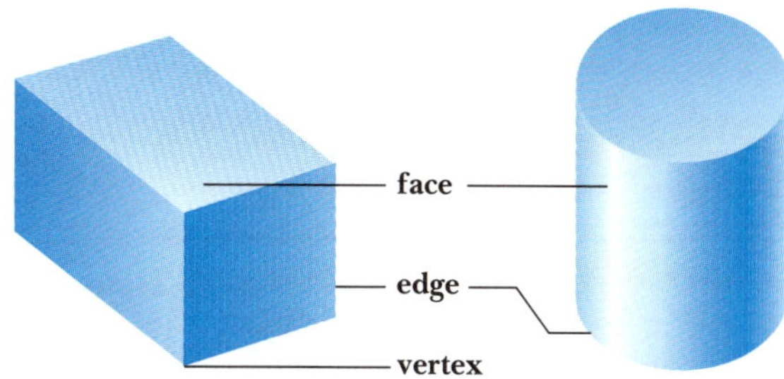

Fig. P6

Formulae for the **surface area** and **volume** of common solids are given in the table on page 209.

b) **Angle** is a measure of rotation or turning.

1 **revolution** = 360 **degrees** (1 rev = 360°)
1 **degree** = 60 **minutes** (1° = 60')

The names of angles change with their size. See Fig. P7.

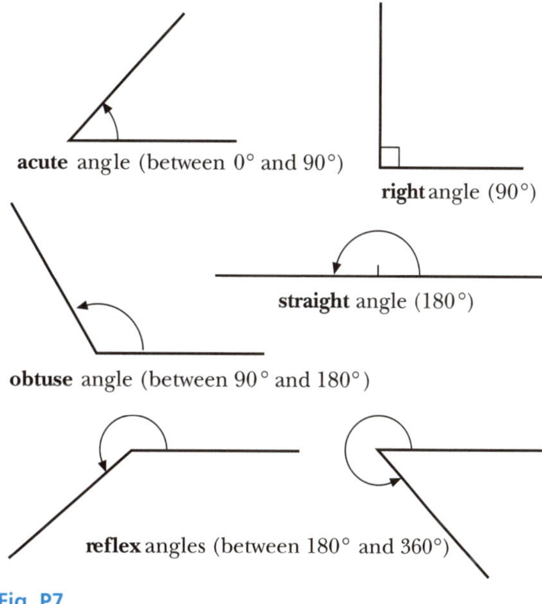

Fig. P7

Angles are measured and constructed using a **protractor**.

Fig. P8 shows some properties of angles formed when straight lines meet.

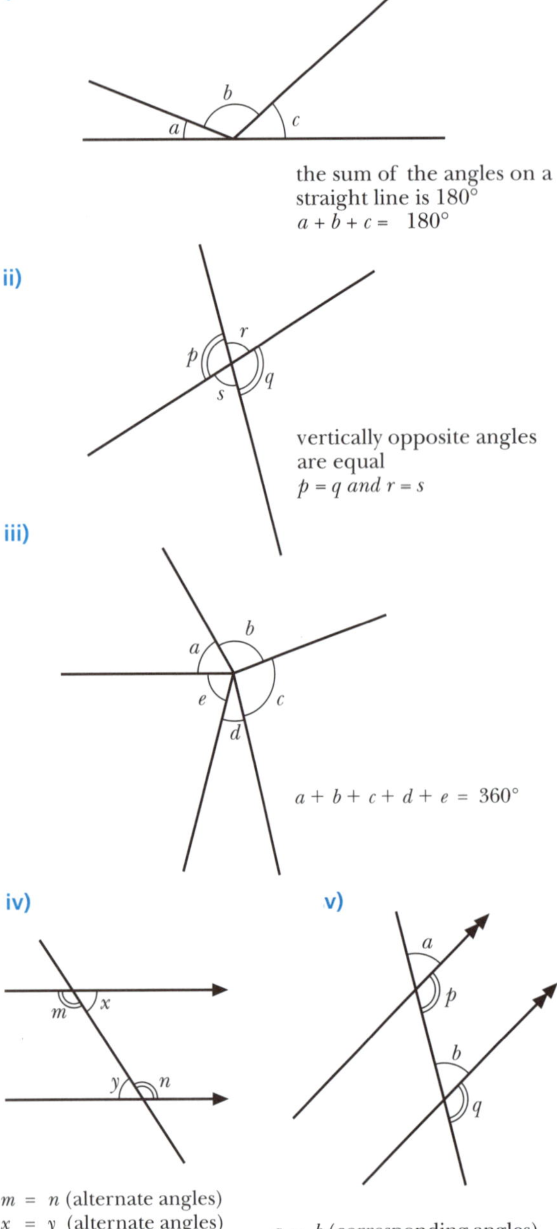

Fig. P8

c) Fig. P9 shows the names and properties of some **common triangles**.

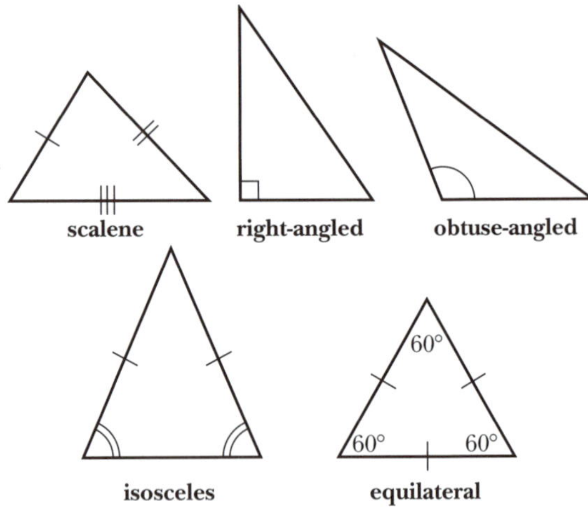

Fig. P9

Fig. P10 shows the names and properties of some **common quadrilaterals**.

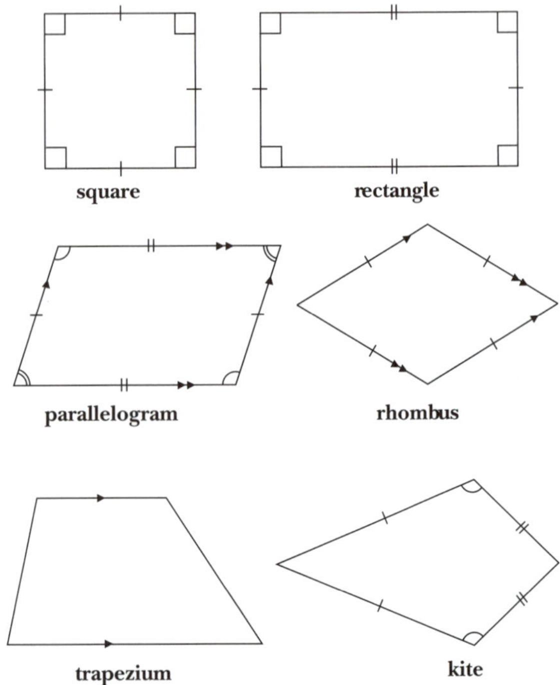

Fig. P10

Fig. P11 gives the names of lines and regions in a **circle**.

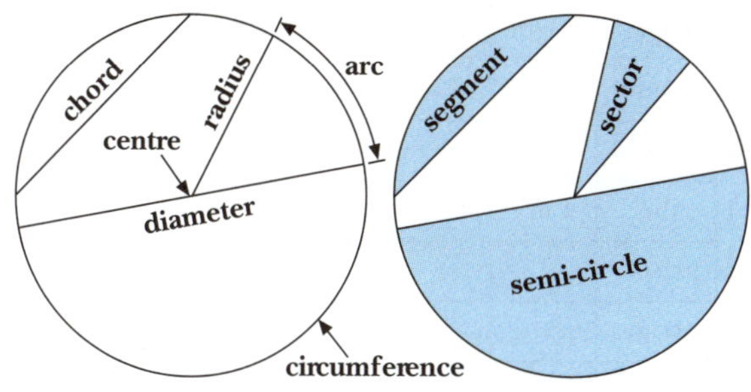

Fig. P11

A **polygon** is a plane shape with three or more straight sides. A **regular polygon** has all its sides of equal length and all its angles of equal size. Fig. P12 gives the names of some common regular polygons.

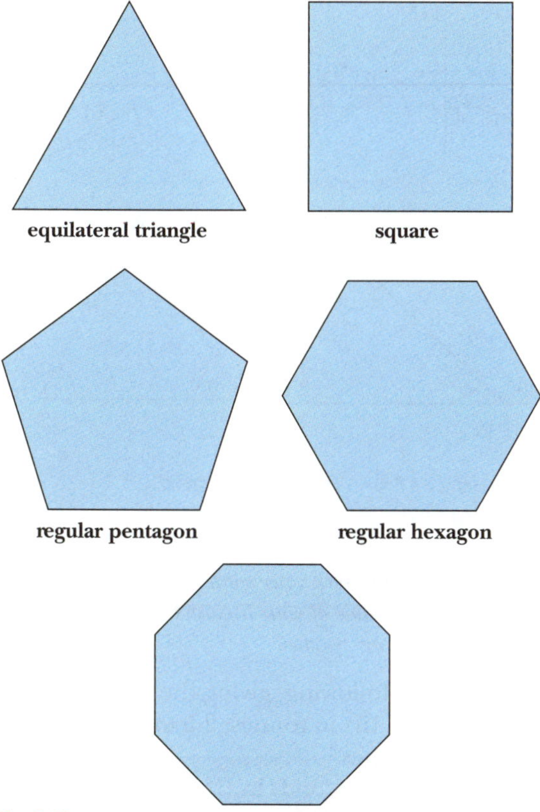

Fig. P12

Formulae for the **perimeter and area of plane shapes** are given in the table on page 209.

The **SI system of units** is given in the tables on pages 207 and 208.

A **ruler** and **set-square** can be used to construct **parallel lines** (Fig. P13) and a **perpendicular** from a point to a line (Fig. P14).

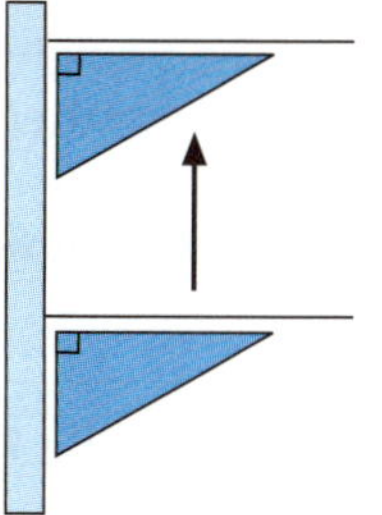

Fig. P13 Parallel lines (ruler and set-square)

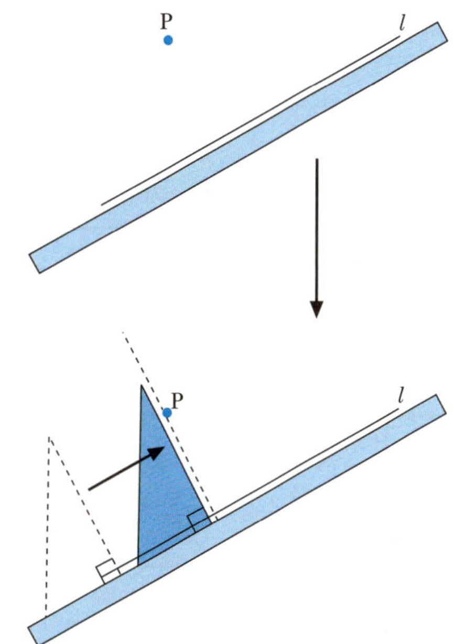

Fig. P14 Perpendicular from point P to line *l* (ruler and set-square)

In Book 1 coverage of geometry and mensuration appears in Chapters 3, 6, 11, 13, 14, 16, 20 and 21.

Review test 5 *(Geometry and mensuration)*

Allow 25 minutes for this test. Use the answers at the back of the book to check your work. If you do not understand why some of your answers were incorrect, ask a friend or your teacher. Then try Test 6.

1 a) Add the following, giving the answer (i) in litres, (ii) in ml: 1·885 litres, 325 ml, 2·04 litres

b) How many minutes in (i) 210 seconds, (ii) 1 day?

2 How many faces, edges and vertices does a hexagonal prism have?

3 In Fig. P9, one of the triangles is marked as 'scalene'. Are there any other scalene triangles in Fig. P9?

4 Copy and complete the following table.

	shape	length	breadth	perimeter	area
a)	rectangle	5 cm	9 cm		
b)	rectangle	8 cm		30 cm	
c)	square			28 cm	
d)	square				64 km^2

5 Copy and complete the following table of circles. Use the value 3 for π.

	radius	diameter	circumference	area
a)	7 cm			
b)		16 cm		
c)			15 cm	
d)				363 cm^2

6 Copy and complete the following table of triangles.

	base	height	area
a)	10 cm	7 cm	
b)	9 cm	3 cm	
c)	6 cm		12 cm^2
d)		9 m	54 m^2

7 Copy the following table. Complete the unshaded boxes.

	shape	length	breadth	height	base area	volume
a)	cuboid	8 cm	3 cm	11 cm		
b)	cuboid	2 cm	6 cm			60 cm^3
c)	cube	4 m				
d)	prism			5·5 cm	6 cm^2	
e)	prism			28 cm		84 cm^3
f)	prism				4 m^2	30 m^3

8 Write down the sizes of the lettered angles in Fig. P15.

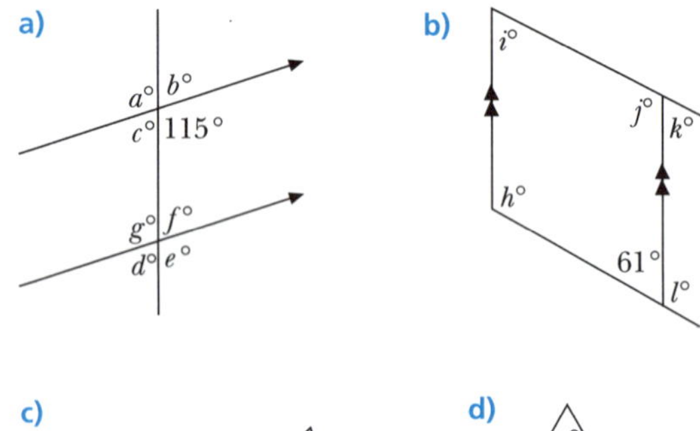

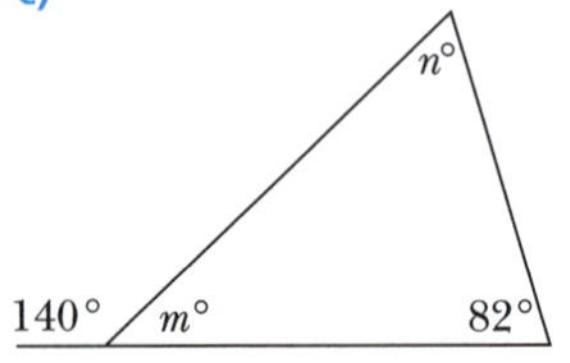

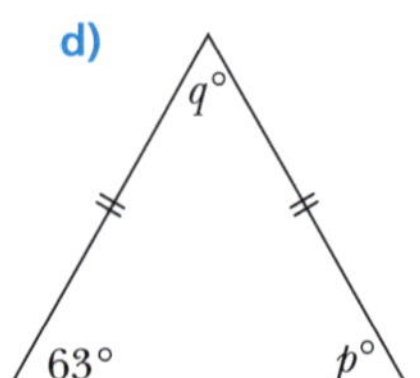

Fig. P15

Review test 6 *(Geometry and mensuration)*

Allow 25 minutes for this test. Use the answers at the back of the book to check your work. If you do not understand why some of your answers were incorrect, ask a friend or your teacher.

1 a) Add the following, giving the answer (i) in kg, (ii) in tonnes: 2·5 tonnes, 850 kg, 4·955 tonnes

b) How many seconds in (i) 5 minutes, (ii) 2 hours?

2 How many faces, edges and vertices does a square-based pyramid have?

3 One of the angles of an isosceles triangle is 22°. What are the sizes of its other two angles? (*Note*: there are two possible answers; give both.)

4 Copy and complete the following table.

	shape	length	breadth	perimeter	area
a)	rectangle	2 km	11 km		
b)	rectangle		12 cm		36 cm^2
c)	square	25 mm			
d)	square			34 m	

5 Copy and complete the following table of circles. Use the value 3 for π.

	radius	diameter	circumference	area
a)	4·5 cm			
b)		10 cm		
c)			84 m	
d)				3 m^2

6 Copy and complete the following table of triangles.

	base	height	area
a)	11 cm	8 cm	
b)	5 cm	15 cm	
c)		2 m	20 m^2
d)	4 cm		22 cm^2

7 Copy the following table. Complete the unshaded boxes.

	shape	length	breadth	height	base area	volume
a)	cuboid	7 cm	4 cm	10 cm		
b)	cuboid	3 cm	6 cm			54 cm^3
c)	cube					216 cm^3
d)	prism			8 cm	3·5 cm^2	
e)	prism				12·5 cm^2	100 cm^3
f)	prism			2 m		26 m^3

8 Write down the sizes of the lettered angles in Fig. P16.

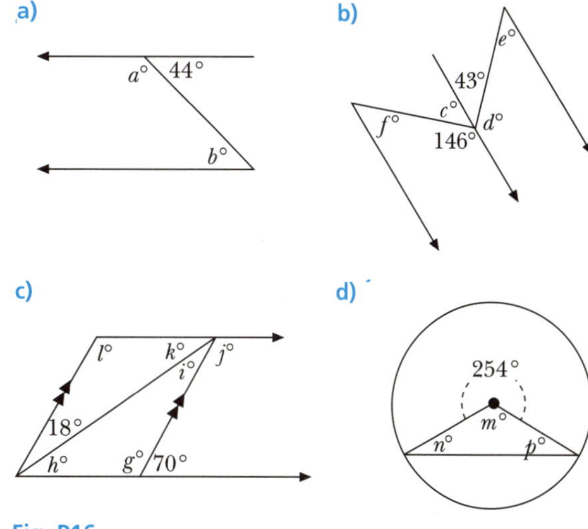

Fig. P16

Statistics

a) Information in numerical form is called **statistics**. Statistical **data** may be given in **rank order** (i.e. in order of increasing size) such as in the following marks obtained in a test out of 5:

0, 1, 1, 2, 2, 2, 3, 3, 5

Data may also be given in a **frequency table** (Table P1).

mark	0	1	2	3	4	5
frequency	1	2	3	2	0	1

Table P1

The **frequency** is the number of times each piece of data occurs.

Statistics can also be presented in graphical form. Fig. P17 shows the above data in a **pictogram**, a **bar chart** and a **pie chart**.

pictogram

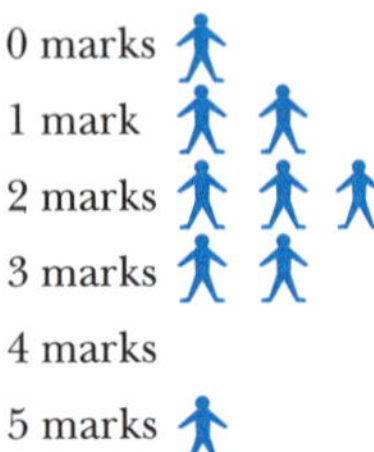

bar chart

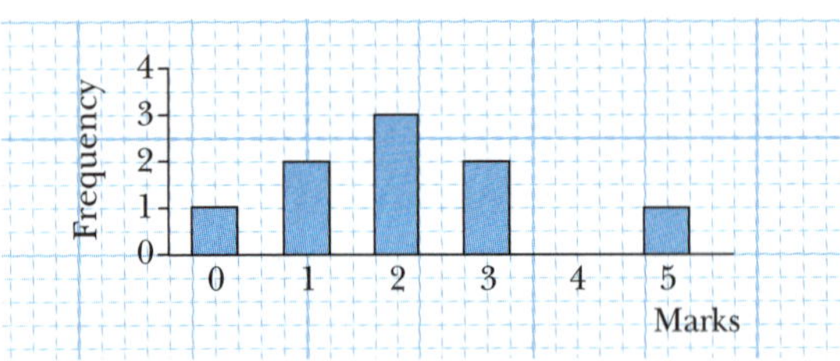

pie chart

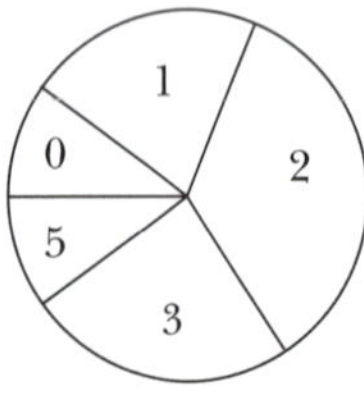

Fig. P17

b) The **average** of a set of statistics is a number which is representative of the whole set. The three most common averages are the **mean**, the **median** and the **mode**. For the nine numbers given in rank order in paragraph a) above,

$$mean = \frac{0 + 1 + 1 + 2 + 2 + 2 + 3 + 3 + 5}{9}$$

$(= 2\frac{1}{9})$;

the *median* is the middle number when the data are arranged in order of size (2);
the *mode* is number with the greatest frequency (also 2 in this case). If a set of data has two modes we say it is **bimodal**.

In Book 1 coverage of statistics appears in Chapters 17, 18 and 22.

Review test 7 (Statistics)

Allow 20 minutes for this test. Use the answers at the back of the book to check your work. If you do not understand why some of your answers were incorrect, ask a friend or your teacher. Then try Test 8.

1 The bar chart in Fig. P18 shows the rainfall for each month in a year.

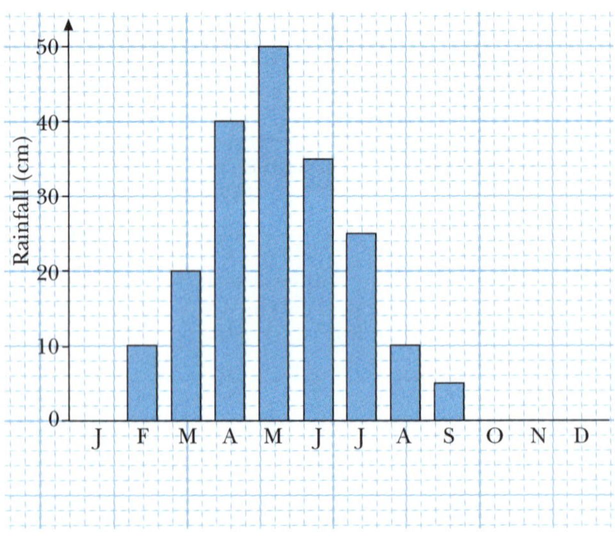

Fig. P18

a) Which month had most rainfall?
b) How many cm of rain fell in the wettest month?
c) Which months had no rainfall?
d) List the four wettest months in rank order.
e) Find in cm the total rainfall for the year.

2 For each set of numbers, calculate the mean:
a) 11, 13, 15 **b)** 8, 9, 13
c) 2, 9, 7, 9, 8 **d)** 5, 5, 1, 0, 9

3 Find the mode, median and mean of each set of numbers:
a) 6, 6, 8, 11, 14
b) 1, 2, 5, 5, 6, 6, 6, 7, 7, 8
c) 8, 6, 3, 10, 6, 9
d) 6, 4, 10, 6, 11, 7, 5, 8, 6

Review test 8 *(Statistics)*

Allow 20 minutes for this test. Use the answers at the back of the book to check your work. If you do not understand why some of your answers were incorrect, ask a friend or your teacher..

1 The marks obtained in a test out of 10 are shown in the following frequency table.

mark	3	4	5	6	7	8
frequency	4	9	6	9	5	2

a) What was the highest mark?

b) How many students scored this mark?

c) Are the data bimodal?

d) How many students scored more than 5 marks?

e) How many students took the test?

2 For each set of numbers, calculate the mean:

a) 17, 5, 7, 11
b) 2, 10, 5, 7
c) 4, 11, 2, 8, 9, 2
d) 7, 8, 10, 11, 14, 16

3 Find the mode, median and mean of each set of numbers:

a) 3, 4, 4, 6, 7, 9
b) 3, 7, 10, 10, 11, 11, 11
c) 2, 0, 16, 0, 7, 11
d) 5, 4, 2, 5, 2, 1, 3, 5, 3, 4, 5, 3

1 Properties of numbers: Number patterns

Factors, prime factors (revision)

$40 \div 8 = 5$ and $40 \div 5 = 8$.
8 and 5 divide into 40 without remainder. 8 and 5 are **factors** of 40.
A **prime number** has only two factors, itself and 1. 2, 3, 5, 7, 11, 13 … are prime numbers. 1 is not a prime number.

Exercise 1a *(Revision)*

In Chapter 2 of Book 1 you used a 1–100 number square to find prime numbers between 1 and 100. This method was called the **sieve of Eratosthenes**. Use this method to find prime numbers between 1 and 200.

Copy Table 1.1 and extend it to include all whole numbers from 1 to 200.

1	2	3	4	5	6	7	8	9	10
11	12	13	14	15	16	17	18	19	20
21	22	23	24	25	26	27	28	29	30
31	32	33	34	35	36				

Table 1.1

a) Shade 1 since it is not a prime number.
b) Shade all the multiples of 2, except 2.
c) Shade all the multiples of 3, except 3.
d) Shade all the multiples of 5, except 5.
e) Shade all the multiples of 7, except 7.
f) Continue in this way with 11 and 13.
All numbers that are left unshaded are prime numbers.

Example 1

a) Write down all the factors of 24.
b) State which of these factors are prime numbers.
c) Express 24 as a product of its prime factors.

a) Factors of 24: 1, 2, 3, 4, 6, 8, 12, 24
b) Prime factors of 24: 2 and 3
c) $24 = 2 \times 2 \times 2 \times 3$

Exercise 1b *(Revision)*

For each number, (a) write down all its factors, (b) state which factors are prime numbers, (c) express the number as a product of its prime factors in index form.

1 18	**2** 28	**3** 33	**4** 45
5 16	**6** 22	**7** 30	**8** 48
9 12	**10** 36	**11** 39	**12** 56
13 42	**14** 50	**15** 63	**16** 72

Example 2

Express 90 as a product of its prime factors in index form.

Method: divide 90 by the prime numbers 2, 3, 5, 7, … in turn until it will not divide further.

Working:

2	90
3	45
3	15
5	5
	1

$90 = 2 \times 3 \times 3 \times 5$
$90 = 2 \times 3^2 \times 5$
Notice that $3 \times 3 = 3^2$ in **index form**.

Exercise 1c *(Revision)*

Express each number as a product of its prime factors in index form.

1 27	**2** 44	**3** 52	**4** 75
5 98	**6** 104	**7** 116	**8** 117
9 200	**10** 279	**11** 364	**12** 444

Highest common factor (revision)

14 is the **highest common factor** (HCF) of 28 and 42. It is the greatest number which will divide exactly into both 28 and 42.

Example 3

Find the HCF of 504 *and* 588.

Method: express each number as a product of its prime factors.

Working:

	504			588
2	504		2	588
2	252		2	294
2	126		3	147
3	63		7	49
3	21		7	7
7	7			1
	1			

$504 = 2^3 \times 3^2 \times 7$
$588 = 2^2 \times 3 \times 7^2$

Find the common prime factors.

$504 = (2^2 \times 3 \times 7) \times 2 \times 3$
$588 = (2^2 \times 3 \times 7) \times 7$

The HCF is the product of the common prime factors.

$\text{HCF} = 2^2 \times 3 \times 7$
$= 4 \times 3 \times 7$
$= 84$

Exercise 1d (Revision)

Find the HCF of the following.

1 28 and 42
2 30 and 45
3 24 and 40
4 18 and 30
5 54 and 105
6 24 and 78
7 60 and 108
8 216 and 168
9 36, 54 and 60
10 72, 108 and 54
11 324, 432 and 540
12 252, 567 and 378

Lowest common multiple (revision)

Multiples of 6:
6, 12, 18, 24, 30, 36, **42**, 48, ...
Multiples of 14:
14, 28, **42**, 56, 70, ...

Notice that 42 is the lowest number which is a multiple of both 6 and 14. 42 is the **lowest common multiple** (LCM) of 6 and 14.

Example 4

Find the LCM of 22, 30 *and* 40.

Method: express each number as a product of its prime factors.

$22 = 2 \times 11$
$30 = 2 \times 3 \times 5$
$40 = 2^3 \times 5$

The prime factors of 22, 30 and 40 are 2, 3, 5 and 11. The highest power of each prime factor must be in the LCM.

These are 2^3, 3, 5 and 11.

Thus, $\text{LCM} = 2^3 \times 3 \times 5 \times 11$
$= 8 \times 3 \times 5 \times 11$
$= 1\,320$

Exercise 1e (Revision)

Find the LCM of the following.

1 9 and 12
2 8 and 10
3 10 and 15
4 20 and 24
5 15 and 33
6 42 and 56
7 2, 3 and 7
8 4, 5 and 6
9 8, 10 and 12
10 12, 15 and 18
11 36, 45 and 60
12 20, 28 and 35

Rules for divisibility

Any whole number is exactly divisible by	
2	if its last digit is even or 0
3	if the sum of its digits is divisible by 3
4	if its last two digits form a number divisible by 4
5	if its last digit is 5 or 0
6	if its last digit is even and the sum of its digits is divisible by 3
8	if its last three digits form a number divisible by 8
9	if the sum of its digits is divisible by 9
10	if its last digit is 0

Table 1.2

There is no easy rule for division by 7. Notice the following:

a) If a number m is divisible by another number n, m is also divisible by the factors of n. For example, a number divisible by 8 is also divisible by 2 and 4.

b) If a number is divisible by two or more numbers, it is also divisible by the LCM of these numbers. For example, a number divisible by both 6 and 9 is also divisible by 18. 18 is the LCM of 6 and 9.

Example 5

Test the following numbers to see which are exactly divisible by 9. *a)* 51 066 *b)* 9 039 *c)* 48 681

Method: find the sum of the digits of each number.

a) $5 + 1 + 0 + 6 + 6 = 18$
18 is divisible by 9.
Thus 51 066 is divisible by 9.

b) $9 + 0 + 3 + 9 = 21$
21 is *not* divisible by 9.
Thus 9 039 is *not* divisible by 9.

c) $4 + 8 + 6 + 8 + 1 = 27$
27 is divisible by 9.
Thus 48 681 is divisible by 9.

Example 6

Which of the numbers 5, 6 *and* 8 *will divide into* 2 328 *without remainder?*

a) Test for division by 5.
2 328 does not end in 5 or 0.
2 328 is not divisible by 5.

b) Test for division by 6.
$2 + 3 + 2 + 8 = 15$
15 is divisible by 3 and 2 328 is even.
2 328 is divisible by 6.

c) Test for division by 8.
The last three digits of 2 328 form the number 328.
$328 \div 8 = 41$
328 is divisible by 8.
Thus 2 328 is divisible by 8.
2 328 is divisible by 6 and 8; it is not divisible by 5. Notice that since 2 328 is divisible by 6 and 8, it is also divisible by 24. 24 is the LCM of 6 and 8.

Exercise 1f

1 Copy and complete Table 1.3. Make a tick in a box if the number at the left of the box is divisible by the number above the box. Make a cross if it is not. The first row of boxes has been done.

		divisors							
	number	2	3	4	5	6	8	9	10
a)	13 545	✘	✔	✘	✔	✘	✘	✔	✘
b)	32 550								
c)	83 241								
d)	2 005								
e)	6 328								
f)	3 240								
g)	51 294								
h)	4 770								
i)	435								
j)	360								
k)	7 138								
l)	l) 1 848								

Table 1.3

2 a) Find out which of the numbers 5, 8 and 9 will divide into 51 768 exactly.

b) Hence state which of the numbers 36, 40, 45, 72 will also divide into 51 768 exactly.

3 76 356 36 116 16 869 22 374

a) Which of the numbers are divisible by 3?

b) Which of the numbers are divisible by 4?

c) Which of the numbers are divisible by 6?

d) Hence state which of the numbers are divisible by 12.

4 a) A student writes $5\,044 \times 9 = 45\,295$. Explain how the teacher immediately knows that the student has made a mistake.

b) Show that $141 \times 19 = 2\,699$ is false without doing the multiplication.

5 In the number 81 34*, the * stands for a missing digit.

a) Find the digit which will make the number divisible by 9.

b) Find the digit which will make the number divisible by 8.

c) Find the digit which will make the number divisible by 15.

Number patterns

The multiples of 3 can be given in a row, or sequence: 3, 6, 9, 12, 15, 18, 21, ...
They can also be shown by shading on a 1–100 number square as in Fig. 1.1.

1	2	3	4	5	6	7	8	9	10
11	12	13	14	15	16	17	18	19	20
21	22	23	24	25	26	27	28	29	30
31	32	33	34	35	36	37	38	39	40
41	42	43	44	45	46	47	48	49	50
51	52	53	54	55	56	57	58	59	60
61	62	63	64	65	66	67	68	69	70
71	72	73	74	75	76	77	78	79	80
81	82	83	84	85	86	87	88	89	90
91	92	93	94	95	96	97	98	99	100

Fig. 1.1

These are both examples of **number patterns**.

Extending number patterns

Example 7

Find the next four terms in the sequence 1, 2, 4, 7, 11, 16, ...

Method: find the differences between one number and the next.

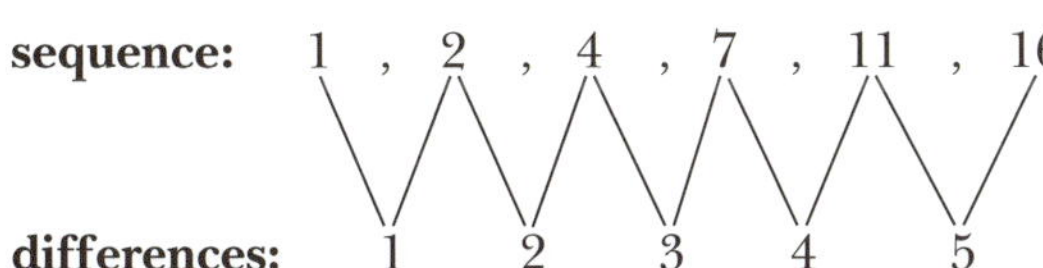

Notice the pattern in the differences. The differences increase by 1 each time. The next term in the sequence is found by adding 6 to 16. This gives 22. The next term is found by adding 7 to 22, and so on. The next four terms are: ..., 22, 29, 37, 46.

Exercise 1g

1 Complete the gaps in the following sequences.

a) Multiples of 4: 4, 8, 12, 16, ..., 100

b) Multiples of 6: 6, 12, 18, 24, ..., 96

c) Multiples of 8: 8, 16, 24, 32, ..., 96

d) Multiples of 9: 9, 18, 27, 36, ..., 99

2 Make four 1–100 number squares.
On the first number square, shade all the multiples of 4 which you found in question 1.
Repeat on the other number squares for the multiples of 6, 8 and 9.

3 Find the next four terms of the following sequences.

a) 2, 5, 8, 11, 14, ...

b) 1, 6, 11, 16, 21, ...

c) 1, 12, 23, 34, 45, ...

d) 10, 9, 8, 7, 6, ...

e) 0, 1, 3, 6, 10, ...

f) 1, 2, 4, 8, 16, ...

g) 1, 3, 7, 13, 21, ...

h) 1, 2, 5, 10, 17, ...

i) 1, 4, 9, 16, 25, ...

j) 1, 1, 2, 3, 5, 8, 13, 21, ...

4 A trader stacks some tins in triangles as shown in Fig. 1.2.

Fig. 1.2

a) Copy and complete Table 1.4.

no. of tins in bottom row	1	2	3	4
no. of tins altogether	1	3		

Table 1.4

b) Extend the table for 5, 6, 7, 8 tins in the bottom row.

5 a) Copy and complete the sequence of square numbers shown in Table 1.5.

index form	1^2	2^2	3^3	4^2	…	10^2
number	1	4	9	16	…	100

Table 1.5

b) Copy the pattern in Fig. 1.3 on to squared paper.

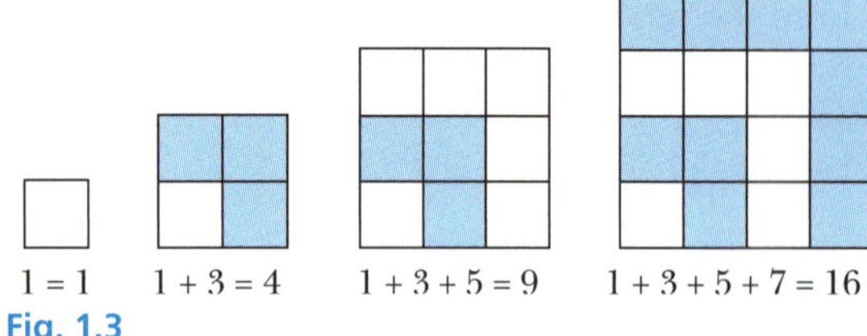

Fig. 1.3

Extend the pattern by drawing 5×5, 6×6 and 7×7 squares. Is it true that 7^2 = sum of the first seven odd numbers?

c) Copy the pattern in Table 1.6 and complete it for the numbers 5, 6 and 7. Write down the sequence formed by the total column. What do you notice?

number	pattern	total
1	1	1
2	1 + 2 + 1	4
3	1 + 2 + 3 + 2 + 1	9
4	1 + 2 + 3 + 4 + 3 + 2 + 1	16
5		
6		
7		

Table 1.6

Graphs of number patterns

A **graph** is a picture. The pictograms, bar charts and pie charts you drew when working with Book 1 were all examples of graphs.

Graphs are usually drawn on graph paper. There are two common kinds of graph paper as shown in Figs 1.4 and 1.5.

Fig. 1.4 2 mm graph paper; the small squares are 2 mm by 2 mm

Fig. 1.5 1 mm graph paper; the small squares are 1 mm by 1 mm

The lines on the graph paper are either thick, medium or thin. These make big, medium and small squares. On your graph paper, find out the following:

1 the length of side of the big, medium and small squares;
2 the number of small squares inside a big square;
3 the width, in big squares, of your graph paper;
4 the length, in big squares, of your graph paper.

In this book most graphs will be drawn on 2 mm by 2 mm graph paper.

The following example shows how to draw a simple graph of a number pattern.

Example 8

Draw a graph to show the sequence 1, 2, 4, 7, 11, 16.

The graph is given in Fig. 1.6.

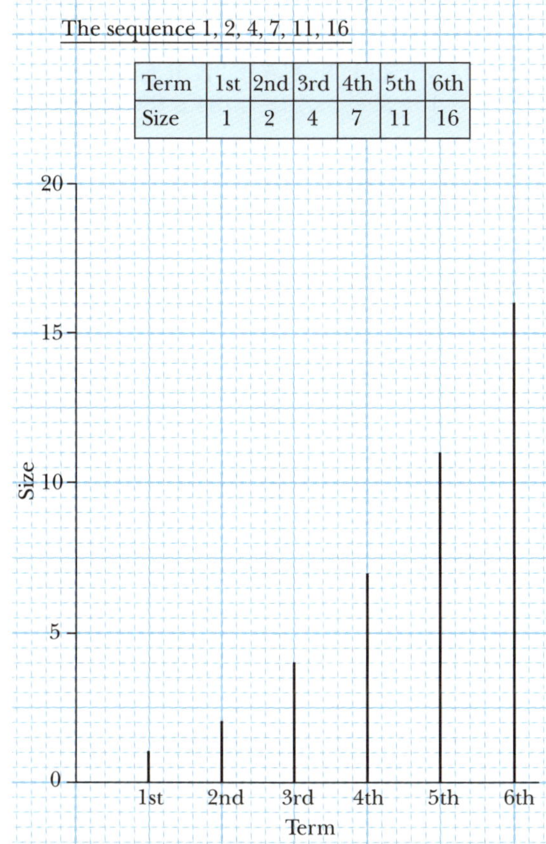

Fig. 1.6

Notice the following in Fig. 1.6.

a) The lines represent the terms of the sequence.

b) The length of each line represents the size of each term. For example, the fifth term, 11, is a line 11 units long.

c) Two lines are labelled with numbers. These are called **axes**.

d) The axis along the bottom of the graph shows the numbers of the terms. This is called the **horizontal axis**.

e) The axis at the left-hand side of the graph gives a scale, or measure, of the sizes of the terms. This is called the **vertical axis**. In this case the scale uses 2 cm to represent 5 units.

f) A table showing the data of the graph is given.

g) The title, or name, of the graph is given at the top.

Every graph should show the following:

1 a title;
2 a table giving the data of the graph;
3 labelled axes with suitable scales;*
4 lines or points giving a picture of the data.

*Look at the highest numbers in the data when choosing scales. Chapter 14 contains further advice on choosing scales.

Exercise 1h

In questions 1–6, use the same scales as those in Fig. 1.6.

1 Table 1.7 gives the factors of 18 in numerical order.

numerical order	1st	2nd	3rd	4th	5th	6th
factors of 18	1	2	3	6	9	18

Table 1.7

Draw a graph of the factors of 18.

2 Draw a graph of the first five multiples of 4: 4, 8, 12, 16, 20.

3 The numbers 1, 3, 6, 10, 15, 21, ... are known as the **triangle numbers** (see Exercise 1g, question 4). Draw a graph of the first six triangle numbers.

4 The numbers 1, 4, 9, 16, 25, ... are known as the **square numbers** (see Exercise 1g, question 5). Draw a graph of the first five square numbers.

5 Draw a graph of the first 10 odd numbers.

6 Draw a graph of the first 10 even numbers.

7 The sequence 1, 1, 2, 3, 5, 8, ... is known as the **Fibonacci sequence**. Each term is the sum of the previous two terms.

a) Write down the first 10 terms of the Fibonacci sequence.

b) Draw a graph of the first 10 terms of the Fibonacci sequence. (Use a scale of 2 cm to 10 units on the vertical axis.)

8 Draw a graph of the factors of 30.

9 Draw a graph of the decreasing sequence 16, 8, 4, 2, 1, $\frac{1}{2}$. Use a scale of 1 cm to 1 unit on the vertical axis.

10 Draw a graph of the sequence 32, 21, 12, 5, 0, 5, 12, 21, 32.

Squares and square roots

$7^2 = 7 \times 7 = 49$.
In words 'the square of 7 is 49'. We can turn this statement round and say, '**the square root** of 49 is 7'.

In symbols, $\sqrt{49} = 7$. The symbol $\sqrt{}$ means the square root of.

To find the square root of a number, first find its factors.

Example 9

Find $\sqrt{11\,025}$.

Method: Try the prime numbers 2, 3, 5, 7, ... in turn.

Working:

3	11 025
3	3 675
5	1 225
5	245
7	49
7	7
	1

$$\begin{aligned} 11\,025 &= 3^2 \times 5^2 \times 7^2 \\ &= (3 \times 5 \times 7) \times (3 \times 5 \times 7) \\ &= 105 \times 105 \end{aligned}$$

Thus $\sqrt{11\,025} = 105$

It is not always necessary to write a number in its prime factors.

Example 10

Find $\sqrt{6\,400}$.

$$\begin{aligned} 6\,400 &= 64 \times 100 \\ &= 8^2 \times 10^2 \end{aligned}$$

Thus $\sqrt{6\,400} = 8 \times 10 = 80$

The rules for divisibility can be useful when finding square roots.

Example 11

Find $\sqrt{5\,184}$.

Use the rules for divisibility.
Since 84 is divisible by 4, 5 184 is divisible by 4.
Since $5 + 1 + 8 + 4 = 18$, 5 184 is divisible by 9.

Working:

4	5 184
4	1 296
4	324
9	81
9	9
	1

$$\begin{aligned} 5\,184 &= 4^2 \times 4 \times 9^2 \\ &= 4^2 \times 2^2 \times 9^2 \end{aligned}$$

Thus $\sqrt{5\,184} = 4 \times 2 \times 9 = 72$

Exercise 1i

Find by factors the square roots of the following.

1 225	**2** 196	**3** 324
4 441	**5** 484	**6** 400
7 900	**8** 1 600	**9** 2 500
10 4 900	**11** 576	**12** 784
13 729	**14** 625	**15** 1 225
16 1 936	**17** 1 764	**18** 2 025
19 2 304	**20** 2 916	**21** 3 025
22 3 600	**23** 3 969	**24** 8 100
25 3 136	**26** 4 356	**27** 5 625
28 6 561	**29** 7 056	**30** 7 744

Perfect squares

$9 = 3 \times 3 \qquad \sqrt{9} = 3$

$25 = 5 \times 5 \qquad \sqrt{25} = 5$

$225 = 15 \times 15 \qquad \sqrt{225} = 15$

$9\,216 = 96 \times 96 \qquad \sqrt{9\,216} = 96$

We say that 9, 25, 225, 9 216 are **perfect squares** because their square roots are whole numbers. A perfect square is a whole number whose square root is also a whole number.

It is always possible to express a perfect square in factors with even indices. For example,

$$\begin{aligned} 9\,216 &= 96^2 = 3^2 \times 32^2 \\ &= 3^2 \times 4^2 \times 8^2 \\ &= 3^2 \times 2^{10} \end{aligned}$$

Example 12

Find the smallest number by which 540 must be multiplied so that the product is a perfect square.

2	540
2	270
3	135
3	45
3	15
5	5
	1

$540 = 2^2 \times 3^3 \times 5$

The index of 2 is even.

The indices of 3 and 5 are odd.

One more 3 and one more 5 will make all the indices even. The product will then be a perfect square.

The number required $= 3 \times 5 = 15$.

Exercise 1j

Find the smallest numbers by which the following must be multiplied so that their products are perfect squares.

1 24	**2** 54	**3** 45
4 99	**5** 84	**6** 162
7 405	**8** 240	**9** 432
10 147	**11** 252	**12** 504

To find the square root of a fraction, find the square roots of its numerator and denominator.

Example 13

Find the values of the following.

a) $\sqrt{\frac{4}{25}}$ *b)* $\sqrt{\frac{27}{48}}$ *c)* $\sqrt{5\frac{4}{9}}$

a) $\sqrt{\frac{4}{25}} = \frac{\sqrt{4}}{\sqrt{25}} = \frac{2}{5}$

b) Reduce the given fraction to its lowest terms.

$$\sqrt{\frac{27}{48}} = \sqrt{\frac{9 \times 3}{16 \times 3}} = \frac{\sqrt{9}}{\sqrt{16}} = \frac{3}{4}$$

c) Express the mixed number as an improper fraction.

$$\sqrt{5\frac{4}{9}} = \sqrt{\frac{49}{9}} = \frac{\sqrt{49}}{\sqrt{9}} = \frac{7}{3} = 2\frac{1}{3}$$

Exercise 1k

Find the square roots of the following.

1 $\frac{9}{25}$	**2** $\frac{16}{49}$	**3** $\frac{1}{4}$
4 $\frac{36}{81}$	**5** $\frac{9}{16}$	**6** $\frac{48}{75}$
7 $\frac{8}{18}$	**8** $\frac{72}{200}$	**9** $\frac{72}{98}$
10 $\frac{75}{108}$	**11** $2\frac{1}{4}$	**12** $1\frac{7}{9}$
13 $1\frac{9}{16}$	**14** $3\frac{6}{25}$	**15** $20\frac{1}{4}$

Chapter summary

① *Patterns* occur when a *sequence of numbers* obeys a certain rule. For example:
- **a)** 1, 3, 6, 10, 15, ... are triangle numbers
- **b)** 1, 4, 9, 16, 25, ... are square numbers
- **c)** 1, 1, 2, 3, 5, 8, 13, ... is a Fibonacci sequence
- **d)** 3, 6, 9, 12, 15, ... are multiples of 3

② Number patterns can be shown in a *diagram* (e.g. Figs 1.2 and 1.3) or in a simple *graph* (Fig. 1.6).

③ If $a \times a = b$, then b is the *square* of a and a is the *square root* of b. For example, since $4 \times 4 = 16$, 16 is the square of 4 and 4 is the square root of 16.

④ If the square root of a number, p, is a whole number then p is a *perfect square*. For example, 121 is a perfect square because its square root is 11 (a whole number).

2 Large and small numbers

Large numbers

There is no such thing as 'the biggest number in the world'. It is always possible to count higher. Science and economics use very large numbers. Thus we need special names for large numbers. Table 2.1 gives the names and values of some large numbers.

name	value				
thousand	1 000				
million	1 000 thousand	=	1 000 000	=	$1\,000^2$
billion	1 000 million	=	1 000 000 000	=	$1\,000^3$

Table 2.1

How big is a million?

The following examples may give you some idea of the size of a million.

1 A 1 cm by 1 cm square of 1 mm graph paper contains 100 small 1 mm × 1 mm squares.

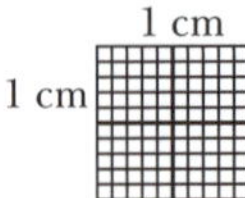

Fig. 2.1 100 small squares

A 1 m by 1 m square of the same graph paper contains 1 million of these small squares.

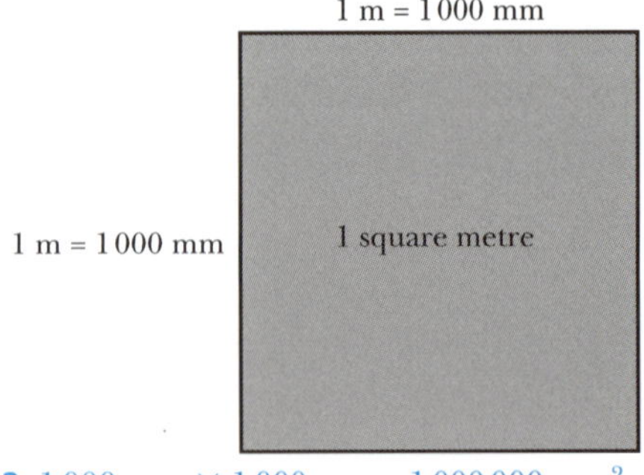

Fig. 2.2 1 000 mm × 1 000 mm = 1 000 000 mm^2

2 A cubic metre measures 100 cm by 100 cm by 100 cm.

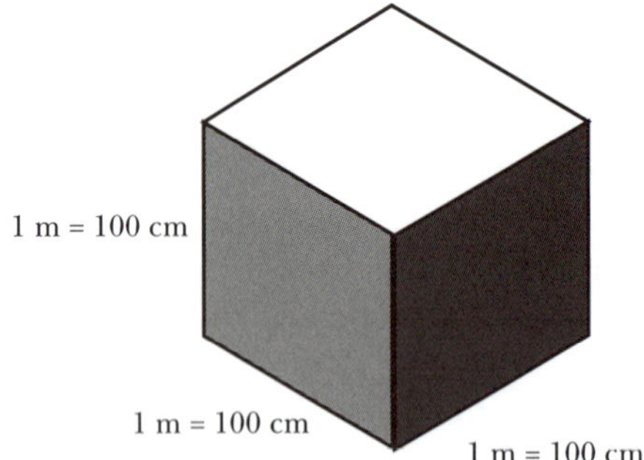

Fig. 2.3 1 cubic metre

Volume of a cubic metre
= 100 cm × 100 cm × 100 cm
= 1 000 000 cm^3
Thus 1 million cubic centimetres, cm^3, will exactly fill a 1 cubic metre box.

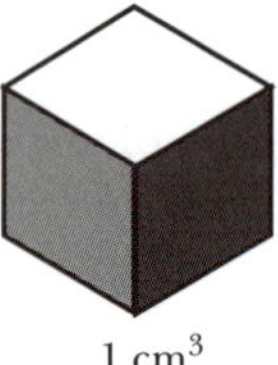

Fig. 2.4 One million of these make 1 cubic metre

Exercise 2a

1 What is the correct name for **(a)** a thousand thousand, **(b)** a thousand million?

2 A football field measures 80 m by 50 m.
   a) Change the dimensions in cm and calculate the area of the field in cm^2.
   b) A bar of soap measures 8 cm by 5 cm. Calculate how many soap bars would be needed to cover the football field.

3 A library has about 4 000 books. Each book has about 250 pages. Approximately how many pages are there in the library?

4 How long would it take to count to 1 million if it takes an average of 1 second to say each number? Give your answer to the nearest $\frac{1}{2}$ day.

5 Find out which of the following is nearest to the number of seconds in a year.

a) 500 000
b) 1 000 000
c) 3 000 000
d) 30 000 000
e) 2 000 000 000

Writing large numbers

Grouping digits

Read the number 31556926 out aloud. Was it easy to do? It may have been quite difficult. You had to decide, 'Is the number bigger than a million or not?', 'Does it begin with 3 million, 31 million or 315 million?'.

It is necessary to write large numbers in a helpful way. It is usual to group the digits of large numbers in threes from the decimal point. A small gap is left between each group.

31556926 should be written as 31 556 926. Now it is easy to see that the number begins with 31 million.

We no longer use commas between the groups of digits. Many countries use a comma as a decimal point, thus to avoid confusion commas are not used for grouping the digits.

Exercise 2b

Write the following numbers, grouping digits in threes from the decimal point. (Use spaces, not commas.)

1 1 million	**2** 59244	**3** 721,568,397
4 2,312,400	**5** 8 million	**6** 3 billion
7 9215	**8** 14682053	**9** 108,412
10 12345	**11** 100000000	**12** 987654

Digits and words

Editors of newspapers know that large numbers sometimes confuse readers. They often use a mixture of digits and words when writing large numbers.

Example 1

What do the numbers in the following headlines stand for?

a) FOOD IMPORTS RISE TO Le1 BILLION
b) OIL PRODUCTION NOW 2·3 MILLION BARRELS DAILY
c) FLOODS IN INDIA – 0·6 MILLION HOMELESS
d) NEW ROAD TO COST Le2$\frac{1}{4}$ BILLION

a) Le1 billion is short for Le1 000 000 000

b) 2·3 million = 2·3 × 1 000 000
= 2 300 000

c) 0·6 million = 0·6 × 1 000 000
= 600 000

d) Le2$\frac{1}{4}$ billion = Le2·25 billion
= Le2 250 000 000

Example 2

Express the following in a mixture of digits and words.

a) Le3 000 000 *b)* 6 800 000 000
c) 240 000 000 *d)* Le500 000

a) Le3 000 000 = Le3 × 1 000 000
= Le3 million

b) 6 800 000 000 = 6·8 × 1 000 000 000
= 6·8 billion

c) 240 000 000 = 240 × 1 000 000
= 240 million

or

240 000 000 = 0·24 × 1 000 000 000
= 0·24 billion (or 240 million)

d) Le500 000 = Le0·5 × 1 000 000
= Le0·5 million or Le$\frac{1}{2}$ million

Exercise 2c

1 Express the following numbers in digits only.

a) Le2 million **b)** 150 million km
c) 3 billion **d)** 5$\frac{1}{2}$ million
e) Le2·1 billion **f)** 4·2 million litres
g) 0·4 billion **h)** Le1$\frac{1}{4}$ million
i) 0·7 million tonnes **j)** Le$\frac{3}{4}$ million
k) 0·45 million **l)** Le0·58 billion

2 Imagine you are a newspaper editor. Write the following numbers using a mixture of digits and words.

a) 8 000 000 tonnes **b)** Le6 000 000
c) 2 000 000 000 **d)** Le3 700 000 000
e) Le7 400 000 **f)** Le1 750 000

g) 200 000 litres h) 500 000 000
i) 300 000 tonnes j) 250 000
k) 980 000 barrels l) 490 000 000

Standard form

Numbers such as 1 000, 1 000 000, 1 000 000 000 can easily be expressed as powers of 10. For example,

$$1\,000\,000 = 10 \times 10 \times 10 \times 10 \times 10 \times 10 = 10^6$$

Other numbers can be expressed as a product of two terms, one of which is a power of 10. For example,

$$2\,000\,000 = 2 \times 1\,000\,000 = 2 \times 10^6$$
$$7\,000 = 7 \times 1\,000 = 7 \times 10^3$$
$$2\,500\,000 = 2{\cdot}5 \times 1\,000\,000 = 2{\cdot}5 \times 10^6$$
$$8\,600\,000\,000 = 8{\cdot}6 \times 1\,000\,000\,000 = 8{\cdot}6 \times 10^9$$

The numbers 2×10^6, 7×10^3, $2{\cdot}5 \times 10^6$ and $8{\cdot}6 \times 10^9$ are all in the form $A \times 10^n$ such that A is a number between 1 and 10 and n is a whole number. Such numbers are said to be in **standard form**.

Scientists often use standard form when writing numbers. Standard form makes it easy to tell the size of a number. There is also less chance of making a mistake with zeros when using standard form.

Example 3

Express the following numbers in standard form.
a) 60 000 *b)* 650 *c)* 480 000 000 *d)* 320 000

a) $60\,000 = 6 \times 10\,000 = 6 \times 10^4$
b) $650 = 6{\cdot}5 \times 100 = 6{\cdot}5 \times 10^2$
c) $480\,000\,000 = 4{\cdot}8 \times 100\,000\,000 = 4{\cdot}8 \times 10^8$
d) $320\,000 = 3{\cdot}2 \times 100\,000 = 3{\cdot}2 \times 10^5$

Exercise 2d

Express the following numbers in standard form.

1 9 000 000 **2** 4 000
3 4 000 000 000 **4** 600
5 300 000 **6** 60 000
7 5 000 000 000 **8** 70
9 20 000 000 **10** 89 000
11 720 000 000 **12** 2 300 000
13 55 **14** 170 000
15 5 400 **16** 25 000 000
17 6 300 **18** 9 400 000 000
19 410 000 **20** 85 000 000
21 950 **22** 3 600
23 360 **24** 36

Example 4

Express the following in ordinary form.
a) 4×10^4 *b)* $4{\cdot}3 \times 10^4$ *c)* $7{\cdot}8 \times 10^7$

a) $4 \times 10^4 = 4 \times 10\,000 = 40\,000$
b) $4{\cdot}3 \times 10^4 = 4{\cdot}3 \times 10\,000 = 43\,000$
c) $7{\cdot}8 \times 10^7 = 7{\cdot}8 \times 10\,000\,000 = 78\,000\,000$

Exercise 2e

Change the following from standard form to ordinary form.

1 6×10^4 **2** 8×10^3 **3** 9×10^5
4 4×10^2 **5** 7×10^1 **6** 3×10^2
7 5×10^7 **8** 2×10^6 **9** 6×10^8
10 $6{\cdot}3 \times 10^4$ **11** $8{\cdot}4 \times 10^3$ **12** $9{\cdot}8 \times 10^5$
13 $7{\cdot}2 \times 10^1$ **14** $3{\cdot}6 \times 10^2$ **15** $4{\cdot}4 \times 10^2$
16 $5{\cdot}1 \times 10^7$ **17** $2{\cdot}5 \times 10^6$ **18** $6{\cdot}7 \times 10^8$
19 $3{\cdot}7 \times 10^3$ **20** $5{\cdot}9 \times 10^7$ **21** $8{\cdot}5 \times 10^4$
22 $3{\cdot}4 \times 10^3$ **23** $3{\cdot}4 \times 10^2$ **24** $3{\cdot}4 \times 10^1$

Small numbers

Decimal fractions

Decimal fractions also have names.

8 tenths = 0·8
8 hundredths = 0·08
8 thousandths = 0·008
8 ten thousandths = 0·000 8
8 hundred thousandths = 0·000 08

Notice that digits are grouped in threes from the decimal point as before.

Example 5

Write the following as decimal fractions.
a) 28 *thousandths* *b)* $\frac{865}{100\,000}$
c) 350 *millionths* *d)* $\frac{400}{10\,000}$

a) 28 thousandths = 1 thousandth × 28
= 0·001 × 28
= 0·028

b) $\frac{865}{100\,000} = 0{\cdot}008\,65$

There are five zeros in the denominator. The

decimal fraction is obtained by moving the digits in the numerator five places to the right.

c) 350 millionths = 1 millionth × 350
= 0·000 001 × 350
= 0·000 350 = 0·000 35

In a decimal fraction it is not necesary to write any zeros after the last non-zero digit.

d) $\frac{400}{10\,000}$ = 0·0400
= 0·04

Exercise 2f

Write the following as decimal fractions.

1 6 hundredths
2 4 thousandths
3 9 tenths
4 8 millionths
5 4 ten thousandths
6 6 hundred thousandths
7 $\frac{3}{1\,000}$
8 $\frac{9}{100\,000}$
9 $\frac{7}{10\,000}$
10 16 hundredths
11 34 thousandths
12 26 ten thousandths
13 $\frac{28}{100\,000}$
14 $\frac{84}{1\,000}$
15 $\frac{756}{10\,000}$
16 27 tenths
17 65 hundredths
18 402 thousandths
19 20 hundredths
20 240 thousandths
21 700 thousandths
22 $\frac{620}{100\,000}$
23 $\frac{330}{100\,000}$
24 $\frac{4\,020}{100\,000}$
25 90 hundredths
26 900 thousandths
27 300 ten thousandths
28 $\frac{720}{1\,000}$
29 $\frac{720}{10\,000}$
30 $\frac{720}{100\,000}$

Laws of indices

10^3 is short for $10 \times 10 \times 10$.
Similarly, x^5 is short for $x \times x \times x \times x \times x$.
x can be any number.

Example 6

Multiply a) x^5 *by* x^3 *b)* a^3 *by* a^2 *c)* y *by* y^4.

a) $x^5 \times x^3 = (x \times x \times x \times x \times x) \times (x \times x \times x)$
$= x \times x \times x \times x \times x \times x \times x \times x$
$= x^8$

b) $a^3 \times a^2 = (a \times a \times a) \times (a \times a)$
$= a \times a \times a \times a \times a$
$= a^5$

c) $y \times y^4 = y \times (y \times y \times y \times y)$
$= y \times y \times y \times y \times y$
$= y^5$

Notice that the index in the result is the sum of the given indices:

$$x^5 \times x^3 = x^{5+3} = x^8$$
$$a^3 \times a^2 = a^{3+2} = a^5$$
$$y \times y^4 = y^1 \times y^4 = y^{1+4} = y^5$$

In general: $x^a \times x^b = x^{a+b}$

Example 7

Simplify the following. a) $10^4 \times 10^2$ *b)* $4c^3 \times 7c^2$

In fully expanded form:

a) $10^4 \times 10^2 = (10 \times 10 \times 10 \times 10) \times (10 \times 10)$
$= 10 \times 10 \times 10 \times 10 \times 10 \times 10$
$= 10^6$

b) $4c^3 \times 7c^2 = 4 \times c \times c \times c \times 7 \times c \times c$
$= 4 \times 7 \times c \times c \times c \times c \times c$
$= 28c^5$

Or, more quickly, by adding indices:

a) $10^4 \times 10^2 = 10^{4+2} = 10^6$
b) $4c^3 \times 7c^2 = 4 \times 7 \times c^{3+2} = 28c^5$

Exercise 2g

1 Simplify the following by fully expanding the terms.

a) $x^2 \times x^3$ **b)** $10^2 \times 10^5$
c) $a^4 \times a^3$ **d)** $10^5 \times 10$
e) $n^5 \times n$ **f)** $10^4 \times 10^5$
g) $3a^2 \times 8a^4$ **h)** $5x^3 \times 4x^7$
i) $3c^2 \times 2c^5$ **j)** $4y^6 \times 7y$

2 Simplify the following by adding the indices.

a) $m^3 \times m^5$ **b)** $a^6 \times a^4$
c) $c^5 \times c^9$ **d)** $10^2 \times 10^7$
e) $b^8 \times b^7$ **f)** $x^7 \times x$
g) $2e^4 \times 5e^{10}$ **h)** $3 \times 10^6 \times 5 \times 10^3$
i) $5y^5 \times 3y^3$ **j)** $4x \times 5x^5$

Example 8

Divide a) x^5 *by* x^3 *b)* a^7 *by* a^4 *c)* p^6 *by* p^5.

a) $x^5 \div x^3 = \dfrac{x^5}{x^3} = \dfrac{x \times x \times x \times x \times x}{x \times x \times x}$

$= \dfrac{x \times x \times (x \times x \times x)}{(x \times x \times x)}$

$= x^2$

$$b)\ a^7 \div a^4 = \frac{a^7}{a^4} = \frac{a \times a \times a \times a \times a \times a \times a}{a \times a \times a \times a}$$

$$= \frac{a \times a \times a \times (a \times a \times a \times a)}{(a \times a \times a \times a)}$$

$$= a^3$$

$$c)\ p^6 \div p^5 = \frac{p^6}{p^5} = \frac{p \times p \times p \times p \times p \times p}{p \times p \times p \times p \times p}$$

$$= \frac{p \times (p \times p \times p \times p \times p)}{(p \times p \times p \times p \times p)}$$

$$= p$$

Notice that the index in the result is the index of the divisor subtracted from the index of the dividend:

$$x^5 \div x^3 = x^{5-3} = x^2$$
$$a^7 \div a^4 = a^{7-4} = a^3$$
$$p^6 \div p^5 = p^{6-5} = p^1 = p$$

In general: $x^a \div x^b = x^{a-b}$

Example 9

Divide a) 10^6 *by* 10^2, *b)* $12a^7$ *by* $3a^2$.

In fully expanded form:

$$a)\ 10^6 \div 10^2 = \frac{10^6}{10^2}$$

$$= \frac{10 \times 10 \times 10 \times 10 \times 10 \times 10}{10 \times 10}$$

$$= 10 \times 10 \times 10 \times 10 = 10^4$$

$$b)\ 12a^7 \div 3a^2 = \frac{12 \times a \times a \times a \times a \times a \times a \times a}{3 \times a \times a}$$

$$= \frac{4 \times (3 \times a \times a) \times a \times a \times a \times a \times a}{(3 \times a \times a)}$$

$$= 4 \times a \times a \times a \times a \times a = 4a^5$$

Or, more quickly, by subtracting indices:

$a)\ 10^6 \div 10^2 = 10^{6-2} = 10^4$
$b)\ 12a^7 \div 3a^2 = \frac{12}{3} \times a^{7-2} = 4a^5$

Exercise 2h

1 Simplify the following by fully expanding the terms.

a) $a^7 \div a^3$ **b)** $10^5 \div 10^2$

10^6

c) $c^4 \div c$ **d)** $\frac{\quad}{10^3}$

e) $\frac{d^6}{d^5}$ **f)** $\frac{10^5}{10^3}$

g) $12x^7 \div 4x^3$ **h)** $10a^8 \div 5a^6$

i) $4x^6 \div 4x$ **j)** $51m^9 \div 3m$

2 Simplify the following by subtracting indices.

a) $x^6 \div x^4$ **b)** $b^8 \div b^5$

c) $c^9 \div c^3$ **d)** $\frac{a^{11}}{a^9}$

e) $10^9 \div 10^7$ **f)** $\frac{x^7}{x}$

g) $18x^5 \div 9x^4$ **h)** $\frac{24x^8}{6x^5}$

i) $\frac{8 \times 10^9}{4 \times 10^6}$ **j)** $(3{\cdot}6 \times 10^7) \div (1{\cdot}2 \times 10^3)$

Example 10

Simplify $x^3 \div x^3$
a) by fully expanding each term,
b) by subtracting indices.

$$a)\ x^3 \div x^3 = \frac{x \times x \times x}{x \times x \times x} = 1$$

$$b)\ x^3 \div x^3 = x^{3-3} = x^0$$

From the results of parts *a)* and *b)* in Example 10, $x^0 = 1$.

In general: **any number raised to the power 0 has the value 1.**

Example 11

Simplify $x^2 \div x^5$
a) by fully expanding each term,
b) by subtracting indices.

$$a)\ x^2 \div x^5 = \frac{x \times x}{x \times x \times x \times x \times x}$$

$$= \frac{1}{x \times x \times x} = \frac{1}{x^3}$$

$$b)\ x^2 \div x^5 = x^{2-5} = x^{-3}$$

From the results of parts *a)* and *b)* in Example 11,

$$x^{-3} = \frac{1}{x^3}$$

In general, $x^{-a} = \dfrac{1}{x^a}$

Example 12

Simplify the following.

a) 10^{-3} *b)* $x^0 \times x^4 \times x^{-2}$

c) $a^{-3} \div a^{-5}$ *d)* $\left(\frac{1}{4}\right)^{-2}$

a) $10^{-3} = \dfrac{1}{10^3} = \dfrac{1}{1\,000}$

b) $x^0 \times x^4 \times x^{-2} = 1 \times x^4 \times \dfrac{1}{x^2} = \dfrac{x^4}{x^2}$

$= x^{4-2} = x^2$

or

$x^0 \times x^4 \times x^{-2} = x^{0+4+(-2)} = x^2$

c) $a^{-3} \div a^{-5} = \dfrac{1}{a^3} \div \dfrac{1}{a^5} = \dfrac{1}{a^3} \times \dfrac{a^5}{1}$

$= a^{5-3} = a^2$

or

$a^{-3} \div a^{-5} = a^{(-3)-(-5)}$

$= a^{-3+5} = a^2$

d) $\left(\frac{1}{4}\right)^{-2} = \dfrac{1}{\left(\frac{1}{4}\right)^2} = \dfrac{1}{\frac{1}{16}} = 16$

Exercise 2i

Simplify the following.

1 10^{-2} **2** 10^{-4}

3 10^{-6} **4** $x^5 \times x^{-2}$

5 $a^{-2} \times a^{-3}$ **6** $m^0 \times n^0$

7 $a^2 \div a^7$ **8** $x^2 \div x^{-7}$

9 $p^{-2} \div p^{-7}$ **10** $b^3 \div b^0$

11 $r^7 \div r^7$ **12** $c^{-1} \times c^{-1}$

13 $\left(\frac{1}{2}\right)^{-3}$ **14** $\left(\frac{1}{3}\right)^{-2}$

15 $\left(\frac{1}{9}\right)^{-1}$ **16** $2a^{-1} \times 3a^2$

17 $(2a)^{-1} \times 3a^2$ **18** $2a^{-1} \times (3a)^2$

Decimal fractions in standard form

Decimal fractions such as 0·001 and 0·000 001 can be expressed as powers of 10. For example,

$$0{\cdot}000\,001 = \frac{1}{1\,000\,000} = \frac{1}{10^6} = 10^{-6}$$

Thus any decimal fraction can be expressed in standard form. For example,

$$0{\cdot}008 = \frac{8}{1\,000} = \frac{8}{10^3} = 8 \times 10^{-3}$$

$$0{\cdot}000\,03 = \frac{3}{100\,000} = \frac{3}{10^5} = 3 \times 10^{-5}$$

$$0{\cdot}000\,25 = \frac{2{\cdot}5}{10\,000} = \frac{2{\cdot}5}{10^4} = 2{\cdot}5 \times 10^{-4}$$

The numbers 8×10^{-3}, 3×10^{-5} and $2{\cdot}5 \times 10^{-4}$ are all in standard form $A \times 10^n$, where A is a number between 1 and 10 and n is an integer. Notice that for decimal fractions, n is a negative integer.

Example 13

Express the following fractions in standard form.

a) 0·000 07 *b)* 0·075

c) 0·000 000 022 *d)* 0·000 006 3

a) $0{\cdot}000\,07 = \dfrac{7}{100\,000} = \dfrac{7}{10^5} = 7 \times 10^{-5}$

b) $0{\cdot}075 = \dfrac{7{\cdot}5}{100} = \dfrac{7{\cdot}5}{10^2} = 7{\cdot}5 \times 10^{-2}$

c) $0{\cdot}000\,000\,022 = \dfrac{2{\cdot}2}{100\,000\,000} = \dfrac{2{\cdot}2}{10^8} = 2{\cdot}2 \times 10^{-8}$

d) $0{\cdot}000\,006\,3 = \dfrac{6{\cdot}3}{1\,000\,000} = \dfrac{6{\cdot}3}{10^6} = 6{\cdot}3 \times 10^{-6}$

Exercise 2j

Express the following in standard form.

1 0·005 **2** 0·08

3 0·000 6 **4** 0·000 004

5 0·000 02 **6** 0·000 0009

7 0·3 **8** 0·003

9 0·000 03 **10** 0·038

11 0·006 2 **12** 0·71

13 0·000 88 **14** 0·000 45

15 0·000 026 **16** 0·000 072

17 0·000 005 5 **18** 0·011

19 0·000 000 91 **20** 0·000 000 067

21 0·005 7 **22** 0·000 15

23 0·001 5 **24** 0·015

Example 14

Express the following numbers as decimal fractions.

a) 9×10^{-4} *b)* $9{\cdot}4 \times 10^{-4}$ *c)* $5{\cdot}3 \times 10^{-7}$

a) $9 \times 10^{-4} = \dfrac{9}{10\,000} = 0{\cdot}000\,9$

b) $9{\cdot}4 \times 10^{-4} = \dfrac{9{\cdot}4}{10\,000} = 0{\cdot}000\,94$

c) $5{\cdot}3 \times 10^{-7} = \dfrac{5{\cdot}3}{10\,000\,000} = 0{\cdot}000\,000\,53$

Exercise 2k

Express the following as decimal fractions.

1 2×10^{-4}	**2** 8×10^{-6}
3 5×10^{-3}	**4** 4×10^{-2}
5 7×10^{-1}	**6** 3×10^{-5}
7 6×10^{-3}	**8** 9×10^{-5}
9 2×10^{-7}	**10** $2{\cdot}8 \times 10^{-4}$
11 $8{\cdot}3 \times 10^{-6}$	**12** $5{\cdot}1 \times 10^{-3}$
13 $4{\cdot}5 \times 10^{-2}$	**14** $7{\cdot}9 \times 10^{-1}$
15 $3{\cdot}3 \times 10^{-5}$	**16** $6{\cdot}2 \times 10^{-3}$
17 $9{\cdot}4 \times 10^{-5}$	**18** $2{\cdot}6 \times 10^{-4}$
19 $1{\cdot}8 \times 10^{-1}$	**20** $8{\cdot}8 \times 10^{-3}$
21 $4{\cdot}1 \times 10^{-2}$	**22** $2{\cdot}4 \times 10^{-3}$
23 $2{\cdot}4 \times 10^{-2}$	**24** $2{\cdot}4 \times 10^{-1}$

Rounding off numbers

In Book 1 you learned how to round off numbers to the nearest thousand, hundred, ten, etc. Remember that the digits 1, 2, 3, 4 are rounded down and the digits 5, 6, 7, 8, 9 are rounded up.

Exercise 2l *(Oral revision)*

1 Round off the following to the nearest i) thousand, ii) hundred, iii) ten.

a) 12 835	**b)** 46 923	**c)** 28 006
d) 9 785	**e)** 30 637	**f)** 13 067
g) 8 615	**h)** 4 517	**i)** 16 560
j) 59 094	**k)** 5 555	**l)** 19 503

2 Round off the following to the nearest i) whole number ii) tenth iii) hundredth.

a) 2·517	**b)** 7·994	**c)** 3·125
d) 0·945	**e)** 0·493	**f)** 9·507

Significant figures

Significant figures begin from the first non-zero digit at the left of a number. As before, the digits 5, 6, 7, 8, 9 are rounded up and 1, 2, 3, 4 are rounded down. Digits should be written with their correct place value.

Read the following examples carefully.

a) 546·52 = 500 to 1 significant figure (s.f.)
546·52 = 550 to 2 s.f.
546·52 = 547 to 3 s.f.
546·52 = 546·5 to 4 s.f.

b) 8·029 6 = 8 to 1 s.f.
8·029 6 = 8·0 to 2 s.f.

In this case the zero must be given after the decimal point. It is significant.

8·029 6 = 8·03 to 3 s.f.
8·029 6 = 8·030 to 4 s.f.

Notice that the fourth digit is zero. It is significant and must be written down.

c) 0·009 25 = 0·009 to 1 s.f.

9 is the first non-zero digit. The two zeros after the decimal point are not significant figures. However, they must be written down to keep the place value correct.

0·009 25 = 0·009 3 to 2 s.f.

Exercise 2m (Oral)

1 Round off the following to i) 1 s.f., ii) 2 s.f., iii) 3 s.f.

a) 7 284	**b)** 6 035	**c)** 14 612
d) 3 604	**e)** 8 009	**f)** 5 050
g) 28 336	**h)** 9 852	**i)** 9 395
j) 26 002	**k)** 69 625	**l)** 19 340

2 Round off the following to i) 1 s.f., ii) 2 s.f., iii) 3 s.f., iv) 4 s.f.

a) 7·038 4	**b)** 18·502	**c)** 12·675
d) 3·779 8	**e)** 234·06	**f)** 79·405
g) 62·469	**h)** 1·994 2	**i)** 780·88
j) 678·45	**k)** 25·205	**l)** 2·005 67

3 Round off the following to i) 1 s.f., ii) 2 s.f., iii) 3 s.f.

a) 0·067 52	**b)** 0·305 9	**c)** 0·006 307
d) 0·000 666 6	**e)** 0·033 55	**f)** 0·880 4
g) 0·002 583	**h)** 0·009 009	**i)** 0·000 220 8
j) 0·900 4	**k)** 0·606 06	**l)** 0·042 429

4 Round off the following to i) 1 s.f., ii) 2 s.f., iii) 3 s.f.

a) 25·25	**b)** 3·906	**c)** 168·8
d) 0·701 8	**e)** 0·007 775	**f)** 0·000 387 5
g) 109·8	**h)** 40·65	**i)** 5·753
j) 0·008 088	**k)** 694·9	**l)** 0·047 45

5 Assume the following numbers have been rounded off. State the number of significant figures in each.

a) 78	**b)** 5·65	**c)** 0·003
d) 295·4	**e)** 0·055	**f)** 10·5
g) 0·044	**h)** 39·9	**i)** 788·3
j) 0·000 6	**k)** 0·6	**l)** 5·45

Decimal places

Decimal places are counted from the decimal point. Zeros after the point are significant and are also counted. Digits are rounded up or down as before. Place values must be kept.

Read the following examples carefully.

a) 14·902 8 = 14·9 to 1 decimal place (d.p.)
14·902 8 = 14·90 to 2 d.p.
14·902 8 = 14·903 to 3 d.p.

b) 2·397 5 = 2·4 to 1 d.p.
2·397 5 = 2·40 to 2 d.p.
2·397 5 = 2·398 to 3 d.p.

c) 0·007 2 = 0·0 to 1 d.p.
0·007 2 = 0·01 to 2 d.p.
0·007 2 = 0·007 to 3 d.p.

Exercise 2n (Oral)

Round off the following to
a) 1 d.p. **b)** 2 d.p. **c)** 3 d.p.

1 12·934 8	**2** 24·117 7	**3** 5·072 5
4 1·937 5	**5** 1·987 5	**6** 0·584 6
7 0·062 5	**8** 0·037 5	**9** 0·900 2
10 0·008 9		

Problems with large and small numbers

Example 15

A light year is a distance of 9·456 × 10¹² *km. Express this number to two significant figures, then write it out in full.*

$9{\cdot}456 \times 10^{12}$ km = $9{\cdot}5 \times 10^{12}$ km to 2 s.f.
$9{\cdot}5 \times 10^{12}$ km = 9 500 000 000 000 km

Example 16

The pages of a book are numbered from 1 *to* 400. *The thickness of the book is* 24 *mm. Calculate the thickness of one leaf (i.e. two pages) of the book. Give the answer in metres in standard form.*

A book with 400 pages contains 200 leaves of paper.
Thickness of 200 leaves = 24 mm
Thickness of one leaf = $\frac{24}{200}$ mm

$$\text{Thickness of one leaf in metres} = \frac{24}{200 \times 1\,000}\text{ m}$$
$$= \frac{12}{100\,000}\text{ m}$$
$$= \frac{1{\cdot}2}{10\,000}\text{ m}$$
$$= 1{\cdot}2 \times 10^{-4}\text{ m}$$

Exercise 2p

1 In the following statements, round each number to two significant figures, then write it out in full.

a) It will cost Le3·18 billion to renovate the classrooms of some schools.

b) The area of Sierra Leone is 71·740 thousand km^2.

c) It was estimated that the population of Freetown was about 2 million at the end of 1999.

d) One can of oil has a volume of $1{\cdot}589\,9 \times 10^{-1} m^3$.

e) The light from the moon is $2{\cdot}15 \times 10^{-6}$ times the light from the sun.

f) The sun is about $1{\cdot}496 \times 10^8$ km from the earth.

2 In the following statements, round each number to two significant figures, then write it in standard form.

a) The budget of Western Area was Le892·46 billion.

b) Le289 000 000 000 was allocated to Northern Province.

c) £28 500 000 worth of goods was imported from the UK.

d) The density of air is $0{\cdot}001\,293\text{ g cm}^{-3}$.

e) The land area of Africa is 30 280 000 km^2.

f) 1 watt is equivalent to 0·001 341 horsepower.

3 In an election there were 2·277 million registered male voters and 2·447 million registered female voters. How many registered voters were there altogether?

4 In successive years the crude oil production in Nigeria was $7{\cdot}580 \times 10^9$ and $7{\cdot}677 \times 10^9$ barrels. How many barrels were produced altogether in those two years? Give your answer in standard form.

Chapter summary

① To avoid confusion, when writing large numbers or small decimal fractions, group the digits in threes from the decimal point: e.g. 49 560 216 and 0·003 48.

② A number in *standard form* is written as $A \times 10^n$, where A is a number between 1 and 10 (inclusive) and n is a positive or negative integer.

③ The *laws of indices* are:

$$x^a \times x^b = x^{a+b}$$
$$x^a \div x^b = x^{a-b}$$
$$x^0 = 1$$
$$x^{-a} = \frac{1}{x^a}$$

④ *Significant figures* (s.f.) begin from the first non-zero digit at the left of a number. For example:

18 329 = 18 000 to 2 significant figures
0·092 752 = 0·092 8 to 3 significant figures

⑤ *Decimal places* (d.p.) are counted from the decimal point. Zeros after the point are taken into consideration. For example:

2·081 6 = 2·1 to 1 decimal place
= 2·08 to 2 decimal places
= 2·082 to 3 decimal places

5 The height of Mount Everest is $8{\cdot}85 \times 10^3$ m. The height of Mount Kilimanjaro is $5{\cdot}89 \times 10^3$ m. Write these heights in ordinary form and find the difference in height between the two mountains.

6 In 1920 the population of the world was 1·8 billion. By 2000 the world's population was 6 billion. Find the increase in world population during those 80 years.

7 The area of Liberia is approximately 10 times the area of The Gambia. If the area of The Gambia is approximately $1{\cdot}1 \times 10^4$ km^2, find the approximate area of Liberia.

8 The distance between two points is $2{\cdot}54 \times 10^{-2}$ m. Express this distance in km in standard form.

3 Plane shapes (2) Quadrilaterals and patterns

Quadrilateral means four-sided. A quadrilateral is a shape with four sides. Thus squares and rectangles are quadrilaterals.

You will need a pencil, a set-square, a ruler, a protractor, and scissors or a sharp knife for the work of this chapter.

Parallelogram

Use a ruler and set-square to draw any pair of parallel lines.

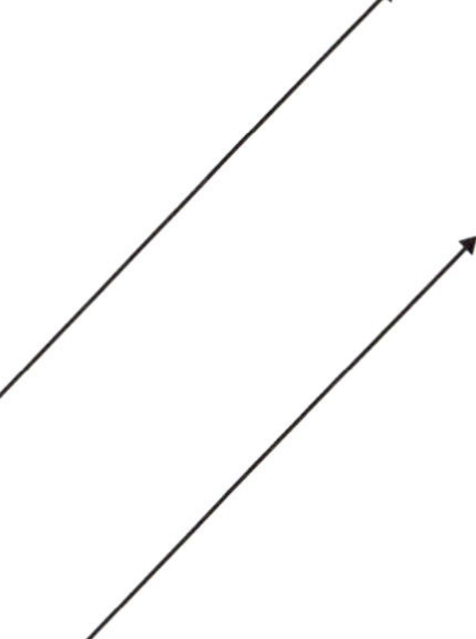

Fig. 3.1

Draw another pair of parallel lines so that both lines cross the first pair.

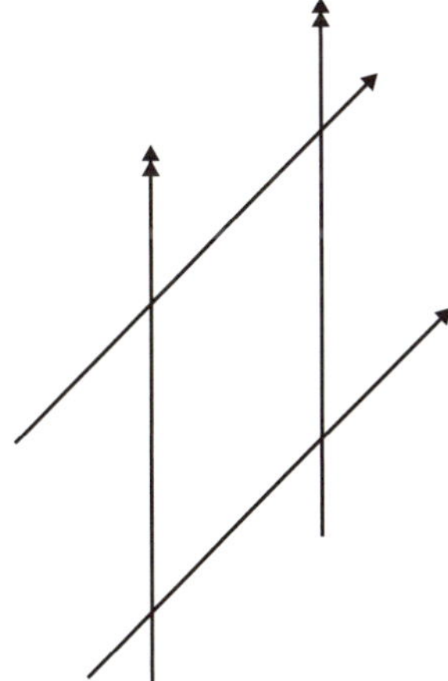

Fig. 3.2

The shape inside the four lines is a **parallelogram**.

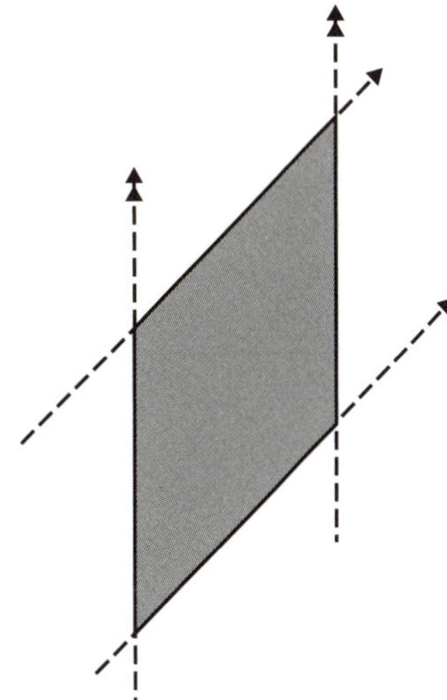

Fig. 3.3

A parallelogram is a quadrilateral which has opposite sides parallel.

Exercise 3a *(Class activity)*

1 Try to name a few things in your home, class or town which have the shape of a parallelogram.

2 How many sides has a parallelogram?

3 How many angles has a parallelogram?

4 **a)** Draw a parallelogram with sides at least 5 cm long.

b) Draw a parallelogram on a sheet of newspaper. Cut out the parallelogram.

5 Use the parallelograms you made in question 4 to do the following.

a) Measure the lengths of the sides of the parallelograms. What do you notice?

b) Measure the angles of the parallelograms. What do you notice?

c) Find the total of the four angles of each parallelogram.

d) Draw the diagonals of the parallelograms.

Fig. 3.4

e) Measure the lengths of both diagonals of each parallelogram. What do you notice?
f) In each parallelogram, measure the distance from the centre to each corner. What do you notice?
g) At the centre, where the diagonals cross, there are four angles. How many are acute? What kind of angles are the others?
h) Try to fold the newspaper parallelogram so that opposite sides meet. Do they meet completely? Do the folded parts of the parallelogram cover each other completely?
i) Try to fold the newspaper parallelogram so that opposite angles meet. Do this for both pairs of opposite angles. Do the folded parts cover each other completely?
j) Do any of your parallelograms have a line of symmetry?

6 Fig. 3.5 shows a parallelogram PQRS with four angles marked a, b, c, d.

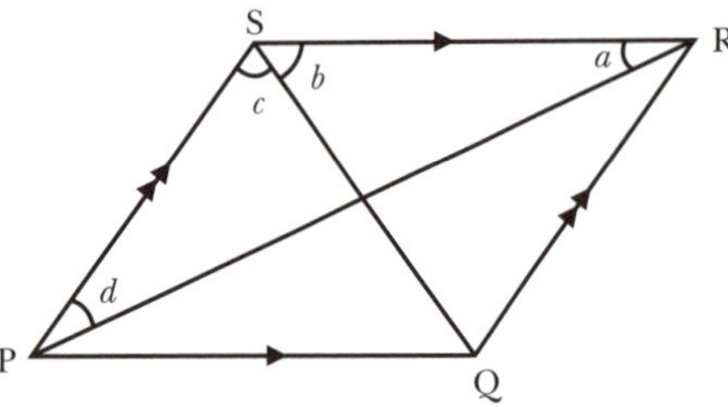

Fig. 3.5

a) $S\hat{R}P = a$; name another angle which is the same size as a.
b) $R\hat{S}Q = b$; name another angle which is the same size as b.
c) $P\hat{S}Q = c$; name another angle which is the same size as c.
d) $S\hat{P}R = d$; name another angle which is the same size as d.

Rhombus

Fig. 3.6

Fig. 3.6 shows a playing card, the ace of diamonds. The shape of the diamond is called a **rhombus**. The rhombus is a quadrilateral which has all four sides equal.

Fig. 3.7 Rhombus

Exercise 3b *(Class activity)*

1 Try to name a few things in your home, class or town which have the shape of a rhombus.
2 How many sides has a rhombus?
3 How many angles has a rhombus?
4 Use the following method to make a rhombus from a sheet of paper.

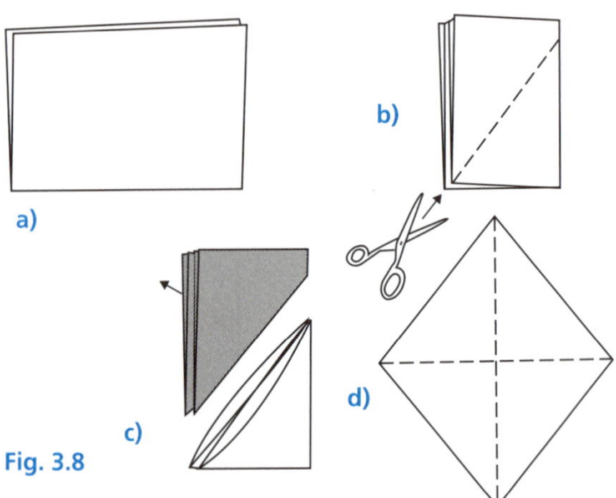

Fig. 3.8

a) Fold a rectangular sheet of paper so that opposite sides meet.
b) Fold the paper again. Draw a line as shown in Fig. 3.8(b).
c) Cut along the line through all four thicknesses of paper.
d) Unfold the triangular part. This gives a rhombus.

5 Use the rhombus you made in question 4 and the rhombus in Fig. 3.7 (or Fig. 3.9) to do the following.
a) Measure the lengths of the sides of the rhombuses. What do you notice?
b) Measure the angles of the rhombuses. What do you notice?
c) Find the total of the four angles of each rhombus.
d) Draw the diagonals of each rhombus.

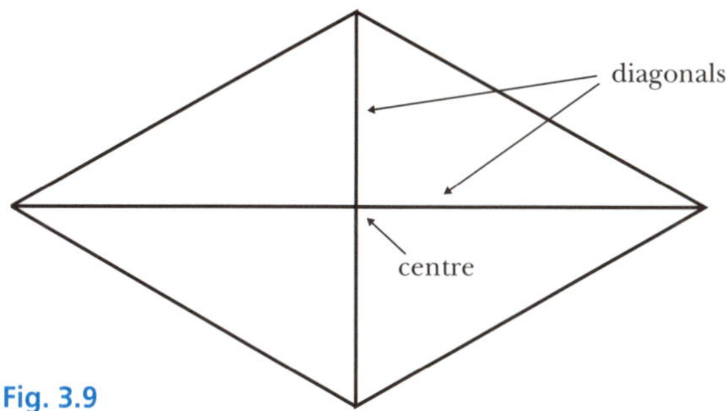

Fig. 3.9

e) Measure the lengths of both diagonals of each rhombus. What do you notice?
f) In each rhombus, measure the distance from the centre to each corner. What do you notice?
g) At the centre, where the diagonals cross, there are four angles. What kind of angles are they?
h) How many lines of symmetry has a rhombus? Check by folding your paper rhombus.
i) Fig. 3.10 shows angles a and b between the short diagonal and the sides. In each rhombus, measure the angles a and b. What do you notice?

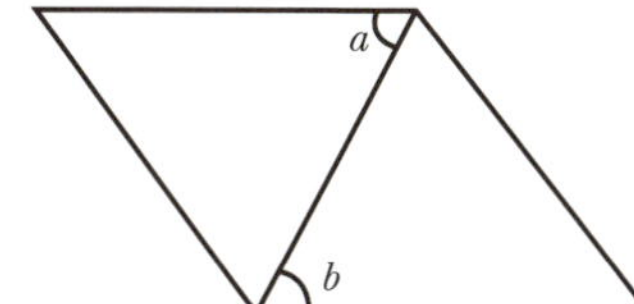

Fig. 3.10

j) Fig. 3.11 shows angles x and y between the long diagonal and the sides. In each rhombus, measure the angles x and y. What do you notice?

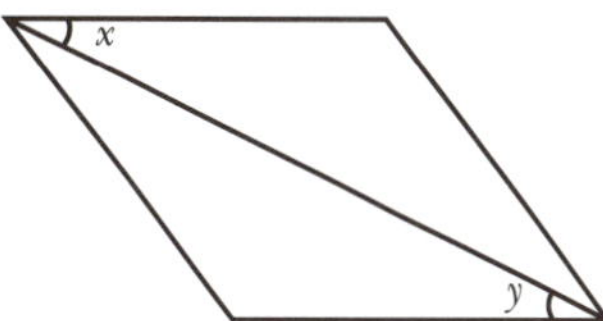

Fig. 3.11

6 Fig. 3.12 shows a rhombus with an angle marked 27°. Copy the figure and fill in the sizes of all the other angles.

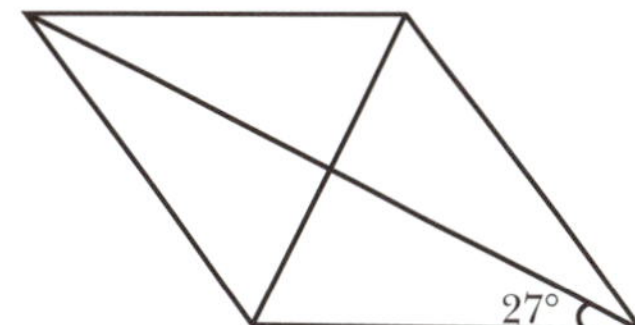

Fig. 3.12

7 Write down three properties shown by both a rhombus and a parallelogram.
8 Write down three differences between a rhombus and a parallelogram.
9 What is the difference between a square and a rhombus? Is a square a rhombus?

Kite

A **kite** is a quadrilateral in which one diagonal is a line of symmetry. Fig. 3.13 shows some kites and their lines of symmetry.

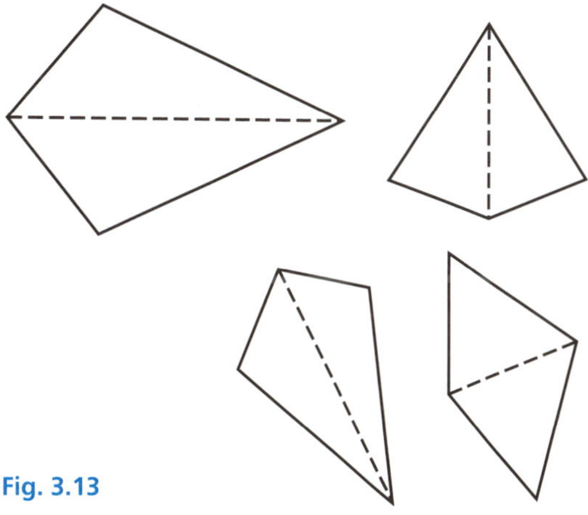
Fig. 3.13

Exercise 3c *(Class activity)*

1 Try to name a few things in your home, class or town which have the shape of a kite.
2 How many sides and angles has a kite?
3 Use the following method to make a kite from a piece of paper.

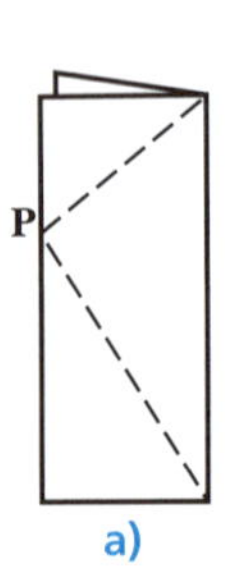

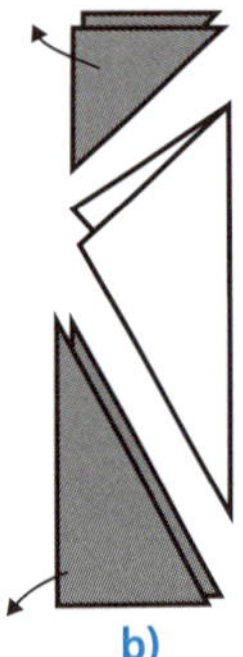

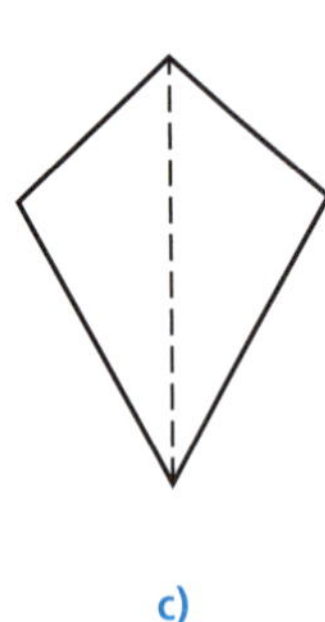

Fig. 3.14

a) Fold a rectangular sheet of paper so that opposite sides meet. Mark a point, P, on the long edge such that it is not at the mid-point of the long edge. Draw lines from the point to each end of the fold.
b) Cut off the four corners along the lines you have drawn.
c) Unfold the remaining part. This gives a kite shape.

4 Use the kite you made in question 3 and those in Fig. 3.13.
a) Measure the lengths of the sides of the kites. What do you notice?
b) Measure the angles of the kites. What do you notice?
c) Find the total of the four angles of each kite.
d) Measure the lengths of both diagonals of each kite. What do you notice?
e) At the centre, where the diagonals cross, there are four angles. What kind of angles are they?
f) How many lines of symmetry has a kite?

5 Fig. 3.15 shows a kite with two angles marked 40° and 112°. Copy the figure and fill in the sizes of the two other angles of the kite.
6 Fig. 3.16 shows a kite with two angles marked 31° and 52°. Copy the figure and fill in the sizes of all the other angles.
7 Write down two properties which a kite and a rhombus both have.
8 Write down three things that are different between a kite and a rhombus. Is a rhombus a kite?

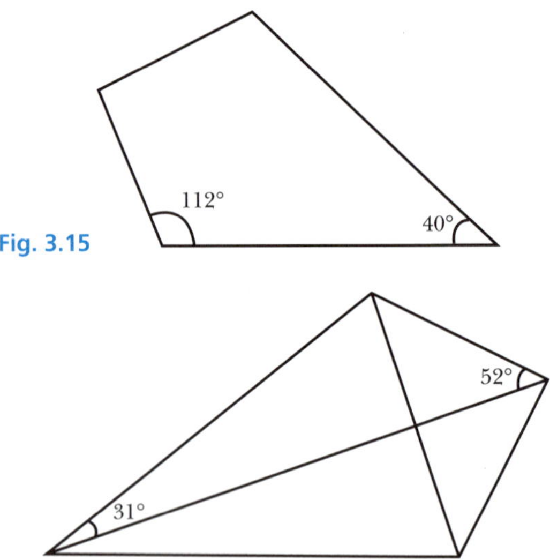

Fig. 3.15

Fig. 3.16

Connections between quadrilaterals

Definitions

Table 3.1 gives sketches and definitions of the common quadrilaterals.

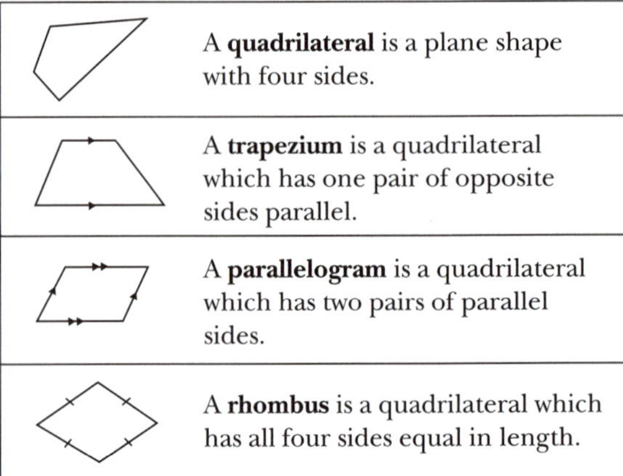

	A **quadrilateral** is a plane shape with four sides.
	A **trapezium** is a quadrilateral which has one pair of opposite sides parallel.
	A **parallelogram** is a quadrilateral which has two pairs of parallel sides.
	A **rhombus** is a quadrilateral which has all four sides equal in length.

Table 3.1

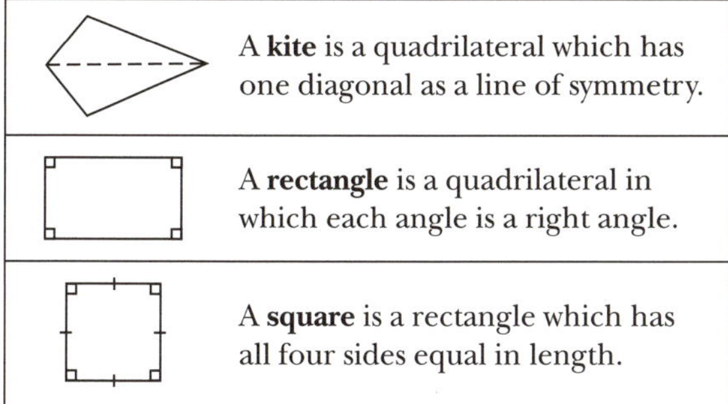

	A **kite** is a quadrilateral which has one diagonal as a line of symmetry.
	A **rectangle** is a quadrilateral in which each angle is a right angle.
	A **square** is a rectangle which has all four sides equal in length.

Table 3.1 (continued)

Connections

The definitions show that squares are special rectangles. Thus all squares are also rectangles. However, some rectangles are not squares.

Parallelograms have two pairs of sides parallel. This is also true of squares, rectangles and rhombuses. Thus squares, rectangles and rhombuses are special parallelograms. However, there are many parallelograms which are not squares, rectangles or rhombuses. Connections between the quadrilaterals are shown in Fig. 3.17.

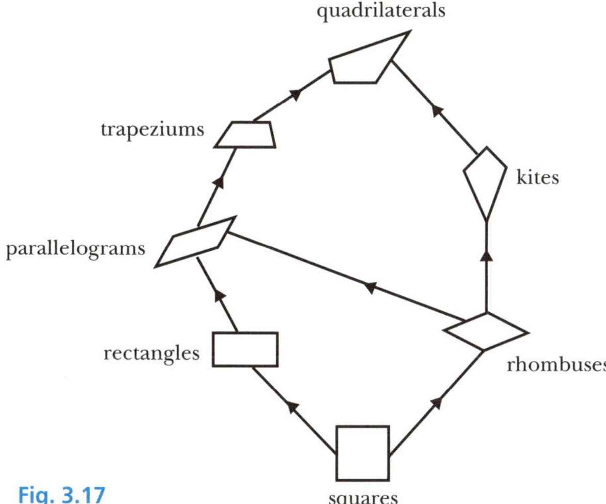

Fig. 3.17

In Fig. 3.17, look at the arrow which goes from rhombuses to kites. Read this as 'all rhombuses are kites'. Read all the arrows in the same way. Notice, following the arrows, all squares are rhombuses and all rhombuses are kites. Thus all squares are kites. There is no arrow which goes from kites to rhombuses. Thus it is not true to say that all kites are rhombuses.

Exercise 3d

1 Name four shapes which are special examples of trapeziums.

2 Name three shapes which are special examples of parallelograms.

3 Name two shapes which are special examples of kites.

4 The diagonals of a kite cross at right angles. Name other shapes for which this is always true.

5 The diagonals of a parallelogram bisect each other. Name other shapes for which this is always true.

6 The diagonals of a square are equal in length. Name another shape for which this is always true.

7 In Fig. 3.17,
   a) touch every shape that is a trapezium;
   b) touch every shape that is a kite.
   c) Which shape(s) did you touch twice?

8 In Fig. 3.17,
   a) touch every shape that is a kite;
   b) touch every shape that is a parallelogram.
   c) Which shape(s) did you touch twice?

9 In Fig. 3.17,
   a) touch every shape that is a rhombus;
   b) touch every shape that is a square.
   c) Which shape(s) did you touch twice?

10 Discuss whether each statement is true or false.
   a) All parallelograms are trapeziums.
   b) All trapeziums are parallelograms.
   c) All squares are kites.
   d) All rhombuses are both parallelograms and kites.
   e) All kites are rhombuses.
   f) Some kites are rhombuses.
   g) Some trapeziums are rectangles.
   h) All parallelograms are squares.
   i) All squares are trapeziums.

Patterns with shapes

Look at the patterns in Fig. 3.18. They all have something in common. They are all made by taking a **basic shape** and repeating it to build up the pattern.

a) brick wall

b) wall pattern

c) cloth pattern

d) print pattern (M. C. Escher's 'Symmetry Drawing E124' © 2000 Cordon Art B. V. – Baarn – Holland. All rights reserved.)

Fig. 3.18

Look at the patterns in Fig. 3.19.

a)

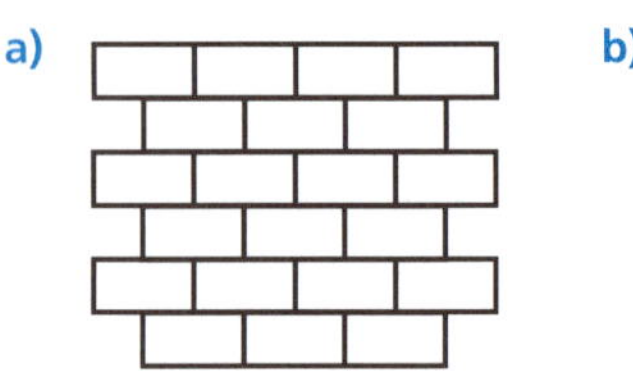

b)

c)

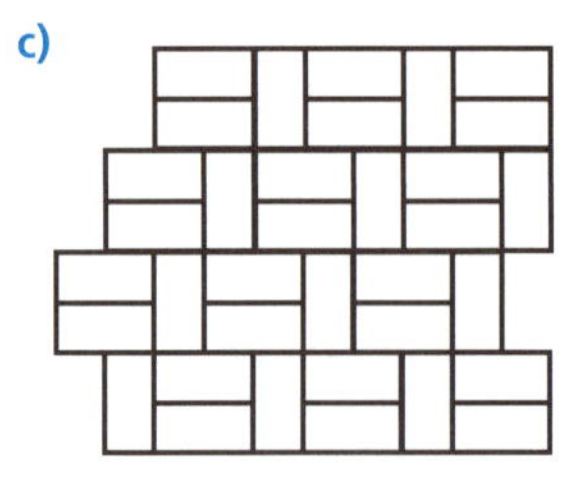

d)

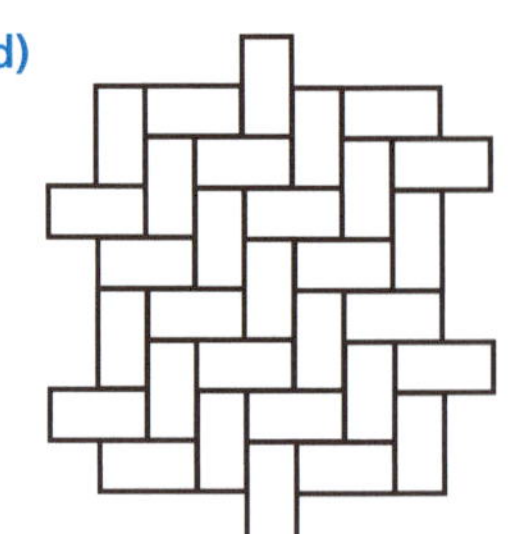

Fig. 3.19

The basic shape which makes each pattern is a 2×1 rectangle. The patterns are different because the rectangles have been arranged in different ways.

Exercise 3e

You will need graph paper, a ruler and a pencil for this exercise.

1 Copy patterns a), b) and c) of Fig. 3.19 on to graph paper. Make each rectangle 2 cm by 1 cm. Draw enough rectangles so that each pattern is at least 10 cm wide and 8 cm long.

2 Copy the patterns of Fig. 3.20 on to graph paper. Extend each pattern by repeating the sequence of basic shapes.

a)

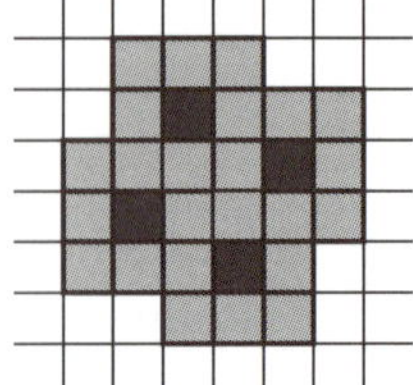

b)

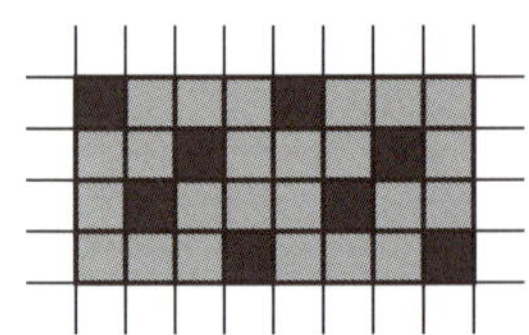

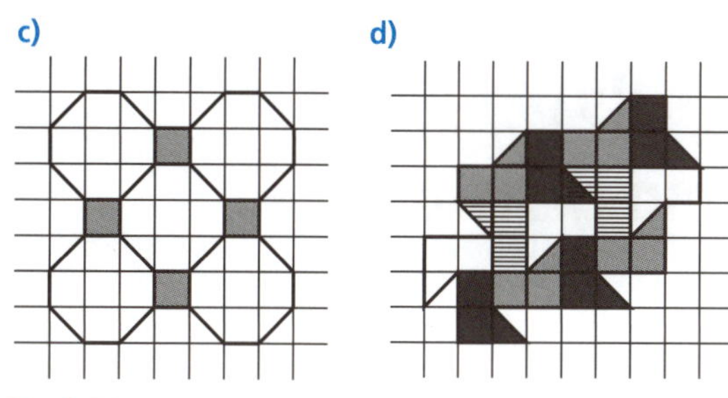

Fig. 3.20

Chapter summary

1. *Quadrilateral* means four-sided. Table 3.1 gives sketches and definitions of the common quadrilaterals.
2. Plane shapes can be repeated to give geometric patterns (see Figs 3.18, 3.19 and 3.20).

4 Directed numbers (2) Multiplication and division

Adding and subtracting directed numbers (revision)

Numbers can be shown on a number line which extends above and below zero. This gives positive and negative numbers. See Fig. 4.1.

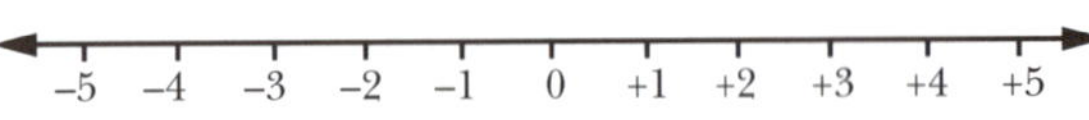

Fig. 4.1

The signs + and – show the directions from 0. Positive and negative numbers are called **directed numbers**.

You learned how to add and subtract directed numbers in Book 1.

To add a positive number, move to the right on the number line.

Example 1

$(+1) + (+3) = +4$
$(-3) + (+5) = +2$

To subtract a positive number, move to the left on the number line.

Example 2

$(+5) - (+3) = +2$
$(+3) - (+7) = -4$
$(-1) - (+2) = -3$

To add a negative number, move to the left on the number line. This is equivalent to subtracting a positive number of the same value.

Example 3

$(+1) + (-4) = (+1) - (+4) = -3$
$(-3) + (-2) = (-3) - (+2) = -5$
$(+8) + (-2) = (+8) - (+2) = +6$

To subtract a negative number, move to the right on the number line. This is equivalent to adding a positive number of the same value.

Example 4

$(+1) - (-4) = (+1) + (+4) = +5$
$(-5) - (-8) = (-5) + (+8) = +3$
$(-3) - (-2) = (-3) + (+2) = -1$

Exercise 4a *(Oral revision)*

Simplify the following.

1 $(+1) + (+8)$
2 $(-3) + (+9)$
3 $0 + (+11)$
4 $(+11) - (+6)$
5 $(+6) - (+10)$
6 $(-3) - (+7)$
7 $(+8) + (-5)$
8 $(-3) + 0$
9 $(-2) + (-4)$
10 $(+7) - (-5)$
11 $0 - (-10)$
12 $(-3) - (-1)$
13 $(+4) + (+4) + (+4)$
14 $(-6) + (-6) + (-6)$
15 $(-6) + (+6) + 0$
16 $12 - (+3) - 8$
17 $8 - (+8) + 8$
18 $3 - 5 - 7$
19 $(-7) + (+6) + (+1)$
20 $10 + (-4) + (-6)$
21 $(-5) + (-5) + (-5)$
22 $6 - (-3) - (-4)$
23 $-8 - (-12) + (-2)$
24 $-3 + (-3) - (-11)$

If you had difficulty with Exercise 4a, revise Chapter 12 in Book 1.

Multiplication of directed numbers

Positive multipliers

Multiplication is a short way of writing repeated additions. For example,

$$\begin{aligned} 3 \times 4 &= 3 \text{ lots of } 4 \\ &= 4 + 4 + 4 \\ &= 12 \end{aligned}$$

With directed numbers,

$$\begin{aligned} (+4) + (+4) + (+4) &= 3 \text{ lots of } (+4) \\ &= 3 \times (+4) \end{aligned}$$

The multiplier is 3. It is positive. Thus,

$$(+3) \times (+4) = (+4) + (+4) + (+4) = +12$$
$$(+3) \times (+4) = +12$$

Fig. 4.2 shows $1 \times (+4)$ and $(+3) \times (+4)$ as movements on the number line. The movements are in the same direction from 0.

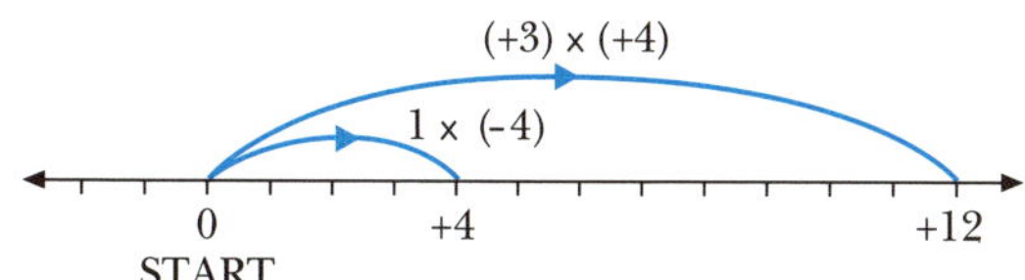

Fig. 4.2

Similarly,

$$\begin{aligned} (-2) + (-2) + (-2) + (-2) + (-2) \\ &= 5 \text{ lots of } (-2) \\ &= 5 \times (-2) \end{aligned}$$

The multiplier is 5. It is positive. Thus,

$$(+5) \times (-2) = (-2) + (-2) + (-2) + (-2) + (-2) = -10$$
$$(+5) \times (-2) = -10$$

Fig. 4.3 shows $1 \times (-2)$ and $(+5) \times (-2)$ as movements on the number line. The movements are in the same direction from 0.

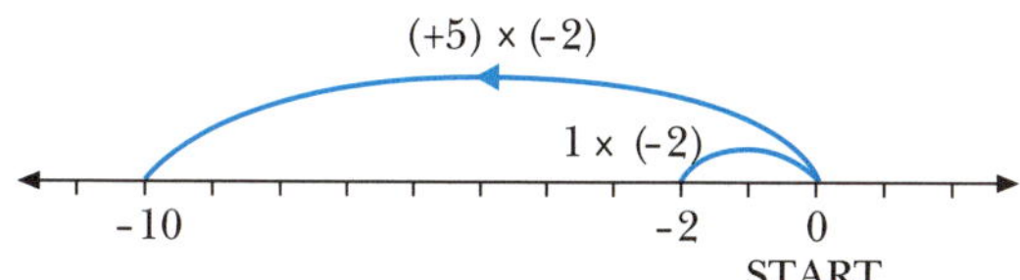

Fig. 4.3

In general: $(+a) \times (+b) = +(a \times b)$
$(+a) \times (-b) = -(a \times b)$

Example 5

Simplify the following.

a) $(+9) \times (+4)$ *b)* $(+17) \times (-3)$
c) $(+\frac{1}{2}) \times (+\frac{1}{4})$ *d)* $3 \times (-1{\cdot}2)$

a) $(+9) \times (+4) = +(9 \times 4) = +36$
b) $(+17) \times (-3) = -(17 \times 3) = -51$
c) $(+\frac{1}{2}) \times (+\frac{1}{4}) = +(\frac{1}{2} \times \frac{1}{4}) = +\frac{1}{8}$
d) $3 \times (-1{\cdot}2) = (+3) \times (-1{\cdot}2)$
$= -(3 \times 1{\cdot}2) = -3{\cdot}6$

Exercise 4b

1 Continue the following number patterns as far as the seventh term.

a) $+15, +10, +5, 0, -5, \ldots$
b) $+6, +4, +2, 0, \ldots$
c) $+30, +20, +10, \ldots$

2 Complete the following.

a) $(+5) \times (+3) = \ldots$
$(+5) \times (+2) = \ldots$
$(+5) \times (+1) = \ldots$
$(+5) \times 0 = \ldots$
$(+5) \times (-1) = \ldots$
$(+5) \times (-2) = \ldots$
$(+5) \times (-3) = \ldots$

b) $(+2) \times (+3) = \ldots$
$(+2) \times (+2) = \ldots$
$(+2) \times (+1) = \ldots$
$(+2) \times 0 = \ldots$
$(+2) \times (-1) = \ldots$
$(+2) \times (-2) = \ldots$
$(+2) \times (-3) = \ldots$

c) $(+10) \times (+3) = \ldots$
$(+10) \times (+2) = \ldots$
$(+10) \times (+1) = \ldots$
$(+10) \times 0 = \ldots$
$(+10) \times (-1) = \ldots$
$(+10) \times (-2) = \ldots$
$(+10) \times (-3) = \ldots$

3 Simplify the following.

a) $(+6) \times (+3)$ **b)** $(+5) \times (+10)$
c) $(+5) \times (-8)$ **d)** $(+4) \times (-7)$
e) $(+17) \times (+2)$ **f)** $(+20) \times (+6)$
g) $(+10) \times (-10)$ **h)** $(+15) \times (-4)$
i) $(+3) \times (+2\frac{1}{2})$ **j)** $(+1\frac{1}{4}) \times (+\frac{1}{5})$
k) $(+2) \times (-3\frac{1}{2})$ **l)** $(+1) \times (-\frac{2}{3})$
m) $(+1{\cdot}5) \times (+2)$ **n)** $(+5{\cdot}1) \times (+3)$
o) $(+4) \times (-1{\cdot}2)$ **p)** $(+3{\cdot}2) \times (-5)$
q) $8 \times (+7)$ **r)** $8 \times (-7)$
s) $7 \times (+8)$ **t)** $7 \times (-8)$

Negative multipliers

Work through Exercise 4c very carefully and discuss with your teacher.

Exercise 4c *(Oral)*

1 Find the next four terms in each of the following patterns.

a) $+15, +12, +9, +6, \ldots, \ldots, \ldots, \ldots$
b) $(+5) \times (+3), (+4) \times (+3), (+3) \times (+3), (+2) \times (+3), \ldots, \ldots, \ldots, \ldots$

c) $(+5) \times (+3) = +15$
$(+4) \times (+3) = +12$
$(+3) \times (+3) = +9$
$(+2) \times (+3) = +6$
$\ldots \times \ldots = \ldots$
$\ldots \times \ldots = \ldots$
$\ldots \times \ldots = \ldots$
$\ldots \times \ldots = \ldots$

2 Find the next four terms in each of the following patterns.

a) $-15, -12, -9, -6, \ldots, \ldots, \ldots, \ldots$

b) $(+5) \times (-3), (+4) \times (-3), (+3) \times (-3), (+2) \times (-3), \ldots, \ldots, \ldots, \ldots$

c) $(+5) \times (-3) = -15$
$(+4) \times (-3) = -12$
$(+3) \times (-3) = -9$
$(+2) \times (-3) = -6$
$\ldots \times \ldots = \ldots$
$\ldots \times \ldots = \ldots$
$\ldots \times \ldots = \ldots$
$\ldots \times \ldots = \ldots$

Look at your results in question 1 of Exercise 4c. The last row of 1(c) is:

$(-2) \times (+3) = -6.$

(-2) is the multiplier. It is negative.
The number being multiplied, $(+3)$, is positive.

The result is negative. This result may not be surprising. We already know that

$(+3) \times (-2) = -6.$

Thus we would expect that

$(-2) \times (+3) = -6.$

Fig. 4.4 shows $1 \times (+3)$ and $(-2) \times (+3)$ as movements on the number line. The movements are in opposite directions from 0.

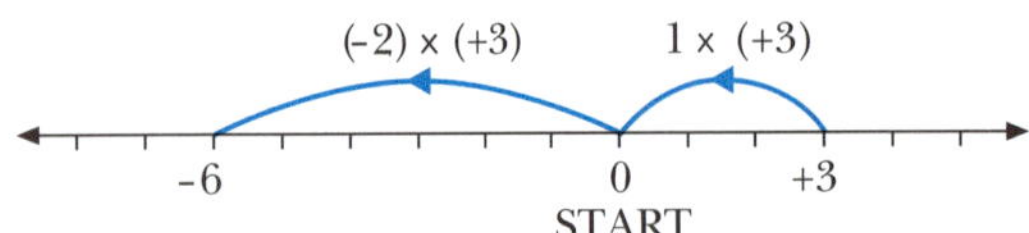

Fig. 4.4

Look at your results in question 2 of Exercise 4c. The last row of 2(c) is:

$(-2) \times (-3) = +6$

(-2) is the multiplier. It is negative.

The number being multiplied, (-3), is also negative.

The result is *positive.* This result is quite surprising. However, on the number line the movements are again in opposite directions from 0. Fig. 4.5 shows $1 \times (-3)$ and $(-2) \times (-3)$ as movements on the number line.

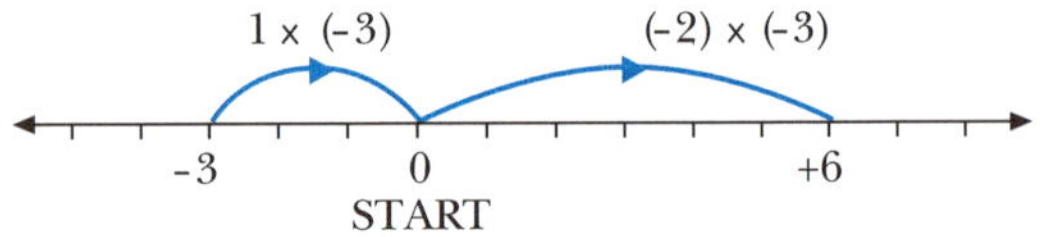

Fig. 4.5

In general: $(-a) \times (+b) = -(a \times b)$
$(-a) \times (-b) = +(a \times b)$

Example 6

Simplify the following.

a) $(-7) \times (+4)$ *b)* $(-5) \times (-18)$
c) $(-\frac{1}{3}) \times (+\frac{2}{5})$ *d)* $(-4) \times (-2{\cdot}2)$

a) $(-7) \times (+4) = -(7 \times 4) = -28$
b) $(-5) \times (-18) = +(5 \times 18) = +90$
c) $(-\frac{1}{3}) \times (+\frac{2}{5}) = -(\frac{1}{3} \times \frac{2}{5}) = -\frac{2}{15}$
d) $(-4) \times (-2{\cdot}2) = +(4 \times 2{\cdot}2) = +8{\cdot}8$

Exercise 4d

1 Continue the following number patterns as far as the seventh term.

a) $+15, +10, +5, 0, \ldots$

b) $-6, -4, -2, \ldots$

c) $-30, -20, -10, \ldots$

2 Complete the following.

a) $(+3) \times (+5) = \ldots$
$(+2) \times (+5) = \ldots$
$(+1) \times (+5) = \ldots$
$0 \times (+5) = \ldots$
$(-1) \times (+5) = \ldots$
$(-2) \times (+5) = \ldots$
$(-3) \times (+5) = \ldots$

b) $(+3) \times (-2) = \ldots$
$(+2) \times (-2) = \ldots$
$(+1) \times (-2) = \ldots$
$0 \times (-2) = \ldots$
$(-1) \times (-2) = \ldots$
$(-2) \times (-2) = \ldots$
$(-3) \times (-2) = \ldots$

c) $(+3) \times (-10) = \ldots$
$(+2) \times (-10) = \ldots$
$(+1) \times (-10) = \ldots$
$0 \times (-10) = \ldots$
$(-1) \times (-10) = \ldots$
$(-2) \times (-10) = \ldots$
$(-3) \times (-10) = \ldots$

3 Simplify the following.

a) $(-6) \times (+3)$ **b)** $(+5) \times (+10)$
c) $(-5) \times (-8)$ **d)** $(-4) \times (-7)$
e) $(-16) \times (+2)$ **f)** $(-20) \times (+4)$
g) $(-8) \times (-8)$ **h)** $(-13) \times (-5)$
i) $(-2) \times (+1\frac{1}{2})$ **j)** $(-1\frac{1}{3}) \times (+1)$
k) $(-\frac{1}{3}) \times (-3)$ **l)** $(-4) \times (-\frac{1}{2})$
m) $(-5) \times (+1{\cdot}2)$ **n)** $(-2{\cdot}4) \times (+3)$
o) $(-0{\cdot}3) \times (-9)$ **p)** $(-6) \times (-3{\cdot}1)$
q) -8×6 **r)** $8 \times (-6)$
s) $-8 \times (-6)$ **t)** $-6 \times (-8)$

Division with directed numbers

When directed numbers are multiplied together,

two **like** signs give a **positive** result;
two **unlike** signs give a **negative** result.

For example,

$$(+3) \times (+8) = +24$$
$$(-3) \times (-8) = +24$$
$$(+3) \times (-8) = -24$$
$$(-3) \times (+8) = -24$$

The same rule is true for division. For example,

$$(+24) \div (+3) = (+8)$$
$$(-24) \div (-3) = (+8)$$
$$(+24) \div (-3) = (-8)$$
$$(-24) \div (+3) = (-8)$$

Example 7

Divide a) -36 *by* 9, *b)* -4 *by* -12.

a) $-36 \div 9 = \dfrac{-36}{+9} = -\left(\dfrac{36}{9}\right) = -4$

b) $-4 \div (-12) = \dfrac{-4}{-12} = +\left(\dfrac{4}{12}\right) = +\frac{1}{3}$

Example 8

Simplify $\dfrac{(-6) \times (-5)}{-10}$.

$$\frac{(-6) \times (-5)}{-10} = \frac{+30}{-10} = -\left(\frac{30}{10}\right) = -3$$

Exercise 4e

1 Divide the following.

a) -18 by 3 **b)** -18 by -3
c) 18 by -3 **d)** 36 by $+4$
e) -20 by -4 **f)** -8 by -1
g) -22 by -11 **h)** 24 by -8
i) 33 by -3 **j)** -3 by -18
k) -6 by 12 **l)** -5 by -15

2 Simplify the following.

a) $\dfrac{(-2) \times (+12)}{-6}$ **b)** $\dfrac{(-6) \times (-10)}{-4}$

c) $\dfrac{36}{(-2) \times (-9)}$ **d)** $\dfrac{(-3) \times (-15)}{9}$

e) $\dfrac{9 \times 20}{-3}$ **f)** $\dfrac{-28 \times (-3)}{21}$

g) $\dfrac{30}{(-5) \times (-4)}$ **h)** $\dfrac{(-1) \times (-5)}{-10}$

i) $\dfrac{4 \times (-3)}{-24}$

Exercise 4f

1 Write down the next four terms of the following patterns.

a) $+6, +4, +2, 0, -2, \ldots, \ldots, \ldots, \ldots$

b) $2 \times (+3), 2 \times (+2), 2 \times (+1), 2 \times 0,$
$2 \times (-1), \ldots, \ldots, \ldots, \ldots$

c)
$2 \times (+3) = +6$
$2 \times (+2) = +4$
$2 \times (+1) = +2$
$2 \times 0 = 0$
$2 \times (-1) = -2$
$\ldots \times \ldots = \ldots$
$\ldots \times \ldots = \ldots$
$\ldots \times \ldots = \ldots$
$\ldots \times \ldots = \ldots$

d) $+16, +12, +8, +4, 0, \ldots, \ldots, \ldots, \ldots$

e) $(+4) \times 4, (+3) \times 4, (+2) \times 4, (+1) \times 4,$
$0 \times 4, \ldots, \ldots, \ldots, \ldots$

f)
$(+4) \times 4 = +16$
$(+3) \times 4 = +12$
$(+2) \times 4 = +8$
$(+1) \times 4 = +4$
$0 \times 4 = 0$
$\ldots \times \ldots = \ldots$
$\ldots \times \ldots = \ldots$
$\ldots \times \ldots = \ldots$
$\ldots \times \ldots = \ldots$

g) $-15, -10, -5, 0, +5, \ldots, \ldots, \ldots, \ldots$

h) $(+3) \times (-5), (+2) \times (-5), (+1) \times (-5),$
$0 \times (-5), (-1) \times (-5), \ldots, \ldots, \ldots, \ldots$

i) $(+3) \times (-5) = -15$
$(+2) \times (-5) = -10$
$(+1) \times (-5) = -5$
$0 \times (-5) = 0$
$(-1) \times (-5) = +5$
$\ldots \times \ldots = \ldots$
$\ldots \times \ldots = \ldots$
$\ldots \times \ldots = \ldots$
$\ldots \times \ldots = \ldots$

2 Copy and complete the multiplication table in Fig. 4.6.

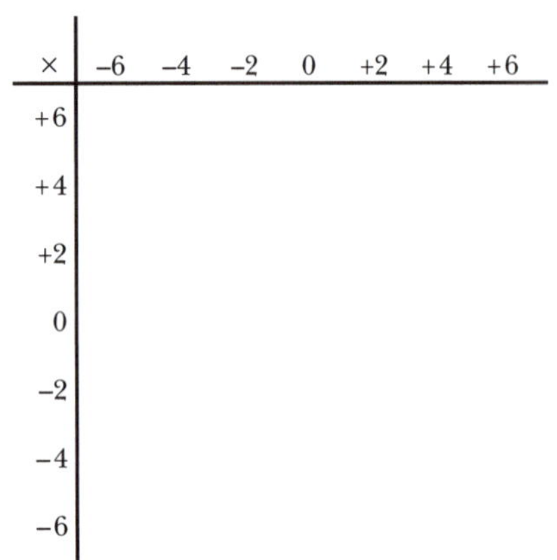

Fig. 4.6

3 Simplify the following.
a) $(-3) \times 4$ **b)** $(-4) \times (-7)$
c) $5 \times (-3)$ **d)** $(-6) \times (-1)$
e) $24 \times (-2)$ **f)** $(-8) \times (-7)$
g) $(-1) \times (-1)$ **h)** $0 \times (-3)$
i) $(-1) \times 1$

4 The bottom of a water well is -6 metres from ground level. An oil well is 15 times deeper. Find the distance of the bottom of the oil well from ground level.

5 What must be multiplied by:
a) 5 to make 40? **b)** 1 to make -7?
c) -2 to make 12? **d)** -3 to make -30?
e) 4 to make -36? **f)** -9 to make 27?

6 Simplify the following.
a) $(+20) \div (-10)$ **b)** $(-26) \div (+2)$
c) $(-6) \div (-6)$ **d)** $(+18) \div (-3)$
e) $(-27) \div (+3)$ **f)** $(+30) \div (+15)$
g) $\frac{-14}{-7}$ **h)** $\frac{+50}{-25}$ **i)** $\frac{-60}{+12}$

7 What must be divided by:
a) 6 to make 2? **b)** 6 to make -2?
c) -3 to make 5? **d)** 8 to make -3?
e) -2 to make 11? **f)** -3 to make 30?

8 Simplify the following.
a) $(-7) \times (-3) \times (-2)$
b) $(-1) \times (-1) \times (-1)$
c) $\frac{(-8) \times (+5)}{-10}$ **d)** $\frac{+60}{(-3) \times (-5)}$
e) $(-3) \times (-2)^2$ **f)** $\frac{(-2) \times (-12)}{(+6)^2}$

9 Simplify the following.
a) $(-1\frac{1}{2}) \times 3\frac{2}{3}$ **b)** $(-2{\cdot}8) \times (-0{\cdot}2)$
c) $\frac{4}{9}$ of $(-2\frac{4}{7})$ **d)** $7 \times (-6{\cdot}2)$

10 Simplify the following.
a) $1\frac{3}{4} \div (-2\frac{1}{4})$ **b)** $(-4{\cdot}8) \div (-6)$
c) $-7\frac{1}{5} \div (-9\frac{3}{5})$ **d)** $-8{\cdot}4 \div 7$

Chapter summary

① *Directed numbers* can be multiplied and divided.

② When *two numbers of the same sign* are multiplied or divided, the result is positive.

③ When *two numbers of different signs* are multiplied or divided, the result is negative.

5 Inverse and identity

Additive inverse

If we add 0 (zero) to any number, the result is the same as the given number. For example,

$3 + 0 = 3, \qquad 0 + 8 = 8.$

We say that **0 is the identity for addition.**

If the sum of two numbers is 0, we say that each number is the **additive inverse** of the other.

For example, $(+3) + (-3) = 0$.
(-3) is the additive inverse of $(+3)$.
$(+3)$ is the additive inverse of (-3).
$(-8) + (+8) = 0$.
$(+8)$ is the additive inverse of (-8).
(-8) is the additive inverse of $(+8)$.

Example 1

State the additive inverses of

a) -19 *b)* $0{\cdot}32$ *c)* $-\frac{7}{8}$
d) 6×10^7 *e)* $-3{\cdot}1 \times 10^{-5}$

Given number	*Additive inverse*
a) -19	$+19$
b) $0{\cdot}32$	$-0{\cdot}32$
c) $-\frac{7}{8}$	$+\frac{7}{8}$
d) 6×10^7	-6×10^7
e) $-3{\cdot}1 \times 10^{-5}$	$+3{\cdot}1 \times 10^{-5}$

In parts (d) and (e) of Example 1, remember that the power of 10 in a number in standard form places the decimal point. It is not significant in deciding whether the number is positive or negative.

Exercise 5a (Oral)

State the additive inverses of the following.

1 $+2$	**2** -5	**3** $+7$
4 -6	**5** $+13$	**6** -13
7 $+117$	**8** -312	**9** $+1$
10 $-\frac{1}{4}$	**11** $+0{\cdot}27$	**12** 0
13 $+0{\cdot}77$	**14** $-1\,000$	**15** $-\frac{11}{12}$
16 $-7{\cdot}7$	**17** $+5\frac{3}{4}$	**18** $+0{\cdot}3$
19 $+5 \times 10^2$	**20** $+9{\cdot}7 \times 10^6$	**21** -3×10^{-4}
22 $-2{\cdot}1 \times 10^3$	**23** $+7{\cdot}9 \times 10^{-2}$	**24** $+\pi$

Additive inverses can be used when solving equations.

Example 2

Solve the following equations.

a) $x + 7 = 2$ *b)* $a - 8 = 4$ *c)* $y - 2 = -9$

a) $x + 7 = 2$ is the same as $x + (+7) = 2$
Add (-7) to both sides.

$$x + (+7) + (-7) = 2 + (-7)$$
$$x + 0 = 2 - 7$$
$$x = -5$$

b) $a - 8 = 4$ is the same as $a + (-8) = 4$
Add $(+8)$ to both sides.

$$a + (-8) + (+8) = 4 + (+8)$$
$$a + 0 = 4 + 8$$
$$a = 12$$

c) $y - 2 = -9$ is the same as $y + (-2) = -9$
Add $(+2)$ to both sides.

$$y + (-2) + (+2) = -9 + (+2)$$
$$y + 0 = -9 + 2$$
$$y = -7$$

When solving equations, you may prefer to use ordinary addition and subtraction as shown in Chapter 19 of Book 1.

Exercise 5b (Oral or written)

Solve the following equations.

1 $a + 8 = 15$	**2** $x + 9 = 5$	**3** $x + 1 = 0$
4 $y - 1 = 4$	**5** $m - 3 = 7$	**6** $n - 12 = 12$
7 $d + 3 = -4$	**8** $x - 7 = -6$	**9** $a - 3 = -10$
10 $c - 9 = -9$	**11** $h + 8 = 8$	**12** $k - 5 = -6$
13 $b - 10 = 0$	**14** $c + 2 = -22$	**15** $d - 4 = -4$
16 $p + 8 = -7$	**17** $q - 13 = 0$	**18** $r + 18 = 7$
19 $2 + x = 8$	**20** $-7 + y = 11$	**21** $12 + z = 5$
22 $6 - a = 1$	**23** $8 - b = 10$	**24** $-5 - c = 14$

Multiplicative inverse

If we multiply any number by 1 the result is the same as the given number. For example,

$1 \times 9 = 9, \qquad -5 \times 1 = -5, \qquad 1 \times \frac{3}{4} = \frac{3}{4}.$

We say that **1 is the identity for multiplication**. If the product of two numbers is 1, we say that each number is the **multiplicative inverse** of the other. For example,

$9 \times \frac{1}{9} = 1$

$\frac{1}{9}$ is the multiplicative inverse of 9.
9 is the multiplicative inverse of $\frac{1}{9}$.

$(-5) \times (-\frac{1}{5}) = 1$

$-\frac{1}{5}$ is the multiplicative inverse of -5.
-5 is the multiplicative inverse of $-\frac{1}{5}$.

$\frac{3}{4} \times \frac{4}{3} = 1$

$\frac{4}{3}$ is the multiplicative inverse of $\frac{3}{4}$.

$\frac{3}{4}$ is the multiplicative inverse of $\frac{4}{3}$.

You have already used multiplicative inverses. In Book 1 you used **reciprocals**. The reciprocal of a fraction is that fraction turned upside down. The reciprocal of $\frac{2}{3}$ is $\frac{3}{2}$. Thus the multiplicative inverse of a number is the same as its reciprocal. $\frac{1}{8}$ is the reciprocal of $\frac{8}{1}$ or 8. $\frac{1}{8}$ is the multiplicative inverse of 8.

Example 3

Find the multiplicative inverses of the following.

a) $-\frac{3}{2}$ *b)* $0{\cdot}3$ *c)* $2\frac{1}{2}$ *d)* n *e)* $\frac{a}{2b}$

a) Reciprocal of $-\frac{3}{2} = -\frac{2}{3}$.
$-\frac{2}{3}$ is the multiplicative inverse of $-\frac{3}{2}$.
Check: $(-\frac{3}{2}) \times (-\frac{2}{3}) = +(\frac{3}{2} \times \frac{2}{3}) = 1$.

b) $0{\cdot}3 = \frac{3}{10}$
Reciprocal of $\frac{3}{10} = \frac{10}{3}$.
$\frac{10}{3}$ (or $3\frac{1}{3}$) is the multiplicative inverse of $0{\cdot}3$.
Check: $0{\cdot}3 \times 3\frac{1}{3} = \frac{3}{10} \times \frac{10}{3} = 1$.

c) $2\frac{1}{2} = \frac{5}{2}$
$\frac{2}{5}$ is the multiplicative inverse of $2\frac{1}{2}$.
The check is left as an exercise.

d) $\frac{1}{n}$ is the multiplicative inverse of n.

$n \times \frac{1}{n} = 1$

e) Reciprocal of $\frac{a}{2b} = \frac{2b}{a}$.

$\frac{2b}{a}$ is the multiplicative inverse of $\frac{a}{2b}$.

Exercise 5c

Find the multiplicative inverses of the following.

1 3	**2** 8	**3** $\frac{1}{7}$
4 $\frac{1}{6}$	**5** $\frac{2}{3}$	**6** $\frac{5}{3}$
7 $\frac{9}{10}$	**8** $\frac{8}{7}$	**9** -2
10 $-\frac{1}{4}$	**11** -1	**12** $-\frac{5}{6}$
13 $0{\cdot}8$	**14** $0{\cdot}27$	**15** $-0{\cdot}7$
16 $-0{\cdot}1$	**17** a	**18** $\frac{1}{t}$
19 $\frac{p}{q}$	**20** 2π	**21** $\frac{16}{\pi}$
22 $\frac{2a}{b}$	**23** $\frac{1}{2r}$	**24** $5x$

Multiplicative inverses can be used when solving equations.

Example 4

Solve $-5x = 20$.

Method I:
Notice that -5 is multiplying x. Multiply both sides by the multiplicative inverse of -5. Multiply both sides by $-\frac{1}{5}$.

$$(-\tfrac{1}{5}) \times (-5) \times x = (-\tfrac{1}{5}) \times (+20)$$
$$1 \times x = -(\tfrac{1}{5} \times 20)$$
$$x = -4$$

Method II:
Notice that multiplying by $-\frac{1}{5}$ is equivalent to dividing by -5. The example can be solved as follows.

$$-5x = 20$$

Divide both sides by -5.

$$\frac{(-5) \times x}{(-5)} = \frac{+20}{-5}$$
$$1 \times x = -(\tfrac{20}{5})$$
$$x = -4$$

The second method is usually quicker.

Exercise 5d

Solve the following equations.

1 $4x = 28$ **2** $3x = 18$ **3** $5y = 40$

4 $-2r = 18$ **5** $-4d = 20$ **6** $-6x = 12$
7 $5s = 1\frac{1}{4}$ **8** $9m = 13\frac{1}{2}$ **9** $7x = 4\frac{2}{3}$
10 $-3t = 2\frac{1}{4}$ **11** $-8n = 5\frac{5}{7}$ **12** $-2x = 7$
13 $-5a = -15$ **14** $-6c = -36$ **15** $-9x = 9$
16 $-9y = -9$ **17** $-36 = 9a$ **18** $-22 = -2b$

Example 5

Solve the following equations.

a) $\frac{a}{5} = \frac{4}{15}$ *b)* $\frac{4y}{7} = 2\frac{2}{3}$ *c)* $9 = -1\frac{2}{7}c$

a) $\frac{a}{5} = \frac{4}{15}$

$\frac{a}{5}$ is the same as $\frac{1}{5}a$

$$\frac{1}{5}a = \frac{4}{15}$$

Multiply both sides by $\frac{5}{1}$.

$$\frac{5}{1} \times \frac{1}{5} \times a = \frac{4}{15} \times \frac{5}{1}$$
$$1 \times a = \frac{4 \times 5}{15}$$
$$a = \frac{4}{3} = 1\frac{1}{3}$$

b) $\frac{4y}{7} = 2\frac{2}{3}$

Change mixed numbers to common fractions.

$$\frac{4}{7} \times y = \frac{8}{3}$$

Multiply both sides by $\frac{7}{4}$.

$$\frac{7}{4} \times \frac{4}{7} \times y = \frac{8}{3} \times \frac{7}{4}$$
$$1 \times y = \frac{8 \times 7}{3 \times 4}$$
$$y = \frac{14}{3} = 4\frac{2}{3}$$

c) $9 = -1\frac{2}{7}c$

Change mixed numbers to common fractions.

$$9 = -\frac{9}{7}c$$

Multiply both sides by $-\frac{7}{9}$.

$$-\frac{7}{9} \times 9 = \left(-\frac{7}{9}\right) \times \left(-\frac{9}{7}\right) \times c$$
$$-\left(\frac{7 \times 9}{9}\right) = 1 \times c$$
$$-7 = c$$
$$c = -7$$

Exercise 5e

Solve the following equations.

1 $\frac{1}{4}x = 9$ **2** $\frac{1}{3}a = 2$ **3** $\frac{1}{9}y = 1$

4 $\frac{1}{5}r = \frac{7}{30}$ **5** $\frac{m}{2} = \frac{3}{4}$ **6** $\frac{t}{6} = \frac{7}{12}$

7 $\frac{z}{8} = 2\frac{1}{2}$ **8** $\frac{x}{4} = \frac{3}{5}$ **9** $\frac{a}{5} = 1\frac{1}{2}$

10 $\frac{c}{10} = \frac{1}{7}$ **11** $\frac{e}{7} = \frac{1}{10}$ **12** $\frac{x}{3} = \frac{1}{3}$

13 $\frac{3}{4}x = \frac{21}{32}$ **14** $\frac{5a}{2} = \frac{15}{16}$ **15** $\frac{7x}{12} = \frac{35}{48}$

16 $\frac{4s}{5} = 1\frac{1}{3}$ **17** $\frac{9}{10}r = 3\frac{3}{5}$ **18** $\frac{11x}{6} = 16\frac{1}{2}$

19 $1\frac{1}{2}x = 5\frac{1}{4}$ **20** $1\frac{2}{3}x = 4\frac{1}{6}$ **21** $2\frac{3}{5}a = 26$

22 $-\frac{1}{3}x = 6$ **23** $-\frac{a}{2} = -7$ **24** $\frac{n}{5} = -4$

25 $-\frac{m}{4} = 1\frac{3}{4}$ **26** $\frac{t}{10} = -\frac{3}{5}$ **27** $-\frac{s}{7} = -\frac{1}{8}$

28 $-\frac{3x}{5} = -\frac{9}{10}$ **29** $-\frac{8}{9}k = \frac{2}{3}$ **30** $-3\frac{1}{2}x = 42$

Inverse operations

Do the following.

1 Stand up. Sit down.
2 Add 3 to 15. Subtract 3 from the result.
3 Multiply 7 by 2. Divide the result by 2.

In each case you should end where you start. When this happens, we say that the two actions are **inverse operations**.

Sitting down is the inverse operation of standing up. Adding a number is the inverse operation of subtracting the same number. Multiplying by a number and dividing by the same number are inverse operations (Table 5.1).

operation	inverse operation
shut the door	open the door
add 20	subtract 20
subtract -3	add -3
multiply by 4	divide by 4
divide by 0·3	multiply by 0·3

Table 5.1

Exercise 5f *(Oral)*

Find the inverses of the following operations.

1 shut your eyes
2 go up 2 steps
3 add 16
4 add -5
5 subtract $4\frac{1}{2}$
6 subtract -1
7 multiply by 1·8
8 multiply by 9
9 divide by 7
10 divide by -4

Inverse operations are helpful when solving problems.

Example 6

I think of a number. 14 added to the number gives 29. What number am I thinking of?

Either:

my number $\xrightarrow{\text{add 14}}$ 29

thus, 29 $\xrightarrow{\text{subtract 14}}$ my number

my number $= 29 - 14 = 15$

Or:

let my number be x, then

$$x + 14 = 29$$

subtract 14 from both sides

$$x + 14 - 14 = 29 - 14$$
$$x = 15$$

Example 7

Find the number which, when 8 is subtracted from it, gives -3.

Either:

the number $\xrightarrow{\text{subtract 8}}$ -3

thus, -3 $\xrightarrow{\text{add 8}}$ the number

the number $= -3 + 8 = 5$

Or:

let n be the number, then

$$n - 8 = -3$$

add 8 to both sides

$$n - 8 + 8 = -3 + 8$$
$$n = 5$$

Exercise 5g

1 I think of a number. 7 added to the number gives 9. What number am I thinking of?

2 Find the number which, when 10 is added to it, gives 31.

3 I think of a number. 4 subtracted from the number gives 12. What number am I thinking of?

4 Find the number which, when 5 is subtracted from it, gives 7.

5 When 12 is added to a number the result is 23. What is the number?

6 When 15 is taken from a number the result is 5. What is the number?

7 A boy has some money. He spends Le18 000. He is left with Le32 000. How much money did he have at first?

8 A woman needs Le200 000. Her son gives her Le110 000 and her daughter gives her the rest. How much does the daughter give?

9 When 8 is added to a number the result is -5. What is the number?

10 When $2\frac{1}{4}$ is subtracted from a number the result is 2. What is the number?

11 Find the number which, when 9 is subtracted from it, gives -8.

12 A motorist is 7 km east of O. She drives westwards for 18 km. Where does she finish? (Distances west of O are negative.)

Example 8

Three-quarters of a certain number is 12. What is the number?

Either:

the number $\xrightarrow{\times \frac{3}{4}}$ 12

thus, 12 $\xrightarrow{\div \frac{3}{4}}$ the number

$$\text{the number} = 12 \div \frac{3}{4}$$
$$= 12 \times \frac{4}{3} = 16$$

Or:
let the number be a

$$\tfrac{3}{4} \text{ of } a = 12$$
$$\tfrac{3}{4} \times a = 12$$

divide both sides by $\frac{3}{4}$

$$\tfrac{3}{4} \div \tfrac{3}{4} \times a = 12 \div \tfrac{3}{4}$$
$$\tfrac{3}{4} \times \tfrac{4}{3} \times a = 12 \times \tfrac{4}{3}$$
$$1 \times a = 4 \times 4$$
$$a = 16$$

Example 9

When a sum of money is equally shared between nine people, each person gets Le1 500. *What is the sum of money?*

Either:

sum of money $\xrightarrow{\div 9}$ Le1 500

thus, Le1 500 $\xrightarrow{\times 9}$ sum of money

sum of money = Le1 500 × 9 = Le13 500

Or:
let the sum of money be Lem

Le$m \div 9$ = Le1 500

$$\frac{m}{9} = 1\,500$$

Multiply both sides by 9.

$$\frac{m}{9} \times 9 = 1\,500 \times 9$$
$$m = 13\,500$$

The sum of money is Le13 500.

Exercise 5h

1 6 times a number is 48. What is the number?
2 Find the number which, when multiplied by 10, gives 70.
3 A number divided by 5 gives 9. What is the number?
4 A number divided by 3 gives 12. What is the number?
5 Find the cost of a car if four of the cars cost $123 000.
6 A television set is paid for in 12 equal instalments. Each payment is Le6 000. How much does the television set cost?
7 Find the mass of one dictionary if 35 dictionaries have a mass of 52·5 kg.
8 When a length of wood is cut into 18 equal lengths, each piece is 12·2 cm long. How long was the wood before it was cut?
9 Two-fifths of a number is 12. What is the number?
10 Find the number which, when divided by $\frac{2}{3}$, gives 27.
11 A bottle is $\frac{3}{4}$ full and contains 723 ml. How much will the bottle hold when completely full?
12 $2\frac{1}{2}$ times a number is $4\frac{1}{6}$. What is the number?
13 Find the number which, when divided by 0·7, gives 0·8.
14 14 times a certain number gives −84. What is the number?
15 When a number is divided by $-\frac{1}{2}$ the result is $\frac{4}{7}$. What is the number?

Chapter summary

1. *Zero (0)* is the *identity for addition*, i.e. if we add 0 to any number the result is the same as the given number.
2. If the sum of two numbers is 0, one is the *additive inverse* of the other. For example, 5 is the additive inverse of −5 since −5 + 5 = 0.
3. *One (1)* is the *identity for multiplication*, i.e. if we multiply any number by 1 the result is the same as the given number.
4. If the product of two numbers is 1, one is the *multiplicative inverse* of the other. For example, $\frac{1}{2}$ is the multiplicative inverse of 2 since $\frac{1}{2} \times 2 = 1$. Similarly, −8 and $-\frac{1}{8}$ are multiplicative inverses because $-8 \times (-\frac{1}{8}) = 1$.
5. The multiplicative inverse of a number is the same as its *reciprocal*, e.g. $\frac{1}{2}$ is the reciprocal of 2, and −8 is the reciprocal of $-\frac{1}{8}$.
6. If two operations cancel each other, they are inverse operations, e.g. add 2 then subtract 2, or multiply by $\frac{1}{4}$ then multiply by 4.
7. Inverses and inverse operations can be used to solve equations.

6 Angles (3) Angles in a polygon

Angles between lines (revision)

1 The sum of the angles on a straight line is 180°.

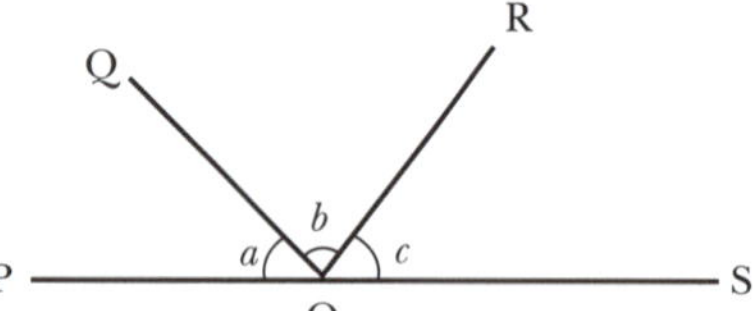

Fig. 6.1

In Fig. 6.1, PÔQ + QÔR + RÔS = 180°
i.e. $a + b + c = 180°$

2 Vertically opposite angles are equal.

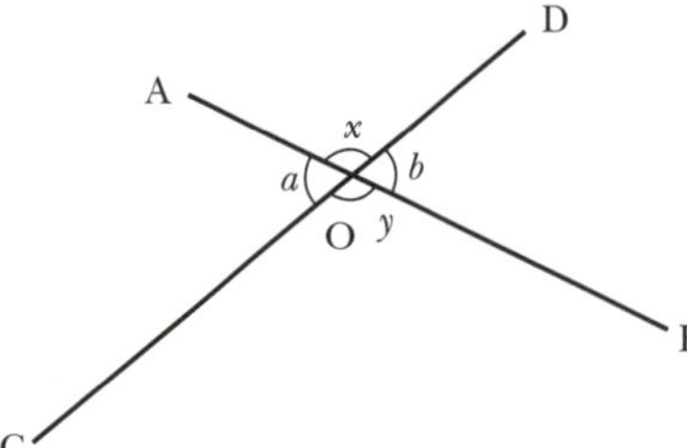

Fig. 6.2

In Fig. 6.2, AÔC = DÔB and AÔD = CÔD
i.e. $a = b$ and $x = y$

3 The sum of the angles at a point is 360°.

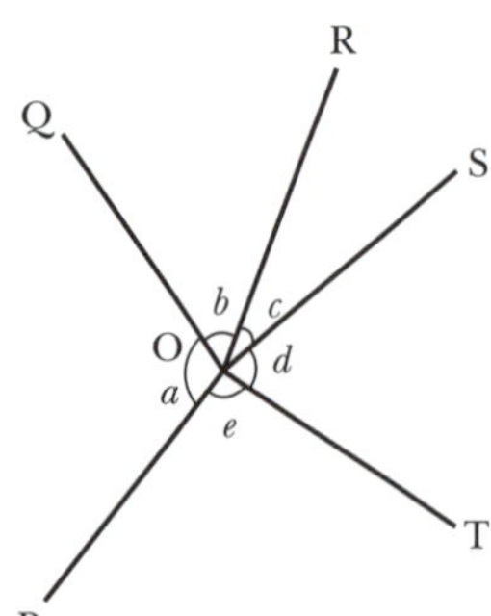

Fig. 6.3

In Fig. 6.3,
PÔQ + QÔR + RÔS + SÔT + TÔP = 360°
$a + b + c + d + e = 360°$

4 When a transversal crosses parallel lines, corresponding angles are equal.

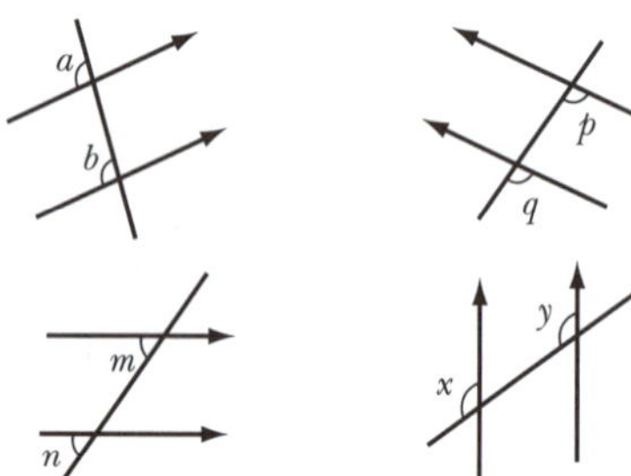

Fig. 6.4

In each figure, the marked angles are equal.
$a = b$, $p = q$, $m = n$, $x = y$

5 When a transversal crosses parallel lines, alternate angles are equal.

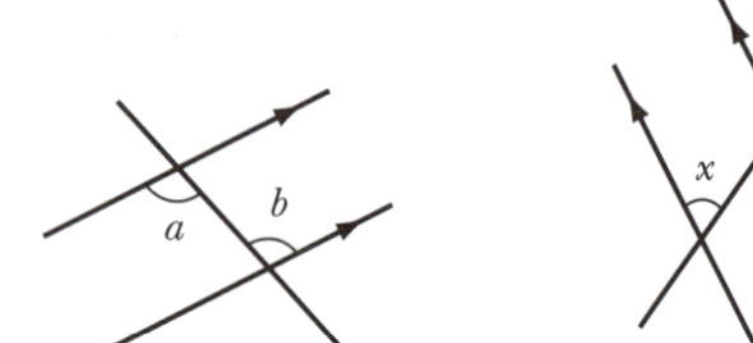

Fig. 6.5

In each figure, the marked angles are equal.
$a = b$ and $x = y$

Exercise 6a *(Oral revision)*

Find the sizes of the lettered angles in Fig. 6.6. Give reasons.

1 **2**

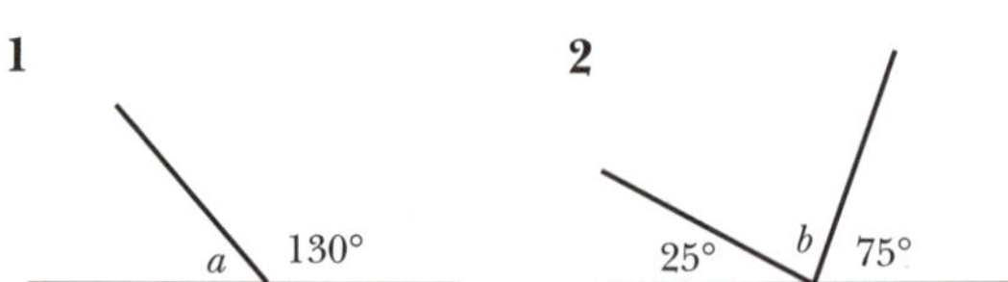

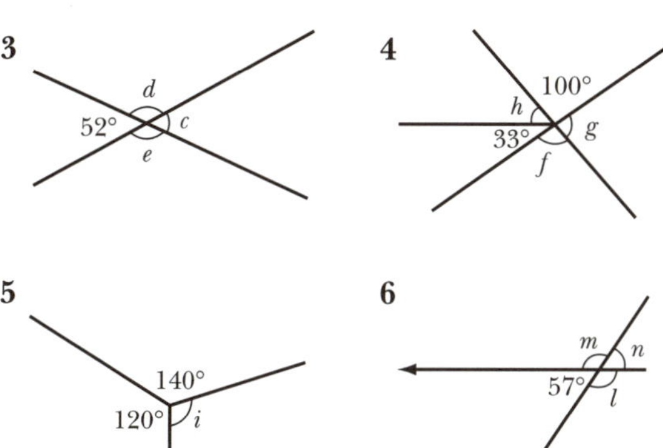

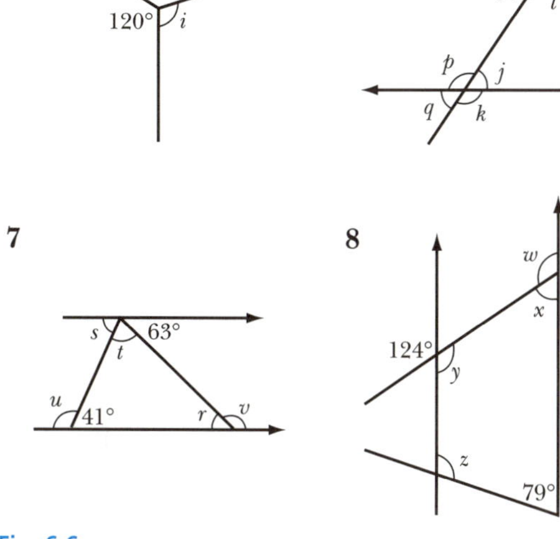

Fig. 6.6

Angles in a triangle (revision)

1 The sum of the angles of a triangle is 180°.

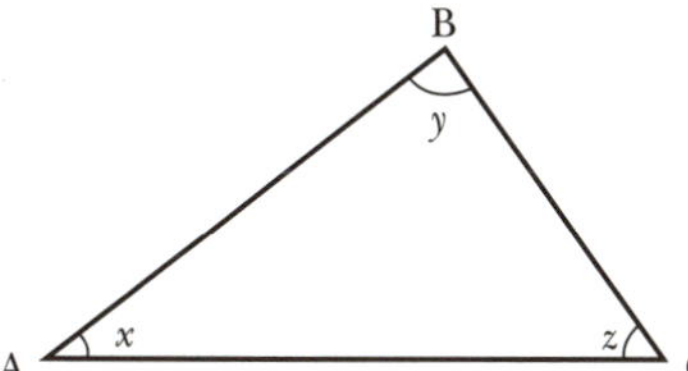

Fig. 6.7

In Fig. 6.7, $\hat{A} + \hat{B} + \hat{C} = 180°$

$x + y + z = 180°$

2 In an isosceles triangle, the angles opposite the equal sides are equal.

In Fig. 6.8, AB = AC, thus $\hat{C} = \hat{B}$

or $x = y$

BC is the **base** of isosceles ΔBAC.

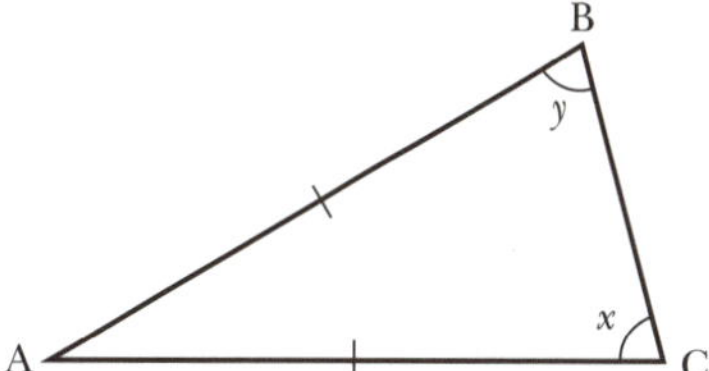

Fig. 6.8

3 In an equilateral triangle, each angle is 60°.

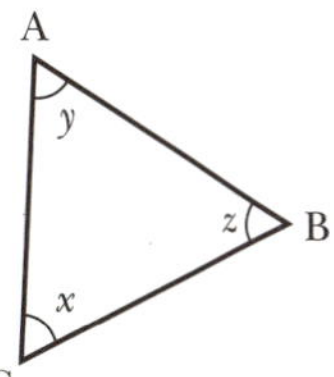

Fig. 6.9

In Fig. 6.9, AB = BC = CA

thus $\hat{C} = \hat{A} = \hat{B} = 60°$

or $x = y = z = 60°$

Example 1

Find the lettered angles in Fig. 6.10. Give reasons.

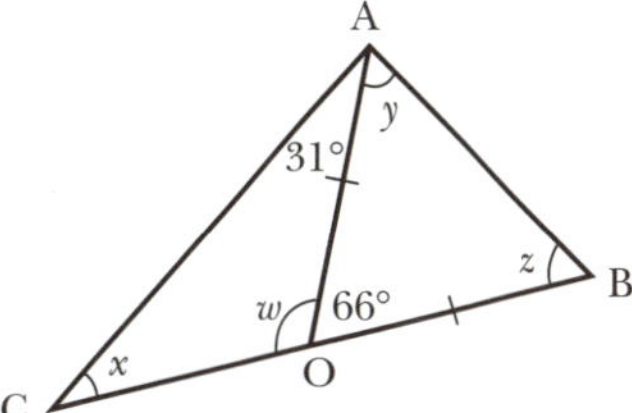

Fig. 6.10

In ΔAOC,

$w = 180° - 66°$ (angles on straight line COB)

$w = 114°$

$x = 180° - (114° + 31°)$ (angles of ΔAOC)

$= 180° - 145°$

$= 35°$

ΔAOB is isosceles, thus $y = z$

$y + z = 180° - 66°$ (angles of ΔAOC)

$y + z = 114°$

$y = z = \frac{114°}{2} = 57°$

Exercise 6b *(Revision)*

Find the sizes of the lettered angles in Fig. 6.11. Give reasons.

Note: in any diagram, lines marked with a small line are equal in length.

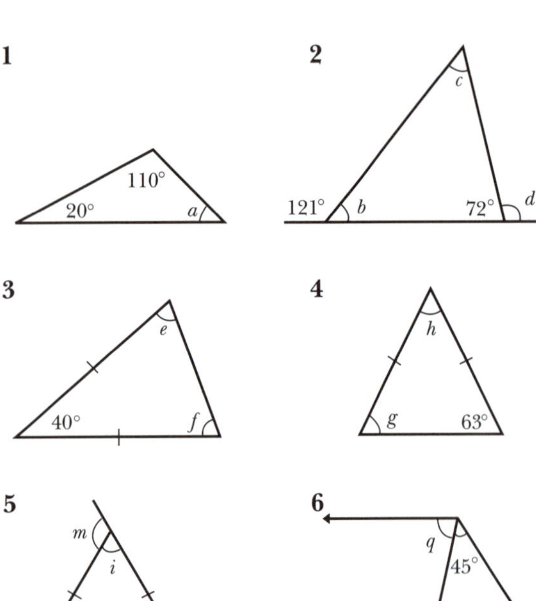

Fig. 6.11

Angles in a quadrilateral

Any quadrilateral can be divided into two triangles by drawing its diagonals (Fig. 6.12).

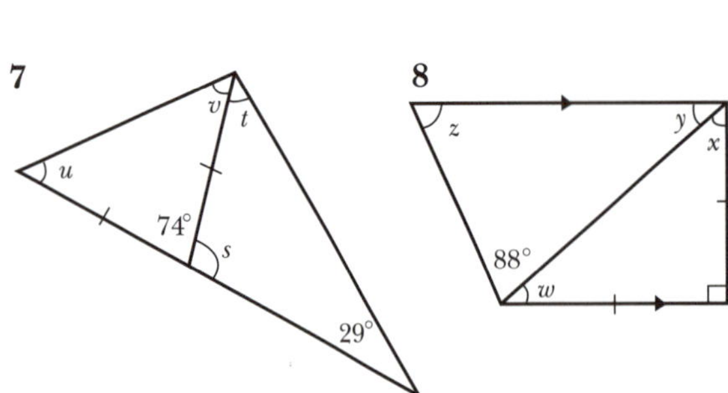

Fig. 6.12

The sum of the angles in each triangle is 180°. Thus the sum of the angles in the quadrilateral is 360°. For example, with the lettering of Fig. 6.13,

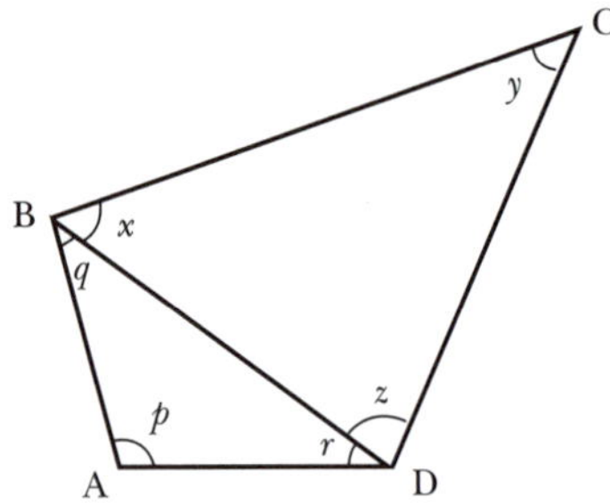

Fig. 6.13

$$p + q + r = 180° \text{ (angles of } \Delta\text{ABD)}$$
$$x + y + z = 180° \text{ (angles of } \Delta\text{BCD)}$$

Thus

$$p + q + r + x + y + z = 180° + 180°$$
$$= 360°$$

In the quadrilateral,

$$\hat{A} = p, \quad \hat{B} = q + x, \quad \hat{C} = y, \quad \hat{D} = r + z$$
$$\hat{A} + \hat{B} + \hat{C} + \hat{D} = p + (q + x) + y + (r + z)$$
$$= p + q + r + x + y + z$$
$$= 360°$$

Thus, **the sum of the angles of any quadrilateral = 360°.**

Example 2

Find the value of x in Fig. 6.14. Hence find the other two angles of the quadrilateral.

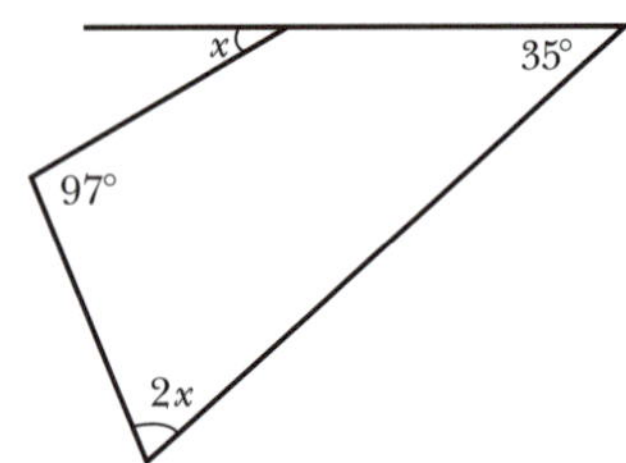

Fig. 6.14

The fourth angle of the quadrilateral $= 180° - x$ (angles on straight line)

Thus, $(180° - x) + 2x + 97° + 35° = 360°$ (sum of angles of quadrilateral)

$$2x - x + 180° + 97° + 35° = 360°$$
$$x + 312° = 360°$$
$$x = 360° - 312°$$
$$x = 48°$$

$2x = 2 \times 48° = 96°$
$180° - x = 180° - 48° = 132°$
The other two angles of the quadrilateral are 96° and 132°.
Check: $96° + 132° + 97° + 35° = 360°$.

Exercise 6c

1 Find the sizes of all the angles of the quadrilaterals in Fig. 6.15.

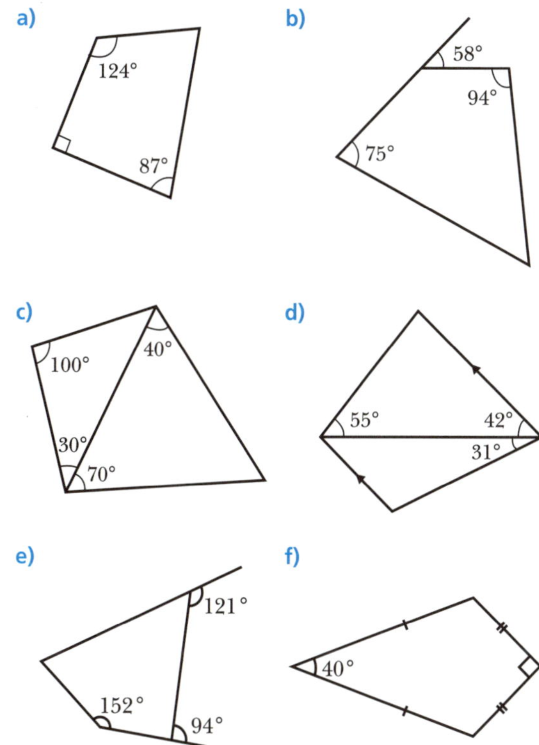

Fig. 6.15

2 Calculate the fourth angle of the quadrilaterals whose other three angles, in order, are:

a) 100°, 60°, 80° **b)** 58°, 117°, 122°
c) 95°, 85°, 90° **d)** 109°, 71°, 109°
e) 114°, 95°, 114° **f)** 118°, 64°, 75°
g) 58°, 113°, 156° **h)** 90°, 110°, 85°
i) 97°, 85°, 107° **j)** 111°, 111°, 111°

3 Make rough sketches of quadrilaterals c) and d) of question 2. What types of quadrilaterals are they?

4 In Fig. 6.16, first find the value of x, then find the unknown angles of the quadrilaterals.

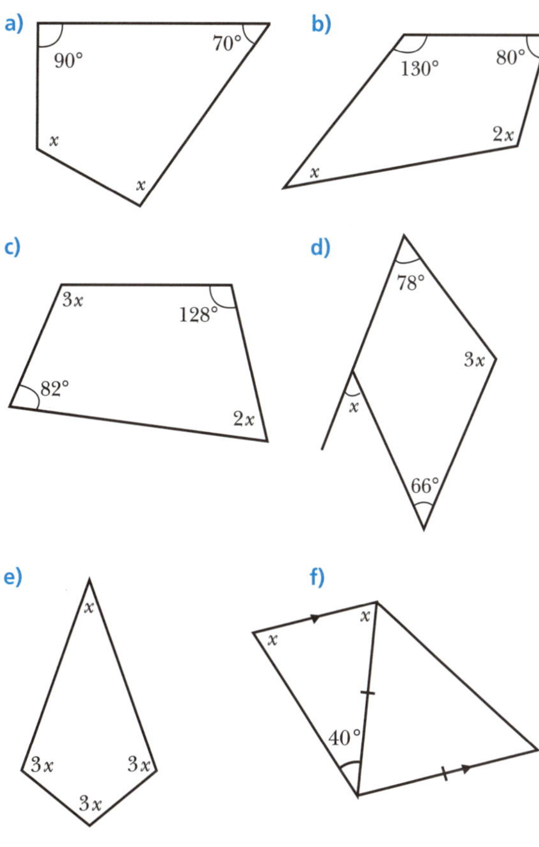

Fig. 6.16

5 The angles of a quadrilateral are x, $2x$, $3x$ and $4x$ in that order.

a) Make an equation in x.
b) Find x.
c) Find the angles of the quadrilateral.
d) Make a rough drawing of the quadrilateral.
e) What kind of quadrilateral is it?

Polygons

A **polygon** is any plane figure with straight sides. Thus a triangle is a three-sided polygon and a quadrilateral is a four-sided polygon. Polygons are named after the number of sides they have. Table 6.1 gives the names of the first eight polygons.

triangle	3 sides
quadrilateral	4 sides
pentagon	5 sides
hexagon	6 sides
heptagon	7 sides
octagon	8 sides
nonagon	9 sides
decagon	10 sides

Table 6.1

A regular polygon has all sides and all angles equal. Fig. 6.17 shows the first six regular polygons.

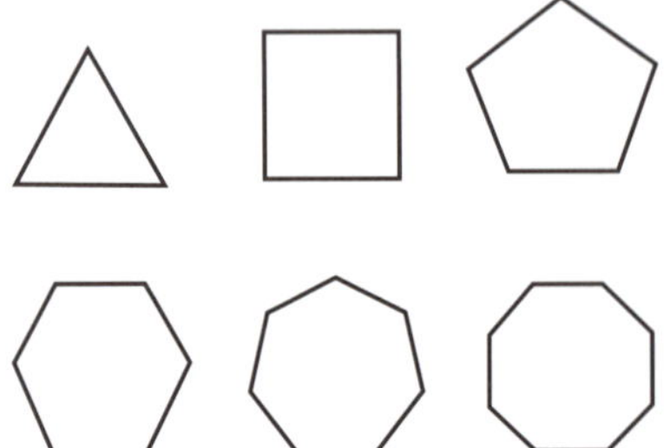

Fig. 6.17

Sum of the interior angles of a polygon

Look at the quadrilateral a), the pentagon b) and the hexagon c) in Fig. 6.18.

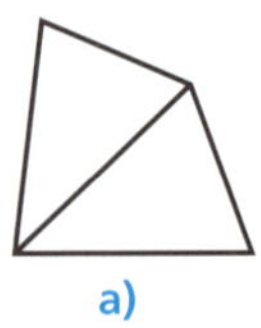

a)

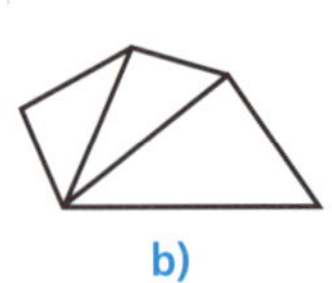

b)

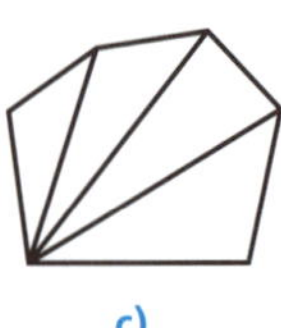

c)

Fig. 6.18

In each polygon, one vertex is joined to all the other vertices. This divides the polygons into triangles. The number of triangles depends on the number of sides of the polygon. Table 6.2 shows the number of triangles for the polygons in Fig. 6.18.

polygon	**number of sides**	**number of triangles**
quadrilateral	4	2
pentagon	5	3
hexagon	6	4

Table 6.2

In each case, the number of triangles is two less than the number of sides. For a polygon with n sides there will be $n - 2$ triangles. The sum of the angles of a triangle is 180°. Thus,

the sum of the angles of an n-sided polygon $= (n - 2) \times 180°$

Notice that this formula is true for the polygons we know. In a triangle, $n = 3$.

Sum of angles $= (3 - 2) \times 180°$
$= 1 \times 180° = 180°$

In a quadrilateral, $n = 4$.

Sum of angles $= (4 - 2) \times 180°$
$= 2 \times 180° = 360°$

Example 3

Calculate the size of each angle of a regular heptagon.

A regular heptagon has seven equal sides and seven equal angles.

Use the formula,

sum of angles of polygon $= (n - 2) \times 180°$

In a heptagon, $n = 7$.

Sum of angles $= (7 - 2) \times 180°$
$= 5 \times 180° = 900°$

There are seven angles.

Each angle $= \frac{900°}{7} = 128\frac{4}{7}°$

Example 4

The sum of seven of the angles of a nonagon is 1 000°. The other two angles are equal to each other. Calculate the sizes of the other two angles.

A nonagon has nine sides and nine angles.

Use the formula,

sum of angles of polygon $= (n - 2) \times 180°$

In a nonagon, $n = 9$.

$$\begin{aligned}\text{Sum of angles} &= (9 - 2) \times 180^\circ \\ &= 7 \times 180^\circ = 1\,260^\circ \\ \text{Sum of seven of the angles} &= 1\,000^\circ \\ \text{Sum of two other angles} &= 1\,260^\circ - 1\,000^\circ \\ &= 260^\circ \\ \text{Size of each angle} &= \frac{260^\circ}{2} = 130^\circ\end{aligned}$$

Example 5

The sum of the angles of a polygon is 1 980°. How many sides has the polygon?

Let the polygon have n sides.

Thus, $(n - 2) \times 180^\circ = 1\,980^\circ$

Divide both sides by 180.

$$(n - 2) \times \frac{180}{180} = \frac{1980}{180}$$

$$n - 2 = 11$$

Add 2 to both sides.

$$n = 13$$

The polygon has 13 sides.

Exercise 6d

1 a) In Fig. 6.19, O is any point inside each polygon. Straight lines join O to the vertices of each polygon. This divides the polygons into triangles.

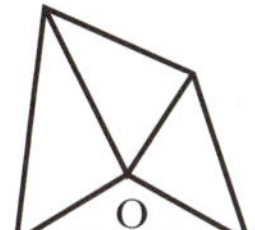

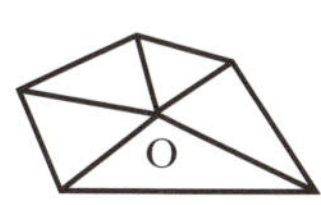

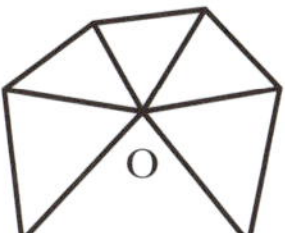

Fig. 6.19

Draw a heptagon (seven sides) and an octagon (eight sides). Divide these into triangles in the same way as shown in Fig. 6.19.

b) Copy and complete Table 6.3.

c) Hence find a formula for the sum of the angles of an n-sided polygon.

2 Calculate the size of each angle of **a)** a regular hexagon, **b)** a regular decagon.

3 In Fig. 6.20, O is the centre of regular pentagon ABCDE.

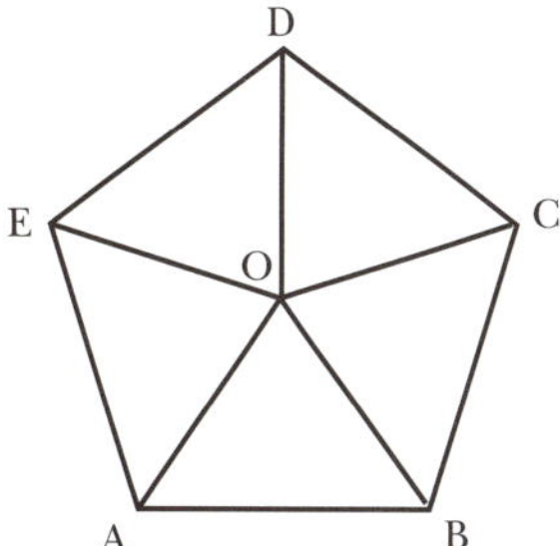

Fig. 6.20

a) Calculate the size of each angle at O.

b) What kind of triangle is ΔAOB?

c) Calculate the size of $O\hat{A}B$ and $O\hat{B}A$.

d) Hence find the size of each angle of ABCDE.

e) Check your answer to d) by using the $(n - 2) \times 180^\circ$ formula for the sum of the angles of a pentagon.

4 Fig. 6.21 shows a pattern made with squares and regular octagons.

Find the sizes of the three angles at point A,

polygon	number of sides	number of triangles	sum of angles at O	sum of angles of polygon
quadrilateral	4	4	360°	4 × 180° − 360°
pentagon	5	5	360°	5 × 180° − 360°
hexagon				
heptagon				
octagon				
n-gon	n			

Table 6.3

a) from knowledge of the sum of the angles at a point,

b) by calculating the sizes of the angles of a regular octagon using the $(n - 2) \times 180°$ formula.

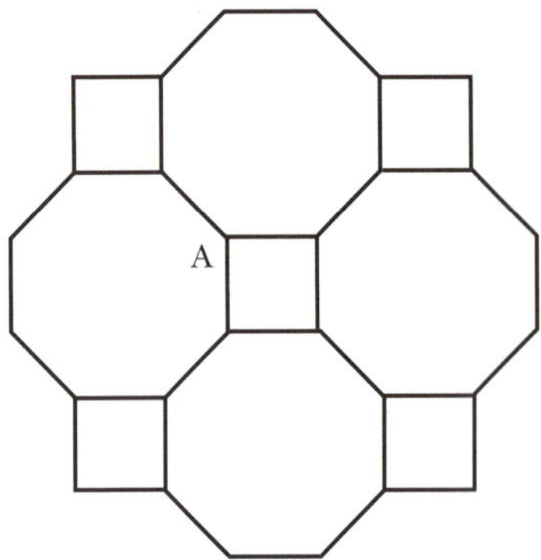

Fig. 6.21

5 The pattern in Fig. 6.22 is made from four regular pentagons.

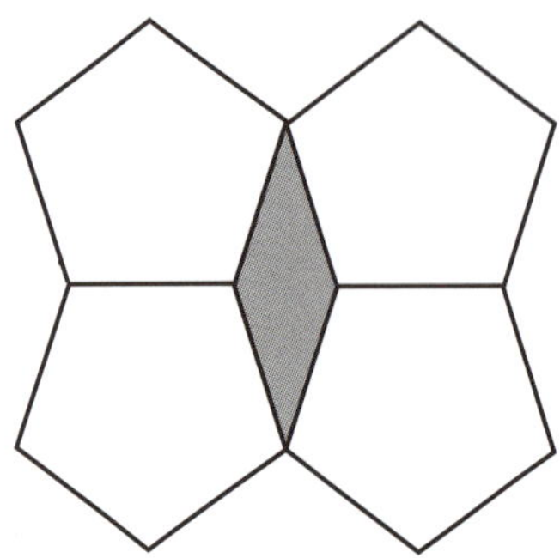

Fig. 6.22

a) What kind of quadrilateral is shown shaded?

b) Calculate the sizes of the four angles of the shaded quadrilateral.

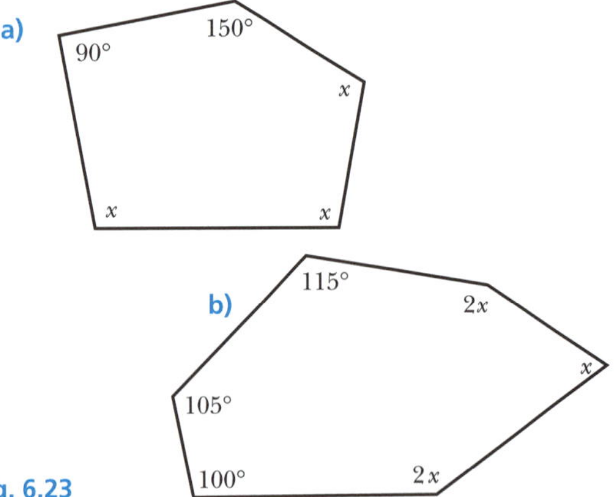

Fig. 6.23

6 In Fig. 6.23, first find the value of x, then find the unknown angles in each polygon.

7 The sum of seven of the angles of a decagon is 1 170°. The other three angles are all equal to each other. Calculate the sizes of the other three angles.

8 If the angles of a pentagon could be x, $2x$, $3x$, $4x$ and $5x$, what would be the value of x? Calculate the size of the largest angle. What do you notice? Sketch the pentagon. What type of shape is it?

9 How many sides has a polygon if the sum of its angles is **a)** 3 240°, **b)** 2 340°?

10 a) How many sides has a polygon if the sum of its angles is 3 960°?

b) If the polygon is regular, what is the size of each angle?

Chapter summary

1. A *polygon* is any plane shape with straight sides. Polygons are mostly named after the number of sides they have (Table 6.1).
2. A *regular polygon* has all sides and all angles equal.
3. The *sum of the angles of an n-sided polygon* $= (n - 2) \times 180°$

   For example, the sum of the angles of a quadrilateral is 360°.

7 Expansion of algebraic expressions

Remember that in algebra, letters stand for numbers. The numbers can be whole or fractional, positive or negative.

Directed algebraic terms

1 Just as $5a$ is short for $5 \times a$, so $-5a$ is short for $(-5) \times a$.

2 Just as m is short for $1 \times m$, so $-m$ is short for $(-1) \times m$.

3 Algebraic terms and numbers can be multiplied together. For example,

$$\begin{aligned} 4 \times (-3x) &= (+4) \times (-3) \times x \\ &= -(4 \times 3) \times x = -12 \times x \\ &= -12x \\ (-2y) \times (-8y) &= (-2) \times y \times (-8) \times y \\ &= (-2) \times (-8) \times y \times y \\ &= +(2 \times 8) \times y^2 \\ &= +16y^2 \text{ or just } 16y^2 \end{aligned}$$

4 Division with directed numbers is also possible. For example,

$$18a \div (-6) = \frac{(+18) \times a}{(-6)} = -\left(\frac{18}{6}\right) \times a$$
$$= (-3) \times a = -3a$$
$$\frac{-33x^2}{-3x} = \frac{(-33) \times x \times x}{(-3) \times x} = +\left(\frac{33}{3}\right) \times x = 11x$$

Read example 1 carefully.

Example 1

	simplify	working	result
a)	$-5 \times 2y$	$= (-5) \times (+2) \times y$ $= -(5 \times 2) \times y$	$= -10y$
b)	$-6 \times -4x$	$= (-6) \times (-4) \times x$ $= +(6 \times 4) \times x$	$= 24x$
c)	$-3a \times 7$	$= (-3) \times a \times (+7)$ $= (-3) \times (+7) \times a$	$= -21a$
d)	$4y \times -5$	$= (+4) \times y \times (-5)$ $= (+4) \times (-5) \times y$	$= -20y$
e)	$-3a \times -6b$	$= (-3) \times a \times (-6) \times b$ $= (-3) \times (-6) \times a \times b$	$= 18ab$
f)	$\frac{-14a}{7}$	$= \frac{(-14) \times a}{(+7)}$ $= -\left(\frac{14}{7}\right) \times a$ $= -2 \times a$	$= -2a$
g)	$-\frac{1}{3}$ of $36x^2$	$= \frac{(+36) \times x^2}{(-3)}$ $= -\left(\frac{36}{3}\right) \times x^2$	$= -12x^2$

Exercise 7a

Simplify the following.

1 $(-5) \times a$
2 $x \times (-4)$
3 $(-x) \times 3$
4 $3 \times (-c)$
5 $(-6) \times (-x)$
6 $(-y) \times (-9)$
7 $3 \times (-2a)$
8 $(-3) \times (-2a)$
9 $(-3) \times 2a$
10 $(-9) \times 4x$
11 $(-5x) \times -8$
12 $(-5x) \times 8$
13 $7a \times (-6)$
14 $2 \times (-11y)$
15 $4 \times (-4c)$
16 $(-10) \times (-3y)$
17 $(-2x) \times (-9y)$
18 $3a \times (-7b)$
19 $(-8x) \times (-3x)$
20 $6d \times (-3d)$
21 $21a \div (-7)$
22 $(-6x) \div (-2)$
23 $20y \div (-10)$
24 $18z \div (-3)$
25 $\frac{-16x}{8}$
26 $\frac{28x}{-4}$
27 $\frac{17x}{-17}$
28 $\frac{-49x}{-7}$
29 $\frac{1}{5}$ of $(-45y)$
30 $(-\frac{1}{10})$ of $100z$
31 $(-\frac{1}{8})$ of $(-48t)$
32 $\frac{1}{4}$ of $(-36n)$

33 $\frac{-36x^2}{-12x}$ **34** $\frac{22ab}{-2a}$

35 $\frac{-39xy}{3y}$ **36** $\frac{-63m^2}{-21m}$

Substitution

Example 2

Find the value of a) 4x, b) xy − 5y when x = 2 and y = 3.

a) Substitute the value 2 for x, i.e. use the value 2 instead of x.

When $x = 2$, $4x = 4 \times x$
$= 4 \times 2$
$= 8$

b) $xy - 5y = x \times y - 5 \times y$

When $x = 2$ and $y = 3$,

$xy - 5y = 2 \times 3 - 5 \times 3$
$= 6 - 15$
$= -9$

Exercise 7b

Find the value of the following when $a = 1$, $b = 2$ and $c = 3$.

1 $5a$	**2** $6b$	**3** $9c$
4 $6a$	**5** $7b$	**6** $2c$
7 $-4a$	**8** $-b$	**9** $-3c$
10 $a + b$	**11** $a + c$	**12** $b + c$
13 $b - a$	**14** $a - b$	**15** $c - a$
16 $a - c$	**17** ab	**18** bc
19 $ac - b$	**20** $a - bc$	**21** $2a + b$
22 $3b + 2c$	**23** $7a - 2b$	**24** $4c - 3b$

Example 3

What is the value of $\frac{p - q}{p}$ *when* $p = -5$ *and* $q = +10$?

Notice that $\frac{p - q}{p}$ is the same as $\frac{(p - q)}{p}$.

Simplify the top line *before* dividing.

When $p = -5$ and $q = +10$,

$$\frac{p - q}{p} = \frac{(-5) - (+10)}{(-5)} = \frac{-15}{-5} = +\left(\frac{15}{5}\right) = +3$$

Exercise 7c

Find the value of the following when $x = 4$, $y = -5$ and $z = -3$.

1 $2x$	**2** $4y$	**3** $10z$
4 $-8x$	**5** $-y$	**6** $-2z$
7 xy	**8** xz	**9** yz
10 x^2	**11** y^2	**12** z^2
13 xyz	**14** $x + y$	**15** $x - y$
16 $x + z$	**17** $z - x$	**18** $x - z$
19 $\frac{y + z}{x}$	**20** $\frac{x - y}{z}$	**21** $\frac{x + y}{z}$
22 $\frac{x + z}{x + y}$	**23** $\frac{y + 5z}{x}$	**24** $\frac{x}{z - y}$

Removing brackets

$3 \times (7 + 5)$ means first add 7 and 5, then multiply the result by 3. Suppose a pencil costs 7 leones and a rubber costs 5 leones.

Cost of a pencil and rubber

= 7 leones + 5 leones
= (7 + 5) leones = 12 leones

If three students each buy a pencil and a rubber, then,

total cost = $3 \times (7 + 5)$ leones
= 3×12 leones
= 36 leones.

There is another way to find the total cost. Three pencils cost 3×7 leones. Three rubbers cost 3×5 leones. Altogether,

total cost = 3×7 leones + 3×5 leones
= 21 leones + 15 leones
= 36 leones

Thus, $3 \times (7 + 5) = 3 \times 7 + 3 \times 5$.

This shows that brackets can be removed by multiplying the 3 into both the 7 and the 5.

Usually we do not write the multiplication sign. We just write $3(7 + 5)$.

$3(7 + 5)$ is short for $3 \times (7 + 5)$.

Say $3(7 + 5)$ as '3 multiplied into (7 + 5)' or just '3 into (7 + 5)'.

Thus,

$3(7 + 5) = 3 \times 7 + 3 \times 5$

In general, using letters for numbers,

$$\boldsymbol{a(x + y) = ax + ay}$$

Notice also that

$$3(7 - 5) = 3 \times 2 = 6$$
$$\text{and } 3 \times 7 - 3 \times 5 = 21 - 15 = 6$$
$$\text{Thus, } 3(7 - 5) = 3 \times 7 - 3 \times 5$$

Again, using letters for numbers,

$$\boldsymbol{a(x - y) = ax - ay}$$

Exercise 7d

Simplify each of the following in two ways. Question 1 shows you how to do this.

1 $9(7-3)$ *a)* $9(7-3) = 9 \times 4 = 36$
b) $9(7-3) = 9 \times 7 - 9 \times 3$
$= 63 - 27 = 36$

2 $3(7+2)$	**3** $10(6-4)$	**4** $9(4+3)$
5 $6(4-2)$	**6** $7(1+9)$	**7** $3(8-2)$
8 $3(8+2)$	**9** $4(11-3)$	**10** $5(10+2)$

Example 4

Remove brackets from the following.

a) $8(2c + 3d)$ *b)* $4y(3x - 5)$ *c)* $(7a - 2b)3a$

a) $8(2c + 3d) = 8 \times 2c + 8 \times 3d$
$= 16c + 24d$

b) $4y(3x - 5) = 4y \times 3x - 4y \times 5$
$= 12xy - 20y$

c) $(7a - 2b)3a$

Notice that we can multiply into the bracket from the right.

$(7a - 2b)3a = 7a \times 3a - 2b \times 3a$
$= 21a^2 - 6ab$

Exercise 7e

Remove brackets from the following.

1 $3(x+y)$	**2** $4(9-n)$	**3** $2(a-7)$
4 $5(2p-q)$	**5** $6(3a+4b)$	**6** $7(7x+2y)$
7 $2a(4+7c)$	**8** $4y(6x-8)$	**9** $3x(7-8p)$
10 $3q(-p+q)$	**11** $2a(-a-b)$	**12** $5d(-b-2c)$
13 $(a+2b)2$	**14** $(u-v)5$	**15** $(3a+b)3$
16 $(5-3d)3a$	**17** $(7c-2)7c$	**18** $(4s+t)6s$

The multiplier outside the bracket can be a directed number.

Example 5

Remove brackets from the following.

a) $-7(2n + 3)$ *b)* $-5z(x - 9y)$ *c)* $(3 - 5a)(-2a)$

a) $-7(2n + 3)$
$= (-7) \times (+2) \times n + (-7) \times (+3)$
$= (-14n) + (-21)$
$= -14n - 21$

Notice that $+(-21) = -(+21) = -21$. Adding a negative number is equivalent to subtracting a positive number of the same value.

b) $-5z(x - 9y)$
$= (-5z) \times (+1) \times x - (-5z) \times (+9) \times y$
$= (-5xz) - (-45yz)$
$= -5xz + 45yz = 45yz - 5xz$

Notice that $-(-45yz) = +(+45yz) = +45yz$.

c) $(3 - 5a)(-2a)$
$= (+3) \times (-2a) - (+5) \times (-2a) \times a$
$= (-6a) - (-10a^2)$
$= -6a + 10a^2 = 10a^2 - 6a$

Example 5 shows that **when the multiplier is negative, the signs inside the bracket are changed when the bracket is removed.**

Exercise 7f

Remove brackets from the following.

1 $-3(m+n)$	**2** $-2(u+v)$
3 $-4(a+b)$	**4** $-5(a-b)$
5 $-8(x-y)$	**6** $-9(p-q)$
7 $-4n(3m+2)$	**8** $-7y(3-5y)$
9 $-a(4a+6)$	**10** $-2a(-a-3b)$
11 $-5x(11x-2y)$	**12** $-p(p-5q)$
13 $(2c+8d)(-2)$	**14** $(-5m+2n)(-9m)$
15 $(10+3t)(-7t)$	**16** $-x(2x-11y)$
17 $-3(12a-5)$	**18** $-5a(-5x-7y)$

Example 6

Remove brackets and simplify the following.

a) $3(6a + 3b) + 5(2a - b)$

b) $2(3x - y) - 3(2x - 3y)$

c) $x(x - 7) + 4(x - 7)$

a) $3(6a + 3b) + 5(2a - b)$
$= 18a + 9b + 10a - 5b$
$= 18a + 10a + 9b - 5b$
$= 28a + 4b$

Notice that like terms are grouped.

b) $2(3x - y) - 3(2x - 3y)$
$= (+2)(3x - y) + (-3)(2x - 3y)$*
$= 6x - 2y + (-6x) + (+9y)$*
$= 6x - 2y - 6x + 9y$
$= 6x - 6x - 2y + 9y$
$= 7y$

*You will be able to leave out the first two steps after trying a few exercises.

c) $x(x - 7) + 4(x - 7)$
$= x \times x - x \times 7 + 4 \times x - 28$
$= x^2 - 7x + 4x - 28$
$= x^2 - 3x - 28$

Exercise 7g

Remove brackets and simplify the following.

1 $3a + 2(a + 2b)$
2 $6x + 3(2y - x)$
3 $7p + 5(p - q)$
4 $5c + 3(1 + 2c)$
5 $8a + 5(2a - b)$
6 $11x + 3(3x + 2y)$
7 $12x - 2(4x + 5)$
8 $9r - 4(3 + r)$
9 $14a - 3(2b + 5a)$
10 $4a - 5(a - 2)$
11 $3 - 7(5 - 4x)$
12 $10t - 8(3 - t)$
13 $5(a + 2) + 4(a + 1)$
14 $2(5x + 8y) + 3(2x - y)$
15 $2(3x - y) + 3(x + 2y)$
16 $2(a - 3b) + 3(a - b)$
17 $6(4x + y) - 7(3x + 5y)$
18 $4(x - 2y) - 3(2x - y)$
19 $7(a - b) - 8(a - 2b)$
20 $6(a - 2b) - 3(2a + b)$
21 $x(x - 2) + 3(x + 2)$
22 $x(x + 4) + 5(x + 4)$
23 $x(x - 2) + 7(x - 2)$
24 $x(x - 8) + 4(x - 8)$
25 $a(a + 5) - 2(a + 5)$
26 $a(a + 2) - 9(a + 2)$
27 $y(y - 3) - 6(y - 3)$
28 $z(z - 1) - 10(z - 1)$
29 $x(x + a) + a(x + a)$
30 $a(a + b) - b(a + b)$

Expanding algebraic expressions

The expression $(a + 2)(b - 5)$ means $(a + 2) \times (b - 5)$. The terms in the first bracket, $(a + 2)$, multiply each term in the second bracket, $(b - 5)$. Just as

$x(b - 5) = bx - 5x$

so, writing $(a + 2)$ instead of x,

$(a + 2)(b - 5) = b(a + 2) - 5(a + 2)$

The brackets on the right-hand side can now be removed.

$(a + 2)(b - 5) = b(a + 2) - 5(a + 2)$
$= ab + 2b - 5a - 10$

$ab + 2b - 5a - 10$ is the product of $(a + 2) \times (b - 5)$. We often say that the **expansion** of $(a + 2)(b - 5)$ is $ab + 2b - 5a - 10$.

Example 7

Expand the following. *a)* $(a + b)(c + d)$ *b)* $(6 - x)(3 + y)$ *c)* $(2p - 3q)(5p - 4)$

a) $(a + b)(c + d) = c(a + b) + d(a + b)$
$= ac + bc + ad + bd$

b) $(6 - x)(3 + y) = 3(6 - x) + y(6 - x)$
$= 18 - 3x + 6y - xy$

c) $(2p - 3q)(5p - 4) = 5p(2p - 3q) - 4(2p - 3q)$
$= 10p^2 - 15pq - 8p + 12q$

In general, using letters for numbers,

$$\mathbf{(a + b)(x + y) = x(a + b) + y(a + b) = ax + bx + ay + by}$$

When expanding brackets it is very important to be careful with the signs of the terms in the final product.

Exercise 7h

Expand the following.

1 $(p + q)(r + s)$
2 $(x + 8)(y + 3)$
3 $(4 + 5a)(3b + a)$
4 $(a - b)(c + d)$
5 $(x - 7)(y + 1)$
6 $(2 - p)(3p + q)$
7 $(w + x)(y - z)$
8 $(a + 6)(b - 9)$
9 $(2m + 5n)(p - 3q)$
10 $(a - b)(c - d)$
11 $(x - 4)(y - 5)$
12 $(5x - y)(x - 3y)$

It is often possible to simplify terms in the final product.

Example 8

Expand $(x + 8)(x + 5)$.

$$(x + 8)(x + 5) = x(x + 8) + 5(x + 8)$$
$$= x^2 + 8x + 5x + 40$$

Notice that the middle two terms are both terms in x. They can be collected together.

$$(x + 8)(x + 5) = x^2 + 13x + 40$$

Example 9

Expand the following.

a) $(6 + x)(3 - x)$ *b)* $(2a - 3b)(a + 4b)$

a) $(6 + x)(3 - x) = 3(6 + x) - x(6 + x)$
$= 18 + 3x - 6x - x^2$
$= 18 - 3x - x^2$

b) $(2a - 3b)(a + 4b) = a(2a - 3b) + 4b(2a - 3b)$
$= 2a^2 - 3ab + 8ab - 12b^2$
$= 2a^2 + 5ab - 12b^2$

Example 10

Expand $(x - 3)^2$.

$$(x - 3)^2 = (x - 3)(x - 3)$$
$$= x(x - 3) - 3(x - 3)$$
$$= x^2 - 3x - 3x + 9$$
$$= x^2 - 6x + 9$$

Exercise 7i

Expand the following.

1 $(a + 3)(a + 4)$ **2** $(b + 2)(b + 5)$
3 $(m + 3)(m - 2)$ **4** $(n - 7)(n + 2)$
5 $(x + 2)^2$ **6** $(y + 1)(y - 4)$
7 $(c - 2)(c + 5)$ **8** $(d - 3)(d - 4)$
9 $(p - 2)(p - 5)$ **10** $(x - 4)^2$
11 $(y + 1)(y + 7)$ **12** $(a - 4)(a + 6)$
13 $(b - 3)(b - 7)$ **14** $(c + 5)(c - 1)$
15 $(3 + d)(2 + d)$ **16** $(5 - x)(2 + x)$
17 $(3 - y)(4 - y)$ **18** $(m + 2n)(m + 3n)$
19 $(a - 3b)(a + 2b)$ **20** $(x - 4y)(x - 3y)$
21 $(p + 2q)^2$ **22** $(m + 5n)(m - 3n)$
23 $(a + 5)(2a - 3)$ **24** $(3x + 4)(x - 2)$
25 $(2h - k)(3h + 2k)$ **26** $(5x + 2y)(3x + 4y)$
27 $(3a - 2b)^2$ **28** $(5h + k)^2$
29 $(5a - 2b)(2a - 3b)$ **30** $(7m - 5n)(5m + 3n)$

Chapter summary

① *Directed algebraic terms* behave like directed numbers, e.g.

just as $(-3) \times (-7) = +21$, so
$(-a) \times (-5a) = 5a^2$ and
just as $\frac{-28}{2} = -14$, so $\frac{-7x^2}{x} = -7x$.

② In an algebraic expression,
$3b$ is short for $3 \times b$
pq is short for $p \times q$
m^2 is short for $m \times m$

③ $a(x + y)$ is short for $a \times (x + y)$.

④ To *expand (or remove) brackets*, use the following rules:

$a(x + y) = ax + ay$
$a(x - y) = ax - ay$
$-a(x - y) = -ax + ay$
(notice the effect of the negative term outside the bracket)
$(a + b)(x + y) = x(a + b) + y(a + b)$
$= ax + bx + ay + by$

8 Everyday arithmetic (3) Approximation and estimation

Approximation

Rounding off numbers (revision)

When numbers are rounded off, the digits 1, 2, 3, 4 are rounded down and the digits 5, 6, 7, 8, 9 are rounded up.

Example 1

Round off 124·25 *a) to* 2 *significant figures, b) to* 1 *decimal place.*

124·25 = 120 to 2 s.f.
124·25 = 124·3 to 1 d.p.

Example 2

In a national budget it was decided to spend Le1 971 117 000 *on agricultural research. How might the Finance Minister say this amount in a speech?*

The Le1 117 000 at the end of Le1 971 117 000 would be a lot of money for a student to spend. However, in terms of a national budget, Le1 117 000 is insignificant. The Minister is more likely to say the amount as:

Le1·97 billion
or, about Le1·97 billion
or, just over Le1·97 billion

Another way might be to say:

about Le2 billion
or, just under Le2 billion

In the first case the amount has been rounded to 3 significant figures (3 s.f.).
In the second case the amount has been rounded to 2 s.f.

If a newspaper says, 'Nation to spend Le1·97 billion on agricultural research', we take this to mean that the Nation will spend between Le1·965 billion and Le1·975 billion.

Exercise 8a

1 a) There are four 1s in the amount Le1 971 117 000. Write down the amounts of money that each 1 represents.
b) There are two 7s in the amount Le1 971 117 000. Write down the amounts of money that each 7 represents.

2 Round off the following to 3 significant figures.
a) 6 568 **b)** 51 065 **c)** 241 269
d) 2 345 **e)** 73·354 **f)** 729 504

3 Round off the following to 2 significant figures.
a) 193 **b)** 279 **c)** 86 512
d) 3·92 **e)** 3·97 **f)** 22·5

4 Round off the following to 1 decimal place.
a) 0·666 **b)** 0·54 **c)** 7·825
d) 6·09 **e)** 8·03 **f)** 19·95

5 Round off the following to the nearest whole number.
a) 36·8 cm **b)** 13·47 kg **c)** Le28·65
d) 29·8 litres **e)** 62·5 mm **f)** Le8·09

6 The actual age of a hospital patient is 39 years, 8 months, 29 days. A doctor asks the patient's age. What will be the reply?

7 In a budget it was decided to spend Le779 362 610 on school libraries. Give at least three different ways in which an Education Minister might say this amount in a speech.

8 A newspaper headline reads 'Nation to spend Le30·5 million on Science and Technology'. Between what amounts will the Nation spend?

9 Table 8.1 gives the provisional amounts for Sierra Leone's external trade accounts in two successive quarters.

	1st quarter	2nd quarter
exports (Le billion)	19·16	13·82
imports (Le billion)	15·72	18·08

Table 8.1

a) How might a Finance Minister give the 1st quarter export figure in a speech?
b) How might a newspaper print the 2nd quarter import figure?
c) If exports are greater than imports, there is a **surplus**. Find the amount of the surplus for the 1st quarter to 2 significant figures.
d) If imports are greater than exports, there is a **deficit**. Find the amount of the deficit for the 2nd quarter to 2 significant figures.

10 Some cars were timed over 100 km of untarred road. Their average time for the journey was 1 h 28 min 14 s.
a) Round the average time to the nearest $\frac{1}{4}$ hour.
b) Use the rounded time to find the approximate average speed for the journey in km/h. Give your answer to 1 significant figure.

False accuracy

Consider the following:

1 A student measures a line with a ruler and says it is 162·83 mm long. It is impossible to measure 0·83 mm on an ordinary ruler. The answer is an example of **false accuracy**. It is more realistic to say that the line is 163 mm long.

2 A report says that the estimated population of a city was 3 012 773. Since this number is an estimate it would have been more realistic to give the population to 3 significant figures: 3·01 million.

Most measuring instruments, such as a ruler, protractor, thermometer, balance, measuring cylinder, give results which are correct only to 2 or 3 significant figures. The answers to calculations using measurements from such instruments should likewise only be given to 2 or 3 significant figures.

Some instruments can measure very accurately. Ask your science teacher to show you a micrometer screw gauge, a travelling microscope, a chemical beam balance, a Vernier gauge or any other highly accurate measuring instrument.

Exercise 8b *(Oral)*

1 Give the measures which will complete Table 8.2.

instrument	can measure accurately to the nearest
ruler	mm
protractor	
thermometer	
spring balance	
measuring cylinder	
clock	

Table 8.2

2 Each of the following is an example of false accuracy. Round the digits in each quantity to 3 significant figures.
a) The line is 185·39 mm long.
b) The teacher is 175·778 cm tall.
c) The radius of the earth is about 6 383·4 km.
d) The bank is 985·372 m from the market.
e) Mount Everest is 8 847·73 m high.
f) The villages are 14·275 km apart.
g) The nurse had a mass of 67·883 kg.
h) Each biscuit has a mass of 6·629 5 g.
i) The parcel weighed 2·865 5 kg.
j) The lorry carried a load of 7·643 21 tonnes.
k) The tin contained 125·108 g of coffee.
l) The letter was 11·319 g in mass.
m) The population of a State was 3 656 487.
n) The area of the Atlantic Ocean is 86 563 680 km^2.
o) The cup held 240·862 ml of tea.
p) The capital budget was Le5 198 424.28.
q) It took 14 h 22 min 39·63 s to fly from London to Freetown.
r) A full petrol tank holds 40·117 5 litres.
s) A house cost Le812 436 400.
t) The mean temperature was 26·247 7°C.

3 Table 8.3 gives some estimated populations. Round each number to a suitable degree of accuracy.

a country	32 837 541
a large city	1 325 062
a large town	385 460
a small town	7 825
a village	683

Table 8.3

Estimation

Estimating numbers

Example 3

A school has 21 classes. One of the second-year classes has 34 students. Estimate the number of students in the school.

First method

Round off the numbers to 1 s.f.

Number of classes $\simeq$ 20

Number of students per class $\simeq$ 30

Number of students in school $\simeq 20 \times 30$

$= 600$

Second method

Assume the second-year class represents every class in the school.

Number of students in school

$\simeq 21 \times 34$

$\simeq 714$

$= 700$ to 1 significant figure.

Notice that there can be varying answers when estimating. In Example 3, different methods give 600 or 700 students. However, both numbers are of the *same order of size*. Knowing that the school contains 600 or 700 students gives a good idea of the size of the school. Thus, either number is a good estimate.

Example 4

A student writes 47 *words in five lines of writing. His exercise book has* 28 *lines on each page.*

a) Approximately how many words does he write on one page?

b) How many pages will a 750-word essay take up?

a) Five lines of writing contain 47 words.
One line of writing contains $\frac{47}{5} \simeq 9$ words.
28 lines of writing contain approximately
$9 \times 28 = 252$ words.
Approximately 250 words are written on each page.

b) Number of pages for 750 words $\simeq \frac{750}{250} = 3$.
A 750-word essay will take up about three pages.

Exercise 8c

1 A school has 27 classes. One of the classes has 33 students. Estimate the number of students in the school.

2 A college has 689 students. The average mass of a student is approximately 51 kg. Estimate the total mass, in tonnes, of all the students in the school.

3 A book has 598 pages. It is approximately 3 cm thick. A bookshelf is 75 cm long and is full of books. Estimate the total number of pages in the books on the shelf.

4 A shop buys a stock of 1 440 pencils at Le100 each. Estimate the total cost of the pencils in leones.

5 On average a student writes about eight words per line.

a) Approximately how many lines will she take to write 1 000 words?

b) If her exercise book has 28 lines per page, estimate the number of pages a 1 000-word essay will take.

6 **a)** Count the number of words in 10 lines of your literature or history exercise book.

b) Find the average number of words you write on each line. Give your answer to the nearest whole number.

c) Count the number of lines per page in your exercise book. Estimate the number of words you write per page.

d) Estimate, to the nearest $\frac{1}{2}$ page, the number of pages it takes you to write a 1000-word essay.

7 In history exams, some students fill as many as 18 pages of writing. If 73 students enter for a history exam, estimate the maximum number of pages of paper that will be used.

8 A copy typist types about 32 words per minute. Estimate how long it will take to type a letter of 279 words.

Estimating quantities using body measures

In Book 1 you were asked to measure your hand span and pace.

The hand span and pace are useful body measures. Body measures can be used to estimate other distances.

Exercise 8d (Class activity)

1 Use the method given in Chapter 24 of Book 1 to find the lengths of your hand span and pace. Have they changed since last year?

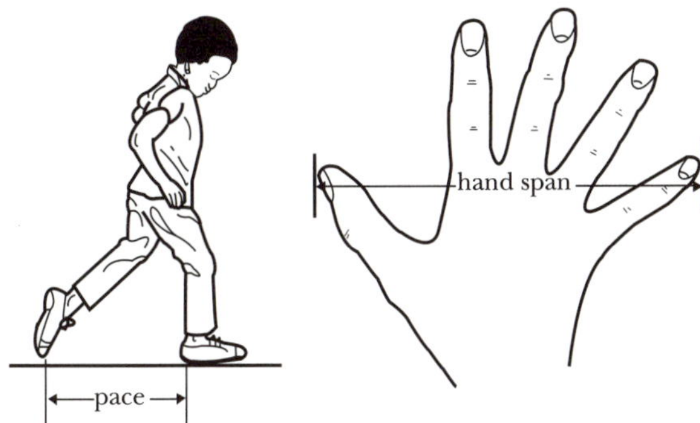

Fig. 8.1

2 Use your hand span to estimate the following.
  - a) the height of the classroom door
  - b) the width of the nearest window
  - c) your own height
  - d) the diameter of a bicycle wheel
  - e) the length and breadth of this book
  - f) the diameter of a shot-put circle

3 Use a metre-rule to check the accuracy of your estimates in question 2.

4 Use your pace to estimate the following.
  - a) the width of the school hall
  - b) the length of the school football field
  - c) the distance of your classroom door from the school gate
  - d) the width of a road near your school
  - e) the perimeter of your school compound
  - f) the length of your classroom

5 If possible, use a tape measure to check some of your estimates in question 4.

6 Two students, A and B, walked across the width of a school assembly area. A took 30 paces. B took 36 paces. Which of the following could be reasons why their results are different?
  - a) A is lazy
  - b) B is a girl
  - c) A is quicker than B
  - d) B has longer legs than A
  - e) A has a longer pace than B
  - f) B was carrying a bucket of water

Estimating quantities using traditional measures

Market traders often use traditional measures to estimate quantities. For example, dry measures such as rice and beans are sometimes measured in cups, basins and sacks.

Fig. 8.2

Liquids such as palm oil, groundnut oil and kerosene are measured in jars, bottles and tins. Medicine is often measured in teaspoons.

Exercise 8e

1 Assume that for dry rice and beans,

20 cups ≃ 1 basin
40 basins ≃ 1 sack

  - a) A sack contains 100 kg of rice. Estimate the number of kilograms of rice in 1 basin. Estimate the number of grams of rice in 1 cup.
  - b) A trader buys a sack of rice for Le60 000. She sells it at Le300 per cup . Estimate her profit on a sack of rice.
  - c) When selling beans, a trader charges Le300 000 for a sack and Le600 for a cup. Four women buy a sack of beans between them. They share the beans equally. How many cups does each woman get? How much does each woman save by buying the beans in this way?

2 Assume that for palm oil, groundnut oil and kerosene,

30 mentholatum jars ≃ 1 bottle
24 bottles ≃ 1 tin

  - a) A tin contains 25 litres of groundnut oil. Estimate the capacity, in litres, of a bottle. Estimate the capacity, in ml, of a mentholatum jar.

b) A trader pays Le30 000 for a tin of kerosene. He sells it in bottles. If he makes a profit of just over Le8 400 on each tin, what is the selling price per bottle? Give the answer to the nearest leone.

c) When selling palm oil, a trader charges Le1 152 for a tin and Le2 for a mentholatum jar. Express both selling prices as a selling price per bottle. Hence find the ratio of the two selling prices.

3 It takes 40 cups of water to fill a large bucket. A dining hall contains 329 students. How many buckets of water are needed so that each student gets at least 1 cup of water?

4 A box of 45 matches costs Le4 000. A petty trader splits a box into bundles of five matches and sells them for Le500 per bundle. Find the profit on two boxes of matches.

5 A bottle contains 150 ml of medicine. The label says, 'Take 2 teaspoonfuls 3 times a day'. If 1 teaspoon ≈ 5 ml, estimate how many days the medicine will last.

Chapter summary

① To *round off numbers*, round digits 1, 2, 3, 4 down and 5, 6, 7, 8, 9 up.

② There are various ways of rounding off:

a) to the nearest whole number, nearest ten, nearest hundred and so on;
b) to one, two or three significant figures;
c) to a given number of decimal places.

See the Summary for Chapter 2 for further details on rounding off.

③ Use *estimations* to obtain a rough idea of the outcome of a calculation. When estimating, use rounded numbers: one significant figure is usually enough.

④ Body measures and other local and traditional methods are very useful when estimating quantities in day-to-day situations.

Revision exercises and tests

Chapters 1–8

Revision exercise 1 *(Chapters 1, 2, 8)*

1 Find the HCF and LCM of 84 and 210.

2 Which of the numbers 5, 6 and 8 will divide into 6 320 without leaving a remainder?

3 Find the next four terms of the following number patterns.

a) 6, 13, 20, 27, 34, ...
b) 5, 6, 8, 11, 15, 20, ...
c) 3, 6, 12, 24, ...
d) 0, 2, 6, 12, 20, ...

4 Find the smallest number by which 350 must be multiplied to give a perfect square.

5 Express the following numbers in standard form.

a) 3 500 000 **b)** 5 700 **c)** 28
d) 0·47 **e)** 0·085 **f)** 0·000 003

6 Simplify the following.

a) $10^2 \times 10^5$ **b)** $3x^2 \times 5x^3$
c) $9a^3 \times 2a^{-2}$ **d)** $10^7 \div 10^3$
e) $16y^5 \div 8y^3$ **f)** $42x^{-3} \div 14x^{-7}$

7 Divide 2·647 by 0·9 and give the answer correct to 2 d.p.

8 A school has 34 classes. One of the classes has 36 students. Estimate to 1 s.f. the number of students in the school.

9 It takes a student about 1 hour to read 29 pages of a book. The book contains 326 pages. Estimate the number of hours it takes the student to read the whole book.

10 A packet of 200 air letters is 1·2 cm thick. Calculate the thickness of one air letter. Give your answer in metres in standard form.

Revision test 1 *(Chapters 1, 2, 8)*

1 The next term in the sequence 2, 3, 5, 8, 12, 17, ... is

A 18 **B** 19 **C** 22 **D** 23 **E** 24

2 Which of the following statements is (are) true?

a) 1 089 is divisible by 6
b) 1 089 is divisible by 9
c) 1 089 is a perfect square

A *a)* only **B** *b)* only **C** *c)* only
D *a)* and *b)* only **E** *b)* and *c)* only

3 The square root of $12\frac{1}{4}$ is

A $1\frac{3}{4}$ **B** $3\frac{1}{2}$ **C** $3\frac{3}{4}$ **D** $6\frac{1}{4}$ **E** $6\frac{1}{8}$

4 Write 0·000 263 in standard form.

A $2{\cdot}63 \times 10^{-6}$ **B** $2{\cdot}63 \times 10^{-5}$
C $2{\cdot}63 \times 10^{-4}$ **D** $2{\cdot}63 \times 10^{4}$
E $2{\cdot}63 \times 10^{5}$

5 What is 0·003 867 to 3 significant figures?

A 0·004 **B** 0·003 86 **C** 0·003 87
D 386 **E** 387

6 If
$1 \times 2 = 2^2 - 2$
$2 \times 3 = 3^2 - 3$
$3 \times 4 = 4^2 - 4$
$4 \times 5 = 5^2 - 5$
. . . = . . .

a) complete $n \times (n + 1) = \ldots$;
b) use this to calculate $1\,001^2 - 1\,001$.

7 Draw graphs to show **a)** the first six multiples of 3, **b)** the factors of 42.

8 Write 1 296 as a product of its prime factors.

Hence find $\sqrt{1\,296}$.

9 The following numbers are in standard form. Change them to ordinary form.

a) 9×10^2 **b)** $3{\cdot}6 \times 10^5$ **c)** $6{\cdot}1 \times 10^7$
d) 8×10^{-4} **e)** 6×10^{-1} **f)** $3{\cdot}4 \times 10^{-3}$

10 A student writes 78 words in 8 lines of writing.

a) Find, to the nearest whole number, the average number of words per line.
b) Estimate how many lines of writing it will take to write a 1 500-word essay.

Revision exercise 2 *(Chapters 3, 6)*

1 In Fig. R1, ABCD is a kite with angles as shown. Find the sizes of angles x and y.

2 In Fig. R2, ABCD and CDEF are squares and CFXY and BCYZ are rectangles. Their

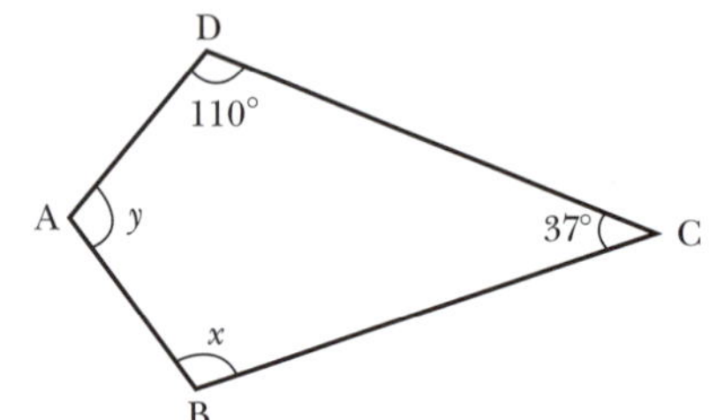

Fig. R1

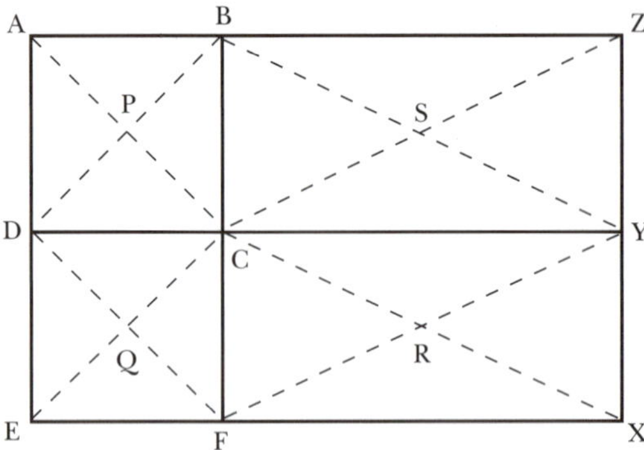

Fig. R2

diagonals cross at P, Q, R, S respectively. What kind of quadrilateral is

a) BPCS **b)** CQFR **c)** PDQC
d) SCRY **e)** SCFY **f)** BDFY
g) PDEC **h)** PQRS **i)** XYBF?

3 In Fig. R3, WXYZ is a rhombus. Its diagonals have been drawn and $W\hat{Y}Z = 26°$. Find the sizes of angles *a* and *b*.

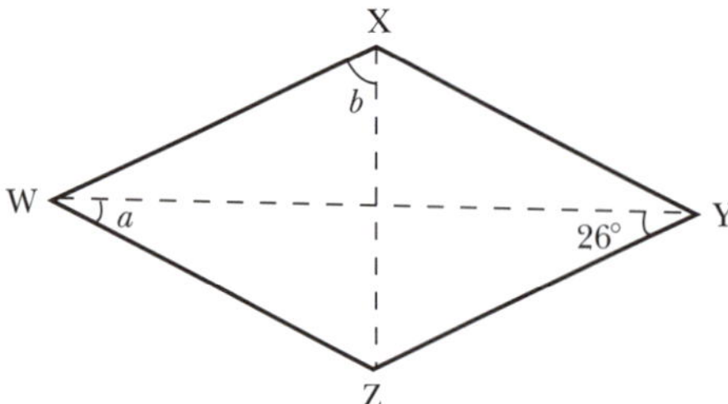

Fig. R3

4 In Fig. R4, AB = AC = CD and $C\hat{A}D = 28°$. If BCD is a straight line, find the sizes of angles *a*, *b*, *c*, *d*, *e*.

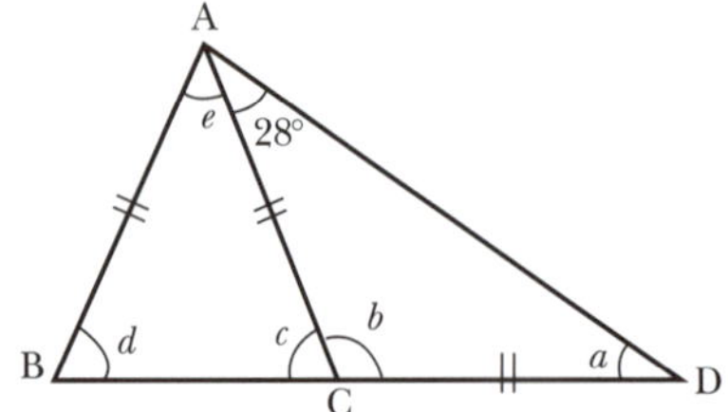

Fig. R4

5 In Fig. R5, ABCD is a parallelogram and ABXY is a rhombus. If BC = 3 cm and CD = 5 cm, find the perimeter of the whole figure.

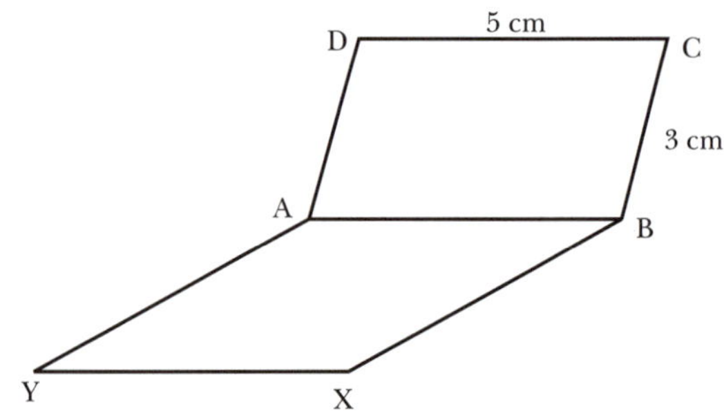

Fig. R5

6 A quadrilateral has angles of 117°, 42°, 146° and $x°$. Find the value of *x*.

7 Calculate the size of each angle of a regular 15-sided polygon.

8 **a)** Find the sum of the angles of a hexagon.
b) Hence calculate the value of *x* in Fig. R6.

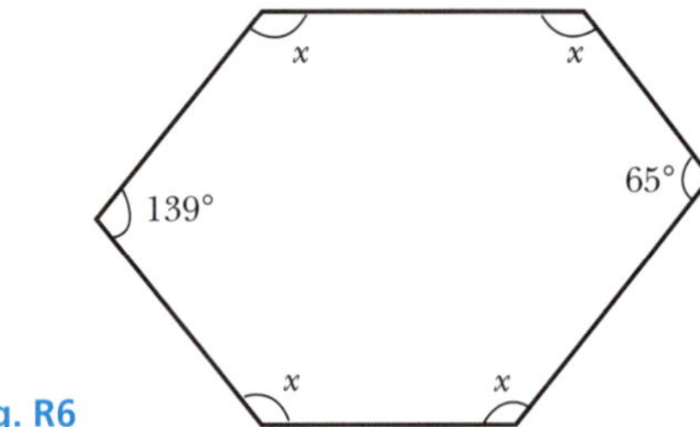

Fig. R6

9 The sum of three of the angles of a nonagon is 462°. The other six angles are all equal to each other. Calculate the size of each of the other angles.

10 Copy patterns *a)* and *b)* of Fig. R7 on to graph paper. Extend each pattern by repeating the sequence of basic shapes.

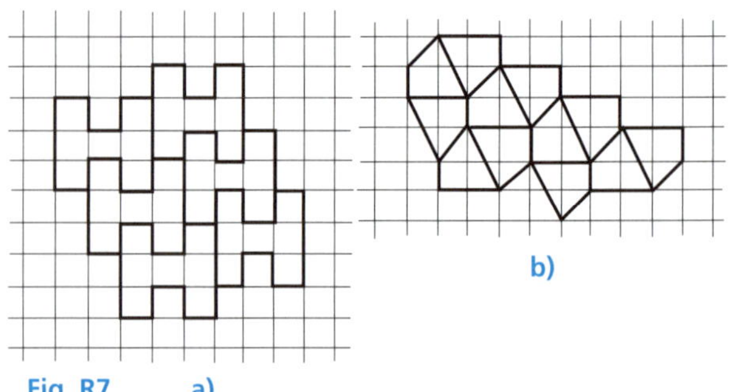

Fig. R7 a)

Revision test 2 *(Chapters 3, 6)*

1 In Fig. R8, PQRT and TQRS are parallelograms.

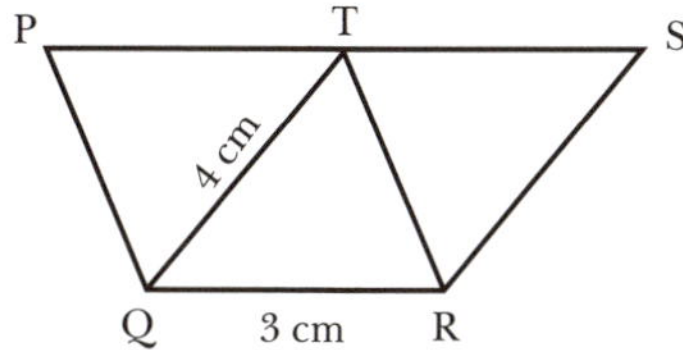

Fig. R8

QR = 3 cm and TQ = 4 cm. What is PS?

A 3 cm **B** 4 cm **C** 5 cm **D** 6 cm **E** 7 cm

2 Which one of the following statements is false?

A All rhombuses are parallelograms.
B All trapeziums are parallelograms.
C All squares are kites.
D All squares are rectangles.
E All rectangles are trapeziums.

3 In Fig. R9, PQ is parallel to RS and the line LM crosses PQ and RS at F and G respectively.

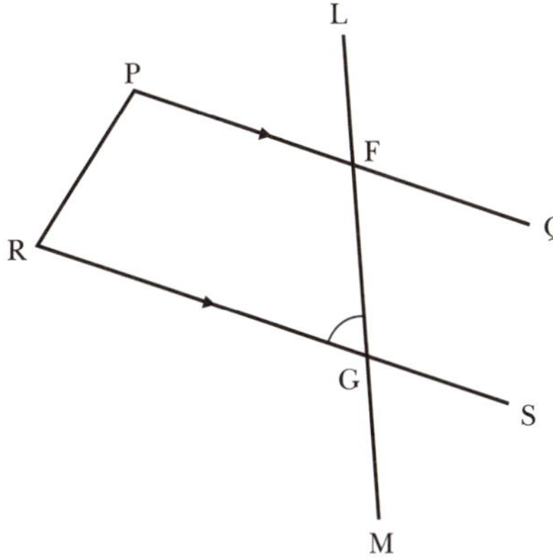

Fig. R9

Which angle is a corresponding angle to $F\hat{G}R$?

A $Q\hat{F}G$ **B** $P\hat{F}G$ **C** $F\hat{G}S$ **D** $P\hat{R}G$ **E** $L\hat{F}P$

4 In Fig. R10, POQ and SOR are straight lines. If $P\hat{O}S = 40°$ and $T\hat{O}Q = 65°$, calculate $T\hat{O}R$.

A 105° **B** 35° **C** 30° **D** 25° **E** 15°

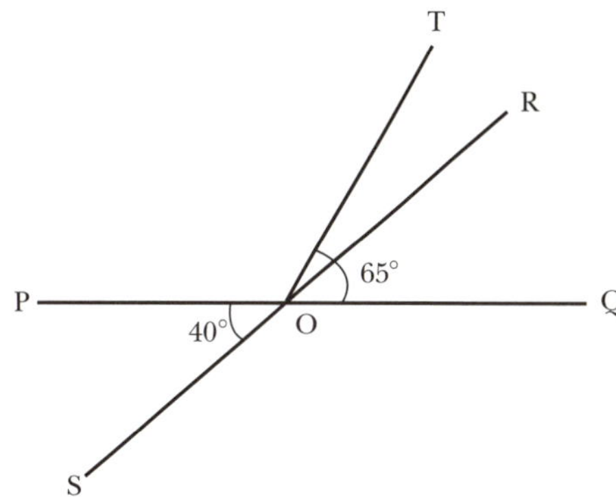

Fig. R10

5 In Fig. R11, the size of angle x is

A 29° **B** 32° **C** 58° **D** 61° **E** 64°

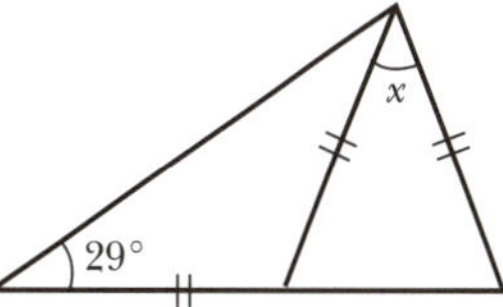

Fig. R11

6 A quadrilateral has angles of 128°, 91°, $a°$ and $2a°$. Find the value of a.

7 The sum of the angles of a polygon is 1 620°. Calculate the number of sides that the polygon has.

8 a) Find the sum of the angles of a pentagon.

b) Hence calculate the value of y in Fig. R12.

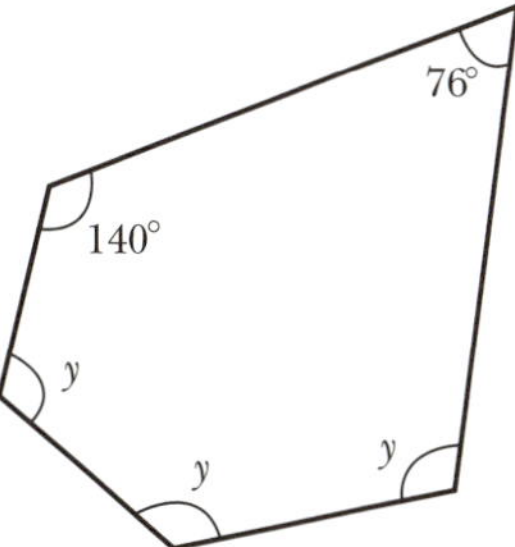

Fig. R12

9 The sum of four of the angles of a heptagon (seven sides) is 600°. The other three angles are of sizes $4x°$, $5x°$ and $6x°$. Find the value of x and hence find the sizes of the three angles.

10 Sketch a quadrilateral which has only one line of symmetry.

Revision exercise 3 *(Chapters 4, 5, 7)*

1 Simplify the following.

a) $(-5) \times 3$ **b)** $(-8) \times (-2)$
c) $6 \times (-5)$ **d)** $(-1) \times (-9)$
e) $(-7) \times (-3)$ **f)** $29 \times (-2)$
g) $(+18) \div (-6)$ **h)** $(-8) \div (-4)$
i) $(-30) \div (-10)$ **j)** $\dfrac{-19}{-1}$
k) $\dfrac{-100}{25}$ **l)** $\dfrac{48}{-8}$

2 Write down

a) the additive inverses of $+6, -18, -48, +2\frac{1}{2}$;
b) the multiplicative inverses of $+\frac{3}{4}, -\frac{2}{3}, \dfrac{x}{3a}, 2y$;
c) the inverse operations of *add 5, subtract 3, multiply by 1·2, divide by −4.*

3 Simplify the following.

a) $5 \times (-2a)$ **b)** $\frac{1}{2}$ of $-8c$
c) $-45x \div (-9)$ **d)** $\dfrac{-33ab}{11b}$

4 Remove brackets from the following.

a) $4(5x - 9)$ **b)** $(7 - 2g)3$
c) $-8(a + 9b)$ **d)** $(6 + 3x)(-2)$
e) $-3(x - 5y)$ **f)** $(2 - 7a)(-4)$
g) $-5(-3 + 9a)$ **h)** $-2(-x - 6y)$

5 Find the value of the following when $a = 3$, $b = -1$ and $c = 4$.

a) $-2b$ **b)** $\dfrac{a+b}{c}$ **c)** $\dfrac{c}{a-b}$

6 Solve the following.

a) $-3x = 12$ **b)** $8n = -32$
c) $-5d = -35$ **d)** $\dfrac{1}{6}m = \dfrac{5}{36}$
e) $\dfrac{3a}{2} = \dfrac{9}{14}$ **f)** $-2\frac{1}{3}x = -14$

7 Remove brackets and simplify the following.

a) $3x - 2(2x - y)$
b) $3(3x - 7) + (5x - 9)$
c) $7(x - 2y) - 5(x - 3y)$
d) $8(x + y) - 7(2x - y)$

8 Expand the following.

a) $(a + b)(x + y)$ **b)** $(5 - x)(6 + y)$
c) $(m + 4)(n - 8)$ **d)** $(2p + q)(3r - 5s)$

9 Expand the following.

a) $(u + 2v)(u + 3v)$
b) $(2c - 5)(c - 3)$
c) $(3x + 2y)(2x - y)$
d) $(2a - 9b)(4a + 5b)$

10 Expand the following.

a) $(a + 3)^2$ **b)** $(b - 5)^2$
c) $(2x + 1)^2$ **d)** $(m + 4n)^2$

Revision test 3 *(Chapters 4, 5, 7)*

1 If $(-3) \div (-24) = y$, then $y =$

A $+72$ **B** $+8$ **C** $+\frac{1}{8}$ **D** $-\frac{1}{8}$
E -8

2 Which one of the following is the inverse operation of add 8?

A subtract -8 **B** add $-\frac{1}{8}$ **C** subtract $-\frac{1}{8}$
D add $\frac{1}{8}$ **E** subtract 8

3 Simplify $\dfrac{-5a^2}{15a}$.

A $\dfrac{5a}{3}$ **B** $-\frac{2}{3}$ **C** -2 **D** $-\dfrac{a}{3}$ **E** $-\dfrac{a}{5}$

4 Find the value of $\dfrac{b}{2a + b}$ when $a = 5$ and $b = -2$.

A $-\frac{1}{3}$ **B** $-\frac{1}{4}$ **C** $-\frac{1}{9}$ **D** $\frac{1}{6}$ **E** $\frac{1}{10}$

5 Simplify $(a + (-a)) + b$.

A $2b$ **B** b **C** $2a$ **D** $2a - b$ **E** $2a + b$

6 Simplify the following.

a) $(-6) \times 8$ **b)** $(-2\frac{1}{2}) \times (-2\frac{2}{5})$
c) $\frac{7}{8}$ of $(-5\frac{1}{3})$ **d)** $38 \div (-2)$
e) $(-3{\cdot}6) \div (-9)$ **f)** $(-3\frac{2}{3}) \div 6\frac{3}{5}$

7 Solve the following.

a) $-3x = 18$ **b)** $\frac{1}{5}a = \frac{7}{15}$
c) $\dfrac{n}{2} = -5$ **d)** $\frac{27}{2}d = 42$
e) $-\dfrac{7m}{10} = -2\frac{4}{5}$ **f)** $\frac{5}{8}y = -1\frac{1}{4}$

8 I think of a number. 19 subtracted from the number gives -2. What number am I thinking of?

9 Find the value of the following when $x = -2$, $y = 5$, $z = -1$.

a) $x^2 + y^2$ **b)** $(x + y)^2$
c) $\dfrac{x + y}{y + z}$ **d)** $\dfrac{x}{y} + \dfrac{y}{z}$

10 Expand the following.

a) $(v-4)(v-9)$ **b)** $(b+4)(3b+2)$
c) $(5x+2)(2x-3)$ **d)** $(4m-n)(3m-2n)$

General revision test A (Chapters 1–8)

1 What is the next term in the sequence 1, 3, 7, 15, 31, ...?

A 33 **B** 47 **C** 51 **D** 59 **E** 63

2 Find the least number by which 112 must be multiplied to give a perfect square.

A 2 **B** 3 **C** 5 **D** 7 **E** 11

3 Express 526 000 in standard form.

A $5{\cdot}26 \times 10^{-5}$ **B** $5{\cdot}26 \times 10^{-4}$
C $5{\cdot}26 \times 10^{3}$ **D** $5{\cdot}26 \times 10^{4}$
E $5{\cdot}26 \times 10^{5}$

4 A length of wire is given as 6·8 cm correct to 2 significant figures. What is the least possible length of the wire?

A 6·7 cm **B** 6·74 cm **C** 6·75 cm
D 6·8 cm **E** 6·85 cm

5 In Fig. R13, ABCD is a kite. $B\hat{A}C = 26°$ and $A\hat{D}C = 105°$. $A\hat{C}D =$

A 26° **B** 41° **C** 49° **D** 62° **E** 64°

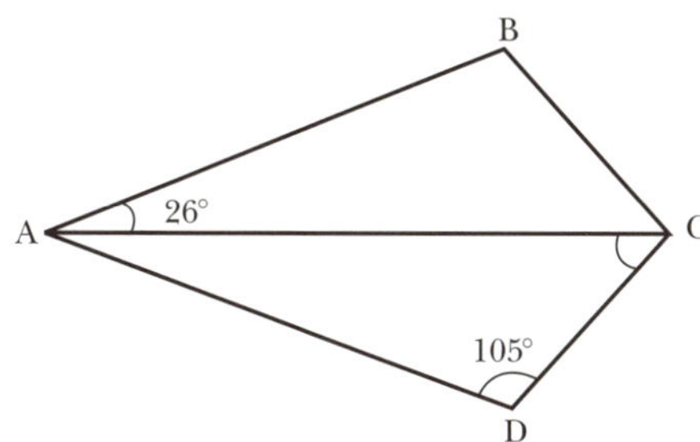

Fig. R13

6 Simplify $(y+z)^2 - 2yz$.

A $y^2 + z^2 + 4yz$ **B** $y^2 - z^2$
C $y^2 + z^2$ **D** $y^2 + z^2 - 2yz$
E $y^2 + z^2 - 4yz$

7 If $m \times (-2) = 12$, then $m =$

A +24 **B** +14 **C** +6 **D** −6
E −24

8 If $\frac{5}{6}$ of a certain number is $-6\frac{2}{3}$, the number is

A $-\frac{1}{8}$ **B** $-5\frac{1}{3}$ **C** $-5\frac{5}{9}$ **D** $-7\frac{1}{2}$
E −8

9 In Fig. R14, ABCDE is a pentagon such that △ABD is equilateral.

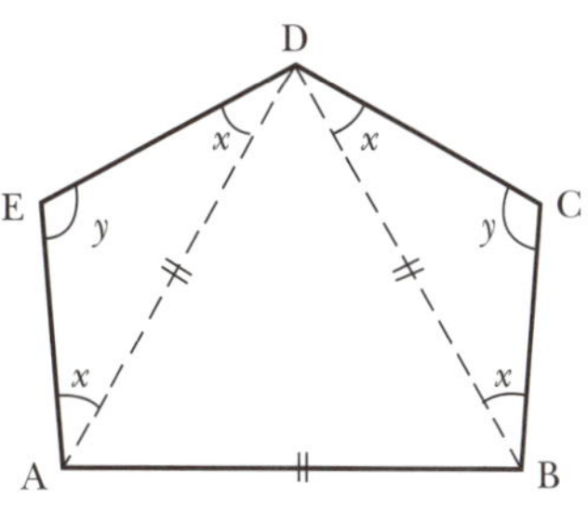

Fig. R14

If $x = 35°$, then $y =$

A 95° **B** 110° **C** 120° **D** 130°
E 145°

10 What is the value of $p^2q - q^2p$ if $p = 3$ and $q = 1$?

A −12 **B** −6 **C** 0 **D** 6 **E** 12

11 Express the following as products of their prime factors.

a) 800 **b)** 126 **c)** 198

12 If

$$\begin{aligned} 1 &= 1^2 \\ 1 + 3 &= 2^2 \\ 1 + 3 + 5 &= 3^2 \\ 1 + 3 + 5 + 7 &= 4^2 \\ \ldots &= \ldots \end{aligned}$$

a) what will be the value of x if $1 + 3 + 5 + \ldots + x = 23^2$,
b) what will be the value of y if $1 + 3 + 5 + \ldots + 99 = y^2$?

13 Express $1{\cdot}56 \times 10^4$ as a whole number correct to 2 significant figures.

14 Express 0·504 6 correct to **a)** 3 decimal places, **b)** 2 significant figures, **c)** the nearest $\frac{1}{10}$.

15 Simplify the following.

a) $(-6) \times (+5)$ **b)** $(+7) \times (-0{\cdot}9)$
c) $(-10)^2$ **d)** $(-5) \div (-40)$
e) $(-5{\cdot}4) \div (+0{\cdot}6)$ **f)** $\dfrac{+34}{-17}$

16 Solve the following.

a) $\frac{3}{4}m = \frac{15}{44}$ **b)** $1\frac{2}{3}x = 5\frac{5}{6}$
c) $\frac{x}{5} = -\frac{5}{8}$ **d)** $-1\frac{3}{7} = -3\frac{1}{3}y$

17 Find the value of k in Fig. R15.

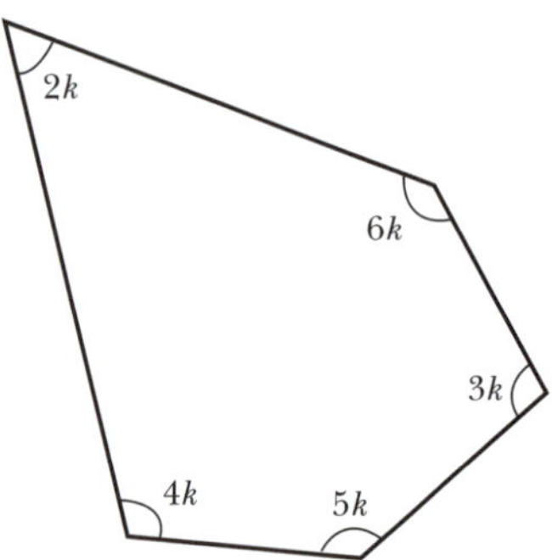

Fig. R15

18 Expand the following.

a) $(x - 5)(x - 6)$ **b)** $(2p - 3q)(2p - 5q)$
c) $(m + 4)(m - 4)$ **d)** $(t - 8)^2$

19 Fig. R16 shows part of a pattern. Make a sketch of the basic shape which makes the pattern.

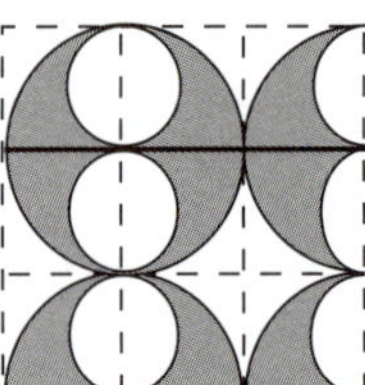

Fig. R16

20 10 nails have a mass of about 63 g. Estimate the number of nails in 1 kg to the nearest 10 nails.

9 Proportion, ratio, rate

Fractions and percentages (revision)

To change a common fraction to a decimal fraction

Divide the numerator of the fraction by its denominator. For example,

$\frac{5}{8} = 5{\cdot}000 \div 8$
$= 0{\cdot}625$ (a terminating decimal)

$\frac{1}{9} = 1{\cdot}000 \div 9$
$= 0{\cdot}111\ldots$
$= 0{\cdot}\dot{1}$ (a recurring decimal)

To change a decimal fraction to a common fraction

Write the decimal fraction as a fraction with a denominator which is a power of 10. Simplify if possible.

For example,

$$0{\cdot}85 = \frac{85}{100} = \frac{85 \div 5}{100 \div 5} = \frac{17}{20}$$

To change a fraction to a percentage

Multiply the fraction by 100.
For example,

$$\frac{4}{7} = (\tfrac{4}{7} \times 100)\% = \tfrac{400}{7}\% = 57\tfrac{1}{7}\%$$
$$0{\cdot}145 = (0{\cdot}145 \times 100)\% = 14{\cdot}5\% = 14\tfrac{1}{2}\%$$

To change a percentage to a fraction

Divide the percentage by 100.
For example,

$92\% = \frac{92}{100}$
$= 0{\cdot}92$ (as a decimal fraction)
$= \frac{23}{25}$ (as a common fraction)

Exercise 9a *(Revision)*

1 Change the following to decimal fractions.

a) $\frac{3}{8}$ **b)** $\frac{12}{25}$ **c)** $\frac{1}{20}$
d) $\frac{1}{3}$ **e)** $\frac{2}{3}$ **f)** $\frac{8}{9}$

2 Change the following to common fractions in their lowest terms.

a) 0·2 **b)** 0·55 **c)** 0·312
d) 0·264 **e)** 0·004 **f)** 0·875

3 Change the following to percentages.

a) $\frac{4}{5}$ **b)** 0·1 **c)** $\frac{5}{6}$
d) 0·222 **e)** $2\frac{1}{2}$ **f)** 0·105

4 Change the following percentages to fractions.

a) 60% **b)** 28% **c)** 4%
d) $2\frac{1}{2}\%$ **e)** 128% **f)** $5\frac{2}{3}\%$

If you had difficulty with Exercise 9a, revise Chapters 4 and 9 in Book 1.

Proportion

Unitary method

Read Examples 1 and 2 carefully.

Example 1

A worker gets Le90 000 *for* 10 *days of work. Find the amount for* *a)* 3 *days* *b)* 24 *days* *c) x days.*

We are to find money. Money comes last in every line of working.
For 10 days the worker gets Le90 000
For 1 day the worker gets Le90 000 ÷ 10 = Le9 000
a) For 3 days the worker gets
3 × Le9 000 = Le270 000
b) For 24 days the worker gets
24 × Le9 000 = Le216 000
c) For x days the worker gets x × Le9 000 = Le9 000x

Notice the following.

1 Each line of working is a complete sentence.
2 The quantity to be found comes last in each sentence.
3 The first sentence states the given facts.

4 The second sentence gives the pay for 1 day, a **unit**.

This is an example of **direct proportion**. The less time worked (3 days), the less money paid (Le27 000). The more time worked (24 days), the more money paid (Le216 000).

Example 2

Seven workers dig a piece of ground in 10 *days. How long would five workers take?*

We are to find time. Time comes last in every line of working.

7 workers take 10 days
1 worker takes 10×7 days = 70 days
5 workers take $70 \div 5$ days = 14 days

Notice the following:

1 We assume that all the workers work at the same rate.
2 The second sentence gives the time for one unit, a single worker.

This is an example of **inverse proportion**. Fewer workers (5) take a longer time (14 days). More workers (7) take a shorter time (10 days).

Example 3

Five people took 8 *days to plant* 1 200 *trees. How long will it take ten people to plant the same number of trees?*

5 people take 8 days
1 person takes 8×5 days = 40 days
10 people take $40 \div 10$ days = 4 days

Notice in Example 3 that the number of trees was not used.

When solving problems by the unitary method, always:

1 write in sentences with the quantity to be found at the end;
2 decide whether the problem is an example of direct or inverse proportion;
3 find the rate for 1 unit before answering the problem. This is where the **unitary method** gets its name from.

Many problems cannot be answered by unitary method. For example, 'If a girl is 1 metre tall when she is 6 years old, how tall will she be when she is 18?' We cannot say. She will certainly *not* be 3 metres tall!

Exercise 9b *(Oral)*

In this exercise, **i)** give the first sentence of working, **ii)** state whether the problem is an example of *direct proportion* or *inverse proportion* or *neither*, **iii)** answer part **a)** only.

1 A woman is paid Le7 500 for 5 days. Find her pay for **a)** 1 day, **b)** 2 days, **c)** 22 days.
2 Six notebooks cost Le6 000. Find the cost of **a)** one notebook, **b)** five notebooks, **c)** 44 notebooks.
3 Five men build a wall in 10 days. How long will it take **a)** one man, **b)** 10 men, **c)** 25 men?
4 A two-year-old boy has six sisters. **a)** How many sisters did he have when he was one year old? How many sisters will he have when he is **b)** three years old, **c)** 21 years old?
5 A car travels 84 km in 2 hours. How far does it travel in **a)** 1 hour, **b)** 3 hours, **c)** x hours?
6 A piece of land has enough grass to feed 15 cows for 4 days. How long would it last **a)** one cow, **b)** six cows, **c)** y cows?
7 The temperature of 6 litres of liquid is 30°C. Find the temperature of **a)** 1 litre, **b)** 8 litres, **c)** 400 ml.
8 Nine equal bottles hold $4\frac{1}{2}$ litres of water altogether. How much water does **a)** one bottle, **b)** five bottles, **c)** x bottles hold?
9 A container has enough water to last nine people for 4 days. How long would it last **a)** one person, **b)** eight people, **c)** z people?
10 A car uses 10 litres of petrol in 80 km. How far will it go on **a)** 1 litre, **b)** 5 litres, **c)** x litres?
11 It takes three lorries 84 trips to carry all the sugar in a warehouse to the market. How many trips will it take **a)** one lorry, **b)** seven lorries, **c)** x lorries?
12 It takes five students 1 hour to sweep their dormitory. Find how long it will take **a)** one student, **b)** three students, **c)** 12 students.

Exercise 9c

1 Where possible, work out parts b) and c) to the questions of Exercise 9b.
2 A man gets Le80 000 for 5 days' work. How much does he get for 14 days?
3 It takes four people 3 days to dig a small field. How long would it take three people to do the same work?
4 A girl buys seven pens for Le2 100. How much would 10 pens cost?

5 A 3-tonne lorry makes 10 journeys to move a pile of earth. How many journeys would a 5-tonne lorry make?

6 A 14-year old boy runs 100 m in 14 seconds. How long would it take a 6-year old boy?

7 A bag of corn can feed 100 chickens for 12 days. How long would the same bag feed 80 chickens?

8 It takes twenty-one 9-litre buckets to fill a drum with water. How many 7-litre buckets would it take?

9 A car travels at 60 km/h and takes 5 hours for a journey. How long would the car take if it travelled at 90 km/h?

10 A 480-page book is 2·4 cm thick (not counting the thickness of the covers). Find the thickness of 380 pages of the book.

11 A bag of rice feeds 15 students for 7 days. How long would the same bag feed 10 students?

12 Five buses need three trips to take 450 students to the stadium to watch a concert. How many trips would three buses need to take the same number of students?

Ratio

Suppose that two chairs cost Le6 000 and Le8 000. The **ratio** of their prices is 6 000 : 8 000, 'six thousand to eight thousand'.

Ratios behave in the same way as fractions. For example,

$$\frac{6\,000}{8\,000} = \frac{3\,000}{4\,000} = \frac{12\,000}{16\,000} = \frac{3}{4}$$

and $6000:8000 = 3000:4000 = 12000:16000 = 3:4$

Thus, both parts of a ratio may be multiplied or divided by the same number. It is usual to express ratios as whole numbers in their lowest terms.

Example 4

Express the ratio of 8 cm *to* 3·5 cm *as simply as possible.*

$$\begin{aligned} 8 \text{ cm to } 3{\cdot}5 \text{ cm} &= 8:3{\cdot}5 \\ &= 8 \times 2 : 3{\cdot}5 \times 2 \\ &= 16:7 \end{aligned}$$

Notice that we do not give units in a ratio.

Example 5

Express the ratio 96c : $1.20 *as simply as possible.*

Express both sums of money in cents.

$$\frac{96\text{c}}{\$1.20} = \frac{96\text{c}}{120\text{c}} = \frac{96}{120} = \frac{96 \div 24}{120 \div 24} = \frac{4}{5}$$

The ratio is 4 : 5.

Notice that quantities must be in the same units before they can be given as a ratio.

Exercise 9d

Express the following ratios as simply as possible.

1 3 : 6
2 20 to 30
3 15 : 12
4 28 to 21
5 Le10 to Le15
6 1 h to 15 min
7 1 mm to 1 cm
8 400 kg : 1 tonne
9 80 s to 2 min
10 18 boys to 12 boys
11 $200 to $150
12 Le1.25 : 75c
13 2 days to 1 week
14 3 days to 3 weeks
15 1 h 30 min: 2 h
16 5 cm to 5 mm
17 Le60 : Le84
18 5 m to $3\frac{1}{2}$ m
19 35° to 90°
20 90 km/h : 120 km/h

Example 6

Fill the gap in the ratio 2 : 7 =   : 28.

Let the missing number be *a*.

Then $2:7 = a:28$

$$\text{or } \frac{2}{7} = \frac{a}{28}$$

$$\text{Thus } a = \frac{2 \times 28}{7} = 8$$

The missing number is 8.

Exercise 9e

Fill the gaps in the following.

1 $\frac{4}{5} = \frac{}{10}$

2 4 : 5 =   : 10

3 $\frac{3}{8} = \frac{9}{}$

4 3 : 8 = 9 :

5 6 : 9 =   : 15

6 10 : 12 = 25 :

7 8 : 12 =   : 9

8   : 9 = 16 : 24

9 120 :   = 84 : 56

10 22 : 18 = 33 :

Sharing

Ratios are often used when sharing quantities.

Example 7

Two students share 35 mangoes in the ratio 2 : 3. How many mangoes does each students get?

Treat the parts of the ratio as shares.
One student gets 2 shares.
The other student gets 3 shares.
There are 5 shares altogether.
Number of mangoes in 5 shares $= 35$
Number of mangoes in 1 share $= \frac{35}{5} = 7$
Number of mangoes in 2 shares $= 2 \times 7 = 14$
Number of mangoes in 3 shares $= 3 \times 7 = 21$
One student gets 14 mangoes and the other student gets 21 mangoes.

Exercise 9f

1 Share the following quantities in the given ratios.
  a) Le15 000 in the ratio 1 : 2
  b) 26 kg in the ratio 5 : 8
  c) 20 cm in the ratio 4 : 1
  d) Le30 000 in the ratio 2 : 3
  e) 80 ml in the ratio 3 : 7
  f) 22 oranges in the ratio 9 : 2
2 Two women share 60 eggs in the ratio 1 to 2. How many eggs does each receive?
3 Juma is 12 years old and Tunde is 8 years old. They share 15 bananas in the ratio of their ages. How many does each get?
4 Two regions have populations of 2 850 000 and 5 030 000 respectively.
  a) Express each population to the nearest million.
  b) Give the rounded populations as a ratio in its simplest terms.
  c) If the regions share Le26 million in the ratios of their populations, find the approximate amount that each region gets.
5 A farmer divides 240 cattle among his three children in the ratio 5 : 4 : 3. How many cattle does each get?

Many problems which can be solved by the unitary method can also be solved by using ratios.

Example 8

If four watches cost Le1 920, find the cost of nine watches.

Cost of 9 watches : cost of 4 watches $= 9 : 4$
Cost of 4 watches $=$ Le1 920
Cost of 9 watches $= \frac{9}{4} \times$ Le1 920
$= 9 \times$ Le480
$=$ Le4 320

Notice that this is an example of direct ratio, or direct proportion.

Example 9

If five men dig a drain in 14 days, how long would seven men take?

Time taken by 7 men : time taken by 5 men = 5 : 7
(More men take less time.)
Time taken by 5 men $=$ 14 days
Time taken by 7 men $= \frac{5}{7} \times 14$ days
$= 10$ days

Notice that this is an example of inverse ratio, or inverse proportion.

Example 10

If 450 g of jam costs Le1 800, how much will $1\frac{1}{2}$ kg cost?

Units must be the same.
Working in grammes,
Cost of 1 500 g : cost of 450 g = 1 500 : 450 = 10 : 3
Cost of 450 g $=$ Le1 800
Cost of $1\frac{1}{2}$ kg $= \frac{10}{3} \times$ Le1 800 $=$ Le6 000

Example 11

A full water tank serves 50 students for 10 days. For how long will the same tank serve 125 students?

Time served for 50 students $= 10$ days
Time served for 125 students $= \frac{50}{125} \times 10$ days
$= 4$ days

Exercise 9g

1 If 10 ball-point pens cost Le3 000 how much will three pens cost?
2 A shelf holds 21 books each 5 cm thick. How many books, each 7 cm thick, will the shelf hold?
3 If 13 light-bulbs cost Le13 000, how much will 17 light-bulbs cost?

4 To pay for a television set it takes 15 monthly payments of Le12 800. How long will it take at Le8 000 per month?

5 It costs Le100 800 to stay at a hotel for 7 days. How much does it cost to stay for 3 days?

6 42% of a lottery is given as first prize and 28% as second prize. If the first prize is Le108 600, what is the second prize? (To the nearest Le100.)

7 A rope can be cut into 18 lengths of 17·5 cm. How many lengths of 15·75 cm can it be cut into?

8 If Le400 is equivalent to 85 fr CFA, approximately how many francs are equivalent to Le250?

9 A lorry can carry 820 bricks each of mass 1·68 kg. How many 1·64 kg bricks can it carry?

10 A cyclist takes 3 h 41 min to cycle to a village at an average speed of 19 km/h. If the next day it takes 4 h 7 min, what is the average speed?

11 A school notice board can take 60 sheets of paper. How many posters could be displayed on the same notice board if each poster is about three times as large as a sheet of paper?

12 81 carpets, each measuring 1 m^2, are required to cover the floor of a hall. How many 9 m^2 carpets are required to cover the same floor?

Percentages

Example 12

Find 15% *of* 2·8 kg.

$$\begin{aligned}15\% \text{ of } 2{\cdot}8\text{ kg} &= \tfrac{15}{100} \times 2{\cdot}8\text{ kg}\\ &= 15 \times 0{\cdot}028\text{ kg}\\ &= 0{\cdot}42\text{ kg} = 420\text{ g}\end{aligned}$$

Example 13

Express 3·3 m *as a percentage of* 7·5 m.

Express the quantities as a fraction: $\dfrac{3{\cdot}3\text{ m}}{7{\cdot}5\text{ m}} = \dfrac{33}{75}$

Express the fraction as a percentage:

$$\begin{aligned}\frac{33}{75} &= \frac{33}{75} \times 100\%\\ &= \frac{33 \times 4}{3}\%\\ &= 44\%\end{aligned}$$

Thus 3·3 m is 44% of 7·5 m.

Example 14

Le646 *is* 85% *of a sum of money. Find the sum of money.*

Using the direct ratio method,

$$\begin{aligned}85\% \text{ of the money} &= \text{Le}646\\ 100\% \text{ of the money} &= \text{Le}646 \times \tfrac{100}{85}\\ &= \text{Le}\tfrac{64\,600}{85} = \text{Le}\tfrac{3\,800}{5}\\ &= \text{Le}760\end{aligned}$$

or, by the unitary method,

$$\begin{aligned}85\% \text{ of the money} &= \text{Le}646\\ 1\% \text{ of the money} &= \frac{\text{Le}646}{85}\\ 100\% \text{ of the money} &= \frac{\text{Le}646}{85} \times 100 = \text{Le}760\end{aligned}$$

Exercise 9h

1 Find the value of the following.

a) 25% of Le100 **b)** 75% of Le300
c) 50% of 3·5 m **d)** $33\frac{1}{3}$% of 8·16 litres
e) $12\frac{1}{2}$% of Le1 136 **f)** 150% of 22 m
g) 19% of 300 **h)** 82% of Le1 500
i) 120% of 15 kg **j)** $2\frac{1}{2}$% of 60 km

2 Express i) as a percentage of ii).

a) i) 37 ii) 50
b) i) 64 ii) 400
c) i) Le1 300 ii) Le10 000
d) i) Le1 900 ii) Le5 700
e) i) 400 g ii) 8 kg
f) i) 1·5 m ii) 2·5 m
g) i) Le2 500 ii) Le1 000
h) i) 850 mm ii) 1 m
i) i) Le15 ii) Le24
j) i) 3·5 kg ii) 2·8 kg

3 Find the quantity of which

a) Le8 000 is 20% **b)** 12 m is 75%
c) 5 g is $33\frac{1}{3}$% **d)** Le9 000 is 30%
e) Le5.50 is 5% **f)** 4·35 kg is 150%
g) 39 is 78% **h)** 2·4 m is $66\frac{2}{3}$%
i) Le50 is 250% **j)** Le221 is 65%

Example 15

Factory X makes 400 *bicycles per week. Factory Y makes* 700 *bicycles per week. They increase their weekly production to* 424 *and* 735. *Which factory increases production at the greater rate per cent?*

Factory *X*: the increase is 24 on 400

Increase per cent $= \frac{24}{400} \times 100\% = 6\%$
Factory Y: the increase is 35 on 700
Increase per cent $= \frac{35}{700} \times 100\% = 5\%$
Factory X increases production at a greater rate per cent.

Notice that factory Y has the greater numerical increase, but the smaller increase per cent.

Exercise 9i

1 Express Le39 as a percentage of Le300.
2 Find $37\frac{1}{2}\%$ of 2 metres.
3 85% of a quantity is 1·19 kg. Find the quantity.
4 Find 46% of $2\frac{1}{2}$ kg.
5 Express 4·2 m^2 as a percentage of 6 m^2.
6 Le56 is $17\frac{1}{2}\%$ of a sum of money. Find the sum of money.
7 Find $8\frac{1}{3}\%$ of 84 g.
8 Find the quantity of which 5·6 kg is 175%.
9 Find 215% of 40 m.
10 Express Le234 as a percentage of Le180.
11 In an examination, a girl gets 336 marks out of 480. What percentage is this?
12 A man earns Le96 000 per month. His monthly rent is Le16 800. What percentage of his wages goes in rent?
13 A school has 575 students. 44% are boys. How many girls are in the school?
14 A farmer sells 99 hectares of land. This represents $37\frac{1}{2}\%$ of his original farm. How big was the original farm?
15 A rubber band is 7·5 cm long when unstretched. It is stretched to a length of 9·75 cm. What percentage is this of the original length?
16 A school has 675 desks. 54 of them are broken. Express the ratio, *number of broken desks : number of desks altogether* as a fraction in its lowest terms. Hence find the percentage of broken desks and the percentage of desks that are not broken.
17 65% of a farmer's trees are paw paw. The remainder are mangoes. What is the ratio, *number of paw paw trees : number of mango trees*? If the farmer has 936 paw paw trees, how many mango trees are there?
18 Last year village X had a population of 875 and village Y had a population of 1 175. This year it was found that X had increased by 16% and Y by 12%. Which village had the greater numerical increase in population?

Rate

45 km/h, Le800/day, 9 km/litre are all examples of **rates**. The first rate tells the distance gone in 1 hour. The second tells how much money is made in 1 day. The third tells the distance travelled on 1 litre. Say 45 km/h as '45 km per hour'.

Example 16

A car goes 160 km *in* 2 hours. *What is its rate in* km/h?

In 2 hours the car travels 160 km.
In 1 hour the car travels $\frac{160}{2}$ km $=$ 80 km
The rate of the car is 80 km/h.

Example 17

A worker gets Le24 000 *for* 5 *days' work. What is the rate of pay per day?*

In 5 days the worker gets Le24 000.
In 1 day the worker gets Le$\frac{24\,000}{5}$ $=$ Le4 800.
The worker's rate of pay is Le4 800/day.

Example 18

A car uses 10 litres *of petrol to travel* 74 km. *Express its petrol consumption as a rate in* km *per* litre.

On 10 litres the car travels 74 km
On 1 litre the car travels $\frac{74}{10}$ km $=$ 7·4 km
Its petrol consumption is 7·4 km/litre.

Example 19

The price of an article is reduced from Le400 *to* Le360. *Express the reduction as a rate of cents in the leone.*

Reduction $=$ Le400 $-$ Le360 $=$ Le40
On Le400 the reduction is Le40
On Le1 the reduction is Le$\frac{40}{400}$ $=$ Le$\frac{1}{10}$ $=$ 10c
The reduction is at the rate of 10c in the leone.

Notice that in every example, the unitary method is used to find rate.

Exercise 9j

1 A car travels 126 km in $1\frac{1}{2}$ hours. Find its rate in km/h.

2 An athlete runs 90 m in 10 seconds. Find this rate in metres per minute.

3 A football player scores 40 goals in 60 games. Find his rate of scoring in goals per game.

4 A car factory made 375 cars in 5 days. Find its production rate in cars per day.

5 The rent of a shop is Le1 128 000 per year. Express this as a monthly rate.

6 A piece of metal has a mass of 630 g and a volume of 70 cm^3. Find the density of the metal. *Note*: density is the rate g/cm^3.

7 A girl cycles at a rate of 16 km/h for $2\frac{1}{2}$ hours. How far does she travel?

8 A car travels 11 km per litre of petrol. Find how much petrol the car uses in going 891 km.

9 A trader reduces all his prices by 15c in the leone. Find the new price of a shirt which originally cost Le4 000.

10 A town with a population of 21 280 registered 633 births in a year. Round both numbers to 1 significant figure and estimate the birth rate per 1 000 population.

Chapter summary

(1) Problems in proportion can be solved by the *unitary method*:

a) Write a sentence with the quantity to be found at the end.

b) Decide whether the problem is an example of *direct* or *inverse* proportion.

c) Find the rate for 1 unit.

d) Then find the required quantity by multiplying (for direct proportion) or dividing (for inverse proportion).

(2) A *ratio* is said as 'three to ten' and written as 3:10.

(3) Ratios behave like fractions. For example:

$\frac{3}{10} = \frac{30}{100} = \ldots$

Similarly, 3:10 = 30:100 and so on.

(4) It is usual to express ratios in their lowest whole-number terms.

(5) The unitary method can be used to solve problems involving ratios. However, it is necessary to be clear about direct and inverse ratios.

(6) The principles of ratios and the unitary method can be used when solving problems with percentages (see Examples 12, 13 and 14).

(7) A *rate* is a ratio that involves a relation between two different quantities (e.g. km per hour, leones per month). Again, the unitary method is very helpful when solving problems with rates (see Examples 16, 17, 18 and 19).

10 Everyday arithmetic (4) Personal, household, civic, commercial

Personal arithmetic

Interest

Bankers want people to save money. They give extra payments to encourage saving. The extra money is called **interest**.

For example, a person saves Le10 000 in a bank for a year. If the **interest rate** is 8% per annum (i.e. 8% per year), the saver will have Le10 800 at the end of the year: the original Le10 000 plus Le800 interest from the bank. Interest that is paid like this is called **simple interest**.

Example 1

Find the simple interest on Le60 000 *for* 5 *years at* 9% *per annum.*

Yearly interest = 9% of Le60 000

$$= \frac{9}{100} \times \text{Le}60\,000 = \text{Le}5\,400$$

Interest for 5 years = Le5 400 × 5 = Le27 000

Exercise 10a

Find the simple interest on the following.

1 Le40 000 for 1 year at 5% per annum
2 Le70 000 for 1 year at 4% per annum
3 Le10 000 for 3 years at 6% per annum
4 Le10 000 for 2 years at 4% per annum
5 Le10 000 for 4 years at $4\frac{1}{2}$% per annum
6 Le10 000 for $3\frac{1}{2}$ years at 4% per annum
7 Le30 000 for 2 years at 5% per annum
8 Le20 000 for 4 years at 6% per annum
9 Le70 000 for 3 years at 5% per annum
10 Le60 000 for $2\frac{1}{2}$ years at 5% per annum
11 Le35 000 for 4 years at 3% per annum
12 Le25 000 for 2 years at 6% per annum
13 Le15 000 for 3 years at 4% per annum
14 Le55 000 for 4 years at 6% per annum
15 Le25 000 for 3 years at 5% per annum

Sometimes people have to borrow money. When someone borrows money that person has to pay interest to the lender.

Example 2

A man borrows Le1 600 000 *to buy a house. He is charged interest at a rate of* 11% *per annum. In the first year he paid the interest on the loan. He also paid back* Le100 000 *of the money he borrowed. How much did he pay back altogether? If he paid this amount by monthly instalments, how much did he pay per month?*

Interest on Le1 600 000

$$\begin{aligned}\text{for 1 year} &= 11\% \text{ of Le}1\,600\,000\\ &= \tfrac{11}{100} \times \text{Le}1\,600\,000\\ &= 11 \times \text{Le}16\,000\\ &= \text{Le}176\,000\end{aligned}$$

Total money paid in

$$\begin{aligned}\text{1st year} &= \text{Le}176\,000 + \text{Le}100\,000\\ &= \text{Le}276\,000\end{aligned}$$

Monthly payments = Le276 000 ÷ 12 = Le23 000
(Notice that the man now owes Le1 500 000. Interest will be paid on this new amount in the second year.)

Exercise 10b

1 Find the total amount to be paid back (i.e. loan+ interest) on the following loans.
   a) Le20 000 for 3 weeks at 10% interest per week
   b) Le10 000 for 1 year at 9% simple interest per annum
   c) Le1 000 000 for 15 years at 8% simple interest per annum
   d) Le600 000 for 3 years at $7\frac{1}{2}$% simple interest per annum
   e) Le860 000 for $2\frac{1}{2}$ years at $8\frac{1}{2}$% simple interest per annum

2 A man borrows Le4 000 on a short term loan. He is charged interest of Le1 on each Le10 per week. How much does he pay back altogether if he borrows the money **a)** for 1 week, **b)** for 3 weeks, **c)** for 10 weeks?

3 A woman borrows Le20 000 for 4 weeks. She agrees to pay Le25 000 back at the end of the 4 weeks.

a) How much interest does she pay over the 4 weeks?

b) How much interest does she pay per week?

c) Find the percentage rate of interest per week that she pays.

4 A man got a Le18 000 000 loan to buy a house. He paid interest at a rate of 9% per annum. In the first year he paid the interest on the loan. He also paid back Le1 400 000 of the money he borrowed.

a) How much did he pay in the first year altogether?

b) If he paid this amount in monthly instalments, how much did he pay each month?

5 A woman borrowed Le300 000 to pay for a bicycle. She agreed to pay the money back over 2 years, paying simple interest at 9% per annum.

a) Calculate the simple interest on Le300 000 at 9% per annum for 2 years.

b) Hence find the total amount she must pay back.

c) If the total money is paid back in monthly instalments over 2 years, how much will she pay each month?

Income tax

Most people have to pay a part of their income to the government. The part they pay is called **income tax**. The government uses taxes to pay for public services such as defence, education, health and transport.

The method of calculating taxes varies in different countries. Here is the Sierra Leone method, and an example to show how it is calculated.

Tax is paid each year on taxable income. The rates of tax on taxable income are given in Table 10.1.

taxable income	rate of tax
not over Le1 000 000 per annum	nil
next Le2 000 000 per annum	20%
next Le2 000 000 per annum	25%
next Le2 500 000 per annum	30%
excess over Le7 500 000 per annum	35%

Table 10.1

Example 3

A man has an income of Le7 200 000 per annum. Calculate the amount of tax he pays in a year.

First Le1 000 000 is **tax free**

taxable income = Le7 200 000 – Le1 000 000
= Le6 200 000

tax on Le2 000 000 + Le2 000 000 + Le2 200 000

$$\frac{20}{100} \text{ of Le2 000 000} = \text{Le400 000}$$

$$+ \frac{25}{100} \text{ of Le2 000 000} = +\text{Le500 000}$$

$$+ \frac{30}{100} \text{ of Le2 200 000} = +\text{Le660 000}$$

$$\text{total tax} = \text{Le1 560 000}$$

Note: Anyone earning below Le1 000 000 will not pay tax.

Exercise 10c

1 Calculate the monthly tax paid on an annual income of Le1 200 000.

2 Calculate the monthly income tax paid by a man who earns Le2 140 000 per annum.

3 Calculate the annual income tax on the salary for a woman who earns Le3 260 000.

4 Calculate the income tax paid per month by a Bank Manager whose annual salary was Le8 760 000.

5 Calculate the annual income tax paid by a doctor who earns annual salary of Le9 624 000.

6 An accountant earns Le13 200 000 in one year. What should he pay as tax
a) for the year
b) in one month?

Household arithmetic

Discount buying

A **discount** is a reduction in price. Discounts are often given for paying in cash.

Example 4

A radio costs Le54 000. *A* $12\frac{1}{2}\%$ *discount is given for cash. What is the cash price?*

Either:

$$\text{discount} = 12\tfrac{1}{2}\% \text{ of Le}54\,000 = \frac{12\frac{1}{2}}{100} \times \text{Le}54\,000$$
$$= \tfrac{1}{8} \times \text{Le}54\,000$$
$$= \text{Le}6\,750$$

$$\text{cash price} = \text{Le}54\,000 - \text{Le}6\,750 = \text{Le}47\,250$$

Or:

$$\text{cash price} = (100\% - 12\tfrac{1}{2}\%) \text{ of Le}54\,000$$
$$= 87\tfrac{1}{2}\% \text{ of Le}54\,000$$
$$= \frac{87\frac{1}{2}}{100} \times \text{Le}54\,000 = \tfrac{7}{8} \times \text{Le}54\,000$$
$$= \text{Le}47\,250$$

Discounts are often given for buying in bulk.

Example 5

A trader sells ball-point pens at Le250 *each or four for* Le800. *How much is saved by buying four pens at once instead of four pens separately?*

$$\text{Normal cost of 4 pens} = 4 \times \text{Le}250 = \text{Le}1\,000$$
$$\text{Discount price of 4 pens} = \text{Le}800$$
$$\text{Saving} = \text{Le}1\,000 - \text{Le}800$$
$$= \text{Le}200$$

Exercise 10d

1 Find the discount price if a discount of
a) 10% is given on a cost price of Le43 000
b) $12\frac{1}{2}\%$ is given on a cost price of Le28 000
c) 8% is given on a cost price of Le108 000
d) 25% is given on a marked price of Le9 200
e) 20% is given on a marked price of Le2 995

2 The selling price of a table is Le140 000. The trader gives a 25% discount for cash. What is the cash price?

3 During a sale a shop takes 12c in the leone off all marked prices. What would be the sale price of a shirt marked Le7 225?

4 A trader sells eggs at Le300 each or Le1 500 for six. How much is saved by buying three dozen eggs in sixes instead of separately?

5 A 500 g bag of salt costs Le500. A 20 kg sack of salt costs Le10 000. Calculate the saving per kg by buying the 20 kg sack of salt.

6 A market trader asks Le15 000 for some cloth. A woman offers Le8 000. After bargaining, they agree a price half-way between the two starting prices. How much does the woman pay? What discount did she get by bargaining?

Instalment buying

An **instalment** is a part payment. Many people find it easier to buy expensive items by paying instalments.

Example 6

The cost of a cassette player is either Le34 000 *in cash or a deposit of* Le4 000 *and* 12 *monthly payments of* Le2 750. *Find the difference between the instalment price and the cash price.*

Instalment price = deposit + instalments
= Le4 000 + 12 × Le2 750
= Le4 000 + Le33 000
= Le37 000

Price difference = Le37 000 − Le34 000 = Le3 000

Buying by instalment is called **hire purchase**. The buyer hires the use of an item before paying for it completely. This is why hire purchase is more costly than paying in cash.

Exercise 10e

1 The hire purchase price of a dressing mirror is Le124 200. This is spread over 12 equal monthly instalments. Calculate each instalment.

2 The hire purchase price of a table is Le84 000. 25% is paid as a deposit. The rest is spread over 12 equal monthly instalments.
   a) Calculate the amount of the deposit.
   b) Calculate the remainder to be paid.
   c) Find the amount of each monthly instalment.

3 To buy a suit, a man can either pay Le112 500 cash or he can pay 16 weekly instalments of Le8 050.
   a) Find the cost of the suit when paying by instalments.
   b) Find the difference between the cash and hire purchase prices.

4 A television set costs either Le494 000 cash or 52 weekly payments of Le11 450. How much more does the television set cost when paid for weekly?

5 The cash price of a car is Le8 970 600. The hire purchase payments require a 10% deposit and 36 monthly payments of Le244 200. Calculate the saving when paying in cash.

6 A refrigerator costs Le445 000. A 5% discount is given for a cash payment. Alternatively, it can be paid for by hire purchase. In this case the price is raised by 11%. Calculate the difference between paying cash and paying by hire purchase.

Civic arithmetic

Value Added Tax (VAT)

A proportion of the money paid for certain goods and services is given to the government. The part which is given to the government is called **Value Added Tax (VAT)**, and the goods and services are called **VATable** items. In Sierra Leone 5% of the cost of VATable items is given to the government as VAT. The government uses money collected as VAT to improve services such as education, health and transport.

Example 7

An advertisement for a table says that its price is 'Le153 000 *plus* 5% *VAT'. How much does the customer pay?*

Amount paid by customer = 105% of Le153 000

$$= \text{Le}153\,000 \times \frac{105}{100}$$

= Le160 650

Note: The difference between Le160 650 and Le153 000 is Le7 650. The Government receives Le7 650 as VAT.

Example 8

One year a company paid a Le945 000 *telephone bill to SIERRATEL. If* 5% *is the rate of VAT, calculate how much money the Government receives as VAT on the telephone bill.*

Since Le945 000 includes 5% VAT, then Le945 000 is 105% of the actual telephone bill. The VAT is 5% of the actual telephone bill.

105% of actual telephone bill = Le945 000
1% of actual telephone bill = Le945 000 ÷ 105
= Le9 000
5% of actual telephone bill = Le9 000 × 5
= Le45 000

The Government receives Le45 000 as VAT.

Exercise 10f

1 Find out how much customers pay for each item in the following advertisement:

TRUE FASHIONS	
(a) Shirts	Le8 000 + 5% VAT
(b) Dresses	Le24 000 + 5% VAT
(c) Jackets	Le29 000 + 5% VAT
(d) Trousers	Le19 000 + 5% VAT
(e) Shoes	Le22 000 + 5% VAT

2 Find the amount of money that the government receives as VAT on each item in the following advertisement:

COMFORT FURNISHING*	
(a) Coffee tables	Le56 700
(b) Mattresses	Le92 400
(c) Beds	Le108 150
(d) 3-piece suites	Le156 450
(e) Kitchen tables	Le69 300
*All prices include 5% VAT	

3 A contractor supplied some items to a school. The contractor's bill is shown below. If each amount includes 5% VAT, calculate how much the government receives as VAT.

(a) Stationery	Le 84 000
(b) Sports equipment	Le 262 500
(c) Desks and chairs	Le672 000
(d) School lockers	Le157 500
(e) Electrical fittings	Le52 500
Total	Le1 228 500

Electricity bills

Electricity bills are charged on the number of units of electricity used, the Demand charge (Le1 500 per bill) and the Value Added Tax (VAT) of 5% of the bill.

Example 9

An electricity meter changes from 45 243 *to* 46 143. *Calculate the bill if the cost of each unit is* Le150.

The difference between the two readings on the meter gives the number of units used.

$$\begin{array}{r} 46\,143 \\ -45\,243 \\ \hline \end{array}$$

Number of units used = 900
900 units at Le150 = Le135 000
Value Added Tax (VAT) = 5% of Le135 000
$= \frac{5}{100} \times$ Le135 000
= Le6 750
Demand charge = Le1 500
Total cost = Le135 000 + Le6 750 + Le1 500
= Le143 250

Exercise 10g

Unless told otherwise, use the rates in Example 9 for this exercise.

1 Find the bill for 296 units of electricity.
2 Find the bill for someone who uses only half as many units as given in question 1.
3 A consumer uses 588 units of electricity. Find the bill if the cost of each unit is Le120, the Demand charge is Le1 200 and VAT is 5%.
4 The reading on an electricity meter changes from 10 819 to 14 027. The charge is 35c per unit. Calculate the bill in dollars if the Demand charge is $5 and VAT is 5%.
5 Consecutive quarterly readings of an electricity meter are 39 125 and 45 223. If each unit costs Le130 calculate the bill in leones.

Post Office charges

Tables 10.3, 10.4 and 10.5 give the charges for letter post, parcel post and postal orders in Sierra Leone (2005).

postage rates: letters	
up to 20 g	Le2 500
for every extra 20 g or part thereof	Le2 500
aerogramme (Africa)	Le2 000
postcard	Le400

Table 10.3

postage rates: parcels	
up to 1 kg	Le57 000
over 1 kg and up to 3 kg	Le72 000
over 3 kg and up to 5 kg	Le112 000
over 5 kg and up to 10 kg	Le147 000
over 10 kg and up to 15 kg	Le183 000
over 15 kg and up to 20 kg	Le218 000
over 20 kg and up to 25 kg	Le273 000

Table 10.4

postal order charges (poundage) denomination	poundage
Le1 000	Le300
Le5 000	Le1 200
Le10 000	Le2 000
Le20 000	Le2 500
Le25 000	Le3 000
Le30 000	Le3 500
Le50 000	Le5 000

Table 10.5

Example 10

Find the cost of posting

a) six letters, each of which is less than 20 g,

b) one letter of mass 23 g,

c) one letter of mass 56 g.

a) six letters, each less than 20 g:
cost = 6 × Le2 500 = Le150 000

b) 23 g letter:

	mass	cost
first	20 g	Le2 500
subsequent	3 g	Le2 500
totals	23 g	Le5 000

The cost is Le5 000.

c) 56 g letter:

	mass	cost
first	20 g	Le2 500
second	20 g	Le2 500
subsequent	16 g	Le2 500
totals	56 g	Le7 500

The cost is Le7 500.

Notice that any letter over 20 g and under 40 g will cost Le5 000. Similarly any letter between 40 g and 60 g will cost Le7 500.

Example 11

Two parcels have masses of 2·2 kg *and* 2·6 kg. *a) Find the cost of posting these parcels. b) If both parcels are to be sent to the same person, find the saving if the two parcels are made into one parcel.*

a) Both parcels come in the range: *over* 1 kg *and up to* 3 kg,
postage = 2 × Le72 000 = Le144 000

b) If the parcels are made into one parcel,
mass of new parcel = 2·2 kg + 2·6 kg = 4·8 kg.
This comes in the range: *over* 3 kg *and up to* 5 kg
postage = Le112 000
saving = Le144 000 − Le112 000 = Le32 000

Example 12

A parent sends a postal order for Le85 000. *How much does the postal order cost?*

Cost of postal order
= value of postal order + poundage.
Postal orders are issued in a limited number of denominations (values). The poundage can be made up in a number of ways. For example,

a)	*b)*	*c)*
Le50 000 : Le5 000	Le50 000 : Le5000	Le30 000 : Le3 500
Le30 000 : Le3 500	Le25 000 : Le3 000	Le30 000 : Le3 500
Le5 000 : Le1 200	Le10 000 : Le2 000	Le25 000 : Le3 000
Le85 000 : Le9 700	Le85 000 : Le10 000	Le85 000 : Le10 000

Of these, *a)* is the cheapest.
Cost of postal order = Le85 000 + Le9 700
= Le94 700

The assistant in the Post Office will usually tell customers the cheapest way of buying postal orders.

Exercise 10h

1 Find the cost of posting letters of the following masses.

a) 14 g b) 9 g c) 18 g d) 20 g
e) 33 g f) 42 g g) 58 g h) 25 g
i) 65 g j) 13 g k) 40 g l) 50 g

2 Find the cost of posting parcels of the following masses.

a) 850 g b) 1·5 kg c) 7·24 kg
d) 8·1 kg e) 9·75 kg f) 2·92 kg
g) 4·92 kg h) 484 g i) 1 484 g
j) 7 kg k) 7·005 kg l) 6·994 kg

3 Find the poundage on postal orders of the following denominations.

a) Le30 000 b) Le5 000 c) Le50 000 d) Le10 000
e) Le25 000 f) Le20 000 g) Le1 000 h) Le100 000

4 Find the cost of posting the following.

a) Three postcards
b) Six aerogrammes
c) One postcard and a 36 g letter
d) Four letters under 20 g each and three aerogrammes
e) Two postcards, an aerogramme and a 52 g letter.

5 A textbook has a mass of 830 g. Find the cost of sending a parcel of 10 of these books. Allow 50 g for wrapping paper and string.

6 A man buys postal orders to the value of Le81 000. Find the total cost if he buys the postal orders in the cheapest possible way.

7 Three parcels have masses of 1·3 kg, 2·5 kg and 3·1 kg.

a) Find the total cost of posting these parcels.
b) If all the parcels are to be sent to the same person, find the saving if the three parcels are made into one parcel.

8 Find the cheapest way of buying postal orders to the value **a)** Le68 000, **b)** Le70 000. Give some reasons why postal orders to the value Le68 000 cost more than postal orders to the value Le70 000.

Commercial arithmetic

Profit and loss

Example 13

A trader buys a kettle for Le8 000 *and sells it at a profit of* 15%. *Find his actual profit and the selling price.*

$$\begin{aligned} \text{Profit} &= 15\% \text{ of Le}8\,000 = \tfrac{15}{100} \times \text{Le}8\,000 \\ &= \text{Le}\,\tfrac{120\,000}{100} \\ &= \text{Le}1\,200 \\ \text{Selling price} &= \text{Le}8\,000 + \text{Le}1\,200 \\ &= \text{Le}9\,200 \end{aligned}$$

Example 14

A hat is bought for Le2 500 *and sold for* Le2 200. *What is the loss per cent?*

Actual loss = Le2 500 − Le2 200 = Le300

The ratio, loss : cost = Le300 : Le2 500 = 300 : 2 500 = $\frac{300}{2500}$

Thus the loss is $\frac{300}{2500}$ of the cost price.

$$\begin{aligned} \text{Percentage loss} &= \tfrac{300}{2500} \times 100\% \\ &= 12\% \end{aligned}$$

Notice that the loss (or gain) is calculated as a percentage of the cost price.

Exercise 10i

1 Find (i) the profit or loss, and (ii) the selling price, for the following cost prices.

a) Le4 000; profit 20%
b) Le10 000; profit 15%
c) Le3 750; loss 8%
d) Le1 440; loss $12\frac{1}{2}$%
e) Le750; profit 60%

2 Find (i) the actual, (ii) the percentage profit or loss, for the following cost and selling prices.

	cost price	selling price
a)	Le3 000	Le3 450
b)	Le1 800	Le2 250
c)	Le360 000	Le324 000
d)	Le96 000	Le132 000
e)	Le4 200	Le3 570

3 A farmer buys a cow for Le400 000 and sells it for Le330 000. What is the percentage loss?

4 A trader bought some hats for Le1 900 each. She sold them at a 30% profit. What was the selling price?

5 A carpenter bought some wood for Le9 000. He used the wood to make a box which he sold for Le30 000. What percentage profit was this?

6 Amadu bought a cap for Le2 500. He sold it to Ali at a 20% profit. What did Ali pay?

7 Ali (in question 6) was short of money. He sold the cap to Daniel at a loss of 20%. What did Daniel pay?

8 A carpet that cost Le336 000 was sold at a loss of $17\frac{1}{2}$%. What was the selling price?
9 A woman buys a car for Le3 500 000 and sells it for Le3 745 000. Her son buys a bicycle for Le80 000 and sells it for Le86 000. Which one makes the greater profit per cent?
10 An article is bought for Le2 250 and sold for Le2 520. Find the profit per cent. Find the price at which it should be sold to make a profit of 16%.
11 A man sells an article for Le21 750 and makes a profit of 16%. What did the article cost? Find how much he should have sold it for to make a profit of 28%.
12 A woman buys yams at Le4 400 a dozen and sells them at Le440 each. Find her profit per cent.
13 A villager paid Le380 000 for 11 goats. He sold them at a profit of 32%. What was the selling price of each goat?
14 A bicycle can be bought either in cash for Le247 000 or by paying 52 weekly payments of Le5 700. By what percentage is the instalment cost greater than the cash price?
15 By selling goods for Le5 350 a trader makes a profit of 7%. She reduces her prices to Le5 150. What is her percentage profit now?

Commission

Commission is payment for selling an item. For example, insurance agents get commission for selling insurance. The more insurance they sell, the more commission they get. Factories often employ sales representatives to sell their goods to shops and traders. The sales representatives often receive a proportion of the value of the goods they sell. This proportion is their commission.

Example 15

A sales representative works for an electric fan company. He gets a commission of 14c *in the leone. In one week he sells four large fans at* Le105 000 *each and nine small fans at* Le54 000 *each. Calculate his commission.*

Total sales = 4 × Le105 000 + 9 × Le54 000
= Le420 000 + Le486 000
= Le906 000

He gets 14c for every leone.

Commission = 906 000 × 14c
= 12 684 000c
= Le126 840

Example 16

A bank charges $2\frac{1}{2}$% commission for issuing a Bank Draft to its customers. If a customer obtained a Bank Draft for Le840 000 *from the bank, calculate the total cost of the Bank Draft.*

Commission paid to the bank = $2\frac{1}{2}$% of Le840 000

$$= \text{Le}2\tfrac{1}{2} \times \frac{1}{100} \times 840\,000$$

$$= \text{Le}\frac{5}{200} \times 840\,000$$

= Le21 000

Total cost of Bank Draft
= value of Bank Draft + commission
= Le840 000 + Le21 000
= Le861 000

Exercise 10j

1 An estate agent gets 2% commission for selling a house. What is the commission for selling a house for Le59 900 000?
2 A car salesman gets 1c in the leone commission. Calculate his commission if he sells Le52 380 000 worth of cars in a month.
3 An agent sells tickets for a pop concert. She gets Le1 000 for every five tickets she sells. How much will she get for selling 285 tickets?
4 An agent for a mail order company gets 10% commission on all monthly payments. How much commission does she get for a monthly payment of Le253 800?
5 An insurance agent sells Le2 840 000 worth of insurance. His commission is 20%. How much money does he get?
6 A rent collector's commission is $4\frac{1}{2}$% of his takings. In one month he collects Le8 428 000 in rent. How much money does he get?
7 A cinema manager gets Le240 commission on every ticket she sells. How much money does she get during a week when she sells 1 318 tickets?
8 An electrical goods salesman gets 14c in the leone commission. How much commission does he get if he sells 20 radios at Le48 000

each and two television sets at Le615 000 each?

9 A history book costs Le4 200. The writers of the book get 10% of the price of each book that is sold. How much will they get if it sells 15 628 copies in one year?

10 A furniture salesperson gets an 8% commission. What is the total commission for selling 44 chairs at Le53 000 each, 11 tables at Le203 000 each and five beds at Le154 000 each?

11 Calculate the commission paid to a bank at $2\frac{1}{2}$% to collect a Bank Draft of Le480 000.

12 A bank charges $2\frac{1}{2}$% commission for issuing a Bank Draft. Calculate the value of the Bank Draft if a person has to pay Le1 230 000 to obtain it from the bank.

13 A customer deposits a cheque for Le500 000. Her bank charges 2% commission for clearing the cheque. Calculate how much money will be credited to her account.

14 Le274 400 is credited to the account of a customer who deposited a cheque meant for another bank. If the bank charges 2% commission for the clearance, calculate the value of the cheque.

Chapter summary

1. *Interest* is a small payment either charged by a bank for services provided or given to savers to encourage saving. Interest is often calculated as a small percentage of the amount of money held in the account.

2. Government provides public services such as education, health and roads. The cost of this is met by *tax*. At a personal level there are two main taxes: *income tax* and *value added tax* (VAT). Income tax is calculated as a proportion of salary. VAT is calculated as a direct tax (e.g. 5%) of the value of certain goods and services.

3. Post Office, electricity and other service charges are paid at agreed rates according to services rendered.

4. Many payments and other commercial transactions involve the use of percentages: e.g. profit and loss accounts; commission.

(The rates given in this chapter are provided for the purposes of explanation and practice. They should be used as a guide only; readers are advised that rates can change frequently and dramatically.)

11 Algebra: Factors, factorisation, fractions

Factors of algebraic terms

All numbers, other than 1, have two or more factors. For example, the factors of 42 are:

1, 2, 3, 6, 7, 14, 21, 42

In the same way, algebraic terms have two or more factors. For example, the expression $6ab$ has 16 factors:

$1, 2, 3, 6, a, 2a, 3a, 6a, b, 2b, 3b, 6b, ab, 2ab, 3ab, 6ab$

Each factor divides exactly into $6ab$. For example,

$$6ab \div 3a = \frac{2 \times 3 \times a \times b}{3 \times a} = 2b$$

$$6ab \div 2ab = \frac{2 \times 3 \times a \times b}{2 \times a \times b} = 3$$

Example 1

Write down all the factors of $5a^2x$.

Expand $5a^2x$ as a product of separate terms:

$5a^2x = 5 \times 1 \times a \times a \times x$

The factors will contain:

numerical terms: 1, 5
terms in a: $a, 5a$
terms in x: $x, 5x$
terms in a^2: $a^2, 5a^2$
terms in ax: $ax, 5ax$
terms in a^2x: $a^2x, 5a^2x$

The factors of $5a^2x$ are: $1, 5, a, 5a, x, 5x, a^2, 5a^2, ax, 5ax, a^2x, 5a^2x$.

Notice that 1 and the term itself are always factors of an algebraic term.

Exercise 11a

Write down all the factors of the following.

1 $3x$	**2** ab	**3** x^2
4 a^2b	**5** $6a$	**6** $5ab$
7 xyz	**8** $10m^2$	**9** $25pq$
10 $8de$	**11** $2a^2b^2$	**12** $14ab^2$

Highest common factor

Algebraic expressions may have common factors.

Example 2

Find the HCF of $12ab^2$ and $30a^2b$.

$$12ab^2 = 2 \times 2 \times 3 \times a \times b \times b$$
$$30a^2b = 2 \times 3 \times 5 \times a \times a \times b$$

The highest product of factors that is contained in both expressions is $2 \times 3 \times a \times b = 6ab$.
$6ab$ is the HCF of $12ab^2$ and $30a^2b$.

With practice the HCF can be found without expanding each expression.

Exercise 11b

Find the HCF of the following.

1 ax and ay	**2** $3d$ and $3e$
3 ax and bx	**4** $3m$ and $5m$
5 $2m$ and $2n$	**6** gp and gq
7 $2xy$ and $7xz$	**8** $4r$ and $12s$
9 abz and xyz	**10** $3mx$ and $10nx$
11 $4pq$ and $4pr$	**12** abc and abd
13 axy and bxy	**14** $9pq$ and $11pq$
15 $4ax$ and $10bx$	**16** amx and anx
17 x^2 and $5x$	**18** $2x^2$ and $8x$
19 $5x^2$ and $10x$	**20** $3a^2$ and $12a$
21 mn^2 and m^2n	**22** $8de$ and $6de$
23 $10m^2$ and $15m^2$	**24** $9ab^2$ and $12a^2b$
25 $18xy$ and $6xy$	**26** $21ad$ and $14bd$
27 $5a^2$ and $20a^2b$	**28** $16xy^2$ and $4xy$
29 $18a^2y$ and $27x^2y^2$	**30** $17ax^2$ and $3by$

Factorisation

Example 3

Complete the brackets in the statement
$15ax + 10a = 5a(\quad)$.

The contents of the bracket multiplied by $5a$ should give $15ax + 10a$. See **Removing brackets** in Chapter 7. Thus, divide each term in $15ax + 10a$ by $5a$ to find the contents of the bracket.

$$\text{Contents of bracket} = \frac{15ax}{5a} + \frac{10a}{5a}$$

$$= 3x + 2$$

Thus $15ax + 10a = 5a(3x + 2)$

Check: RHS $= 5a(3x + 2) = 5a \times 3x + 5a \times 2$
$= 15ax + 10a =$ LHS

In the above example, $5a$ is the HCF of $15ax$ and $10a$. $5a(3x + 2)$ is the factorised form of $15ax + 10a$. $5a$ and $(3x + 2)$ are factors of $15ax + 10a$.

Factorisation means writing an expression in terms of its factors. Think of factorisation as the inverse of removing brackets.

Example 4

Factorise the following.

a) $12y + 8z$ *b)* $4n^2 - 2n$ *c)* $24pq - 16p^2$

a) $12y + 8z$
The HCF of $12y$ and $8z$ is 4.

$$12y + 8z = 4\left(\frac{12y}{4} + \frac{8z}{4}\right) *$$

$$= 4(3y + 2z)$$

b) $4n^2 - 2n$
The HCF of $4n^2$ and $2n$ is $2n$.

$$4n^2 - 2n = 2n\left(\frac{4n^2}{2n} - \frac{2n}{2n}\right) *$$

$$= 2n(2n - 1)$$

c) $24pq - 16p^2$
The HCF of $24pq$ and $16p^2$ is $8p$.

$$24pq - 16p^2 = 8p\left(\frac{24pq}{8p} - \frac{16p^2}{8p}\right) *$$

$$= 8p(3q - 2p)$$

* With practice the first line of working can be left out. The results of factorisation can be checked by removing the brackets.

Exercise 11c

1 Copy the following statements and complete the brackets.

a) $9x + 3y = 3(\quad)$
b) $5a - 15b = 5(\quad)$
c) $ax + ay = a(\quad)$
d) $px + qx = x(\quad)$
e) $8am - 8bm = 8m(\quad)$
f) $a - ay = a(\quad)$
g) $2s - rs = s(\quad)$
h) $3ab + 5ax = a(\quad)$
i) $3abx + 5adx = ax(\quad)$
j) $9xy - 3xz = 3x(\quad)$
k) $12cm + 16dm = 4m(\quad)$
l) $15x^2 - 10x = 5x(\quad)$
m) $18ax + 9x = 9x(\quad)$
n) $4m^2 - 2m = 2m(\quad)$
o) $2pq - 6q^2 = 2q(\quad)$
p) $5a^2 + 2ax = a(\quad)$

2 Factorise the following.

a) $12c + 6d$ b) $4a - 8b$
c) $6z - 3$ d) $9x + 12y$
e) $xy + xz$ f) $bc + dc$
g) $9x + ax$ h) $abc + abd$
i) $xyz - ayz$ j) $pmq + amb$
k) $3ab - 6ac$ l) $12ax + 8bx$
m) $3x^2 - x$ n) $6m^2 - 2$
o) $2abx + 7acx$ p) $3d^2e + 5d^2$
q) $4am^2 - 6am$ r) $-15x^2 - 10$
s) $-18fg - 12g$ t) $-5xy + 10y$

Lowest common multiple

Example 5

Find the LCM of the following.
a) $8a$ *and* $6a$ *b)* $2x$ *and* $3y$

a) $8a = 2 \times 2 \times 2 \times a$
$6a = 2 \times 3 \times a$
LCM $= 2 \times 2 \times 2 \times 3 \times a = 24a$

b) $2x = 2 \times x$
$3y = 3 \times y$
LCM $= 2 \times 3 \times x \times y = 6xy$

Exercise 11d

Find the LCM of the following.

1 a and b 2 x and 5
3 $2a$ and 3 4 $3a$ and $4b$
5 $2x$ and $5y$ 6 $9a$ and a
7 x and $3x$ 8 ab and bc
9 xy and yz 10 $3b$ and $2b$
11 x^2 and x 12 $3a$ and a^2
13 $3m$ and m^2n 14 $2a^2$ and $9ab$
15 $3x^2y$ and $2xy^2$ 16 $6ab$ and $5b^2$

Algebraic fractions

Equivalent fractions

Equivalent fractions can be made by multiplying or dividing the numerator and denominator of a fraction by the same quantity. For example:

multiplication

a) $\frac{a}{2} = \frac{a \times 3}{2 \times 3} = \frac{3a}{6}$

b) $\frac{a}{2} = \frac{a \times a}{2 \times a} = \frac{a^2}{2a}$

c) $\frac{3}{d} = \frac{3 \times 2b}{d \times 2b} = \frac{6b}{2bd}$

division

d) $\frac{4x}{6y} = \frac{4x \div 2}{6y \div 2} = \frac{2x}{3y}$

e) $\frac{5ab}{10b} = \frac{5ab \div 5b}{10b \div 5b} = \frac{a}{2}$

Example 6

Fill the blanks in the following.

a) $\frac{3a}{2} = \frac{}{10}$ *b)* $\frac{5ab}{12a} = \frac{}{12}$ *c)* $\frac{9bc}{12b} = \frac{3c}{}$

a) Compare the two denominators.
$2 \times 5 = 10$
The denominator of the first fraction has been multiplied by 5. The numerator must also be multiplied by 5.

$\frac{3a}{2} = \frac{3a \times 5}{2 \times 5} = \frac{15a}{10}$

b) The denominator of the first fraction has been divided by a. The numerator must also be divided by a.

$\frac{5ab}{12a} = \frac{5ab \div a}{12a \div a} = \frac{5b}{12}$

c) Divide both numerator and denominator by $3b$.

$\frac{9bc}{12b} = \frac{9bc \div 3b}{12b \div 3b} = \frac{3c}{4}$

Exercise 11e

Fill the blanks in the following.

1 $\frac{8b}{5} = \frac{}{15}$ **2** $\frac{a}{b} = \frac{ax}{}$ **3** $\frac{2x}{5} = \frac{}{10}$

4 $\frac{3a}{8} = \frac{6a}{}$ **5** $\frac{3}{12a} = \frac{}{4a}$ **6** $\frac{9c}{21d} = \frac{}{7d}$

7 $\frac{9ah}{6ak} = \frac{3h}{}$ **8** $\frac{bm}{my} = \frac{}{y}$ **9** $\frac{}{3a} = \frac{1}{a}$

10 $\frac{}{8yz} = \frac{3x}{2y}$ **11** $\frac{2c}{a} = \frac{6c^2}{}$ **12** $\frac{3m}{1} = \frac{}{2d}$

Adding and subtracting algebraic fractions

As with common numerical fractions, algebraic fractions must have common denominators before they can be added or subtracted.

Example 7

Simplify the following.

a) $\frac{5a}{8} - \frac{3a}{8}$ *b)* $\frac{5}{2d} + \frac{7}{2d}$ *c)* $\frac{1}{x} - \frac{1}{3x}$

d) $\frac{4}{a} + b$ *e)* $\frac{1}{u} + \frac{1}{v}$ *f)* $\frac{5}{4c} - \frac{4}{3d}$

a) $\frac{5a}{8} - \frac{3a}{8} = \frac{5a - 3a}{8} = \frac{2a}{8} = \frac{2a \div 2}{8 \div 2} = \frac{a}{4}$

b) $\frac{5}{2d} + \frac{7}{2d} = \frac{5 + 7}{2d} = \frac{12}{2d} = \frac{12 \div 2}{2d \div 2} = \frac{6}{d}$

c) $\frac{1}{x} - \frac{1}{3x}$

The LCM of x and $3x$ is $3x$.

$$\frac{1}{x} - \frac{1}{3x} = \frac{3 \times 1}{3 \times x} - \frac{1}{3x} = \frac{3}{3x} - \frac{1}{3x}$$

$$= \frac{3 - 1}{3x} = \frac{2}{3x}$$

d) $\frac{4}{a} + b = \frac{4}{a} + \frac{b}{1}$

The LCM of a and 1 is a.

$$\frac{4}{a} + \frac{b}{1} = \frac{4}{a} + \frac{a \times b}{a} = \frac{4}{a} + \frac{ab}{a}$$

$$= \frac{4 + ab}{a}$$

This does not simplify further.

e) $\dfrac{1}{u} + \dfrac{1}{v}$

The LCM of u and v is uv.

$$\frac{1}{u} + \frac{1}{v} = \frac{1 \times v}{uv} + \frac{1 \times u}{uv}$$

$$= \frac{v}{uv} + \frac{u}{uv}$$

$$= \frac{v + u}{uv}$$

This does not simplify further.

f) $\dfrac{5}{4c} - \dfrac{4}{3d}$

The LCM of $4c$ and $3d$ is $12cd$.

$$\frac{5}{4c} - \frac{4}{3d} = \frac{5 \times 3d}{12cd} - \frac{4 \times 4c}{12cd}$$

$$= \frac{15d}{12cd} - \frac{16c}{12cd}$$

$$= \frac{15d - 16c}{12cd}$$

Exercise 11f

Simplify the following.

1 $\dfrac{7a}{5} - \dfrac{4a}{5}$	**2** $\dfrac{9b}{2} - \dfrac{3b}{2}$	**3** $\dfrac{4x}{9} + \dfrac{8x}{9}$
4 $\dfrac{x}{2} + \dfrac{x}{3}$	**5** $\dfrac{a}{4} - \dfrac{a}{20}$	**6** $\dfrac{6x}{5} - \dfrac{3x}{4}$
7 $\dfrac{2}{a} + \dfrac{5}{a}$	**8** $\dfrac{3}{5y} - \dfrac{1}{5y}$	**9** $\dfrac{5}{2x} + \dfrac{7}{2x}$
10 $\dfrac{4}{3a} - \dfrac{1}{3a}$	**11** $\dfrac{7}{8y} + \dfrac{9}{8y}$	**12** $\dfrac{1}{x} + \dfrac{1}{x}$
13 $\dfrac{1}{3x} + \dfrac{1}{x}$	**14** $\dfrac{1}{a} - \dfrac{1}{5a}$	**15** $\dfrac{1}{z} - \dfrac{1}{2z}$
16 $\dfrac{1}{4a} - \dfrac{1}{6a}$	**17** $\dfrac{1}{3x} + \dfrac{1}{5x}$	**18** $\dfrac{3}{2a} - \dfrac{2}{3a}$
19 $\dfrac{3}{x} + 1$	**20** $2 - \dfrac{b}{a}$	**21** $3 + \dfrac{1}{2d}$
22 $\dfrac{9}{x} + y$	**23** $2b + \dfrac{3}{4}$	**24** $p - \dfrac{3}{2q}$
25 $\dfrac{1}{a} + \dfrac{1}{b}$	**26** $\dfrac{1}{x} - \dfrac{1}{y}$	**27** $\dfrac{1}{3} + \dfrac{1}{m}$
28 $\dfrac{3}{c} - \dfrac{2}{d}$	**29** $\dfrac{5}{4a} - \dfrac{2}{3b}$	**30** $\dfrac{2}{5x} + \dfrac{1}{3y}$

Fractions with brackets

$\dfrac{x+6}{3}$ is a short way of writing $\dfrac{(x+6)}{3}$ or $\frac{1}{3}(x+6)$.

Notice that all the terms of the numerator are divided by 3.

$$\frac{x+6}{3} = \frac{(x+6)}{3} = \tfrac{1}{3}(x+6) = \tfrac{1}{3}x + 2$$

Example 8

Simplify a) $\dfrac{x+3}{5} + \dfrac{4x-2}{5}$, *b)* $\dfrac{7a-3}{6} - \dfrac{3a+5}{4}$.

a) $$\frac{x+3}{5} + \frac{4x-2}{5} = \frac{(x+3)+(4x-2)}{5}$$

$$= \frac{x+3+4x-2}{5}$$

$$= \frac{5x+1}{5}$$

b) The LCM of 6 and 4 is 12.

$$\frac{7a-3}{6} - \frac{3a+5}{4} = \frac{2(7a-3)}{2 \times 6} - \frac{3(3a+5)}{3 \times 4}$$

$$= \frac{2(7a-3) - 3(3a+5)}{12}$$

removing brackets $$= \frac{14a - 6 - 9a - 15}{12}$$

collecting like terms $$= \frac{5a - 21}{12}$$

The next example shows that further simplification is sometimes possible after collecting like terms.

Example 9

Simplify $\dfrac{4x+1}{3} - \dfrac{x-5}{12}$.

The LCM of 3 and 12 is 12.

$$\frac{4x+1}{3} - \frac{x-5}{12} = \frac{4(4x+1)}{12} - \frac{(x-5)}{12}$$

$$= \frac{4(4x+1) - (x-5)}{12}$$

removing brackets $$= \frac{16x + 4 - x + 5}{12}$$

collecting like terms $= \frac{15x + 9}{12}$

factorising the numerator $= \frac{3(5x + 3)}{12}$

dividing numerator and denominator by 3 $= \frac{5x + 3}{4}$

Exercise 11g

1 Simplify the following.

a) $\frac{2a-3}{2} + \frac{a+4}{2}$ **b)** $\frac{3b+4}{3} + \frac{2b-5}{3}$

c) $\frac{4c-3}{5} - \frac{2c+1}{5}$ **d)** $\frac{3x+4}{4} - \frac{x-3}{4}$

e) $\frac{z+5}{4} + \frac{3z-5}{2}$ **f)** $\frac{2n+7}{3} - \frac{5n+6}{4}$

g) $\frac{3a-2}{4} + 2a$ **h)** $3b - \frac{5b-1}{2}$

i) $\frac{5u-3}{4} + \frac{u-3}{6}$ **j)** $\frac{m-1}{6} - \frac{m+1}{8}$

k) $\frac{3c-2d}{10} + \frac{2c-3d}{15}$ **l)** $\frac{2a+3b}{9} + \frac{a-4b}{6}$

2 Simplify the following *as far as possible.*

a) $\frac{3x+1}{4} - \frac{x-5}{4}$ **b)** $\frac{7x-14}{10} - \frac{2x+1}{10}$

c) $\frac{6h+5}{7} - \frac{4h-6}{21}$ **d)** $\frac{a+3b}{3} - \frac{5a-3b}{6}$

Chapter summary

1 As with numbers (other than 1), all algebraic terms have two or more factors. For example, $7pq$ has eight factors:
$1, 7, p, q, 7p, 7q, pq$ and $7pq$
Each factor divides exactly into the term (e.g. $7pq \div 7q = p$). See Example 1.

2 In general, the rules of arithmetic regarding factorisation, highest common factors, least common multiples, equivalent fractions, and the addition and subtraction of fractions also apply to algebraic terms (Examples 2, 3, 4, 5, 6, 7).

3 The process of factorisation of algebraic terms is the inverse of removing brackets (see Chapter 7). For example, $15ab - 12a^2$ factorises as $3a(5b - 4a)$, where $3a$ is the HCF of the first two terms.

4 The process of addition and subtraction of algebraic fractions makes use of the LCM of the denominators of the given fractions (Example 7).

12 The Cartesian plane and coordinates

The position of points on a line

The number line is a **graph**, or picture, of all the positive and negative numbers (Fig. 12.1).

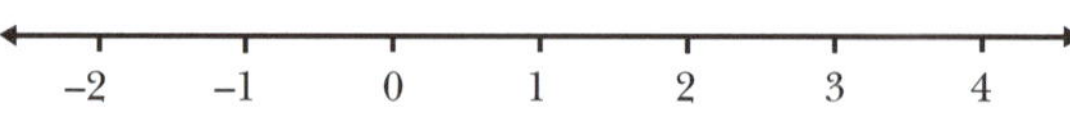

Fig. 12.1

If we draw points on the number line, we can say exactly where they are on the line.

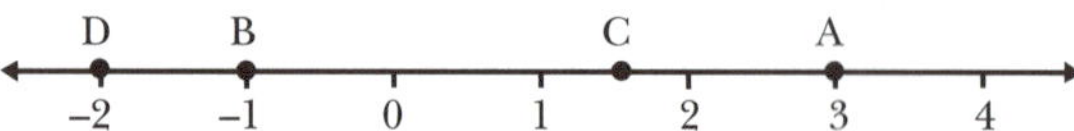

Fig. 12.2

In Fig. 12.2, A is 3 units to the right of zero and B is 1 unit to the left of zero. We can shorten this to A(3) and B(−1). In the same way, C is the point C($1\frac{1}{2}$) and D is the point D(− 2).

A(3) and B(−1) give the **positions** of A and B. Notice that we are using brackets in a different way from the way we use them in algebra and arithmetic.

Exercise 12a

1 In Fig. 12.3 P(2) gives the position of P and Q(−3) gives the position of Q. Give the positions of R, S, T, U and V in the same way.

Fig. 12.3

2 In Fig. 12.4, A(0·7) describes the position of A. Describe the positions of B, C, D, E, F and G in the same way.

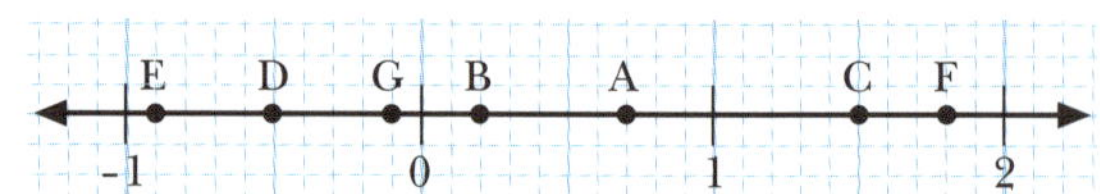

Fig. 12.4

3 Draw a number line from −10 to 10. On the line, mark the points A(6), B(3), C(−4), D(−8), E(9), F(−9), G(0), H($7\frac{1}{2}$) and I($-6\frac{1}{2}$).

4 Use graph paper to draw a number line like that of Fig. 12.4 On the line, mark the points P(0·8), Q(1·3), R(0·4), S(−0·4), T(−0·7), U(1·9) and V(1·0).

The position of points on a plane surface

Exercise 12b *(Discussion)*

1 Try to describe the positions of points P, Q and R in Fig. 12.5.
Hint: one way is to measure the distances of P, Q and R from the edges of the page.

+
Q

Fig. 12.5 R+

2 Fig. 12.6 shows the same points on a cm square grid. Starting at the cross, describe how to get to P, Q and R. Does this make it easier to describe the positions of the points?

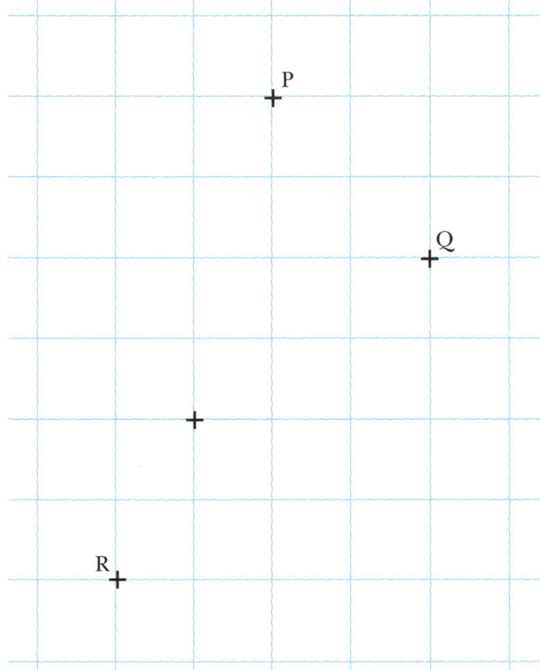

Fig. 12.6

Cartesian plane

The positions of points on a line are found by using a number line. The positions of points on a plane surface are found by using *two* number lines, usually at right angles. See Fig. 12.7.

In Fig. 12.7, starting from the zero point,
P is in position 1 unit to the *right* and 4 units *up*;
Q is in position 3 units to the *right* and 2 units *up*;
R is in position 1 unit to the *left* and 2 units *down*.

We can shorten this to P(1, 4), Q(3, 2) and R(−1, −2). The position of each point is represented by a pair of numbers.

Fig. 12.7 is a graph, or picture, of the three points P, Q and R. In a graph like this, the number lines are called **axes**. They cross at the zero-point of each axis. This point is called the **origin**. The axis going across from left to right is called the ***x*-axis**. It has a positive scale to the right of O and a negative scale to the left of O. The axis going up the page is called the ***y*-axis**. It has a positive scale upwards from O and a negative scale downwards from O.

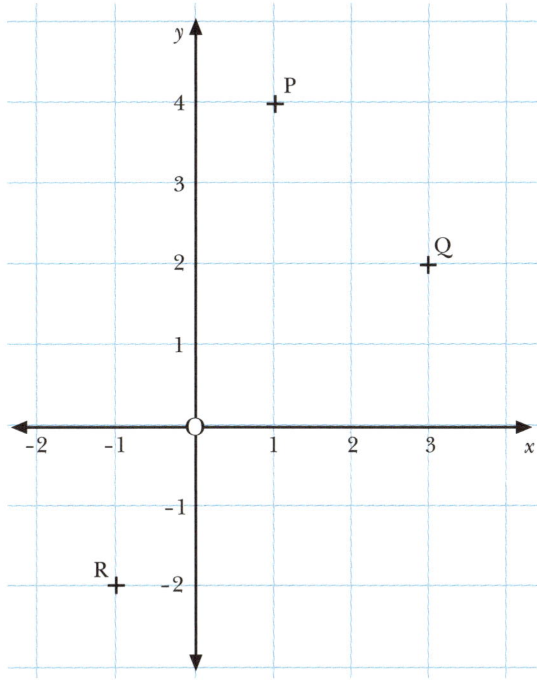

Fig. 12.7

A plane surface with axes drawn on it, such as Fig. 12.7 and Fig. 12.8, is called a **Cartesian plane**. It is named after the French philosopher and mathematician, Descartes. His work made it possible to represent geometry in a numerical way.

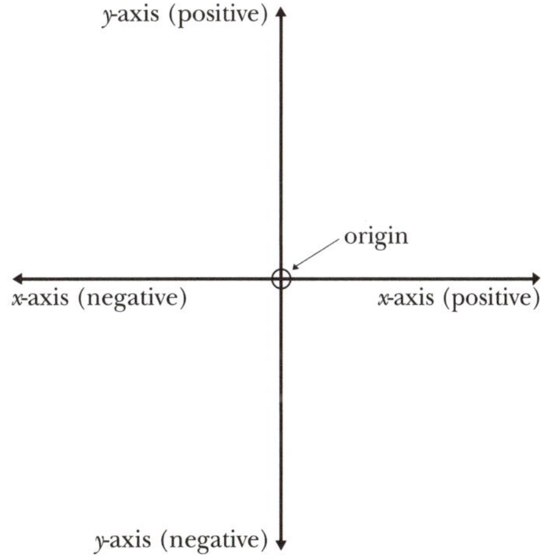

Fig. 12.8

Coordinates

Fig. 12.9 shows a Cartesian plane with points A, B, C and D drawn on it.

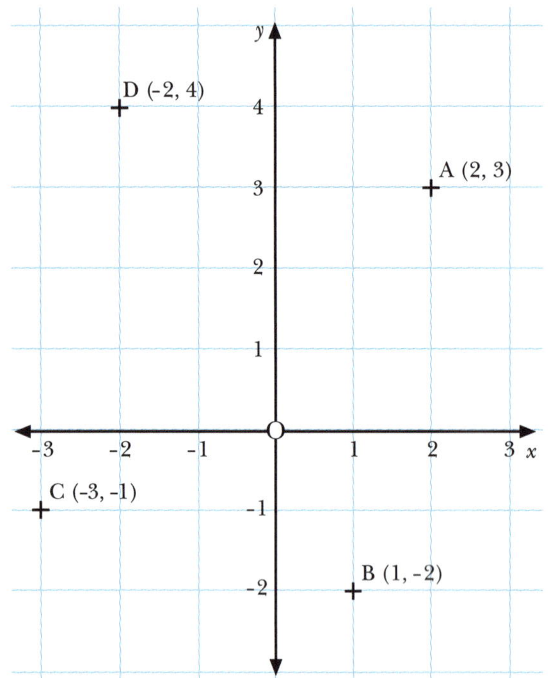

Fig. 12.9

The position of A is found by moving 2 units to the *right* of the origin and then 3 units *up* the page parallel to the *y*-axis. We can shorten this to A(2, 3). C is found by moving 3 units to the *left* of the origin and then 1 unit *down* the page. Its position is C(−3, −1). In the same way, B and D are the points B(1, −2) and D(−2, 4).

The position of each point is given by an **ordered pair of numbers**. These are called the **coordinates** of the point. The first number is called the ***x*-coordinate**. The *x*-coordinate gives the distance of the point along the *x*-axis. The second number is called the ***y*-coordinate**. The *y*-coordinate gives the distance of the point along the *y*-axis. The coordinates are separated by a comma.

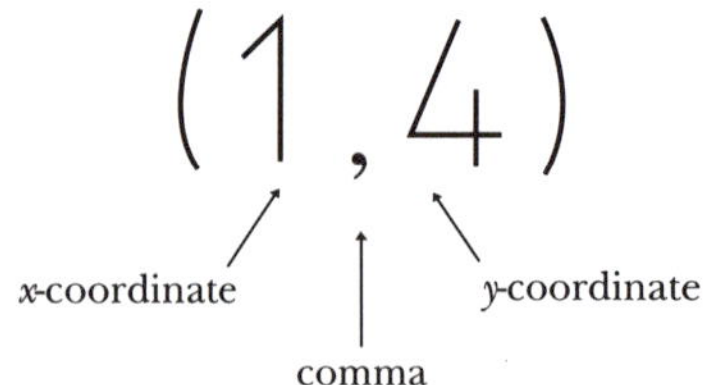

Fig. 12.10

The *order* of the pair of numbers is very important. For example, the point (1, 4) is not the same as the point (4, 1). This is shown in Fig. 12.11.

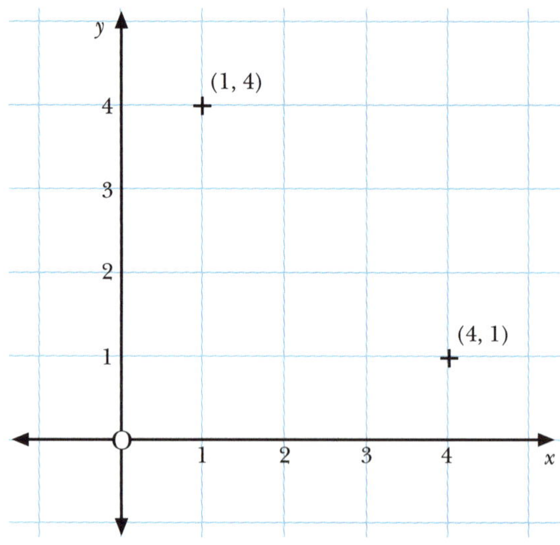

Fig. 12.11

Example 1

Write down the coordinates of the points A, B, C, D, E, F *in Fig. 12.12.*

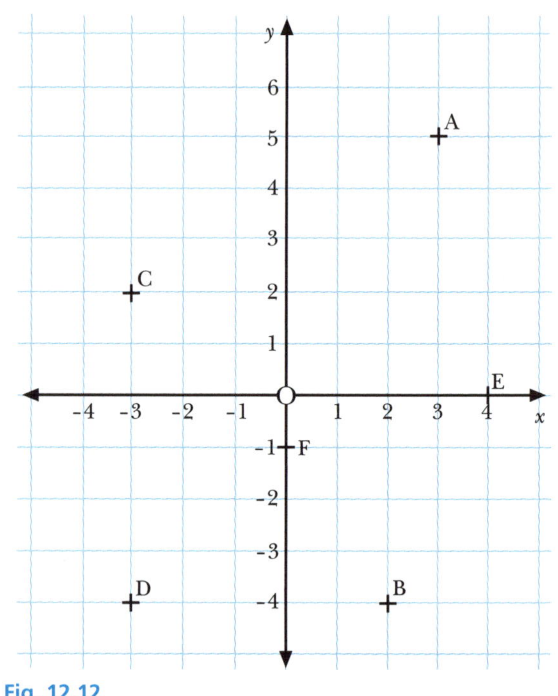

Fig. 12.12

The coordinates of the points are A(3, 5), B(2, −4), C(−3, 2), D(−3, −4), E(4, 0), F(0, −1).

Notice that E is on the *x*-axis; its *y*-coordinate is 0. F is on the *y*-axis; its *x*-coordinate is 0.

Example 2

Write down the coordinates of the vertices of triangle ABC *and parallelogram* PQRS *in Fig. 12.13.*

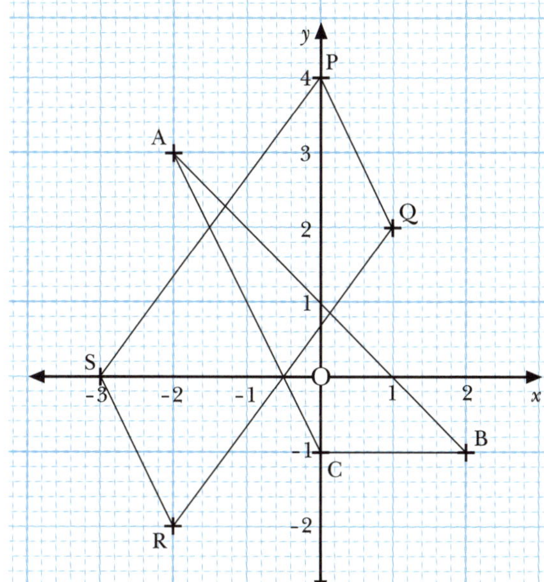

Fig. 12.13

The vertices of triangle ABC are A(−2, 3), B(2, −1) and C(0, −1). The vertices of parallelogram PQRS are P(0, 4), Q(1, 2), R(−2, −2) and S(−3, 0).

Notice that C and P are on the *y*-axis. Their *x*-coordinate is 0 (zero). S is on the *x*-axis. Its *y*-coordinate is 0.

Exercise 12c

1 What are the coordinates of the points A, B, C, D, E, F, G, H, I and J in Fig. 12.14?

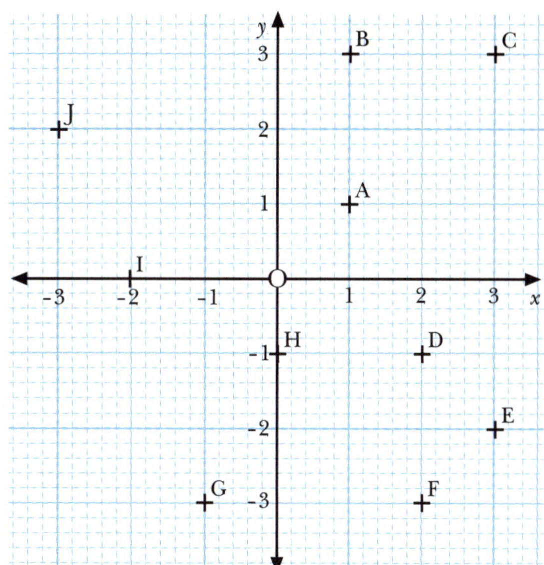

Fig. 12.14

2 In Fig. 12.15 name the points that have the following coordinates.

a) (9, 5) **b)** (5, −8) **c)** (−15, −10)
d) (−5, 8) **e)** (12, 0) **f)** (0, 12)
g) (0, −7) **h)** (−7, 0) **i)** (14, −11)
j) (−13, 15) **k)** (−4, −12) **l)** (14, 14)

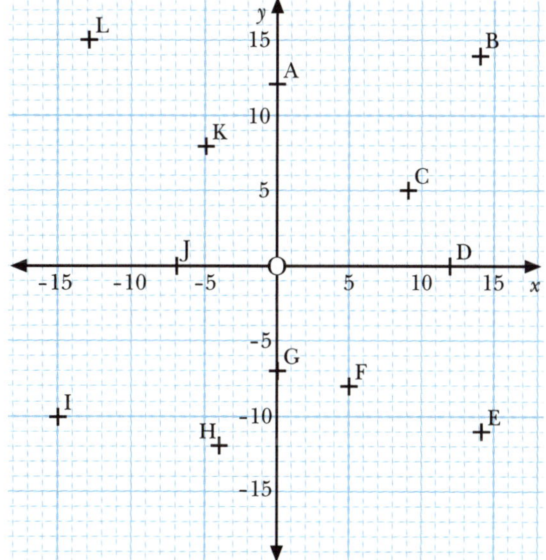

Fig. 12.15

3 Use Fig. 12.16 to complete the coordinates of the following points:

a) A(, 4)	**b)** B(−4,)	**c)** C(, 3)
d) D(−4,)	**e)** E(, 7)	**f)** F(4,)
g) G(, 1)	**h)** H(2,)	**i)** I(, −2)
j) J(3,)	**k)** K(, −2)	**l)** L(−3,)
m) M(, −3)	**n)** N(−3,)	

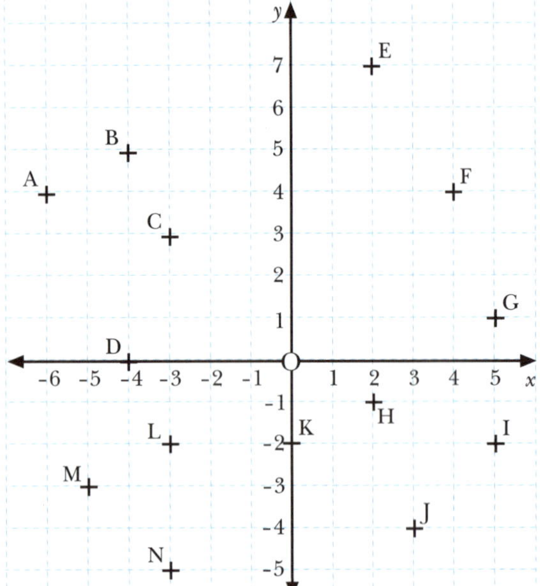

Fig. 12.16

4 What are the coordinates of the vertices T, U, V, W, X, Y and Z of the shape in Fig. 12.17?

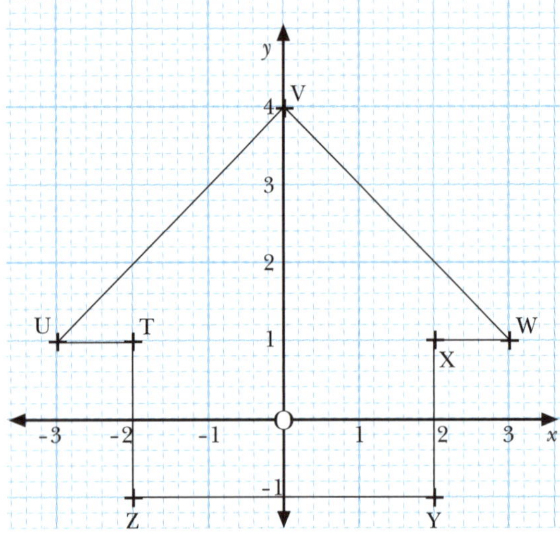

Fig. 12.17

5 What are the coordinates of the vertices of the 'elephant' in Fig. 12.18? Start where shown and work clockwise round the figure.

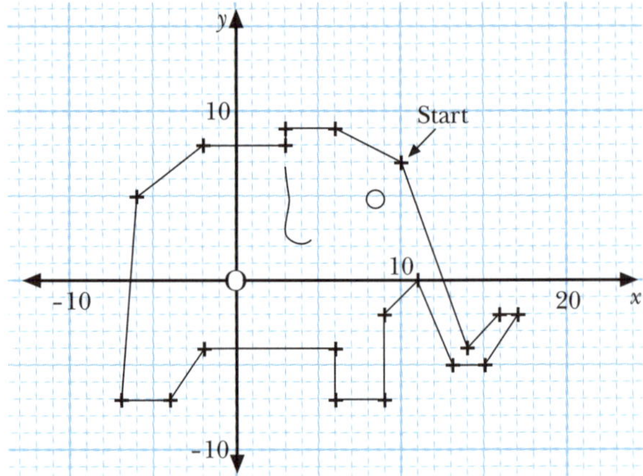

Fig. 12.18

6 Fig. 12.19 shows part of a map drawn on a Cartesian plane.

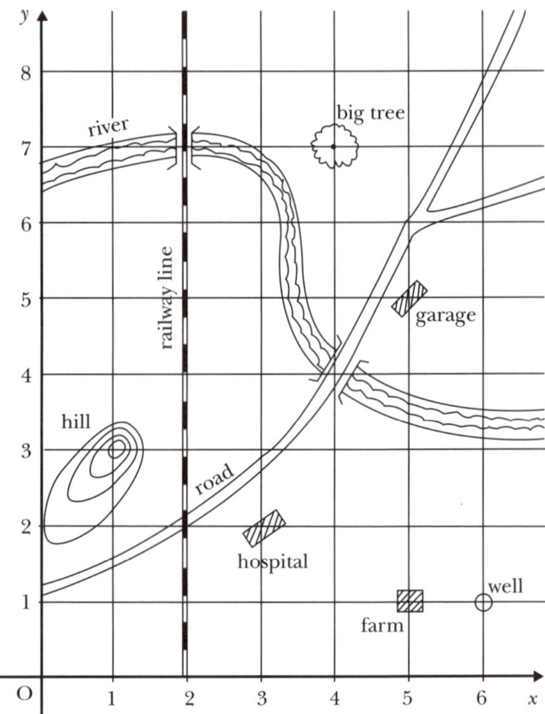

Fig. 12.19

Find the coordinates of

a) the big tree **b)** the garage

c) the farm **d)** the well

e) the hospital **f)** the top of the hill

g) the point where the railway line crosses the road

h) the point where the railway line crosses the river

i) the point where the road crosses the river

j) the point where the road branches to the right.

k) Find the coordinates of any four points on the railway line. What do you notice?

7 Fig. 12.20 is the graph of lines l and m.

a) Write down the coordinates of the points marked + on line l. What do you notice?

b) Write down the coordinates of the points marked + on line m. What do you notice?

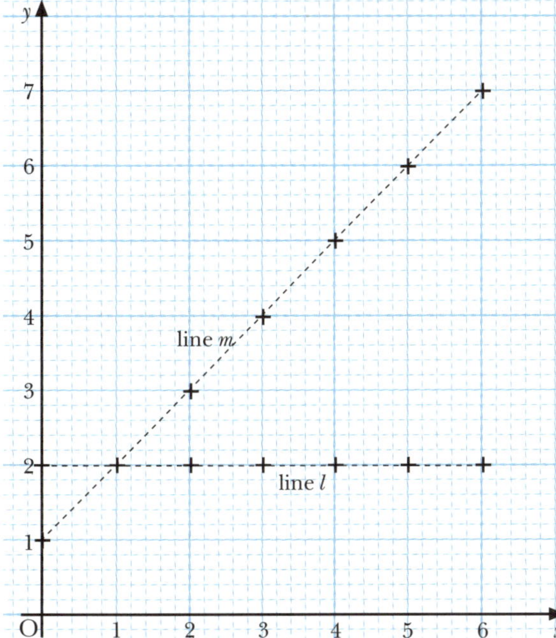

Fig. 12.20

Plotting points

To **plot** a point means to draw its position on a Cartesian plane.

The easiest way to plot a point is as follows:

1 Start at the origin.

2 Move along the x-axis by an amount and in a direction given by the x-coordinate of the point.

3 Move up or down parallel to the y-axis by an amount and in a direction given by the y-coordinate.

Example 3

Plot the points $(-1, 2)$ *and* $(2{\cdot}6, -1{\cdot}8)$ *on a Cartesian plane.*

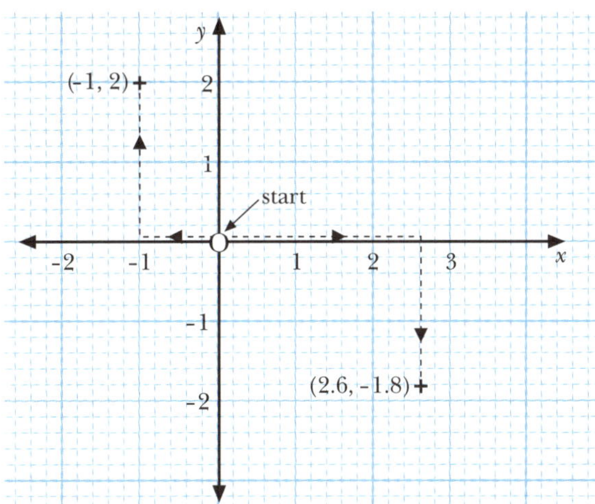

Fig. 12.21

The dotted arrows in Fig. 12.21 show the method of plotting.

For $(-1, 2)$:

Start at the origin. The x-coordinate is -1. Move 1 unit to the left along the x-axis. The y-coordinate is 2. Move 2 units up parallel to the y-axis. Plot the point.

For $(2{\cdot}6, -1{\cdot}8)$:

Start at the origin. The x-coordinate is $2{\cdot}6$. Move $2{\cdot}6$ units to the right on the x-axis. The y-coordinate is $-1{\cdot}8$. Move $1{\cdot}8$ units down parallel to the y-axis. Plot the point.

Note: the dotted arrows in Fig. 12.21 are not normally put on the graph. They are given here to show the method only. Notice that the points are plotted with a small vertical cross: +.

Example 4

The vertices of quadrilateral PQRS *have coordinates* P$(-3, 18)$, Q$(15, 14)$, R$(11, -4)$ *and* S$(-7, 0)$. A *and* B *are the points* A$(-3, -7)$ *and* B$(3, 0)$.

a) Using a scale of 2 cm *represents* 10 *units on both axes, plot points* P, Q, R, S, A *and* B.

b) Join the vertices of quadrilateral PQRS. *What kind of quadrilateral is it?*

c) Find the coordinates of the point where the diagonals of PQRS *cross.*

d) What do you notice about the points A, B *and* Q?

a) The scale is given. The highest x-coordinate is 15 and the lowest is -7. The x-axis must include these numbers. A scale from -10 to 20 on the x-axis will be suitable. The highest

y-coordinate is 18 and the lowest is −7. A scale from −10 to 20 on the y-axis will be suitable. The points are plotted in Fig. 12.22.

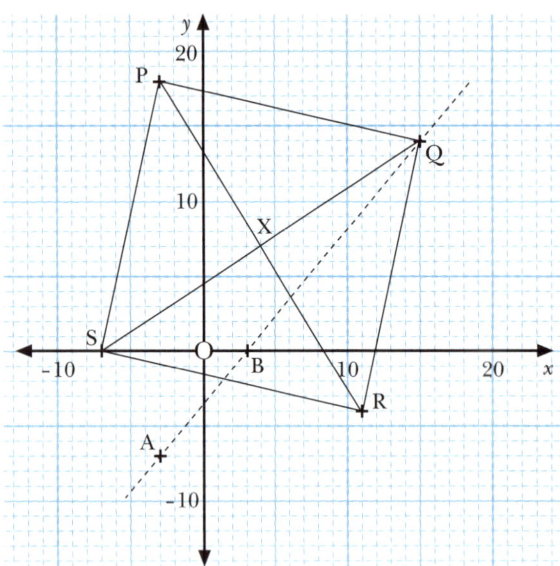

Fig. 12.22

b) PQRS is a square.

c) The diagonals of PQRS cross at X(4, 7).

d) B, A and Q lie on a straight line (dotted in Fig. 12.22).

When drawing Cartesian graphs, *always*:

1 draw the axes;

2 label the origin O;

3 label the axes x and y;

4 write the scales along each axis.

Exercise 12d

Work on graph paper in this exercise.

1 Draw the origin, O, near the middle of a clean sheet of graph paper. Use a scale of 1 cm represents 1 unit on both axes. Plot the following points:
A(8, 10), B(−8, −10), C(3, −5), D(−6, 9), E(−4, −7), F(1, 8), G(2, 0), H(0, −6), I(−2·4, 5·2), J(−4, 3·8), K(0, 6·6), L(0·8, −7·8).

2 Draw the origin, O, near the middle of a sheet of graph paper. Use a scale of 2 cm represents 1 unit on both axes. Plot the following points, then join each point to the next in alphabetical order.
A(0, 1), B(1, 2), C(1, 1), D(2, 1), E(1, 0), F(2, −1), G(1, −1), H(1, −2), I(0, −1), J(−1, −2), K(−1, −1), L(−2, −1), M(−1, 0), N(−2, 1), P(−1, 1), Q(−1, 2).
Finally, join Q to A.

3 Draw the origin, O, near the middle of a sheet of graph paper. Use a scale of 2 cm represents 5 units on both axes. Plot the following points. Join each point to the next in the order they are given.
START (−10, −5), (−5, 10), (0, 15), (5, 17), (3, 14), (3, 12), (15, 6), (14, 3), (11, 3), (13, 2), (5, 3), (6, −6) FINISH
What picture does your graph show?

4 Take O near the middle of your graph paper and let 2 cm represent 1 unit on both axes.

a) Plot the points P(4, 3), Q(4, 1), R(−1, 1), S(−1, 3), W(1, 2), X(1, −1), Y(−2, −1) and Z(−2, 2).

b) Find the areas, in unit^2, of rectangle PQRS, square WXYZ, triangle SXY, triangle PYZ.

5 As in question 4, but plot the points A(0, 4), B(−3, −1), C(−2, −4), D(1, 1), E(3, 2), F(4, 0) and G(2, −1).

a) Draw quadrilateral ABCD. What kind of quadrilateral is it? Let its diagonals cross at X. Find the coordinates of X.

b) What do you notice about points B, X, D and E?

c) Draw quadrilateral DEFG. What kind of quadrilateral is it? Let its diagonals cross at Y. Find the coordinates of Y.

6 a) Complete the ordered pairs in the following pattern:
(0, 0), (1, 1), (2, 4), (3, 9), (4, 16), (5, 25), (6,), (7,), (8,), (9,), (10,).

b) Draw the origin, O, at the bottom left-hand corner of a sheet of graph paper. Draw an x-axis with a scale of 1 cm to 1 unit. Draw a y-axis with a scale of 1 cm to 5 units.

c) Plot the points in part a).

d) Join the points you have plotted by drawing as smooth a curve as you can.

e) Use your graph to find $(8·4)^2$, $(6·5)^2$, $\sqrt{20}$, $\sqrt{90}$.

Chapter summary

1. A *number line* is a picture or *graph* of relative positions of positive and negative numbers.
2. A *Cartesian graph* gives a picture of the relative positions of points on a plane.The *Cartesian plane* is a plane surface with two *axes* drawn on it. The axes are at right angles: the *x-axis* (horizontal) and the *y-axis* (vertical), crossing at the *origin* (the zero point for both axes).
3. Every point on the Cartesian plane has a unique *ordered pair of coordinates* in the form (*a*, *b*), where *a* is the *x-coordinate* (the distance of the point along the *x*-axis) and *b* is the *y-coordinate* (the distance of the point along the *y*-axis).
4. To *plot a point* means to draw its position on a Cartesian graph.
5. When drawing a Cartesian graph, always:

   draw the axes,

   label the origin (O),

   label the *x*- and *y*-axes,

   write the scales along the axes.

13 Solving equations (2)

Solving equations by the balance method (revision)

$2x - 9 = 15$ is an **equation** in x. x is the **unknown** in the equation. $2x - 9$ is on the left-hand side (LHS) of the equals sign and 15 is on the right-hand side (RHS) of the equals sign.

To **solve an equation** means to find the value of the unknown that makes the equation true.

Example 1

Solve $3x = 12$.

$3x = 12$

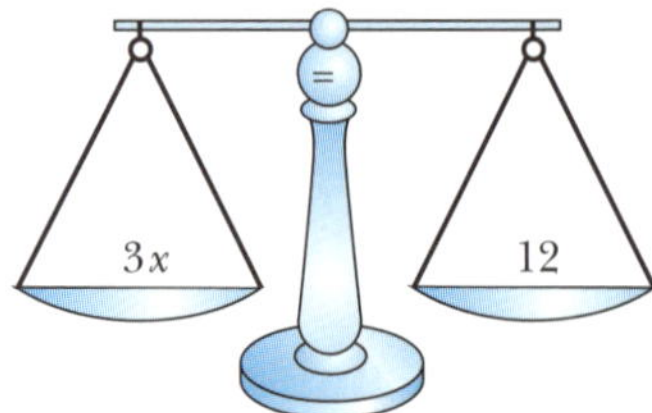

Fig. 13.1

Divide both the LHS and RHS by 3, the coefficient of the unknown. This maintains the balance of the equation.

$\frac{3x}{3} = \frac{12}{3}$

Fig. 13.2

$x = 4$

Fig. 13.3

$x = 4$ is the solution of the equation $3x = 12$.
Check: when $x = 4$, LHS $= 3 \times 4 = 12 =$ RHS

Example 2

Solve $2x - 9 = 15$.

$2x - 9 = 15$

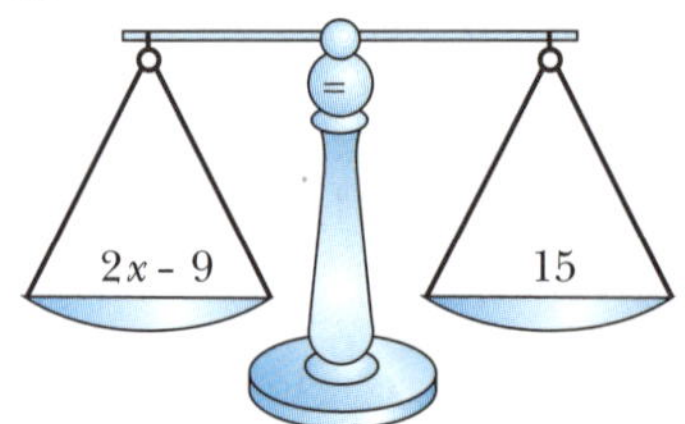

Fig. 13.4

a) The LHS of the equation contains the unknown. Add 9 to $2x - 9$. This leaves $2x$. 9 must also be added to the RHS to keep the balance of the equation.
$2x - 9 = 15$
Add 9 to both sides (+9 is the additive inverse of −9).
$2x - 9 + 9 = 15 + 9$

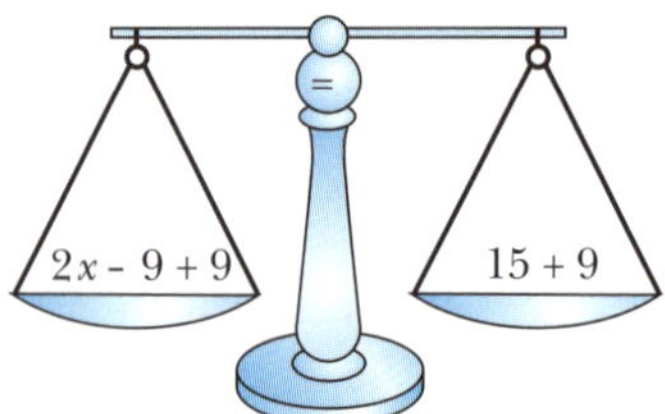

Fig. 13.5

Simplifying,
$2x = 24$

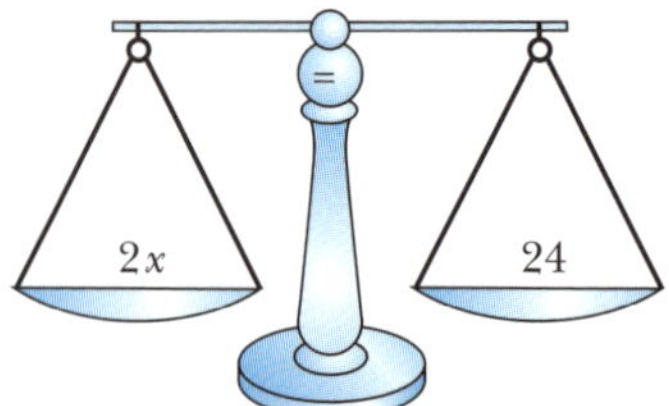

Fig. 13.6

b) The equation is now simpler. Divide the LHS by 2 to leave x. The RHS must also be divided by 2 to keep the balance of the equation.

$2x = 24$
Divide both sides by 2.

$\frac{2x}{2} = \frac{24}{2}$

Fig. 13.7

$x = 12$

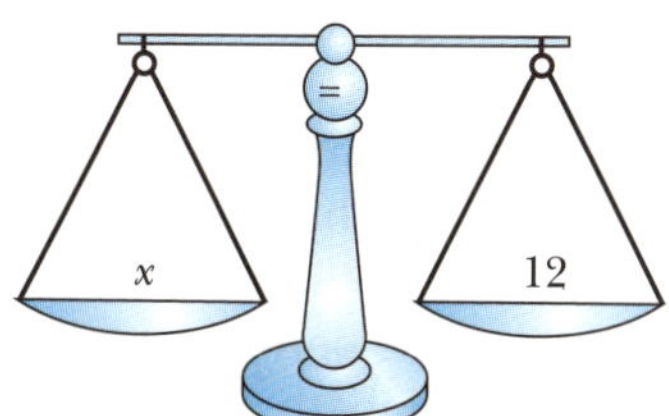

Fig. 13.8

$x = 12$ is the solution of the equation $2x - 9 = 15$.
Check: when $x = 12$, LHS $= 2 \times 12 - 9 = 24 - 9 = 15 =$ RHS

Exercise 13a (Revision)

Use the balance method to solve the following.

1 $3x - 8 = 10$	**2** $2x + 5 = 17$
3 $4x - 1 = 1$	**4** $16 = 7x + 2$
5 $27 = 10x - 3$	**6** $20 = 9x + 11$
7 $4 + 5a = 19$	**8** $37 = 7 + 6z$
9 $51 = 3 + 8n$	**10** $10y - 7 = 27$
11 $9 + 2r = 16$	**12** $2 = 3d - 8$

Word problems

We can use equations to solve many word problems. There is always an unknown in a word problem. The aim is to find the numerical value of the unknown.

When solving a word problem:

1 Choose a letter for the unknown.
2 Write down the information given in the question in algebraic form.
3 Make an equation.
4 Solve the equation.
5 Give the answer in written form.
6 Check the result against the information given in the question.

Example 3

I think of a number. I multiply it by 5. I add 15. The result is 100. What is the number I thought of?

Let the number be n.
I multiply n by 5: $5n$
I add 15: $5n + 15$
The result is 100: $5n + 15 = 100$ (1)
Subtract 15 from both sides of (1).
$5n + 15 - 15 = 100 - 15$
$5n = 85$ (2)
Divide both sides of (2) by 5.

$$\frac{5n}{5} = \frac{85}{5}$$

$$n = 17$$

The number is 17.
Check: $17 \times 5 = 85$; $85 + 15 = 100$

Example 4

A rectangle is 8 m *long and its perimeter is* 30 m. *Find the breadth of the rectangle.*

Let the breadth of the rectangle be b metres.
Perimeter $= 8 + b + 8 + b$ metres
$= 16 + 2b$ metres
Thus $16 + 2b = 30$
Subtract 16 from both sides.
$2b = 30 - 16 = 14$
Divide both sides by 2.
$b = \frac{14}{2} = 7$
The breadth of the rectangle is 7 metres.
Check: 8 m + 7 m + 8 m + 7 m = 30 m

Exercise 13b will help you to change written information into algebraic form.

Exercise 13b

1 How many altogether if
  a) a number x is doubled?
  b) a number n is multiplied by 8?
  c) a number m is multiplied by 6 and then 4 is added?
  d) a number y is doubled and then 5 is taken away?
  e) a number is 3 less than a?
  f) a number d is added to another number four times as big?
  g) Augusta has h leones and Gloria has twice as much?
  h) a number t is trebled and 7 is subtracted?

i) one girl has k leones and another girl has 9 leones less?

j) team X scores g goals and team Y scores 23 goals more than X?

2 What is the perimeter of

a) a square of side x cm?

b) a triangle with sides $2a$ metres, a metres and 4 metres?

c) a regular hexagon of side c cm?

d) a rectangle of breadth b metres and length three times as long?

e) a rectangle of length 10 metres and breadth h metres?

f) an isosceles triangle with two sides of length $2t$ cm and one side of length t cm?

g) an equilateral triangle of side $2b$ metres?

h) a regular pentagon of side k cm?

i) a rectangle of length y metres and breadth 4 m less than the length?

j) a regular heptagon of side $2x$ cm?

Exercise 13c

The questions in this exercise correspond in order to the questions of Exercise 13b.

1 John thinks of a number. He doubles it. His result is 58. What number did John think of?

2 Six boys each have the same number of sweets. The total number of sweets is 78. How many sweets did each boy have?

3 A number is multiplied by 6 and then 4 is added. The result is 34. Find the first number.

4 A woman has two boxes of matches. She uses five matches and has 75 matches left. How many matches were in each box?

5 I am thinking of a number. I take away 5. The result is 14. What number did I think of?

6 When a number is added to another number four times as big, the result is 30. Find the first number.

7 Augusta and Gloria share 21 leones so that Gloria gets twice as much as Augusta. How much does Augusta get?

8 Find the number such that when it is trebled and 7 is subtracted, the result is 8.

9 One girl has 9 leones less than another girl. They have 29 leones between them. How much does each girl have?

10 During a football season, one team scored 23 goals more than another. Between them they scored 135 goals. How many goals did each team score?

11 A square has a perimeter of 32 m. Find the length of one side of the square.

12 A triangle is such that the first side is twice the length of the second side. The third side is 4 m long. If the perimeter of the triangle is 13 m, find the lengths of the first and second sides.

13 A regular hexagon has a perimeter of 90 cm. Find the length of one side of the hexagon.

14 A rectangle is three times as long as it is broad. If the perimeter of the rectangle is 40 m, find its length and breadth.

15 A rectangle is 10 m long and its perimeter is 26 m. Find the breadth of the rectangle.

16 An isosceles triangle has two long sides and one short side. The short side is half the length of a long side. If the perimeter of the triangle is 15 cm, find the length of the short side.

17 An equilateral triangle has a perimeter of 36 cm. What is the length of half of one of its sides?

18 What is the length of a side of a regular pentagon of perimeter 85 mm?

19 A rectangle is such that its breadth is 2 m less than its length. Find the length of the rectangle if the perimeter is 8 m.

20 What is the length of a side of a regular heptagon of perimeter 10·5 cm?

Solving equations – further examples

It is possible to use operations with directed numbers when solving equations. See Chapter 5.

Example 5

Solve $25 - 9x = 2$.

$$25 - 9x = 2$$

Subtract 25 from both sides.

$$25 - 25 - 9x = 2 - 25$$
$$-9x = -23$$

Divide both sides by −9.

$$\frac{-9x}{-9} = \frac{-23}{-9}$$

$$x = \frac{23}{9} = 2\tfrac{5}{9}$$

Check: when $x = \frac{23}{9}$,

LHS $= 25 - 9 \times \frac{23}{9} = 25 - 23 = 2 =$ RHS

If an equation has unknown terms on both sides of the equals sign, collect the unknown terms on one side and the number terms on the other side.

Example 6

Solve $5x - 4 = 2x + 11$.

$5x - 4 = 2x + 11$ (1)

Subtract $2x$ from both sides of (1).

$5x - 2x - 4 = 2x - 2x + 11$

$3x - 4 = 11$ (2)

Add 4 to both sides of (2).

$3x - 4 + 4 = 11 + 4$

$3x = 15$ (3)

Divide both sides of (3) by 3.

$x = 5$

Check: when $x = 5$,

LHS $= 5 \times 5 - 4 = 25 - 4 = 21$

RHS $= 2 \times 5 + 11 = 10 + 11 = 21 =$ LHS

Note that equations (1), (2) and (3) are all equivalent.

Exercise 13d

Solve the following equations and check the solutions.

1 $13 - 6a = 1$
2 $12 + 5a = -3$
3 $4b + 24 = 0$
4 $0 = 25 - 15x$
5 $12 = 9 - 3a$
6 $9 - 8y = 3$
7 $5 - 4n = 8$
8 $7 = 9 - 3m$
9 $7a = 3a + 20$
10 $20 - 2t = 3t$
11 $5n = 12 - n$
12 $7c - 6 = c$
13 $10q = 3q - 7$
14 $3x = 18 - 3x$
15 $3m + 8 = m$
16 $9x + 1 = 7x$
17 $4h - 2 = h + 7$
18 $5a + 6 = 2a + 20$
19 $18 - 5f = 2f + 4$
20 $11 - 3e = 2e - 19$
21 $6x + 1 = 26 - 2x$
22 $4x + 7 = 5x + 6$
23 $x + 7 = 19 + 2x$
24 $11 + 9n = 6n + 13$

Equations with brackets

Always remove brackets before collecting terms.

Example 7

Solve $3(3x - 1) = 4(x + 3)$.

$3(3x - 1) = 4(x + 3)$ (1)

Remove brackets.

$9x - 3 = 4x + 12$ (2)

Subtract $4x$ from both sides, and add 3 to both sides.

$9x - 4x - 3 + 3 = 4x - 4x + 12 + 3$

$5x = 15$ (3)

Divide both sides by 5.

$x = 3$

Check: when $x = 3$,

LHS $= 3(3 \times 3 - 1) = 3(9 - 1) = 3 \times 8 = 24$

RHS $= 4(3 + 3) = 4 \times 6 = 24 =$ LHS

Example 8

Solve $5(x + 11) + 2(2x - 5) = 0$.

$5(x + 11) + 2(2x - 5) = 0$ (1)

Remove brackets.

$5x + 55 + 4x - 10 = 0$ (2)

Collect like terms.

$9x + 45 = 0$ (3)

Subtract 45 from both sides.

$9x = -45$ (4)

Divide both sides by 9.

$x = -5$

Check: when $x = -5$,

LHS $= 5(-5 + 11) + 2(2 \times (-5) - 5)$

$= 5 \times 6 + 2(-10 - 5)$

$= 30 + 2 \times (-15) = 30 - 30 = 0 =$ RHS

Exercise 13e

Solve the following equations and check the solutions.

1 $2(x + 5) = 18$
2 $15 = 3(x - 3)$
3 $55 = 5(2a - 1)$
4 $2(3y + 1) = 14$
5 $4(x + 7) + 12 = 0$
6 $0 = 7(x - 3)$
7 $6(2s - 7) = 5s$
8 $4b = 3(3b + 15)$
9 $3(f + 2) = 2 - f$
10 $3x + 1 = 2(3x + 5)$
11 $5(a + 2) = 4(a - 1)$
12 $5(b + 1) = 3(b + 3)$
13 $7(2e + 3) = 3(4e + 9)$
14 $8(2d - 3) = 3(4d - 7)$
15 $5(x + 1) = 7(2 - x)$
16 $2(4 - x) = 3(2 - x)$
17 $2(y - 2) + 3(y - 7) = 0$
18 $5(y + 8) + 2(y + 1) = 0$
19 $5(x - 4) - 4(x + 1) = 0$

20 $3(2x + 3) - 7(x + 2) = 0$
21 $5(5z - 2) - 9(3z - 2) = 2$
22 $3(6 + 7y) + 2(1 - 5y) = 42$
23 $5(v + 2) + 3(v + 5) = 1$
24 $4(3 - 5n) - 7(5 - 4n) + 3 = 0$

Word problems involving brackets

Example 9

I subtract 3 from a certain number, multiply the result by 5 and then add 9. If the final result is 54, find the original number.

Let the original number be x.

I subtract 3: this gives $x - 3$
I multiply by 5: this gives $5(x - 3)$
I add 9: this gives $5(x - 3) + 9$
The result is 54.
Thus, $5(x - 3) + 9 = 54$ (1)

Clear brackets.
$5x - 15 + 9 = 54$ (2)
Collect terms.
$5x = 54 + 15 - 9 = 60$ (3)
thus $x = 60 \div 5 = 12$

The original number is 12.

Example 10

Find two consecutive even numbers such that seven times the smaller number subtracted from nine times the greater number makes 46.

Note: 1, 2, 3, 4, 5, ... are consecutive whole numbers
2, 4, 6, 8, 10, ... are consecutive even numbers
1, 3, 5, 7, 9, ... are consecutive odd numbers

Let the numbers be x and $(x + 2)$.
Multiply x by 7: this gives $7x$
Multiply $(x + 2)$ by 9: this gives $9(x + 2)$
Subtract: this gives $9(x + 2) - 7x$
The result is 46:

$9(x + 2) - 7x = 46$ (1)
$9x + 18 - 7x = 46$ (2)
$9x - 7x = 46 - 18$ (3)
$2x = 28$ (4)

$$x = \frac{28}{2} = 14$$

If $x = 14$
$(x + 2) = 14 + 2 = 16$
The numbers are 14 and 16.

Example 11

Mohammed and Alie sell ballpoint pens at the same price. One day Mohammed increases his price by Le2 *and Alie reduces her price by* Le4*. Mohammed sells six pens and Alie sells nine pens. If they both take in the same amount of money, what was the original price of a pen?*

Let the original price of a pen be Lex.

Mohammed's new price = Le$(x + 2)$
Alie's new price = Le$(x - 4)$
Mohammed's income = Le$6(x + 2)$
Alie's income = Le$9(x - 4)$

They both take in the same money,
thus, $6(x + 2) = 9(x - 4)$

Clear brackets.
$6x + 12 = 9x - 36$
Collect terms.
$12 + 36 = 9x - 6x$
$48 = 3x$
$16 = x$

The original price of a pen was Le16.

Exercise 13f

1 I add 12 to a certain number and then double the result. The answer is 42. Find the original number.
2 I subtract 8 from a certain number. I then multiply the result by 3. The final answer is 21. Find the original number.
3 I think of a number. I multiply it by 5. I then subtract 19. Finally, I double the result. The final number is 22. What number did I think of?
4 Find two consecutive whole numbers such that five times the smaller number added to three times the greater number makes 59. (*Hint*: let the numbers be x and $x + 1$.)
5 Find two consecutive odd numbers such that six times the smaller added to four times the greater comes to 138. (*Hint*: let the numbers be x and $x + 2$.)
6 A rectangular room is 2 m longer than it is wide. Its perimeter is 70 m. If the width of the room is w m, express the length of the room in terms of w. Hence find the width of the room.
7 A man has a body mass of m kg. He is 30 kg

heavier than each of his twin children. Express the body mass of each child in terms of m. If the mass of the father and children comes to 156 kg, find the mass of the father.

8 Black pencils cost Le100 each and coloured pencils cost Le200 each. If 24 mixed pencils cost Le3 100, how many of them were black? (*Hint*: let there be x black pencils. Thus there are $(24 - x)$ coloured pencils.)

9 A worker gets Le6 000 per hour for ordinary time and Le9 000 per hour for overtime. If she gets Le32 400 for a 50-hour week, how many hours were overtime?

10 The cost of petrol rises by Le100 per gallon. Last week a motorist bought 8 gallons at the old price. This week she bought 6 gallons at the new price. Altogether, the petrol cost Le104 000. What was the old price for 1 gallon?

11 A trader bought some oranges at Le50 each. He finds that six of them are rotten. He sells the rest at Le100 each and makes a profit of Le950. How many oranges did he buy? (*Hint*: let the number of oranges be x.)

12 Two years ago an egg cost Le50 less than last year. This year an egg costs Le50 more than last year. The cost of 12 eggs two years ago was the same as the cost of eight eggs this year. What was the cost of an egg last year? (*Hint*: let last year's cost be n leones. Express the cost for the other years in terms of n.)

Equations with fractions

Always clear fractions before collecting terms. To clear fractions, multiply both sides of the equation by the LCM of the denominators of the fractions.

Example 12

Solve the equation $\frac{4m}{5} - \frac{2m}{3} = 4$.

$$\frac{4m}{5} - \frac{2m}{3} = 4$$

The LCM of 5 and 3 is 15.
Multiply both sides of the equation by 15, i.e. multiply *every* term by 15.

$$15 \times \left(\frac{4m}{5}\right) - 15 \times \left(\frac{2m}{3}\right) = 15 \times 4$$

$$3 \times 4m - 5 \times 2m = 15 \times 4$$
$$12m - 10m = 60$$
$$2m = 60$$

Divide both sides by 2.

$$m = 30$$

Check: when $m = 30$

$$\text{LHS} = \frac{4 \times 30}{5} - \frac{3 \times 30}{3} = \frac{120}{5} - \frac{60}{3}$$
$$= 24 - 20 = 4 = \text{RHS}$$

Example 13

Solve the equation $\frac{3x-2}{6} - \frac{2x+7}{9} = 0$.

The LCM of 6 and 9 is 18.
Multiply both sides of the equation by 18.

$$\frac{18(3x-2)}{6} - \frac{18(2x+7)}{9} = 18 \times 0$$

$$3(3x-2) - 2(2x+7) = 0$$

Clear brackets.

$$9x - 6 - 4x - 14 = 0$$

Collect terms.

$$5x - 20 = 0$$

Add 20 to both sides.

$$5x = 20$$

Divide both sides by 5.

$$x = 4$$

Check: when $x = 4$,

$$\text{LHS} = \frac{3 \times 4 - 2}{6} - \frac{2 \times 4 + 7}{9} = \frac{12-2}{6} - \frac{8+7}{9}$$

$$= \frac{10}{6} - \frac{15}{9} = \frac{5}{3} - \frac{5}{3} = 0 = \text{RHS}$$

Exercise 13g

Solve the following equations.

1 $\frac{x}{3} = 5$	**2** $\frac{x}{5} = \frac{1}{2}$
3 $4 = \frac{a}{9}$	**4** $\frac{7a}{2} - 21 = 0$
5 $\frac{4}{3} = \frac{2z}{15}$	**6** $1\frac{1}{2} - \frac{3x}{4} = 0$
7 $\frac{x-2}{3} = 4$	**8** $\frac{5+a}{4} = 6$

9 $\dfrac{2-a}{5} = 1$

10 $5 = \dfrac{2y-3}{7}$

11 $\dfrac{3n+1}{8} = 2$

12 $4 = \dfrac{9+5a}{6}$

13 $\dfrac{x+18}{2} = 5x$

14 $x = \dfrac{x-24}{9}$

15 $\dfrac{5x-8}{2} = 2x$

16 $\dfrac{22-3x}{4} = 2x$

17 $\dfrac{4-z}{7} = z$

18 $\dfrac{2(8x+7)}{3} = 5x$

19 $\dfrac{x}{2} - \dfrac{x}{3} = 2$

20 $\dfrac{x}{2} + \dfrac{3x}{4} = 5$

21 $\dfrac{3m}{5} - \dfrac{m}{3} = \dfrac{8}{5}$

22 $\dfrac{3x}{7} = \dfrac{2x}{3} - \dfrac{1}{3}$

23 $\dfrac{x-5}{2} = \dfrac{x-4}{3}$

24 $\dfrac{4t+3}{5} = \dfrac{t+3}{2}$

25 $\dfrac{5e-1}{4} - \dfrac{7e+4}{8} = 0$

26 $\dfrac{2d+7}{6} + \dfrac{d-5}{3} = 0$

27 $\dfrac{6m-3}{7} = \dfrac{2m+1}{7}$

28 $\dfrac{3(2a+1)}{4} = \dfrac{5(a+5)}{6}$

29 $\dfrac{2a-1}{3} - \dfrac{a+5}{4} = \dfrac{1}{2}$

30 $\dfrac{4x-3}{2} = \dfrac{9x-6}{8} + 2\frac{3}{4}$

Word problems involving fractions

Example 14

I add 55 to a certain number and then divide the sum by 3. The result is four times the first number. Find the number.

Let the number be n.

I add 55 to n: this gives $n + 55$

I divide the sum by 3: this gives $\dfrac{n+55}{3}$

The result is $4n$.

Thus $\dfrac{n+55}{3} = 4n$ (1)

Multiply both sides by 3.

$$\frac{3(n+55)}{3} = 3 \times 4n \qquad (2)$$

$$n + 55 = 12n \qquad (3)$$

Collect terms.

$$55 = 12n - n$$
$$55 = 11n \qquad (4)$$

Thus,

$$n = 5$$

The number is 5.

Example 15

The body mass of a man is x kg. The body masses of his two children are five-sixths and four-fifths that of their father.

a) Express the children's masses in terms of x.

b) If the difference between the masses of the children is 2·3 kg find the mass of the father.

a) One child is $\frac{5}{6}$ of x kg $= \dfrac{5x}{6}$ kg

The other is $\frac{4}{5}$ of x kg $= \dfrac{4x}{5}$ kg

b) $\dfrac{5x}{6} - \dfrac{4x}{5} = 2{\cdot}3$

The LCM of 5 and 6 is 30.
Multiply both sides by 30.

$$30 \times \frac{5x}{6} - 30 \times \frac{4x}{5} = 30 \times 2{\cdot}3$$

$$5 \times 5x - 6 \times 4x = 69$$
$$25x - 24x = 69$$
$$x = 69$$

The mass of the father is 69 kg.

Exercise 13h

1 I think of a number. I double it. I divide the result by 5. My answer is 6. What number did I think of?

2 I subtract 17 from a certain number and then divide the result by 5. My final answer is 3. What was the original number?

3 I add 9 to a certain number and then divide the sum by 16. Find the number if my final answer is 1.

4 I add 45 to a certain number and then divide the sum by 2. The result is five times the original number. Find the original number.

5 One-fifth of an even number added to one-sixth of the next even number makes a total of 15. Find the two numbers. (*Hint*: let the numbers be x and $x + 2$.)

6 A mother is 24 years older than her daughter. If the daughter's age is x years,

a) express the mother's age in terms of x;

b) find x when the daughter's age is one-third of her mother's age.

7 The price of a packet of salt goes up by Le200. The old price is four-fifths of the new price. Find the old and new prices. (*Hint*: let the old price be n leones. Thus the new price is $n + 200$ leones.)

8 A man's weekly pay is \$$x$. He spends half of his pay on food and one-third on rent.

a) Express the amount he spends on food in terms of x.

b) Express the amount he spends on rent in terms of x.

c) Find his weekly pay if he spends a total of \$80 on food and rent.

9 The distance between two villages is d km.

a) Express four-fifths of that distance in terms of d.

b) Express three-quarters of the distance in terms of d.

c) If the difference between these distances is 1·5 km, find the value of d.

10 Juma is y years old.

a) How old was she 3 years ago?

b) How old will she be in 4 years' time?

c) Find her age, if half of what she was 3 years ago is equal to one-third of what she will be in 4 years' time.

11 I think of a number. I subtract 14 from the number and then treble the difference. The result is two-thirds of the number. Find the original number.

12 If the price of petrol is increased by Le15 per litre, find the old price per litre if one-third of the new price is equal to three-quarters of the old price.

13 The price of a television set is Ley and the price of a video recorder is two-thirds the price of a television set. If a customer pays Le1 000 000 for the two items, find the price of a television set.

14 I subtract 13 from a certain number and then divide the result by 3. The result is the same as adding 3 to the number and then dividing by 5. Find the number.

15 A student has x sweets. She gives 20 to her friends. If one-third of the remainder is equal to one-fifth of the original number of sweets, find the original number of sweets.

16 A man shares y cows between his two children in the ratio of 5:3. If the difference between their shares is 16 cows, what is the value of y?

Chapter summary

1. To *solve an equation* means to find the value of the unknown that makes the equation true.

2. When *solving equations*:
   - **a)** remove any brackets before collecting terms,
   - **b)** clear any fractions before collecting terms (by multiplying both sides of the equation by the LCM of the denominators of the fractions),
   - **c)** collect unknown terms on one side of the equals sign and number terms on the other (using the balance method).

3. When *solving word problems*:
   - **a)** choose a letter for the unknown,
   - **b)** write the given information in algebraic form,
   - **c)** make an equation and solve it,
   - **d)** check the answer against the given information,
   - **e)** give the answer in written form in terms of the given problem.

14 Straight line graphs (1)

Continuous graphs

Consider the following example.

If 1 m of string costs Le50, then 2 m costs Le100, 3 m costs Le150, and so on. We can show lengths and costs in a **table of values** (Table 14.1). The values in the table form a set of ordered pairs:

(1, 50), (2, 100), (3, 150), (4, 200), (5, 250)

length (m)	1	2	3	4	5
cost (Le)	50	100	150	200	250

Table 14.1

We can plot the ordered pairs on a Cartesian plane. Fig. 14.1 shows the graph of the five points. Length (m) is on the horizontal axis and cost (Le) is on the vertical axis.

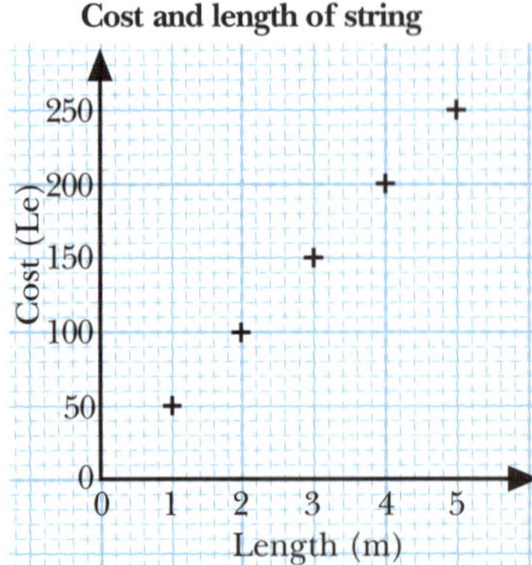

Fig. 14.1

It can be seen that the points in the graph lie in a straight line.

Other lengths of string, such as 10 m, 1·4 m, 3·75 m, would have corresponding costs. Thus it is possible to plot more points. Instead of this, we can draw a **continuous line** through the points which have been plotted. Starting at (0, 0) (no string costs nothing!) we can continue the line as far as we want. Fig. 14.2 shows the graph extended as far as the cost of 10 m of string.

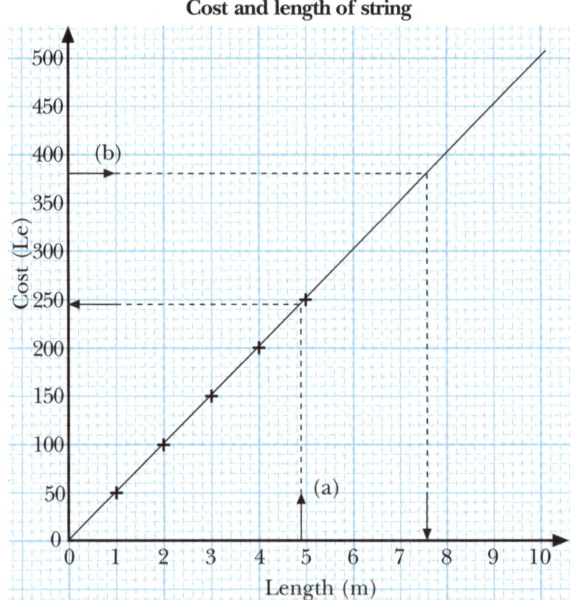

Fig. 14.2

The graph can be used to answer questions like these.

1 How much would 4·9 m of string cost?

Follow the dashed line (a) in Fig. 14.2. Start at 4·9 m on the length axis. Read the cost which corresponds to 4·9 m: Le245.

2 How much string can be bought for Le380?

Follow the dashed line (b) in Fig. 14.2. Start at Le380 on the cost axis. Read the length which corresponds to Le380 : 7·6 m.

Example 1

A student walks along a road at a speed of 120 m *per minute.*

a) *Make a table of values showing how far the student has walked after* 0, 1, 2, 3, 4, 5, *minutes.*

b) Using a scale of 1 cm *to* 1 min *on the horizontal axis and* 1 cm *to* 100 m *on the vertical axis, draw a graph of this information.*

c) Use the graph to find i) how far the student has walked after 2·6 min, *ii) how long it takes the student to walk* 500 m.

a) Table 14.2 is the table of values.

time (min)	0	1	2	3	4	5
distance (m)	0	120	240	360	480	600

Table 14.2

b)

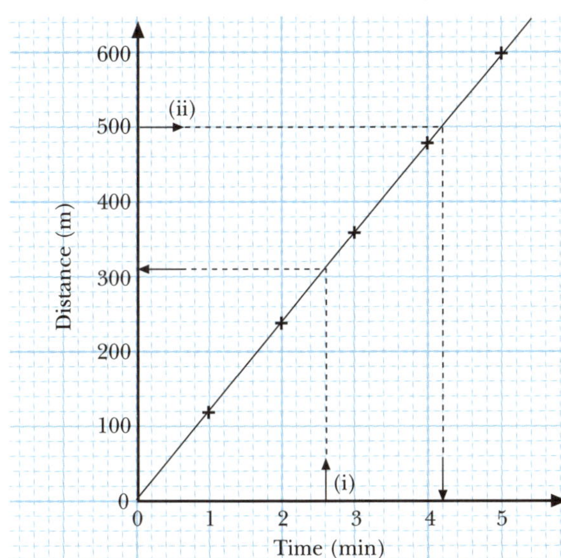

Fig. 14.3

c) i) See dashed line (i) on Fig. 14.3. 2·6 min corresponds to 310 m (approximately). The student has walked about 310 m after 2·6 min.

ii) See dashed line (ii) on Fig. 14.3. 500 m corresponds to 4·2 min (approximately). The student takes about 4·2 min to walk 500 m.

Notice that graphs usually only give approximate results.

When drawing graphs, *always*

1 draw and name the two axes;

2 give a title to the graph.

Exercise 14a

1 Use the graph in Fig. 14.2 to find the following.

a) The cost of 6 m, 3·5 m, 9 m, 8·2 m, 2·6 m, 7·1 m of string.

b) How much string can be bought for Le350, Le400, Le210, Le90, Le125, Le465.

2 A car increases its speed steadily over 6 seconds as shown in Table 14.3.

time (s)	0	1	2	3	4	5	6
speed (km/h)	0	15	30	45	60	75	90

Table 14.3

a) Use a scale of 2 cm represents 1 second on the horizontal axis and 2 cm represents 10 km/h on the vertical axis. Draw a graph of the information in Table 14.3.

b) Use your graph to find i) the speed of the car after 2·5 s, ii) the time taken to reach a speed of 80 km/h.

3 A girl walks along a road at a speed of 100 m per minute.

a) Copy and complete Table 14.4.

time (min)	0	1	2	3	4	5	6
distance (m)	0	100	200				

Table 14.4

b) Using a scale of 2 cm to 1 min on the horizontal axis and 2 cm to 100 m on the vertical axis, draw a graph of the information.

c) Use your graph to find i) how far the girl has walked after 5·7 min, ii) how long it takes her to walk 335 m.

4 Cloth costs Le6 000 for 1 metre.

a) Copy and complete Table 14.5.

length (m)	1	2	3	4	5	6
cost (Le)	6 000	12 000	18 000			

Table 14.5

b) Using a scale of 2 cm to 1 metre on the horizontal axis and 2 cm to Le5 000 on the vertical axis, draw a graph of the information.

c) Use your graph to find i) the cost of 3·8 m of cloth, ii) how much cloth can be bought for Le14 000?

5 A car travels 7 km on 1 litre of petrol.

a) Copy and complete Table 14.6.

petrol (litres)	0	10	20	30	40	50
distance (km)	0	70	140	210		

Table 14.6

b) Using a scale of 2 cm to 10 litres on the horizontal axis and 2 cm to 100 km on the vertical axis, draw a graph of the information.

c) Use your graph to find i) the distance that the car will travel on 22 litres, ii) how much petrol the car uses in travelling 230 km.

6 1 gallon of fuel costs Le8 000.

a) Copy and complete Table 14.7.

fuel (gallons)	0	1	2	3	4	5	6
cost (Le)	0	8000	16000	24000			

Table 14.7

b) Using a scale of 2 cm to 1 litre on the horizontal axis and 2 cm to Le5 000 on the vertical axis, draw a graph of this information.

c) Use the graph to find i) the cost of 4·5 gallons of fuel, ii) how much fuel can be bought for Le60 000.

7 Sugar costs Le2 000 per kg.

a) Copy and complete Table 14.8.

sugar (kg)	1	2	3	4	5	6
cost (Le)	2000	4000	6000			

Table 14.8

b) Using a scale of 2 cm to 1 kg on the horizontal axis and 2 cm to Le1 000 on the vertical axis, draw a graph of this information.

c) Use your graph to find i) the cost of $2\frac{1}{2}$ kg of sugar, ii) how much sugar can be bought for Le7 500.

8 The drill of an oil well drills downwards at a rate of 7·5 m/h.

a) Copy and complete Table 14.9.

time (h)	0	1	2	3	4	5
distance (m)	0	−7.5	−15	−22·5		

Table 14.9

b) Draw the origin near the top left corner of your graph paper. Using a scale of 2 cm represents 1 hour on the horizontal axis and 1 cm represents 5 m on the vertical axis, draw a graph of the information.

c) Use the graph to find i) how long it takes the drill to drill down through 25 m, ii) the distance of the drill from ground level after 90 min.

9 A car travelling at 90 km/h covers 3 km in 2 min, 6 km in 4 min, 9 km in 6 min, and so on.

a) Make a table of values showing how far the car travels in 2 min, 4 min, 6 min, 8 min, 10 min.

b) Using a scale of 1 cm to 1 min on the horizontal axis and 1 cm to 1 km on the vertical axis, draw a graph of the information in your table.

c) Use the graph to find i) how far the car travels in $3\frac{1}{2}$ min, ii) how long it takes the car to travel 10 km.

10 A man cycles at a speed of 18 km/h.

a) Make a table of values showing how far the man travels in $\frac{1}{2}$, 1, $1\frac{1}{2}$, 2, $2\frac{1}{2}$, 3 hours.

b) Using a scale of 2 cm represents 1 hour on the horizontal axis and 2 cm represents 10 km on the vertical axis, draw a graph of the information.

c) Use the graph to find i) how far the man cycles in 1·6 hours, ii) how long it takes him to cycle 40 km.

Discontinuous graphs

Example 2

Glasses cost Le900 *each.*

a) Make a table of values showing the cost of 1, 2, 3, 4, 5 *glasses.*

b) Draw a graph to show this information.

a) See Table 14.10.

number of glasses	1	2	3	4	5
cost (Le)	900	1 800	2 700	3 600	4 500

Table 14.10

b) See Fig. 14.4.

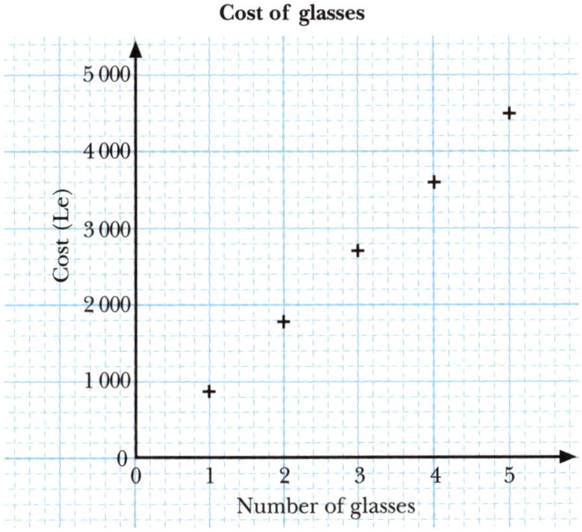

Fig. 14.4

The points in the graph in Fig. 14.4 lie in a straight line. However, we do *not* connect them. This is because it is impossible to buy a fraction of a glass such as $1\frac{1}{2}$ or 3·2. Thus there is no part of the graph which corresponds to fractions. A graph like this is called a **discontinuous graph**.

Exercise 14b

The graphs in this exercise are discontinuous. Plot the points only.

1 Cinema tickets cost Le2 000 each.

a) Copy and complete Table 14.11.

number of tickets	0	1	2	3	4	5
cost (Le)	0	2 000	4 000			

Table 14.11

b) Using a scale of 2 cm to 1 ticket on the horizontal axis and 1 cm to Le1 000 on the vertical axis, draw a graph of this information.

2 A bottle of 60 pills costs Le4 800.

a) Copy and complete Table 14.12.

number of pills	10	20	30	40	50	60
cost (Le)	800					4800

Table 14.12

b) Using a scale of 2 cm represents 10 pills on the horizontal axis and 2 cm represents Le1 000 on the vertical axis, draw a graph to show the information.

c) Without doing any more calculation, plot the points representing the cost of 5, 15, 25, 35, 45, 55 pills.

d) Hence *estimate* the cost of 17 pills.

3 In Chapter 6 you learned that the sum of the angles of an n-sided polygon is $(n - 2) \times 180°$.

a) Use this formula to complete Table 14.13.

number of sides of polygon	3	4	5	6	7
sum of interior angles (degrees)	180	360	540		

Table 14.13

b) Using a scale of 2 cm to 1 side on the horizontal and 2 cm to 100° on the vertical axis, draw a graph to show the information in the table.

4 Car tyres cost Le48 000 each.

a) Make a table of values showing the costs of 1, 2, 3, 4, 5 tyres.

b) Using a scale of 2 cm represents 1 tyre on the horizontal axis and 2 cm represents Le50 000 on the vertical axis, draw a graph to show this information.

Choosing scales

Most of the graphs shown in this chapter are drawn to a small scale. This is to fit the sizes of the columns in the book. However, it is better to choose a big scale when drawing graphs. The scales given in exercises 14a and 14b are all of a suitable size.

When choosing scales, first look at your table of values. For example, look at Table 14.14.

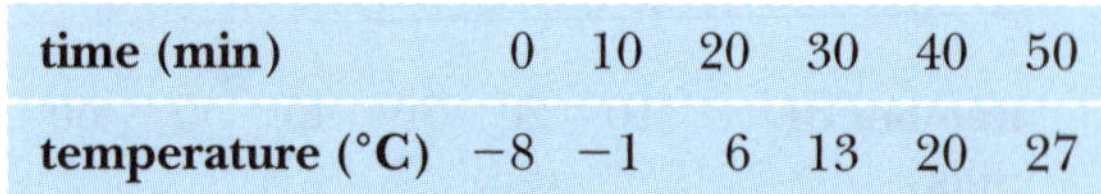

time (min)	0	10	20	30	40	50
temperature (°C)	−8	−1	6	13	20	27

Table 14.14

This shows that the time scale on the horizontal axis must go from 0 min to 50 min, as shown in Fig. 14.5.

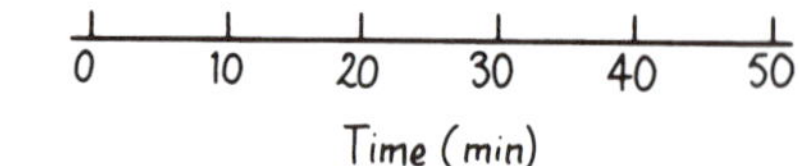

Fig. 14.5

The temperature scale on the vertical axis must go from −8°C to 27°C. It is better to round these values to give a range from −10°C to 30°C, as shown in Fig. 14.6.

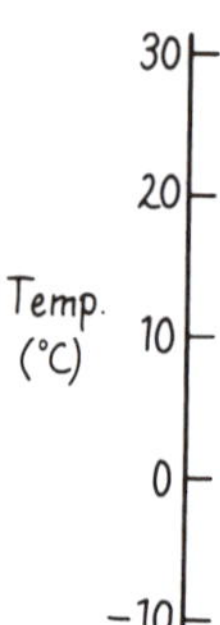

Fig. 14.6

Both axes meet at the origin. A rough sketch of the axes, such as in Fig. 14.7, can be made. Most graph paper is about 24 cm long by 18 cm wide. In this case, a scale of 2 cm to 10 units on both axes will be suitable.

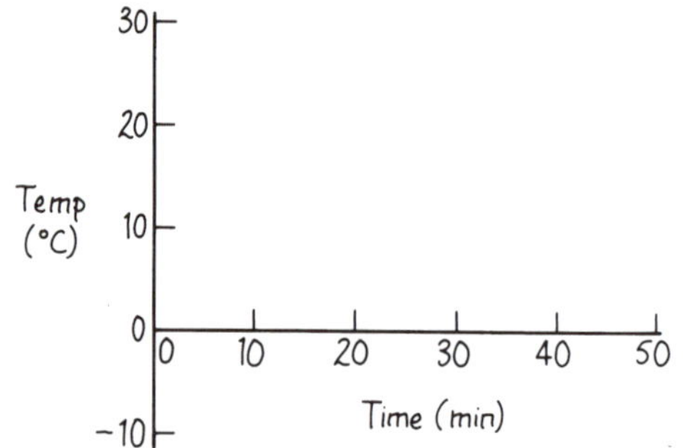

Fig. 14.7

Always look at the data and make a rough sketch as in Fig. 14.7. This will help you to place your graph on your graph paper.

On 2 mm graph paper, it is usual to let 2 cm represent 1, 2, 5, 10, 20, 50, 100, ... units (Fig. 14.8).

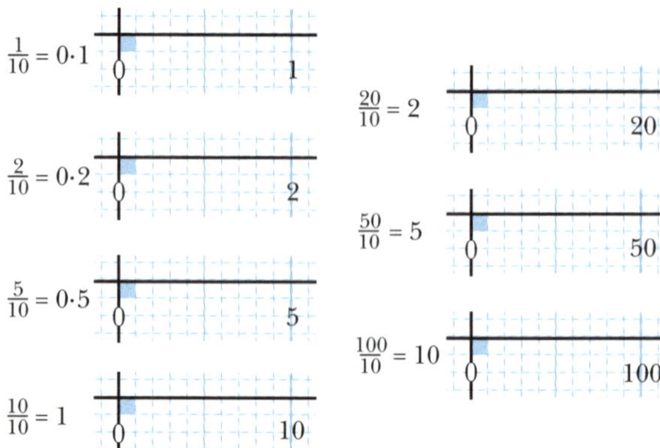

Fig. 14.8

In Fig. 14.8, in each case, a 2 mm square has been filled in and what it represents has been indicated.

In any scale used, you should know what each 2 mm small square represents. This helps in plotting your points and in taking accurate readings from your graphs.

The scale that you use will depend on the data. It is advisable not to use scales in multiples of 3 or 4, for example, because the squares on the paper are in multiples of 5 or 10.

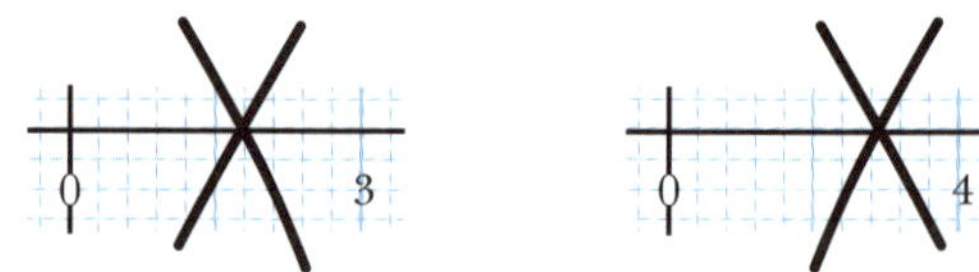

Fig. 14.9

Example 3

The labour charges for repairing a television set consist of a standing charge of Le5 000 *on all bills and an hourly rate of* Le2 000 *per hour.*

a) Make a table showing the total labour charges for jobs which take $\frac{1}{2}$ h, 1 h, 2 h, 3 h, 4 h.

b) Choose a suitable scale and draw a graph of the information.

c) Find the total labour charges for a job which takes i) $2\frac{1}{2}$ hours, *ii)* 24 min.

a) The total labour charges are shown in Table 14.15.

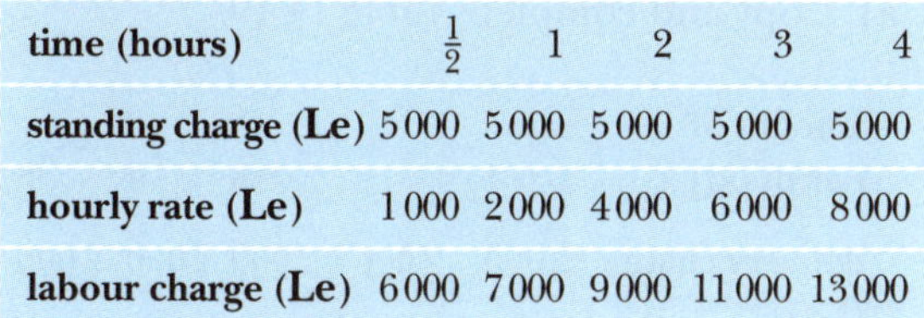

time (hours)	$\frac{1}{2}$	1	2	3	4
standing charge (Le)	5 000	5 000	5 000	5 000	5 000
hourly rate (Le)	1 000	2 000	4 000	6 000	8 000
labour charge (Le)	6 000	7 000	9 000	11 000	13 000

Table 14.15

b) Choosing scales:
Time goes from $\frac{1}{2}$ h to 4 h. Use a range 0 to 4 h (Fig. 14.10).

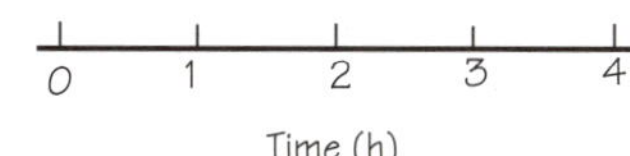

Fig. 14.10

Labour charges go from Le6 000 to Le13 000. Use a range 0 to Le15 000 (Fig. 14.11). Always include the origin if possible.

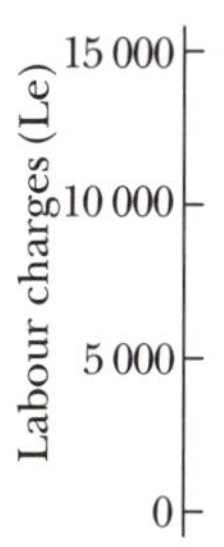

Fig. 14.11

Fig. 14.12 is a sketch of the axes.

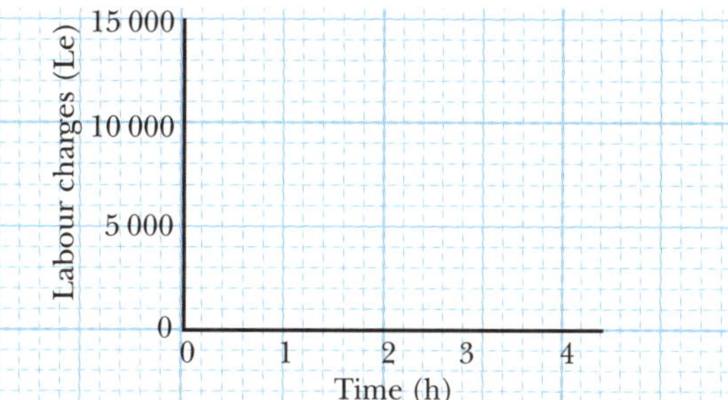

Fig. 14.12

Scales of 2 cm to 1 h on the horizontal axis and 2 cm to Le5 000 on the vertical axis will be suitable. Fig. 14.13 shows the graph.

c) i) Reading up from $2\frac{1}{2}$ h on the time axis corresponds to a charge of Le10 000 on the labour charges axis.

ii) $24 \text{ min} = \frac{24}{60} \text{ hour} = 0{\cdot}4 \text{ h}$

0·4 h corresponds approximately to Le5 750. The charge for a 24-minute job is about Le5 750.

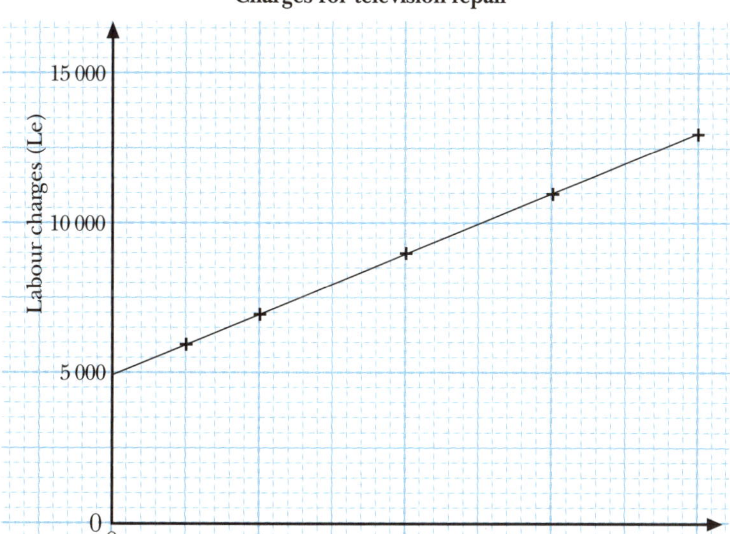

Fig. 14.13

Exercise 14c

1 A piece of meat is taken out of a freezer. Its temperature rises steadily as shown in Table 14.16.

time (min)	0	10	20	30	40	50
temperature (°C)	−6	0	6	12	18	24

Table 14.16

a) Choose a suitable scale and draw a graph of this information.

b) Use the graph to estimate i) the temperature of the meat after 13 min, ii) the time taken for the meat to reach a temperature of 20°C.

2 The unstretched length of a rubber band is 120 mm. When masses were hung on the rubber band, its total length changed as given in Table 14.17.

mass (g)	0	200	400	600	800	1 000
length (mm)	120	170	220	270	320	370

Table 14.17

a) Choose a suitable scale and draw a graph of the data.

b) Use your graph to find i) the length of the rubber band when a mass of 250 g is hung on it, ii) the mass which stretches the rubber band to a length of 300 mm.

3 A baby was 3·4 kg when he was born. For his first 6 weeks, his mass increased by about 0·3 kg per week.

a) Copy and complete Table 14.18.

week number	0	1	2	3	4	5	6
mass (kg)	3·4	3·7	4·0	4·3			

Table 14.18

b) Choose a suitable scale and draw a graph of this information.

c) Approximately how many days old was the baby when his mass was 5 kg?

4 An oil company sells petrol to garages at the rate of Le16 000 per kilolitre. There is also a delivery charge of Le2 000 on all orders.

a) Copy and complete Table 14.19.

amount of petrol (kl)	1	2	3	4	5
delivery charge (Le)	2 000	2 000	2 000	2 000	2 000
basic charge (Le)	16 000	32 000	48 000		
total cost (Le)	18 000	34 000	50 000		

Table 14.19

b) Choose a suitable scale and draw a graph of this information.

c) Use the graph to find i) the cost of 4 500 litres of petrol, ii) how much petrol is delivered for Le90 000.

5 The basic cost of window glass is Le400 per m^2. There is also a handling and cutting charge of Le100 on all orders.

a) Copy and complete Table 14.20.

area of glass (m^2)	$\frac{1}{2}$	1	$1\frac{1}{2}$	2	$2\frac{1}{2}$
handling/cutting (Le)	100	100	100	100	100
basic charge (Le)	200	400	600		
total cost (Le)	300	500	700		

Table 14.20

b) Choose a suitable scale and draw a graph of this information.

c) A window has nine panes of glass. Each pane is 25 cm by 50 cm.

i) Calculate the total area, in m^2, of the glass.

ii) Use the graph to find out how much the glass costs.

Information from graphs

Conversion graphs

A **conversion graph** changes one set of units into another. Fig. 14.14 is a conversion graph for changing Nigerian naira into Ghanaian cedis and cedis into naira.

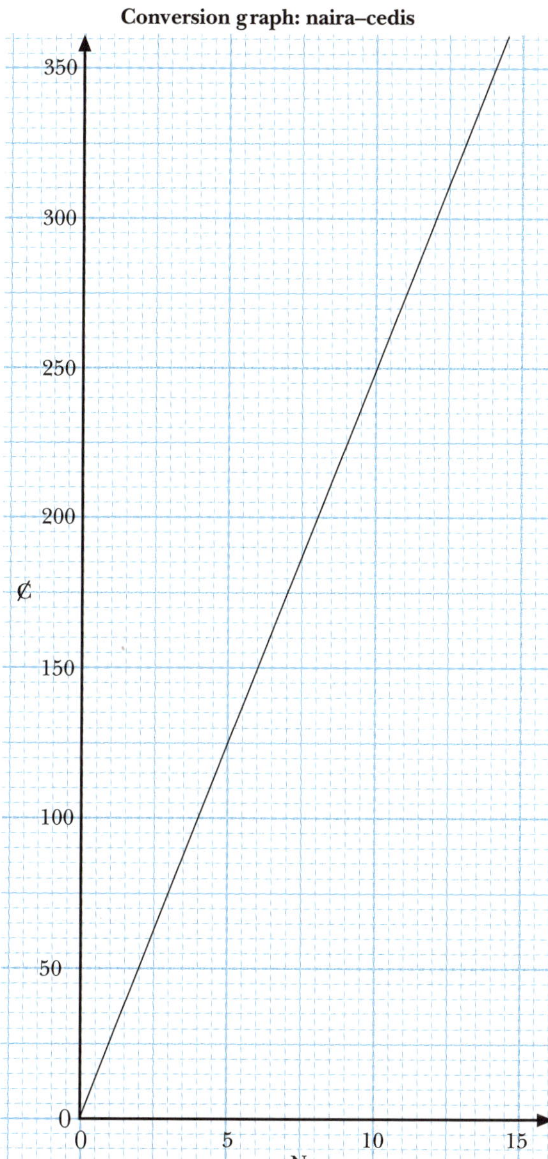

Fig. 14.14

The conversion graph was constructed from the exchange rate. The exchange rate for the graph in Fig. 14.14 is ₦1 = ₵25.00. This is equivalent to ₦10 = ₵250. The ordered pair (10, 250) is joined to the origin. The graph can be extended as far as we like. Fig. 14.14 can be used for values as high as ₦14 and ₵350.

Example 5

Use the conversion graph in Fig. 14.14 to find the following.

a) The Ghanaian equivalent of i) ₦5, *ii)* ₦14.

b) The Nigerian equivalent of i) ₵50, *ii)* ₵310.

From the graph,

a) i) ₦5 is approximately equivalent to ₵125.
   ii) ₦14 is approximately equivalent to ₵350.

b) i) ₵50 is approximately equivalent to ₦2.00.
   ii) ₵310 is approximately equivalent to ₦12.50.

A bigger scale would give a graph which could be read more accurately.

Distance/time graphs

A distance/time graph represents the movement of an object or person in terms of the distance covered and the time taken.

Example 6

Joe and Dan leave home at the same time to walk to school 3 km *away. Their journeys are shown in Fig. 14.15.*

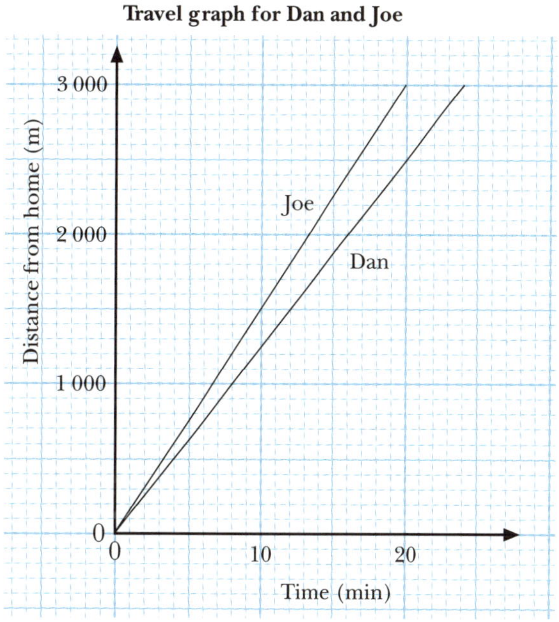

Travel graph for Dan and Joe

Fig. 14.15

a) How long did Joe take to walk to school?

b) How long did Dan take to walk to school?

c) Find Dan's and Joe's speeds in metres per minute.

From the graph,

a) Joe took 20 min.

b) Dan took 24 min.

c) In each case the journey was 3 000 m.
Joe took 20 min to travel 3 000 m.
In 1 min Joe travelled $\frac{3\,000}{20}$ m = 150 m
Joe 's speed was 150 m/min.
Dan took 24 min to travel 3 000 m.
In 1 min Dan travelled $\frac{3\,000}{24} = \frac{1\,000}{8} = 125$ m
Dan's speed was 125 m/min.

A speed is a rate of change. It is the rate of change of distance with time. There is another way to find the speeds in Example 6. Fig. 14.16 is the graph of Dan's journey.

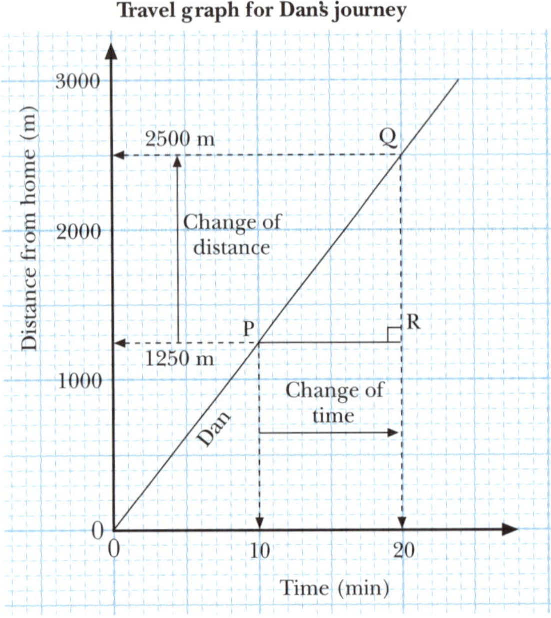

Fig. 14.16

A right-angled triangle PQR has been drawn on part of Dan's line. See Fig. 14.16. In going from P to Q, the time changes from P to R and the distance changes from R to Q.

$$\text{Dan's speed} = \frac{\text{distance travelled}}{\text{time taken}}$$

$$= \frac{\text{change of distance RQ}}{\text{change of time PR}}$$

$$= \frac{(2\,500 - 1\,250)\,\text{m}}{(20 - 10)\text{ min}}$$

$$= \frac{1\,250\text{ m}}{10\text{ min}}$$

$$= 125\text{ m/min}$$

Any right-angled triangle can be drawn. The bigger the triangle, the more accurate the result.

Exercise 14d

1 Use Fig. 14.14 to find the Ghanaian equivalent of: **a)** ₦5, **b)** ₦11.50, **c)** ₦7.50, **d)** ₦3.50, **e)** ₦8.

2 Use Fig. 14.14 to find the Nigerian equivalent of: **a)** ₵250, **b)** ₵140, **c)** ₵60, **d)** ₵95, **e)** ₵325.

3 Refer to the graph in Fig. 14.15 to answer the following.

a) If Joe arrived at school just when the first lesson started, how many minutes late was Dan?

b) At the moment Joe arrived at school, how much further did Dan have to walk?

c) When Joe was halfway to school how far was Dan i) from home, ii) from school?

d) How far had Joe walked after 14 min?

e) How long did it take Dan to walk 1·8 km?

Fig. 14.17 is a conversion graph for changing naira into leones and leones into naira.

4 Use Fig. 14.17 to find how many leones are the equivalent of: **a)** ₦10, **b)** ₦5, **c)** ₦11.50, **d)** ₦2.50, **e)** ₦13, **f)** ₦8.75.

5 Use Fig. 14.17 to find how many naira are the equivalent of: **a)** Le40, **b)** Le80, **c)** Le48, **d)** Le84, **e)** Le78, **f)** Le17.

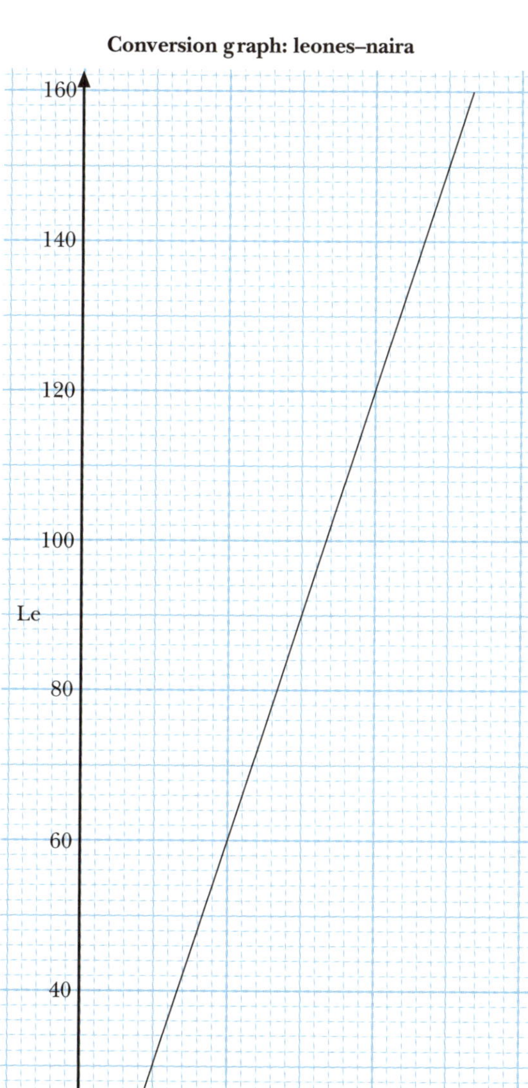

Fig. 14.17

A test is marked out of 30. Fig. 14.18 is a conversion graph for changing the marks into percentages.

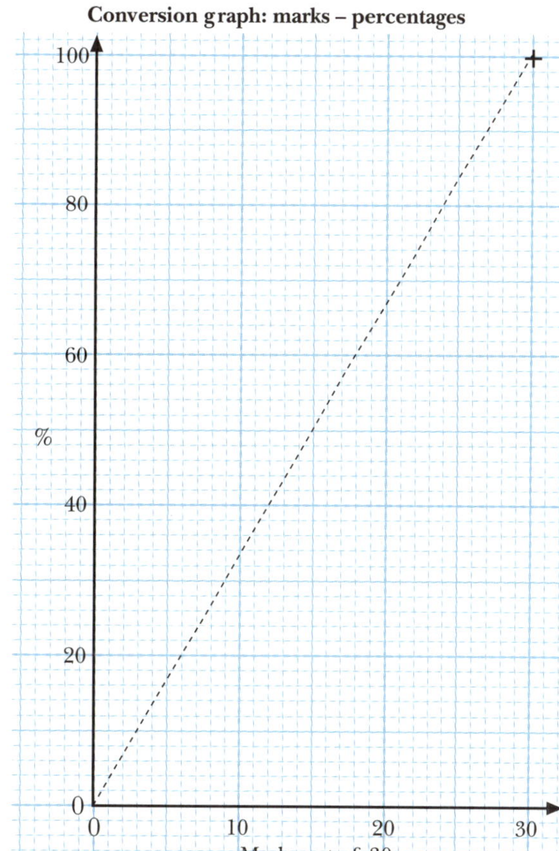

Fig. 14.18

6 Use Fig. 14.18 to change the following marks out of 30 to percentages. Give your answers to the nearest whole per cent.

a) 15	**b)** 12	**c)** 27	**d)** 18
e) 10	**f)** 20	**g)** 5	**h)** 25
i) 4	**j)** 13	**k)** 16	**l)** 29
m) $7\frac{1}{2}$	**n)** $22\frac{1}{2}$	**o)** $11\frac{1}{2}$	**p)** $24\frac{1}{2}$

7 Use Fig. 14.18 to change the following percentages to marks out of 30. Give your answer to the nearest whole mark.

a) 80%	**b)** 20%	**c)** 30%	**d)** 70%
e) 53%	**f)** 47%	**g)** 63%	**h)** 13%

Car A and car B leave Kabala at the same time. They travel 200 km to Bo. Their journeys are shown in Fig. 14.19.

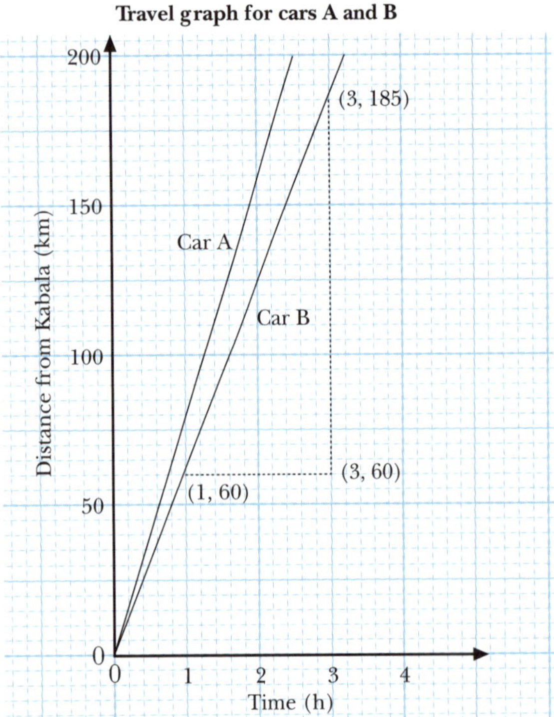

Fig. 14.19

8 Use Fig. 14.19 to answer the following.

a) How long did car A take to get to Bo?

b) How long did car B take to get to Bo?

c) Find the speeds of car A and car B.

d) Use the triangle (dotted) to check your result for car B.

9 Use Fig. 14.19 to answer the following.

a) When car A reached Bo, how far behind was car B?

b) After 1 hour, how far was each car from Bo?

c) After 2 hours, how far were the cars apart?

d) How long did it take each car to travel the first 50 km?

Fig. 14.20 is a graph of the journeys of two students, Mary and Abu. They leave their university at different times and travel 6 km to hospital. Mary walks and the line ABCD shows her journey. Abu cycles and the line FD shows his journey.

10 Use Fig. 14.20 to answer the following questions.

a) What time did Mary leave the university?

b) What time did Mary arrive at the hospital?

c) Mary stopped for a rest during her journey. How long did she stop for?

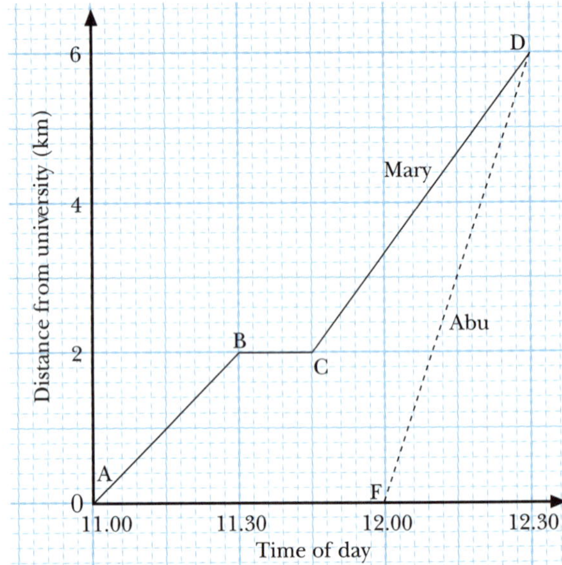

Fig. 14.20

d) During part AB of Mary's journey, how far did she walk? How long did part AB take?

e) During part CD of Mary's journey, how far did she walk? How long did part CD take?

f) How far was Mary from the hospital at 11.15 hours?

g) What time did Abu leave the university?

h) What time did Abu arrive at the hospital?

i) When Abu leaves the university, how far is Mary from the hospital?

j) How far apart were the students at 12.15 hours?

11 Use Fig. 14.20 to find the following speeds.

a) Mary's speed between A and B

b) Mary's speed between C and D

c) Mary's average speed for the whole journey

d) Abu's average speed for his whole journey

12 Use the method of Fig. 14.18 to make a conversion graph for changing marks in a test out of 40 into percentages. Use your graph to change the following marks out of 40 to percentages.

a) 30 **b)** 24 **c)** 16 **d)** 36
e) 18 **f)** 22 **g)** 10 **h)** 26
i) 27 **j)** 5 **k)** 31 **l)** 13

13 Fig. 14.21 is a sketch of a conversion graph for chaging temperature in °F to temperature in °C.

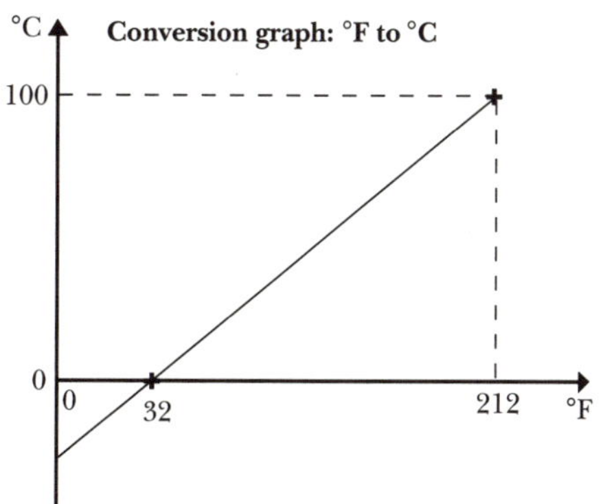

Fig. 14.21

a) Choose a suitable scale and draw an accurate conversion graph for changing °F in the range 0°F to 212°F to °C.

b) Use your graph to change the following temperatures to °C. Give your answers to the nearest whole °C.

i) 50°F ii) 150°F iii) 113°F iv) 185°F
v) 98°F vi) 200°F vii) 0°F viii) 14°F

14 The rate of exchange between Liberian money and Gambian money is $1 = D9·90.

a) Draw a conversion graph for amounts up to $10.

b) Use the graph to find the Gambian equivalents of:
i) $5 ii) $8.50 iii) $4.20 iv) $9.10.

c) Use the graph to find the Liberian equivalents of: i) D76, ii) D32, iii) D70, iv) D59.

Chapter summary

① *Graphs* are used to show the relationship between two quantities.

② Depending on the nature of the quantities, graphs may be *continuous* or *discontinuous*.

③ A *continuous graph* is in the form of a continuous line and shows, for example, the relationship between time taken and distance covered (a *travel graph*) or the cost of items such as lengths of materials, fluids, and substances that can be poured (e.g. granulated sugar, salt).

④ A *discontinuous graph* is in the form of individual points where it is impossible to fill the gaps between them (see Example 2).

⑤ Choose a big *scale* when drawing graphs. Refer to the given data to find the upper and lower limits of the scale. Always show the *origin* if possible. On 2 mm graph paper, use scales of 2 cm to 1, 2, 5, 10, 20, 50, 100, . . . units. Do *not* use scales that are multiples of 3 or 4.

⑥ A *conversion graph* changes one set of units into another. It is often used to show exchange rates.

15 Everyday arithmetic (5) Calculator skills and tables

Know your calculator

There are many kinds of calculators. Some have more buttons or keys than others. Some work in different ways from others. So learn about *your* calculator. Find out what it can do. If you use it well, it will do tedious arithmetic for you. It will save your brain for more important things.

Fig. 15.1 shows the main parts of a four-function calculator which has percentage and square root keys as well as a memory.

Power

A calculator gets its power either from small batteries or, if it is fitted with solar cells, from any light source (e.g. daylight or even candle-light). If your calculator has batteries, switch it off when not in use. Get into the habit of saving your batteries.

Display

The display shows the answers. The digits in the display are a little unusual. They are made of small line segments.

Keyboard

The keyboard has four main sets of keys or buttons:

1 *Number keys*
Press these keys: [0], [1], [2], [3], [4], [5], [6], [7], [8], [9] and the decimal point key (usually shown as a dot [·]) to enter numbers into the calculator.

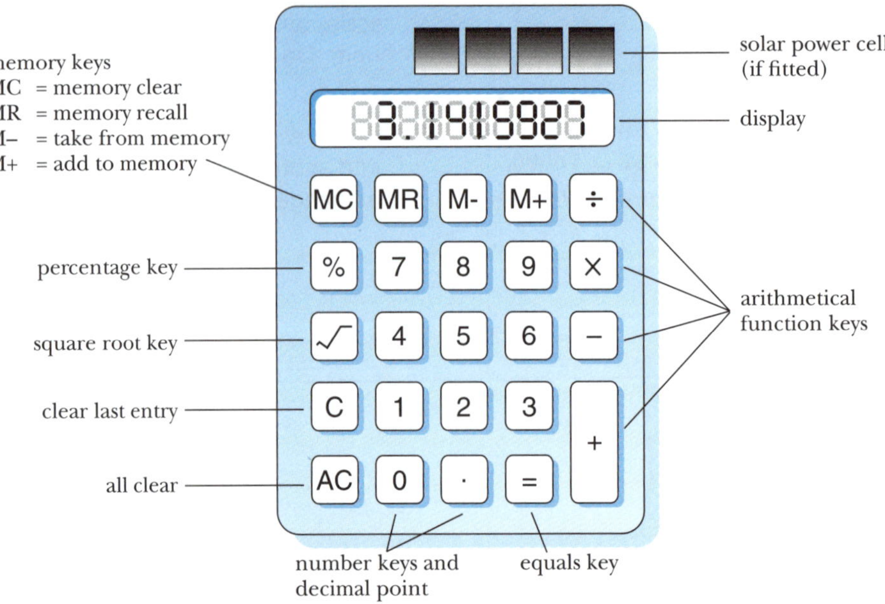

Fig. 15.1

2 *Basic calculation keys*
Press these keys: [+], [−], [×], [÷], [%], [√] and [=] to operate on the numbers you have entered, and to display answers.

3 *Clearing keys*
The [C] key clears the last number you entered. Press [C] If you enter a wrong number by mistake. On some calculators [CE] is written instead of [C]. The [AC] key clears the whole calculation that you are working on. Use this if you want to start from the beginning again. Often the [AC] key is linked to the calculator's [ON] key and is written as [ON/AC] or just as [AC], as in Fig. 15.1. Press [AC] before starting any calculation and 0 is shown on the display.

4 *Memory keys*

a) Memory plus key
Press [M+] to store the displayed number in the memory of the calculator. If there is any previous number in the memory, it adds the displayed number to it.

b) Memory minus key
Press [M−] to subtract the displayed number from the number in the memory. The answer obtained from the addition or subtraction will be the new number in the memory.

c) Memory recall key
If there is a number in the memory, the calculator usually shows a small M in one corner of the display.
Press [MR] to display the number in the memory.

d) Memory clear key
Press [MC] to clear the number stored in the memory.

Exercise 15a *(Class activity)*

1 Copy and complete Table 15.1 on page 120. For each key sequence, first guess what you think the outcome will be. Then use your calculator to get a result. If anything unexpected happens, make a note in the right-hand column.

2 Display on your calculator
a) the highest possible number,
b) the lowest positive number.

3 To find what a snail lives in:
a) calculate $5 \times 31 \times 499$;
b) turn your calculator upside down and read the display.

4 To find out what plants grow in:
a) calculate $\sqrt{50\,481\,025}$;
b) turn your calculator upside down and read the display.

5 **a)** Use your calculator to complete Table 15.2.

powers of 7	value
7^1	7
7^2	49
7^3	343
7^4	
7^5	
7^6	
7^7	
7^8	

Table 15.2

b) Look at the final digits of the value displayed in Table 15.2. Is there a pattern? If so, what is it?
c) Is there a recognisable pattern in the final two digits?
d) Try the above with a different starting number, e.g. 3, 6, 11, or 13. Are there any patterns?

6 '100 up' is a game for one person.
To start: Enter any 2-digit prime number into your calculator.
Aim: To get the calculator to display a number in the form 100· ***** where * may be any digit.
Rule: You must *multiply* the number shown in the calculator display by any number of your choice.
Scoring: Record each multiplication as a trial. Try to achieve your aim in as few trials as possible, i.e. you should keep your score as *low as possible.*

	key sequence	guess	result on calculator	notes
a)	[2] [3] [+] [4] [5] [=]			
	[1] [2] [−] [5] [=]			
	[6] [×] [4] [=]			
	[3] [6] [÷] [9] [=]			
b)	[5] [+] [2] [=] [=] [=]			
	[1] [9] [−] [3] [=] [=] [=]			
	[5] [×] [2] [=] [=] [=]			
	[3] [2] [÷] [2] [=] [=] [=]			
c)	[1] [÷] [4] [×] [4] [=]			
	[1] [÷] [3] [×] [3] [=]			
	[2] [÷] [9] [×] [9] [=]			
d)	[5] [×] [×] [=]			
	[5] [×] [×] [=] [=]			
	[7] [+] [+] [=]			
	[7] [+] [+] [=] [=] [=]			
e)	[49] [√]			
	[81] [√] [√]			
	[7] [+] [36] [√] [=]			
	[49] [√] [−] [5] [=]			
f)	[2] [÷] [5] [%]			
	[12] [×] [25] [%]			
	[12] [+] [25] [%]			
	[12] [−] [25] [%]			
g)	[2] [+] [5] [×] [3] [=]			
	[5] [+] [3] [×] [2] [=]			
	[3] [+] [5] [÷] [2] [=]			
	[2] [+] [3] [÷] [5] [=]			
	[2] [×] [5] [+] [3] [=]			
	[5] [×] [3] [+] [2] [=]			
	[5] [÷] [2] [+] [3] [=]			
	[3] [÷] [5] [+] [2] [=]			
h)	[6] [+] [3] [C] [4] [=]			
	[2] [×] [8] [C] [7] [=]			
	[8] [÷] [5] [C] [4] [=]			
	[9] [+] [5] [−] [3] [C] [2] [=]			
	[7] [−] [2] [×] [8] [C] [9] [=]			
i)	[2] [×] [8] [AC] [3] [=]			
	[8] [÷] [5] [AC] [8] [−] [5] [=]			
j)	[7] [−] [−] [3] [=]			
	[7] [−] [+] [3] [=]			
	[7] [−] [×] [3] [=]			
	[7] [+] [−] [3] [=]			
k)	[MC] [2] [M+] [8] [M+] [3] [M+] [MR]			
	[MC] [29] [M+] [8] [M−] [MR]			
	[MC] [25] [M+] [4] [M+] [MC] [MR]			
	[MC] [2] [×] [7] [M+] [5] [×] [3] [M+] [MR]			
	[MC] [8] [×] [×] [M+] [6] [×] [×] [M+] [MR] [√]			

Table 15.1

Here is a sample game:

	display	*press keys*	*trial no. (score)*
START	29	× 3	1
	87	× 1·2	2
	104·4	× 0·9	3
	93·96	× 1·05	4
	98·658	× 1·02	5
FINISH	100·63116		

The score for this game is 5. Starting with 29, can you do better? Try to beat 5, then play some games starting with other prime numbers.

Addition and subtraction

Use the [+], [−] keys to add and subtract and [=] to display the result.

Example 1

Calculate 356 + 717.

Keystrokes:

Display:

0 3 35 356 356 7 71 717 *1073* (answer)

Rough check: 400 + 700 = 1 100

It is a good idea to start any new calculation by pressing the [AC] key. This clears any previous calculation or data which the calculator may contain. When using a calculator it is possible to make keying-in mistakes. So make a habit of doing a rough check. Do the check mentally.

Example 2

Calculate 89 − 54 − 17

Keystrokes:

[AC] [8] [9] [−] [5] [4] [−] [1] [7] [=]

Display:

0 8 89 89 5 54 *35* 1 17 *18* (answer)

Rough check: 90 − 50 − 20 = 20

Notice the value 35 in the display. This is an intermediate result (89 − 54 = 35). It appears when the second operation is entered.

Example 3

Calculate 9 − 16 + 18

Keystrokes:

Display:

0 9 9 1 16 −7 1 8 *11* (answer)

Rough check: 10 − 20 + 20 = 10

Notice that the calculator gives a *negative* outcome if it is programmed to subtract a larger number from a smaller number. Thus 9 − 16 gives −7 as an intermediate result during the above calculation.

Exercise 15b

1 Do the following on your calculator. Write down what appears in the display when you press each key and underline the final answer.

a) 7 + 2 **b)** 9 − 5
c) 57 − 29 **d)** 38 + 48
e) 94 − 38 − 26 **f)** 18 + 37 + 42
g) 123 + 456 − 543 **h)** 38 − 82 + 71
i) 32·7 − 8·4 **j)** 3·4 + 7·8 + 4·3

2 Look at the following. Six of them are incorrect.

i) 6 + 7 = 14 ii) 48 + 19 = 912
iii) 22 − 12 = 10 iv) 950 − 42 = 53
v) 235 + 680 = 3 015 vi) 8·9 + 4·5 = 13·4
vii) 87 − 59 = 82 viii) 36 + 48 = −12

a) Decide which ones appear to be incorrect.
b) Use your calculator to correct them.

3 Look at the following before doing them. What kind of answer do you expect? Do the calculations.

a) 2 − 7 **b)** 5 − 15
c) 16 − 49 **d)** 36 − 73
e) 8 − 75 **f)** 44 − 260
g) 256 − 911 **h)** 56 − 46 − 66

4 An athlete buys some clothes. The bill is shown in Fig. 15.2. Check that the shop assistant has added up everything correctly.

Sports World

Tracksuit	Le5 999
Sweatshirt	Le1 990
Shorts	Le1 490
Running shoes	Le3 645
Total	Le13 124

Fig. 15.2

5 What will the shopping in Fig. 15.3 cost?

Bottle orange juice	Le429
Jar coffee	Le582
Packet of tea	Le195
Sugar	Le180
Margarine	Le299
Jar peanut butter	Le265
Oranges	Le389
Packet of bacon	Le409
Shampoo	Le405
Bottle apple juice	Le376
Chicken	Le1 450

Fig. 15.3

Multiplication and division

Use the [×] and [÷] buttons to multiply and divide numbers. Given a multiplication (or a division) in the form $a \times b$ (or $a \div b$), press the keys [a] [×] [b] (or [a] [÷] [b]) then either [+], [−], [×], [÷] or [=] will display the answer.

Example 4

Calculate 68 × 29.

Keystrokes:

[AC] [6] [8] [×] [2] [9] [=]

Display:

0 6 68 68 2 29 *1972* (answer)

Rough check: 70 × 30 = 2 100

Example 5

Calculate 725 ÷ 25 × 14.

Keystrokes:

[AC] [7] [2] [5] [÷] [2] [5] [×] [1] [4] [=]

Display:

0 7 72 725 725 2 25 *29* 1 14 *406* (answer)

Rough check: 700 ÷ 20 × 10 = 350

Notice that 725 ÷ 25 = 29. 29 appears in the display at an intermediate stage of the calculation.

Calculators have a limited number of spaces in the display (usually eight spaces). Because of this there is a limit to the size of answer they can display. Try the calculation 68 000 × 29 000 on a calculator. Fig. 15.4 shows what could result on some eight-digit calculators.

a)

b)

c)

d)

Fig. 15.4

Note that 68 000 × 29 000 = 1 972 000 000 (requiring 10 digits).

The calculators in **a)** and **b)** show the digits

1972 but are unable to display the full number properly. So they print a small E (error) to warn the user.

The calculators in **c)** and **d)** group the display into two parts: 1·972 and 09. This is short for 1·972 × 1 000 000 000. Note the nine zeros in the second number. They correspond to the 09. This type of calculator is called a *scientific calculator*. Scientific calculators can cope with very large numbers, because they give the outcome in *standard form*: 68 000 × 29 000 = 1·972 × 10^9.

Example 6

How many seconds are there in a 31-day month?

Number of seconds
= 60 × 60 × 24 × 31
= 2 678 400 [calculator]

Exercise 15c

1 Do the following on your calculator. Write down what appears in the display as you press each button. Underline your final answer.
   a) 67 × 88 **b)** 4 234 ÷ 58
   c) 513 ÷ 19 **d)** 46^2
   e) 49 × 67 × 13 **f)** 7938 ÷ 81 ÷ 14
   g) 102 × 104 ÷ 78 **h)** 495 ÷ 33 × 41

2 Do the following calculations.
   Give each answer i) as displayed on the calculator, ii) rounded off to 2 decimal places.
   a) 6·74 × 9·08 **b)** 51·73 × 24·79
   c) 28 341 ÷ 85 **d)** 74·184 ÷ 40·08
   e) 4 ÷ 3 × 6 **f)** 7 ÷ 11 × 44
   g) 773 ÷ 4·17 × 5·308
   h) 3·142 × 4·5 × 4·5

3 Look at the following. Six of them are incorrect.
   i) 5 × 9 = 30
   ii) 100 000 ÷ 100 = 1 000
   iii) 67 × 84 = 3 216
   iv) 690 ÷ 15 = 45
   v) 1 000 ÷ 30 = 33
   vi) 1·7 × 1·5 × 1·3 = 33·15
   vii) 360 ÷ 18 ÷ 5 = 4
   viii) 4 123 ÷ 814 = 5
   a) Decide which ones appear to be incorrect.
   b) Use your calculator to correct them.

4 Multiply 30 000 by 50 000 on your calculator. What is displayed?

5 **a)** Calculate 10 000 000 ÷ 0·9.
   b) Calculate 10 000 000 ÷ 0·9 ÷ 0·9.

6 How many seconds are there in a 365-day year?

7 **a)** Write your age to the nearest year.
   b) Calculate how many days you have lived (assume 365 days in a year).
   c) Calculate how many hours you have lived.
   d) Calculate how many minutes you have lived.
   e) Is it possible for your calculator to calculate the number of seconds you have lived?

8 A health inspector gets a salary of Le173 220 per annum. How much does this represent **a)** per month, **b)** per day? Give answers to the nearest leone.

9 Twelve members of a club hired a bus to visit Bo. If the bus company charged Le3 150 000, how much did each member have to pay?

10 An aeroplane travels 550 km in 1 hour.
   a) How many km does it travel in one minute?
   b) How many metres does it travel in one minute?
   c) How many metres does it travel in one second?

Mixed operations, brackets

Look back to Exercise 15a, question 1, part (g). In some cases calculators appear to give two answers to the same problem. According to the rules of precedence in arithmetic:

2 + 5 × 3 = 2 + 15 = 17
and 5 × 3 + 2 = 15 + 2 = 17.

However, the calculator gives on the one hand:

Keystrokes: [2] [+] [5] [×] [3] [=]

Display: 2 2 5 7 3 *21* (answer)

and on the other:

Keystrokes: [3] [×] [5] [+] [2] [=]

Display: 3 3 5 15 2 *17* (answer)

This is because the calculator follows the operations in the order it receives them.

Example 7

Calculate $34 + 8 \times 52$.

There are no brackets, but multiplication is done before addition. Rearrange the numbers as follows:

$$34 + 8 \times 52 = 8 \times 52 + 34$$
$$= (8 \times 52) + 34$$
$$= 450 \text{ [calculator]}$$

Example 8

Calculate $2{\cdot}3 \times (8{\cdot}9 - 2{\cdot}1)$.

The brackets show that the subtraction is to be done first. Rearrange the numbers so that the subtraction comes before the multiplication:

$$2{\cdot}3 \times (8{\cdot}9 - 2{\cdot}1)$$
$$= (8{\cdot}9 - 2{\cdot}1) \times 2{\cdot}3$$
$$= 15{\cdot}64 \text{ [calculator]}$$

In the above examples it is possible to 'turn the calculation round' because in general $a \times b = b \times a$. However, with division this is not possible. Read the following example carefully.

Example 9 *(Optional)*

Calculate $84 \div (37 - 23)$.

The subtraction in the brackets must be done first. The outcome is held in memory, to be recalled when it is needed. The sequence of working is as follows:

37 [−] 23 [M+] 84 [÷] [MR] [=] 6

Check the above sequence on your own calculator and note the changes in display.

It is essential to enter numbers and operations in an order which will enable the calculator to give correct results. This means doing calculations in brackets first and storing them if necessary. Thereafter, do multiplications and divisions before additions and subtractions.

Exercise 15d

1 In six of the following cases, calculators will give incorrect results if the numbers and operations are entered in the given order. In those cases rearrange the numbers so that calculators will compute correct results.

a) $89 \times 6 - 231$ **b)** $45 + 68 \div 17$
c) $22 + 42 \div 3$ **d)** $63 + 18 \times 5$
e) $18 \times (17 - 15)$ **f)** $(19 + 9) \div 7$
g) $487 \times (6 + 3)$ **h)** $100 \times (31 - 14)$

2 Calculate the following, rearranging the order *where necessary.*

a) $95 \times 7 - 436$ **b)** $101 + 51 \times 9$
c) $55 + 75 \div 5$ **d)** $666 \div 36 + 2{\cdot}5$
e) $49 \times (19 - 3)$ **f)** $(434 - 343) \div 13$
g) $8{\cdot}438 + 36{\cdot}2 \div 2{\cdot}6$
h) $8{\cdot}8 \times (6{\cdot}12 - 3{\cdot}47)$

3 *Optional*

All of the following require part of the calculation to be stored (either on paper or in memory).

a) $68 - 14 \times 3$ **b)** $216 \div (25 - 7)$
c) $708 \div (28 + 31)$ **d)** $444 - 261 \div 29$
e) $46{\cdot}7 \div (15{\cdot}28 - 3{\cdot}59)$
f) $381{\cdot}04 - 12{\cdot}6 \times 7{\cdot}8$

Squares and square root tables

Using tables

If calculators are not available, then calculations can be done by using tables.

Table of squares

Table 15.3 on page 125 can be used to convert 2-digit numbers to squares of those numbers.

Example 10

Use the table of squares to find $6{\cdot}7^2$.

6 is the first digit. Look for 6 in the left-hand column of Table 15.3.
7 is the second digit. Look for the column headed ·7.
Find the number which is across from 6 and under ·7. See Fig. 15.5.

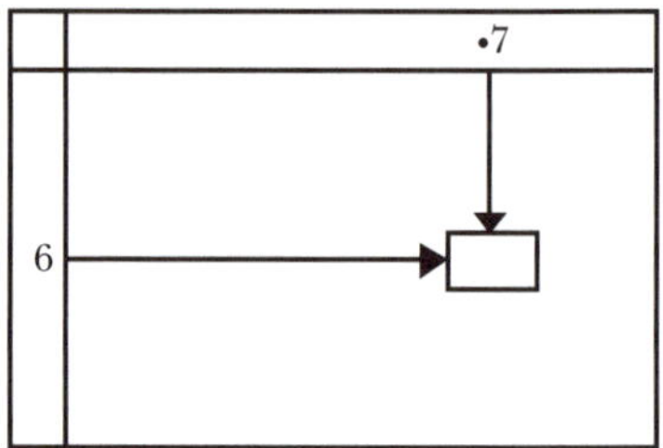

Fig. 15.5

The number is 44·89
Thus $6{\cdot}7^2 = 44{\cdot}89$

	·0	·1	·2	·3	·4	·5	·6	·7	·8	·9
1	1·00	1·21	1·44	1·69	1·96	2·25	2·56	2·89	3·24	3·61
2	4·00	4·41	4·84	5·29	5·76	6·25	6·76	7·29	7·84	8·41
3	9·00	9·61	10·24	10·89	11·56	12·25	12·96	13·69	14·44	15·21
4	16·00	16·81	17·64	18·49	19·36	20·25	21·16	22·09	23·04	24·01
5	25·00	26·01	27·04	28·09	29·16	30·25	31·36	32·49	33·64	34·81
6	36·00	37·21	38·44	39·69	40·96	42·25	43·56	44·89	46·24	47·61
7	49·00	50·41	51·84	53·29	54·76	56·25	57·76	59·29	60·84	62·41
8	64·00	65·61	67·24	68·89	70·56	72·25	73·96	75·69	77·44	79·21
9	81·00	82·81	84·64	86·49	88·36	90·25	92·16	94·09	96·04	98·01

Table 15.3 Squares from 1·0 to 9·9

Examples 10 and 11 show how to use Table 15.3.

	0	1	2	3	4	5	6	7	8	9
1	100 316	105 332	110 346	114 361	118 374	122 387	126 400	130 412	134 424	138 436
2	141 447	145 458	148 469	152 480	155 490	158 500	161 510	164 520	167 529	170 539
3	173 548	176 557	179 566	182 574	184 583	187 592	190 600	192 608	195 616	197 624
4	200 632	202 640	205 648	207 656	210 663	212 671	214 678	217 686	219 693	221 700
5	224 707	226 714	228 721	230 728	232 735	235 742	237 748	239 755	241 762	243 768
6	245 775	247 781	249 787	251 794	253 800	255 806	257 812	259 819	261 825	263 831
7	265 837	266 843	268 849	270 854	272 860	274 866	276 872	277 877	279 883	281 889
8	283 894	285 900	286 906	288 911	290 917	292 922	293 927	295 933	297 938	298 943
9	300 949	302 954	303 959	305 964	307 970	308 975	310 980	311 985	313 990	315 995

Table 15.4 Square roots from 1 to 99

Examples 14 and 15 show how to use Table 15.4.

Notice the following about this square root table.

1 There are no decimal points. These have to be put in by inspection.

2 There are two sets of digits for each number.

Example 11

Use the table of squares to find a) 19^2, b) 190^2.

a) $19 = 1{\cdot}9 \times 10$

$19^2 = (1{\cdot}9 \times 10)^2$

$= 1{\cdot}9^2 \times 10^2$

From the table,

$1{\cdot}9^2 = 3{\cdot}61$

Thus, $19^2 = 3{\cdot}61 \times 100$

$= 361$

b) $190 = 1{\cdot}9 \times 100$

$190^2 = (1{\cdot}9 \times 100)^2$

$= 1{\cdot}9^2 \times 100^2$

$= 3{\cdot}61 \times 10\,000$

$= 36\,100$

In Example 11, notice that

$1{\cdot}9^2 = 3{\cdot}61$

$19^2 = 361$

$190^2 = 36\,100$

When a number is multiplied by increasing powers of 10, its square is multiplied by increasing powers of 100.

Example 12

Use the table of squares to find a) $0{\cdot}8^2$, b) $0{\cdot}25^2$.

a) $0{\cdot}8 = 8{\cdot}0 \times 10^{-1}$

$(0{\cdot}8)^2 = (8{\cdot}0 \times 10^{-1})^2$

$= 8^2 \times 10^{-2}$

From the tables

$8^2 = 64{\cdot}00$

Thus $0{\cdot}8^2 = 64 \times \frac{1}{10^2}$

$= 0{\cdot}64$

b) $0{\cdot}25 = 2{\cdot}5 \times 10^{-1}$

$(0{\cdot}25)^2 = (2{\cdot}5 \times 10^{-1})^2$

$= 2{\cdot}5^2 \times 10^{-2}$

From the tables

$2{\cdot}5^2 = 6{\cdot}25$

Thus $0{\cdot}25^2 = 6{\cdot}25 \times \frac{1}{100}$

$= 0{\cdot}0625$

Exercise 15e

Use the table of squares (Table 15.3) for this exercise.

1 Find the value of the following.

a) $1{\cdot}4^2$ **b)** $2{\cdot}3^2$ **c)** $6{\cdot}8^2$
d) $7{\cdot}2^2$ **e)** $4{\cdot}9^2$ **f)** $8{\cdot}5^2$
g) $5{\cdot}6^2$ **h)** $9{\cdot}8^2$ **i)** $3{\cdot}1^2$
j) $1{\cdot}8^2$ **k)** $5{\cdot}7^2$ **l)** $4{\cdot}3^2$

2 Find the value of the following.

a) 18^2 **b)** 31^2 **c)** 32^2
d) 15^2 **e)** 29^2 **f)** 44^2
g) 70^2 **h)** 20^2 **i)** 62^2
j) 59^2 **k)** 81^2 **l)** 99^2

3 Round off the following to 2 s.f. and then find the approximate square of each number.

a) $1{\cdot}73^2$ **b)** $2{\cdot}88^2$ **c)** $78{\cdot}6^2$
d) $52{\cdot}1^2$ **e)** $9{\cdot}647^2$ **f)** $4{\cdot}975^2$
g) $63{\cdot}62^2$ **h)** $80{\cdot}53^2$ **i)** $36{\cdot}03^2$

4 Find the value of the following.

a) 130^2 **b)** 410^2 **c)** 870^2
d) 500^2 **e)** $2\,700^2$ **f)** $8\,300^2$

5 Look at the following pattern.

$1{\cdot}5^2 = 2{\cdot}25 = 1 \times 2 + 0{\cdot}25$

$2{\cdot}5^2 = 6{\cdot}25 = 2 \times 3 + 0{\cdot}25$

$3{\cdot}5^2 = 12{\cdot}25 = 3 \times 4 + 0{\cdot}25$

Find out if the pattern continues in the same way.

6 Find the squares of **a)** 12 and 21, **b)** 13 and 31. What do you notice?

7 A square has a side of length 4·3 cm. Calculate its area in **a)** cm^2, **b)** m^2.

8 A square plot has a side of length 240 m. Calculate its area in **a)** m^2, **b)** hectares. (1 hectare $= 10\,000\ m^2$)

9 A square has a perimeter of 30 cm. Find **a)** the length of one of its sides, **b)** its area.

10 Find out which of the following are true.

a) $65^2 = 16^2 + 63^2$ **b)** $65^2 = 25^2 + 60^2$
c) $65^2 = 30^2 + 35^2$ **d)** $65^2 = 33^2 + 56^2$
e) $65^2 = 36^2 + 43^2$ **f)** $65^2 = 39^2 + 52^2$

11 *(Optional)* Find the values of the following:

a) $0{\cdot}4^2$ **b)** $0{\cdot}7^2$ **c)** $0{\cdot}5^2$
d) $0{\cdot}11^2$ **e)** $0{\cdot}48^2$ **f)** $0{\cdot}31^2$
g) $0{\cdot}65^2$ **h)** $0{\cdot}83^2$ **i)** $0{\cdot}27^2$
j) $0{\cdot}19^2$ **k)** $0{\cdot}58^2$ **l)** $0{\cdot}77^2$

Square roots of numbers

$5^2 = 5 \times 5 = 25$

Thus $\sqrt{25} = 5$.

Numbers that have exact square roots are said to be **perfect squares**. We can find the approximate square root of a number by knowing the perfect squares immediately before and after it.

Example 13

Between what whole numbers do the square roots of the following numbers lie:
a) 3·6 *b)* 9·4 *c)* 40 *d)* 78

a) $\sqrt{3{\cdot}6}$

3·6 lies between 1 and 4

thus $\sqrt{3{\cdot}6}$ lies between $\sqrt{1}$ and $\sqrt{4}$

i.e. $\sqrt{3{\cdot}6}$ lies between 1 and 2.

b) $\sqrt{9{\cdot}4}$

9·4 lies between 9 and 16

thus $\sqrt{9{\cdot}4}$ lies between $\sqrt{9}$ and $\sqrt{16}$

i.e. $\sqrt{9{\cdot}4}$ lies between 3 and 4.

c) $\sqrt{40}$

40 lies between 36 and 49

thus $\sqrt{40}$ lies between $\sqrt{36}$ and $\sqrt{49}$

i.e. $\sqrt{40}$ lies between 6 and 7.

d) $\sqrt{78}$

78 lies between 64 and 81

thus $\sqrt{78}$ lies between $\sqrt{64}$ and $\sqrt{81}$

i.e. $\sqrt{78}$ lies between 8 and 9.

Square root tables

With our approximations we can find the square roots of numbers using square root tables.

Table 15.4 on page 125 can be used to find the square roots of 2-digit numbers.

Examples 14 and 15 show how to put in the decimal point and how to choose the correct set of digits.

Example 14

Use the square root table on page 125 to find

a) $\sqrt{5{\cdot}7}$ *b)* $\sqrt{57}$.

a) $\sqrt{5{\cdot}7}$

5·7 lies between 4 and 9

thus, $\sqrt{5{\cdot}7}$ lies between $\sqrt{4}$ and $\sqrt{9}$

i.e. $\sqrt{5{\cdot}7}$ lies between 2 and 3

thus, $\sqrt{5{\cdot}7}$ = 2 point something.

In the table, look for 5 in the left-hand column. The next digit is 7. Look for the column headed 7. Find the digits across from 5 and under 7. See Fig. 15.6.

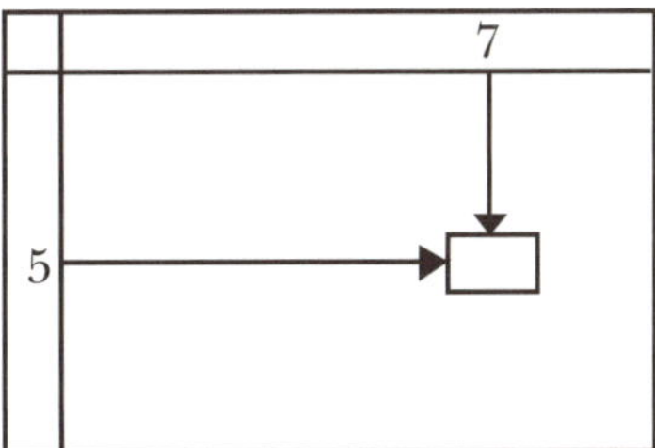

Fig. 15.6

This gives $\begin{matrix}239\\755\end{matrix}$

Since the required result begins with a 2, the required digits are 239. Ignore 755.

Thus $\sqrt{5{\cdot}7}$ = 2·39

b) $\sqrt{57}$

57 lies between 49 and 64

thus, $\sqrt{57}$ lies between $\sqrt{49}$ and $\sqrt{64}$

i.e. $\sqrt{57}$ lies between 7 and 8.

Thus, $\sqrt{57}$ = 7 point something.
Use the table as in part *a)*.
The required digits are 755. Ignore 239.

Thus $\sqrt{57}$ = 7·55

Notice that the square root table only gives results rounded to 3 significant figures. Thus

$\sqrt{5{\cdot}7}$ = 2·39 to 3 s.f.

On a calculator $\sqrt{5{\cdot}7}$ = 2·387 467 3.
However, 3 significant figures are accurate enough for most purposes.

Example 15

Use the square root table on page 125 to find

a) $\sqrt{940}$, *b)* $\sqrt{3\,998}$.

a)
$$940 = 9{\cdot}4 \times 100$$
$$\sqrt{940} = \sqrt{9{\cdot}4} \times \sqrt{100}$$
$$= \sqrt{9{\cdot}4} \times 10$$
9·4 is just over 9

thus, $\sqrt{9{\cdot}4}$ is just over 3

thus, $\sqrt{9{\cdot}4} = 3$ point something.
From the table,
$$\sqrt{9{\cdot}4} = 3{\cdot}07$$
thus, $\sqrt{940} = 3{\cdot}07 \times 10$
$= 30{\cdot}7$ to 3 s.f.

b) The square root table can only be used for 2-digit numbers. Round off 3 998 to 2 s.f.
$$3\,998 = 4\,000 \text{ to 2 s.f.}$$
thus, $\sqrt{3\,998} \simeq \sqrt{4\,000}$
$$\simeq \sqrt{40} \times \sqrt{100}$$
$$\simeq \sqrt{40} \times 10$$
40 is between 36 and 49.

Thus $\sqrt{40}$ is between 6 and 7

i.e. $\sqrt{40} = 6$ point something.
From the table,
$$\sqrt{40} = 6{\cdot}32$$
thus, $\sqrt{3\,998} \simeq 6{\cdot}32 \times 10$
$\simeq 63{\cdot}2$

Notice again that the final results are not exact.

For example, $\sqrt{3\,998} = 63{\cdot}229\,74$ (calculator).

Example 16 *(Optional)*

Use the square root table to find a) $\sqrt{0{\cdot}28}$, *b)* $\sqrt{0{\cdot}47}$.

a)
$$0{\cdot}28 = 28 \times 10^{-2}$$
$$\sqrt{0{\cdot}28} = \sqrt{28 \times 10^{-2}}$$
$$= \sqrt{28} \times \sqrt{10^{-2}}$$
$$= \sqrt{28} \times 10^{-1}$$
$\sqrt{28}$ lies between $\sqrt{25}$ and $\sqrt{36}$.

Thus $\sqrt{28}$ lies between 5 and 6.
From the table:
$$\sqrt{28} = 5{\cdot}29$$
Thus $\sqrt{0{\cdot}28} = 5{\cdot}29 \times \frac{1}{10} = \frac{5{\cdot}29}{10}$
$$= 0{\cdot}529$$

b)
$$0{\cdot}47 = 47 \times 10^{-2}$$
$$\sqrt{0{\cdot}47} = \sqrt{47 \times 10^{-2}}$$
$$= \sqrt{47} \times \sqrt{10^{-2}}$$
$$= \sqrt{47} \times 10^{-1}$$
$\sqrt{47}$ lies between $\sqrt{36}$ and $\sqrt{49}$.

Thus $\sqrt{47}$ lies between 6 and 7.
From the tables
$$\sqrt{47} = 6{\cdot}86$$
Thus $\sqrt{0{\cdot}47} = 6{\cdot}86 \times \frac{1}{10} = \frac{6{\cdot}86}{10}$
$$= 0{\cdot}686$$

Exercise 15f

Use the square root table (Table 15.4) for this exercise.

1 Between what whole numbers do the square roots of the following numbers lie?

a) 7·6	**b)** 9·6	**c)** 17
d) 27	**e)** 34	**f)** 30
g) 48	**h)** 60	**i)** 75
j) 69	**k)** 54	**l)** 83

2 Find the square roots of the following.

a) 9	**b)** 90	**c)** 2·8
d) 28	**e)** 4·7	**f)** 47
g) 36	**h)** 3·6	**i)** 25
j) 2·5	**k)** 6·3	**l)** 63

3 Find the square roots of the following.

a) 7	**b)** 70	**c)** 700
d) 7 000	**e)** 2·9	**f)** 29
g) 290	**h)** 2 900	**i)** 29 000
j) 250	**k)** 2 500	**l)** 38
m) 380	**n)** 3 800	**o)** 38 000
p) 10	**q)** 100	**r)** 1 000
s) 2	**t)** 430	**u)** 500
v) 72 000	**w)** 8 400	**x)** 960

4 Round off the following to 2 s.f. Then find their approximate square roots.

a) 9·28	**b)** 78·3	**c)** 463
d) 8·45	**e)** 61·3	**f)** 613
g) 59·4	**h)** 5·86	**i)** 5·003
j) 500·3	**k)** 6 394	**l)** 1 982

5 Find out if $\sqrt{10}$ is a good approximation for π.

6 A square has an area of about 45 cm^2. Find the length of one of its sides. Hence find its perimeter to the nearest cm.

7 a) Use the square root table to find m if

$m = \sqrt{41}$.

b) Using the value of m found in part **a)**, use the table of squares (Table 15.3) to find the value of m^2.

c) What do you notice?

8 (*Optional*) Find the square roots of the following.

a) 0·21	**b)** 0·34	**c)** 0·43
d) 0·62	**e)** 0·55	**f)** 0·73
g) 0·86	**h)** 0·92	**i)** 0·69
j) 0·78	**k)** 0·59	**l)** 0·98

Chapter summary

(1) In many circumstances people nowadays use calculators to do calculations.

(2) Where calculators are not available, it is possible to use tables to make calculations easier.

(3) Whether using calculators or tables, it is very useful to be able to estimate the size of the likely outcome of a calculation and where the decimal point is likely to be. This helps to detect errors (either from pressing the wrong button, or from using a table incorrectly).

16 Scale drawing (1)

Scale

Fig. 16.1

Fig. 16.1 is a **scale drawing** of the front cover of this book. The only difference between Fig. 16.1 and the front cover is size and colour. The scale drawing is smaller.

Check the following measurements:

width of Fig. 16.1 $\simeq$ 6·2 cm
width of front cover $\simeq$ 18·6 cm

We can write the ratio of the two widths as follows.

$$6{\cdot}2\ \text{cm} : 18{\cdot}6\ \text{cm} = 1:3$$

We say that the **scale** of Fig. 16.1 is **1 to 3** or **1 cm represents 3 cm**. We have already used scales when drawing graphs.

The scale of a drawing is found by comparing a length on the drawing with the corresponding actual length on the object which has been drawn.

$$\text{Scale} = \frac{\text{any length on scale drawing}}{\text{corresponding length on actual object}}$$

For example, the scale of Fig. 16.1 can be found by comparing the heights instead of the widths.

$$\text{Scale} = \frac{\text{height of Fig. 16.1}}{\text{height of front cover}}$$

$$\simeq \frac{8{\cdot}0\ \text{cm}}{24{\cdot}0\ \text{cm}} = \frac{1}{3}$$

Example 1

Fig. 16.2a) is a scale drawing of Fig. 16.2b). Use measurement to find the scale of the drawing.

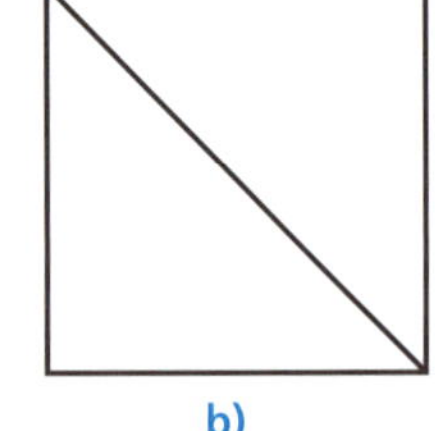

Fig. 16.2 a) b)

Fig. 16.2 a): length of diagonal of □ = 9 mm
Fig. 16.2 b): length of diagonal of □ = 36 mm

$$\text{Scale} = \frac{9\ \text{mm}}{36\ \text{mm}} = \frac{1}{4}$$

The scale is 1 to 4, or 1 mm represents 4 mm.

The result in Example 1 can be checked by comparing a different pair of corresponding sides, for example the uprights of the □. Notice that the measurements must be in the same units.

Example 2

An airport runway measuring 6 000 m *is drawn to a scale of* 1 cm *represents* 500 m. *Find its length on the drawing.*

500 m is represented by 1 cm

1 m is represented by $\frac{1}{500}$ cm

6 000 m is represented by $6\,000 \times \frac{1}{500}$ cm = 12 cm

Length on drawing = 12 cm

Example 3

The scale drawing of the length of an advertisement billboard measures 5 cm. *What is the actual length of the billboard if the scale is* 1 cm *represents* 2 m*?*

1 cm represents 2 m
5 cm represents 5 × 2 m = 10 m
Actual length of billboard = 10 m

Example 4

A plan of a school compound is drawn to a scale of 1 cm *represents* 5 m. *a) If the football field is* 80 m *by* 53 m, *find its length and breadth on the drawing.*
b) If the scale drawing of the hall is a 7 cm *by* 3·2 cm *rectangle, find its actual length and breadth.*

In scale drawings, a **plan** is a drawing of the view from above the object.

a) 5 m is represented by 1 cm
1 m is represented by $\frac{1}{5}$ cm
80 m is represented by $80 \times \frac{1}{5}$ cm = 16 cm
53 m is represented by $53 \times \frac{1}{5}$ cm = 10·6 cm

On the drawing, the football field will be 16 cm long and 10·6 cm wide.

b) 1 cm represents 5 m
7 cm represents 7 × 5 m = 35 m
3·2 cm represents 3·2 × 5 m = 16 m

The hall is 35 m long and 16 m wide.

Notice in Example 4 that the scale is given in mixed units. 1 cm represents 5 m is the same as 1 cm represents 500 cm or 1 to 500.

Exercise 16a

1 In each part of Fig. 16.3, the smaller diagram is a scale drawing of the larger diagram. Measure two corresponding lengths and give the scales of the drawings.

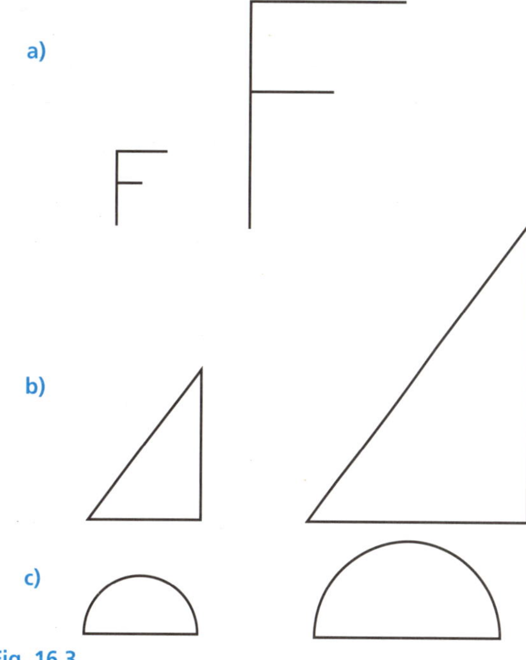

Fig. 16.3

2 Copy and complete Table 16.1. The first part has been done.

	actual length	scale	length on drawing
a)	90 m	1 cm to 10 m	9 cm
b)	20 m	1 cm to 5 m	
c)	8 m	1 cm to 2 m	
d)	73 m	1 cm to 10 m	
e)	65 m	1 cm to 5 m	
f)	3 km	1 cm to 200 m	
g)	450 m	1 cm to 100 m	
h)	375 km	1 cm to 50 km	
i)	1·53 km	10 cm to 1 km	
j)	2·86 km	5 cm to 1 km	
k)	23·8 m	1 cm to 2 m	

Table 16.1

3 Copy and complete Table 16.2. The first part has been done.

	length on drawing	scale	actual length
a)	6 cm	1 cm to 10 m	60 m
b)	11 cm	1 cm to 5 m	
c)	5 cm	1 cm to 2 m	
d)	7·5 cm	1 cm to 10 m	
e)	8·2 cm	1 cm to 100 m	
f)	9·3 cm	1 cm to 2 m	
g)	8·6 cm	1 cm to 50 km	
h)	14·8 cm	2 cm to 1 km	
i)	11·3 cm	5 cm to 1 m	
j)	12·6 cm	2 cm to 1 m	

Table 16.2

Scale drawing

Example 5

A rectangular field measures 45 m *by* 30 m. *Draw a plan of the field. Use measurement to find the distance between opposite corners of the field.*

First, make a rough sketch of the plan. Enter the details on the rough sketch as in Fig. 16.4.

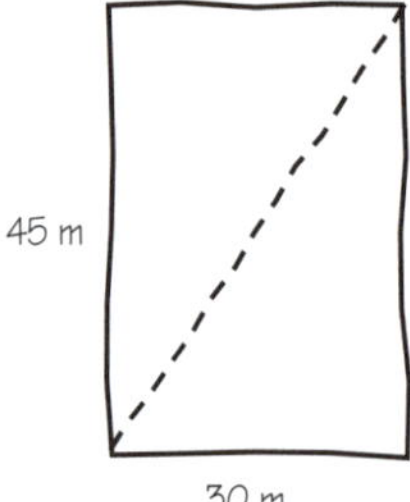

Fig. 16.4

Second, choose a suitable scale. As with graphs, the scale must suit the size of the page.
Using 1 cm represents 1 m will give a 45 cm × 30 cm rectangle. This will be too big for the page.

Using 1 cm represents 5 m will give a 9 cm x 6 cm rectangle. This will be suitable.

Third, make an accurate drawing of the plan. This is shown in Fig. 16.5.

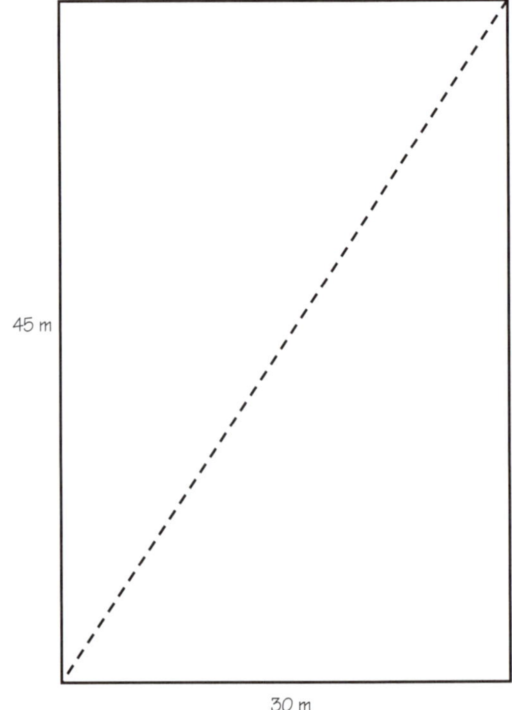

Fig. 16.5 Plan of field
Scale: 1 cm to 5 m

The distance between opposite corners of the field is represented by the dotted line.
Length of dotted line ≃ 10·8 cm
Actual distance ≃ 10·8 × 5 m
= 54 m (to nearest metre)

Notice the following points.

1 Scale drawings should be made on plain paper.
2 Mathematical instruments are needed. For example, a pencil, a ruler and a set-square were used to draw Fig. 16.5.
3 The drawing has a title and the scale is given.
4 The dimensions of the actual object are written on the drawing.

Example 6

Fig. 16.6 shows a sketch of two paths AX *and* BX. *Points* A *and* B *are* 178 m *and* 124 m *from* X *respectively. The distance between* A *and* B *is* 108 m. *Make a scale drawing of the paths and find the angle between the paths at* X.

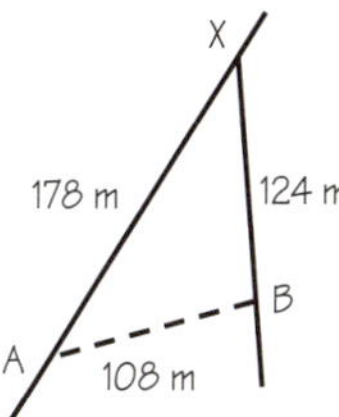

Fig. 16.6

It is necessary to construct a scale drawing of triangle AXB. Using a scale of 1 cm to 20 m, the sides of the triangle in the scale drawing will be as follows.

AX = $\frac{178}{20}$ cm = 8·9 cm

BX = $\frac{124}{20}$ cm = 6·2 cm

AB = $\frac{108}{20}$ cm = 5·4 cm

Using the method of constructing triangles given in Book 1, Chapter 21, Fig. 16.7 is the required scale drawing.

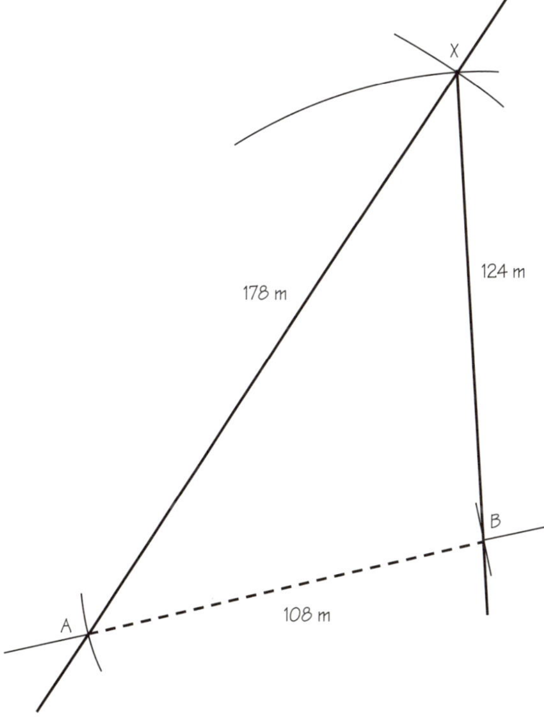

Fig. 16.7 Plan of paths AX and BX
Scale: 1 cm to 20 m

Using a protractor, A$\hat{X}$B= 37° (to the nearest degree). The angle between the paths is 37°.

Exercise 16b

Make sketches where none are given. Choose suitable scales where none are given. All questions should be answered by taking measurements from an accurate scale drawing.

1. Find the distance between the opposite corners of a rectangular room which is 12 m by 9 m. Use a scale of 1 cm to 1 m.
2. A rectangular field measures 55 m by 40 m. Draw a plan of the field. Use measurement to find the distance between opposite corners of the field.
3. *Classwork*: Measure the length and breadth of the top of your desk. Draw a plan of the top of your desk. Find the length of a diagonal from your drawing. Check your work by measuring the actual diagonal on your desk.
4. *Classwork*: Measure the length and breadth of your classroom. Draw a plan of your classroom. Find a way of showing that your drawing is accurate.
5. A square field is 300 m × 300 m. Draw a plan of the field. Find the distance of the centre of the field from one of its corners.
6. Fig. 16.8 shows the plan of a room ABCD. PQ and XY are windows. HK is a door.

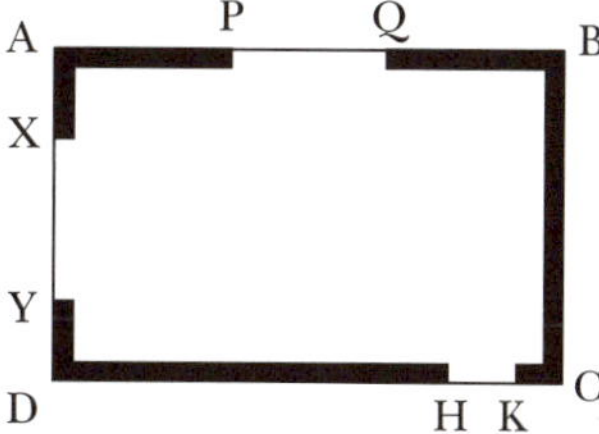

Fig. 16.8

AB = 10 m, BC = 7 m, AX = 1·5 m,
XY = 4 m, AP = 3 m, PQ = 2·5 m,
KC = 0·75 m, HK = 1·5 m.
Draw a plan on a scale of 1 cm to 1 m. Find the distances AC, XK, PH and QY.

7. A rectangular field measures 104 m by 76 m. Use a scale of 1 cm to 10 m to draw a plan of

the field. Find the distance from the centre spot to a corner flag.

8 Fig. 16.9 is a sketch of a cross-section of a round hut. Use the dimensions on the figure to make an accurate scale drawing.

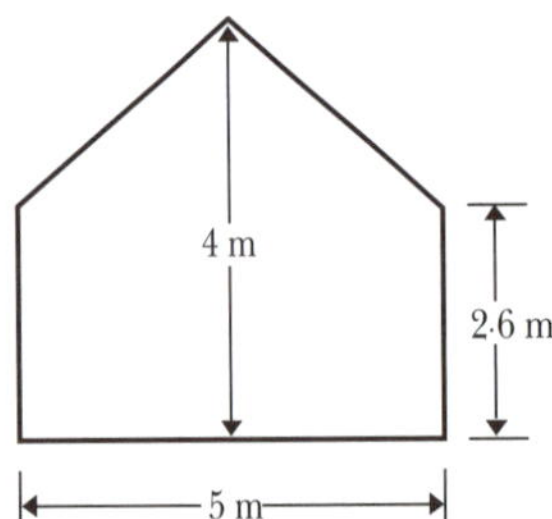

Fig. 16.9

Find the angle at the vertex of the roof.

9 Fig. 16.10 is a sketch of the end view of a house.

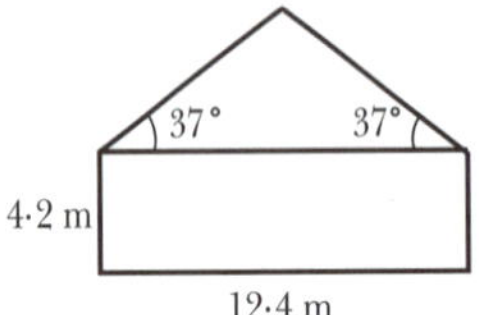

Fig. 16.10

Make a scale drawing and find the greatest height of the house.

10 A triangular plot, ABC, is such that AB = 120 m, BC = 80 m and CA = 60 m. P is the middle point of AB. Find the length of PC. Use a scale of 1 cm to 10 m.

11 In Fig. 16.11, A and D are on opposite sides of a river.

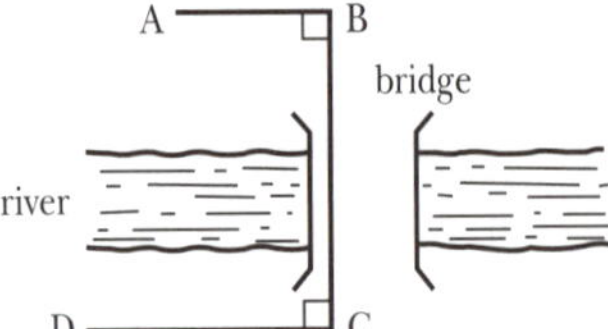

Fig. 16.11

AB = 52 m, BC = 119 m and CD = 86 m. Make a scale drawing and hence find the distance AD.

12 Two straight paths meet at an angle of 55° at a point X. Two students start together at X. One student runs down one path at 4 metres per second. The other student runs down the other path at 5 metres per second. If they start at the same time, how far apart are they after 11 seconds?

Reading scale drawings

Many professions use scale drawings. The most common scale drawings are **maps** and **technical drawings**. Surveyors and cartographers make maps. Maps are used by geographers, navigators, planners, the police and soldiers. Engineers and draughtsmen make technical drawings. Technical drawings are used by builders, mechanics, electricians and other skilled people. A scale drawing is an accurate way of storing and giving information. It is important to be able to read scale drawings.

Maps

A map is an accurately drawn plan of a piece of land. Distances on the map represent the horizontal distances between points on the land. Fig. 16.12 is a small-scale map of Sierra Leone.

Fig. 16.12 Sierra Leone
Scale: 1 cm to 60 km

Try to find a map of Sierra Leone in your school library.

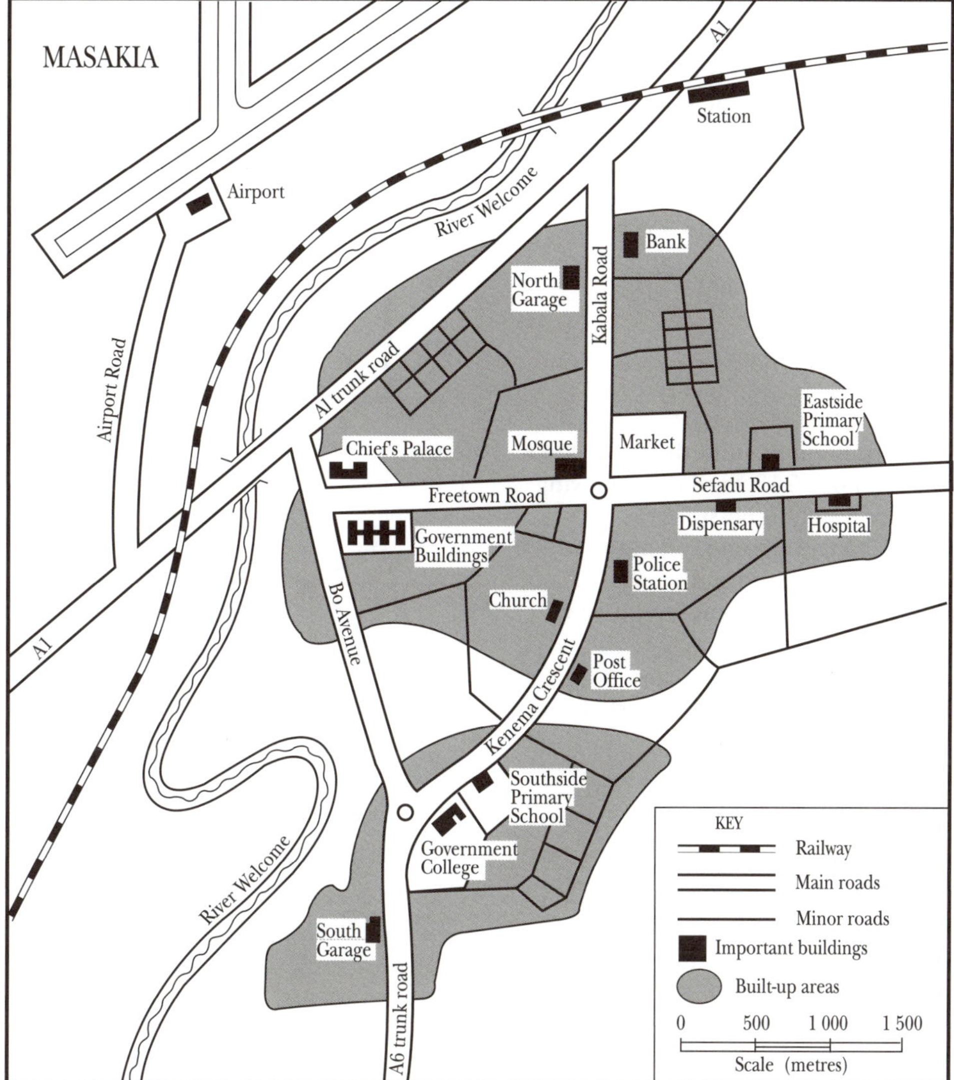

Fig. 16.13 Masakia

Fig. 16.13 is a large-scale map of an imaginary town, Masakia.

Look at the way the scale is given in Fig. 16.13 on page 135. Measure the scale in Fig. 16.14. You will find that 1 cm represents 500 m.

0 500 1 000 1 500

metres

Fig. 16.14

Exercise 16c

1 Use map of Sierra Leone (if available) to find the following distances to the nearest 10 km.

a) Freetown to Bo
b) Makeni to Koidu
c) Kabala to Kenema
d) Freetown to Makeni
e) Kenema to Mile 91
f) Moyamba to Magburaka
g) Kenema to Koidu
h) Kabala to Matru Jong
i) Freetown to Punje through Mile 91 and Bo
j) Freetown to Koidu through Makeni
k) Kenema to Koidu through Bumbuna

2 Use the map in Fig. 16.13. Which roads would you travel on if you took the best route between the following main roads only?

a) The Chief's palace and the hospital
b) The station and the airport
c) The North garage and the South garage
d) The bank and the Post Office
e) Eastside Primary School and Southside Primary School
f) Government College and the dispensary

g) The mosque and the airport
h) The Police Station and the airport
i) The hospital and the airport
j) Government Buildings and the Post Office

3 Use the map in Fig. 16.13. Find the following distances as accurately as possible.

a) From the Chief's palace to the mosque
b) From the church to the bank
c) From Government Buildings to Eastside Primary School
d) From the hospital to the dispensary
e) From the North garage to the market
f) The length of Freetown Road
g) The length of Bo Avenue
h) The width of the river
i) The width of the airport's runway
j) The length of Kabala Road

4 Use the map in Fig. 16.13. Find the following distances, i) in a straight line, ii) by going on main roads, taking the best route.

a) From the Post Office to the Chief's palace
b) From the station to the airport
c) From the dispensary to the Post Office
d) From Southside Primary School to Government Buildings
e) From Government Buildings to the station

Technical drawings

Fig. 16.15 is the plan of the wiring for an electric plug. It is drawn full size.

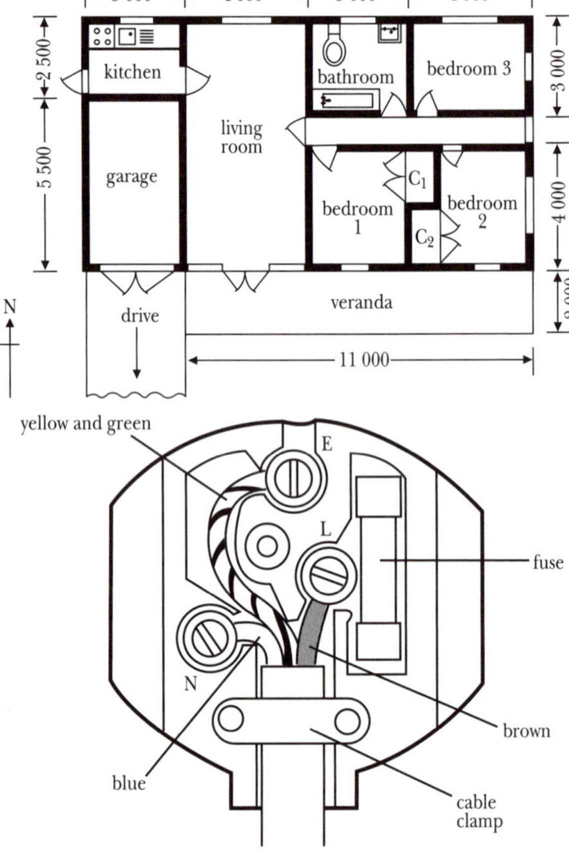

Fig. 16.15 Electric plug: wiring diagram full size

Fig. 16.16 is the ground plan of a house. Some of the important dimensions are given on the drawing. All such dimensions are in mm.

Fig. 16.16 House: ground plan

Exercise 16d

1 Use the wiring diagram in Fig. 16.15 to answer the following.

a) Each wire is connected to a terminal. How many terminals are there?
b) What is the colour of the wire which is connected to the terminal marked L?
c) What is the colour of the wire which is

connected to the terminal marked E?

d) What is the colour of the wire which is connected to the terminal marked N?

e) Which terminal is next to the fuse?

f) How many screws are on the cable clamp?

g) Find the greatest width of the plug.

2 Use the ground plan in Fig. 16.16 to answer the following.

a) How many rooms has the house? (Do not count the garage as a room.)

b) Which is the biggest room in the house?

c) Which is the smallest room in the house?

d) If a person walked from the kitchen to the bathroom, how many doors would he pass through?

e) Which room has most windows?

f) How many windows does the house have altogether?

g) Which room(s) is (are) north of bedroom 2?

h) Which room(s) is (are) west of the bathroom?

i) What do you think C1 and C2 stand for?

j) What is the length and breadth of the living room in metres?

k) What is the length and breadth of the garage in metres?

l) What is the total area that the house covers? Give your answer in m^2 and include the garage and veranda.

Chapter summary

① A *scale drawing* is a pictorial representation of a real object, area or region. The most common scale drawings are maps and technical drawings.

② *Scales* are usually given in the form of a ratio of a length on the drawing to the corresponding actual length on the object. We write a scale as *1 to n* or *1 cm represents n units*, where *n* is usually 2, 5, 10, 50, 100, 1 000 and so on.

③ When presenting a scale drawing:

a) use plain paper

b) give the drawing a title

c) state the scale of the drawing

d) write the dimensions of the actual object on the drawing.

It is helpful to make a rough sketch before starting.

Revision exercises and tests

Chapters 9–16

Revision exercise 4 *(Chapters 9, 10)*

1 A car uses 20 litres of petrol for a journey of 180 km. How many litres will it use for a journey of 108 km? (Assume it travels at the same rate.)

2 The number of boys in a school is 120. If the ratio of boys to girls is 2 : 3, find the total number of students in the school.

3 **a)** Express 15 as a percentage of 40 and simplify.

b) Increase 80 by 20 per cent.

c) The price of an article decreased from \$125 to \$100. Express this as a decrease per cent of the original price.

4 A factory made 1 500 refrigerators in a 40-hour week. Find its production rate in refrigerators/hour.

5 A man borrowed Le12 500 at simple interest. At the end of 8 months he paid back Le13 000 as payment of his debt and the interest on it. Calculate the percentage rate of simple interest per annum.

6 A car costs Le7 600 000. A 9% discount is given for payment in cash. The car can also be bought by paying 24 monthly instalments of Le364 000.

Find the cost of the car **a)** when cash is paid, **b)** when it is paid for by instalments. **c)** Find the difference between paying in cash and paying by instalments.

7 The reading on an electricity meter changes from 9 883 to 10 146.

a) How many units of electricity have been used?

b) If the charges are Le1 500 per unit and VAT is charged at 5%, calculate the electricity bill if a demand charge of Le1 500 per bill is added.

8 Use the postage rates given in Table 10.4 (on page 81) to find the total cost of posting two parcels of mass 2·8 kg and 5·7 kg.

If both parcels are being sent to the same person, find the saving if they are made into one parcel.

9 A woman sells a gold ring for Le1 920 000 and makes a profit of 60%. Find the cost of the gold ring. Find the selling price if she is to make a profit of 95%.

10 A bookseller sells Le48 120 worth of books in a month. His commission is 4c in the Le. How much money does he get?

Revision test 4 *(Chapters 9, 10)*

1 In 1990 an electric fan cost Le2 800. In 2000 the same model cost Le5 200. Give the 1990 cost to the 2000 cost as a ratio in its simplest terms.

A 1 : 2 **B** 7 : 13 **C** 28 : 52
D 26 : 14 **E** 199 : 200

2 I travelled at 60 km/h and took 2 h for a journey. How long would it have taken me if I had travelled at 50 km/h?

A $1\frac{1}{5}$ h **B** $1\frac{1}{3}$ h **C** $1\frac{2}{3}$ h **D** $2\frac{2}{5}$ h **E** $2\frac{2}{3}$ h

3 In an exam 154 out of 175 candidates passed. What percentage failed?

A $6\frac{2}{7}$% **B** 12% **C** $13\frac{7}{11}$% **D** 15%
E 88%

4 How much interest does Le400 make in 5 years at 7% per annum?

A Le7 **B** Le20 **C** Le28 **D** Le35 **E** Le140

taxable income	
Le40 000 to Le100 000 per month = 10%	
Le101 000 to Le160 000 per month = 15%	
Le161 000 to Le240 000 per month = 20%	
Le241 000 to Le300 000 per month = 30%	
TAX FREE below Le40 000	
for self	allowance of Le6 000
for each child under 16	allowance of Le2 500

Table R1

5 Douda's salary is Le76 000 per month. He has no children. What is his tax (use Table R1)?

A Le9 000 **B** Le3 000 **C** Le3 600
D Le12 000 **E** Le13 000

6 Calculate the tax paid on a salary of Le137 500 (use Table R1 on page 138).

7 The hire purchase price of a radio is Le68 000. $12\frac{1}{2}\%$ is paid as a deposit. The remainder is spread over 12 equal monthly instalments.

a) Calculate the amount of the deposit.
b) Calculate the remainder to be paid.
c) Find the amount of each monthly instalment to the nearest leone.

8 By selling a house for Le69 million, an agent makes a profit of 15%. How much did the house cost?

9 Use the postal order poundage rates given in Table 10.5 (on page 81). A shirt bought by mail order costs Le179 000.

a) Find the cost of buying a Le179 000 postal order to pay for the shirt.
b) Show that it would be cheaper to send a Le180 000 postal order and find how much is saved.

10 A salesman gets a commission of $8\frac{1}{3}\%$ of the value of the things he sells. Find his commission to the nearest Leone for selling two books at Le11 800 each, five tennis balls at Le3 300 each and
14 spoons at Le850 each.

Revision exercise 5 *(Chapters 11, 13)*

1 Find the HCF and LCM of $6a^2m$ and $3a^3m^2$.

2 Factorise the following.

a) $10 + 15b$ **b)** $x^2 - ax$
c) $4ab - 2a^2$ **d)** $27x^2y - 36xy^2$

3 Complete the following.

a) $\frac{x}{a} = \frac{\quad}{am}$ **b)** $\frac{d}{2e} = \frac{df}{\quad}$

c) $\frac{6xy}{\quad} = \frac{3y}{4ab}$ **d)** $\frac{\quad}{8qr} = \frac{pr}{2q}$

4 Simplify the following.

a) $\frac{7x}{m} - \frac{3x}{m}$ **b)** $\frac{4x}{3} - \frac{2x}{9}$

c) $\frac{5}{a} + \frac{8}{3a}$ **d)** $\frac{1}{p} - \frac{1}{q}$

5 Simplify the following.

a) $\frac{3a+1}{2} + \frac{a+2}{3}$ **b)** $\frac{2b-3}{3} - \frac{2b-5}{4}$

c) $\frac{5a+2}{2} - \frac{2(3a+1)}{3}$

6 Solve the following.

a) $12 - 5a = 2$ **b)** $13 + 3t = 5t$
c) $5h - 2 = 2h + 19$ **d)** $11 - 5x = 4x - 16$

7 One person earns Le1 700 more than another person. Between them, they earn a total of Le10 500. How much does each person earn?

8 Solve the following.

a) $2(3x + 1) = 4(x + 5)$
b) $5(2a - 3) - 3(2a + 1) = 0$
c) $7m - 4(m - 1) = 15$

9 Find two consecutive even numbers such that three times the smaller added to eight times the greater comes to 170.
(*Hint*: let the numbers be x and $x + 2$.)

10 Solve the following.

a) $\frac{3r}{5} - 15 = 0$ **b)** $\frac{3x}{2} - 2 = \frac{2x}{3}$

c) $\frac{m-3}{2} + \frac{m-8}{3} = 0$

d) $\frac{3(2x-1)}{4} = \frac{4(x+2)}{3} - 3$

Revision test 5 *(Chapters 11, 13)*

1 Express $\frac{2}{a} + \frac{7}{b}$ as a single fraction.

A $\frac{2b+7a}{ab}$ **B** $\frac{9ab}{a+b}$ **C** $\frac{9}{ab}$

D $\frac{9}{a+b}$ **E** $\frac{2b+7a}{a+b}$

2 A teacher asks a class to write $\frac{x+8}{4}$ in another way. Three of the answers are:
I $\frac{1}{4}(x + 8)$, II $x + 2$, III $\frac{1}{4}x + 2$.
Which of I, II, III is (are) correct?

A I only **B** II only **C** III only
D I and II only **E** I and III only

3 Simplify $\frac{x-2}{6} - \frac{x-7}{4}$.

A $\frac{8-5x}{6}$ **B** $-\frac{(12-5x)}{6}$

C $\frac{17-x}{12}$ **D** $-\frac{(25-x)}{12}$

E $\frac{x-17}{12}$

4 Express the following statement as an algebraic equation: 'The result of taking 2 from n and multiplying the answer by 4 is the same as multiplying n by 3 and taking away 5.'

A $4(n-2) = 5(n-3)$
B $4(n-2) = 3n-5$
C $4(n-2) = 5-3n$
D $4(2-n) = -2n$
E $4(2-n) = 3(n-5)$

5 Solve the equation $\frac{x+2}{3} + 2x = 10$.

A $x = 9\frac{1}{3}$ **B** $x = 5$ **C** $x = 4\frac{2}{3}$
D $x = 4$ **E** $x = 1\frac{1}{7}$

6 a) Factorise the numerator and denominator of $\frac{-2x-6}{3x+9}$. Hence simplify the expression.

b) Simplify and factorise $2a(b+c) - b(c+2a)$.

c) Solve $3x + 2 = 5 - x$.

7 Solve the following.

a) $9 - 4x = 11 - 7x$
b) $6a - 3 = 25 + 5a$
c) $9 - 5x = 3 - 2x$
d) $13x + 15 = 7x + 17$

8 A mother is 10 times as old as her son. In 6 years time she will be four times as old as her son. Find their present ages. (*Hint*: let the son's present age be x years.)

9 Solve the following.

a) $4(x+2) = 2(3x-1)$
b) $17y - 2(6y+1) = 8$
c) $\frac{7z}{2} - 18 = \frac{z}{2}$
d) $\frac{a+3}{3} - \frac{3a-7}{5} = 0$

10 The height of a boy is x cm. His father is $1\frac{1}{10}$ times his height. His sister is $\frac{7}{8}$ of his height.

a) Express the heights of the father and sister in terms of x.

b) If the difference in height between his father and sister is 36 cm, find the height of the boy.

Revision exercise 6 (Chapters 12, 14)

1 Draw a number line from -10 to 10. On the line mark the points A(8), B(2), C(-5), D(-2), E(0), F($3\frac{1}{2}$), G($-7\frac{1}{2}$), H($5\frac{1}{2}$).

2 Write down the coordinates of the points P, Q, R, S, T, U, V, W, X, Y, Z in Fig. R17.

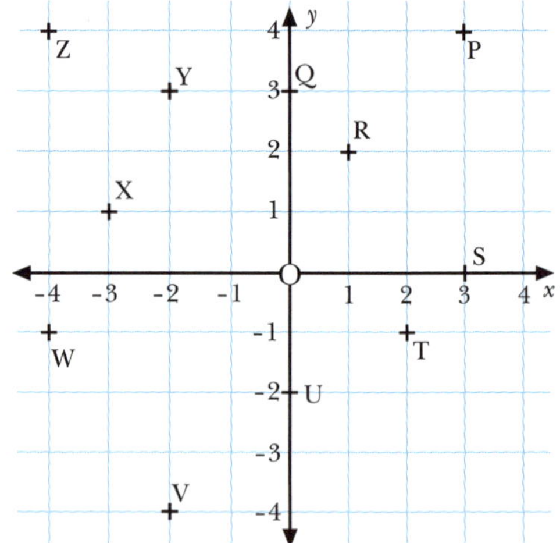

Fig. R17

3 In Fig. R18 name the points which have coordinates (3, -4), (-7, -3), (15, 6), (3, 4), (-4, 3), (6, 9), (-9, 8), (17, -2).

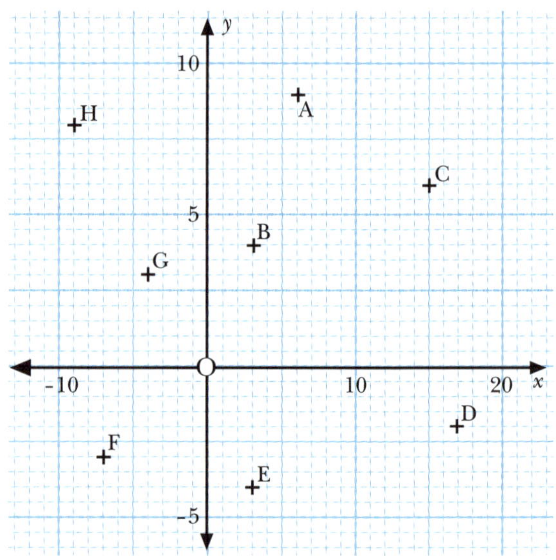

Fig. R18

4 a) Choose a suitable scale and plot the points P(-2, 1), Q(0, 2), R(2, 0) and S(0, -1).

b) What kind of quadrilateral is PQRS?

c) Find the coordinates of the point where the diagonals of PQRS cross each other.

5 Given the following sets of points:

i) A(−2, 2), B(−4, 2), C(−4, −2), D(−2, −2)

ii) E(−1, 2), F(−1, −2), G(1, −2), H(1, 2)

iii) I(2, 0), J(4, 0), K(4, 2), L(2, 2), M(2, −2)

draw an origin O near the middle of a sheet of graph paper. Use a scale of 1 cm represents 1 unit on both axes.

a) Plot the points in i). Join the points by straight lines in alphabetical order A–B–C–D.

b) Repeat for the points in ii) and iii).

c) What word is formed by the joined points?

6 Fig. R19 is part of a conversion graph. It is used for finding the car insurance premiums to be paid according to the value of the cars being insured.

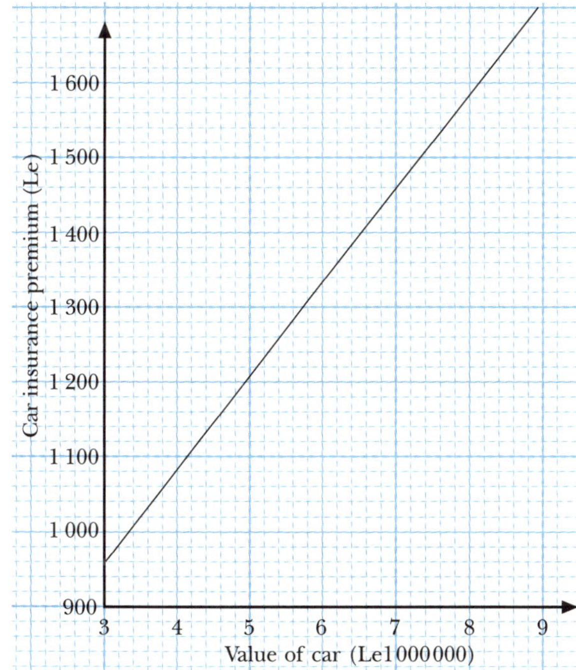

Fig. R19

a) What is the insurance premium for a car of value Le5 500 000?

b) What is the value of a car that belongs to someone who pays an insurance premium of Le1 060?

c) What is the difference in premiums paid by a man who insures his car for Le3 000 000 and a woman who insures her car for Le8 000 000?

7 A new candle is 15 cm long. When lit it burns steadily as shown in Table R2.

burning time (h)	0	1	2	3	4	5
length of candle remaining (cm)	15	13·8	12·6	11·4	10·2	9

Table R2

Choose a suitable scale and draw a graph of the information in Table R2. Use your graph to answer the following.

a) Find the length of the candle remaining after it has burned for 2·6 h.

b) How long does it take to burn 5 cm of candle?

c) Hence estimate how long the candle will last altogether.

8 Fig. R20 is a sketch of a graph which shows the distance from A and the time for a car going from A to B and back again. Find:

a) the distance from A to B,

b) how long the car stops at B,

c) the average speed in km/h from i) A to B, and ii) B to A.

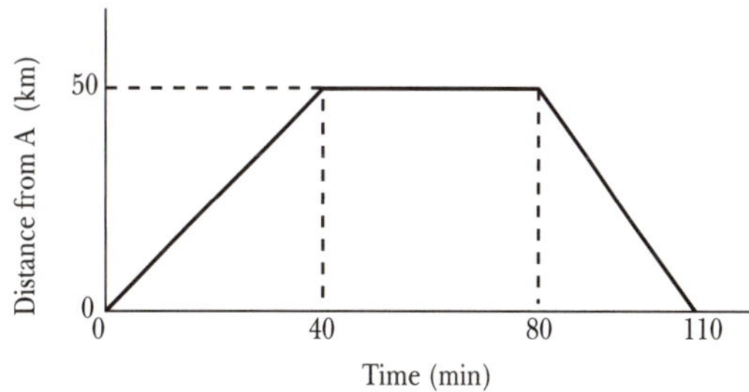

Fig. R20

9 The sum of the angles on a straight line is 180°.

Fig. R21

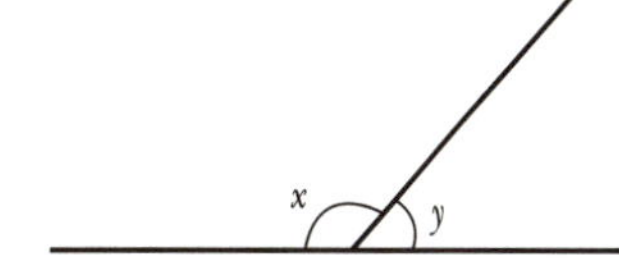

In Fig. R21, $x + y = 180$.

a) Copy and complete Table R3.

x	0	45	90	135	180
y	180	135			

Table R3

b) Choose a suitable scale and draw a graph of the information in your table.

c) Use your graph to find i) y when $x = 40$, ii) x when $y = 128$.

10 Given that 1 fr CFA is equal to Le4.50, draw a conversion graph for amounts up to 10 fr CFA. Find **a)** the number of fr CFA that will be given for Le12.00, **b)** the number of leones equivalent to 8 fr CFA.

Revision test 6 *(Chapters 12, 14)*

1 The position of a point X is given by X($-0{\cdot}9$). Which of the points A, B, C, D, E in Fig. R22 is in the same position as X?

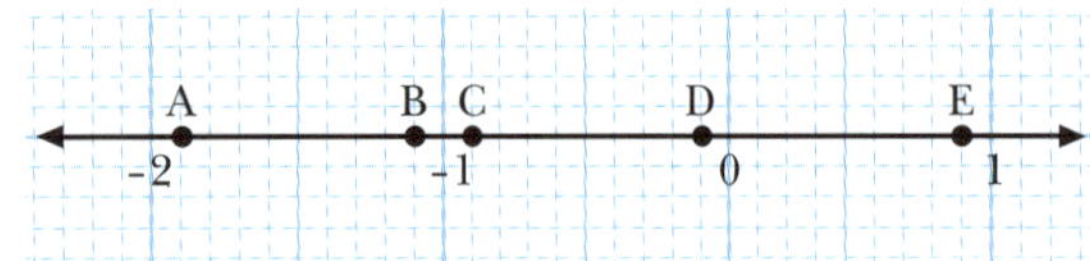

Fig. R22

2 Which of the points A, B, C, D, E in Fig. R23 has coordinates (-2, 3)?

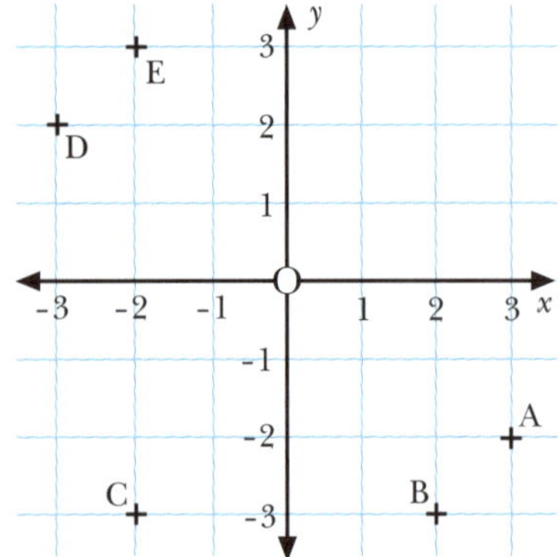

Fig. R23

3 A straight line PO joins the point P(5, -3) to the origin, O. PO is extended to Q so that PO = OQ. What are the coordinates of Q?

A (-5, -3) **B** (-3, -5) **C** (-5, 3)
D (-3, 5) **E** (3, -5)

Fig. R24 is a graph giving the cost (in Le) of cloth (in metres). Use the graph to answer questions 4 and 5.

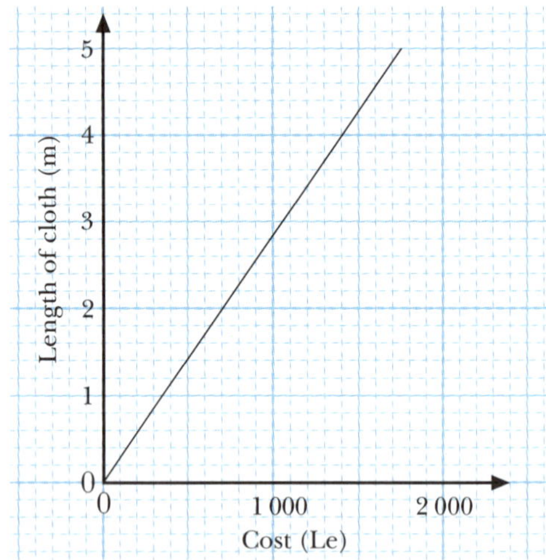

Fig. R24

4 What is the cost of 3 m of cloth?

A Le90 **B** Le180 **C** Le1 050 **D** Le1 100
E Le1 500

5 Approximately what length of cloth can be bought for Le450?

A $1{\cdot}3$ m **B** $2{\cdot}5$ m **C** 4 m **D** $15{\cdot}75$ m
E $17{\cdot}5$ m

6 Choose a suitable scale and plot the points A(1, 3), B(6, 3), C(3, -1), D(-2, -1).

a) AC and BD cross at P. Find the coordinates of P.

b) What is the size of $A\hat{P}D$?

c) What kind of quadrilateral is ABCD?

7 Fig. R25 is a graph showing the cost of hiring a car. The cost is made up of a basic charge and an additional charge for the distance that the car is driven.

a) How much does it cost to hire the car for a journey of i) 100 km, ii) 450 km?

b) What is the basic charge (i.e. the charge if no distance is travelled)?

c) Find the additional charge as a rate in leones/km.

8 A person walks at a speed of 6 km/h.

a) Make a table of values showing how far the person walks in $\frac{1}{4}$, $\frac{1}{2}$, $\frac{3}{4}$, 1, $1\frac{1}{4}$, $1\frac{1}{2}$, $1\frac{3}{4}$, 2 hours.

b) Using scales of 1 cm to $\frac{1}{4}$ hour and 1 cm to 1 km, draw a graph of the information.

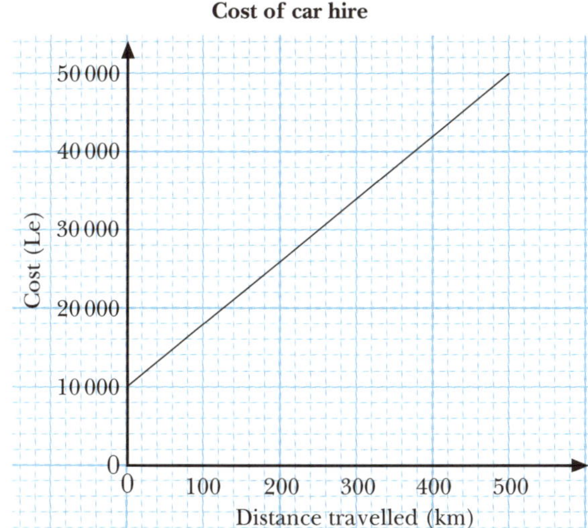

Fig. R25

c) Use the graph to find i) how far the person walks in 69 min, ii) how long it takes the person to walk 10 km.

9 Fig. R26 is a distance/time graph of a walker (A) and a cyclist (B). A walks steadily from the Post Office to the bank. B cycles from the bank to the Post Office but stops to talk to a friend on the way.

a) How long does the journey take both A and B?

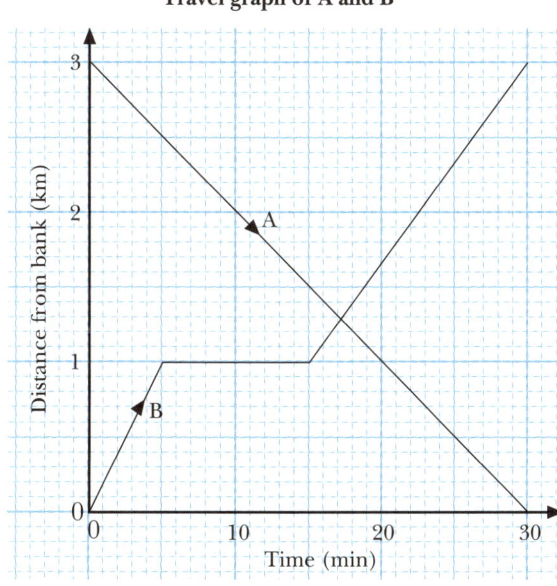

Fig. R26

b) How far is it from the bank to the Post Office?

c) How long does B stop to talk to his friend?

d) How far is B from the bank when he stops?

e) How far are A and B from the Post Office when they meet on the road?

10 Given that 1 Euro is equal to Le3 000, draw a conversion graph for amounts up to 10 Euro. Find **a)** the number of Euro that will be given for Le4 200, **b)** the number of leones equivalent to 5 Euros.

Revision exercise 7 *(Chapters 15, 16)*

1 Copy and complete Table R4.

	true length	scale	length on drawing
a)	120 km	1 cm to 10 km	
b)	1·32 km	5 cm to 1 km	
c)	15·8 m	1 cm to 2 m	

Table R4

2 Copy and complete Table R5.

	length on drawing	scale	true length
a)	5·4 cm	1 cm to 8 km	
b)	7·2 cm	1 cm to 5 km	
c)	14·8 cm	2 cm to 1 m	

Table R5

3 The original price of a motor bike is Le250 000. Find the new price if the original price is increased by 9%.

Find the selling price if the trader then gives a 9% discount on the new price.

4 A tank holds 69 litres of water. During the day 9% is lost due to evaporation. How much water is left in the tank to the nearest 100 ml?

5 Use tables to find the values of **a)** $6{\cdot}3^2$, **b)** $4{\cdot}8^2$, **c)** 48^2, **d)** 340^2.

6 Use tables to find the values of the following.

a) $\sqrt{8}$ **b)** $\sqrt{80}$

c) $\sqrt{42}$ **d)** $\sqrt{420}$

e) $\sqrt{8\,500}$ **f)** $\sqrt{9\,000}$

7 Round each of the given numbers to 2 s.f. Hence use tables to find the approximate values of the following.

a) $5{\cdot}46^2$ **b)** $29{\cdot}38^2$

c) $\sqrt{4{\cdot}37}$ **d)** $\sqrt{628}$

8 A map is drawn to a scale of 5 cm to 1 km. A straight road is 1·58 km long. How long will the road appear on the map?

9 Use measurement to find the scale of triangle a) to triangle b) in Fig. R27.

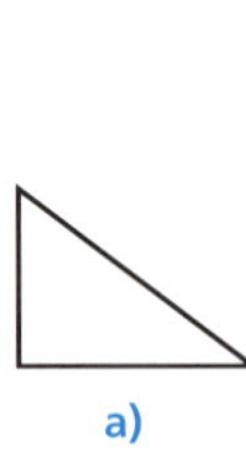

a)

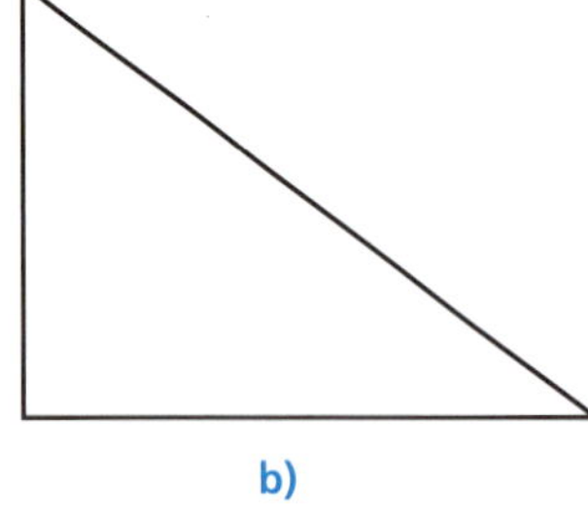

b)

Fig. R27

10 A triangular plot PQR is such that PQ = 100 m, QR = 70 m and PR = 50 m. X is the mid-point of side PQ.

Use a scale of 1 cm to 10 m to make a scale drawing of the plot. Hence find the true length of XR.

Revision test 7 (Chapters 15, 16)

1 The scale drawing of a straight railway track measures 12·5 cm. What is the actual length of the track if the scale is 1 cm to 5 km?

A 6 km **B** 12·5 km **C** 25 km
D 62·5 km **E** 625 km

2 Use tables to find the value of $\sqrt{650}$.

A 2·55 **B** 8·06 **C** 25·5 **D** 80·6
E 255

3 Use tables to find the value of 34^2.

A 5·74 **B** 11·56 **C** 115·6 **D** 1 156
E 11 560

4 A map is drawn to a scale of 2 cm to 100 km. If the actual distance between two towns is 374 km, what is this distance as measured on the map?

A 1·97 cm **B** 3·74 cm **C** 7·48 cm
D 19·7 cm **E** 74·8 cm

5 Refer to the map in Fig. 16.13 on page 135. Which one of the following is on Kenema Crescent?

A Bank **B** Church **C** Dispensary
D Mosque **E** Station

6 Use tables to find the values of the following.

a) $1{\cdot}8^2$ **b)** $3{\cdot}7^2$ **c)** 89^2 **d)** $2\,400^2$

7 Round each of the given numbers to 2 s.f. Hence use tables to find the approximate values of the following.

a) $4{\cdot}052^2$ **b)** $312{\cdot}8^2$

c) $\sqrt{9{\cdot}76}$ **d)** $\sqrt{8\,155}$

8 A photograph measures 8 cm by 10 cm. It is enlarged so that the shorter side becomes 12 cm and the longer side x cm. Find x.

9 A plan of a compound is drawn on a scale of 1 cm to 5 m.

a) If a wall is 24 m long, find its length on the drawing.

b) If the scale drawing of a round house is a circle of diameter 0·7 cm, find the actual diameter of the round house.

10 A rectangular sheet of paper measures 60 cm by 40 cm. Use a scale of 1 cm to 10 cm and make a scale drawing of the sheet of paper. Hence find the length of a diagonal of the sheet of paper.

General revision test B (Chapters 9–16)

1 If five people can do a piece of work in 6 days, how many days, to the nearest whole number, should eight people take to do it? Assume that the rate of work is the same.

A 4 **B** 5 **C** 7 **D** 8 **E** 9

2 What percentage of 4 is 5?

A 125% **B** 120% **C** 80% **D** 25%
E 20%

3 A trader gains Le4 000 on a sale which was equivalent to 8% profit. What was the cost price?

A Le54 000 **B** Le50 000 **C** Le32 000
D Le500 **E** Le320

4 Which of the following are factors of $4x^2y$?

I $2x$ II xy III $4y$

A I only **B** II only **C** III only
D none of them **E** all of them

5 The LCM of $5ab^2$ and $3a^2b$ is

A ab **B** $\frac{3a}{5b}$ **C** $\frac{5b}{3a}$ **D** $15a^2b^2$ **E** $15a^3b^3$

6 In Fig. R28, what are the coordinates of the point where the diagonals of kite PQRS cross?

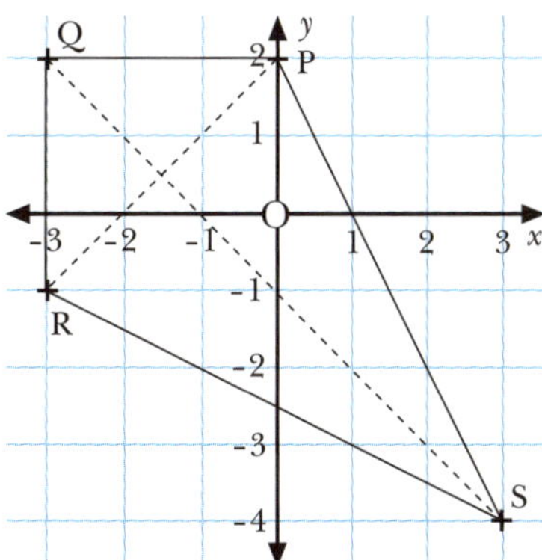

Fig. R28

A $(-1\frac{1}{2}, -\frac{1}{2})$ **B** $(-1\frac{1}{2}, \frac{1}{2})$
C $(-\frac{1}{2}, -1\frac{1}{2})$ **D** $(\frac{1}{2}, -1\frac{1}{2})$
E $(1\frac{1}{2}, -\frac{1}{2})$

7 Solve the equation $5 - \frac{2x}{3} = 1$. $x =$

A 1 **B** 4 **C** 6 **D** 7 **E** 9

8 Fig. R29 is a distance/time graph for a car.

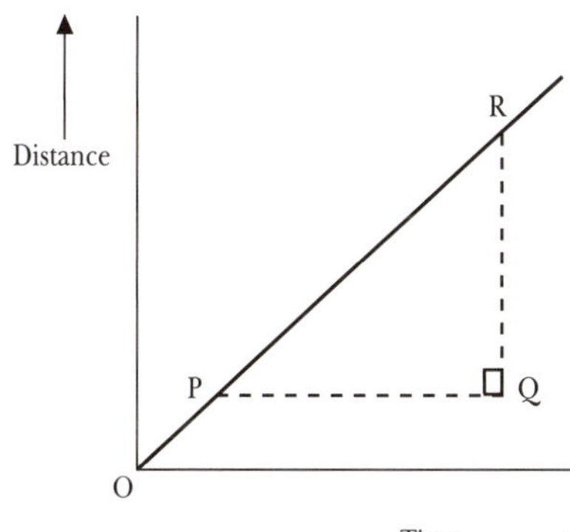

Fig. R29

What does the value of $\frac{QR}{PQ}$ represent?

A the time taken by the car
B the distance the car travels
C the average speed of the car
D the time the car was not moving
E the distance between P and R

9 Find the value of $\sqrt{94}$ to 2 s.f.
A 3·1 **B** 9·7 **C** 31 **D** 32 **E** 47

10 A map is drawn to a scale of 1 : 40 000. What distance, in km, will a line on the map 2·8 cm long represent?
A 11·2 km **B** 7 km **C** 1·12 km
D 0·7 km **E** 0·112 km

11 In one month a man spent Le6 500 on newspapers and Le2 400 on soap. Next month he reduced his newspaper spending by 40% and increased his spending on soap in the ratio 3: 5. How much did he save?

12 A 500 g bag of sugar costs Le3 900. A 25 kg sack of sugar costs Le175 000. Calculate the saving per kg by buying the 25 kg sack.

13 Use Table 10.1 (page 77) to answer this question.
If a woman's income is Le5 160 000 per annum, calculate her taxable income and the amount of tax she pays.

14 a) Complete the brackets:

$5x^2 - 10x = 5x(\quad)$

b) Factorise: $18ax + 12ay$

c) Simplify: $\frac{5-t}{5} - \frac{4-t}{4}$

d) Simplify: $\frac{3(2x-3)}{5} - \frac{1}{3}$

15 a) Choose a suitable scale and plot the following points: A(11, −15), B(−4, 0), C(−7, −3), D(−10, 0), E(−4, 6), F(5, 6), G(−2, 2), H(13, −13).

b) Join the points in alphabetical order and join H to A.

c) What picture have you drawn?

16 a) Solve: $3(x-6) = 4(1-2x)$

b) Solve: $\frac{c-5}{4} - \frac{6-c}{8} = 1$

c) Six times a number added to seven times 4 less than the number comes to 11. Find the number.

17 A man leaves home and cycles to his office 12 km away. His journey is shown on the graph in Fig. R30.

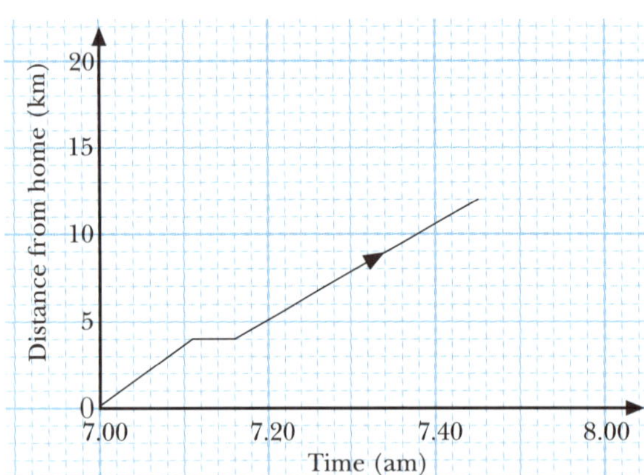

Fig. R30

a) What time did he arrive at his office?
b) How long did the journey take altogether?
c) Find his average speed for the whole journey.
d) During the journey he stopped to replace the chain. How long did this take?
e) How far was he from home when the chain came off?

18 Use the tables on page 125 to find the value of the following.

a) 58^2 b) 140^2 c) $7{\cdot}3^2$

d) $\sqrt{43}$ e) $\sqrt{640}$ f) $\sqrt{3\,900}$

19 Fig. R31 is a scale drawing of the plan of a round house.

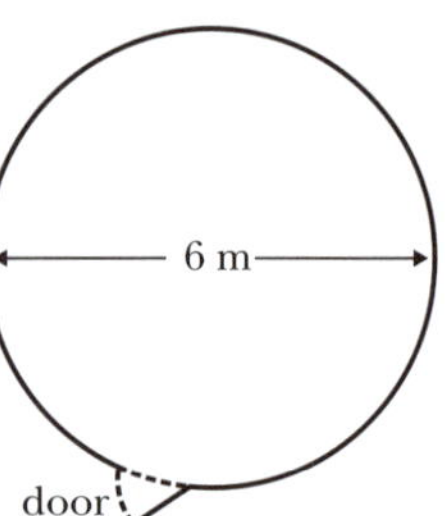

Fig. R31

a) If the actual diameter of the house is 6 m, use measurement to find the scale of the drawing.
b) Hence find the actual width of the door.

20 Fig. R32 is a sketch of a simple bridge. M is the mid-point of the bridge.

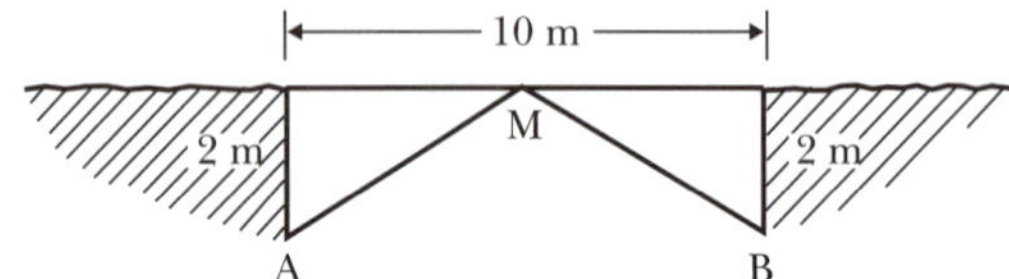

Fig. R32

a) Use a scale of 1 cm to 1 m to draw an accurate scale drawing of the bridge.
b) Hence find the length of the support AM.

17 Solving triangles (1) Pythagoras' rule

To **solve** a triangle means to find the sizes of its sides and angles *by calculation.*

In any triangle, the sum of the angles is 180°. Thus if two angles are known, it is easy to calculate the third angle.

In any right-angled triangle, if two of the sides are known, it is possible to calculate the length of the third side. Work carefully through Exercise 17a.

Exercise 17a

1 The longest side of a right-angled triangle is called the **hypotenuse**. The hypotenuse is opposite to the right angle.

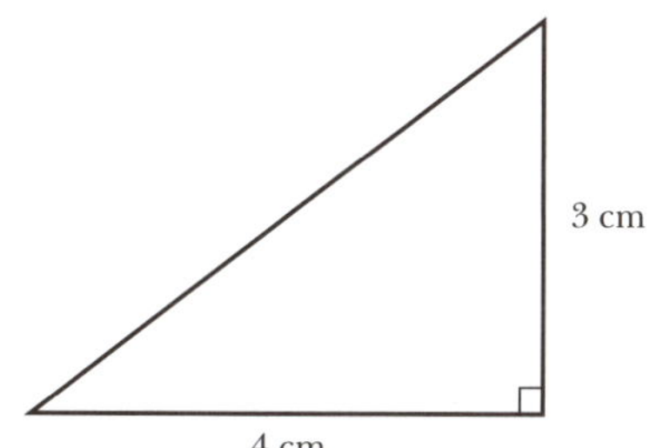

Fig. 17.1

Measure the length of the hypotenuse of the triangle in Fig. 17.1.

2 Fig. 17.2 shows a right-angled triangle with sides of 3, 4 and 5 units. A square has been drawn on each side of the triangle. Each square is divided into small squares of area 1 unit^2.

a) Count the number of unit^2 in the square on the hypotenuse.

b) Count the number of unit^2 in the squares on the other two sides. Add these together.

c) What do you notice?

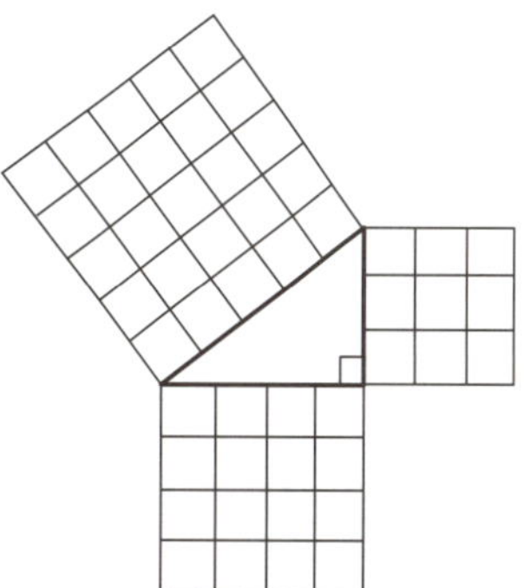

Fig. 17.2

3 Repeat question 2 with the triangle in Fig. 17.3.

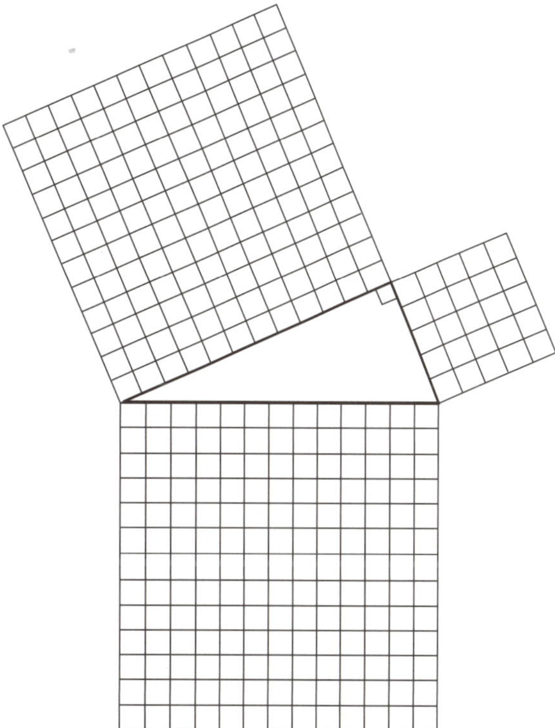

Fig. 17.3

4 *Class project*
   a) On a large sheet of graph paper, draw a right-angled triangle such that the sides containing the right angle are 8 cm and 6 cm.
   b) Measure the hypotenuse.
   c) Draw squares on the three sides of the triangle as in Figs 17.2 and 17.3.
   d) Count the number of 1 cm^2 squares on the hypotenuse.
   e) Count the number of 1 cm^2 squares on the other two sides. Add these together.
   f) What do you notice?

5 Repeat question 4 for a right-angled triangle such that the sides containing the right angle are 8 cm and 15 cm.

Pythagoras' rule

From the work of Exercise 17a, it can be seen that the square on the hypotenuse is equal in area to the sum of the squares on the other two sides. In Fig. 17.4,

$AB^2 = BC^2 + AC^2$

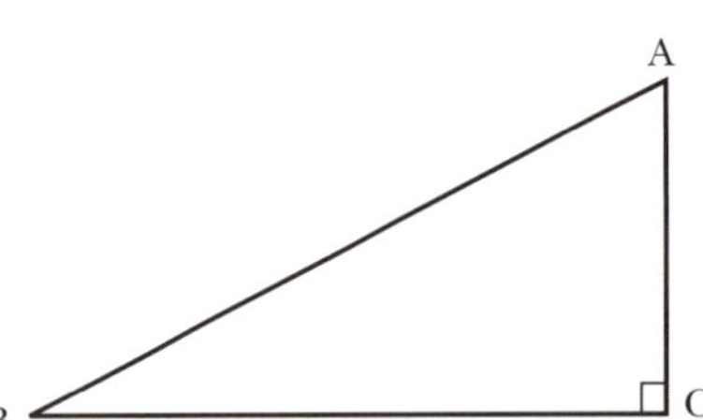

Fig. 17.4

This rule is very famous. It is called **Pythagoras' rule**. Pythagoras was a Greek philosopher who lived about 2 500 years ago. The rule was proved by Pythagoras and his friends at that time. However, the rule was used long before then and has been proved independently in other parts of the world.

There are many ways of proving Pythagoras' rule. The proof which follows is sometimes known as the Chinese proof.

In Fig. 17.5, PQRS is a square of side $a + b$ units. W is a point on PQ such that PW $= a$ units and WQ $= b$ units. Similarly for X, Y and Z. Lines joining these points give a square of side c and four right-angled triangles (shaded) within the large square.

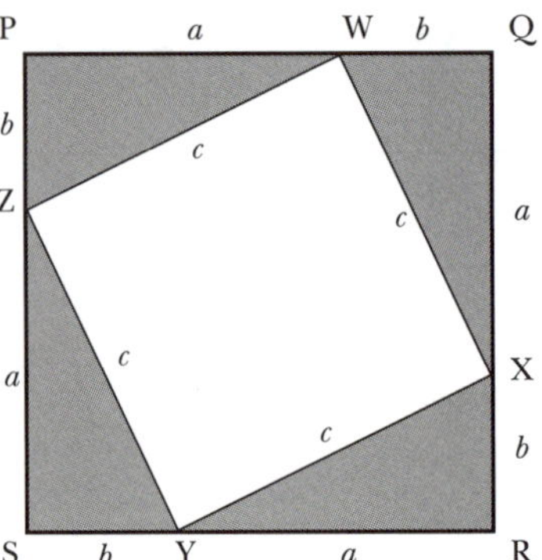

Fig. 17.5

The area of square PQRS can be found in two ways:

1 area of PQRS $=$ length $\times$ breadth
$= (a + b)(a + b)$
Expanding brackets, this gives
area of PQRS $= a^2 + 2ab + b^2$

2 area of PQRS $=$ area of square WXYZ + areas of four triangles
$= c^2 + 4 \times \frac{1}{2}ab$
$= c^2 + 2ab$
Thus, $c^2 + 2ab = a^2 + 2ab + b^2$
Subtract $2ab$ from both sides
$c^2 = a^2 + b^2$

Look at right-angled triangle PWZ in Fig. 17.5. c is the hypotenuse of ΔPWZ and a and b are its other two sides. See Fig. 17.6.

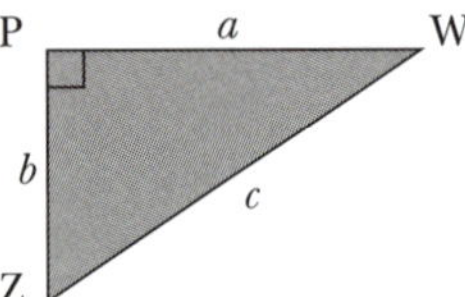

Fig. 17.6

For any right-angled triangle with hypotenuse c and other sides a and b,

$$\boldsymbol{c^2 = a^2 + b^2}$$

Example 1

Given the data of Fig. 17.7, calculate the value of c.

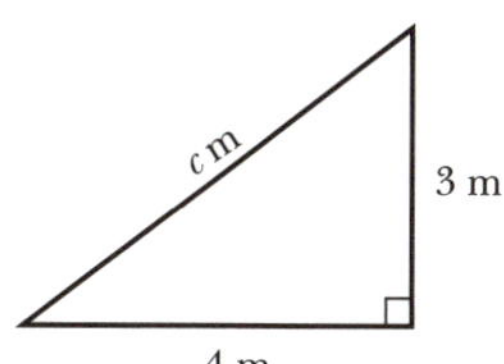

Fig. 17.7

Using Pythagoras' rule,

$$c^2 = 3^2 + 4^2$$
$$= 9 + 16$$
$$= 25$$
$$c = \sqrt{25} = 5$$

The hypotenuse is 5 m long.

Example 2

Calculate the length of the third side of the triangle in Fig. 17.8.

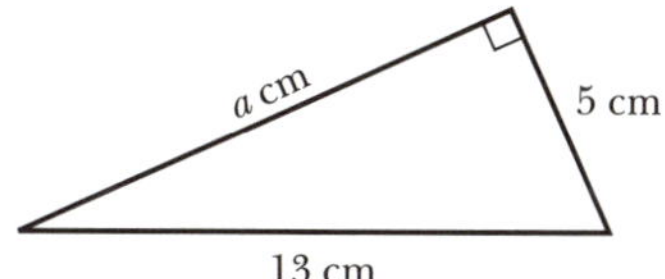

Fig. 17.8

Using Pythagoras' rule,

$$13^2 = a^2 + 5^2$$
$$169 = a^2 + 25$$

Subtract 25 from both sides.

$$169 - 25 = a^2$$
$$a^2 = 144$$
$$a = \sqrt{144} = 12$$

The length of the third side of the triangle is 12 cm.

Example 3

In Fig. 17.9, calculate the length of PS.

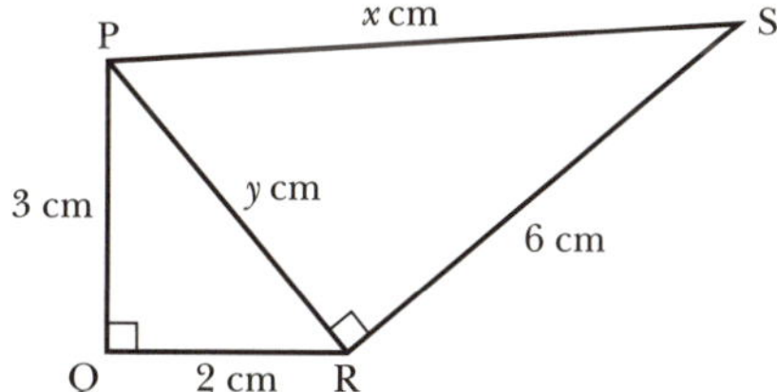

Fig. 17.9

PS is in right-angled triangle PRS.

Let PR be y cm.

In ΔPQR, $y^2 = 3^2 + 2^2$
$$= 9 + 4$$
$$= 13$$

Let PS be x cm.

In ΔPRS, $x^2 = y^2 + 6^2$
$$= 13 + 36$$
$$= 49$$
$$x = \sqrt{49} = 7$$
$$\text{PS} = 7 \text{ cm}$$

Example 4

In Fig. 17.10, calculate the length of AD.

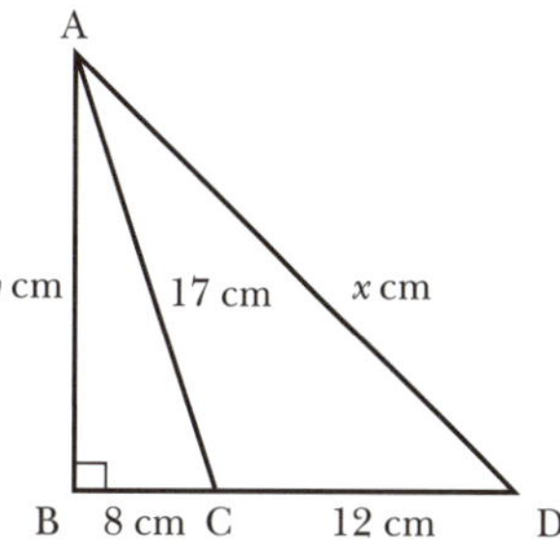

Fig. 17.10

AD is in right-angled triangle ABD.

Let AB be y cm.

In ΔABC, $y^2 = 17^2 - 8^2$
$$= 289 - 64$$
$$= 225$$

Let AD be x cm.

In ΔABD, $x^2 = y^2 + (8 + 12)^2$
$$= 225 + 20^2$$
$$= 225 + 400$$
$$= 625$$
$$x = \sqrt{625} = 25$$
$$\text{AD} = 25 \text{ cm}$$

In Examples 3 and 4, notice that the sides labelled y are *intermediate* sides. We do not have to find their values. When y^2 has been found, there is no need to find y. y^2 is used in the second part of the working.

Exercise 17b

1 ABC is a triangle in which $\hat{B} = 90°$. In each of the following, draw and label a sketch, then calculate the length of the third side of the triangle.

a) AB = 6 m, BC = 8 m
b) AB = 9 cm, BC = 12 cm
c) AB = 5 m, BC = 12 m

d) AB = 15 cm, BC = 8 cm
e) AC = 25 m, BC = 24 m
f) AC = 25 cm, BC = 20 cm
g) AC = 100 m, AB = 80 m
h) AC = 26 cm, AB = 24 cm
i) AC = 41 mm, AB = 40 mm
j) AC = 29 m, BC = 21 m

2 Find the value of x in each of the following figures. It will be necessary to find a value for y^2 before finding x. All measurements are in cm.

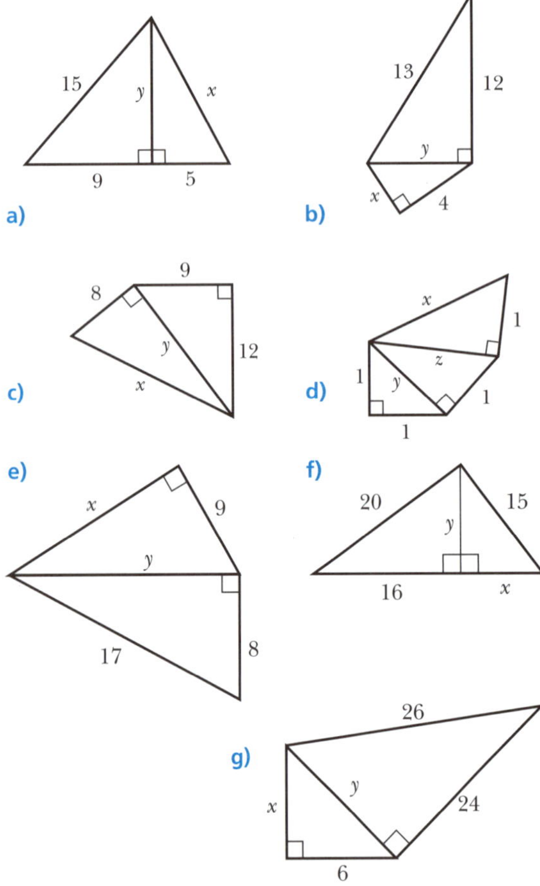

Fig. 17.11

Pythagorean triples

The sides of the triangle in Example 1 are 3 m, 4 m and 5 m. We call this a 3, 4, 5 triangle. The numbers (3, 4, 5) are called a **pythagorean triple**. A pythagorean triple is a set of three whole numbers which give the lengths of the sides of right-angled triangles. (5, 12, 13), (7, 24, 25), (8, 15, 17) are some other common pythagorean triples. You discovered these and others in Exercise 17b.

(6, 8, 10) and (30, 40, 50) are multiples of (3, 4, 5). They are also pythagorean triples.

Example 5

Which of the following is a pythagorean triple?
a) (33, 56, 65) *b)* (15, 30, 35)

Using the table of squares in Chapter 15, Table 15.3,

a) $33^2 + 56^2 = 1\,089 + 3\,136$
$= 4\,225$
$65^2 = 4\,225$
thus, $33^2 + 56^2 = 65^2$
(33, 56, 65) is a pythagorean triple.

b) $15^2 + 30^2 = 225 + 900$
$= 1\,125$
$35^2 = 1\,225$
thus $15^2 + 30^2 \neq 35^2$
(15, 30, 35) is *not* a pythagorean triple.

Exercise 17c

1 Write down four multiples of each of the following pythagorean triples.
a) (3, 4, 5) **b)** (5, 12, 13)
c) (7, 24, 25) **d)** (8, 15, 17)

2 Find out which of the following are pythagorean triples.
a) (20, 21, 29) **b)** (15, 22, 27)
c) (28, 45, 53) **d)** (11, 60, 61)
e) (27, 36, 45) **f)** (20, 22, 26)
g) (18, 24, 30) **h)** (12, 16, 20)
i) (14, 24, 28) **j)** (30, 40, 50)

3 Try to complete the following pattern of pythagorean triples.
$(3, 4, 5) \rightarrow 3^2 = 4 + 5$
$(5, 12, 13) \rightarrow 5^2 = 12 + 13$
$(7, 24, 25) \rightarrow 7^2 = 24 + 25$
$(9, \ldots, \ldots) \rightarrow 9^2 =$
$(11, \ldots, \ldots) \rightarrow 11^2 =$
Hint: notice that the difference between the last two numbers of each triple is 1.

4 Try to complete the following pattern of pythagorean triples.
$(6, 8, 10) \rightarrow \frac{1}{2}$ of $6^2 = 8 + 10$
$(8, 15, 17) \rightarrow \frac{1}{2}$ of $8^2 = 15 + 17$
$(10, 24, 26) \rightarrow \frac{1}{2}$ of $10^2 = 24 + 26$
$(12, \ldots, \ldots) \rightarrow \frac{1}{2}$ of $12^2 =$
$(14, \ldots, \ldots) \rightarrow \frac{1}{2}$ of $14^2 =$
Hint: notice that the difference between the last two terms of each triple is 2.

5 Try to extend the patterns of questions 3 and 4 for five more terms.

Everyday use of Pythagoras' rule

So far, the exercises in this chapter have been arranged so that when a square root of a number was needed, it could be found exactly. However, this does not often happen with numbers in everyday situations. More often we have to find squares and square roots from tables.

Example 6

Fig. 17.12 shows a ladder leaning against a wall. The ladder is 7·3 m *long and the foot of the ladder is* 1·8 m *from the wall. Find how far up the wall the ladder reaches.*

Fig. 17.12

Draw a sketch of the right-angled triangle which contains the ladder (Fig. 17.13).

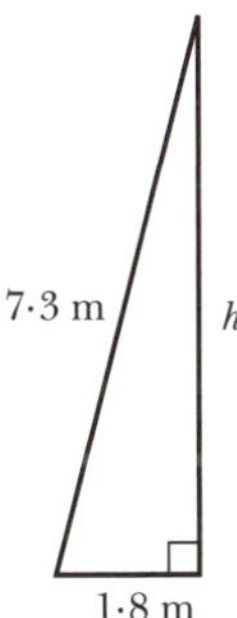

Fig. 17.13

By Pythagoras' rule,

$h^2 = 7{\cdot}3^2 - 1{\cdot}8^2$
$= 53{\cdot}29 - 3{\cdot}24$ (from squares table)
$= 50{\cdot}05$
$h^2 = 50$ to 2 s.f.
$h \simeq \sqrt{50} = 7{\cdot}07$ (from square roots table)
$= 7{\cdot}1$ to 2 s.f.

The ladder reaches about 7·1 m up the wall.

The problem can also be answered by scale drawing. Fig. 17.14 is a scale drawing of the data on a scale 1 cm to 1 m.

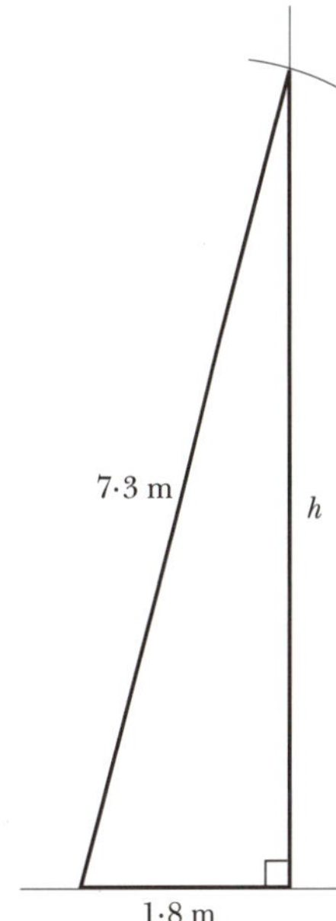

Fig. 17.14 Ladder and wall
Scale: 1 cm to 1 m

From the drawing, $h \simeq 7{\cdot}1$ cm
Height of ladder up the wall $\simeq 7{\cdot}1 \times 1$ m
$\simeq 7{\cdot}1$ m

Exercise 17d

In each question, sketch the right-angled triangle which contains the unknown. Either use Pythagoras' rule or make a scale drawing to solve the triangle.

1 A pencil which has been sharpened at each end just fits along the diagonal of the base of a box. See Fig. 17.15.

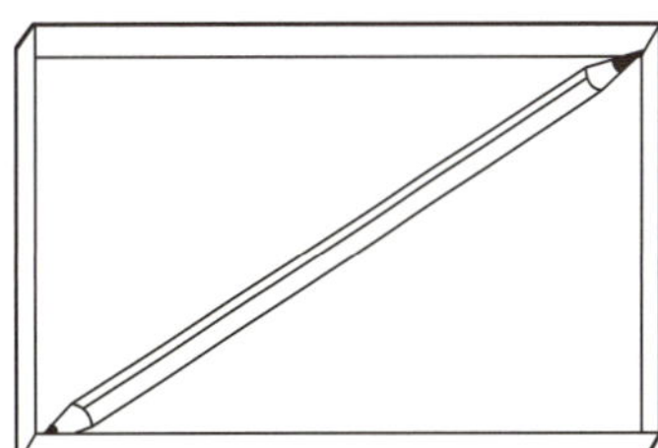

Fig. 17.15

If the box measures 14 cm by 8 cm, find the length of the pencil.

2 A telegraph pole is supported by a wire as shown in Fig. 17.16.

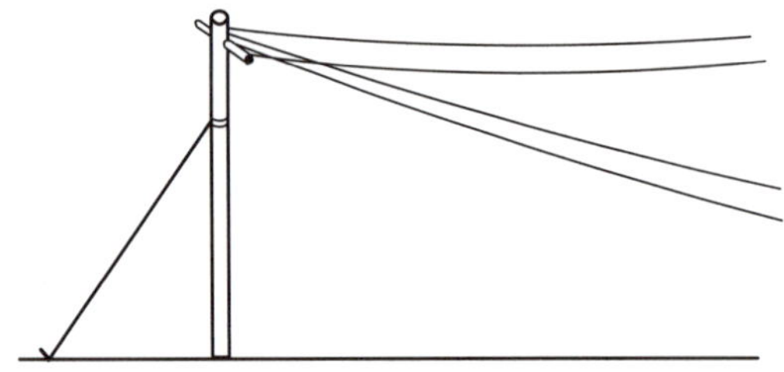

Fig. 17.16

The wire is attached to the pole 6 m above the ground and to a point on the ground 2·5 m from the foot of the pole. Calculate the total length of wire needed if an extra 0·8 m of wire is needed for the attachments.

3 Fig. 17.17 shows a straight pipe which carries water from a reservoir at R to a tap at T.

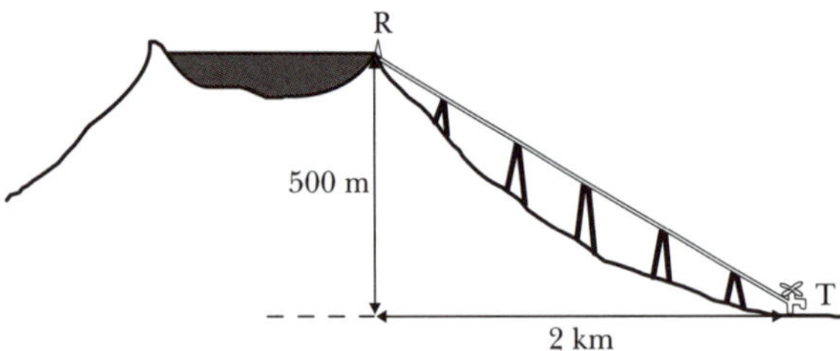

Fig. 17.17

R and T are 2 km apart horizontally and R is 500 m above the level of T. Find the length of the pipe.

4 Find the length of the longest straight line which can be drawn on a rectangular board which measures 2·2 m by 1·2 m.

5 A plane flies northwards for 430 km. It then flies eastwards for 380 km. How far is it from its starting point? (Neglect its height above the ground.)

6 Fig. 17.18 shows a simple bridge over a ditch. The bridge is supported by uprights, u, and diagonals, d. Find the length of a diagonal support, if the upright supports are 4 m long and the bridge is 20 m long.

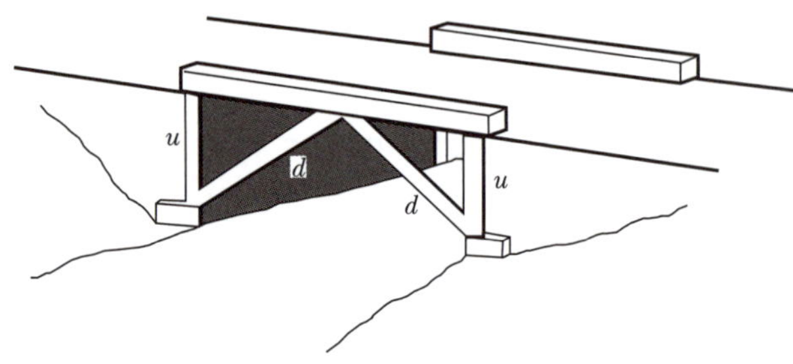

Fig. 17.18

7 A ladder 7 m long leans against a wall as in Fig. 17.19.

Fig. 17.19

Its foot is 2 m from the wall. Calculate how far up the wall the ladder reaches.

8 Fig. 17.20 shows the plan of a road which turns through a right angle to go round a building.

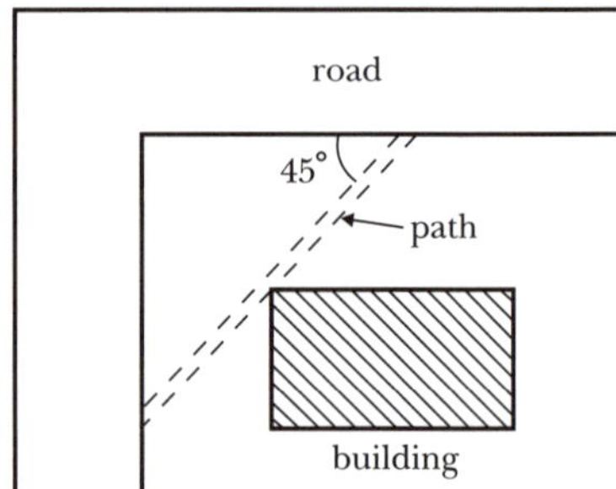

Fig. 17.20

To save time, people on foot cut off the corner. This gives a path which meets the road at 45°. If the path is 24 m long, how much distance is saved?

9 The distance between the opposite corners of a rectangular lawn is 30 m. The length of the lawn is 24 m. Calculate the breadth of the lawn.

10 A wire 15 m long is stretched tight from the top of a radio mast to a point on the horizontal ground. The distance of the point on the ground from the foot of the radio mast is 8 m. How high is the radio mast above the level ground?

11 A student cycles from home to school, first eastwards to a road junction 12 km from home, then southwards to school. If the school is 19 km from home, how far is it from the road junction?

12 A palm wine tapper climbs to a point on a palm tree 9 m above the ground with the aid of a ladder 10 m long, leaning against the palm tree. Calculate the distance of the foot of the ladder from the foot of the palm tree.

Chapter summary

① To *solve a triangle* means to find the sizes of its sides and angles by calculation.

② In a *right-angled triangle*, the longest side is opposite the right angle. It is called the *hypotenuse*.

③ *Pythagoras' rule* states that in a right-angled triangle the square on the hypotenuse is equal in area to the sum of the squares on the other two sides.

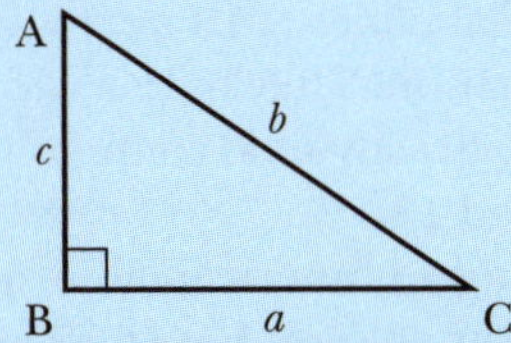

Fig. 17.21

In Fig. 17.21, $AC^2 = AB^2 + BC^2$, or

$b^2 = c^2 + a^2$

④ A *pythagorean triple* is a set of three whole numbers, a, b, c, which obey the above rule.

⑤ Use Pythagoras' rule to solve right-angled triangles (see Example 6).

18 Everyday arithmetic (6) Timetables and charts

Reading tabulated data

Tabulated data means information given in a table. Tabulated data is often in numerical form. Numerical tables are a neat way of storing a lot of information. They have a wide range of uses. You have already seen some of these in Chapters 14 and 15.

When reading a numerical table, always look first at its title, its column headings and its row headings. These show what the table is about. Look at the headings in Table 18.1.

Table 18.1 is a monthly rainfall chart. The column headings show the letters J, F, M, …. These are **abbreviations** for January, February, March, …. Abbreviations are often used in tables. They save space. We often have to use common sense when deciding what the abbreviations are short for.

The row headings give the names of four towns. The table gives the average monthly rainfall in these towns for any month.

We read the table by making a **cross-reference**. For example, to find the rainfall for Bo in September, read across from Bo and down from S. Where the two directions cross, gives the information. On average, Bo gets 178 mm of rain in September.

Exercise 18a *(Oral)*

Refer to Table 18.1 for this exercise.

1 Use the table to find the average rainfall for the following.
   a) Kabala in January
   b) Port Loko in December
   c) Yele in May
   d) Bo in March
   e) Port Loko in June
   f) Kabala in August
   g) Bo in July
   h) Yele in October
   i) Kabala in February
   j) Yele in November
   k) Bo in November
   l) Port Loko in September

2 For each town, name the month which has the highest rainfall.

3 For each town, name the month(s) with the lowest rainfall.

4 Look at the data for August and September for the four towns. Can you see a difference between the figures for Kabala and Yele and those for Bo and Port Loko?

5 In the table, the towns are arranged in order from most northerly (Kabala) to most southerly (Port Loko). What can you say about the rainfall as you go from the north to the south in Sierra Leone?

	J	F	M	A	M	J	J	A	S	O	N	D
Kabala	0	0	0	10	48	91	155	249	145	15	15	0
Yele	3	3	28	56	203	226	330	292	213	41	3	3
Bo	10	23	89	137	150	188	160	84	178	155	46	10
Port Loko	66	109	155	262	404	660	531	318	516	460	213	81

Table 18.1 Mean monthly rainfall (mm)

Timetables

Railway timetables

Railway timetables give the times of arrival and departure of passenger trains for various towns.

Fig. 18.1 is a timetable for passenger services between Ibadan and Offa, in Nigeria.

IBADAN–OFFA				
		201 UP		**202 DN**
Ibadan	**D**	6.00 pm	**A**	11.30 am
Oshogbo	**A**	9.32 pm	**D**	7.58 am
	D	9.42 pm	**A**	7.48 am
Offa	**A**	11.45 pm	**D**	6.00 am

Fig. 18.1

In Fig. 18.1, UP and DN mean *up* and *down*. In Nigeria, UP trains travel in a direction away from the coast. DN trains travel towards the coast. 201 and 202 are the numbers of the train service.

Exercise 18b *(Oral)*

Refer to the timetable in Fig. 18.1.

1 What do the letters D and A stand for?

2 What time does the 201 UP train **a)** depart from Ibadan, **b)** arrive in Offa?

3 How long does the up journey take from Ibadan to Offa?

4 How long does the 201 UP train stay at Oshogbo?

5 What time does the 202 DN train **a)** depart from Offa, **b)** arrive at Ibadan?

6 How long does the 'down journey' take from Offa to Ibadan?

7 How long does the 202 DN train stay at Oshogbo?

8 Find the following.

a) The time taken between Oshogbo and Offa on the up journey

b) The time taken between Offa and Oshogbo on the down journey

c) The difference between these two times

Airline charts and timetables

The chart in Fig. 18.2 shows some of the international routes covered by Nigeria Airways.

Where a line connects two towns, it means that there is a direct route between those towns. For example, there is a direct route between Kano and Niamey (Niger) but there is no direct route between Lagos and Niamey. Notice that the route chart is not a scale drawing of the distances.

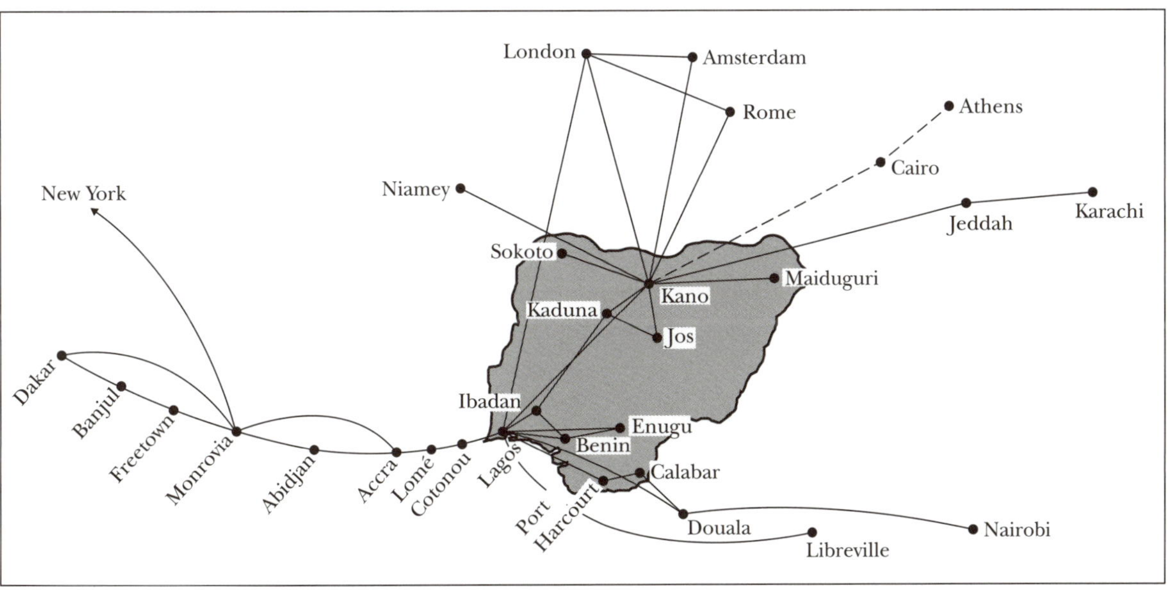

Fig. 18.2

Exercise 18c

Each of the following journeys is made on Nigeria Airways by the most direct route. Use Fig. 18.2 to name the towns that the aircraft will land at during each journey.

1 Lagos to Accra
2 Freetown to Accra
3 Abidjan to Libreville
4 Banjul to New York
5 Nairobi to Lagos
6 Cotonou to Karachi
7 Lagos to Athens
8 Calabar to Amsterdam
9 London to Niamey
10 New York to Kano

Fig. 18.3 is a timetable for Nigeria Airways flights between Lagos and Nairobi.

	LAGOS	DOUALA	NAIROBI
Mon. WT 751	1300 ⟶	a. 1415 d. 1500	⟶ 2055
Thu. WT 753	1300 ⟶	a. 1415 d. 1500	⟶ 2055
Tue. WT 753	1925 ⟵	d. 1810 a. 1725	⟵ 1500
Fri. WT 754	1925 ⟵	d. 1810 a. 1725	⟵ 1500

Fig. 18.3

There are three points to notice:

1 WT is the international code for Nigeria Airways. Thus WT 751 means Nigeria Airways flight number 751.
2 All times are given in terms of the 24-hour clock. Thus 13 00 hours ≡ 1 pm and 19 25 hours ≡ 7.25 pm.
3 All times are local. For example, the Monday plane leaves Lagos at 13 00 hours (Lagos time) and reaches Nairobi at 20 55 hours (Nairobi time). The local time of day in Nairobi is not the same as the local time of day in Lagos. This is because of the rotation of the earth. Your geography or mathematics teacher will be able to explain this fully to you.

Example 1

Express the following times in terms of the 24-hour clock.

a) 5.40 *am* *b)* 2.10 *pm* *c)* 11.55 *am*
d) 9.26 *am* *e)* 7.25 *pm* *f)* 10.10 *pm*

a) 5.40 am = 05 40 hours
b) 2.10 pm = 14 10 hours
c) 11.55 am = 11 55 hours
d) 9.26 am = 09 26 hours
e) 7.25 pm = 19 25 hours
f) 10.10 pm = 22 10 hours

Example 2

Express the following 24-hour clock times as am or pm times.

a) 04 15 *hours* *b)* 08 30 *hours* *c)* 16 10 *hours*
d) 22 25 *hours* *e)* 02 55 *hours* *f)* 19 45 *hours*

a) 04 15 hours = 4.15 am
b) 08 30 hours = 8.30 am
c) 16 10 hours = 4.10 pm
d) 22 25 hours = 10.25 pm
e) 02 55 hours = 2.55 am
f) 19 45 hours = 7.45 pm

Exercise 18d

1 Express the following times in terms of the 24-hour clock.
a) 2 pm **b)** 8.30 pm
c) 9 am **d)** 3 pm
e) 1.30 pm **f)** 5.45 am
g) 4.15 am **h)** 11.55 pm
i) 5 to 9 at night
j) 10 past 6 in the morning
k) midday
l) 3 minutes past midnight

2 Express the following 24-hour clock times as am or pm times.
a) 05 00 hours **b)** 23 00 hours
c) 10 00 hours **d)** 15 00 hours
e) 17 30 hours **f)** 02 15 hours
g) 21 45 hours **h)** 14 15 hours
i) 09 25 hours **j)** 18 19 hours
k) 07 40 hours **l)** 23 57 hours

3 A businessman flew from Lagos to Nairobi on Thursday 31st May.
a) What was his flight number?
b) How long was the aircraft on the ground in Douala?
c) If the actual journey time, including the stop at Douala, was 6 h 10 min, what time will the man's watch show when he lands at Nairobi?
d) What is the difference in local times between Lagos and Nairobi?

4 The businessman in question 3 returned to Lagos on 1st June.

a) What was his flight number?
b) How long was the aircraft on the ground at Douala?
c) If the man had adjusted his watch to give Nairobi time, what will his watch show when he reaches Lagos? Assume that the return journey takes 6 h 10 min.

Exercise 18e contains a mixture of charts and timetables. Remember to read the titles and column headings very carefully. These will tell you what they are about.

Exercise 18e

1 Fig. 18.4 is a distance chart giving the distances, in km, by road between some of the larger settlements in Sierra Leone.

a) Find the following road distances.

i) Mano to Kamakwei

Bo										
27	Bumpe									
304	331	Falaba								
77	104	387	Hangha							
251	277	54	341	Kabala						
218	243	264	307	214	Kamakwei					
189	214	243	280	189	134	Lunsar				
125	150	179	216	125	91	64	Makeni			
61	35	325	139	272	238	186	146	Mano		
110	136	397	30	342	309	282	218	171	Panguma	
213	238	277	290	224	141	35	98	184	315	Port Loko

Fig. 18.4

ii) Kabala to Bumpe
iii) Panguma to Makeni
iv) Port Loko to Falaba
v) Bo to Hangha
vi) Lunsar to Panguma
vii) Falaba to Panguma
viii) Lunsar to Makeni
ix) Kamakwei to Port Loko
x) Bumpe to Falaba

b) Which two cities are furthest apart?

c) Which two cities are nearest to each other?

d) Find the distance from Kabala to Bo:
i) directly,
ii) via Mano,
iii) via Lunsar.

e) Find the total distance travelled on the following round trip: Port Loko → Makeni → Mano → Lunsar → Port Loko.

2 Fig. 18.5 is a school timetable for a Form 2 class.

time / day	0700 to 0740 1	0740 to 0820 2	0820 to 0900 3		1000 to 1040 4	1040 to 1120 5	1120 to 1200 6		1220 to 1300 7	1300 to 1340 8
MON.	Lang.	Lit.	Maths		Sci.	Sci.	R.K.		Hist.	Econ.
TUE.	Hist.	Geog.	Lang.		Econ.	Maths	Lit.		Comm.	Comm.
WED.	Maths	Comm.	R.K.		Geog.	Hist.	Lit.		Econ.	Lang.
THU.	Maths	Lit.	Geog.		Lang.	Sci.	Sci.		Hist.	Econ.
FRI.	Econ.	Geog.	Lang.		Comm.	R.K.	Maths		Lit.	Sci.

Fig. 18.5

a) How many periods are there in each day?

b) What is the length of each period?

c) There are two breaks each day. How long is each break?

d) Write down the different subjects that the class takes. Find the number of periods that the class gets for each subject.

3 Table 18.2 shows part of the stock records of a shop which sells electrical goods. The table shows the numbers of items in the shop at the end of each month.

a) How many radios were in the shop at the end of July?

b) How many TV sets were sold during April and May?

c) During which month did the shopkeeper buy in more radios?

d) i) During which month were most fans and refrigerators sold?
ii) Can you think of a reason for this?

e) In which month did the shop run out of TV sets?

f) Which items should the shopkeeper buy in November?

g) Give some reasons why a stock record is useful.

4 Fig. 18.6 is a chart of the results of a table tennis competition.

a) How many people entered the competition?

b) How many matches were played altogether?

c) i) Who was the winner?
ii) How many matches did he play?
iii) Name the people he beat.
iv) How many points did he score altogether?

	J	F	M	A	M	J	J	A	S	O	N	D
radios	13	12	10	6	16	14	11	10	8	3		
TV sets	8	8	7	7	7	4	3	0	10	9		
record players	12	10	6	3	14	13	10	8	6	1		
fans	20	18	3	27	15	14	13	12	10	10		
refrigerators	8	7	2	11	8	7	6	5	5	4		

Table 18.2 Monthly stock records

d) How many points did Ojo score altogether and how many points were scored against him?

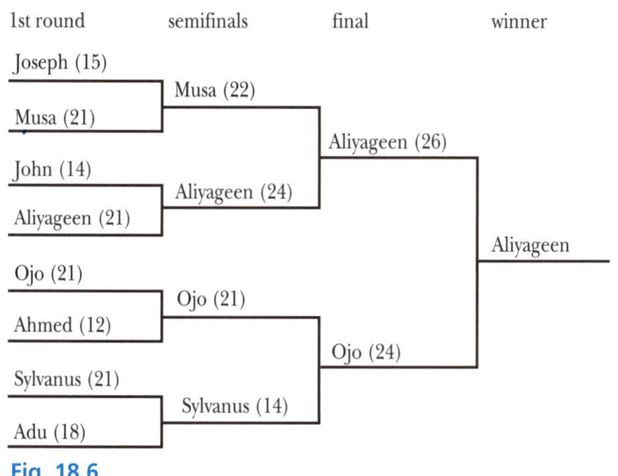

Fig. 18.6

Chapter summary

1. *Tabulated data* is information (usually numbers) given in a table.
2. Tables usually have *column headings* and *row headings*. These tell what the tables are about. There should also be a *title*.
3. Read tables by making a *cross-reference*, i.e. reading across from the column heading and down from the row heading to where the two directions cross.

19 Cylinder: Area and volume

Circumference and area of a circle (revision)

Given a circle, radius r,

diameter of circle $= 2r$

circumference of circle $= 2\pi r$

area of circle $= \pi r^2$

π is a constant number. The value of π is approximately $3{\cdot}14$ or $\frac{22}{7}$.

Exercise 19a *(Revision)*

1 Use the value $\frac{22}{7}$ for π to find the circumference and area of a circle of radius

a) 7 cm **b)** 21 m
c) 35 mm **d)** $1\frac{3}{4}$ m
e) 28 mm **f)** 70 cm
g) 3·5 m **h)** 42 mm
i) 77 cm **j)** 14 cm

2 Use the value 3·14 for π to find the circumference and area of a circle of radius

a) 20 cm **b)** 10 m
c) 6 mm **d)** 40 cm
e) 50 cm **f)** 8 mm
g) 5 cm **h)** 14 cm
i) 8·5 mm **j)** 60 cm

The net of a cylinder (revision)

The surface of a cylinder is in three parts, two circular faces and one curved surface (Fig. 19.1).

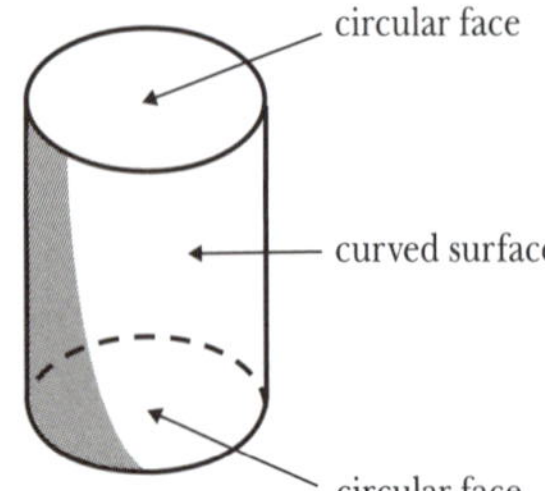

Fig. 19.1

A hollow cylinder can be opened out to give its **net**.

Fig. 19.2 shows that the net of a cylinder is made up of two circles and a rectangle. The total surface area of the cylinder will be the total area of the two circles and the rectangle.

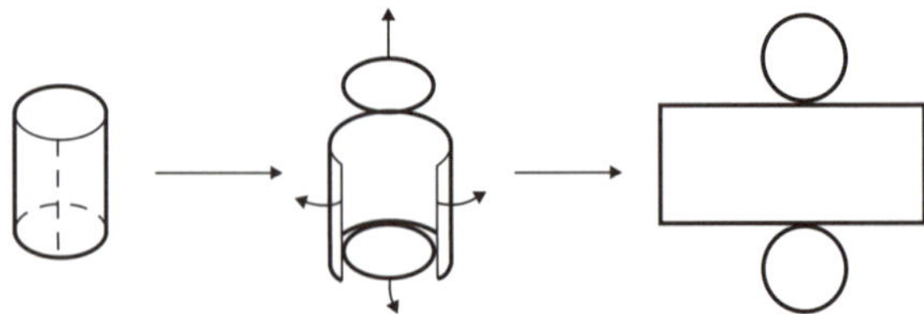

Fig. 19.2

Exercise 19b *(Practical assignment)*

1 a) Cut a strip of paper 5 cm wide by 22 cm long as in Fig. 19.3.

Fig. 19.3

b) Roll the paper to make a cylindrical surface as in Fig. 19.4.

Fig. 19.4

c) What is the height of the cylinder?

d) What is the circumference of each circle at the open ends of the cylinder?

e) Calculate the area of the rectangle you cut out in a).

f) Does this area change when the rectangle is rolled into a cylinder?

g) Measure, to the nearest cm, the diameter of one of the circles at the open end of the cylinder. Use this value to calculate the circumference of the circle. Does your answer agree with your answer to part d)?

2 Fig. 19.5 is a sketch of the net of a cylinder.

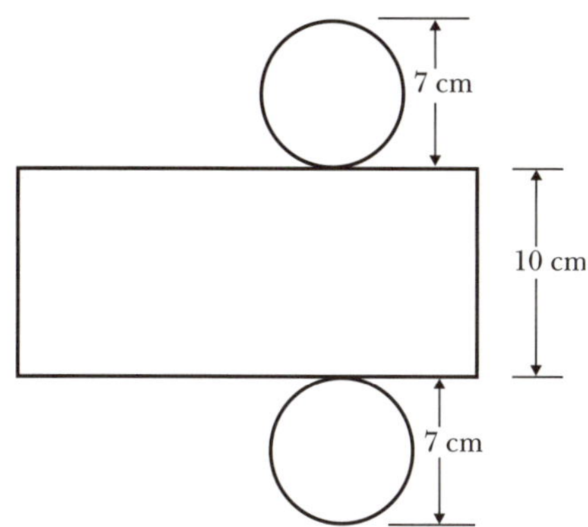

Fig. 19.5

a) What will be the height of the cylinder?
b) What is the diameter of the circular faces of the cylinder?
c) Calculate the circumference of each circle.
d) Hence write down the length of the rectangle in Fig. 19.5.
e) Make an accurate full-size drawing of Fig. 19.5 on thin cardboard. Cut the net out and make it into the shape of a cylinder.

Surface area of a cylinder

Consider a cylinder of height h which has circular faces of radius r.

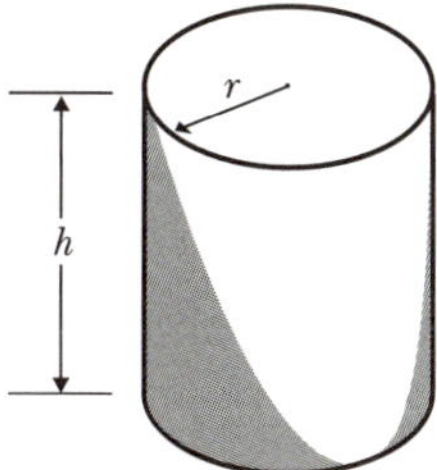

Fig. 19.6

Area of the two circular faces $= \pi r^2 + \pi r^2 = 2\pi r^2$
The curved surface is equivalent to a plane rectangle.

Length of rectangle = Circumference of circular face $= 2\pi r$
breadth of rectangle $= h$
area of rectangle $= 2\pi r \times h = 2\pi rh$
Thus, area of curved surface $= 2\pi rh$
Total surface area of closed cylinder $= \mathbf{2\pi r^2 + 2\pi rh}$

Example 1

A cylindrical cup has a circular base of radius 7 cm *and height of* 10 cm. *Taking the value of* π *to be* $\frac{22}{7}$, *calculate a) its curved surface area, b) the area of its circular base.*

a) The area of the curved surface of a cylinder of radius r and height h is $2\pi rh$.
The curved surface area of the cup

$= 2 \times \frac{22}{7} \times 7 \times 10 \text{ cm}^2$

$= 440 \text{ cm}^2$

b) The area of the circular base of the cup

$= \frac{22}{7} \times 7 \times 7 \text{ cm}^2$

$= 154 \text{ cm}^2$

Example 2

A cylinder of height 12 cm *and radius* 5 cm *is made of cardboard. Use the value of* 3·1 *for* π *to calculate the total area of cardboard needed to make a) a closed cylinder, b) a cylinder open at one end.*

a) Notice that 'radius of a cylinder' is short for 'radius of the circular face of a cylinder'.
Total surface area of closed cylinder
$= 2\pi r^2 + 2\pi rh$
Area of cardboard
$= 2 \times 3{\cdot}1 \times 25 + 2 \times 3{\cdot}1 \times 5 \times 12 \text{ cm}^2$
$= 50 \times 3{\cdot}1 + 120 \times 3{\cdot}1 \text{ cm}^2$
$= 155 + 372 \text{ cm}^2$
$= 527 \text{ cm}^2 = 530 \text{ cm}^2$ to 2 s.f.

b) Surface area of open cylinder
$= \pi r^2 + 2\pi rh$
Area of cardboard
$= 3{\cdot}1 \times 25 + 2 \times 3{\cdot}1 \times 5 \times 12 \text{ cm}^2$
$= 77{\cdot}5 + 372 \text{ cm}^2$
$= 449{\cdot}5 \text{ cm}^2 = 450 \text{ cm}^2$ to 2 s.f.

Note: The data in the question is given to 2 significant figures. The final answers can be rounded to 2 significant figures.

Exercise 19c

In this exercise, round the final answers to 2 significant figures.

1 Calculate the curved surface area of a cylindrical container with the following dimensions. Take the value of π to be 3·14.

a) radius 30 cm, height 36 cm
b) radius 60 cm, height 50 cm
c) diameter 5 cm, height 30 cm
d) radius 15 cm, height 1·2 cm
e) diameter 10 cm, length 18 cm
f) diameter 58 cm, height 86 cm

2 A strip of thin paper is wound eight times round a cylindrical pencil of diameter 7 mm. Use the value $\frac{22}{7}$ for π to find the length of the paper. (Neglect the thickness of the paper.)

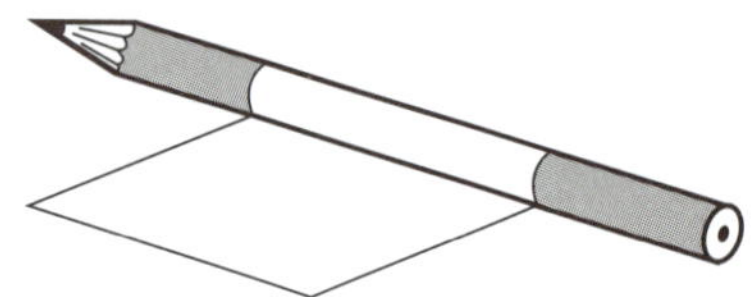

Fig. 19.7

3 A newspaper is rolled into a cylindrical shape of approximate diameter 4 cm. It is wrapped for posting with a strip of paper which goes about $2\frac{1}{2}$ times round the newspaper. Use the value 3 for π to find the approximate length of the wrapping paper.

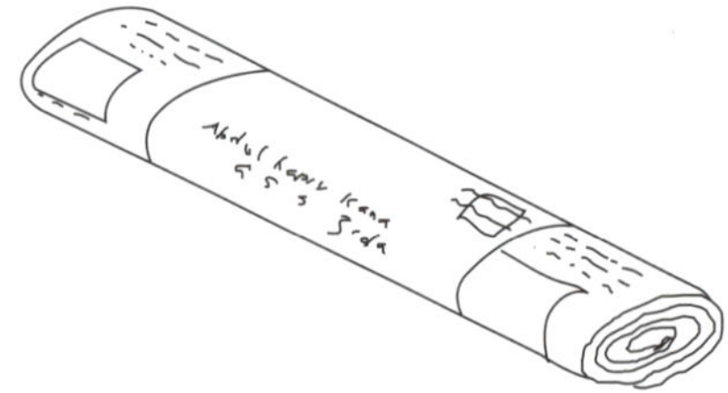

Fig. 19.8

4 In Fig. 19.9 all dimensions are in cm. Use the value $\frac{22}{7}$ for π to calculate the total surface area of each closed cylinder.

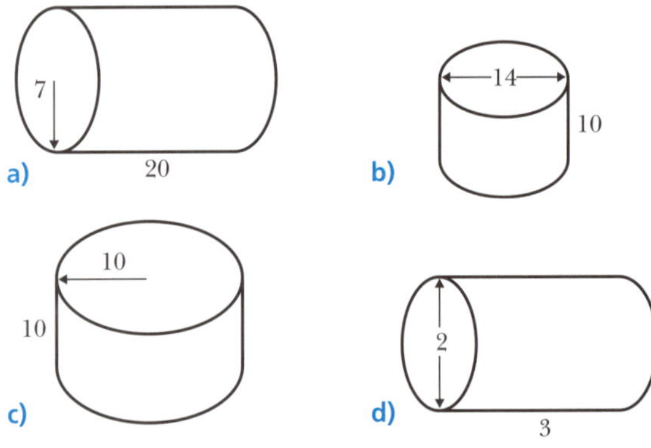

Fig. 19.9

5 A closed tin is in the shape of a cylinder of diameter 10 cm and height 15 cm. Use the value 3·14 for π to find
a) the total surface area of the tin,
b) the value of the tin to the nearest leone if tin plate costs Le15 000 per m^2.

6 A plastic container is in the shape of an open cylinder. It has a lid which is also an open cylinder. The dimensions of the container and lid are given in Fig. 19.10.

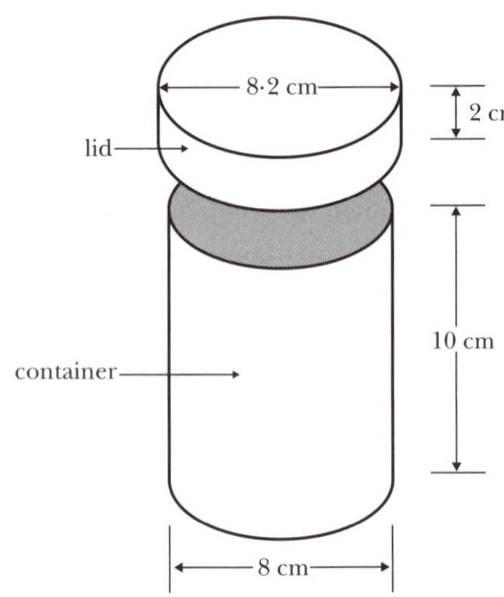

Fig. 19.10

Use the value 3·1 for π to find
a) the surface area of the container,
b) the surface area of the lid,
c) the total area of plastic needed to make both.

Volume of a cylinder

In Book 1 you found that the volume of a prism is given by:

volume of prism
= **area of end face × distance between the end faces**

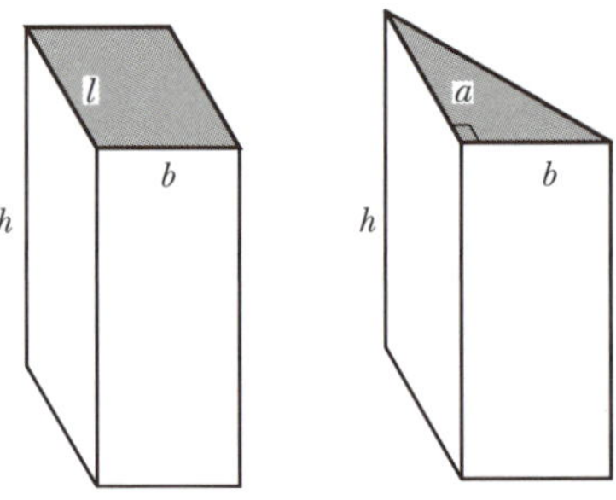

Fig. 19.11

For example, in Fig. 19.11,

$$\text{volume of cuboid} = (l \times b) \times h = lbh$$

$$\text{volume of triangular prism} = (\tfrac{1}{2} \times a \times b) \times h = \tfrac{1}{2}abh$$

A cylinder is a special kind of prism. Its volume can be found in the same way.

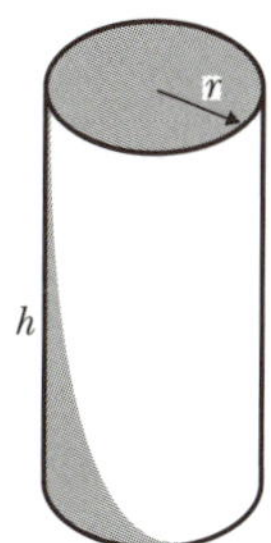

Fig. 19.12

In Fig. 19.12
volume of cylinder =
area of circular face × height of cylinder
$= \pi r^2 \times h$

volume of cylinder $= \boldsymbol{\pi r^2 h}$

Example 3

How many litres can be held by a cylindrical can 14 cm *in diameter and* 20 cm *high? Use the value* $\frac{22}{7}$ *for* π.

$$\begin{aligned} \text{volume of can} &= \pi r^2 h \\ &= \tfrac{22}{7} \times 7 \times 7 \times 20 \\ &= 3\,080 \text{ cm}^3 \\ 1 \text{ litre} &= 1\,000 \text{ cm}^3 \\ \text{capacity of can} &= \tfrac{3\,080}{1\,000} \text{ litres} \\ &= 3{\cdot}08 \text{ litres} \end{aligned}$$

The can holds about 3 litres.

Example 4

88 *litres of oil are poured into a drum* 40 cm *in diameter. Use the value* $\frac{22}{7}$ *for* π *to find out the depth of the oil in the drum.*

Let the depth of the oil in the drum be d cm.
Fig. 19.13 shows the information of the question.

$$\begin{aligned} \text{volume of oil} &= 88 \text{ litres} \\ &= 88 \times 1\,000 \text{ cm}^3 \\ \text{also, volume of oil} &= \pi r^2 d \\ &= \tfrac{22}{7} \times 20 \times 20 \times d \text{ cm}^3 \end{aligned}$$

$$\text{thus, } \tfrac{22}{7} \times 20 \times 20 \times d = 88 \times 1\,000$$

$$d = \frac{88 \times 1\,000 \times 7}{20 \times 20 \times 22} = 70$$

The depth of the oil is 70 cm.

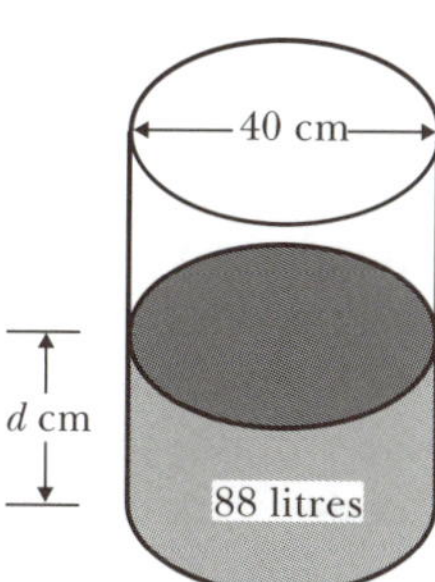

Fig. 19.13

Notice that numerical simplification is left until the last step.

Exercise 19d

Use the value $\frac{22}{7}$ for π in this exercise.

1 Calculate the volume of a cylindrical steel bar which is 8 cm long and 3·5 cm in diameter.

2 The tank on a petrol lorry is a cylinder 2 m in diameter and 7 m long. Calculate its volume in m^3. Find its capacity in kilolitres.

3 A cylindrical storage vessel is 4 m in diameter and $3\frac{1}{2}$ m deep. How many kilolitres will it hold?

4 99 litres of oil are poured into a cylindrical drum 60 cm in diameter. How deep is the oil in the drum?

5 How many litres of water will a cylindrical pipe hold if it is 1 m long and 7 cm in diameter?

6 A wooden roller is 1 m long and 8 cm in diameter. Find
  a) its volume in cm^3,
  b) its mass in grammes if 1 cm^3 of the wood has a mass of 0·7 g.

7 A round brass bar is 5 m long and 14 mm in radius.
  a) Calculate its volume in cm^3.
  b) If the density of the brass is 8 g/cm^3, calculate the mass of the bar in kg.

8 The roof of a building is supported by four cylindrical concrete pillars. Each pillar is 4 m long and 50 cm in diameter.

a) Calculate the total volume of the four pillars in m^3.

b) If 1 m^3 of concrete has a mass of 2·1 tonnes, calculate the total mass of the four pillars in tonnes.

9 A cylindrical container has a diameter of 14 cm and a height of 20 cm and is full of water. The water is poured into another cylinder which has a diameter of 20 cm. How deep is the water in the second cylinder?

10 A cylindrical water tank is 70 cm in diameter. To begin with, it is full of water. A leak starts in the bottom so that it loses 10 litres of water in 1 hour. How long will it take for the water level to fall by 20 cm?

Further exercises on the volume of cylinders are given in Exercise 24e on page 198.

Chapter summary

① A *cylinder* of height h and circular base of radius r has a *curved surface area* of $2\pi rh$. If it is closed, it also has two circular end faces, each of area πr^2.
Therefore,

total surface area of closed cylinder = $2\pi rh + 2\pi r^2$

(The *surface area of an open-ended cylindrical container* will be $2\pi rh + \pi r^2$.)

② In general,

volume of prism = area of end face × distance between end faces

and in particular,

volume of cylinder (height h, radius r) = $\pi r^2 h$

20 Angles of elevation and depression

Horizontal and vertical

Any surface which is parallel to the surface of the earth is said to be **horizontal**. For example, the surface of liquid in a container is always horizontal, even if the container is held at an angle as shown in Fig. 20.1.

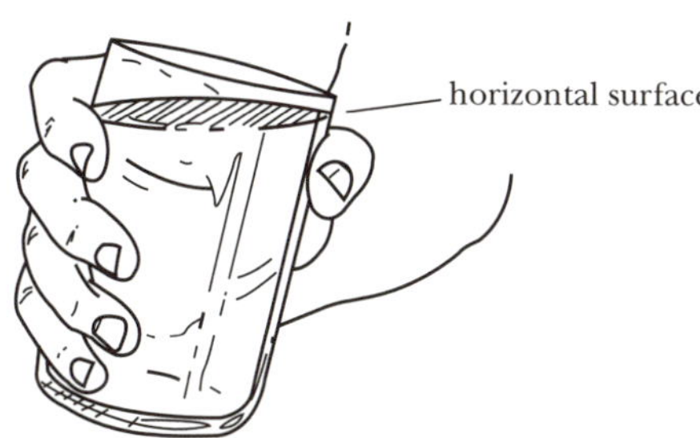

Fig. 20.1

The floor of your classroom is horizontal. Any line drawn on a horizontal surface will also be horizontal. Any line or surface which is perpendicular to a horizontal surface is said to be **vertical**. The walls of your classroom are vertical. The thread on a plumb-line hangs vertically. A plumb-line is a mass which hangs freely on a thread (Fig. 20.2).

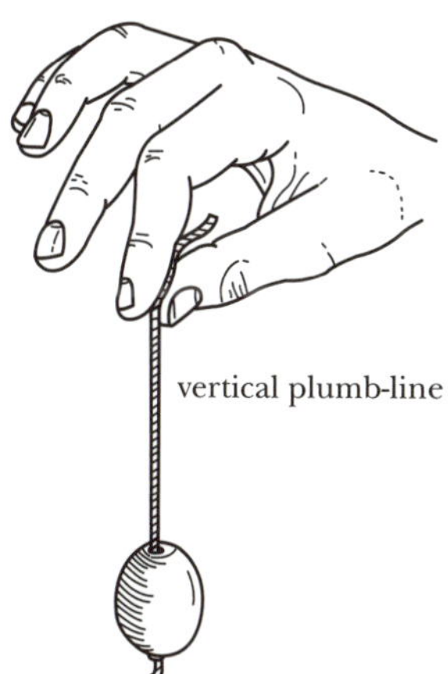

Fig. 20.2

Exercise 20a *(Oral)*

Fig. 20.3 shows a corner of a student's study. Use the picture to answer the questions in this exercise.

Fig. 20.3

1 Say whether the following are horizontal or vertical, or neither.

a) the table top
b) the door
c) the pictures
d) the floor boards
e) the back of the chair
f) the table legs
g) the ruler (on the table)
h) the line where the walls meet
i) the brush handle
j) the top edge of the wall

2 Name a further five things in Fig. 20.3 which are **a)** horizontal, **b)** vertical, **c)** neither horizontal nor vertical.

Angle of elevation

a)

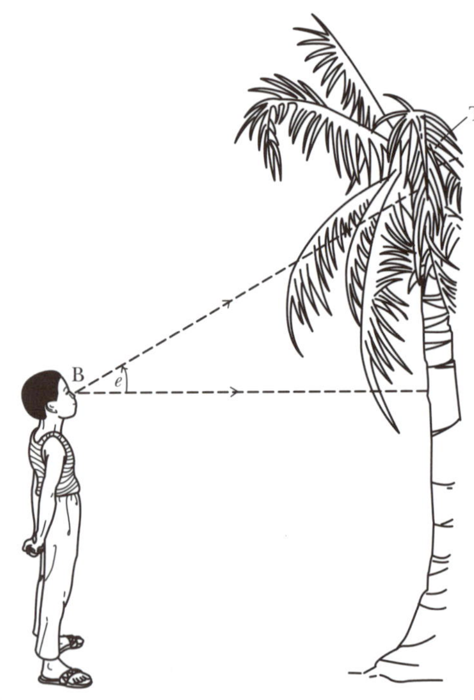

b)

Fig. 20.4

In Fig. 20.4(a) the boy at B looks in a horizontal direction at the palm tree. In Fig. 20.4(b) he looks up at the top of the tree, T. To do this, he has to raise his line of sight from the horizontal through an angle $e°$. The angle $e°$ in Fig. 20.4(b) is called the **angle of elevation** of T from B.

Angle of depression

Fig. 20.5

In Fig. 20.5, the girl in the window at G is looking down at her friend at F. To do this she has to lower her line of sight from the horizontal through an angle $d°$. The angle $d°$ in Fig. 20.5 is called the **angle of depression** of F from G.

Fig. 20.6 shows that there is a connection between angles of elevation and depression.

The angle of elevation of the cat, C, from the dog, D, is equal in size to the angle of depression of D from C. They are alternate angles.

Exercise 20b

You will need a protractor for this exercise.

1 Assume that Figs 20.4, 20.5 and 20.6 are all scale drawings. Measure the following:

a) the angle of elevation, $e°$, in Fig. 20.4(b)

b) the angle of depression, $d°$, in Fig. 20.5

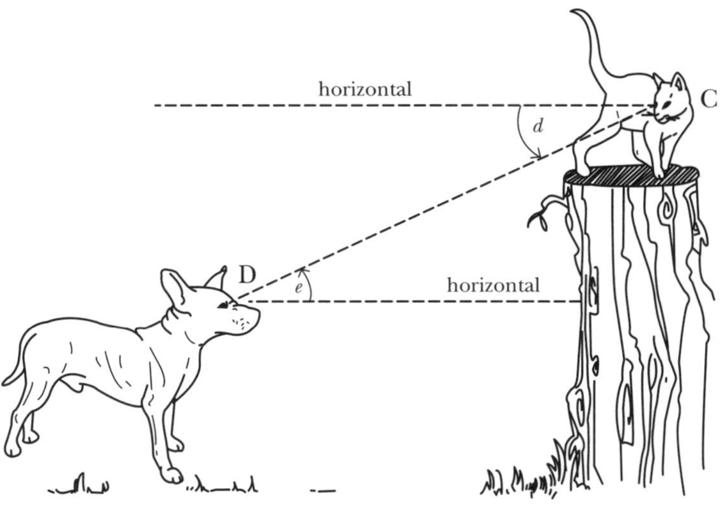

Fig. 20.6

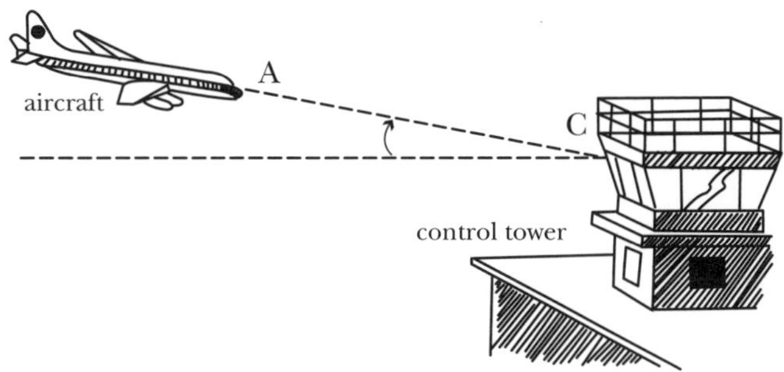

Fig. 20.7

Fig. 20.8

c) the angle of elevation of C from D in Fig. 20.6

d) the angle of depression of D from C in Fig. 20.6.

2 a) Measure the angle of elevation of A from C in Fig. 20.7.

b) Hence state the angle of depression of C from A.

3 a) Measure the angle of depression of man B from man A in Fig. 20.8.

b) Hence state the angle of elevation of A from B.

4 a) Measure the angle of elevation of the light bulb from student P in Fig. 20.9.

b) Measure the angle of elevation of the light bulb from student Q.

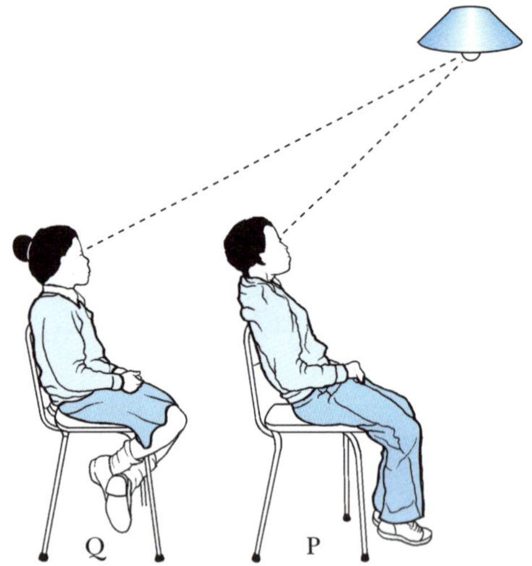

Fig. 20.9

5 In Fig. 20.10, measure the angle of depression of the coin from the man.

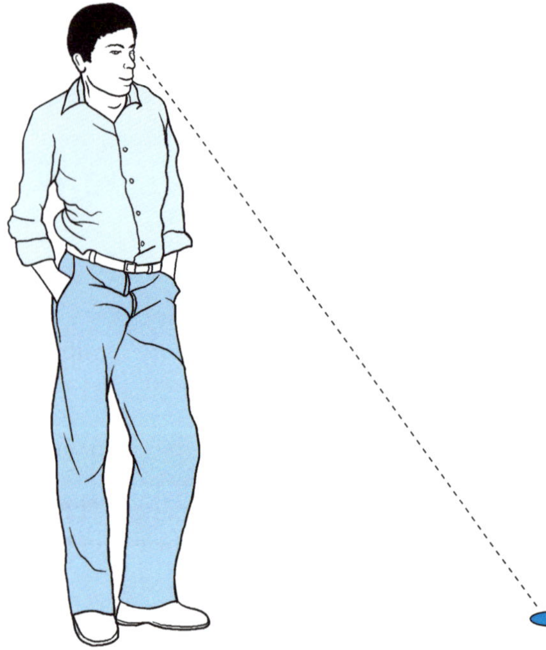

Fig. 20.10

Measuring angles of elevation and depression

Angles of elevation and depression can be measured with a simple instrument called a **clinometer**. Fig. 20.11 shows a clinometer made from a board protractor.

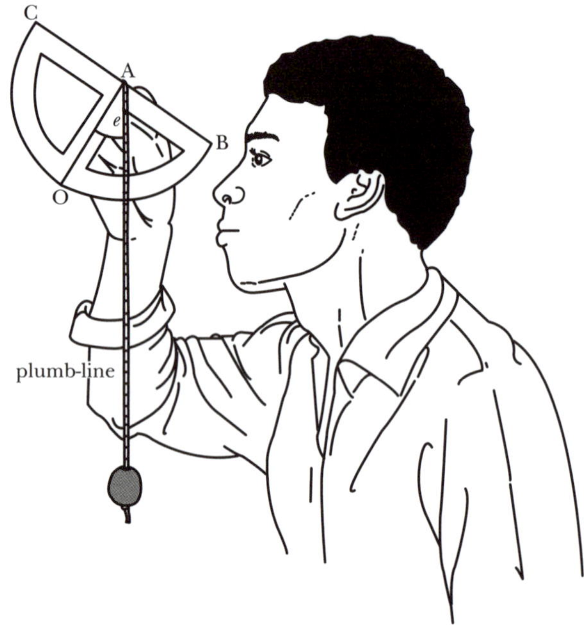

Fig. 20.11

A plumb-line is hung from the centre of the protractor at A. The observer sights an object along the line BAC. The angle of elevation, $e°$, is the angle between AO and the plumb-line. The size of $e°$ can be read from the scale. Notice that $e°$ increases from 0° at O to 90° at B. If a board protractor is used as a clinometer, it may be helpful if the angle markings are changed.

Exercise 20c *(Class project)*

You will need a clinometer and a tape measure for this exercise. A clinometer can be made from a board protractor as shown in Fig. 20.11.

1 Stand at a point X on level ground, where the top of the highest building in your school has an angle of elevation of 45°.
Using a tape measure, find the distance from X to the base of the building. Record the height of the top of the building.

2 Use a similar method as in question 1 above to find the height of the tallest tree in your school compound.

3 Identify a flagpole in your neighbourhood. Using a clinometer and a measuring tape as in question 1, find the height of the flagpole.

4 Use a similar method as in question 1 to find the height of a water tower (or other tall building) in your school.

Fig. 20.12 shows how a clinometer is used to find the angle of elevation of the top of a tree. An observer uses the clinometer and a recorder takes down the reading of $e°$.

Example 1

Two girls use a clinometer to find the angle of elevation of the top of a tree as in Fig. 20.12. They also measure the distance of the tree from the observer and the height of the observer's eye above the ground. Their results are shown in the sketch in Fig. 20.13.

Fig. 20.12

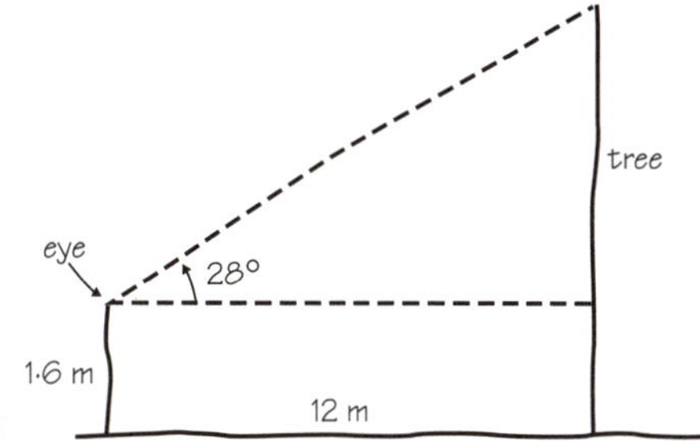

Fig. 20.13

Use the data of the sketch to make an accurate drawing. Hence find the height of the tree.

Fig. 20.14 is a scale drawing using a scale 1 cm to 2 m.

In Fig. 20.14, HT represents the full height of the tree.

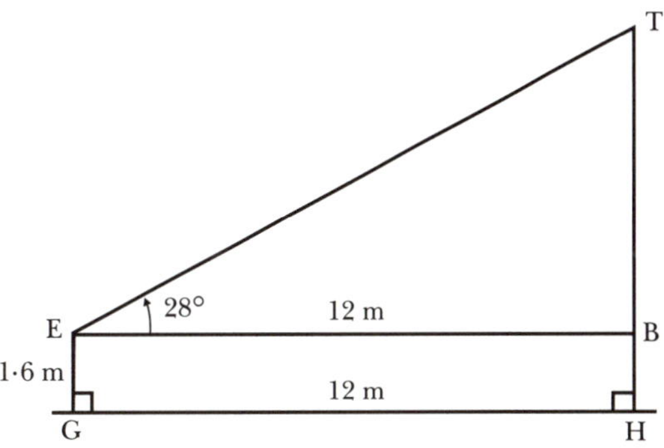

Fig. 20.14

HT = 3·95 cm

height of tree = 3·95 × 2 m

= 7·9 m

There are likely to be small errors in measurements and drawing. It is more sensible to say that the height of the tree is about 8 m to the nearest metre.

Notice that EG is the height of the observer's eye above the ground. Another way to find the height of the tree is to construct triangle TEB. The length BT can be found. The height of the tree will be BT + EG.

Exercise 20d

You will need a protractor, a set-square and a ruler. All questions can be answered by making a scale drawing. Choose a suitable scale in each case.

1 Find the height of the flagpole in Fig. 20.15 to the nearest $\frac{1}{2}$ m.

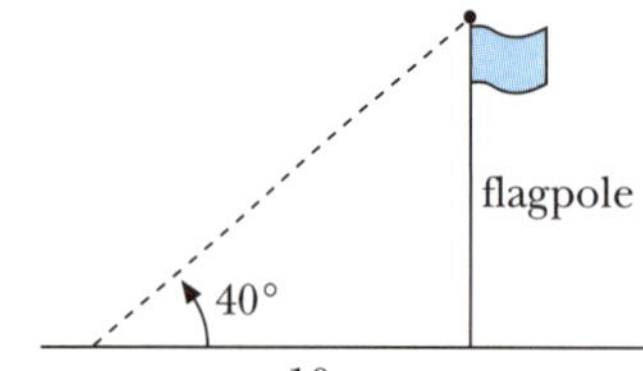

Fig. 20.15

2 Find the height of the observer in Fig. 20.16 above ground level to the nearest metre.

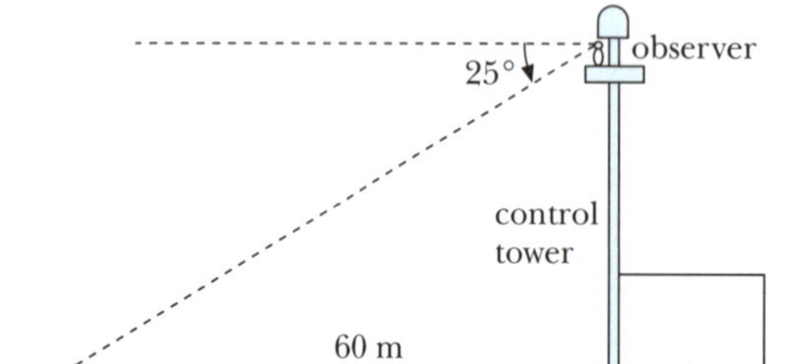

Fig. 20.16

3 Find the height of the water tower in Fig. 20.17 to the nearest $\frac{1}{2}$ m.

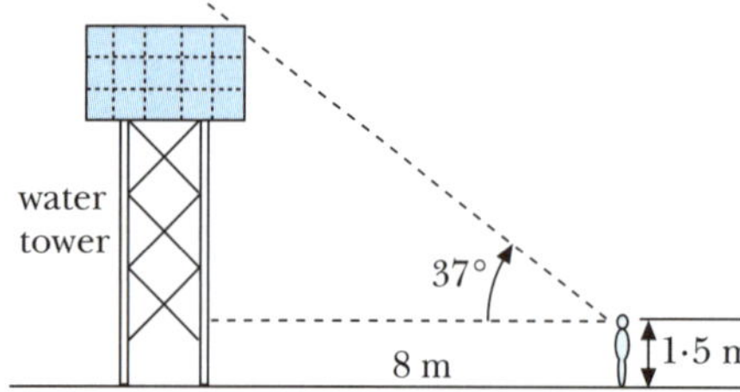

Fig. 20.17

4 Find the width of the river in Fig. 20.18 to the nearest metre.

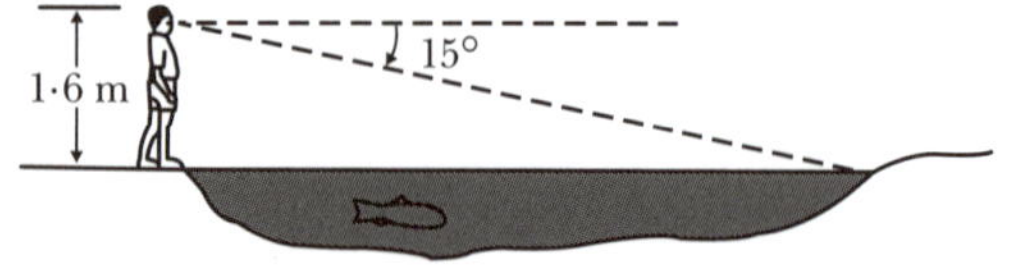

Fig. 20.18

5 Find the height of the tree in Fig. 20.19 to the nearest $\frac{1}{2}$ m.

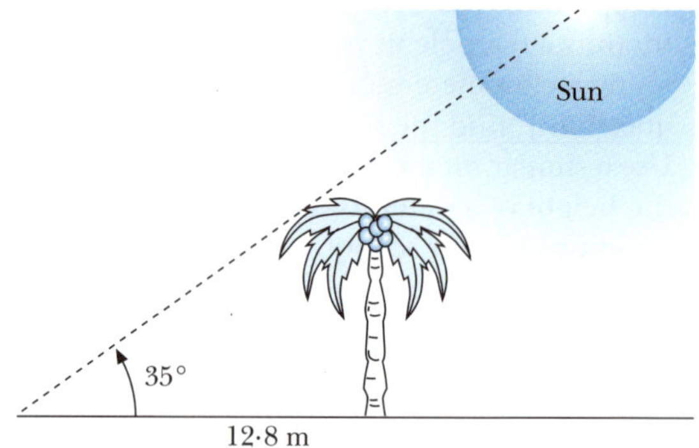

Fig. 20.19

6 Find the height of the building in Fig. 20.20 to the nearest metre.

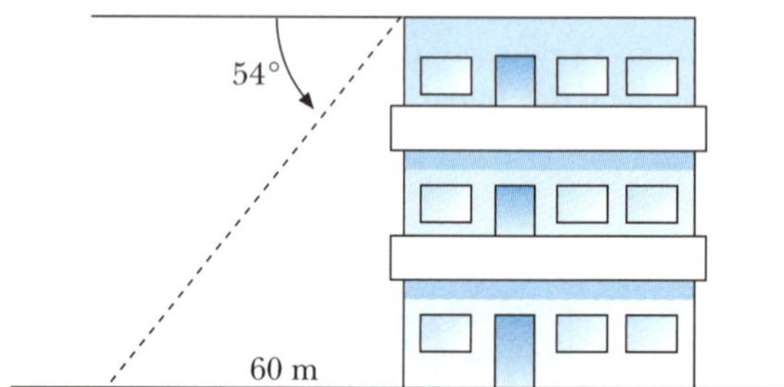

Fig. 20.20

7 The angle of elevation of the top of a tower from a point 42 m away from its base on level ground is 36°. Find the height of the tower.

8 From the top of a building 50 m high, the angle of depression of a car is 55°. Find the distance of the car from the foot of the building.

9 The angle of elevation of the sun is 45°. A tree has a shadow 12 m long. Find the height of the tree.

10 The angle of elevation of the sun is 27°. A man is 180 cm tall. How long is his shadow? Give your answer to the nearest 10 cm.

11 The angle of elevation of the top of a radio mast from a point 53 m from its base on level ground is 61°. Find the height of the mast to the nearest 5 m.

12 Fig. 20.21 shows the angles of elevation of an aircraft from two points 1 100 m apart.

Find the height of the aircraft above the ground to the nearest 100 m.

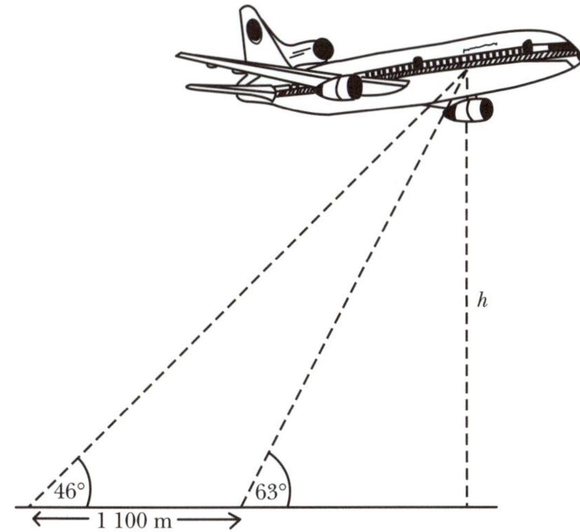

Fig. 20.21

Chapter summary

1. Any line or surface parallel to the surface of the earth is *horizontal*. Any line or surface perpendicular to a horizontal surface is *vertical* (see Figs 20.1 and 20.2).
2. If a line of sight is raised through an angle $e°$ from the horizontal, then $e°$ is called an *angle of elevation* (see Fig. 20.4).
3. If a line of sight is lowered through an angle $d°$ from the horizontal, then $d°$ is called an *angle of depression* (see Fig. 20.5).
4. Angles of elevation and depression can be measured with *a clinometer*.
5. Scale drawing can often be used to find heights and distances that involve angles of elevation and depression (see Example 1).

21 Probability

Experimental probability

A farmer asks, 'Will it rain this month?'

The answer to the farmer's question depends on three things: the month, the place where the farmer is, and what has happened in the past in that month at that place. Table 21.1 gives some answers to the question for different places and months. Compare Table 21.1 with Table 18.1 on page 154.

place	month	answer to question
Kabala	February	no
Yele	July	yes
Bo	January	maybe
Port Loko	June	yes

Table 21.1 'Will it rain this month?'

Is it possible to give a more accurate answer to a farmer in Bo in January? Table 18.1 shows that *on average,* 10 mm of rain falls in Bo in January. However, this is an average found by keeping records over 12 years. The actual rainfall for Bo in January over the 12 years was as follows.

18 mm	0 mm	17 mm	9 mn
11 mm	22 mm	14 mm	0 mm
16 mm	0 mm	7 mm	6 mm

From the above data it can be seen that rain fell in nine of the 12 months of January. If future years follow the pattern of the past, it is likely that in Bo, rain will fall in nine out of the next 12 Januaries. We say that the **probability** of rain falling in Bo in January is $\frac{9}{12}$ (or $\frac{3}{4}$ or 0·75). This probability can never be exact. However, it is the best measure we can give from the data we have. The number $\frac{9}{12}$ is based on experimental records. We say that it is **experimental probability**.

Example 1

A girl writes down the number of male and female children of her mother and father. She also writes down the number of male and female children of her parents' brothers and sisters. Her results are shown in Table 21.2.

	number of children male	female
mother and father	2	5
mother's brothers	6	8
mother's sisters	4	8
father's brothers	5	8
father's sisters	7	7
totals	**24**	**36**

Table 21.2

a) Find the experimental probability that when the girl has children of her own, her first born will be a girl.

b) If the girl eventually has 5 children, how many are likely to be male?

a) In the girl's family there is a total of 60 children. 36 of these are female. If the girl's own children follow the pattern of her family, then the experimental probability that her first born will be a girl is $\frac{36}{60} = \frac{3}{5}$.

b) Following the family pattern, $\frac{3}{5}$ of the girl's children will be female and $\frac{2}{5}$ will be male. The number of male children that the girl is likely to have $= \frac{2}{5}$ of $5 = 2$.

Notice that the results in Example 1 are based on experimental probability. Thus we are using the past to predict the future. Events can easily turn out differently. The answers in Example 1 are no more than calculated guesses.

Exercise 21a *(Discussion)*

1 A woman has four children. They are all males. The children of the rest of her family are equally divided between males and females. What is the woman's next child likely to be, male or female?

2 A 'rainmaker' throws some kola nuts on the ground. From the pattern of the kola nuts, he says that rain will fall next week. Is this a good method? Does it always work? Compare this method with the use of rainfall records. Can rainfall records always tell us when rain will fall?

Exercise 21b *(Experiments)*

1 A bottle top rests either with its mouth up or with its mouth down. See Fig. 21.1.

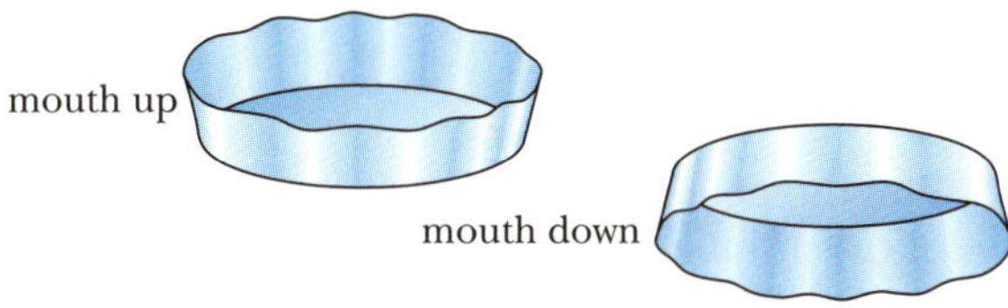

Fig. 21.1

Find a bottle top and drop it 100 times on your desk. Count the number of times it lands mouth up and the number of times it lands mouth down. Record your results in a tally table.

mouth up	𝍸 II
mouth down	𝍸 IIII

Table 21.3

Complete the following.

a) The bottle top landed mouth up … times out of 100 throws.

b) The experimental probability that a bottle top will land mouth up is … .

Compare your results with other people's results. Give some reasons why your results may be different.

2 A drawing pin rests with its point either up or down. See Fig. 21.2.

Fig. 21.2

a) Repeat the experiment in question 1 using a drawing pin.

b) Find the experimental probability that the drawing pin will land point up if dropped on the floor.

c) Compare your results with other people's.

3 A coin, when tossed, lands with either its head up or its tail up.

a) Repeat the experiment in question 1 using a coin.

b) Find the experimental probability that if a coin is tossed it will land tail up.

c) Compare your results with other people's.

4 A die has its six faces numbered 1 to 6.

a) Roll the die 50 times.

b) How many times did you roll a 6?

c) What is the experimental probability of obtaining a 6 on the die?

5 Cut four pieces of string so that three are 15 cm long and one is 10 cm long. Hold all four pieces in your hand so that all four lengths look the same (Fig. 21.3).

Fig. 21.3

Ask a friend to choose one piece. Write down whether a long piece or the shorter piece is chosen. Put the string back, mix them up and ask someone else. Repeat 20 times.

Find the experimental probability that someone will choose the short piece of string.

6 Draw a circle of radius 5 cm on a large sheet of paper. Get 10 paper clips. Hold the paper clips about 30 cm above the centre of the circle and drop them on the paper.

Count the number of paper clips inside the circle and the number outside the circle. (If a paper clip falls on the circumference, count it as being inside the circle.)

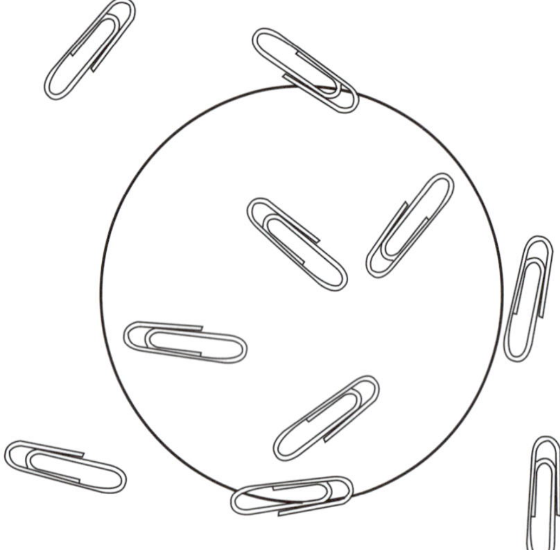

Fig. 21.4

In Fig. 21.4 there are six paper clips inside the circle and four outside. The results can be recorded as shown in Table 21.4.

number of paper clips inside	6
number of paper clips outside	4

Table 21.4

Repeat 10 times. Find the experimental probability that a paper clip dropped from a height of 30 cm will stay within 5 cm of the point where it falls.

7 Write down the numbers of male and female children in your family. Follow the method of Example 1. Hence find the experimental probability that your first-born child will be a boy.

8 Make a survey of the first 10 vehicles that pass your school gates. How many were cars? Use your result to predict how many of the next 10 vehicles will be cars. Check your prediction on the next 10 vehicles.

9 Open this book at any page. Read the right-hand page number. Write down whether the page number includes a 5 or not.

Repeat 50 times, recording your results as shown in Table 21.5.

page number has a 5 in it	
page number has no 5s in it	

Table 21.5

Find the experimental probability that if this book is opened anywhere, the right-hand page number will have a 5 in it.

10 Number the faces of a hexagonal pencil from 1 to 6 (Fig. 21.5).

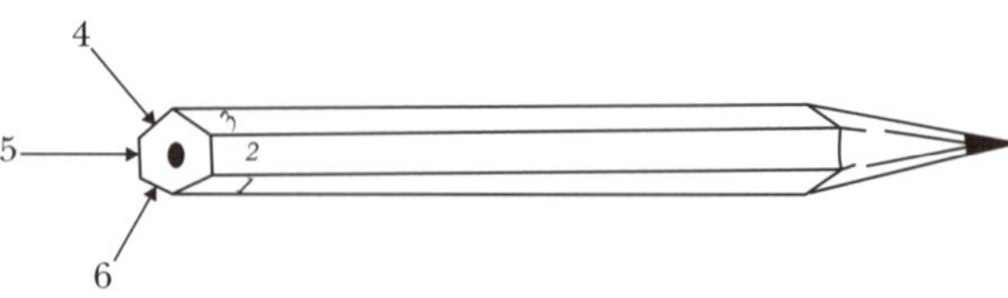

Fig. 21.5

Roll the pencil across your desk. Make a note of the number on the top face when it stops. Repeat 100 times.

How many times did you roll a number 4? What is the experimental probability of rolling a number 4?

Probability as a fraction

Probability is a measure of the likelihood of a **required outcome** happening. It is usually given as a fraction:

$$\text{probability} = \frac{\text{number of required outcomes}}{\text{number of possible outcomes}}$$

In Example 1, the required outcomes were female children and the possible outcomes were both male and female children. Thus, the probability of having a female child

$$= \frac{\text{number of female children}}{\text{number of male and female children}}$$

$$= \frac{36}{60} = \frac{3}{5} = 0{\cdot}6$$

If we are completely sure that something will happen, the probability is 1. For example, if today is Tuesday, the probability that tomorrow is Wednesday is 1.

If we are sure that something *cannot* happen, the probability is 0. For example, the probability of rolling a 7 on the pencil in Fig. 21.5 is 0, because there is no number 7 on the pencil.

If the probability of something happening is x, then the probability of it *not* happening is $1 - x$. For example, if the probability of it raining next month is $\frac{9}{12}$, then the probability of it *not* raining is $\frac{3}{12}$.

Example 2

It is known that out of every 1 000 new cars, 50 develop a mechanical fault in the first 3 months. What is the probability of buying a car that will develop a mechanical fault within 3 months?

$$\begin{aligned} \text{Number of cars developing faults} &= 50 \\ \text{Number of cars altogether} &= 1\,000 \\ \text{Probability of buying a faulty car} &= \frac{50}{1\,000} = \frac{1}{20} \end{aligned}$$

Example 3

A market trader has 100 oranges for sale. Four of them are bad. What is the probability that an orange chosen at random is good?

'At random' means 'without carefully choosing'.

Either:

Four out of 100 oranges are bad,

thus 96 out of 100 oranges are good.

Probability of getting a good orange $= \frac{96}{100} = \frac{24}{25}$

or:

probability of getting a bad orange $= \frac{4}{100} = \frac{1}{25}$

thus,

probability of getting a good orange $= 1 - \frac{1}{25} = \frac{24}{25}$

Example 4

A tray of eggs contains 18 large-sized eggs and 12 small-sized eggs. An egg is selected at random. Find the probability of selecting

a) a small-sized egg

b) either a small-sized or a large-sized egg

c) neither a small-sized nor a large-sized egg.

a) There are 12 small-sized eggs out of 30 eggs in the tray.

Probability of selecting a small-sized egg

$$= \frac{12}{30}$$
$$= \frac{2}{5} = 0{\cdot}4$$

b) It is certain that either a small-sized or a large-sized egg will be selected.

Probability $= \frac{30}{30} = 1$

c) The eggs are either large or small. It is impossible to select any other size.

Probability of neither large nor small $= \frac{0}{30} = 0$

Example 5

The Grammar School enters candidates for the WASSCE. The results for the years 1996 to 2000 are given in

Table 21.6.

year	1996	1997	1998	1999	2000
number of candidates	86	93	102	117	116
number gaining WASSCE passes	51	56	57	65	70

Table 21.6

a) Find the school's success rate as a percentage.

b) What is the approximate probability of a student at The Grammar School getting a WASSCE pass?

a) Total number of passes

$$= 51 + 56 + 57 + 65 + 70$$
$$= 299$$

Total number of candidates

$$= 86 + 93 + 102 + 117 + 116$$
$$= 514$$

$$\begin{aligned} \text{Success rate as a fraction} &= \frac{299}{514} \\ &= 0{\cdot}58 \text{ to 2 s.f.} \\ \text{Success rate as a percentage} &= 0.58 \times 100\% \\ &= 58\% \end{aligned}$$

b) The probability of a student getting a WASSCE pass $\simeq$ 0.58

$= 0{\cdot}6$ to 1 s.f.

In part *b)* it is assumed that the student's chances of success are the same as the school's success rate.

Exercise 21c

1 Answer the following questions:

a) The probability of passing an examination is 0·8. What is the probability of failing the examination?

b) The probability that a girl wins a race is 0·6. What is the probability that she loses?

c) The probability that a pen does not write is 0·05. What is the probability that it writes?

2 A die has six faces numbered 1 to 6. If the die is rolled once, find the probability of

a) obtaining the number 6,

b) obtaining the number 10,

c) not obtaining the number 6,

d) obtaining one of the numbers 1, 2, 3, 4, 5 or 6.

3 A collection of books consists of six maths books and four English books. A book is chosen at random from the collection. Find the probability of choosing

a) a maths book

b) an English book

c) either a maths or an English book

d) neither a maths nor an English book.

4 There are six red balls and nine blue balls in a box. A ball is selected at random. Find the probability that the ball is

a) red, **b)** blue, **c)** red or blue, **d)** yellow.

5 Out of 10 students, the favourite drink of seven is Coke and the favourite drink of the rest is Fanta. One of the students is chosen at random. What is the probability that the favourite drink of the student is

a) Coke,

b) Fanta,

c) neither Coke nor Fanta,

d) either Coke or Fanta?

6 A coin is tossed once. What is the probability of obtaining.

a) a head,

b) a head or a tail,

c) neither a head nor a tail?

7 Statistics show that four out of every 100 new radios break down within the first year. What is the probability of buying a radio which does not break down in the first year?

8 It has rained on 5th June 18 times in the last 20 years. What is the probability that it will rain on 5th June next year?

9 The midday temperatures in Bo for a week in February were 26°C, 26°C, 27°C, 27°C, 26°C, 27°C, 27°C. What is the probability that the midday temperature on the next day will be

a) 2°C, **b)** 35°C, **c)** 26°C, **d)** 27°C?

10 A matchbox contains 15 used sticks and 25 unused sticks.

a) How many sticks are in the box altogether?

b) What is the probability that a stick chosen at random is unused?

11 A statistical survey shows that four out of every 10 women wear a size 16 dress. What is the probability that a woman chosen at random does not wear a size 16 dress?

12 An advertisement says, 'seven out of every 10 people prefer *Red Ring* margarine.' Fifty people were asked which margarine they preferred. If the advertisement is true, approximately how many people will say *Red Ring*?

13 A trader has 100 mangoes for sale. Twenty of them are unripe. Another five of them are bad. If a mango is picked at random, find the probability that it is **a)** unripe, **b)** bad, **c)** neither unripe nor bad?

If 20 of the mangoes were chosen at random, how many would you expect to be **d)** unripe, **e)** bad?

14 It is known that one in 40 of the light-bulbs sold by a certain trader is faulty. If one bulb is taken at random from a large number, what is the probability of it being a good one?

15 Adu and Ebenezer play table tennis together. They have already played 10 games and Adu has won nine of them. What is the probability that he will win the 11th game?

16 Given the data of question 15, Ebenezer wins the 11th and 12th games. What is the probability that he will win the 13th game?

17 A crate contains 15 bottles of Coke and nine bottles of Sprite. If I choose a bottle at random, what is the probability that it is **a)** Coke, **b)** Sprite, **c)** either Coke or Sprite, **d)** neither Coke nor Sprite?

18 Twenty cards are numbered from 1 to 20. A card is chosen at random. What is the probability that it does *not* have the digit 1 in its number?

19 Table 21.7 shows the numbers of pupils getting a place in secondary school from Model Primary School for the years 1996 to 2000.

a) Find Model Primary School's success rate

as a percentage.

b) Find the approximate probability that a pupil chosen at random from Model Primary School will gain a secondary school place.

	1996	1997	1998	1999	2000
number of pupils leaving Model Primary School	54	58	60	63	65
number of pupils gaining a secondary school place	25	26	31	28	34

Table 21.7

20 Table 21.8 gives the results of a traffic survey on a city road one morning. The table shows the total number of vehicles per hour and those that were cars and lorries.

	total number of vehicles	number of cars	number of lorries
0800–0900	46	28	3
0900–1000	37	14	10
1000–1100	32	13	14
1100–1200	35	20	12

Table 21.8

a) For the whole morning, find the total number of vehicles, cars and lorries.

b) Find the percentage of the vehicles that were cars.

c) Find the percentage of the vehicles that were lorries.

d) Find the probability that the next vehicle to come along the road is a car.

e) Of the next 20 vehicles on the road, how many would you expect to be lorries?

Chapter summary

1. When experimental data are used to predict further events, the prediction is called *experimental probability*.

2. If there are n possible outcomes and r required outcomes, the *probability*, p, of obtaining a required outcome is given as a fraction

$$\text{probability, } p = \frac{\text{number of required outcomes}}{\text{number of possible outcomes}} = \frac{r}{n}$$

   where p lies between 0 and 1. p may be expressed as a common fraction, a decimal fraction or a percentage.

3. If an *outcome is certain to happen*, its probability is 1.

4. If an *outcome is certain* **not** *to happen*, its probability is 0 (zero).

5. If the probability of an event happening is p, then the *probability of the event not happening* is $1 - p$.

22 Inequalities (1)

Greater than and less than

In mathematics, we probably use the equals sign, =, more than any other. For example, $5 + 3 = 8$.

However, many quantities are *not* equal:

$5 + 5 \neq 8$

where $\neq$ means *is not equal to.* We can also write:

$5 + 5 > 8$

where > means *is greater than.* Similarly we can write the following:

$3 + 3 \neq 8$
$3 + 3 < 8$

where < means *is less than.*

$\neq$, > and < are **inequality symbols**. They tell us that quantities are not equal. The > and < symbols are more helpful than $\neq$. They tell us more. For example, $x \neq 0$ tells us that x does not have the value 0; x can be any positive or negative number. However, $x < 0$ tells us that x is less than 0; x must be a negative number.

Exercise 22a

1 Rewrite each of the following, using either > or < instead of the words.

a) 6 is less than 11
b) −1 is greater than −5
c) 0 is greater than −2·4
d) −3 is less than +3
e) x is greater than 12
f) y is less than −2
g) 4 is greater than a
h) a is less than 4
i) 15 is less than b
j) b is greater than 15

2 State whether each of the following is true or false.

a) $13 > 5$ b) $19 < 21$
c) $-2 < -4$ d) $-15 > 7$
e) $3 + 9 < 10$ f) $0 > -4 - 3$
g) $14 - 6 > 8$ h) $30 > -50 + 20$

3 Find which symbol, > or <, goes in the box to make each statement true.

a) $9 + 8 \square 10$ b) $7 - 2 \square 7$
c) $6 \square 12 - 5$ d) $0 \square 3 - 6$
e) $16 \square 2 \times 10$ f) $29 \div 7 \square 3.6$
g) $13 \square 3 \times 4{\cdot}9$ h) $(-5)^2 \square (2)^2$

The symbols > and < can be used to change word statements into algebraic statements.

Example 1

The distance between two villages is over 18 km. *Write this as an algebraic statement.*

Let the distance between the villages be d km.
Then, $d > 18$

A statement like $d > 18$ is called an **inequality**.

Example 2

I have x leones. I spend Le20. *The amount I have left is less than* Le5. *Write an inequality in x.*

I spend Le20 out of x leones.
Thus I have $x - 20$ leones left.
Thus $x - 20 < 5$

Example 3

The area of a square is less than 25 cm². *What can be said about a) the length of one of its sides, b) its perimeter?*

a) Let the length of a side of the square be a cm.
Then, $a^2 < 25$

Thus $\sqrt{a^2} < \sqrt{25}$
$a < 5$

b) Perimeter $= 4a$
$a < 5$
Thus, $4a < 4 \times 5$
$4a < 20$

The length of a side of the square is less than 5 cm. Its perimeter is less than 20 cm.

Exercise 22b

1 For each of the following, write an inequality in terms of the given unknown.
   a) The height of the building, h m, is less than 5 m.
   b) The mass of the student, m kg, is less than 50 kg.
   c) The cost of the meal, Lex, was over Le5.
   d) The time taken, t min, was under 5 minutes.
   e) The number of pages, n, was less than 24.
   f) The mass of the letter, m g, was under 20 g.
   g) The cost of the stamp, n leones, was less than Le2 500.
   h) The time for the journey, t min, was over 2 hours.

2 For each of the following, choose a letter for the unknown and write an inequality.
   a) The student is less than 1·5 m tall.
   b) The capacity of the bottle is less than 800 ml.
   c) The book cost more than Le1 200.
   d) The student got over 60% in the exam.
   e) The car used more than 28 litres of petrol.
   f) Her mass was less than 55 kg.
   g) The light was on for over 6 hours.

3 Seven lorries each carry a load of over 4 tonnes. The total mass carried by the lorries is m tonnes. Write an inequality in m.

4 A boy saved over Le500. His father gave him another Le200. The boy now had Ley altogether. Write an inequality in y.

5 In 3 years' time a girl will be over 18 years of age. If her age now is x years, write an inequality in x.

6 There are x goats on a field of area 3 ha. There are less than 20 goats on each hectare. Write an inequality in x.

7 A square has an area of more than 36 cm^2. What can be said about **a)** the length of one of its sides, **b)** its perimeter?

8 The perimeter of a square is less than 28 cm. What can be said about **a)** the length of one of its sides, **b)** its area?

Not greater than and not less than

In most towns there is a speed limit of 50 km/h. If a car, travelling at s km/h, is within the limit, then s is not greater than 50. If $s < 50$ or if $s = 50$, the speed limit will not be broken. This can be written as one inequality:

$s \leqslant 50$

where $\leqslant$ means *is less than or equal to*. Thus, *not greater than* means the same as *less than or equal to.*

In most countries, voters in elections must not be less than 18 years of age. If a person of age a years is able to vote, then a is not less than 18. The person can vote if $a > 18$ or if $a = 18$. This can be written as one inequality:

$a \geqslant 18$

where $\geqslant$ means *is greater than or equal to*. Thus, *not less than* means the same as *greater than or equal to.*

Example 4

Notebooks cost Le600 *each. Deborah has d leones. It is not enough to buy a notebook. Taiwo has t leones. He is able to buy a notebook. What can be said about the values of d and t?*

The question tells us that d is less than 600.
$d < 600$
If Taiwo gets no change, then $t = 600$
If Taiwo gets some change, then $t > 600$
It is not known if Taiwo gets change or not.
Thus, $t \geqslant 600$
Finally, Taiwo clearly has more money than Deborah.
Thus, $t > d$
Similarly,
$d < t$
In conclusion, the following can be said about d and t:

$d < 600 \qquad t \geqslant 600$
$t > d \qquad d < t$

Notice that $t > d$ and $d < t$ are two ways of saying the same thing. It is like saying $9 > 4$ and $4 < 9$.

Exercise 22c

1 For each of the following, write an inequality in terms of the given unknown.

a) The age of the student, a years, was 12 years or less.
b) The number of goals, n, was five or more.
c) The temperature, t°C, was not greater than 38°C.
d) The selling price, Les, was not less than Le2 400.
e) The number of students, n, was less than 36.
f) The speed of the car, v km/h, was never more than 120 km/h.

2 For each of the following, choose a letter for the unknown and then write an inequality.
a) The lorry can carry a load of not more than 7 tonnes.
b) My car cannot go faster than 140 km/h.
c) To join the police force, you must be not less than 160 cm tall.
d) The taxi cannot carry more than five passengers.
e) The well must be not less than 6 m deep.
f) Each cow needs at least 100 m^2 of grazing land.

3 The pass mark in a test was 27. One person got x marks and failed. Another got y marks and passed. What can be said about x and y?

4 Pencils cost 12c each. a cents is not enough to buy a pencil. A person with b cents is able to buy a pencil. Write down three different inequalities in terms of a or b or both.

5 The radius of a circle is not greater than 3 m. What can be said about **a)** its circumference, **b)** its area? Give any inequalities in terms of π.

Graphs of inequalities

The inequality $x < 2$ means that x can have any value less than 2. We can show these values on the number line in Fig. 22.1.

Fig. 22.1

The heavy arrowed line in Fig. 22.1 shows the range of values that x can have. The empty circle at 2 shows that the value 2 is not included. x can have any value to the left of 2.

The inequality $x \geqslant -1$ means that x can have the value -1 or any value greater than -1. Its graph is given in Fig. 22.2.

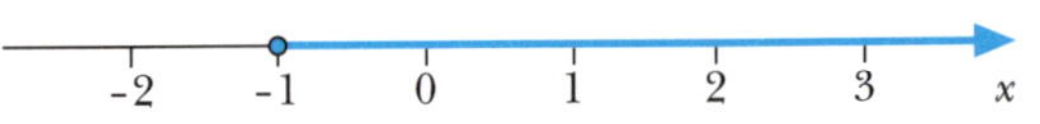

Fig. 22.2

The shaded circle in Fig. 22.2 shows that the value -1 is included. x can have the value -1 and any value to the right of -1.

Example 5

Fig. 22.3 shows the graph of an inequality. What is the inequality?

Fig. 22.3

The shaded circle above 4 shows that the value $x = 4$ is included. The heavy line to the left of 4 shows that x can have values in the range $x < 4$. Thus Fig. 22.3 is the graph of $x \leqslant 4$.

Exercise 22d

1 Write down the inequalities shown in the following graphs.

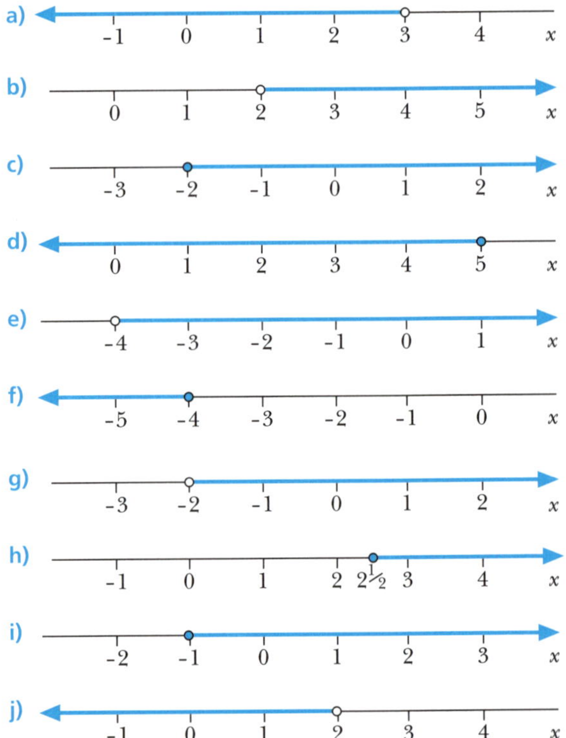

Fig. 22.4

2 Sketch graphs of the following inequalities.

a) $x > 1$	**b)** $x < -2$
c) $x \geqslant -3$	**d)** $x \leqslant 0$
e) $x < 3$	**f)** $x \geqslant -2$
g) $x \geqslant 4$	**h)** $x < -1$
i) $x \leqslant -2$	**j)** $x > 0$

Solution of inequalities

Consider a compound in which 23 people live. At any one time there may be x people in the compound. If all 23 people are in the compound, then $x = 23$. This is an equation.

If some people have left the compound, then $x < 23$. This is an inequality.

The equation has only one solution: $x = 23$.

The inequality has many solutions: if $x < 23$, then x can have the values

0, 1, 2, 3, ..., 20, 21, 22.

Notice that negative and fractional values of x are impossible in this example.

Inequalities are solved in much the same way as equations. We can use the balance method. However, there is one important difference. This will be shown in Examples 9 and 10. Meanwhile, read the following examples carefully.

Example 6

Solve the inequality $x + 4 < 6$.

$x + 4 < 6$

Subtract 4 from both sides.

$x + 4 - 4 < 6 - 4$

$x < 2$

$x < 2$ is the solution. We do not normally try to list the values of the unknown. Fig. 22.1 is the graph of the solution of $x + 4 < 6$.

Example 7

Solve $6 \leqslant 2x - 1$ *and show the solution on a graph.*

$6 \leqslant 2x - 1$

Add 1 to both sides.

$7 \leqslant 2x$

Divide both sides by 2.

$\frac{7}{2} \leqslant \frac{2x}{2}$

$3\frac{1}{2} \leqslant x$

If $3\frac{1}{2} \leqslant x$ then $x \geqslant 3\frac{1}{2}$

$x \geqslant 3\frac{1}{2}$ is the solution of $6 \leqslant 2x - 1$. The graph of the solution is given in Fig. 22.5.

Fig. 22.5

Normally we arrange for the unknown to be on the left-hand side of the inequality. This makes it easier to sketch the graph.

Exercise 22e

Solve the following inequalities. Sketch a graph of each solution.

1 $x - 2 < 3$	**2** $x + 3 \geqslant 6$
3 $a + 5 > 7$	**4** $y - 3 \leqslant 5$
5 $2 > x - 4$	**6** $7 < x + 2$
7 $x + 9 \leqslant 3$	**8** $0 > x + 5$
9 $2x < 6$	**10** $5x \geqslant 45$
11 $12 \geqslant 3x$	**12** $-10 < 5x$
13 $4x \geqslant -9$	**14** $8 \leqslant 3x$
15 $3x + 1 < 13$	**16** $5x - 2 \geqslant 8$
17 $-5 > 4x + 15$	**18** $3 \leqslant 17 + 2x$
19 $4x - 2 > 19$	**20** $3 \leqslant 3x + 5$

Example 8

Find the values of x that satisfy the inequality $3x - 3 > 7$*, such that x is an integer.*

Note: an **integer** is any whole number. $-3, 0, 22$ are examples of integers.

$3x - 3 > 7$

Add 3 to both sides.

$3x > 10$

Divide both sides by 3.

$x > 3\frac{1}{3}$

But x must be an integer.

Thus x can have values 4, 5, 6, ...

$x = 4, 5, 6, \ldots$ is the solution.

Exercise 22f

Solve the following inequalities, given that x is an integer in each case.

1 $x \leqslant 0$	**2** $x > 5\frac{1}{2}$
3 $2x > 9$	**4** $3x < 7$
5 $4x < -11$	**6** $4x > -14$
7 $3 > 5x$	**8** $-8 < 3x$
9 $2x + 1 < 12$	**10** $5x - 7 > 9$
11 $7x > 5x - 9$	**12** $8x < 5x - 10$

13 $6 > 4x + 1$
14 $3x + 20 > 4$
15 $2x + 4 \leqslant 2$
16 $5x - 8 \geqslant 12$
17 $1 \geqslant 6x - 11$
18 $3x - 8 \leqslant 5x$
19 $8x + 16 \leqslant 0$
20 $x + 4 \geqslant 10x - 23$

Multiplication and division by negative numbers

Consider the following true statement: $5 > 3$.

Multiply both sides of the inequality by -2. This gives $-10 > -6$.

But this is a false statement. In fact, -10 is less than -6.

Similarly, if both sides of $5 > 3$ are divided by -2, the result is $-2\frac{1}{2} > -1\frac{1}{2}$. This is also false.

In general, if both sides of an inequality are multiplied or divided by a negative number, the inequality sign must be reversed. For example, if $-2x > 10$ is true, then, on division throughout by -2, $x < -5$ will be true.

Example 9

Solve $5 - x > 3$.

Either:

$$5 - x > 3$$

Subtract 5 from both sides.

$$-x > -2$$

Multiply both sides by -1 and reverse the inequality.

$$(-1) \times (-x) < (-1) \times (-2)$$
$$x < 2$$

Or:

$$5 - x > 3$$

Add x to both sides.

$$5 > 3 + x$$

Subtract 3 from both sides.

$$2 > x$$

thus, $x < 2$

The second method in Example 9 shows that the rule of reversing the inequality sign when multiplying by a negative number is correct.

Example 10

Solve $19 \geqslant 4 - 5x$.

$$19 \geqslant 4 - 5x$$

Subtract 4 from both sides.

$$15 \geqslant -5x$$

Divide both sides by -5 and reverse the inequality sign.

$$\frac{15}{-5} \leqslant \frac{-5x}{-5}$$

$$-3 \leqslant x$$

or $x \geqslant -3$

Example 11

Solve the following inequalities:

a) $y + 8 > 3$
b) $\frac{1}{3}x < -1$
c) $3 - 2x < 8$

a) $y + 8 > 3$
Subtract 8 from both sides.
$y + 8 - 8 > 3 - 8$
$y > -5$

b) $\frac{1}{3}x < -1$
Multiply both sides by 3.
$\frac{1}{3}x \times 3 < -1 \times 3$
$x < -3$

c) $3 - 2x < 8$
Subtract 3 from both sides.
$3 - 2x - 3 < 8 - 3$
$-2x < 5$
Divide both sides by -2 and reverse the inequality sign.

$$\frac{-2x}{-2} > \frac{5}{-2}$$

$$x > -2\frac{1}{2}$$

Exercise 22g

Solve the following inequalities.

1 $-2x < 8$
2 $-3a < -6$
3 $12 \geqslant -4m$
4 $40 \leqslant -5d$
5 $-m \geqslant 7$
6 $-3x > 21$
7 $-\frac{1}{2}y \leqslant 7$
8 $\frac{2}{3} \geqslant -16a$
9 $4 \geqslant -3t$
10 $-2n < -8$
11 $3 - y \leqslant 7$
12 $5 - y \geqslant 1$
13 $5 - 2a > 1$
14 $2 - n \leqslant 3$
15 $-6 - x > 10$
16 $-2x + 4 \geqslant 6$
17 $10 - 3x \leqslant -11$
18 $15 \leqslant 3 - 4x$
19 $2r \geqslant 5r + 6$
20 $9 \leqslant 3 - 4t$

Word problems involving inequalities

Example 11

A triangle has sides of x cm, $(x + 4)$ cm *and* 11 cm, *where* x *is a whole number of* cm. *If the perimeter of the triangle is less than* 32 cm, *find the possible values of* x.

Perimeter of triangle $= x + (x + 4) + 11$

Thus, $x + (x + 4) + 11 < 32$

$2x + 15 < 32$

$2x < 17$

$x < 8\frac{1}{2}$

Also, in any triangle the sum of the lengths of any two sides must be greater than the length of the third side.

Thus, $x + (x + 4) > 11$

$2x + 4 > 11$

$2x > 7$

$x > 3\frac{1}{2}$

Thus $x < 8\frac{1}{2}$ and $x > 3\frac{1}{2}$. But x must be a whole number of cm. Thus the possible values of x are 4, 5, 6, 7, or 8.

Check:

when $x = 4$, perimeter $= 4 + 8 + 11$ cm $= 23$ cm

when $x = 8$, perimeter $= 8 + 12 + 11$ cm $= 31$ cm

The lowest and highest values of x have been checked. The perimeters in both cases are less than 32 cm. There is no need to check the other values.

Exercise 22h

In each question, first make an inequality, then solve the inequality.

1 If 9 is added to a number x, the result is greater than 17. Find the values of x.

2 If 7·3 is subtracted from y, the result is less than 3·4. Find the values of y.

3 Three times a certain number is not greater than 54. Find the range of values of the number.

4 Five times a whole number, x, is subtracted from 62. The result is less than 40. Find the three lowest values of x.

5 x is a whole number. If three-quarters of x is subtracted from 1, the result is always greater than 0. Find the four highest values of x.

6 A man gets a monthly pay of Lex. His monthly rent is Le80 000. After paying his rent, he is left with less than Le2 00 000. Find the range of values of x.

7 A book contains 192 pages. A boy reads x complete pages every day. If he has not finished the book after 10 days, find the highest possible value of x.

8 A rectangle is x cm long and 10 cm wide. Find the range of values of x if the area of the rectangle is not less than 120 cm^2.

9 A triangle has a base of length 6 cm and an area of less than 12 cm^2. What can be said about its height?

10 Last month a woman had a body mass of 53 kg. She reduced this by x kg so that she is now below 50 kg. Assuming that $x < 6$, find the range of values of x.

11 A rectangle is 8 cm long and b cm broad. Find the range of values of b if the perimeter of the rectangle is not greater than 50 cm and not less than 18 cm.

12 The sides of a triangle are x cm, $x + 3$ cm and 10 cm. If x is a whole number of cm, find the lowest value of x.
Hint: the sum of the lengths of any two sides of a triangle must be greater than the length of the third side.

13 An isosceles triangle has sides of length x cm, x cm and 9 cm. Its perimeter is less than 24 cm and x is a whole number.
a) Find the lowest value of x.
b) Find the highest value of x.

14 On a journey of 120 km, a motorist averages less than 60 km/h. Will the journey take more or less than 2 hours?

15 A student cycles a distance of 63 km in less than 3 hours. What is the average speed?

Chapter summary

(1) The common inequality symbols and their meanings are:

$\neq$ is not equal to
$>$ is greater than
$<$ is less than
$\geqslant$ is greater than or equal to
$\leqslant$ is less than or equal to

(2) Inequalities can be shown on graphs (see Figs 22.1 and 22.2 where the unshaded circle shows that the value 2 is not included and the shaded circle shows that the value -1 is included).

(3) The balance method for solving equations can be applied to inequalities. However, there is *one important exception* (shown at **c)** below). An inequality will remain the same:

a) if the same number is added to or subtracted from both sides,

b) if both sides are multiplied or divided by the same positive number,

c) if both sides are multiplied or divided by the same negative number *and the inequality sign is reversed*.

23 Bearings and distances

Direction

The four main directions

There are four main **directions**: north (N), south (S), east (E) and west (W). The sun rises in the east and sets in the west.

If you face east and turn through an angle of 90° to your left, you will face north.

If you face north and turn through an angle of 90° to the left, you will face west.

To face south, face east, then turn through an angle of 90° to the right. See Fig. 23.1.

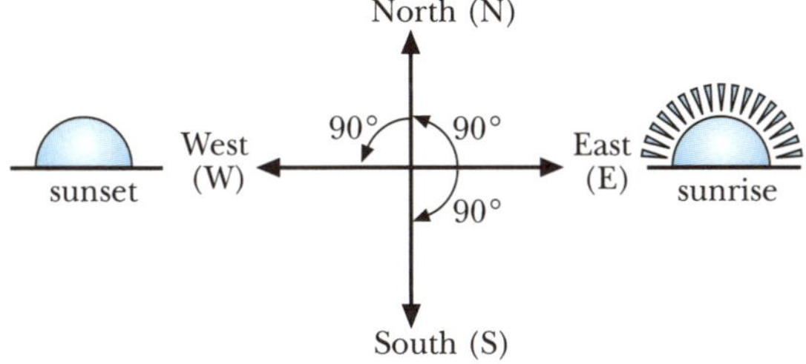

Fig. 23.1

In Fig. 23.2, the four main directions are shown on a map of Sierra Leone.

Fig. 23.2

The magnetic compass

Fig. 23.3 is a photograph of a **magnetic compass**.

Fig. 23.3

The magnetic compass is used for finding **direction**. It has a magnetic needle which always points in the direction **north**.

Points of the compass

Fig. 23.4 shows the main **points** of the compass.

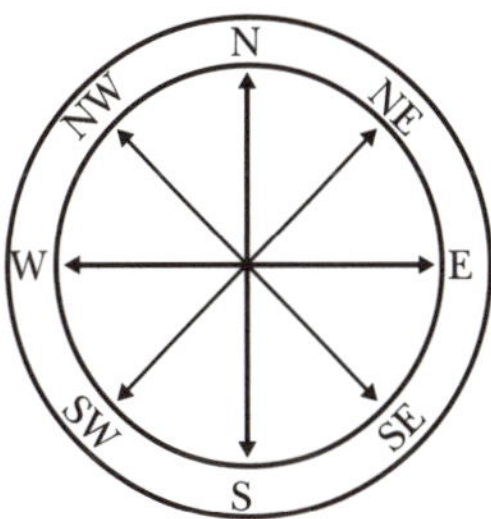

Fig. 23.4

Apart from the four main points, or directions: north (N), south (S), east (E) and west (W), there are also four secondary directions: north-east (NE), south-east (SE), south-west (SW) and north-west (NW). The angle between the directions N and E is 90°. NE is the direction mid-way between N and E. Thus the angle between N and NE is 45°.

Exercise 23a *(Oral)*

1 Do the following and state the final direction that you face.

a) Face east, turn through an angle of 180°
b) Face east, turn through 45° to your right
c) Face east, turn through 90° to your right
d) Face east, turn through 90° to your left.

2 What is the angle between the following directions:

a) N and S **b)** W and E
c) NE and E **d)** N and W
e) E and SW **f)** SW and W
g) N and NW **h)** NE and SW?

Compass bearings

Fig. 23.5 shows two compasses placed at points A and B.

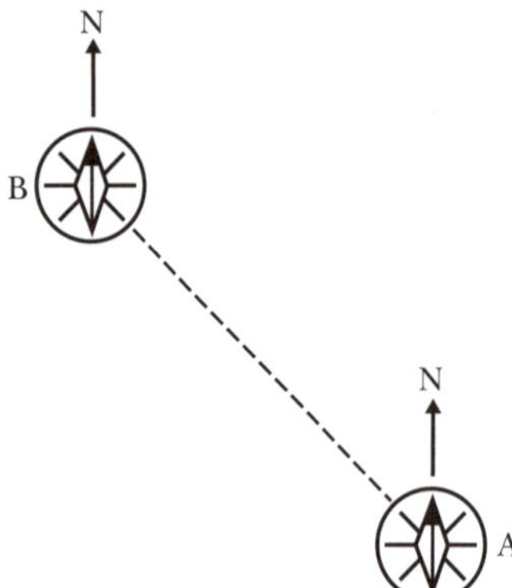

Fig. 23.5

The pointers of both compasses point northwards (N). The compass at B is in a direction NW of A. We say that the **bearing of B from A** is NW. Similarly, the compass at A is in a direction SE of B. The bearing of A from B is SE.

Exercise 23b *(Oral)*

In each of the following diagrams, state **a)** the bearing of B from A, **b)** the bearing of A from B.

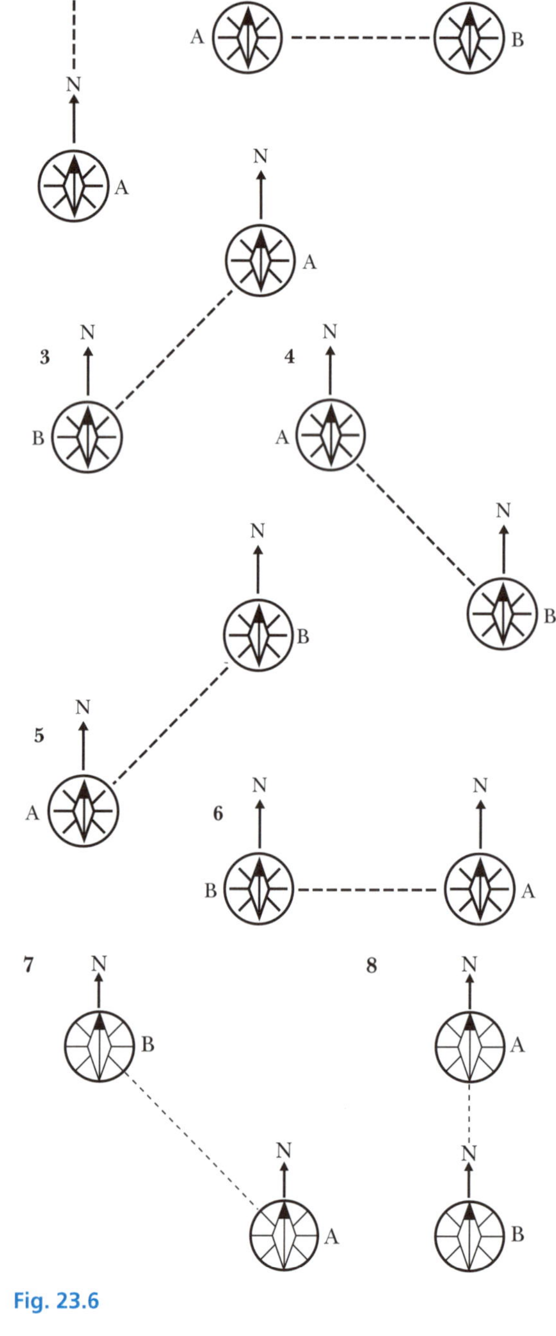

Fig. 23.6

How to state bearings

Bearings can be stated in two ways: **acute-angle bearing** and **three-figure bearing**. The first method is described here, with an exercise, then the second method is described, with a practical assignment.

Acute-angle bearings

In this section, bearings are given as acute angles measured from the north (N) or south (S).

Fig. 23.7 shows the plan of a tree, a round house, a well and a flagpole. Imagine you are standing at A with a compass.

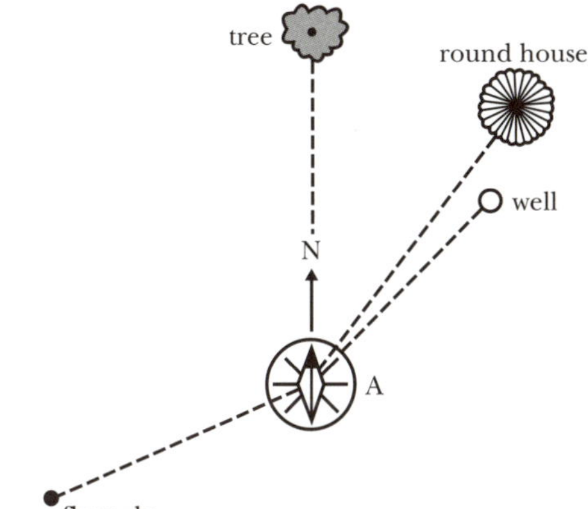

Fig. 23.7

The compass bearing of the tree from A is N. The compass bearing of the well from A is NE. It is not possible to give an exact compass bearing for the round house and the flagpole.

Fig. 23.8 shows that the direction of the round house from A makes an angle of 37° with north.

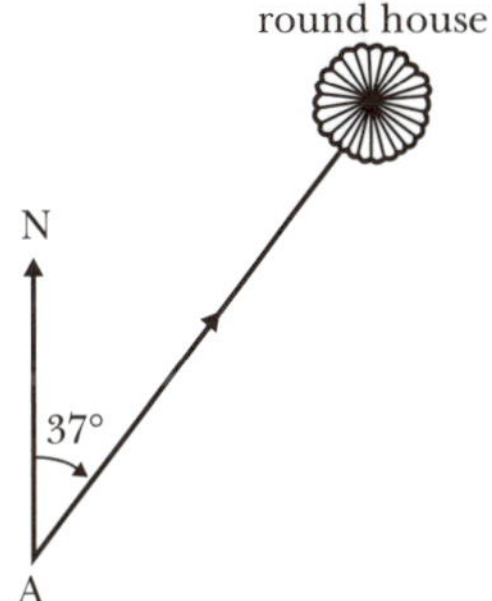

Fig. 23.8

Instead of using the directions N, NE, E, etc., we can give the bearing of the round house as the acute angle it makes with the direction North, i.e. North 37° East, or N37°E. Note that 37° is an *acute angle.*

Fig. 23.9 shows that the direction of the flagpole from A makes an angle of 66° with South.

The bearing of the flagpole is stated as S66°W, i.e. the acute angle it makes with South is 66° on the West side.

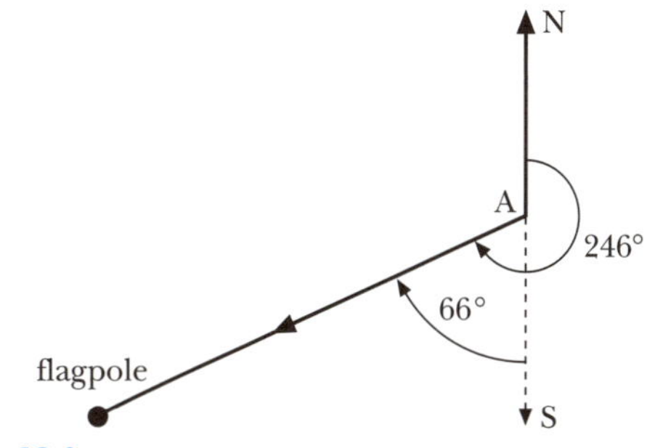

Fig. 23.9

Exercise 23c *(Oral)*

State the bearings of A from B in the following diagrams.

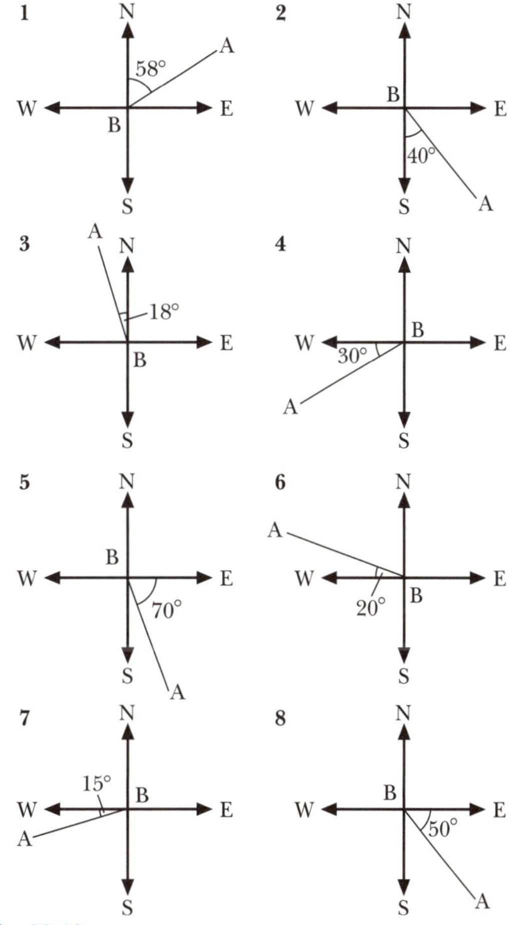

Fig. 23.10

Three-figure bearings

The second method of stating bearings is given in this section.

Three-figure bearings are given as the number of degrees from north, measured in a clockwise direction. Any direction can be given as a three-figure bearing. Three digits are always given. For angles less than 100°, zeros must be written in front of the digits. For example, the direction east is given as a bearing of 090°. The three-figure bearing of north is 000° or 360°. The three-figure bearing for N37°E is 037° and for S66°W it is 246° (Fig. 23.9).

Exercise 23d *(Practical assignment)*

1 a) Mark a point O on a piece of cardboard. With O as centre, draw round a protractor. If necessary, move the protractor so as to make a complete circle with O as centre. Use the protractor to mark off the circle in 30° intervals as shown in Fig. 23.11. Cut out the circle. The circle is a compass face.

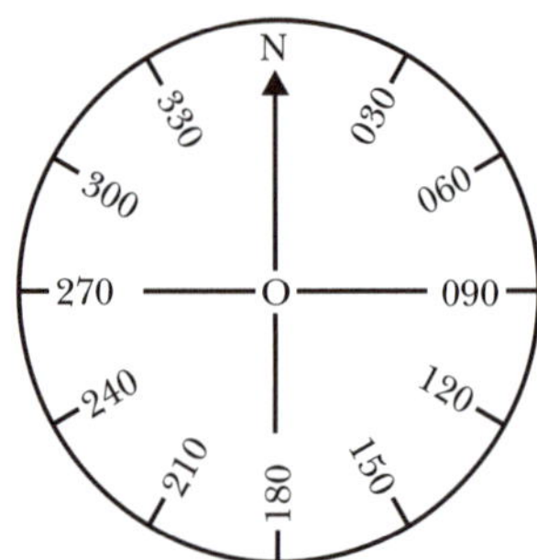

Fig. 23.11

b) Cut a pointer from a thin strip of cardboard. Push a drawing pin through the centre of the compass and the pointer as shown in Fig. 23.12. This gives a model compass. The model compass can be used for estimating the sizes of three-figure bearings.

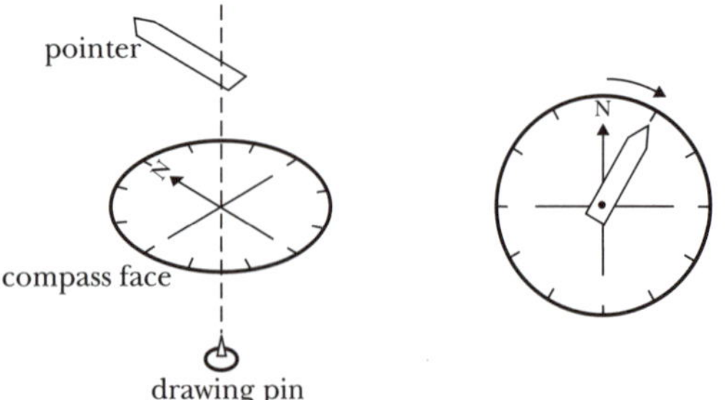

Fig. 23.12

2 For this exercise, take the front of your classroom to be north. Place your model compass so that N points towards the front of your classroom.

a) Turn the pointer and estimate the three-figure bearings of the four corners of the room to the nearest 10°. See Fig. 23.13.

b) Estimate the three-figure bearings of the following:

i) the centre of the door

ii) the centre of each window

iii) the teacher's chair

iv) the friend who is closest to you.

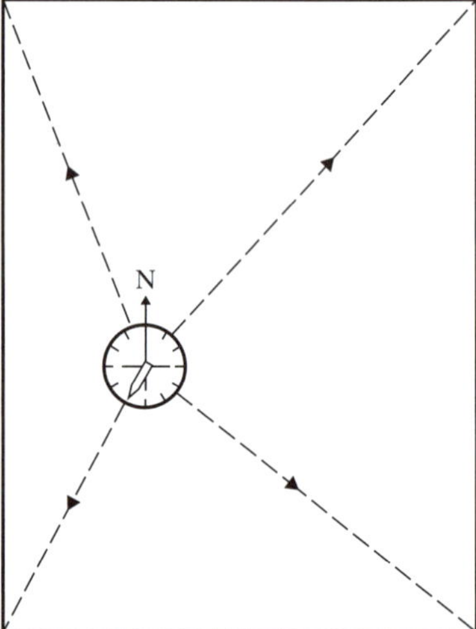

Fig. 23.13

3 Take your desk outside. Place your compass on your desk so that it points northwards (*to find north without a compass*: face the direction the sun rises (east); make a quarter turn to the left; you are now facing north). Estimate the three-figure bearings of some things in your school compound, for example: a flag-pole, the Principal's office, the corner of a classroom block, some big trees, the school gate.

Calculating bearings using three-figure method

Example 1

In Fig. 23.14, find the three-figure bearings of A, B, C *and* D *from* X.

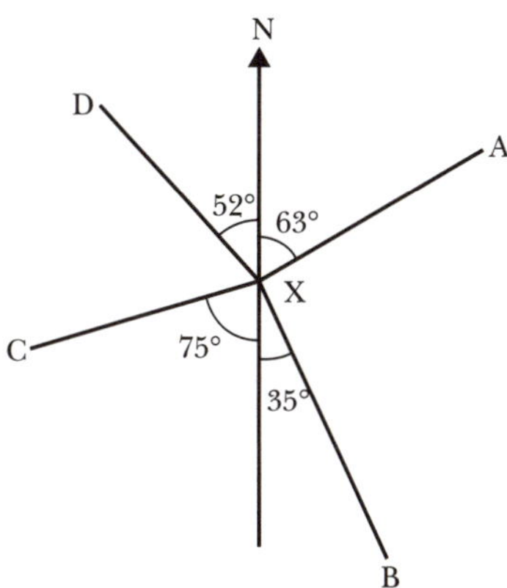

Fig. 23.14

The arrow N shows the direction north.

$N\hat{X}A = 63°$

The bearing of A from X is 063°.

$N\hat{X}B = 180° - 35° = 145°$

The bearing of B from X is 145°.

$N\hat{X}C$ clockwise $= 180° + 75° = 255°$

The bearing of C from X is 255°.

$N\hat{X}D$ clockwise $= 360° - 52° = 308°$

The bearing of D from X is 308°.

Example 2

If the bearing of X *from* Y *is* 247°, *find the bearing of* Y *from* X.

The question gives the bearing of X *from* Y. Start by drawing a point Y. Draw a line pointing north from Y. See Fig. 23.15.

Fig. 23.15

X is on a bearing 247° from Y. Sketch a line YX such that $N_1\hat{Y}X$ is 247° clockwise from the line YN_1. Mark a point X on this line. From X, draw a line pointing north. See the sketch in Fig. 23.16. The two lines pointing north are parallel. Angle N_2XY is the bearing of Y from X.

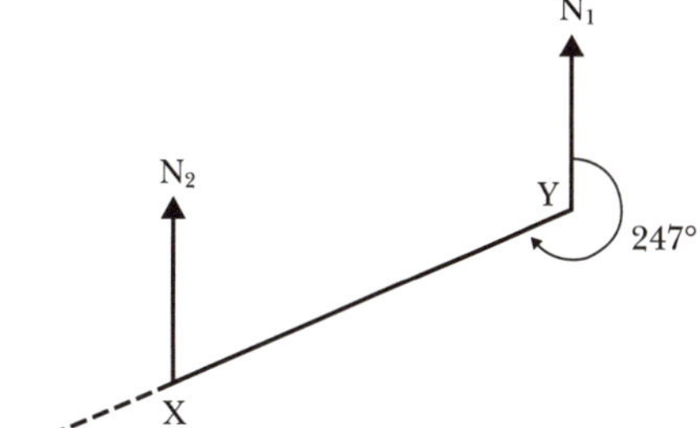

Fig. 23.16

There are many ways of finding the angle. Fig. 23.17 shows two ways. The bearing of Y from X is 067°.

a)

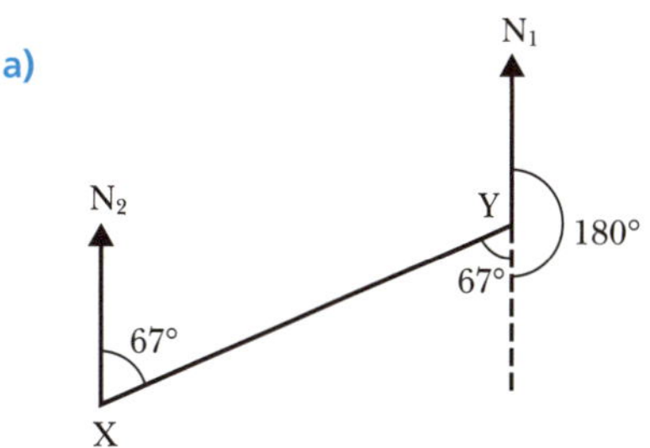

b)

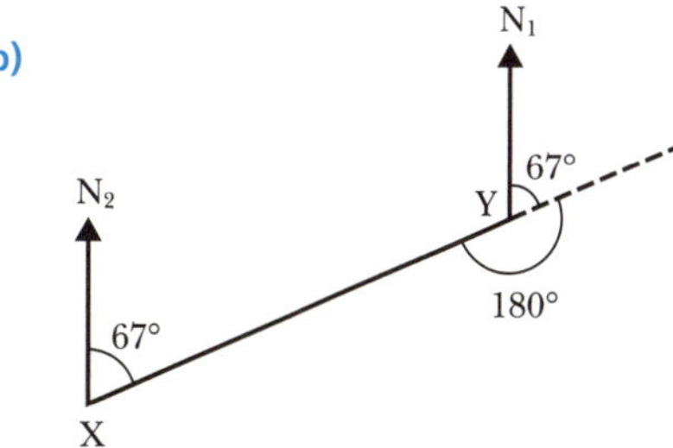

Fig. 23.17

Notice that when making sketches, it is usual to take the top of the page as north.

Exercise 23e

1 For each sketch in Fig. 23.18 state the three-figure bearing of B from A.

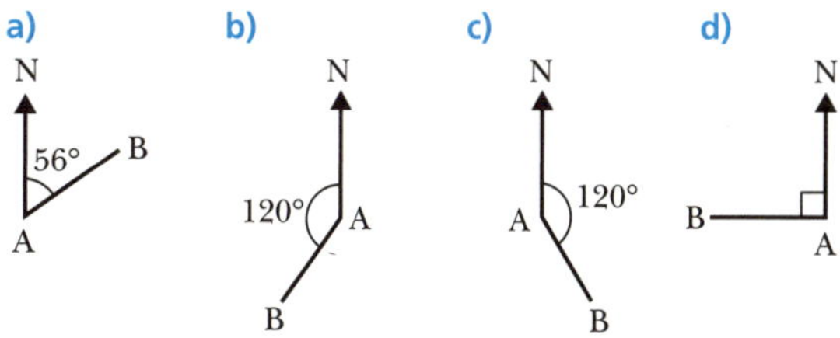

Fig. 23.18

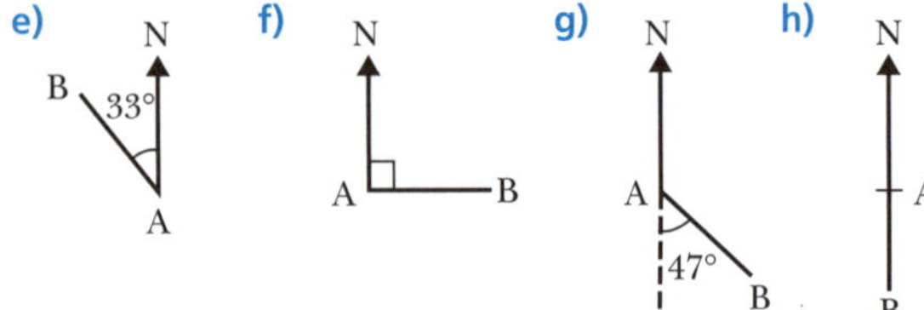

Fig. 23.18 (continued)

2 In Fig. 23.19, find the bearings of A, B, C and D from X.

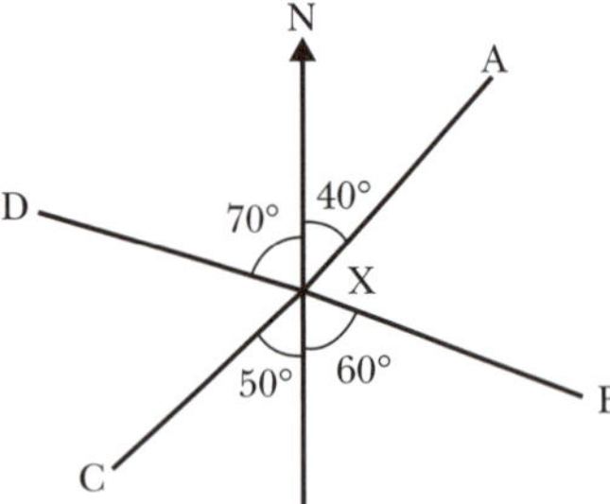

Fig. 23.19

3 In Fig. 23.20, find the bearings of U, V, X, Y, Z from O.

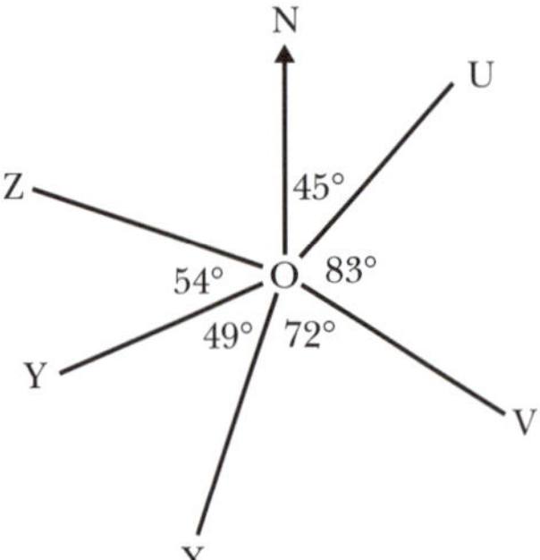

Fig. 23.20

4 Make a sketch of the following bearings. Each sketch should show all the data and must contain a line pointing north.
   a) The bearing of B from A is 040°.
   b) X is on a bearing 160° from Y.
   c) P is on a bearing 320° from Q.
   d) L is on a bearing 200° from K.
   e) The bearing of G from H is 180°.

5 In each diagram in Fig. 23.21, calculate (i) the bearing of A from B, (ii) the bearing of B from A.

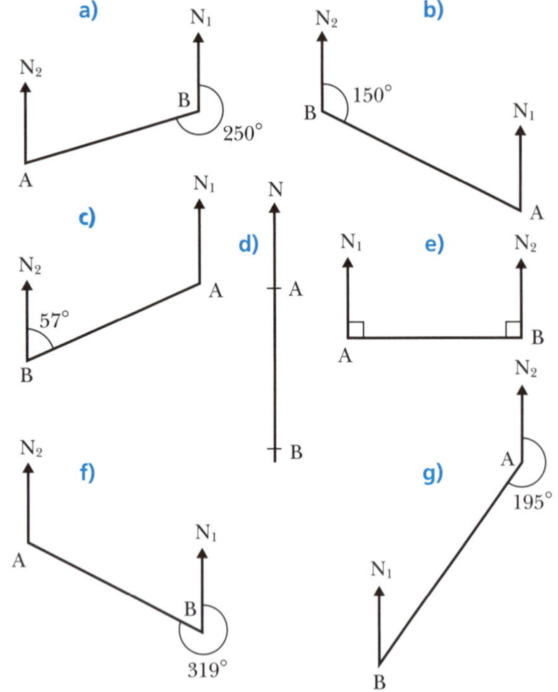

Fig. 23.21

Surveying

To **survey** an area means to take measurements so that a scale drawing of the area can be made. Fig. 23.22 shows a sketch that a student made while surveying a classroom block and a tree.

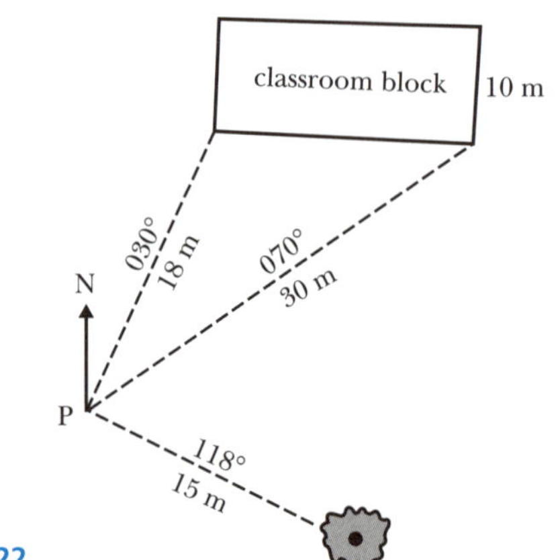

Fig. 23.22

The student has measured the bearings and distances of the tree and two corners of the classroom block from a point P. Thus, for the tree, (118°, 15 m) means that the tree is on a bearing of 118° and a distance 15 m from P. The width of the classroom block has also been measured.

Fig. 23.23 is a scale drawing of the tree and the classroom block.

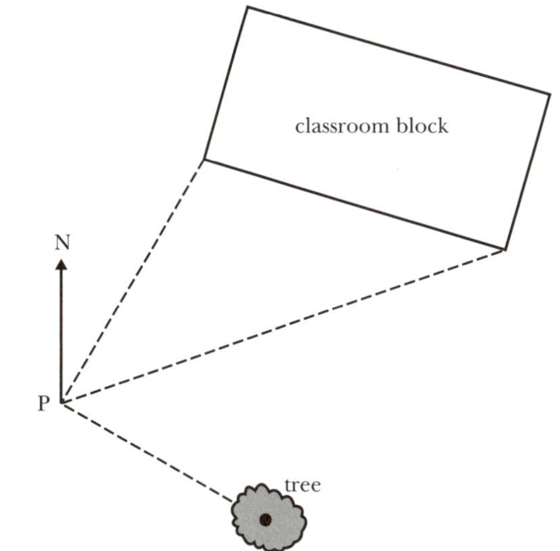

Fig. 23.23 Scale: 1 cm represents 5 m

Method: P is any point. A line pointing north is drawn from P. Lines are drawn on bearings 030°, 070° and 118° from P. These are shown dotted in Fig. 23.23. Distances of 18 m, 30 m and 15 m are marked on these lines respectively. These give the positions of the front corners of the classroom block and the centre of the tree. The rest of the classroom block is drawn, using the fact that it is 10 m wide.

Exercise 23f

1 By taking measurements on Fig. 23.23, find **a)** the length of the classroom block, **b)** the perpendicular distance of the tree from the classroom block.

2 Fig. 23.24 is a sketch and notes from a survey of three trees, A, B and C. Choose a suitable scale and draw an accurate plan of the three trees. Hence find the distance and bearing of A from C.

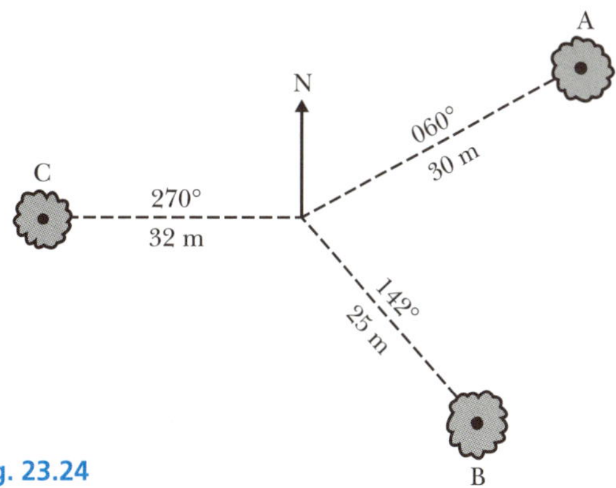

Fig. 23.24

3 Fig. 23.25 is a sketch of part of a river. A and B are 100 m apart. The bearing of the tree from A is 000°. The bearing of the tree from B is 290°. The edges of the river are roughly straight and parallel.

Make a scale drawing of points A and B and the tree. Hence find the approximate width of the river.

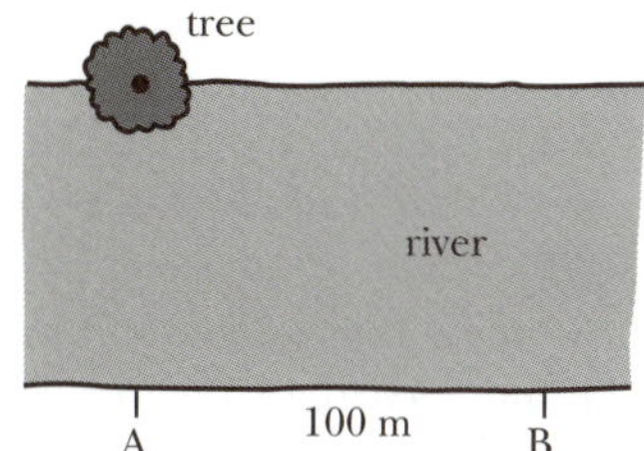

Fig. 23.25

4 Fig. 23.26 is a sketch and notes from a survey of a road. The road is in two straight parts, AB and BC. It is 5 m wide.

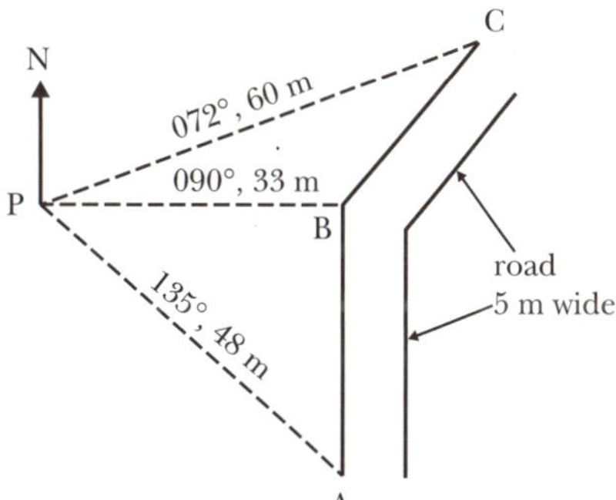

Fig. 23.26

Draw an accurate plan of the road to a suitable scale. Hence find the bearing of B from A and the bearing of C from B.

5 Fig. 23.27 is a sketch and notes from a survey of a straight length of railway line.

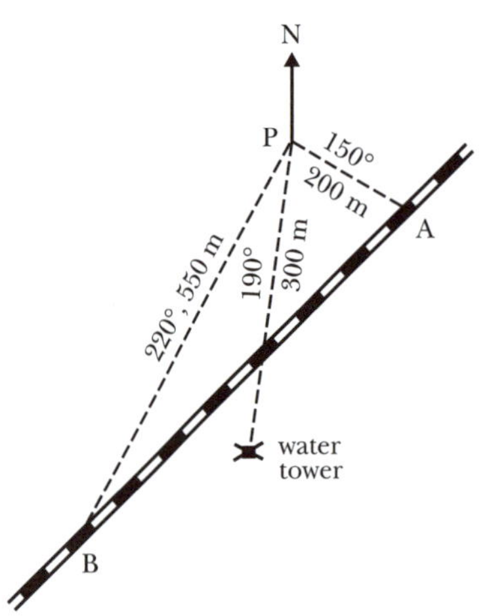

Fig. 23.27

Draw an accurate plan to show the position of the railway line and the water tower. Find the bearing of A from B. Find the distance, to the nearest 10 m, of the water tower from the railway line.

Example 3

A student starts from A and walks 3 km *east to* B. *She then walks* 5 km *on a bearing* 152° *from* B. *She reaches a point* C. *Find the distance and bearing of* C *from* A.

First make a sketch of the information. See Fig. 23.28.

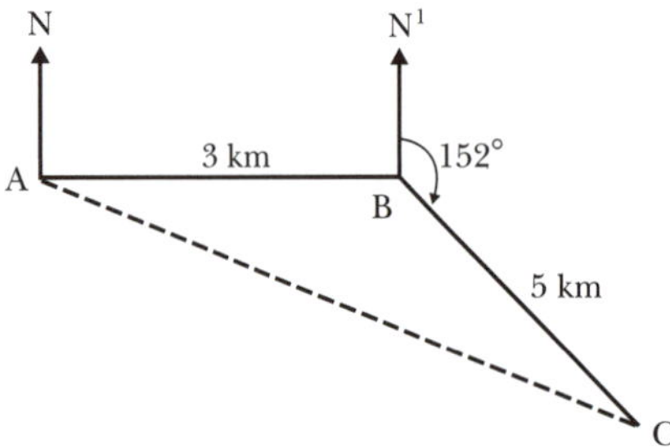

Fig. 23.28

Then make the scale drawing. See Fig. 23.29.

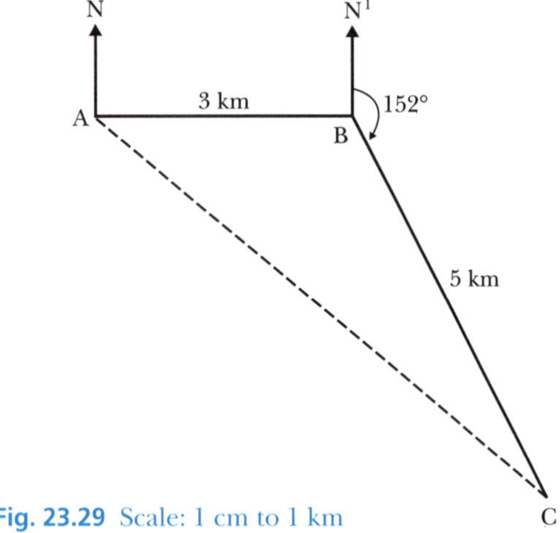

Fig. 23.29 Scale: 1 cm to 1 km

Join AC.

By measurement, AC $\simeq$ 6·9 cm.

Distance of C from A $\simeq$ 6·9 × 1 km = 6·9 km

By measurement, N$\hat{A}$C = 130°.

Bearing of C from A is 130°.

Example 4

Makeni is 116 km *on a bearing* 027° *from Koidu. How far north of Koidu is Makeni? How far west of Makeni is Koidu?*

Make a scale drawing of the data (Fig. 23.30).

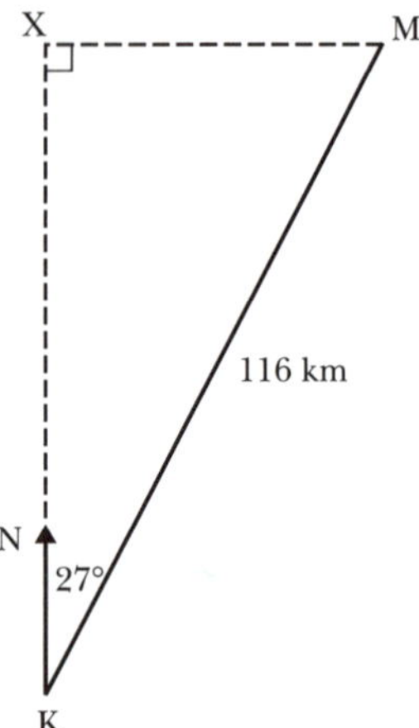

Fig. 23.30 Scale: 1 cm to 20 km

X is the point which is due north of Koidu and due west of Makeni. KX represents the distance that Makeni is north of Koidu.

By measurement, KX ≃ 5·2 cm

The true distance KX ≃ 5·2 × 20 km
= 104 km

MX represents the distance that Koidu is west of Makeni.

By measurement, MX ≃ 2·6 cm

The true distance MX ≃ 2·6 × 20 km
= 52 km

Thus Makeni is approximately 104 km north of Koidu and Koidu is approximately 52 km west of Makeni.

Exercise 23g

Answer each question by making a scale drawing. Always make a rough sketch first.

1 A boy starts at A and walks 3 km east to B. He then walks 4 km north to C. Find the distance and bearing of C from A.

2 A girl starts at A and walks 2 km south to B. She then walks 3 km west to C. Find the distance and bearing of C from A.

3 An aeroplane flies 400 km west then 100 km north. Find its distance and bearing from its starting point.

4 A student cycles 14 km east from A and then 10 km south-east to B. Find the distance and bearing of B from A.

5 A road starts at a college and goes due north for 2 000 m. It then goes 2 000 m on a bearing 040° and ends at a market. How far is the market from the college? What is the bearing of the market from the college?

6 Blama is 450 km due south of Lunsar. Koidu is due west of Blama and on a bearing 225° from Lunsar. Find the distances between
- **a)** Koidu and Blama,
- **b)** Koidu and Lunsar.

7 Talama is 180 km from Kambia. The bearing of Talama from Kambia is 121°.
- **a)** How far south of Kambia is Talama?
- **b)** How far west of Talama is Kambia?

8 A ship is 3 km due east of a harbour. Another ship is also 3 km from the harbour but on a bearing 042° from it.
- **a)** Find the distance between the two ships.
- **b)** Find the bearing of the second ship from the first ship.

9 A plane flies 200 km on a bearing 032°. It then flies 350 km on a bearing 275°.
- **a)** Find the bearing and distance of the plane from its starting point.
- **b)** Find how far north and how far west the plane is from its starting point.

Chapter summary

① The four main directions are North (N), South (S), East (E) and West (W), with secondary directions NE (north-east), SE (south-east), SW (south-west) and NW (north-west). See Fig. 23.4.

② To find the main directions, face the direction that the sun rises (East). Then stretch your arms out by your sides. Your left hand points North and your right hand points South. Turn through 180° and you are facing West (where the sun sets).

③ The magnetic compass is used for finding directions. See Fig. 23.3.

④ A *bearing* is a compass direction. There are two common methods for giving bearings:
- **a)** *acute angle* with North or South: for example, N30°E, S50°W,
- **b)** *three-figure bearing*, measured clockwise from North: for example, 030°, 230°.

⑤ To *survey* an area means to take bearings and distances from which a scale drawing can be made. When surveying, first make a rough sketch (see Example 3).

24 Cone: Area and volume

The net of a cone

Fig. 24.1 shows examples of shapes which contain **cone** shapes. Some are solid and some are hollow.

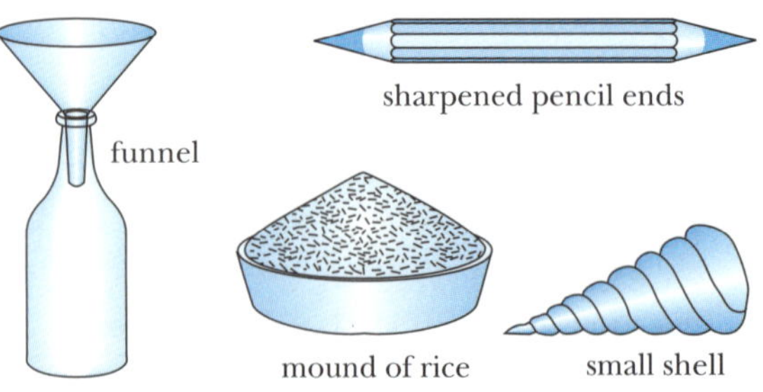

Fig. 24.1

The surface of a cone is in two parts: a circular face and a curved surface (Fig. 24.2).

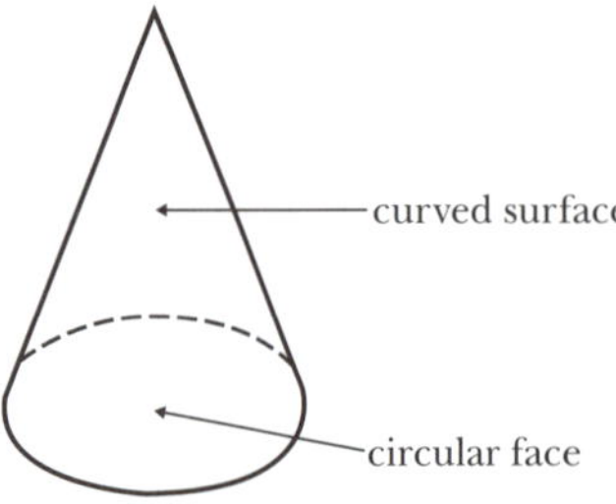

Fig. 24.2

A hollow cone can be opened out to give its net.

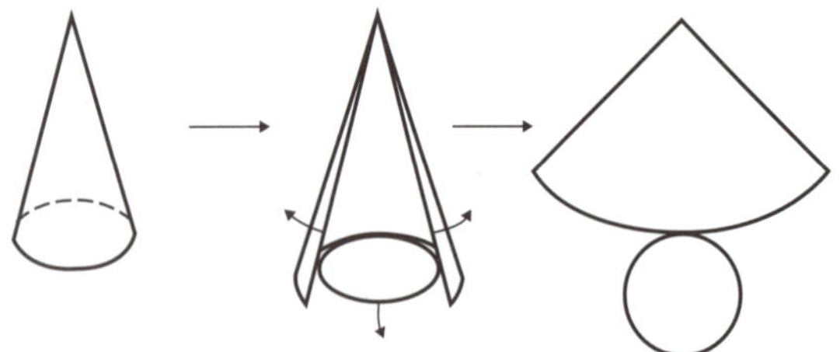

Fig. 24.3

Fig. 24.3 shows that the net of a cone is made up of a circle and a sector of a circle. The total surface area of the cone will be the total area of the circle and the sector.

Exercise 24a *(Practical assignment)*

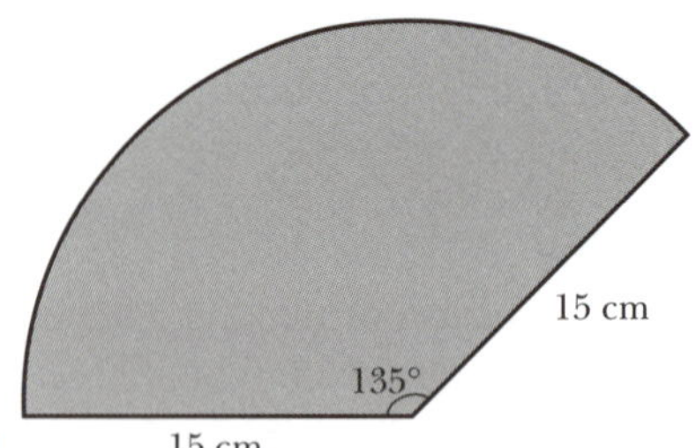

Fig. 24.4

a) Make an accurate full size drawing of Fig. 24.4 on thin cardboard or thick paper. Cut out the shape of the sector.

b) Shape the sector to a cone as in Fig. 24.5.

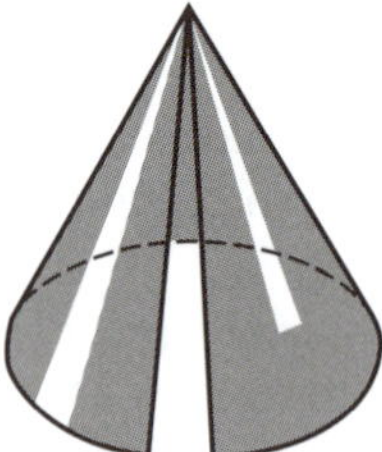

Fig. 24.5

c) What shape is the base of the cone?

d) Using thread, measure the perimeter of the base of the cone.

e) Using thread, measure the length of the arc of the sector in Fig. 24.4.

f) Compare your results in d) and e).

g) What can you say about the perimeter of the base of the cone and the length of the arc of the sector in Fig. 24.4?

Surface area of a cone

The work of Exercise 24a shows that a sector of a circle can be bent to form the curved surface of an open cone.

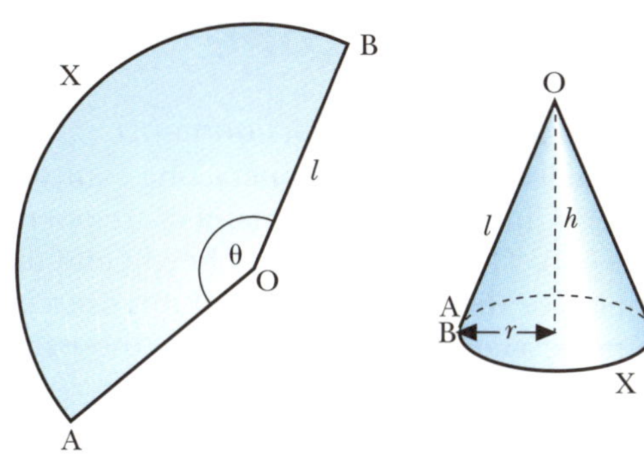

Fig. 24.6

In Fig. 24.6, the sector OAXB is of radius l and angle θ. It is bent into a cone of base radius r. In the cone, the distance from the vertex to the circumference is l. This is called the **slant height**.

Since $A\hat{O}B = \theta$, arc AXB $= \dfrac{\theta}{360}$ of $2\pi l$

$$\text{Circumference of base} = 2\pi r$$
$$= \text{length of arc AXB.}$$

Thus, $$2\pi r = \frac{\theta}{360} \times 2\pi l$$

Dividing both sides by 2π,

$$r = \frac{\theta l}{360} \qquad (1)$$

$$\text{Curved surface area} = \text{area of sector OAXB}$$
$$= \frac{\theta}{360} \text{ of } \pi l^2$$
$$= \frac{\theta l}{360} \times \pi l$$
$$= r \times \pi l \quad [\text{from (1)}]$$
$$= \pi r l$$

Curved surface area of cone = πrl

Total surface area of cone
= curved surface area + area of base circle

Total surface area of cone = $\pi rl + \pi r^2$

where r is the radius of the base and l is the slant height.

Example 1

A cone has a base radius of 5 cm *and a height of* 12 cm. *Calculate a) its slant height, b) its total surface area. Leave the answers in terms of* π *if* π *is involved.*

a) Fig. 24.7 is a sketch of the information.

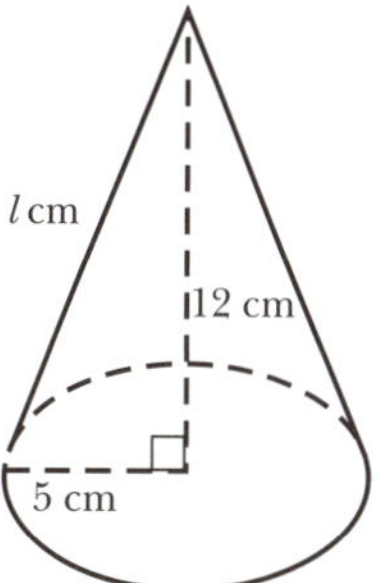

Fig. 24.7

The slant height, l, can be found by using Pythagoras' rule.

$$l^2 = 5^2 + 12^2$$
$$= 25 + 144$$
$$= 169$$
$$l = \sqrt{169} = 13$$

The slant height is 13 cm.

b) Surface area of cone

$$= \pi rl + \pi r^2$$
$$= \pi \times 5 \times 13 + \pi \times 5^2 \text{ cm}^2$$
$$= 65\pi + 25\pi \text{ cm}^2$$
$$= 90\pi \text{ cm}^2$$

Notice that the final answer to part *b)* is left in terms of π.

Example 2

A sector of a circle of radius 10 cm *and angle* 216° *is bent to form a cone. Find the following.*

a) The radius of the base of the cone

b) The curved surface area of the open cone

a) Fig. 24.8 is a sketch of the information.

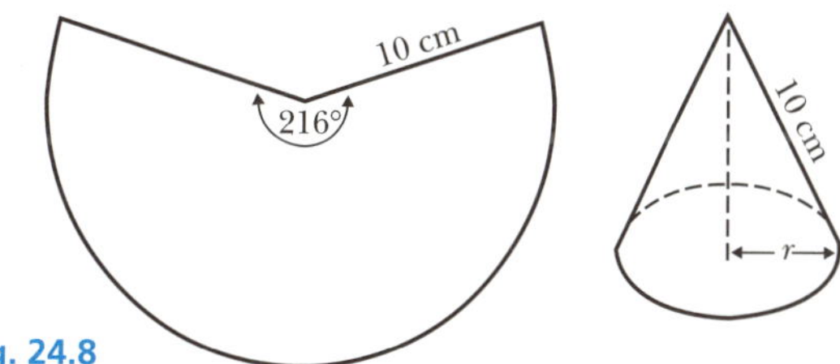

Fig. 24.8

Let the radius of the base of the cone be r cm.

Circumference of base of cone
= length of arc of sector

$2\pi r = \frac{216}{360}$ of $2\pi \times 10$

Dividing both sides by 2π,

$r = \frac{216}{360} \times 10 = \frac{3}{5} \times 10 = 6$

The radius of the base of the cone is 6 cm.

b) Curved surface area of cone $= \pi rl$

$= \pi \times 6 \times 10 \text{ cm}^2$

$= 60\pi \text{ cm}^2$

Exercise 24b

Make a sketch of the information in each question. Give answers to 2 s.f.

1 Use Pythagoras' rule to find the slant height of a cone which has
- **a)** a base radius of 4 cm and a height of 3 cm,
- **b)** a height of 8 cm and a base radius of 6 cm,
- **c)** a height of 12 cm and a base diameter of 10 cm,
- **d)** a base diameter of 16 cm and a height of 15 cm.

2 Find the base radius of a cone made from
- **a)** a semi-circle of radius 12 cm,
- **b)** a sector of a circle of radius 10 cm and angle 144°,
- **c)** a sector of a circle of radius 6 cm and angle 300°,
- **d)** a quarter circle of radius 8 cm.

3 Find the areas of the curved surfaces of the cones in question 1. Leave your answers in terms of π.

4 Find the total surface areas of the solid cones in question 2. Leave your answers in terms of π.

5 Calculate the total surface area of a solid cone of slant height 10 cm and base diameter 10 cm. Use the value 3·14 for π.

6 Calculate the total surface area of a solid cone of vertical height 24 cm and base diameter 14 cm. Use the value $\frac{22}{7}$ for π.

7 Calculate the total surface area of a solid cone of:
- **a)** base radius 6 cm and slant height 10 cm,
- **b)** base radius 8 cm and vertical height 6 cm,
- **c)** vertical height 12 cm and base radius 5 cm,
- **d)** slant height 25 cm and vertical height 24 cm.

Use the value 3·14 for π and give answers to the nearest cm^2.

Volume of a cone

Exercise 24c *(Practical assignment)*

1 Fig. 24.9 shows two containers, one conical, the other cylindrical. Both containers are open at one end. They have the same height and the same base diameter. The aim of this exercise is to make a cone and a cylinder like those in Fig. 24.9.

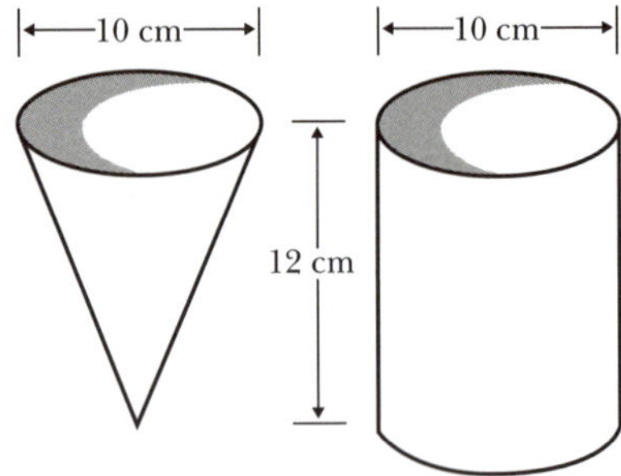

Fig. 24.9

2 Fig. 24.10 gives sketches of the nets of a cone and cylinder. Draw the nets full size on thin cardboard. Cut out the nets and shape them to make a cone and a cylinder. Use sticky tape to join the edges of the nets together.

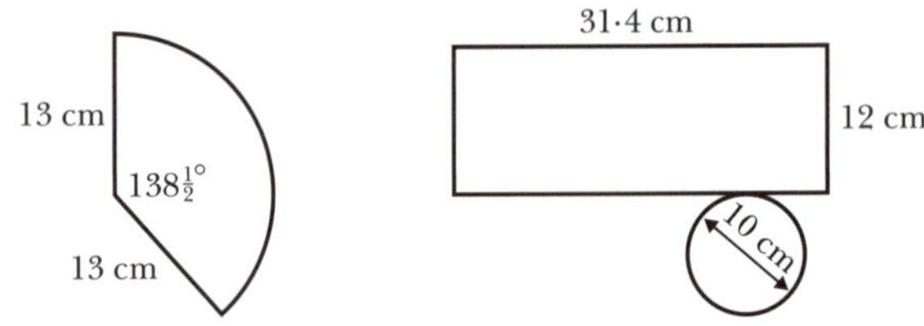

Fig. 24.10

3 Fill the cone full of sand. The sand must be level with the top of the cone. Then pour the sand from the cone into the cylinder.

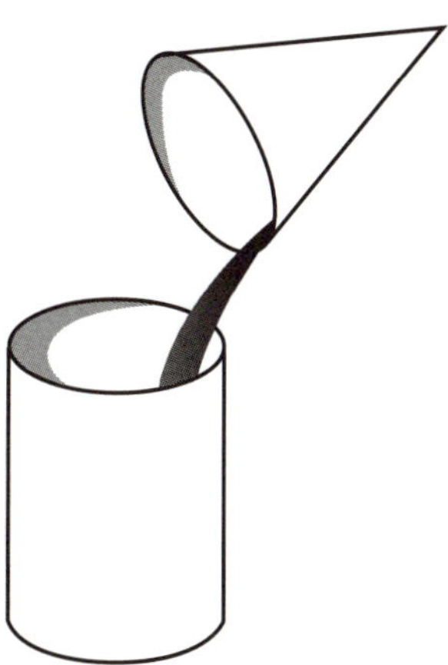

Fig. 24.11

4 Repeat **3** until the cylinder is full. How many full cones are needed to fill the cylinder?

5 a) What fraction of the volume of the cylinder is the volume of the cone?

b) How many times the volume of the cone is the volume of the cylinder?

In Exercise 24c, the cone and the cylinder both had the same base area, πr^2, and the same height, h. If you did Exercise 24c carefully, you will have found that:

volume of cone $= \frac{1}{3} \times$ volume of cylinder with same base area and height

volume of cone $= \frac{1}{3} \times \pi r^2 h$

Any solid which rises to a point, such as a cone or a pyramid, has a volume given by:

volume of pointed solid $= \frac{1}{3} \times$ base area $\times$ height

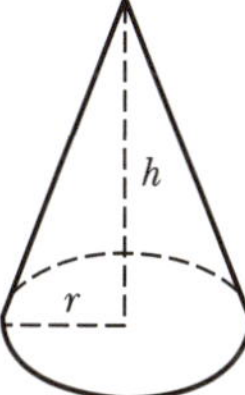

Fig. 24.12

For a cone of height h and base radius r,

Volume of cone $= \frac{1}{3}\pi r^2 h$

Example 3

Fig. 24.13 shows a machine part made from two cones of base radius 3 cm. *The heights of the cones are* 10 cm *and* 4 cm.

a) Calculate the volume of the machine part in cm^3.

b) If the machine part is made of brass of density 8 g/cm^3, *calculate its mass in* kg.

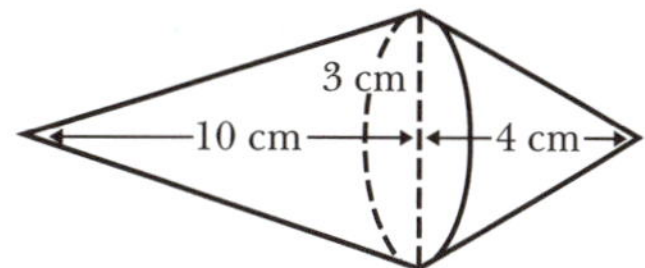

Fig. 24.13

a) Volume of machine part

$= \frac{1}{3}\pi r^2 h_1 + \frac{1}{3}\pi r^2 h_2$

$= \frac{1}{3} \times \pi \times 9 \times 10 + \frac{1}{3} \times \pi \times 9 \times 4 \text{ cm}^3$

$= \frac{1}{3} \times \pi \times 9(10 + 4) \text{ cm}^3$

$= \frac{1}{3} \times \frac{22}{7} \times 9 \times 14 \text{ cm}^3$

$= 132 \text{ cm}^3$

b) Mass of machine part $= 132 \times 8$ g

$= \frac{132 \times 8}{1\,000}$ kg

$= 1{\cdot}056$ kg

Notice how factorisation in part *a)* simplified the arithmetic.

Exercise 24d

1 Use the value $\frac{22}{7}$ for π to calculate the volumes of cones with the following dimensions.

a) height 6 cm, base radius 7 cm

b) base diameter 1·4 cm, height 1·8 cm

c) base radius 1 m, height 1·5 m

d) height 21 cm, base diameter 10 cm

2 A mound of beans is roughly in the shape of a cone of height 20 cm and base diameter 60 cm. Use the value 3 for π to find the approximate volume of beans.

3 A cone and a cylinder have equal volumes and bases of the same diameter. If the height of the cone is 27 cm, what is the height of the cylinder?

4 Rice is sold in cups. A good cupful of rice has a cone-shaped mound of rice on top (Fig. 24.14). Use the value 3 for π to find the approximate volume of rice in the cup shown in Fig. 24.14.

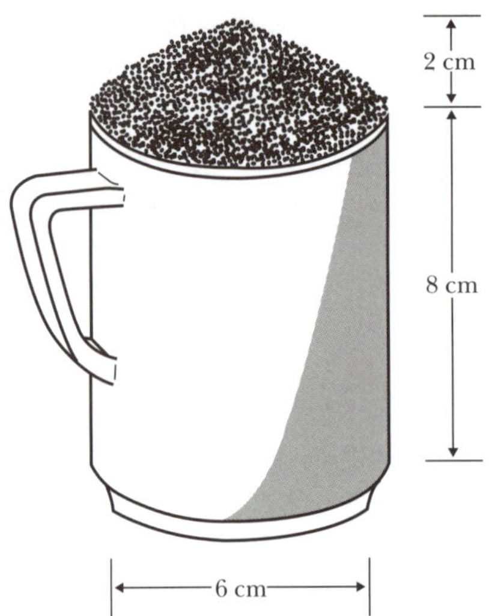

Fig. 24.14

5 A round house is made of two basic shapes, a cylinder and a cone.

Calculate the volume of air in a round house with dimensions as given in Fig. 24.15. Use the value $\frac{22}{7}$ for π.

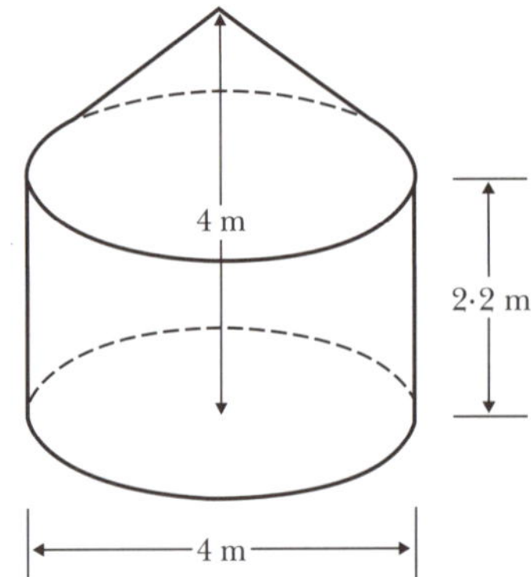

Fig. 24.15

6 A round pencil is sharpened to a cone shape at both ends (Fig. 24.16).

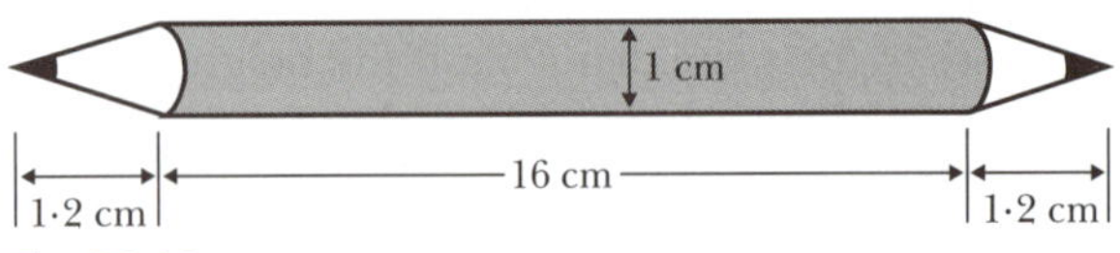

Fig. 24.16

Use the data in Fig. 24.16 and the value $\frac{22}{7}$ for π to find the volume of the pencil.

Estimation using mensuration formulae

Example 4

Fig. 24.17 shows a basin filled with rice. All measurements are approximate. Estimate the volume of rice in the basin.

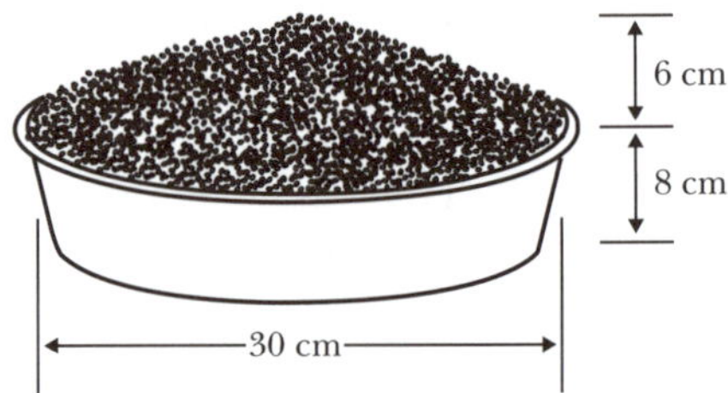

Fig. 24.17

Assume that the basin is a cylinder of height 8 cm and diameter 30 cm. Assume that the rice on top is a cone of height 6 cm.

Volume of rice in basin

$\approx \pi r^2 h$

$\approx \pi \times 15^2 \times 8 \text{ cm}^3$

Volume of rice in 'cone'

$\approx \frac{1}{3}\pi r^2 h$

$\approx \frac{1}{3}\pi \times 15^2 \times 6 \text{ cm}^3$

$\approx \pi \times 15^2 \times 2 \text{ cm}^3$

Total volume of rice

$\approx \pi \times 15^2 \times 8 + \pi \times 15^2 \times 2 \text{ cm}^3$

$\approx \pi \times 15^2(8 + 2) \text{ cm}^3$

$\approx \pi \times 15^2 \times 10 \text{ cm}^3$

$\approx 2\,250\pi \text{ cm}^3$

Using the value 3 for π, total volume of rice

$\approx 2\,250 \times 3 \approx 6\,750 \text{ cm}^3$

$\approx 7\,000 \text{ cm}^3$ to 1 s.f.

The value 3 for π is sufficiently accurate for estimation purposes. The final answer is given to 1 significant figure. There is so much approximation in the question that it would be false accuracy to give any more significant figures.

Exercise 24e

Use the value 3 for π where necessary. Give all answers to 1 significant figure unless told otherwise.

1 The floor of a rectangular room is 5·22 m by 3·91 m. The room is 2·76 m high. Round the

given data to the nearest whole metre and hence estimate

a) the area of the floor in m^2,

b) the volume of the room in m^3.

2 A circular room has a floor of diameter 590 cm. Estimate

a) the perimeter of the room in metres,

b) the area of the floor in m^2.

3 Table 24.1 gives the approximate lengths of some cars.

car	length (m)
VW beetle	3·5
Ford Cortina	4·3
Peugeot 504	4·5
Volvo 244	4·9

Table 24.1

a) Use Table 24.1 to estimate the average length of a car to the nearest tenth of a metre.

b) Estimate the number of cars that can be parked along a street which is 300 m long. Allow a space of about 1 m between each car.

4 A door is made of planks of wood which are 146 mm wide.

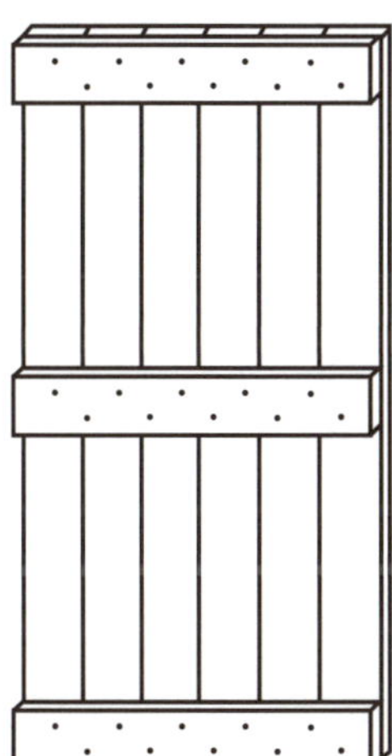

Fig. 24.18

a) Use Fig. 24.18 to estimate the width of the door.

If the door is 2 m high, estimate

b) the area of the door in m^2,

c) the total length of planks used to the nearest metre.

5 A car is approximately 4·5 m long and 1·7 m wide. At the factory where they are made, the cars are parked as closely as possible on a rectangular parking area 200 m by 150 m. Estimate the total number of cars that can be stored on the area.

6 The inside dimensions of a cup are given in Fig. 24.19.

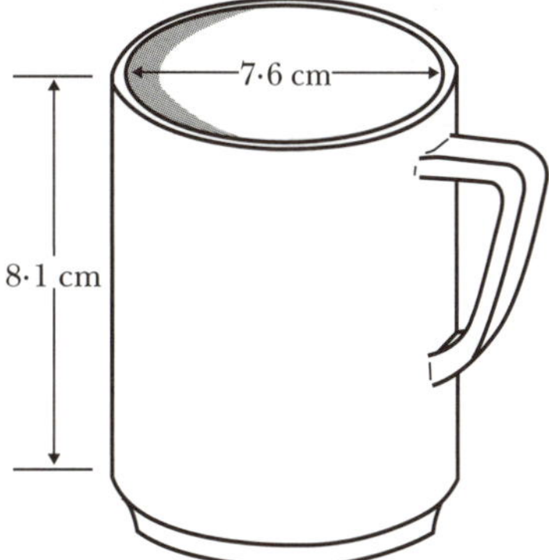

Fig. 24.19

Consider the cup to be a cylinder. Estimate its capacity to the nearest 100 ml.

7 The cup in Fig. 24.19 is filled with rice so that it has a 'cone' of height 2 cm on top. Estimate the total volume of rice that the cup holds to the nearest 10 cm^3.

8 A small bucket has dimensions as shown in Fig. 24.20.

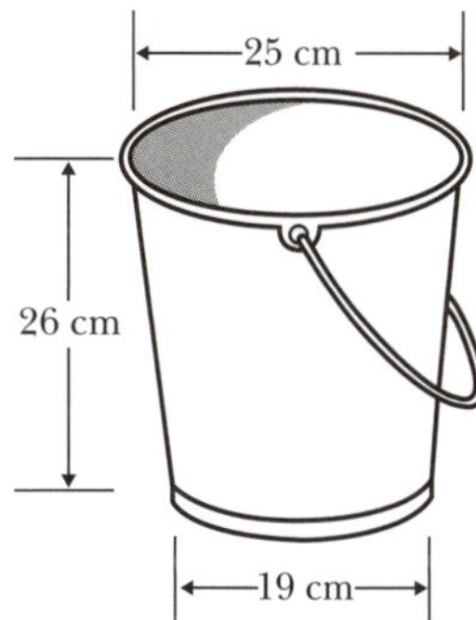

Fig. 24.20

a) Find the average of the top and bottom diameters of the bucket. Let the average be *d*.

b) Consider the bucket to be equivalent to a cylinder of diameter *d*. Estimate the capacity of the bucket to the nearest whole litre.

9 Use the method of the previous question to estimate the capacity of a large bucket of height 30 cm with top and bottom diameters of 30 cm and 22 cm respectively.

10 An oil drum is cut in half. One half is used as a water trough as shown in Fig. 24.21.

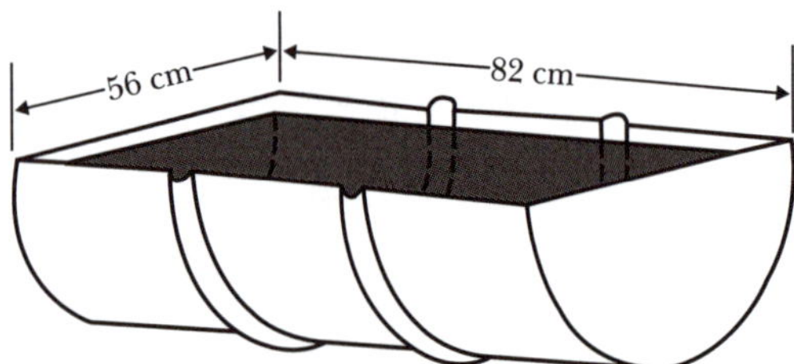

Fig. 24.21

Use the dimensions in Fig. 24.21 to estimate the capacity of the water trough in litres.

Chapter summary

① For a solid cone with base radius r, slant height ℓ and vertical height h (as in Fig. 24.6):

a) curved surface area = $\pi r\ell$

b) total surface area = $\pi r\ell + \pi r^2$

c) volume = $\frac{1}{3}\pi r^2 h$

② When *estimating answers* to mensuration problems, always round off the final answers to a number of significant figures *not more than* the number of significant figures in the given data. In many cases, one significant figure is sufficient.

Revision exercises and tests Chapters 17–24

Revision exercise 8 *(Chapters 17, 19, 24)*

1 A rectangle measures 8 cm by 15 cm. Make a sketch and use Pythagoras' rule to calculate the length of one of its diagonals.

2 In Fig. R33, calculate XY.

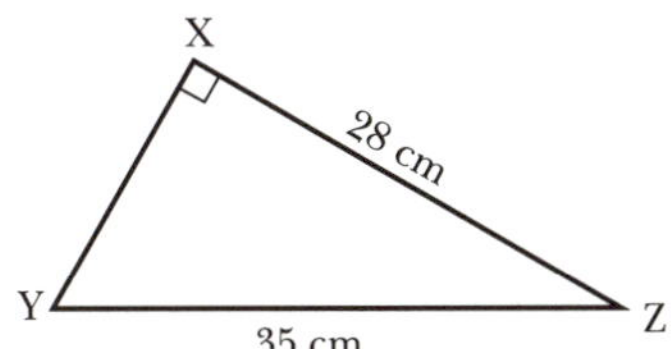

Fig. R33

3 Which of the following are Pythagorean triples?

a) (10, 24, 26) **b)** (12, 29, 31)
c) (14, 49, 50) **d)** (16, 30, 34)

4 In Fig. R34, AP is perpendicular to BC. AB = 13 cm, BP = 5 cm, AC = 15 cm.

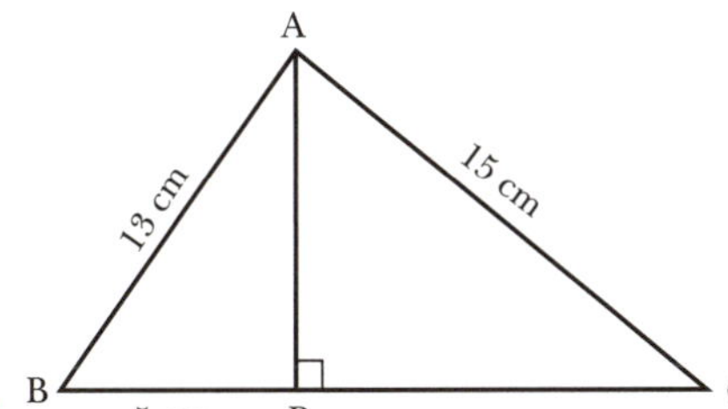

Fig. R34

Calculate the lengths of **a)** AP, **b)** BC.

5 A ladder 9·6 m long leans against a wall. It touches the wall at a point 9 m above the ground. Find the distance of the foot of the ladder from the wall.

6 Use the value $\frac{22}{7}$ for π to find the surface area of a closed cylinder of radius 7 cm and height 30 cm.

7 Take π to be 3·1 and calculate the volume of a cylinder of height 10 cm and radius 4 cm.

8 Calculate the total surface area of a cone of slant height 19 cm and base radius 4 cm. Leave your answer in terms of π.

9 Use the value $\frac{22}{7}$ for π to calculate the volume of a cone of height 14 cm and base radius 6 cm.

10 The base of a refrigerator measures 59 cm by 63 cm. Approximately how many of these can be stored in a room which measures 4 m by 3 m?

Revision test 8 *(Chapters 17, 19, 24)*

1 Which of the following are Pythagorean triples?
I (3, 4, 5), II (5, 12, 13), III (8, 13, 17)

A I only **B** I and II only **C** II only
D II and III only **E** III only

2 PQRS is a rectangle with sides 3 cm and 4 cm. If its diagonals cross at O, calculate the length of PO.

A 2·5 cm **B** 3·0 cm **C** 3·5 cm
D 4·0 cm **E** 5·0 cm

3 The diagonals of a rhombus measure 8 cm by 6 cm. What is the length of a side of the rhombus?

A 5 cm **B** 6 cm **C** 7 cm
D 8 cm **E** 10 cm

4 The volume of a cone of height h and base radius r is given by

A $\frac{1}{3}\pi rh$ **B** $\frac{1}{3}\pi r^2 h$ **C** πrh
D $\pi r^2 h$ **E** $2\pi rh$

5 A cone is 8 cm high and has a base diameter of 12 cm. Its slant height is

A 6 cm **B** 8 cm **C** 10 cm
D 12 cm **E** 20 cm

6 In Fig. R35 (on page 202), $\triangle$PQR is right-angled at Q and QR = 5 cm.

a) If the area of $\triangle$PQR is 30 cm^2, find the length of PQ.

b) Hence find the length of PR.

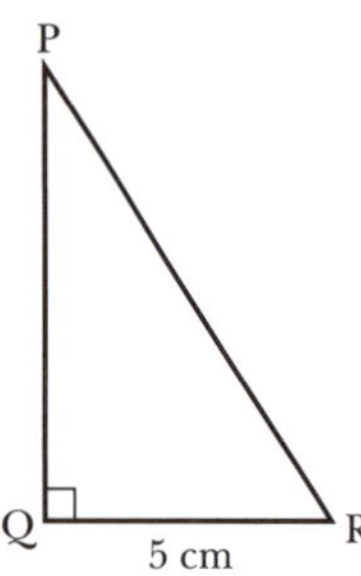

Fig. R35

7 Fig. R36 shows the net of an open cylinder.

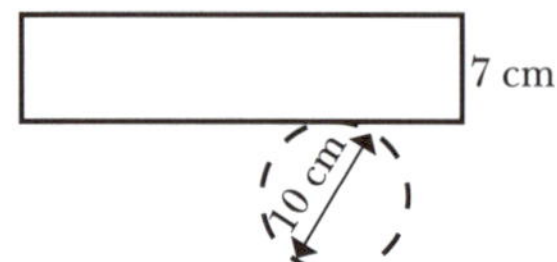

Fig. R36

If the net is folded to make the cylinder,

a) what is the radius of the cylinder,

b) what is the height of the cylinder?

Use the value $\frac{22}{7}$ for π to find

c) the curved surface area of the open cylinder,

d) the volume of the cylinder.

8 A mound of rice is roughly in the shape of a cone of height 12 cm and base diameter 40 cm. Use the value 3 for π to find the approximate volume of rice.

9 62 litres of water are poured into a cylinder of diameter 40 cm. Use the value 3·1 for π to find how deep the water is in the cylinder.

10 Estimate the capacity in litres of a cylindrical drum which is 45 cm in diameter and 66 cm high. Use $\pi = 3{\cdot}1$

Revision exercise 9 *(Chapters 18, 21, 22)*

1 Express the following times in terms of the 24-hour clock.

a) 6.25 am **b)** 6.45 pm

c) 5 to 8 pm **d)** 10 to midnight

2 Use Fig. 18.4 on page 157 to find the total distance travelled on the following journey: Falaba → Kabala → Makeni → Mano.

3 In every full box of 50 new ball-point pens, it is found that five do not work properly.

a) If a pen is picked at random from a full box, what is the probability that it works properly?

b) A box has 30 new ball-point pens. How many of these would you expect to work properly?

4 Statistics show that about 13 people in every 100 are born left-handed. In a village of 2 125 people, approximately how many were probably born left-handed?

5 Yvonne has Le300 000. She wants to buy x blouses and y skirts. A blouse costs Le80 000 and a skirt costs Le110 000. If she gets change, write down an inequality in x and y.

6 Find the range of values of x for which:

a) $x - 3 < 2$ **b)** $2 - x > 5$

c) $2x - 2 < \frac{x + 2}{2}$ **d)** $\frac{x + 2}{5} \geqslant \frac{x - 3}{3} + 1$

7 Use number lines to draw graphs of the solutions of the following.

a) $x - 2 \leqslant 0$ **b)** $2x + 5 \leqslant 3$

8 A class contains 18 girls and 12 boys. A student is chosen at random from the class. What is the probability that the student is **a)** a girl, **b)** a boy, **c)** a boy or a girl?

Fig. R37 is a timetable for flights to Amsterdam from Accra and Lungi. Use Fig. R37 to answer questions 9 and 10.

		Plane 1 Tues./Sat.	Plane 2 Thurs.	Plane 3 Sat.
ACCRA	Dep.	09 50 hours	–	–
LUNGI	Dep.	–	08 45 hours	10 10 hours
TUNIS	Arr.	–	12 30 hours	–
	Dep.	–	13 25 hours	–
AMSTERDAM	Arr.	16 10 hours	17 10 hours	16 10 hours

Fig. R37

9 a) Which plane flies from Accra on a Saturday?

b) What time does the plane leave Accra on Tuesdays?

c) How long is Plane 2 on the ground in Tunis?

10 a) How long does it take to fly from Accra to Amsterdam?

b) How long does it take to fly from Lungi to Amsterdam on i) Saturdays, ii) Thursdays?

Revision test 9 *(Chapters 18, 21, 22)*

1 It has rained on 6th January twice in the last 20 years. What is the probability that it will rain on 6th January next year?

A 0 **B** $\frac{1}{10}$ **C** $\frac{3}{10}$ **D** $\frac{1}{3}$ **E** $\frac{9}{10}$

2 A card is picked at random from a pack of 52 playing cards. The probability that it is a 6 is

A $\frac{1}{52}$ **B** $\frac{1}{13}$ **C** $\frac{3}{26}$ **D** $\frac{1}{26}$ **E** $\frac{1}{4}$

3 A boy has more than Le900. He spends Le300 and has Lem left. Which one of the following inequalities gives m?

A $m > 500$ **B** $m < 600$ **C** $m > 600$
D $m < 1\,200$ **E** $m > 1\,200$

Fig. R38 is a railway timetable for passenger services between Makurdi, Kafanchan and Jos, in Nigeria. Use Fig. R38 to answer questions 4, 5 and 6.

MAKURDI–KAFANCHAN–JOS				
		401 UP		**402 DN**
Makurdi	D	6.40 am	A	6.15 pm
Kafanchan	A	5.05 pm	D	9.20 am
	D	5.35 pm	A	8.50 am
Jos	A	9.50 pm	D	5.00 am

Fig. R38

4 What time does the 402 DN train depart from Kafanchan?

A 5.05 pm **B** 5.35 pm **C** 6.40 am
D 8.50 am **E** 9.20 am

5 How long does the journey from Makurdi to Jos take?

A 1 h 15 min **B** 3 h 10 min **C** 8 h 50 min
D 15 h 10 min **E** 20 h 50 min

6 Find the following.

a) The time taken between Kafanchan and Jos on the up journey.
b) The time taken between Jos and Kafanchan on the down journey.
c) The difference between these two times.

7 A book contains pages numbered from 1 to 48. A page is chosen at random. What is the probability that its page number contains a 3?

8 A letter is chosen at random from the word *trapezium*. Find the probability that it is **a)** a vowel, **b)** one of the letters of the word *permit*, **c)** one of the letters of the word *hollow*.

9 Find the range of values of x for which:

a) $x + 9 > 14$ **b)** $6 - x > 7$
c) $7 \geqslant 28 - 3x$ **d)** $\frac{3}{4}x - 1 \leqslant 1\frac{1}{2} - \frac{1}{2}x$

10 Three times a whole number, n, is subtracted from 38. The result is less than 20.

a) Make an inequality in n.
b) Find the four lowest values of n.

Revision exercise 10 *(Chapters 20, 23)*

1 Fig. R39 shows a right triangular prism ABCDEF. It is resting so that its base is horizontal.

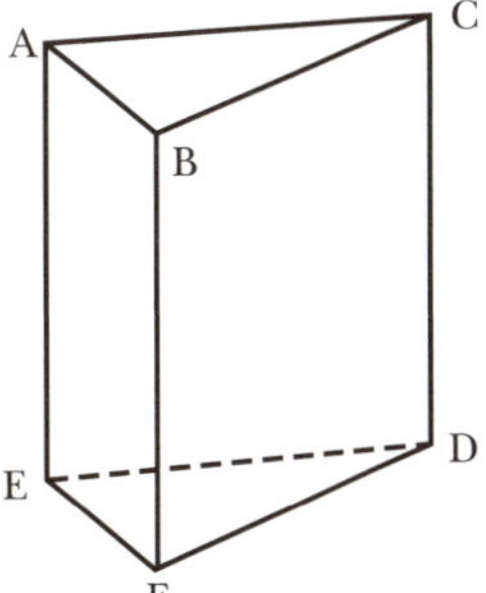

Fig. R39

a) Name four edges which are horizontal.
b) Name two edges which are vertical.

2 Find the angle measured clockwise between the following directions.

a) NE and SE **b)** N and SW
c) NW and E **d)** NE and NW

3 In Fig. R40, state the bearings of I, J, K, L, M from X.

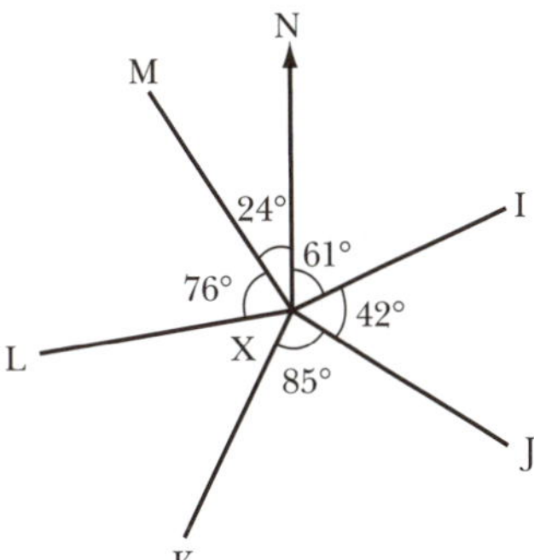

Fig. R40

4 Draw sketches to show the following bearings of X from Y.

a) 215° **b)** 298° **c)** 018° **d)** 125°

5 a) Make a scale drawing of the information in Fig. R41.

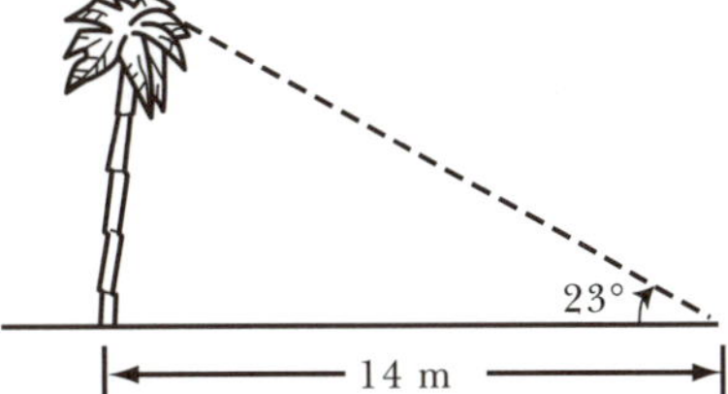

Fig. R41

b) Hence find the height of the tree to the nearest $\frac{1}{2}$ metre.

6 a) Make a scale drawing of the information in Fig. R42.

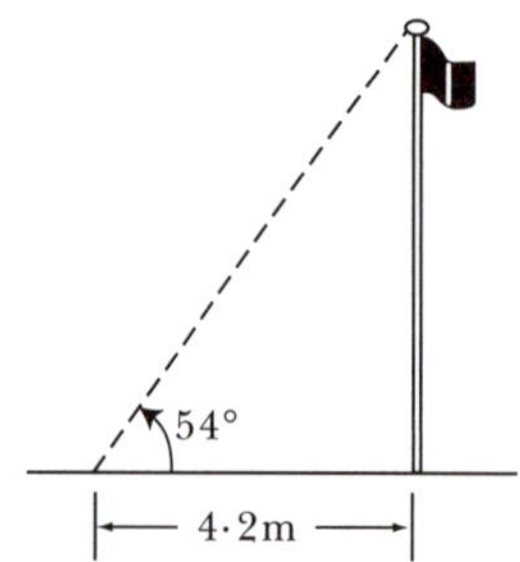

Fig. R42

b) Hence find the height of the flagpole to the nearest 0·1 m.

7 From the top of a tower 14 m high, the angle of depression of a man is 32°. Make a scale drawing and find the distance of the man from the foot of the tower to the nearest $\frac{1}{2}$ m.

8 A woman travels 3 km south, then 4 km south-west and finally 5 km west. Make a scale drawing and find the final distance and bearing from her starting point.

9 A boy cycles south for a distance of 4 km. He then cycles 7 km on a bearing 036°. Make a scale drawing of his journey. Hence find **a)** how far east, **b)** how far north he is from his starting point.

10 When the elevation of the sun is 33°, a girl has a shadow 2·8 m long. Make a scale drawing and hence find the height of the girl to the nearest 5 cm.

Revision test 10 *(Chapters 20, 23)*

1 Fig. R43 shows a right square-based pyramid resting so that its base is horizontal.

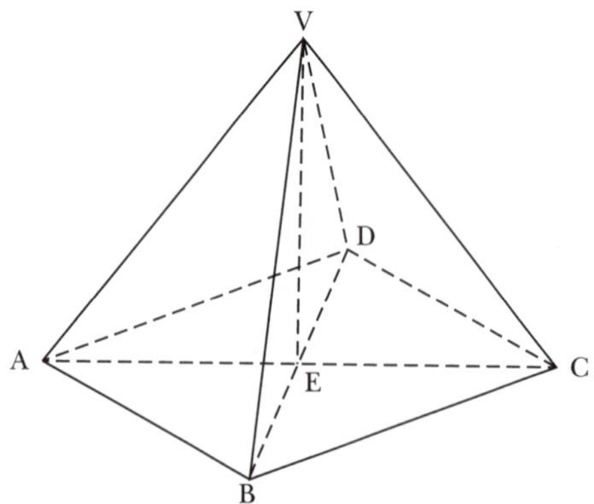

Fig. R43

Which of the points A, B, C, D, E is vertically below V?

2 If the angle of elevation of P from Q is 38°, then the angle of depression of Q from P is
A 19° **B** 38° **C** 52° **D** 128° **E** 142°

3 A vertical fence post has a shadow 1 m long when the angle of elevation of the sun is 45°. The height of the fence post is
A 0·5 m **B** 0·7 m **C** 1 m **D** 1·4 m **E** 2 m

4 Which of the points A, B, C, D, E in Fig. R44 is on a bearing 230° from O?

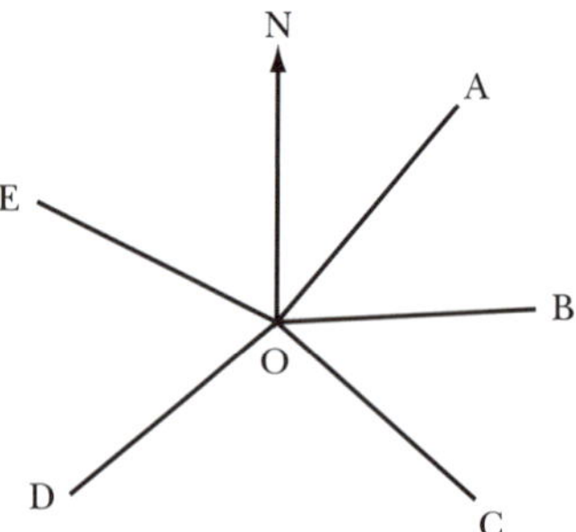

Fig. R44

5 The bearing of P from Q is 063°. The bearing of Q from P is
A 027° **B** 063° **C** 117° **D** 153° **E** 243°

6 From a point P the bearing of a church is 060°. From a point Q 100 m due east of P, the bearing is 330°. Draw a labelled sketch to show the positions of P, Q and the church.

7 The angle of elevation of the top of a tower from a point 23 m from its base on level ground is 50°. Make a scale drawing to find the height of the tower to the nearest metre.

8 Two posts are 1 800 m apart on a road running east and west. A tree is north of one post and on a bearing 304° from the other. Make a scale drawing and find the distance of the tree from each post.

9 A woman walks 2 km N, 3 km NE and finally 2 km E. Make a scale drawing of her journey. Find **a)** how far north, **b)** how far east she is from her starting point.

10 From the top of a tree, the angle of depression of a stone on horizontal ground is 55°. If the stone is 8 m from the foot of the tree, find, by scale drawing, the height of the tree.

General revision test C *(Chapters 17–24)*

1 In Fig. R45, which one of the following equations gives the value of a^2?

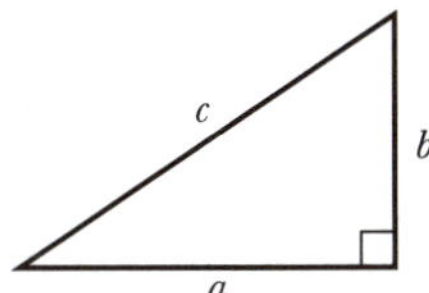

Fig. R45

A $a^2 = b^2 - c^2$ **B** $a^2 = (b - c)^2$
C $a^2 = b^2 + c^2$ **D** $a^2 = c^2 - b^2$
E $a^2 = (c - b)^2$

2 What is the length of the longest rod that can lie flat in a rectangular box which is 2 m long and $1\frac{1}{2}$ m wide?
A 7 m **B** $5\frac{1}{2}$ m **C** 5 m **D** $3\frac{1}{2}$ m **E** $2\frac{1}{2}$ m

3 Table R6 shows the numbers of students getting grades A, B, C, D, E in an essay.

grade	A	B	C	D	E
number	5	11	24	10	6

Table R6

Which grade did the least number of students get?

4 Which one of the following curved surfaces is Fig. R46 the net of?
A open cylinder **B** sphere
C open cone **D** half cylinder
E open hemisphere

Fig. R46

5 A cylinder is of height 5 cm and base radius 2 cm. Use the value 3·14 for π to calculate the area of its curved surface to the nearest cm^2.
A 13 cm^2 **B** 25 cm^2 **C** 31 cm^2 **D** 63 cm^2
E 126 cm^2

6 The height of a man is equal to the length of his shadow. The angle of elevation of the sun is
A 0° **B** 30° **C** 45° **D** 60° **E** 90°

7 A student is picked at random from a class containing 17 boys and 13 girls. What is the probability that the student is a girl?
A $\frac{1}{30}$ **B** $\frac{1}{13}$ **C** $\frac{13}{30}$ **D** $\frac{17}{30}$ **E** $\frac{13}{17}$

8 The range of values of a for which $11 - 2a \geqslant 1$ is
A $a \geqslant 5$ **B** $a \geqslant -5$ **C** $a = 5$
D $a \leqslant 5$ **E** $a \leqslant -5$

Fig. R47

Fig. R47 is the graph of which one of the following inequalities?
A $x > 5$ **B** $x \geqslant 5$ **C** $x < 5$
D $x \leqslant 5$ **E** $x < -5$

10 The bearing of X from Y is 196°. The bearing of Y from X is
A 016° **B** 074° **C** 106° **D** 164° **E** 196°

11 In Fig. R48, **a)** find the length of AC, **b)** hence find the area of △ABC.

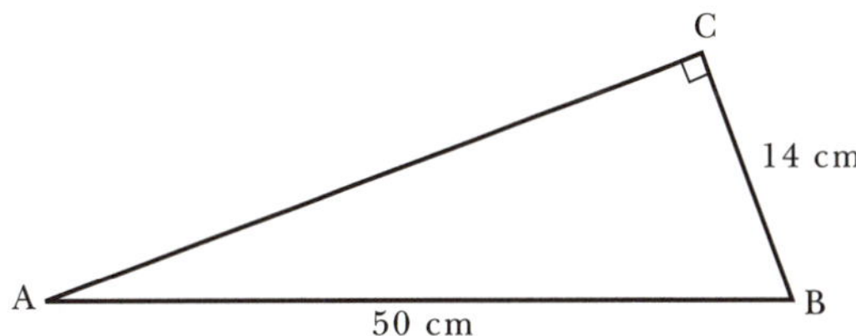

Fig. R48

12 Table R7 shows the number of students in each form of a school for the years 1996 to 2000.

	1996	1997	1998	1999	2000
Form 1	(90)	90	118	121	119
Form 2	87	88	90	118	120
Form 3	60	87	88	89	120
Form 4	57	61	89	85	89
Form 5	58	58	59	89	84

Table R7

a) How many students were in the school in 1999?

b) A girl entered Form 1 in 1996. She is one of the 90 ringed. If she is promoted at the end of each year, i) in what year is she in Form 3, and ii) how many students were in Form 3 in that year?

c) At the beginning of which year in the table did the school increase its Form 1 intake?

d) In which previous year (not in the table) did the school probably increase its Form 1 intake?

13 A cone and a cylinder have equal volumes and radii. The height of the cone is 12 cm. Find the height of the cylinder.

14 A cup is in the shape of a cone of height 12 cm and base diameter 12 cm. It is filled with water. The water is then poured into a cylinder of diameter 8 cm. Calculate the depth of water in the cylinder.

15 Fig. R49 shows sketch notes that a student made of a survey of a tree.

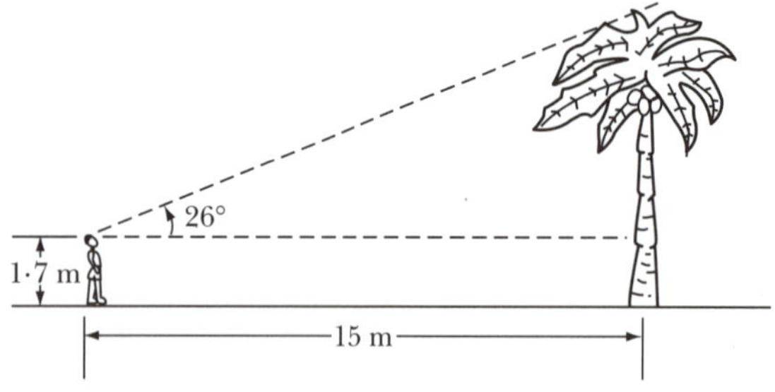

Fig. R49

Make a scale drawing and hence find the height of the tree to the nearest $\frac{1}{2}$ metre.

16 Find the probability of selecting a shape which is a parallelogram from one square, one rectangle, one rhombus, one kite and one trapezium.

17 Find the range of values of x for which

a) $4x + 4 > 7$ **b)** $28 - 5x < 2x + 9$

c) $\frac{3}{2}x - \frac{7}{6} \leqslant \frac{5}{2} - \frac{1}{3}x$

18 Use number lines to draw graphs of the solutions of the following.

a) $x + \frac{5}{2} > 0$ **b)** $9 \geqslant 1 - 2x$

19 Freetown is approximately 1 820 km on a bearing 275° from Lagos. Use a scale of 1 cm to 200 km to make a scale drawing of the positions of Freetown and Lagos. Hence find

a) how far Freetown is north of Lagos,

b) how far Lagos is east of Freetown.

20 A boy has a hand-span of about 21 cm. The diameter of his bicycle wheel is approximately three hand-spans. Estimate, to the nearest 100, the number of times the wheel turns round in travelling 1 km.

Tables

SI units

Length

The **metre** is the basic unit of length.

unit	abbreviation	basic units
1 kilometre	1 km	1 000 m
1 hectometre	1 hm	100 m
1 decametre	1 dam	10 m
1 metre	1 m	1 m
1 decimetre	1 dm	0·1 m
1 centimetre	1 cm	0·01 m
1 millimetre	1 mm	0·001 m

The most common measures are the millimetre, the metre and the kilometre.

1 m = 1 000 mm
1 km = 1 000 m = 1 000 000 mm

Mass

The **gramme** is the basic unit of mass.

unit	abbreviation	basic units
1 kilogramme	1 kg	1 000 g
1 hectogramme	1 hg	100 g
1 decagramme	1 dag	10 g
1 gramme	1 g	1 g
1 decigramme	1 dg	0·1 g
1 centigramme	1 cg	0·01 g
1 milligramme	1 mg	0·001 g

The **tonne** (t) is used for large masses. The most common measures of mass are the milligramme, the gramme, the kilogramme and the tonne.

1 g = 1 000 mg
1 kg = 1 000 g = 1 000 000 mg
1 t = 1 000 kg = 1 000 000 g

Time

The **second** is the basic unit of time. Units of time are not metric.

unit	abbreviation	basic units
1 second	1 s	1 s
1 minute	1 min	60 s
1 hour	1 h	3 600 s

Area

The **square metre** is the basic unit of area. Units of area are derived from units of length.

unit	abbreviation	relation to other units of area
square millimetre	mm^2	
square centimetre	cm^2	$1\ cm^2 = 100\ mm^2$
square metre	m^2	$1\ m^2 = 10\,000\ cm^2$
square kilometre	km^2	$1\ km^2 = 1\,000\,000\ m^2$
hectare (for land measure)	ha	$1\ ha = 10\,000\ m^2$

Volume

The **cubic metre** is the basic unit of volume. Units of volume are derived from units of length.

unit	abbreviation	relation to other units of volume
cubic millimetre	mm^3	
cubic centimetre	cm^3	$1\ cm^3 = 1\,000\ mm^3$
cubic metre	m^3	$1\ m^3 = 1\,000\,000\ cm^3$

Capacity

The **litre** is the basic unit of capacity. 1 litre takes up the same space as $1\,000\ cm^3$.

unit	abbreviation	relation to other units of capacity	relation to units of volume
millilitre	ml		1 ml = $1\ cm^3$
litre	l	1 l = 1 000 ml	1 l = $1\,000\ cm^3$
kilolitre	kl	1 kl = 1 000 l	1 kl = $1\ m^3$

Money

Some divided currencies

Germany	100 cents (c)	= 1 Euro(€)
Kenya	100 cents (cts)	= 1 shilling (KSh)
Nigeria	100 kobo (k)	= 1 naira (₦)
Sierra Leone	100 cents (c)	= 1 leone (Le)
South Africa	100 cents (c)	= 1 rand (R)
The Gambia	100 bututs (b)	= 1 dalasi (D)
UK	100 pence (p)	= 1 pound (£)
USA	100 cents (c)	= 1 dollar ($)
Zimbabwe	100 cents (c)	= 1 dollar (Z$)

Some undivided currencies

Francophone countries	franc CFA
Ghana	cedi (₵)
Japan	yen (¥)
Tanzania	shilling (TSh)
Uganda	shilling (USh)

The calendar

Remember this poem:

Thirty days have September,
April, June and November.
All the rest have thirty-one,
Excepting February alone;
This has twenty-eight days clear,
And twenty-nine in each Leap Year.

For a Leap Year, the year date must be divisible by 4.
Thus 1996 was a Leap Year.
Century year dates, such as 1900 and 2000, are Leap Years only if they are divisible by 400. Thus 2000 was a Leap Year, but 2100 will not be a Leap Year.

Multiplication table

×	1	2	3	4	5	6	7	8	9	10
1	1	2	3	4	5	6	7	8	9	10
2	2	4	6	8	10	12	14	16	18	20
3	3	6	9	12	15	18	21	24	27	30
4	4	8	12	16	20	24	28	32	36	40
5	5	10	15	20	25	30	35	40	45	50
6	6	12	18	24	30	36	42	48	54	60
7	7	14	21	28	35	42	49	56	63	70
8	8	16	24	32	40	48	56	64	72	80
9	9	18	27	36	45	54	63	72	81	90
10	10	20	30	40	50	60	70	80	90	100

Divisibility tests

Any whole number is exactly divisible by

2	if its last digit is even or 0
3	if the sum of its digits is divisible by 3
4	if its last two digits form a number divisible by 4
5	if its last digit is 5 or 0
6	if its last digit is even and the sum of its digits is divisible by 3
8	if its last three digits form a number divisible by 8
9	if the sum of its digits is divisible by 9
10	its last digit is 0

Mensuration formulae

	perimeter	area	volume
square side s	$4s$	s^2	
rectangle length l, breadth b	$2(l+b)$	lb	
circle radius r	$2\pi r$	πr^2	
triangle base b, height h		$\frac{1}{2}bh$	
parallelogram base b, height h		bh	
cube edge s		$6s^2$	s^3
cuboid length l, breadth b, height h			lbh
triangular prism height h, base area A			Ah
cylinder base radius r, height h		$2\pi rh + 2\pi r^2$	$\pi r^2 h$
cone base radius r, slant height l		$\pi rl + \pi r^2$	$\frac{1}{3}\pi r^2 h$

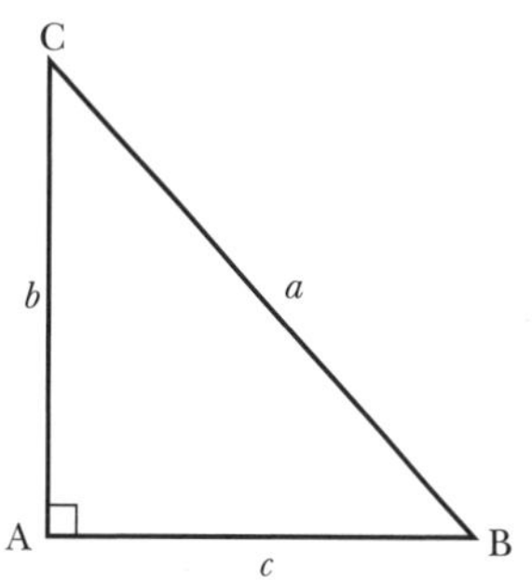

Fig. T1

Angle and length

In an n-sided polygon,
sum of angles = $(n-2) \times 180°$
In the right-angled triangle shown in Fig. T1,
$a^2 = b^2 + c^2$ (Pythagoras' rule)

Symbols

symbol	meaning
$=$	is equal to
$\neq$	is not equal to
$\simeq$	is approximately equal to
$\equiv$	is equivalent to
$>$	is greater than
$<$	is less than
$\geqslant$	is greater than or equal to
$\leqslant$	is less than or equal to
$°$	degrees (size of angle)
°C	degrees Celsius (temperature)
A, B, C, ...	points
AB	the line joining the point A and the point B *or* the distance between points A and B
ΔABC	triangle ABC
$\hat{ABC}$	the angle ABC
⊥	lines meeting at right angles
π	pi (3·14. . . . . . .)
%	per cent

Squares

$x \rightarrow x^2$

x	0	1	2	3	4	5	6	7	8	9	Diff. 1	2	3	4	5	6	7	8	9
10	1000	1020	1040	1061	1082	1103	1124	1145	1166	1188	2	4	6	8	10	13	15	17	19
11	1210	1232	1254	1277	1300	1323	1346	1369	1392	1416	2	5	7	9	11	14	16	18	21
12	1440	1464	1488	1513	1538	1563	1588	1613	1638	1664	2	5	7	10	12	15	17	20	22
13	1690	1716	1742	1769	1796	1823	1850	1877	1904	1932	3	5	8	11	13	16	19	22	24
14	1960	1988	2016	2045	2074	2103	2132	2161	2190	2220	3	6	9	12	14	17	20	23	26
15	2250	2280	2310	2341	2372	2403	2434	2465	2496	2528	3	6	9	12	15	19	22	25	28
16	2560	2592	2624	2657	2690	2723	2756	2789	2822	2856	3	7	10	13	16	20	23	26	30
17	2890	2924	2958	2993	3028	3063	3098	3133	3168	3204	3	7	10	14	17	21	24	28	31
18	3240	3276	3312	3349	3386	3423	3460	3497	3534	3572	4	7	11	15	18	22	26	30	33
19	3610	3648	3686	3725	3764	3803	3842	3881	3920	3960	4	8	12	16	19	23	27	31	35
20	4000	4040	4080	4121	4162	4203	4244	4285	4326	4368	4	8	12	16	20	25	29	33	37
21	4410	4452	4494	4537	4580	4623	4666	4709	4752	4796	4	9	13	17	21	26	30	34	39
22	4840	4884	4928	4973	5018	5063	5108	5153	5198	5244	4	9	13	18	22	27	31	36	40
23	5290	5336	5382	5429	5476	5523	5570	5617	5664	5712	5	9	14	19	23	28	33	38	42
24	5760	5808	5856	5905	5954	6003	6052	6101	6150	6200	5	10	15	20	24	29	34	39	44
25	6250	6300	6350	6401	6452	6503	6554	6605	6656	6708	5	10	15	20	25	31	36	41	46
26	6760	6812	6864	6917	6970	7023	7076	7129	7182	7236	5	11	16	21	26	32	37	42	48
27	7290	7344	7398	7453	7508	7563	7618	7673	7728	7784	5	11	16	22	27	33	38	44	49
28	7840	7896	7952	8009	8066	8123	8180	8237	8294	8352	6	11	17	23	28	34	40	46	51
29	8410	8468	8526	8585	8644	8703	8762	8821	8880	8940	6	12	18	24	29	35	41	47	53
30	9000	9060	9120	9181	9242	9303	9364	9425	9486	9548	6	12	18	24	30	37	43	49	55
31	9610	9672	9734	9797	9860	9923	9986	–	–	–	6	13	19	25	31	38	44	50	57
31	–	–	–	–	–	–	–	1005	1011	1018	1	1	2	3	3	4	5	5	6
32	1024	1030	1037	1043	1050	1056	1063	1069	1076	1082	1	1	2	3	3	4	5	5	6
33	1089	1096	1102	1109	1116	1122	1129	1136	1142	1149	1	1	2	3	3	4	5	5	6
34	1156	1163	1170	1176	1183	1190	1197	1204	1211	1218	1	1	2	3	3	4	5	6	6
35	1225	1232	1239	1246	1253	1260	1267	1274	1282	1289	1	1	2	3	4	4	5	6	6
36	1296	1303	1310	1318	1325	1332	1340	1347	1354	1362	1	1	2	3	4	4	5	6	7
37	1369	1376	1384	1391	1399	1406	1414	1421	1429	1436	1	2	2	3	4	5	5	6	7
38	1444	1452	1459	1467	1475	1482	1490	1498	1505	1513	1	2	2	3	4	5	5	6	7
39	1521	1529	1537	1544	1552	1560	1568	1576	1584	1592	1	2	2	3	4	5	6	6	7
40	1600	1608	1616	1624	1632	1640	1648	1656	1665	1673	1	2	2	3	4	5	6	6	7
41	1681	1689	1697	1706	1714	1722	1731	1739	1747	1756	1	2	2	3	4	5	6	7	7
42	1764	1772	1781	1789	1798	1806	1815	1823	1832	1840	1	2	3	3	4	5	6	7	8
43	1849	1858	1866	1875	1884	1892	1901	1910	1918	1927	1	2	3	3	4	5	6	7	8
44	1936	1945	1954	1962	1971	1980	1989	1998	2007	2016	1	2	3	4	5	5	6	7	8
45	2025	2034	2043	2052	2061	2070	2079	2088	2098	2107	1	2	3	4	5	5	6	7	8
46	2116	2125	2134	2144	2153	2162	2172	2181	2190	2200	1	2	3	4	5	6	7	7	8
47	2209	2218	2228	2237	2247	2256	2266	2275	2285	2294	1	2	3	4	5	6	7	8	9
48	2304	2314	2323	2333	2343	2352	2362	2372	2381	2391	1	2	3	4	5	6	7	8	9
49	2401	2411	2421	2430	2440	2450	2460	2470	2480	2490	1	2	3	4	5	6	7	8	9
50	2500	2510	2520	2530	2540	2550	2560	2570	2581	2591	1	2	3	4	5	6	7	8	9
51	2601	2611	2621	2632	2642	2652	2663	2673	2683	2694	1	2	3	4	5	6	7	8	9
52	2704	2714	2725	2735	2746	2756	2767	2777	2788	2798	1	2	3	4	5	6	7	8	9
53	2809	2820	2830	2841	2852	2862	2873	2884	2894	2905	1	2	3	4	5	6	7	9	10
54	2916	2927	2938	2948	2959	2970	2981	2992	3003	3014	1	2	3	4	5	7	8	9	10

x	0	1	2	3	4	5	6	7	8	9	Diff. 1	2	3	4	5	6	7	8	9
55	3025	3036	3047	3058	3069	3080	3091	3102	3114	3125	1	2	3	4	6	7	8	9	10
56	3136	3147	3158	3170	3181	3192	3204	3215	3226	3238	1	2	3	5	6	7	8	9	10
57	3249	3260	3272	3283	3295	3306	3318	3329	3341	3352	1	2	3	5	6	7	8	9	10
58	3364	3376	3387	3399	3411	3422	3434	3446	3457	3469	1	2	4	5	6	7	8	9	10
59	3481	3493	3505	3516	3528	3540	3552	3564	3576	3588	1	2	4	5	6	7	8	10	11
60	3600	3612	3624	3636	3648	3660	3672	3684	3697	3709	1	2	4	5	6	7	8	10	11
61	3721	3733	3745	3758	3770	3782	3795	3807	3819	3832	1	2	4	5	6	7	9	10	11
62	3844	3856	3869	3881	3894	3906	3919	3931	3944	3956	1	2	4	5	6	7	9	10	11
63	3969	3982	3994	4007	4020	4032	4045	4058	4070	4083	1	3	4	5	6	8	9	10	11
64	4096	4109	4122	4134	4147	4160	4173	4186	4199	4212	1	3	4	5	6	8	9	10	12
65	4225	4238	4251	4264	4277	4290	4303	4316	4330	4343	1	3	4	5	7	8	9	10	12
66	4356	4369	4382	4396	4409	4422	4436	4449	4462	4476	1	3	4	5	7	8	9	11	12
67	4489	4502	4516	4529	4543	4556	4570	4583	4597	4610	1	3	4	5	7	8	9	11	12
68	4624	4638	4651	4665	4679	4692	4706	4720	4733	4747	1	3	4	5	7	8	10	11	12
69	4761	4775	4789	4802	4816	4830	4844	4858	4872	4886	1	3	4	6	7	8	10	11	13
70	4900	4914	4928	4942	4956	4970	4984	4998	5013	5027	1	3	4	6	7	8	10	11	13
71	5041	5055	5069	5084	5098	5112	5127	5141	5155	5170	1	3	4	6	7	9	10	11	13
72	5184	5198	5213	5227	5242	5256	5271	5285	5300	5314	1	3	4	6	7	9	10	11	13
73	5329	5344	5358	5373	5388	5402	5417	5432	5446	5461	1	3	4	6	7	9	10	12	13
74	5476	5491	5506	5520	5535	5550	5565	5580	5595	5610	1	3	4	6	7	9	10	12	13
75	5625	5640	5655	5670	5685	5700	5715	5730	5746	5761	2	3	5	6	8	9	11	12	14
76	5776	5791	5806	5822	5837	5852	5868	5883	5898	5914	2	3	5	6	8	9	11	12	14
77	5929	5944	5960	5975	5991	6006	6022	6037	6053	6068	2	3	5	6	8	9	11	12	14
78	6084	6100	6115	6131	6147	6162	6178	6194	6209	6225	2	3	5	6	8	9	11	13	14
79	6241	6257	6273	6288	6304	6320	6336	6352	6368	6384	2	3	5	6	8	10	11	13	14
80	6400	6416	6432	6448	6464	6480	6496	6512	6529	6545	2	3	5	6	8	10	11	13	14
81	6561	6577	6593	6610	6626	6642	6659	6675	6691	6708	2	3	5	7	8	10	11	13	15
82	6724	6740	6757	6773	6790	6806	6823	6839	6856	6872	2	3	5	7	8	10	12	13	15
83	6889	6906	6922	6939	6956	6972	6989	7006	7022	7039	2	3	5	7	8	10	12	13	15
84	7056	7073	7090	7106	7123	7140	7157	7174	7191	7208	2	3	5	7	8	10	12	14	15
85	7225	7242	7259	7276	7293	7310	7327	7344	7362	7379	2	3	5	7	9	10	12	14	15
86	7396	7413	7430	7448	7465	7482	7500	7517	7534	7552	2	3	5	7	9	10	12	14	16
87	7569	7586	7604	7621	7639	7656	7674	7691	7709	7726	2	3	5	7	9	10	12	14	16
88	7744	7762	7779	7797	7815	7832	7850	7868	7885	7903	2	4	5	7	9	11	12	14	16
89	7921	7939	7957	7974	7992	8010	8028	8046	8064	8082	2	4	5	7	9	11	13	14	15
90	8100	8118	8136	8154	8172	8190	8208	8226	8245	8263	2	4	5	7	9	11	13	14	16
91	8281	8299	8317	8336	8354	8372	8391	8409	8427	8446	2	4	5	7	9	11	13	15	16
92	8464	8482	8501	8519	8538	8556	8575	8593	8612	8630	2	4	6	7	9	11	13	15	17
93	8649	8668	8686	8705	8724	8742	8761	8780	8798	8817	2	4	6	7	9	11	13	15	17
94	8836	8855	8874	8892	8911	8930	8949	8968	8987	9006	2	4	6	8	9	11	13	15	17
95	9025	9044	9063	9082	9101	9120	9139	9158	9178	9197	2	4	6	8	10	11	13	15	17
96	9216	9235	9254	9274	9293	9312	9332	9351	9370	9390	2	4	6	8	10	12	14	15	17
97	9409	9428	9448	9467	9487	9506	9526	9545	9565	9584	2	4	6	8	10	12	14	16	18
98	9604	9624	9643	9663	9683	9702	9722	9742	9761	9781	2	4	6	8	10	12	14	16	18
99	9801	9821	9841	9860	9880	9900	9920	9940	9960	9980	2	4	6	8	10	12	14	16	18

Square roots from 1 to 10

X	0	1	2	3	4	5	6	7	8	9	Differences 1	2	3	4	5	6	7	8	9
1·0	1·000	1·005	1·010	1·015	1·020	1·025	1·030	1·034	1·039	1·044	0	1	1	2	2	3	3	4	4
1·1	1·049	1·054	1·058	1·063	1·068	1·072	1·077	1·082	1·088	1·091	0	1	1	2	2	3	3	4	4
1·2	1·095	1·100	1·105	1·109	1·114	1·118	1·123	1·127	1·131	1·136	0	1	1	2	2	3	3	4	4
1·3	1·140	1·145	1·149	1·153	1·158	1·162	1·166	1·171	1·175	1·179	0	1	1	2	2	3	3	3	4
1·4	1·183	1·187	1·192	1·196	1·200	1·204	1·208	1·212	1·217	1·221	0	1	1	2	2	2	3	3	4
1·5	1·225	1·229	1·233	1·237	1·241	1·245	1·249	1·253	1·257	1·261	0	1	1	2	2	2	3	3	4
1·6	1·265	1·269	1·273	1·277	1·281	1·285	1·288	1·292	1·296	1·300	0	1	1	2	2	2	3	3	3
1·7	1·304	1·308	1·312	1·315	1·319	1·323	1·327	1·330	1·334	1·338	0	1	1	2	2	2	3	3	3
1·8	1·342	1·345	1·349	1·353	1·357	1·360	1·364	1·368	1·371	1·375	0	1	1	1	2	2	3	3	3
1·9	1·378	1·382	1·386	1·389	1·393	1·396	1·400	1·404	1·407	1·411	0	1	1	1	2	2	3	3	3
2·0	1·414	1·418	1·421	1·425	1·428	1·432	1·435	1·439	1·442	1·446	0	1	1	1	2	2	2	3	3
2·1	1·449	1·453	1·456	1·460	1·463	1·466	1·470	1·473	1·477	1·480	0	1	1	1	2	2	2	3	3
2·2	1·483	1·487	1·490	1·493	1·497	1·500	1·503	1·507	1·510	1·513	0	1	1	1	2	2	2	3	3
2·3	1·517	1·520	1·523	1·526	1·530	1·533	1·536	1·539	1·543	1·546	0	1	1	1	2	2	2	3	3
2·4	1·549	1·552	1·556	1·559	1·562	1·565	1·568	1·572	1·575	1·578	0	1	1	1	2	2	2	3	3
2·5	1·581	1·584	1·587	1·591	1·594	1·597	1·600	1·603	1·606	1·609	0	1	1	1	2	2	2	3	3
2·6	1·612	1·616	1·619	1·622	1·625	1·628	1·631	1·634	1·637	1·640	0	1	1	1	2	2	2	2	3
2·7	1·643	1·646	1·649	1·652	1·655	1·658	1·661	1·664	1·667	1·670	0	1	1	1	2	2	2	2	3
2·8	1·673	1·676	1·679	1·682	1·685	1·688	1·691	1·694	1·697	1·700	0	1	1	1	1	2	2	2	3
2·9	1·703	1·706	1·709	1·712	1·715	1·718	1·720	1·723	1·726	1·729	0	1	1	1	1	2	2	2	3
3·0	1·732	1·735	1·738	1·741	1·744	1·746	1·749	1·752	1·755	1·758	0	1	1	1	1	2	2	2	3
3·1	1·761	1·764	1·766	1·769	1·772	1·775	1·778	1·780	1·783	1·786	0	1	1	1	1	2	2	2	3
3·2	1·789	1·792	1·794	1·797	1·800	1·803	1·806	1·808	1·811	1·814	0	1	1	1	1	2	2	2	2
3·3	1·817	1·819	1·822	1·825	1·828	1·830	1·833	1·836	1·839	1·841	0	1	1	1	1	2	2	2	2
3·4	1·844	1·847	1·849	1·852	1·855	1·857	1·860	1·863	1·866	1·868	0	1	1	1	1	2	2	2	2
3·5	1·871	1·874	1·876	1·879	1·882	1·884	1·887	1·889	1·892	1·895	0	1	1	1	1	2	2	2	2
3·6	1·897	1·900	1·903	1·905	1·908	1·911	1·913	1·916	1·918	1·921	0	1	1	1	1	2	2	2	2
3·7	1·924	1·926	1·929	1·931	1·934	1·937	1·939	1·942	1·944	1·947	0	1	1	1	1	2	2	2	2
3·8	1·949	1·952	1·955	1·957	1·960	1·962	1·965	1·967	1·970	1·972	0	1	1	1	1	2	2	2	2
3·9	1·975	1·977	1·980	1·982	1·985	1·988	1·990	1·993	1·995	1·998	0	1	1	1	1	2	2	2	2
4·0	2·000	2·003	2·005	2·008	2·010	2·013	2·015	2·017	2·020	2·022	0	0	1	1	1	1	2	2	2
4·1	2·025	2·027	2·030	2·032	2·035	2·037	2·040	2·042	2·045	2·047	0	0	1	1	1	1	2	2	2
4·2	2·049	2·052	2·054	2·057	2·059	2·062	2·064	2·066	2·069	2·071	0	0	1	1	1	1	2	2	2
4·3	2·074	2·076	2·078	2·081	2·083	2·086	2·088	2·091	2·093	2·095	0	0	1	1	1	1	2	2	2
4·4	2·098	2·100	2·102	2·105	2·107	2·110	2·112	2·114	2·117	2·119	0	0	1	1	1	1	2	2	2
4·5	2·121	2·124	2·126	2·128	2·131	2·133	2·135	2·138	2·140	2·142	0	0	1	1	1	1	2	2	2
4·6	2·145	2·147	2·149	2·152	2·154	2·156	2·159	2·101	2·163	2·166	0	0	1	1	1	1	2	2	2
4·7	2·168	2·170	2·173	2·175	2·177	2·179	2·132	2·184	2·186	2·189	0	0	1	1	1	1	2	2	2
4·8	2·191	2·193	2·195	2·196	2·200	2·202	2·205	2·207	2·209	2·211	0	0	1	1	1	1	2	2	2
4·9	2·214	2·216	2·218	2·220	2·223	2·225	2·227	2·229	2·232	2·234	0	0	1	1	1	1	2	2	2
5·0	2·236	2·238	2·241	2·243	2·245	2·247	2·249	2·252	2·254	2·256	0	0	1	1	1	1	2	2	2
5·1	2·258	2·261	2·263	2·265	2·267	2·269	2·272	2·274	2·276	2·278	0	0	1	1	1	1	2	2	2
5·2	2·280	2·283	2·285	2·287	2·289	2·291	2·294	2·296	2·298	2·300	0	0	1	1	1	1	2	2	2
5·3	2·302	2·304	2·307	2·309	2·311	2·313	2·315	2·317	2·320	2·322	0	0	1	1	1	1	2	2	2
5·4	2·324	2·326	2·328	2·330	2·332	2·335	2·337	2·339	2·341	2·343	0	0	1	1	1	1	1	2	2

X	0	1	2	3	4	5	6	7	8	9	Differences 1	2	3	4	5	6	7	8	9
5·5	2·345	2·347	2·350	2·352	2·354	2·356	2·358	2·360	2·362	2·364	0	0	1	1	1	1	1	2	2
5·6	2·366	2·369	2·371	2·373	2·375	2·377	2·379	2·381	2·383	2·385	0	0	1	1	1	1	1	2	2
5·7	2·388	2·390	2·392	2·394	2·396	2·398	2·400	2·402	2·404	2·406	0	0	1	1	1	1	1	2	2
5·8	2·408	2·410	2·412	2·415	2·417	2·419	2·421	2·423	2·425	2·427	0	0	1	1	1	1	1	2	2
5·9	2·429	2·431	2·433	2·435	2·437	2·439	2·441	2·443	2·445	2·447	0	0	1	1	1	1	1	2	2
6·0	2·450	2·452	2·454	2·456	2·458	2·460	2·462	2·464	2·466	2·468	0	0	1	1	1	1	1	2	2
6·1	2·470	2·472	2·474	2·476	2·478	2·480	2·482	2·484	2·485	2·488	0	0	1	1	1	1	1	2	2
6·2	2·490	2·492	2·494	2·496	2·498	2·500	2·502	2·504	2·506	2·508	0	0	1	1	1	1	1	2	2
6·3	2·510	2·512	2·514	2·516	2·518	2·520	2·522	2·524	2·526	2·528	0	0	1	1	1	1	1	2	2
6·4	2·530	2·532	2·534	2·536	2·538	2·540	2·542	2·544	2·546	2·548	0	0	1	1	1	1	1	2	2
6·5	2·550	2·551	2·553	2·555	2·557	2·559	2·561	2·563	2·565	2·567	0	0	1	1	1	1	1	2	2
6·6	2·569	2·571	2·573	2·575	2·577	2·579	2·581	2·583	2·585	2·587	0	0	1	1	1	1	1	2	2
6·7	2·588	2·590	2·592	2·594	2·596	2·598	2·600	2·602	2·604	2·606	0	0	1	1	1	1	1	2	2
6·8	2·608	2·610	2·612	2·613	2·615	2·617	2·619	2·621	2·623	2·625	0	0	1	1	1	1	1	2	2
6·9	2·627	2·629	2·631	2·632	2·634	2·636	2·638	2·640	2·642	2·644	0	0	1	1	1	1	1	2	2
7·0	2·646	2·648	2·650	2·651	2·653	2·655	2·657	2·659	2·661	2·663	0	0	1	1	1	1	1	2	2
7·1	2·665	2·667	2·668	2·670	2·672	2·674	2·676	2·678	2·680	2·681	0	0	1	1	1	1	1	2	2
7·2	2·683	2·685	2·687	2·689	2·691	2·693	2·694	2·696	2·698	2·700	0	0	1	1	1	1	1	2	2
7·3	2·702	2·704	2·706	2·707	2·709	2·711	2·713	2·715	2·717	2·719	0	0	1	1	1	1	1	2	2
7·4	2·720	2·722	2·724	2·726	2·728	2·729	2·731	2·733	2·735	2·737	0	0	1	1	1	1	1	2	2
7·5	2·739	2·740	2·742	2·744	2·746	2·748	2·750	2·751	2·753	2·755	0	0	1	1	1	1	1	2	2
7·6	2·757	2·759	2·760	2·762	2·764	2·766	2·768	2·769	2·771	2·773	0	0	1	1	1	1	1	2	2
7·7	2·775	2·777	2·778	2·780	2·782	2·784	2·786	2·787	2·789	2·791	0	0	1	1	1	1	1	2	2
7·8	2·793	2·795	2·796	2·798	2·800	2·802	2·804	2·805	2·807	2·809	0	0	1	1	1	1	1	2	2
7·9	2·811	2·812	2·814	2·816	2·818	2·820	2·821	2·823	2·825	2·827	0	0	1	1	1	1	1	2	2
8·0	2·828	2·830	2·832	2·834	2·835	2·837	2·839	2·841	2·843	2·844	0	0	1	1	1	1	1	2	2
8·1	2·846	2·848	2·850	2·851	2·853	2·855	2·857	2·858	2·860	2·862	0	0	1	1	1	1	1	2	2
8·2	2·864	2·865	2·867	2·869	2·871	2·872	2·874	2·876	2·877	2·879	0	0	1	1	1	1	1	2	2
8·3	2·881	2·883	2·884	2·886	2·888	2·890	2·891	2·893	2·895	2·897	0	0	1	1	1	1	1	2	2
8·4	2·898	2·900	2·902	2·903	2·905	2·907	2·909	2·910	2·912	2·914	0	0	1	1	1	1	1	2	2
8·5	2·915	2·917	2·919	2·921	2·922	2·924	2·926	2·927	2·929	2·931	0	0	1	1	1	1	1	1	2
8·6	2·933	2·934	2·936	2·938	2·939	2·941	2·943	2·944	2·946	2·948	0	0	1	1	1	1	1	1	2
8·7	2·950	2·951	2·953	2·955	2·956	2·958	2·960	2·961	2·963	2·965	0	0	1	1	1	1	1	1	2
8·8	2·966	2·968	2·970	2·972	2·973	2·975	2·977	2·978	2·980	2·982	0	0	1	1	1	1	1	1	2
8·9	2·983	2·985	2·987	2·988	2·990	2·992	2·993	2·995	2·997	2·998	0	0	1	1	1	1	1	1	2
9·0	3·000	3·002	3·003	3·005	3·007	3·008	3·010	3·012	3·013	3·015	0	0	1	1	1	1	1	1	1
9·1	3·017	3·018	3·020	3·022	3·023	3·025	3·027	3·028	3·030	3·032	0	0	1	1	1	1	1	1	1
9·2	3·033	3·035	3·036	3·038	3·040	3·041	3·043	3·045	3·046	3·048	0	0	1	1	1	1	1	1	1
9·3	3·050	3·051	3·053	3·055	3·056	3·058	3·059	3·061	3·063	3·064	0	0	1	1	1	1	1	1	1
9·4	3·066	3·068	3·069	3·071	3·072	3·074	3·076	3·077	3·079	3·081	0	0	1	1	1	1	1	1	1
9·5	3·082	3·084	3·085	3·087	3·089	3·090	3·092	3·094	3·095	3·097	0	0	1	1	1	1	1	1	1
9·6	3·098	3·100	3·102	3·103	3·105	3·106	3·108	3·110	3·111	3·113	0	0	1	1	1	1	1	1	1
9·7	3·115	3·116	3·118	3·119	3·121	3·123	3·124	3·126	3·127	3·129	0	0	1	1	1	1	1	1	1
9·8	3·131	3·132	3·134	3·135	3·137	3·139	3·140	3·142	3·143	3·145	0	0	1	1	1	1	1	1	1
9·9	3·146	3·148	3·150	3·151	3·153	3·154	3·156	3·158	3·159	3·161	0	0	1	1	1	1	1	1	1

Square roots from 10 to 100

$x \rightarrow \sqrt{x}$

x	0	1	2	3	4	5	6	7	8	9	Differences								
											1	2	3	4	5	6	7	8	9
10	3·162	3·178	3·194	3·209	3·225	3·240	3·256	3·271	3·286	3·302	2	3	5	6	8	9	11	12	14
11	3·317	3·332	3·347	3·362	3·376	3·391	3·395	3·421	3·435	3·450	1	3	4	6	7	9	10	12	13
12	3·464	3·479	3·493	3·507	3·521	3·536	3·550	3·564	3·578	3·592	1	3	4	6	7	8	10	11	13
13	3·606	3·619	3·633	3·647	3·661	3·674	3·688	3·701	3·715	3·728	1	3	4	5	7	8	10	11	12
14	3·742	3·755	3·768	3·782	3·795	3·808	3·821	3·834	3·847	3·860	1	3	4	5	7	8	9	11	12
15	3·873	3·886	3·899	3·912	3·924	3·937	3·950	3·962	3·975	3·988	1	3	4	5	6	8	9	10	11
16	4·000	4·012	4·025	4·037	4·050	4·062	4·074	4·087	4·099	4·111	1	2	4	5	6	7	9	10	11
17	4·123	4·135	4·147	4·159	4·171	4·183	4·195	4·207	4·219	4·231	1	2	4	5	6	7	8	10	11
18	4·243	4·254	4·266	4·278	4·290	4·301	4·313	4·324	4·336	4·347	1	2	3	5	6	7	8	9	10
19	4·359	4·370	4·382	4·393	4·405	4·416	4·427	4·438	4·450	4·461	1	2	3	5	6	7	8	9	10
20	4·472	4·483	4·494	4·506	4·517	4·528	4·539	4·550	4·561	4·572	1	2	3	4	6	7	8	9	10
21	4·583	4·594	4·604	4·615	4·626	4·637	4·648	4·658	4·669	4·680	1	2	3	4	5	6	8	9	10
22	4·690	4·701	4·712	4·722	4·733	4·743	4·754	4·765	4·775	4·785	1	2	3	4	5	6	7	8	9
23	4·796	4·806	4·817	4·827	4·837	4·848	4·858	4·868	4·879	4·889	1	2	3	4	5	6	7	8	9
24	4·899	4·909	4·919	4·930	4·940	4·950	4·960	4·970	4·980	4·990	1	2	3	4	5	6	7	8	9
25	5·000	5·010	5·020	5·030	5·040	5·050	5·060	5·070	5·079	5·089	1	2	3	4	5	6	7	8	9
26	5·099	5·109	5·119	5·128	5·138	5·148	5·158	5·167	5·177	5·187	1	2	3	4	5	6	7	8	9
27	5·196	5·206	5·215	5·225	5·235	5·244	5·254	5·263	5·273	5·282	1	2	3	4	5	6	7	8	9
28	5·292	5·301	5·310	5·320	5·329	5·339	5·343	5·357	5·367	5·376	1	2	3	4	5	6	7	7	8
29	5·385	5·394	5·404	5·413	5·422	5·431	5·441	5·450	5·459	5·468	1	2	3	4	5	5	6	7	8
30	5·477	5·486	5·495	5·503	5·514	5·523	5·522	5·514	5·550	5·359	1	2	3	4	4	5	6	7	8
31	5·568	5·577	5·586	5·595	5·604	5·612	5·621	5·630	5·639	5·648	1	2	3	3	4	5	6	7	8
32	5·657	5·666	5·675	5·683	5·692	5·701	5·710	5·718	5·727	5·736	1	2	3	3	4	5	6	7	8
33	5·745	5·753	5·762	5·771	5·779	5·788	5·793	5·805	5·814	5·822	1	2	3	3	4	5	6	7	8
34	5·831	5·840	5·848	5·857	5·865	5·874	5·832	5·891	5·899	5·903	1	2	3	3	4	5	6	7	8
35	5·916	5·925	5·933	5·941	5·950	5·958	5·957	5·975	5·683	5·902	1	2	2	3	4	5	6	7	8
36	6·000	6·008	6·017	6·025	6·033	6·042	6·050	6·058	6·066	6·075	1	2	2	3	4	5	6	7	7
37	6·083	6·091	6·099	6·107	6·118	6·124	6·132	6·140	6·148	6·156	1	2	2	3	4	5	6	7	7
38	6·164	6·173	6·181	6·189	6·197	6·205	6·213	6·221	6·229	6·237	1	2	2	3	4	5	6	6	7
39	6·245	6·253	6·261	6·269	6·277	6·285	6·283	6·301	6·309	6·317	1	2	2	3	4	5	6	6	7
40	6·325	6·332	6·340	6·348	6·356	6·364	6·372	6·380	6·387	6·395	1	2	2	3	4	5	6	6	7
41	6·403	6·411	6·419	6·427	6·434	6·442	6·450	6·458	6·465	6·473	1	2	2	3	4	5	5	6	7
42	6·481	6·488	6·496	6·504	6·512	6·519	6·527	6·535	6·542	6·550	1	2	2	3	4	5	5	6	7
43	6·557	6·565	6·573	6·580	6·588	6·595	6·603	6·611	6·618	6·628	1	2	2	3	4	5	5	6	7
44	6·633	6·641	6·648	6·656	6·663	6·671	6·678	6·686	6·693	6·701	1	2	2	3	4	5	5	6	7
45	6·708	6·716	6·723	6·731	6·738	6·745	6·753	6·760	6·768	6·775	1	1	2	3	4	4	5	6	7
46	6·782	6·790	6·797	6·804	6·812	6·819	6·828	6·834	6·841	6·848	1	1	2	3	4	4	5	6	7
47	6·856	6·863	6·870	6·878	6·885	6·892	6·890	6·907	6·914	6·921	1	1	2	3	4	4	5	6	7
48	6·928	6·935	6·943	6·950	6·957	6·964	6·971	6·979	6·986	6·993	1	1	2	3	4	4	5	6	6
49	7·000	7·007	7·014	7·021	7·029	7·033	7·043	7·050	7·057	7·064	1	1	2	3	4	4	5	6	6
50	7·071	7·078	7·085	7·092	7·099	7·106	7·113	7·120	7·127	7·134	1	1	2	3	4	4	5	6	6
51	7·141	7·148	7·155	7·162	7·169	7·176	7·183	7·190	7·197	7·204	1	1	2	3	4	4	5	6	6
52	7·211	7·218	7·225	7·232	7·239	7·246	7·253	7·259	7·260	7·273	1	1	2	3	3	4	5	6	6
53	7·280	7·287	7·294	7·301	7·308	7·314	7·321	7·328	7·335	7·342	1	1	2	3	3	4	5	5	6
54	7·349	7·355	7·362	7·369	7·376	7·382	7·389	7·396	7·403	7·410	1	1	2	3	3	4	5	5	6

x	0	1	2	3	4	5	6	7	8	9	Differences								
											1	2	3	4	5	6	7	8	9
55	7·416	7·423	7·430	7·436	7·443	7·450	7·457	7·463	7·470	7·477	1	1	2	3	3	4	5	5	6
56	7·483	7·490	7·497	7·503	7·510	7·517	7·523	7·530	7·537	7·543	1	1	2	3	3	4	5	5	6
57	7·550	7·556	7·563	7·570	7·576	7·583	7·589	7·596	7·603	7·609	1	1	2	3	3	4	5	5	6
58	7·616	7·622	7·629	7·635	7·642	7·649	7·655	7·662	7·668	7·675	1	1	2	3	3	4	5	5	6
59	7·681	7·688	7·694	7·701	7·707	7·714	7·720	7·727	7·733	7·740	1	1	2	3	3	4	4	5	6
60	7·746	7·752	7·759	7·765	7·772	7·778	7·785	7·791	7·797	7·804	1	1	2	3	3	4	4	5	6
61	7·810	7·817	7·823	7·829	7·836	7·842	7·849	7·855	7·861	7·868	1	1	2	3	3	4	4	5	6
62	7·874	7·880	7·887	7·893	7·899	7·906	7·912	7·918	7·925	7·931	1	1	2	3	3	4	4	5	6
63	7·937	7·944	7·950	7·956	7·962	7·969	7·975	7·981	7·987	7·994	1	1	2	3	3	4	4	5	6
64	8·000	8·006	8·012	8·019	8·025	8·031	8·037	8·044	8·050	8·056	1	1	2	2	3	4	4	5	6
65	8·062	8·068	8·075	8·081	8·087	8·093	8·099	8·106	8·112	8·118	1	1	2	2	3	4	4	5	6
66	8·124	8·130	8·136	8·142	8·149	8·155	8·161	8·167	8·173	8·179	1	1	2	2	3	4	4	5	5
67	8·185	8·191	8·198	8·204	8·210	8·216	8·222	8·228	8·234	8·240	1	1	2	2	3	4	4	5	5
68	8·246	8·252	8·258	8·264	8·270	8·276	8·283	8·289	8·295	8·301	1	1	2	2	3	4	4	5	5
69	8·307	8·313	8·319	8·325	8·331	8·337	8·343	8·349	8·355	8·361	1	1	2	2	3	4	4	5	5
70	8·367	8·373	8·379	8·385	8·390	8·396	8·402	8·408	8·414	8·420	1	1	2	2	3	4	4	5	5
71	8·426	8·432	8·438	8·444	8·450	8·456	8·462	8·468	8·473	8·479	1	1	2	2	3	4	4	5	5
72	8·485	8·491	8·497	8·503	8·509	8·515	8·521	8·526	8·532	8·538	1	1	2	2	3	3	4	5	5
73	8·544	8·550	8·556	8·562	8·567	8·573	8·579	8·585	8·591	8·597	1	1	2	2	3	3	4	5	5
74	8·602	8·608	8·614	8·620	8·623	8·631	8·637	8·643	8·649	8·654	1	1	2	2	3	3	4	5	5
75	8·660	8·666	8·672	8·678	8·683	8·689	8·695	8·701	8·706	8·712	1	1	2	2	3	3	4	5	5
76	8·718	8·724	8·729	8·735	8·741	8·746	8·752	8·758	8·764	8·769	1	1	2	2	3	3	4	5	5
77	8·775	8·781	8·786	8·792	8·798	8·803	8·809	8·815	8·820	8·826	1	1	2	2	3	3	4	4	5
78	8·832	8·837	8·843	8·849	8·854	8·860	8·866	8·871	8·877	8·883	1	1	2	2	3	3	4	4	5
79	8·888	8·894	8·899	8·905	8·911	8·916	8·922	8·927	8·933	8·939	1	1	2	2	3	3	4	4	5
80	8·944	8·950	8·955	8·961	8·967	8·972	8·978	8·983	8·989	8·994	1	1	2	2	3	3	4	4	5
81	9·000	9·006	9·011	9·017	9·022	9·028	9·033	9·039	9·044	9·050	1	1	2	2	3	3	4	4	5
82	9·055	9·061	9·066	9·072	9·077	9·083	9·088	9·094	9·099	9·105	1	1	2	2	3	3	4	4	5
83	9·110	9·116	9·121	9·127	9·132	9·138	9·143	9·149	9·154	9·160	1	1	2	2	3	3	4	4	5
84	9·165	9·171	9·176	9·182	9·187	9·192	9·198	9·203	9·209	9·214	1	1	2	2	3	3	4	4	5
85	9·220	9·225	9·230	9·236	9·241	9·247	9·252	9·257	9·263	9·268	1	1	2	2	3	3	4	4	5
86	9·274	9·279	9·284	9·290	9·295	9·301	9·306	9·311	9·317	9·322	1	1	2	2	3	3	4	4	5
87	9·327	9·333	9·338	9·343	9·349	9·354	9·359	9·365	9·370	9·375	1	1	2	2	3	3	4	4	5
88	9·381	9·386	9·391	9·397	9·402	9·407	9·413	9·418	9·423	9·429	1	1	2	2	3	3	4	4	5
89	9·434	9·439	9·445	9·450	9·455	9·460	9·466	9·471	9·476	9·482	1	1	2	2	3	3	4	4	5
90	9·487	9·492	9·497	9·503	9·508	9·513	9·518	9·524	9·529	9·534	1	1	2	2	3	3	4	4	5
91	9·539	9·545	9·550	9·555	9·560	9·566	9·571	9·576	9·581	9·586	1	1	2	2	3	3	4	4	5
92	9·592	9·597	9·602	9·607	9·613	9·618	9·623	9·628	9·633	9·638	1	1	2	2	3	3	4	4	5
93	9·644	9·649	9·654	9·659	9·664	9·670	9·675	9·680	9·685	9·690	1	1	2	2	3	3	4	4	5
94	9·695	9·701	9·706	9·711	9·716	9·721	9·726	9·731	9·737	9·742	1	1	2	2	3	3	4	4	5
95	9·747	9·752	9·757	9·762	9·767	9·772	9·778	9·783	9·788	9·793	1	1	2	2	3	3	4	4	5
96	9·798	9·803	9·808	9·813	9·818	9·823	9·829	9·834	9·839	9·844	1	1	2	2	3	3	4	4	5
97	9·849	9·854	9·859	9·864	9·869	9·874	9·879	9·884	9·889	9·894	1	1	1	2	3	3	4	4	5
98	9·900	9·905	9·910	9·915	9·920	9·925	9·930	9·935	9·940	9·945	0	1	1	2	2	3	3	4	4
99	9·950	9·955	9·960	9·965	9·970	9·975	9·980	9·985	9·990	9·995	0	1	1	2	2	3	3	4	4

Answers

Preliminary chapter

Review test 1 (Number and numeration)

1 a) 7 tenths b) 5 hundreds
2 a) 3 b) 14
3 a) 20 b) 180
4 a) $\frac{5}{7}$ b) $\frac{8}{11}$
5 a) $\frac{7}{24}$ b) $14\frac{7}{20}$
c) 6 d) $\frac{3}{4}$
6 a) 40% b) 8%
c) 4% d) 18%

7

common fraction	decimal fraction	percentage
$\frac{1}{2}$	0·5	50%
$\frac{2}{5}$	0·4	40%
$\frac{3}{4}$	0·75	75%
$\frac{3}{5}$	0·6	60%
$\frac{7}{25}$	0·28	28%
$\frac{5}{8}$	0·625	62·5%

8 a) 2 b) $2y$
c) −90 d) $20x$
9 a) i) 28 000, ii) 27 500, iii) 27 540
b) i) 14 000, ii) 13 700, iii) 13 710
10 a) i) 1, ii) 0·9, iii) 0·87
b) i) 7, ii) 7·0, iii) 7·01

Review test 2 (Number and numeration)

1 a) 3 hundredths b) 9 units
2 a) 11 b) 18
3 a) 60 b) 360
4 a) $\frac{4}{5}$ b) $\frac{5}{7}$
5 a) $\frac{11}{9} = 1\frac{2}{9}$ b) $1\frac{31}{40}$
c) $\frac{2}{3}$ d) $1\frac{1}{2}$
6 a) 53·3% b) 7%
c) 7% d) 0·65%

7

common fraction	decimal fraction	percentage
$\frac{1}{2}$	0·5	50%
$\frac{7}{10}$	0·7	70%
$\frac{11}{20}$	0·55	55%
$\frac{23}{25}$	0·92	92%
$\frac{2}{3}$	0·6667	$66\frac{2}{3}$%
$\frac{21}{40}$	0·525	52·5%

8 a) −2 b) $-19y$
c) 450 d) $-2x$
9 a) i) 6 000, ii) 6 000, iii) 5 980
b) i) 20 000, ii) 20 100, iii) 20 070
10 a) i) 2, ii) 2·4, iii) 2·39
b) i) 4, ii) 4·3, iii) 4·30

Review test 3 (Algebraic processes)

1 a) $p = 22$ b) $q = 28$
c) $r = 13$ d) $s = 4$
2 a) 15 b) 38
c) 7 d) 7
3 a) $3p$ b) $11q$
c) $5r + 11$ d) $2w + 4y + 14z$
4 a) i) 4, ii) $\frac{d}{7}$
b) i) 4, ii) $b - 2$
5 a) $11 - 6a$ b) $4a - 5$
c) $5 + a$ d) $7x + 13y$
6 a) $a = 2$ b) $b = 7$
c) $c = 8$ d) $k = 1$

Review test 4 (Algebraic processes)

1 a) $f = 5$ b) $g = 9$
c) $m = 36$ d) $n = 9$
2 a) 22 b) −1
c) 27 d) −5

3 a) $14f$ **b)** $5g$
c) $3m - 4n$ **d)** $2y - 5$

4 a) i) 200, ii) $100m$
b) i) 7, ii) $6 + n$

5 a) $a - 8$ **b)** $5b - 7$
c) $4x + y$ **d)** $8y - 7$

6 a) $a = 7$ **b)** $b = 8$
c) $c = 2{\cdot}5$ **d)** $d = 2$

Review test 5 *(Geometry and mensuration)*

1 a) i) 4·25 litres, ii) 4 250 ml
b) i) 3·5, ii) 1 440

2 8 faces, 18 edges, 12 vertices

3 Yes: the right-angled triangle and obtuse-angled triangle are also scalene (their three sides are of different lengths)

4

	shape	length	breadth	perimeter	area
a)	rectangle	5 cm	9 cm	28 cm	45 cm^2
b)	rectangle	8 cm	7 cm	30 cm	56 cm^2
c)	square	7 cm		28 cm	49 cm^2
d)	square	8 km		32 km	64 km^2

5

	radius	diameter	circumference	area
a)	7 cm	14 cm	42 cm	147 cm^2
b)	8 cm	16 cm	48 cm	192 cm^2
c)	2·5 cm	5 cm	15 cm	18·75 cm^2
d)	11 cm	22 cm	66 cm	363 cm^2

6

	base	height	area
a)	10 cm	7 cm	35 cm^2
b)	9 cm	3 cm	13·5 cm^2
c)	6 cm	4 cm	12 cm^2
d)	12 m	9 m	54 m^2

7

	shape	length	breadth	height	base area	volume
a)	cuboid	8 cm	3 cm	11 cm		264 cm^3
b)	cuboid	2 cm	6 cm	5 cm		60 cm^3
c)	cube	4 m				64 m^3
d)	prism			5·5 cm	6 cm^2	33 cm^3
e)	prism			28 cm	3 cm^2	84 cm^3
f)	prism			7·5 m	4 m^2	30 m^3

8 $a = 115°$, $b = 65°$, $c = 65°$, $d = 65°$, $e = 115°$, $f = 65°$, $g = 115°$; $h = 119°$, $i = 61°$, $j = 119°$, $k = 61°$, $l = 119°$; $m = 40°$, $n = 58°$; $p = 63°$, $q = 54°$

Review test 6 *(Geometry and mensuration)*

1 a) i) 8 305 kg, ii) 8·305 tonnes
b) i) 300, ii) 7 200

2 5 faces, 8 edges, 5 vertices

3 *either* 22° and 136° *or* 79° and 79°

4

	shape	length	breadth	perimeter	area
a)	rectangle	2 km	11 km	26 km	22 km^2
b)	rectangle	3 cm	12 cm	30 cm	36 cm^2
c)	square	25 mm		100 mm	625 mm^2
d)	square	8·5 m		34 m	72·25 m^2

5

	radius	diameter	circumference	area
a)	4·5 cm	9 cm	27 cm	60·75 cm^2
b)	5 cm	10 cm	30 cm	75 cm^2
c)	14 m	28 m	84 m	588 m^2
d)	1 m	2 m	6 m	3 m^2

6

	base	height	area
a)	11 cm	8 cm	44 cm^2
b)	5 cm	15 cm	37·5 cm^2
c)	20 m	2 m	20 m^2
d)	4 cm	11 cm	22 cm^2

7

	shape	length	breadth	height	base area	volume
a)	cuboid	7 cm	4 cm	10 cm		280 cm^3
b)	cuboid	3 cm	6 cm	3 cm		54 cm^3
c)	cube	6 cm				216 cm^3
d)	prism			8 cm	3·5 cm^2	28 cm^3
e)	prism			8 cm	12·5 cm^2	100 cm^3
f)	prism			2 m	13 m^2	26 m^3

8 $a = 136°$, $b = 44°$; $c = 34°$, $d = 137°$, $e = 43°$, $f = 34°$; $g = 110°$, $h = 52°$, $i = 18°$, $j = 110°$, $k = 52°$, $l = 110°$; $m = 106°$, $n = p = 37°$

Review test 7 (Statistics)

1 a) May **b)** 50 cm
c) January, October, November, December
d) May, April, June, July **e)** 195 cm
2 a) 13 **b)** 10
c) 7 **d)** 4
3 a) 6, 8, 9 **b)** 6, 6, 5·3
c) 6, 7, 7 **d)** 6, 6, 7

Review test 8 (Statistics)

1 a) 8 **b)** 2
c) Yes (the marks 4 and 6 have a frequency of 9)
d) 16 **e)** 35
2 a) 10 **b)** 6
c) 6 **d)** 11
3 a) 4, 5, 5·5 **b)** 11, 10, 9
c) 0, 4·5, 6 **d)** 5, 3·5, 3·5

Chapter 1

Exercise 1b (page 12)

1 a) 1, 2, 3, 6, 9, 18 **b)** 2, 3 **c)** 2×3^2
2 a) 1, 2, 4, 7, 14, 28 **b)** 2, 7 **c)** $2^2 \times 7$
3 a) 1, 3, 11, 33 **b)** 3, 11 **c)** 3×11
4 a) 1, 3, 5, 9, 15, 45 **b)** 3, 5 **c)** $3^2 \times 5$
5 a) 1, 2, 4, 8, 16 **b)** 2 **c)** 2^4
6 a) 1, 2, 11, 22 **b)** 2, 11 **c)** 2×11
7 a) 1, 2, 3, 5, 6, 10, 15, 30 **b)** 2, 3, 5 **c)** $2 \times 3 \times 5$
8 a) 1, 2, 3, 4, 6, 8, 12, 16, 24, 48 **b)** 2, 3 **c)** $2^4 \times 3$
9 a) 1, 2, 3, 4, 6, 12 **b)** 2, 3 **c)** $2^2 \times 3$
10 a) 1, 2, 3, 4, 6, 9, 12, 18, 36 **b)** 2, 3 **c)** $2^2 \times 3^2$
11 a) 1, 3, 13, 39 **b)** 3, 13 **c)** 3×13
12 a) 1, 2, 4, 7, 8, 14, 28, 56 **b)** 2, 7 **c)** $2^3 \times 7$
13 a) 1, 2, 3, 6, 7, 14, 21, 42 **b)** 2, 3, 7 **c)** $2 \times 3 \times 7$
14 a) 1, 2, 5, 10, 25, 50 **b)** 2, 5 **c)** 2×5^2
15 a) 1, 3, 7, 9, 21, 63 **b)** 3, 7 **c)** $3^2 \times 7$
16 a) 1, 2, 3, 4, 6, 8, 9, 12, 18, 24, 36, 72 **b)** 2, 3 **c)** $2^3 \times 3^2$

Exercise 1c (page 12)

1 3^3 **2** $2^2 \times 11$
3 $2^2 \times 13$ **4** 3×5^2
5 2×7^2 **6** $2^3 \times 13$
7 $2^2 \times 29$ **8** $3^2 \times 13$
9 $2^3 \times 5^2$ **10** $3^2 \times 31$
11 $2^2 \times 7 \times 13$ **12** $2^2 \times 3 \times 37$

Exercise 1d (page 13)

1 14 **2** 15 **3** 8 **4** 6
5 3 **6** 6 **7** 12 **8** 24
9 6 **10** 18 **11** 108 **12** 63

Exercise 1e (page 13)

1 36 **2** 40 **3** 30 **4** 120
5 165 **6** 168 **7** 42 **8** 60
9 120 **10** 180 **11** 180 **12** 140

Exercise 1f (page 14)

1 × ✔ × ✔ × × ✔ ×
✔ ✔ × ✔ ✔ × × ✔
× ✔ × × × × ✔ ×
× × × ✔ × × × ×
✔ × ✔ × × ✔ × ×
✔ ✔ ✔ ✔ ✔ ✔ ✔ ✔
✔ ✔ × × ✔ × × ×
✔ ✔ × ✔ ✔ × ✔ ✔
× ✔ × ✔ × × × ×
✔ ✔ ✔ ✔ ✔ ✔ ✔ ✔
✔ × × × × × × ×
✔ ✔ ✔ × ✔ ✔ × ×

2 a) 8, 9 **b)** 36, 72
3 a) 76 356, 16 869, 22 374
b) 76 356, 36 116
c) 76 356, 22 374
d) 76 356

4 a) 45 295 is not even *or* the sum of its digits is not divisible by 9
b) 141 is divisible by 3 but 2 699 is not divisible by 3

5 a) 2 **b)** 4 **c)** 5

Exercise 1g *(page 15)*

1 a) 20, 24, 28, 32, 36, 40, 44, 48, 52, 56, 60, 64, 68, 72, 76, 80, 84, 88, 92, 96
b) 30, 36, 42, 48, 54, 60, 66, 72, 78, 84, 90
c) 40, 48, 56, 64, 72, 80, 88
d) 45, 54, 63, 72, 81, 90

3 a) 17, 20, 23, 26 **b)** 26, 31, 36, 41
c) 56, 67, 78, 89 **d)** 5, 4, 3, 2
e) 15, 21, 28, 36 **f)** 32, 64, 128, 256
g) 31, 43, 57, 73 **h)** 26, 37, 50, 65
i) 36, 49, 64, 81 **j)** 34, 55, 89, 144

4

1	2	3	4	5	6	7	8
1	3	6	10	15	21	28	36

5 a)

5^2	6^2	7^2	8^2	9^2
25	36	49	64	81

b) If n is any whole number, n^2 = sum of the first n odd numbers.
c) The total column contains square numbers.

Exercise 1i *(page 18)*

1 15 **2** 14 **3** 18 **4** 21
5 22 **6** 20 **7** 30 **8** 40
9 50 **10** 70 **11** 24 **12** 28
13 27 **14** 25 **15** 35 **16** 44
17 42 **18** 45 **19** 48 **20** 54
21 55 **22** 60 **23** 63 **24** 90
25 56 **26** 66 **27** 75 **28** 81
29 84 **30** 88

Exercise 1j *(page 19)*

1 6 **2** 6 **3** 5 **4** 11
5 21 **6** 2 **7** 5 **8** 15
9 3 **10** 3 **11** 7 **12** 14

Exercise 1k *(page 19)*

1 $\frac{3}{5}$ **2** $\frac{4}{7}$ **3** $\frac{1}{2}$
4 $\frac{6}{9}$ $(= \frac{2}{3})$ **5** $\frac{3}{4}$ **6** $\frac{4}{5}$
7 $\frac{2}{3}$ **8** $\frac{6}{10}$ $(= \frac{3}{5})$ **9** $\frac{6}{7}$
10 $\frac{5}{6}$ **11** $1\frac{1}{2}$ **12** $1\frac{1}{3}$
13 $1\frac{1}{4}$ **14** $1\frac{4}{5}$ **15** $4\frac{1}{2}$

Chapter 2

Exercise 2a *(page 20)*

1 a) million **b)** billion
2 a) 40 000 000 cm^2 **b)** 1 million
3 1 million
4 just over $11\frac{1}{2}$ days
5 d) (there are over $31\frac{1}{2}$ million seconds in a year)

Exercise 2b *(page 21)*

1 1 000 000 **2** 59 244
3 721 568 397 **4** 2 312 400
5 8 000 000 **6** 3 000 000 000
7 9 215 **8** 14 682 053
9 108 412 **10** 12 345
11 100 000 000 **12** 987 654

Exercise 2c *(page 21)*

1 a) Le2 000 000 **b)** 150 000 000 km
c) 3 000 000 000 **d)** 5 500 000
e) Le2 100 000 000 **f)** 4 200 000 litres
g) 400 000 000 **h)** Le1 250 000
i) 700 000 tonnes **j)** Le750 000
k) 450 000 **l)** Le580 000 000

2 a) 8 million tonnes **b)** Le6 million
c) 2 billion **d)** Le3·7 billion
e) Le7·4 million
f) Le$1\frac{3}{4}$ million
g) 0·2 million litres
h) $\frac{1}{2}$ billion or 500 million
i) 0·3 million tonnes
j) $\frac{1}{4}$ million
k) 0·98 million barrels
l) 0·49 billion or 490 million

Exercise 2d *(page 22)*

1 9×10^6 **2** 4×10^3
3 4×10^9 **4** 6×10^2
5 3×10^5 **6** 6×10^4
7 5×10^9 **8** 7×10^1
9 2×10^7 **10** $8{\cdot}9 \times 10^4$
11 $7{\cdot}2 \times 10^8$ **12** $2{\cdot}3 \times 10^6$
13 $5{\cdot}5 \times 10^1$ **14** $1{\cdot}7 \times 10^5$
15 $5{\cdot}4 \times 10^3$ **16** $2{\cdot}5 \times 10^7$
17 $6{\cdot}3 \times 10^3$ **18** $9{\cdot}4 \times 10^9$
19 $4{\cdot}1 \times 10^5$ **20** $8{\cdot}5 \times 10^7$
21 $9{\cdot}5 \times 10^2$ **22** $3{\cdot}6 \times 10^3$
23 $3{\cdot}6 \times 10^2$ **24** $3{\cdot}6 \times 10^1$

Exercise 2e (page 22)

1 60 000
2 8 000
3 900 000
4 400
5 70
6 300
7 50 000 000
8 2 000 000
9 600 000 000
10 63 000
11 8 400
12 980 000
13 72
14 360
15 440
16 51 000 000
17 2 500 000
18 670 000 000
19 3 700
20 59 000 000
21 85 000
22 3 400
23 340
24 34

Exercise 2f (page 23)

1 0·06
2 0·004
3 0·9
4 0·000 008
5 0·000 4
6 0·000 06
7 0·003
8 0·000 09
9 0·000 7
10 0·16
11 0·034
12 0·002 6
13 0·000 28
14 0·084
15 0·075 6
16 2·7
17 0·65
18 0·402
19 0·2
20 0·24
21 0·7
22 0·006 2
23 0·003 3
24 0·040 2
25 0·9
26 0·9
27 0·03
28 0·72
29 0·072
30 0·007 2

Exercise 2g (page 23)

1 a) x^5 **b)** 10^7 **c)** a^7
d) 10^6 **e)** n^6 **f)** 10^9
g) $24a^6$ **h)** $20x^{10}$ **i)** $6c^7$
j) $28y^7$

2 a) m^8 **b)** a^{10} **c)** c^{14}
d) 10^9 **e)** b^{15} **f)** x^8
g) $10e^{14}$ **h)** 15×10^9 **i)** $15y^8$
j) $20x^6$

Exercise 2h (page 24)

1 a) a^4 **b)** 10^3 **c)** c^3
d) 10^3 **e)** d **f)** 10^2
g) $3x^4$ **h)** $2a^2$ **i)** x^5
j) $17m^8$

2 a) x^2 **b)** b^3 **c)** c^6
d) a^2 **e)** 10^2 **f)** x^6
g) $2x$ **h)** $4x^3$ **i)** 2×10^3
j) 3×10^4

Exercise 2i (page 25)

1 $\frac{1}{100}$ **2** $\frac{1}{10\,000}$ **3** $\frac{1}{1\,000\,000}$
4 x^3 **5** $\frac{1}{a^5}$ **6** 1
7 $\frac{1}{a^5}$ **8** x^9 **9** p^5
10 b^3 **11** 1 **12** $\frac{1}{c^2}$
13 8 **14** 9 **15** 9
16 $6a$ **17** $\frac{3a}{2}$ **18** $18a$

Exercise 2j (page 25)

1 5×10^{-3}
2 8×10^{-2}
3 6×10^{-4}
4 4×10^{-6}
5 2×10^{-5}
6 9×10^{-7}
7 3×10^{-1}
8 3×10^{-3}
9 3×10^{-5}
10 $3{\cdot}8 \times 10^{-2}$
11 $6{\cdot}2 \times 10^{-3}$
12 $7{\cdot}1 \times 10^{-1}$
13 $8{\cdot}8 \times 10^{-4}$
14 $4{\cdot}5 \times 10^{-4}$
15 $2{\cdot}6 \times 10^{-5}$
16 $7{\cdot}2 \times 10^{-5}$
17 $5{\cdot}5 \times 10^{-6}$
18 $1{\cdot}1 \times 10^{-2}$
19 $9{\cdot}1 \times 10^{-7}$
20 $6{\cdot}7 \times 10^{-8}$
21 $5{\cdot}7 \times 10^{-3}$
22 $1{\cdot}5 \times 10^{-4}$
23 $1{\cdot}5 \times 10^{-3}$
24 $1{\cdot}5 \times 10^{-2}$

Exercise 2k (page 26)

1 0·000 2
2 0·000 008
3 0·005
4 0·04
5 0·7
6 0·000 03
7 0·006
8 0·000 09
9 0·000 000 2
10 0·000 28
11 0·000 008 3
12 0·005 1
13 0·045
14 0·79
15 0·000 033
16 0·006 2
17 0·000 094
18 0·000 26
19 0·18
20 0·008 8
21 0·041
22 0·002 4
23 0·024
24 0·24

Exercise 2l (page 26)

	i)	ii)	iii)
1 a)	13 000	12 800	12 840
b)	47 000	46 900	46 920
c)	28 000	28 000	28 010
d)	10 000	9 800	9 790
e)	31 000	30 600	30 640
f)	13 000	13 100	13 070
g)	9 000	8 600	8 620
h)	5 000	4 500	4 520

i) i) 17 000 ii) 16 600 iii) 16 560
j) i) 59 000 ii) 59 100 iii) 59 090
k) i) 6 000 ii) 5 600 iii) 5 560
l) i) 20 000 ii) 19 500 iii) 19 500
2 a) i) 3 ii) 2·5 iii) 2·52
b) i) 8 ii) 8·0 iii) 7·99
c) i) 3 ii) 3·1 iii) 3·13
d) i) 1 ii) 0·9 iii) 0·95
e) i) 0 ii) 0·5 iii) 0·49
f) i) 10 ii) 9·5 iii) 9·51

Exercise 2m *(page 26)*

1 a) i) 7 000 ii) 7 300 iii) 7 280
b) i) 6 000 ii) 6 000 iii) 6 040
c) i) 10 000 ii) 15 000 iii) 14 600
d) i) 4 000 ii) 3 600 iii) 3 600
e) i) 8 000 ii) 8 000 iii) 8 010
f) i) 5 000 ii) 5 100 iii) 5 050
g) i) 30 000 ii) 28 000 iii) 28 300
h) i) 10 000 ii) 9 900 iii) 9 850
i) i) 9 000 ii) 9 400 iii) 9 400
j) i) 30 000 ii) 26 000 iii) 26 000
k) i) 70 000 ii) 70 000 iii) 69 600
l) i) 20 000 ii) 19 000 iii) 19 300
2 a) i) 7 ii) 7·0 iii) 7·04 iv) 7·038
b) i) 20 ii) 19 iii) 18·5 iv) 18·50
c) i) 10 ii) 13 iii) 12·7 iv) 12·68
d) i) 4 ii) 3·8 iii) 3·78 iv) 3·780
e) i) 200 ii) 230 iii) 234 iv) 234·1
f) i) 80 ii) 79 iii) 79·4 iv) 79·41
g) i) 60 ii) 62 iii) 62·5 iv) 62·47
h) i) 2 ii) 2·0 iii) 1·99 iv) 1·994
i) i) 800 ii) 780 iii) 781 iv) 780·9
j) i) 700 ii) 680 iii) 678 iv) 678·5
k) i) 30 ii) 25 iii) 25·2 iv) 25·21
l) i) 2 ii) 2·0 iii) 2·01 iv) 2·006
3 a) i) 0·07 ii) 0·068 iii) 0·067 5
b) i) 0·3 ii) 0·31 iii) 0·306
c) i) 0·006 ii) 0·006 3 iii) 0·006 31
d) i) 0·000 7 ii) 0·000 67 iii) 0·000 667
e) i) 0·03 ii) 0·034 iii) 0·033 6
f) i) 0·9 ii) 0·88 iii) 0·880
g) i) 0·003 ii) 0·002 6 iii) 0·002 58
h) i) 0·009 ii) 0·009 0 iii) 0·009 01
i) i) 0·000 2 ii) 0·000 22 iii) 0·000 221
j) i) 0·9 ii) 0·90 iii) 0·900
k) i) 0·6 ii) 0·61 iii) 0·606
l) i) 0·04 ii) 0·042 iii) 0·042 4
4 a) i) 30 ii) 25 iii) 25·3
b) i) 4 ii) 3·9 iii) 3·91
c) i) 200 ii) 170 iii) 169
d) i) 0·7 ii) 0·70 iii) 0·702
e) i) 0·008 ii) 0·007 8 iii) 0·007 78
f) i) 0·000 4 ii) 0·000 39 iii) 0·000 388
g) i) 100 ii) 110 iii) 110
h) i) 40 ii) 41 iii) 40·7
i) i) 6 ii) 5·8 iii) 5·75
j) i) 0·008 ii) 0·008 1 iii) 0·008 09
k) i) 700 ii) 690 iii) 695
l) i) 0·05 ii) 0·047 iii) 0·047 5
5 a) 2 b) 3 c) 1 d) 4 e) 2 f) 3
g) 2 h) 3 i) 4 j) 1 k) 1 l) 3

Exercise 2n *(page 27)*

1 a) 12·9 b) 12·93 c) 12·935
2 a) 24·1 b) 24·12 c) 24·118
3 a) 5·1 b) 5·07 c) 5·073
4 a) 1·9 b) 1·94 c) 1·938
5 a) 2·0 b) 1·99 c) 1·988
6 a) 0·6 b) 0·58 c) 0·585
7 a) 0·1 b) 0·06 c) 0·063
8 a) 0·0 b) 0·04 c) 0·038
9 a) 0·9 b) 0·90 c) 0·900
10 a) 0·0 b) 0·01 c) 0·009

Exercise 2p *(page 27)*

1 a) Le3 200 000 000 b) 72 000 km^2
c) 2 000 000 d) 0·16 m^3
e) 0·000 002 2 f) 150 000 000 km
2 a) Le$8{\cdot}9 \times 10^{11}$ b) Le$2{\cdot}9 \times 10^{11}$
c) £$2{\cdot}9 \times 10^7$ d) $1{\cdot}3 \times 10^{-3}$ g cm^{-3}
e) $3{\cdot}0 \times 10^7$ km^2 f) $1{\cdot}3 \times 10^{-3}$
3 4.724 million
4 $1{\cdot}525\,7 \times 10^{10}$
5 8 850 m, 5 890 m, 2 960 m
6 4·2 billion
7 $1{\cdot}1 \times 10^5$ km^2
8 $2{\cdot}54 \times 10^{-5}$ km

Chapter 3

Exercise 3a *(page 29)*

2 4
3 4
5 a) opposite sides are equal in length
b) opposite angles are equal in size
c) the angles should total 360°
e) the diagonals are of different lengths

f) each diagonal is bisected by the other
g) 2 acute, 2 obtuse
j) a parallelogram has no lines of symmetry

6 a) $R\hat{P}Q$ **b)** $S\hat{Q}P$ **c)** $S\hat{Q}R$ **d)** $P\hat{R}Q$

Exercise 3b *(page 30)*

2 4
3 4
5 a) all four sides are of equal length
b) opposite angles are equal in size
c) the angles should total 360°
e) the diagonals are of different lengths
f) each diagonal is bisected by the other
g) right angles (90°)
h) 2
i) $a = b$
j) $x = y$
6

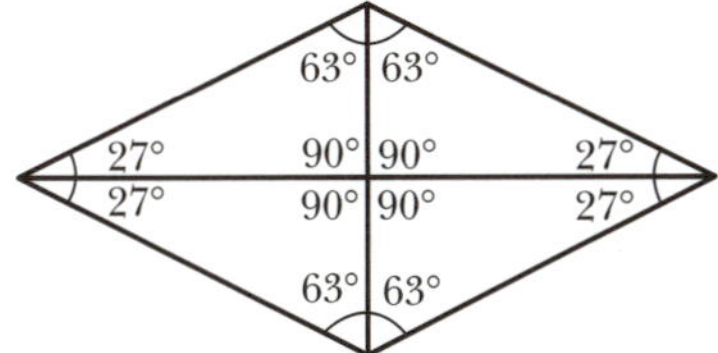

Fig. A1

7 opposite sides are parallel; opposite angles are equal; diagonals bisect each other
8 in a rhombus all four sides are equal in length, the diagonals cross at right angles and there are two lines of symmetry; none of these is true for a parallelogram
9 each angle of a square is a right angle; a square is a special kind of rhombus

Exercise 3c *(page 32)*

2 four of each
4 a) a kite has two pairs of sides of the same length
b) one pair of opposite angles are of equal size
c) 360°
d) the diagonals are of different lengths
e) right angles (90°)
f) 1
5

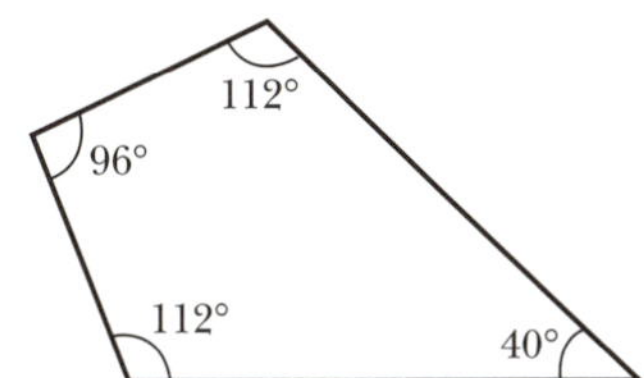

Fig. A2

6

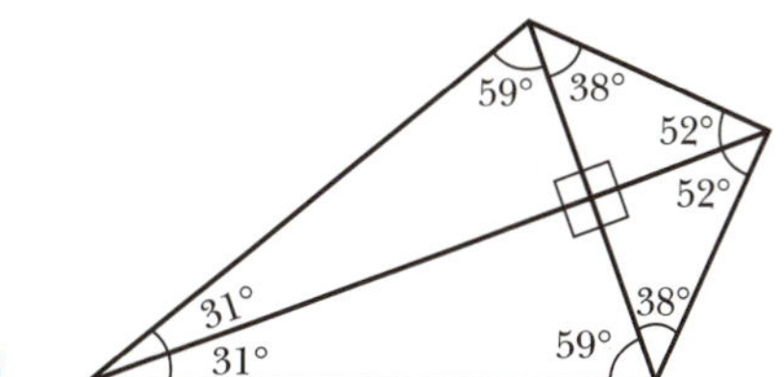

Fig. A3

7 their diagonals cross at right angles; they have bilateral symmetry
8 in a rhombus all four sides are equal in length, there are two pairs of opposite angles equal and there are two lines of symmetry; none of these is true for a kite; a rhombus is a special kind of kite

Exercise 3d *(page 33)*

1 parallelogram, rectangle, rhombus, square
2 rhombus, rectangle, square
3 rhombus, square **4** rhombus, square
5 rectangle, rhombus, square
6 rectangle **7 c)** rhombus, square
8 c) rhombus, square **9 c)** square
10 a) true **b)** false **c)** true
d) true **e)** false **f)** true
g) true **h)** false **i)** true

Chapter 4

Exercise 4a *(page 36)*

1 +9	**2** +6	**3** +11	**4** +5
5 −4	**6** −10	**7** +3	**8** −3
9 −6	**10** +12	**11** +10	**12** −2
13 +12	**14** −18	**15** 0	**16** 1
17 8	**18** −9	**19** 0	**20** 0
21 −15	**22** 13	**23** 2	**24** 5

Exercise 4b *(page 37)*

1 a) +15, +10, +5, 0, −5, −10, −15
b) +6, +4, +2, 0, −2, −4, −6
c) +30, +20, +10, 0, −10, −20, −30

2 a)
$(+5) \times (+3) = +15$
$(+5) \times (+2) = +10$
$(+5) \times (+1) = +5$
$(+5) \times 0 = 0$
$(+5) \times (-1) = -5$
$(+5) \times (-2) = -10$
$(+5) \times (-3) = -15$

b)
$(+2) \times (+3) = +6$
$(+2) \times (+2) = +4$
$(+2) \times (+1) = +2$
$(+2) \times 0 = 0$
$(+2) \times (-1) = -2$
$(+2) \times (-2) = -4$
$(+2) \times (-3) = -6$

c) $(+10) \times (+3) = +30$
$(+10) \times (+2) = +20$
$(+10) \times (+1) = +10$
$(+10) \times 0 = 0$
$(+10) \times (-1) = -10$
$(+10) \times (-2) = -20$
$(+10) \times (-3) = -30$

3 **a)** $+18$ **b)** $+50$ **c)** -40 **d)** -28
e) $+34$ **f)** $+120$ **g)** -100 **h)** -60
i) $+7\frac{1}{2}$ **j)** $+\frac{1}{4}$ **k)** -7 **l)** $-\frac{2}{3}$
m) $+3$ **n)** $+15{\cdot}3$ **o)** $-4{\cdot}8$ **p)** -16
q) 56 **r)** -56 **s)** 56 **t)** -56

Exercise 4c (page 37)

1 **a)** $+3, 0, -3, -6$
b) $(+1) \times (+3), 0 \times (+3), (-1) \times (+3), (-2) \times (+3)$
c) $(+1) \times (+3) = +3$
$0 \times (+3) = 0$
$(-1) \times (+3) = -3$
$(-2) \times (+3) = -6$

2 **a)** $-3, 0, +3, +6$
b) $(+1) \times (-3), 0 \times (-3), (-1) \times (-3), (-2) \times (-3)$
c) $(+1) \times (-3) = -3$
$0 \times (-3) = 0$
$(-1) \times (-3) = +3$
$(-2) \times (-3) = +6$

Exercise 4d (page 38)

1 **a)** $+15, +10, +5, 0, -5, -10, -15$
b) $-6, -4, -2, 0, +2, +4, +6$
c) $-30, -20, -10, 0, +10, +20, +30$

2 **a)** $(+3) \times (+5) = +15$
$(+2) \times (+5) = +10$
$(+1) \times (+5) = +5$
$0 \times (+5) = 0$
$(-1) \times (+5) = -5$
$(-2) \times (+5) = -10$
$(-3) \times (+5) = -15$

b) $(+3) \times (-2) = -6$
$(+2) \times (-2) = -4$
$(+1) \times (-2) = -2$
$0 \times (-2) = 0$
$(-1) \times (-2) = +2$
$(-2) \times (-2) = +4$
$(-3) \times (-2) = +6$

c) $(+3) \times (-10) = -30$
$(+2) \times (-10) = -20$
$(+1) \times (-10) = -10$
$0 \times (-10) = 0$
$(-1) \times (-10) = +10$
$(-2) \times (-10) = +20$
$(-3) \times (-10) = +30$

3 **a)** -18 **b)** $+50$ **c)** $+40$ **d)** $+28$
e) -32 **f)** -80 **g)** $+64$ **h)** $+65$
i) -3 **j)** $-1\frac{1}{3}$ **k)** $+1$ **l)** $+2$
m) -6 **n)** $-7{\cdot}2$ **o)** $+2{\cdot}7$ **p)** $+18{\cdot}6$
q) -48 **r)** -48 **s)** $+48$ **t)** $+48$

Exercise 4e (page 39)

1 **a)** -6 **b)** $+6$ **c)** -6
d) $+9$ **e)** $+5$ **f)** $+8$
g) $+2$ **h)** -3 **i)** -11
j) $+\frac{1}{6}$ **k)** $-\frac{1}{2}$ **l)** $+\frac{1}{3}$

2 **a)** $+4$ **b)** -15 **c)** $+2$
d) $+5$ **e)** -60 **f)** $+4$
g) $+1\frac{1}{2}$ **h)** $-\frac{1}{2}$ **i)** $+\frac{1}{2}$

Exercise 4f (page 39)

1 **a)** $-4, -6, -8, -10$
b) $2 \times (-2), 2 \times (-3), 2 \times (-4), 2 \times (-5)$
c) $2 \times (-2) = -4$
$2 \times (-3) = -6$
$2 \times (-4) = -8$
$2 \times (-5) = -10$
d) $-4, -8, -12, -16$
e) $(-1) \times 4, (-2) \times 4, (-3) \times 4, (-4) \times 4$
f) $(-1) \times 4 = -4$
$(-2) \times 4 = -8$
$(-3) \times 4 = -12$
$(-4) \times 4 = -16$
g) $+10, +15, +20, +25$
h) $(-2) \times (-5), (-3) \times (-5), (-4) \times (-5), (-5) \times (-5)$
i) $(-2) \times (-5) = +10$
$(-3) \times (-5) = +15$
$(-4) \times (-5) = +20$
$(-5) \times (-5) = +25$

2

×	−6	−4	−2	0	+2	+4	+6
+6	−36	−24	−12	0	+12	+24	+36
+4	−24	−16	−8	0	+8	+16	+24
+2	−12	−8	−4	0	+4	+8	+12
0	0	0	0	0	0	0	0
−2	+12	+8	+4	0	−4	−8	−12
−4	+24	+16	+8	0	−8	−16	−24
−6	+36	+24	+12	0	−12	−24	−36

3 **a)** -12 **b)** $+28$ **c)** -15

d) +6 e) −48 f) +56
g) +1 h) 0 i) −1

4 −90 m

5 a) 8 b) −7 c) −6
d) 10 e) −9 f) −3

6 a) −2 b) −13 c) +1
d) −6 e) −9 f) +2
g) 2 h) −2 i) −5

7 a) 12 b) −12 c) −15
d) −24 e) −22 f) −90

8 a) −42 b) −1 c) +4
d) +4 e) −12 f) $+\frac{2}{3}$

9 a) $-5\frac{1}{2}$ b) +0·56 c) $-1\frac{1}{7}$ d) −43·4

10 a) $-\frac{7}{9}$ b) +0·8 c) $+\frac{3}{4}$ d) −1·2

Chapter 5

Exercise 5a (page 41)

1 −2	2 +5	3 −7
4 +6	5 −13	6 +13
7 −117	8 +312	9 −1
10 $+\frac{1}{4}$	11 −0·27	12 0
13 −0·77	14 +1 000	15 $+\frac{11}{12}$
16 +7·7	17 $-5\frac{3}{4}$	18 −0.3
19 -5×10^2	20 $-9{\cdot}7 \times 10^6$	21 $+3 \times 10^{-4}$
22 $+2.1 \times 10^3$	23 $-7{\cdot}9 \times 10^{-2}$	24 $-\pi$

Exercise 5b (page 41)

1 $a = 7$	2 $x = -4$
3 $x = -1$	4 $y = 5$
5 $m = 10$	6 $n = 24$
7 $d = -7$	8 $x = 1$
9 $a = -7$	10 $c = 0$
11 $h = 0$	12 $k = -1$
13 $b = 10$	14 $c = -24$
15 $d = 0$	16 $p = -15$
17 $q = 13$	18 $r = -11$
19 $x = 6$	20 $y = 18$
21 $z = -7$	22 $a = 5$
23 $b = -2$	24 $c = -19$

Exercise 5c (page 42)

1 $\frac{1}{3}$	2 $\frac{1}{8}$	3 7
4 6	5 $\frac{3}{2}$ $(1\frac{1}{2})$	6 $\frac{3}{5}$
7 $\frac{10}{9}$	8 $\frac{7}{8}$	9 $-\frac{1}{2}$
10 −4	11 −1	12 $-\frac{6}{5}$
13 1·25	14 $\frac{100}{27}$	15 $-\frac{10}{7}$
16 −10	17 $\frac{1}{a}$	18 t
19 $\frac{q}{p}$	20 $\frac{1}{2\pi}$	21 $\frac{\pi}{16}$
22 $\frac{b}{2a}$	23 $2r$	24 $\frac{1}{5x}$

Exercise 5d (page 42)

1 $x = 7$	2 $x = 6$
3 $y = 8$	4 $r = -9$
5 $d = -5$	6 $x = -2$
7 $s = \frac{1}{4}$	8 $m = 1\frac{1}{2}$
9 $x = \frac{2}{3}$	10 $t = -\frac{3}{4}$
11 $n = -\frac{5}{7}$	12 $x = -3\frac{1}{2}$
13 $a = 3$	14 $c = 6$
15 $x = -1$	16 $y = 1$
17 $a = -4$	18 $b = 11$

Exercise 5e (page 43)

1 $x = 36$	2 $a = 6$	3 $y = 9$
4 $r = 1\frac{1}{6}$	5 $m = 1\frac{1}{2}$	6 $t = 3\frac{1}{2}$
7 $z = 20$	8 $x = 2\frac{2}{5}$	9 $a = 7\frac{1}{2}$
10 $c = 1\frac{3}{7}$	11 $e = \frac{7}{10}$	12 $x = 1$
13 $x = \frac{7}{8}$	14 $a = \frac{3}{8}$	15 $x = 1\frac{1}{4}$
16 $s = 1\frac{2}{3}$	17 $r = 4$	18 $x = 9$
19 $x = 3\frac{1}{2}$	20 $x = 2\frac{1}{2}$	21 $a = 10$
22 $x = -18$	23 $a = 14$	24 $n = -20$
25 $m = -7$	26 $t = -6$	27 $s = \frac{7}{8}$
28 $x = 1\frac{1}{2}$	29 $k = -\frac{3}{4}$	30 $x = -12$

Exercise 5f (page 44)

1 open your eyes	2 go down 2 steps
3 subtract 16	4 subtract −5
5 add $4\frac{1}{2}$	6 add −1
7 divide by 1·8	8 divide by 9
9 multiply by 7	10 multiply by −4

Exercise 5g (page 44)

1 2	2 21	3 16	4 12
5 11	6 20	7 Le50 000	8 Le90 000
9 −13	10 $4\frac{1}{4}$	11 1	12 −11 km

Exercise 5h (page 45)

1 8	2 7	3 45
4 36	5 $30 750	6 Le72 000
7 1·5 kg	8 219·6 cm	9 30
10 18	11 964 ml	12 $1\frac{2}{3}$
13 0·56	14 −6	15 $-\frac{2}{7}$

Chapter 6

Exercise 6a *(page 46)*

1 $a = 50°$
2 $b = 80°$
3 $c = 52°, d = 128°, e = 128°$
4 $f = 100°, g = 80°, h = 47°$
5 $i = 100°$
6 $n = j = q = 57°,$
$l = m = p = k = 123°$
7 $r = 63°, s = 41°, t = 76°, u = 139°, v = 117°$
8 $w = 124°, x = 56°, y = 124°, z = 101°$

Exercise 6b *(page 47)*

1 $a = 50°$
2 $b = 59°, c = 49°, d = 108°$
3 $e = f = 70°$
4 $g = 63°, h = 54°$
5 $i = j = k = 60°, l = m = n = 120°$
6 $p = 82°, q = 82°, r = 98°$
7 $s = 106°, t = 45°, u = v = 53°$
8 $w = x = 45°, y = 45°, z = 47°$

Exercise 6c *(page 49)*

1 **a)** 59° **b)** 122°, 69°
c) 50°, 70° **d)** 83°, 42°, 107°
e) 59°, 86°, 63° **f)** 115°, 115°
2 **a)** 120° **b)** 63° **c)** 90°
d) 71° **e)** 37° **f)** 103°
g) 33° **h)** 75° **i)** 71°
j) 27°
3 **c)** is a trapezium **d)** is a parallelogram
4 **a)** $x = 100°$; 100°, 100°
b) $x = 50°$; 50°, 100°
c) $x = 30°$; 60°, 90°
d) $x = 18°$; 54°, 162°
e) $x = 36°$; 36°, 108°, 108°, 108°
f) $x = 70°$; 70°, 125°, 55°, 110°
5 **a)** $x + 2x + 3x + 4x = 360°$
b) $x = 36°$
c) 36°, 72°, 108°, 144°
e) a trapezium

Exercise 6d *(page 51)*

1 **c)** $180n - 360$
2 **a)** 120° **b)** 144°
3 **a)** 72° **b)** isosceles
c) both 54° **d)** 108°
e) $5 \times 108° = 540°$
$(5 - 2) \times 180° = 3 \times 180° = 540°$
4 90°, 135°, 135°
5 **a)** rhombus **b)** 144°, 144°, 36°, 36°
6 **a)** $x = 100°$; 100°, 100°, 100°
b) $x = 80°$; 80°, 160°, 160°
7 90° each
8 $x = 36°$; largest angle = 180°; the pentagon would look like a quadrilateral; a trapezium
9 **a)** 20 sides **b)** 15 sides
10 **a)** 24 **b)** 165°

Chapter 7

Exercise 7a *(page 53)*

1 $-5a$	**2** $-4x$	**3** $-3x$
4 $-3c$	**5** $6x$	**6** $9y$
7 $-6a$	**8** $6a$	**9** $-6a$
10 $-36x$	**11** $40x$	**12** $-40x$
13 $-42a$	**14** $-22y$	**15** $-16c$
16 $30y$	**17** $18xy$	**18** $-21ab$
19 $24x^2$	**20** $-18d^2$	**21** $-3a$
22 $3x$	**23** $-2y$	**24** $-6z$
25 $-2x$	**26** $-7x$	**27** $-x$
28 $7x$	**29** $-9y$	**30** $-10z$
31 $6t$	**32** $-9n$	**33** $3x$
34 $-11b$	**35** $-13x$	**36** $3m$

Exercise 7b *(page 54)*

1 5	**2** 12	**3** 27	**4** 6
5 14	**6** 6	**7** −4	**8** −2
9 −9	**10** 3	**11** 4	**12** 5
13 1	**14** −1	**15** 2	**16** −2
17 2	**18** 6	**19** 1	**20** −5
21 4	**22** 12	**23** 3	**24** 6

Exercise 7c *(page 54)*

1 8	**2** −20	**3** −30
4 −32	**5** 5	**6** 6
7 −20	**8** −12	**9** 15
10 16	**11** 25	**12** 9
13 60	**14** −1	**15** 9
16 1	**17** −7	**18** 7
19 −2	**20** −3	**21** $\frac{1}{3}$
22 −1	**23** −5	**24** 2

Exercise 7d *(page 55)*

2 $3(7 + 2) = 3 \times 9 = 27$
$3(7 + 2) = 3 \times 7 + 3 \times 2 = 21 + 6 = 27$
3 $10(6 - 4) = 10 \times 2 = 20$
$10(6 - 4) = 10 \times 6 - 10 \times 4 = 60 - 40 = 20$

4 $9(4+3) = 9 \times 7 = 63$
$9(4+3) = 9 \times 4 + 9 \times 3 = 36 + 27 = 63$
5 $6(4-2) = 6 \times 2 = 12$
$6(4-2) = 6 \times 4 - 6 \times 2 = 24 - 12 = 12$
6 $7(1+9) = 7 \times 10 = 70$
$7(1+9) = 7 \times 1 + 7 \times 9 = 7 + 63 = 70$
7 $3(8-2) = 3 \times 6 = 18$
$3(8-2) = 3 \times 8 - 3 \times 2 = 24 - 6 = 18$
8 $3(8+2) = 3 \times 10 = 30$
$3(8+2) = 3 \times 8 + 3 \times 2 = 24 + 6 = 30$
9 $4(11-3) = 4 \times 8 = 32$
$4(11-3) = 4 \times 11 - 4 \times 3 = 44 - 12 = 32$
10 $5(10+2) = 5 \times 12 = 60$
$5(10+2) = 5 \times 10 + 5 \times 2 = 50 + 10 = 60$

Exercise 7e (page 55)

1 $3x + 3y$ **2** $36 - 4n$ **3** $2a - 14$
4 $10p - 5q$ **5** $18a + 24b$ **6** $49x + 14y$
7 $8a + 14ac$ **8** $24xy - 32y$ **9** $21x - 24px$
10 $-3pq + 3q^2$ **11** $-2a^2 - 2ab$ **12** $-5bd - 10cd$
13 $2a + 4b$ **14** $5u - 5v$ **15** $9a + 3b$
16 $15a - 9ad$ **17** $49c^2 - 14c$ **18** $24s^2 + 6st$

Exercise 7f (page 55)

1 $-3m - 3n$ **2** $-2u - 2v$ **3** $-4a - 4b$
4 $-5a + 5b = 5b - 5a$
5 $-8x + 8y = 8y - 8x$
6 $-9p + 9q = 9q - 9p$ **7** $-12mn - 8n$
8 $-21y + 35y^2 = 35y^2 - 21y$
9 $-4a^2 - 6a$ **10** $2a^2 + 6ab$
11 $10xy - 55x^2$ **12** $5pq - p^2$
13 $-4c - 16d$ **14** $45m^2 - 18mn$
15 $-70t - 21t^2$ **16** $11xy - 2x^2$
17 $15 - 36a$ **18** $25ax + 35ay$

Exercise 7g (page 56)

1 $5a + 4b$ **2** $3x + 6y$
3 $12p - 5q$ **4** $11c + 3$
5 $18a - 5b$ **6** $20x + 6y$
7 $4x - 10$ **8** $5r - 12$
9 $-a - 6b$ **10** $10 - a$
11 $28x - 32$ **12** $18t - 24$
13 $9a + 14$ **14** $16x + 13y$
15 $9x + 4y$ **16** $5a - 9b$
17 $3x - 29y$ **18** $-2x - 5y$
19 $9b - a$ **20** $-15b$
21 $x^2 + x + 6$ **22** $x^2 + 9x + 20$
23 $x^2 + 5x - 14$ **24** $x^2 - 4x - 32$
25 $a^2 + 3a - 10$ **26** $a^2 - 7a - 18$
27 $y^2 - 9y + 18$ **28** $z^2 - 11z + 10$
29 $x^2 + 2ax + a^2$ **30** $a^2 - b^2$

Exercise 7h (page 56)

1 $pr + qr + ps + qs$
2 $xy + 8y + 3x + 24$
3 $12b + 15ab + 4a + 5a^2$
4 $ac - bc + ad - bd$
5 $xy - 7y + x - 7$
6 $6p - 3p^2 + 2q - pq$
7 $wy + xy - wz - xz$
8 $ab + 6b - 9a - 54$
9 $2mp + 5np - 6mq - 15nq$
10 $ac - bc - ad + bd$
11 $xy - 4y - 5x + 20$
12 $5x^2 - xy - 15xy + 3y^2$ $(= 5x^2 - 16xy + 3y^2)$

Exercise 7i (page 57)

1 $a^2 + 7a + 12$ **2** $b^2 + 7b + 10$
3 $m^2 + m - 6$ **4** $n^2 - 5n - 14$
5 $x^2 + 4x + 4$ **6** $y^2 - 3y - 4$
7 $c^2 + 3c - 10$ **8** $d^2 - 7d + 12$
9 $p^2 - 7p + 10$ **10** $x^2 - 8x + 16$
11 $y^2 + 8y + 7$ **12** $a^2 + 2a - 24$
13 $b^2 - 10b + 21$ **14** $c^2 + 4c - 5$
15 $6 + 5d + d^2$ **16** $10 + 3x - x^2$
17 $12 - 7y + y^2$ **18** $m^2 + 5mn + 6n^2$
19 $a^2 - ab - 6b^2$ **20** $x^2 - 7xy + 12y^2$
21 $p^2 + 4pq + 4q^2$ **22** $m^2 + 2mn - 15n^2$
23 $2a^2 + 7a - 15$ **24** $3x^2 - 2x - 8$
25 $6h^2 + hk - 2k^2$ **26** $15x^2 + 26xy + 8y^2$
27 $9a^2 - 12ab + 4b^2$ **28** $25h^2 + 10hk + k^2$
29 $10a^2 - 19ab + 6b^2$ **30** $35m^2 - 4mn - 15n^2$

Chapter 8

Exercise 8a (page 58)

1 **a)** Le10 000, Le100 000, Le1 000 000, Le1 000 000 000 **b)** Le7 000, Le70 000 000
2 **a)** 6 570 **b)** 51 100 **c)** 241 000
d) 2 350 **e)** 73·4 **f)** 730 000
3 **a)** 190 **b)** 280 **c)** 87 000
d) 3·9 **e)** 4·0 **f)** 23
4 **a)** 0·7 **b)** 0·5 **c)** 7·8
d) 6·1 **e)** 8·0 **f)** 20·0
5 **a)** 37 cm **b)** 13 kg **c)** Le29
d) 30 litres **e)** 63 mm **f)** Le8
6 39 years (although 39 years 8 months 29 days is nearer 40 years, it is more usual to round ages down)

7 Le779 million, Le780 million, just under Le800 million

8 between Le30 450 000 and Le30 550 000

9 **a)** Le2 000 billion
b) Le1 800 billion
c) Le340 billion
d) Le430 billion

10 **a)** $1\frac{1}{2}$ h **b)** 70 km/h

Exercise 8b *(page 59)*

1 in order: degree, °C, gramme, ml, minute or second

2 **a)** 185 mm **b)** 176 cm **c)** 6 380 km
d) 985 m **e)** 8 850 m **f)** 14·3 km
g) 67·9 kg **h)** 6·63 g **i)** 2·87 kg
j) 7·64 t **k)** 125 g **l)** 11·3 g
m) 3 660 000 **n)** 86 600 000 **o)** 241 ml
p) Le5 200 000 **q)** 7 h 20 min
r) 40·1 litres **s)** Le8 120 000 **t)** 26·2°C

3

country	33 000 000
large city	1 300 000
large town	390 000
small town	8 000
village	680

Exercise 8c *(page 60)*

1 900 students
2 35 t
3 15 000 pages
4 Le144 000
5 **a)** 125 **b)** 4 pages
7 1 400
8 8, 9 or 10 min

Exercise 8d *(page 61)*

6 **e)**

Exercise 8e *(page 61)*

1 **a)** $2\frac{1}{2}$ kg, 125 g
b) Le180 000
c) 200 cups, Le45 000

2 **a)** approximately 1 litre, 35 ml
b) Le900
c) Le48 000, Le60 000; 4: 5

3 9 buckets
4 Le1 000
5 5 days

Revision exercises 1–3

Revision exercise 1 *(page 63)*

1 HCF: 42, LCM: 420
2 5 and 8 only
3 **a)** 41, 48, 55, 62 **b)** 26, 33, 41, 50
c) 48, 96, 192, 384 **d)** 30, 42, 56, 72
4 14
5 **a)** $3{\cdot}5 \times 10^6$ **b)** $5{\cdot}7 \times 10^3$ **c)** $2{\cdot}8 \times 10^1$
d) $4{\cdot}7 \times 10^{-1}$ **e)** $8{\cdot}5 \times 10^{-2}$ **f)** 3×10^{-6}
6 **a)** 10^7 **b)** $15x^5$ **c)** $18a$
d) 10^4 **e)** $2y^2$ **f)** $3x^4$
7 2·94 8 1 000 9 11 hours
10 6×10^{-5} m

Revision exercise 2 *(page 63)*

1 $x = 110°$, $y = 103°$
2 **a)** kite **b)** kite **c)** square
d) rhombus **e)** trapezium **f)** kite
g) trapezium **h)** rectangle **i)** trapezium
3 $a = 26°$, $b = 64°$
4 $a = 28°$, $b = 124°$, $c = 56°$, $d = 56°$, $e = 68°$
5 26 cm 6 $x = 55°$ 7 156°
8 **a)** 720° **b)** $x = 129°$
9 133° each

Revision exercise 3 *(page 66)*

1 **a)** −15 **b)** +16 **c)** −30
d) +9 **e)** +21 **f)** −58
g) −3 **h)** +2 **i)** +3
j) +19 **k)** −4 **l)** −6

2 **a)** $-6, +18, +48, -2\frac{1}{2}$
b) $+\frac{4}{3}, -\frac{3}{2}, \frac{3a}{x}, \frac{1}{2y}$
c) subtract 5, add 3, divide by 1·2, multiply by −4

3 **a)** $-10a$ **b)** $-4c$ **c)** $5x$ **d)** $-3a$

4 **a)** $20x - 36$ **b)** $21 - 6g$
c) $-8a - 72b$ **d)** $-12 - 6x$
e) $15y - 3x$ **f)** $28a - 8$
g) $15 - 45a$ **h)** $2x + 12y$

5 **a)** 2 **b)** $\frac{1}{2}$ **c)** 1

6 **a)** $x = -4$ **b)** $n = -4$ **c)** $d = 7$
d) $m = \frac{5}{6}$ **e)** $a = \frac{3}{7}$ **f)** $x = 6$

7 **a)** $2y - x$ **b)** $14x - 30$
c) $2x + y$ **d)** $15y - 6x$

8 **a)** $ax + bx + ay + by$
b) $30 - 6x + 5y - xy$

c) $mn + 4n - 8m - 32$
d) $6pr + 3qr - 10ps - 5qs$

9 a) $u^2 + 5uv + 6v^2$
b) $2c^2 - 11c + 15$
c) $6x^2 + xy - 2y^2$
d) $8a^2 - 26ab - 45b^2$

10 a) $a^2 + 6a + 9$
b) $b^2 - 10b + 25$
c) $4x^2 + 4x + 1$
d) $m^2 + 8mn + 16n^2$

Chapter 9

Exercise 9a (page 69)

1 a) 0·375 b) 0·48 c) 0·05
d) $0{\cdot}\dot{3}$ e) $0{\cdot}\dot{6}$ f) $0{\cdot}\dot{8}$

2 a) $\frac{1}{5}$ b) $\frac{11}{20}$ c) $\frac{39}{125}$
d) $\frac{33}{125}$ e) $\frac{1}{250}$ f) $\frac{7}{8}$

3 a) 80% b) 10% c) $83\frac{1}{3}$%
d) 22·2% e) 250% f) $10\frac{1}{2}$%

4 a) $\frac{3}{5}$ b) $\frac{7}{25}$ c) $\frac{1}{25}$
d) $\frac{1}{40}$ e) $1\frac{7}{25}$ f) $\frac{17}{300}$

Exercise 9b (page 70)

1 i) for 5 days the pay is Le7 500 ii) direct
iii) Le1 500
2 i) 6 notebooks cost Le6 000 ii) direct
iii) Le1 000
3 i) 5 men take 10 days ii) indirect iii) 50 days
4 i) a 2-year-old boy has 6 sisters ii) neither
iii) impossible
5 i) in 2 hours a car travels 84 km ii) direct
iii) 42 km
6 i) 15 cows have grass for 4 days ii) indirect
iii) 60 days
7 i) 6 litres are at a temperature of 30°C
ii) neither iii) 30°C
8 i) 9 bottles hold $4\frac{1}{2}$ litres ii) direct
iii) $\frac{1}{2}$ litre
9 i) 9 people have water for 4 days ii) indirect
iii) 36 days
10 i) 10 litres are used in 80 km ii) direct
iii) 8 km
11 i) 3 lorries take 84 trips ii) indirect
iii) 252 trips
12 i) 5 students take 1 hour ii) indirect
iii) 5 hours

Exercise 9c (page 70)

1
1 b) Le3 000 c) Le33 000
2 b) Le5 000 c) Le44 000
3 b) 5 days c) 2 days
5 b) 126 km c) 42x km
6 b) 10 days c) $\frac{60}{y}$ days
8 b) $2\frac{1}{2}$ litres c) $\frac{1}{2}x$ litres
9 b) $4\frac{1}{2}$ days c) $\frac{36}{z}$ days
10 b) 40 km c) 8x km
11 b) 36 trips c) $\frac{252}{x}$ trips
12 b) 1 h 40 min c) 25 min

2 Le224 00 **3** 4 days
4 Le3 000 **5** 6 journeys
6 impossible to say
7 15 days **8** 27 buckets
9 3 h 20 min **10** 1·9 cm
11 $10\frac{1}{2}$ days **12** 5 trips

Exercise 9d (page 71)

1 1 : 2 **2** 2 : 3 **3** 5 : 4 **4** 4 : 3 **5** 2 : 3
6 4 : 1 **7** 1 : 10 **8** 2 : 5 **9** 2 : 3 **10** 3 : 2
11 4 : 3 **12** 5 : 3 **13** 2 : 7 **14** 1 : 7 **15** 3 : 4
16 10 : 1 **17** 5 : 7 **18** 10 : 7 **19** 7 : 18 **20** 3 : 4

Exercise 9e (page 71)

1 8 **2** 8 **3** 24 **4** 24 **5** 10
6 30 **7** 6 **8** 6 **9** 80 **10** 27

Exercise 9f (page 72)

1 a) Le5 000, Le10 000 b) 10 kg, 16 kg
c) 16 cm, 4 cm d) Le12 000, Le18 000
e) 24 ml, 56 ml f) 18, 4
2 20 eggs, 40 eggs
3 Juma: 9 bananas, Tunde: 6 bananas
4 a) 3 million, 5 million b) 3 : 5
c) Le9·75 million, Le16·25 million
5 100 cattle, 80 cattle, 60 cattle

Exercise 9g (page 72)

1 Le900 **2** 15 books **3** Le17 000
4 24 months **5** Le43 200 **6** Le72 400
7 20 **8** 53 fr CFA **9** 840
10 17 km/h **11** 20 posters **12** 9 carpets

Exercise 9h (page 73)

1 a) Le25 b) Le225 c) 1·75 m d) 2·72 litres e) Le142 f) 33 m g) 57 h) Le1 230 i) 18 kg j) 1·5 km
2 a) 74% b) 16% c) 13% d) $33\frac{1}{3}$% e) 5% f) 60% g) 250% h) 85% i) $62\frac{1}{2}$% j) 125%
3 a) Le40 000 b) 16 m c) 15 g d) Le30 000 e) Le110 f) 2·9 kg g) 50 h) 3·6 m i) Le20 j) Le340

Exercise 9i (page 74)

1 13% 2 75 cm 3 1·4 kg
4 1·15 kg 5 70% 6 Le320
7 7 g 8 3·2 kg 9 86 m
10 130% 11 70% 12 $17\frac{1}{2}$%
13 322 14 264 ha 15 130%
16 $\frac{2}{25}$, 8%, 92% 17 13 : 7, 504
18 *Y* (increase of 141) (*X*'s increase = 140)

Exercise 9j (page 74)

1 84 km/h 2 540 m/min
3 $\frac{2}{3}$ goals/game 4 75 cars/day
5 Le94 000/month 6 9 g/cm^3
7 40 km 8 81
9 Le340 10 approx. 30 per 1 000

Chapter 10

Exercise 10a (page 76)

1 Le2 000 2 Le2 800 3 Le1 800
4 Le800 5 Le1 800 6 Le1 400
7 Le3 000 8 Le4 800 9 Le10 500
10 Le7 500 11 Le4 200 12 Le3 000
13 Le1 800 14 Le13 200 15 Le3 750

Exercise 10b (page 76)

1 a) Le26 000 b) Le10 900 c) Le2 200 000 d) Le735 000 e) Le1 042 750
2 a) Le4 400 b) Le5 200 c) Le8 000
3 a) Le5 000 b) Le1 250 c) $6\frac{1}{4}$%
4 a) Le3 020 000 b) Le251 667 (to nearest Le)
5 a) Le54 000 b) Le354 000 c) Le14 750

Exercise 10c (page 78)

1 Le3 333.33
2 Le19 000
3 Le465 000
4 Le174 250
5 Le2 393 400
6 a) Le3 645 000 b) Le303 750

Exercise 10d (page 78)

1 a) Le38 700 b) Le24 500 c) Le99 360 d) Le6 900 e) Le2 396
2 Le105 000 3 Le6 358
4 Le1 800 5 Le500
6 Le11 500, Le3 500 ($23\frac{1}{3}$%)

Exercise 10e (page 79)

1 Le10 350
2 a) Le21 000 b) Le63 000 c) Le5 250
3 a) Le128 800 b) Le16 300
4 Le101 400
5 Le717 660
6 Le71 200

Exercise 10f (page 80)

1 a) Le8 400 b) Le25 200 c) Le30 450 d) Le19 950 e) Le23 100
2 a) Le2 700 b) Le4 400 c) Le5 150 d) Le7 450 e) Le3 300
3 a) Le4000 b) Le12 500 c) Le32 000 d) Le7 500 e) Le2 500

Exercise 10g (page 80)

1 Le48 120 2 Le24 810 3 Le75 288
4 $1 183.94 5 Le833 877

Exercise 10h (page 82)

1 a) Le2 500 b) Le2 500 c) Le2 500 d) Le2 500 e) Le5 000 f) Le47 500 g) Le7 500 h) Le5 000 i) Le10 000 j) Le2 500 k) Le5 000 l) Le7 500
2 a) Le57 000 b) Le72 000 c) Le147 000 d) Le147 000 e) Le147 000 f) Le72 000 g) Le112 000 h) Le57 000 i) Le72 000 j) Le147 000 k) Le147 000 l) Le147 000
3 a) Le3 500 b) Le1 200 c) Le5 000 d) Le2 000 e) Le3 000 f) Le2 500 g) Le300 h) Le10 000
4 a) Le1 200 b) Le12 000 c) Le5 400 d) Le16 000 e) Le103 000
5 Le147 000

6 Le89 800

7 a) Le241 000 b) Le94 000

8 a) cost Le9 100 b) cost Le7 500

a greater number of postal orders are required; the cost of printing these has to be paid for

Exercise 10i (page 82)

1 a) i) Le800 ii) Le4 800

b) i) Le1 500 ii) Le11 500

c) i) Le300 ii) Le3 450

d) i) Le180 ii) Le1 260

e) i) Le450 ii) Le1 200

2 a) i) Le450 profit ii) 15%

b) i) Le450 profit ii) 25%

c) i) Le36 000 loss ii) 10%

d) i) Le36 000 profit ii) $37\frac{1}{2}$%

e) i) Le630 loss ii) 15%

3 $17\frac{1}{2}$%

4 Le2 470

5 $233\frac{1}{3}$%

6 Le3 000

7 Le2 000

8 Le277 200

9 the son ($7\frac{1}{2}$%) (mother's profit = 7%)

10 12%, Le2 610

11 Le18 750, Le24 000

12 20%

13 Le62 700

14 20%

15 3%

Exercise 10j (page 83)

1 Le1 198 000

2 Le523 800

3 Le57 000

4 Le25 380

5 Le568 000

6 Le379 260

7 Le316 320

8 Le306 600

9 Le6 563 760

10 Le426 800

11 Le12 000

12 Le1 200 000

13 Le490 000

14 Le279 888

Chapter 11

Exercise 11a (page 85)

1 1, 3, x, $3x$

2 1, a, b, ab

3 1, x, x^2

4 1, a, b, ab, a^2, a^2b

5 1, 2, 3, 6, a, $2a$, $3a$, $6a$

6 1, 5, a, $5a$, b, $5b$, ab, $5ab$

7 1, x, y, z, xy, xz, yz, xyz

8 1, 2, 5, 10, m, $2m$, $5m$, $10m$, m^2, $2m^2$, $5m^2$, $10m^2$

9 1, 5, 25, p, $5p$, $25p$, q, $5q$, $25q$, pq, $5pq$, $25pq$

10 1, 2, 4, 8, d, $2d$, $4d$, $8d$, e, $2e$, $4e$, $8e$, de, $2de$, $4de$, $8de$

11 1, 2, a, $2a$, b, $2b$, a^2, $2a^2$, b^2, $2b^2$, ab, $2ab$, a^2b, $2a^2b$, ab^2, $2ab^2$, a^2b^2, $2a^2b^2$

12 1, 2, 7, 14, a, $2a$, $7a$, $14a$, b, $2b$, $7b$, $14b$, ab, $2ab$, $7ab$, $14ab$, b^2, $2b^2$, $7b^2$, $14b^2$, ab^2, $2ab^2$, $7ab^2$, $14ab^2$

Exercise 11b (page 85)

1 a	2 3	3 x	4 m
5 2	6 g	7 x	8 4
9 z	10 x	11 $4p$	12 ab
13 xy	14 pq	15 $2x$	16 ax
17 x	18 $2x$	19 $5x$	20 $3a$
21 mn	22 $2de$	23 $5m^2$	24 $3ab$
25 $6xy$	26 $7d$	27 $5a^2$	28 $4xy$
29 $9y$	30 1		

Exercise 11c (page 86)

1 a) $(3x + y)$ b) $(a - 3b)$

c) $(x + y)$ d) $(p + q)$

e) $(a - b)$ f) $(1 - y)$

g) $(2 - r)$ h) $(3b + 5x)$

i) $(3b + 5d)$ j) $(3y - z)$

k) $(3c + 4d)$ l) $(3x - 2)$

m) $(2a + 1)$ n) $(2m - 1)$

o) $(p - 3q)$ p) $(5a + 2x)$

2 a) $6(2c + d)$ b) $4(a - 2b)$

c) $3(2z - 1)$ d) $3(3x + 4y)$

e) $x(y + z)$ f) $c(b + d)$

g) $x(9 + a)$ h) $ab(c + d)$

i) $yz(x - a)$ j) $m(pq + ab)$

k) $3a(b - 2c)$ l) $4x(3a + 2b)$

m) $x(3x - 1)$ n) $2(3m^2 - 1)$

o) $ax(2b + 7c)$ p) $d^2(3e + 5)$

q) $2am(2m - 3)$ r) $-5(3x^2 + 2)$

s) $-6g(3f + 2)$

t) $-5y(x - 2)$ or $5y(2 - x)$

Exercise 11d (page 86)

1 ab	2 $5x$	3 $6a$	4 $12ab$
5 $10xy$	6 $9a$	7 $3x$	8 abc
9 xyz	10 $6b$	11 x^2	12 $3a^2$
13 $3m^2n$	14 $18a^2b$	15 $6x^2y^2$	16 $30ab^2$

Exercise 11e (page 87)

1 $24b$	2 bx	3 $4x$	4 16
5 1	6 $3c$	7 $2k$	8 b
9 3	10 $12xz$	11 $3ac$	12 $6dm$

Exercise 11f (page 88)

1 $\frac{3a}{5}$ 2 $3b$ 3 $\frac{4x}{3}$

4 $\frac{5x}{6}$ 5 $\frac{a}{5}$ 6 $\frac{9x}{20}$

7 $\frac{7}{a}$ 8 $\frac{2}{5y}$ 9 $\frac{6}{x}$

10 $\frac{1}{a}$ 11 $\frac{2}{y}$ 12 $\frac{2}{x}$

13 $\frac{4}{3x}$ 14 $\frac{4}{5a}$ 15 $\frac{1}{2z}$

16 $\frac{1}{12a}$ 17 $\frac{8}{15x}$ 18 $\frac{5}{6a}$

19 $\frac{3+x}{x}$ 20 $\frac{2a-b}{a}$

21 $\frac{6d+1}{2d}$ 22 $\frac{9+xy}{x}$

23 $\frac{8b+3}{4}$ 24 $\frac{2pq-3}{2q}$

25 $\frac{b+a}{ab}$ 26 $\frac{y-x}{xy}$

27 $\frac{m+3}{3m}$ 28 $\frac{3d-2c}{cd}$

29 $\frac{15b-8a}{12ab}$ 30 $\frac{6y+5x}{15xy}$

Exercise 11g (page 89)

1 a) $\frac{3a+1}{2}$ **b)** $\frac{5b-1}{3}$

c) $\frac{2c-4}{5}$ **d)** $\frac{2x+7}{4}$

e) $\frac{7z-5}{4}$ **f)** $\frac{10-7n}{12}$

g) $\frac{11a-2}{4}$ **h)** $\frac{b+1}{2}$

i) $\frac{17u-15}{12}$ **j)** $\frac{m-7}{24}$

k) $\frac{13c-12d}{30}$ **l)** $\frac{7a-6b}{18}$

2 a) $\frac{x+3}{2}$ **b)** $\frac{x-3}{2}$

c) $\frac{2h+3}{3}$ **d)** $\frac{3b-a}{2}$

Chapter 12

Exercise 12a (page 90)

1 R(3), S(−1), T($2\frac{1}{2}$), U($-1\frac{1}{2}$), V(0)

2 B(0·2), C(1·5), D(−0·5), E(−0·9), F(1·8), G(−0·1)

3

F D I C G B A H E
−10 −5 0 5 10

Fig. A4

4

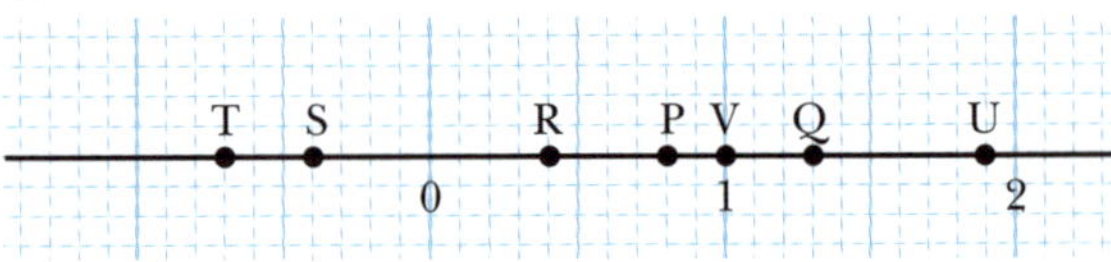

Fig. A5

Exercise 12c (page 93)

1 A(1, 1), B(1, 3), C(3, 3), D(2, −1), E(3, −2), F(2, −3), G(−1, −3), H(0, −1), I(−2, 0), J(−3, 2)

2 a) C **b)** F **c)** I
d) K **e)** D **f)** A
g) G **h)** J **i)** E
j) L **k)** H **l)** B

3 a) A(−6, 4) **b)** B(−4, 5) **c)** C(−3, 3)
d) D(−4, 0) **e)** E(2, 7) **f)** F(4, 4)
g) G(5, 1) **h)** H (2, −1) **i)** I (5, −2)
j) J(3, −4) **k)** K(0, −2) **l)** L(−3, −2)
m) M(−5, −3) **n)** N(−3, −5)

4 T(−2, 1), U(−3, 1), V(0, 4), W(3, 1), X(2, 1), Y(2, −1), Z(−2, −1)

5 (10, 7), (14, −4), (16, −2), (17, −2), (15, −5), (13, −5), (11, 0), (9, −2), (9, −7), (6, −7), (6, −4), (−2, −4), (−4, −7), (−7, −7), (−6, 5), (−2, 8), (3, 8), (3, 9), (6, 9)

6 a) (4, 7) **b)** (5, 5)
c) (5, 1) **d)** (6, 1)
e) (3, 2) **f)** (1, 3)
g) (2, 2) **h)** (2, 7)
i) (4, 4) **j)** (5, 6)
k) for every point, the x-coordinate = 2

7 a) (0, 2), (1, 2), (2, 2), (3, 2), (4, 2), (5, 2), (6, 2) for every point, the y-coordinate = 2
b) (0, 1), (1, 2), (2, 3), (3, 4), (4, 5), (5, 6), (6, 7) for every point, the y-coordinate is 1 more than the x-coordinate

Exercise 12d (page 96)

2 the points join to form a star shape (Fig. A6)

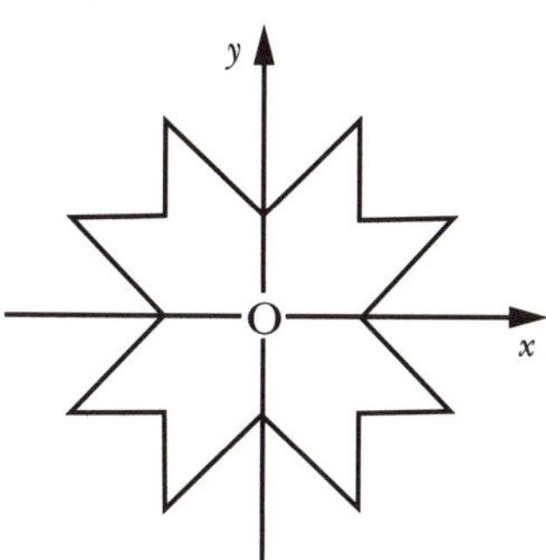

Fig. A6

3 a horse's head

4 **b)** 10 unit^2, 9 unit^2, 6 unit^2, 9 unit^2

5 **a)** parallelogram, X(−1, 0)

b) B, X, D, E lie in a straight line

c) square, Y $(2\frac{1}{2}, \frac{1}{2})$

6 **a)** (6, 36), (7, 49), (8, 64), (9, 81), (10, 100)

c), d) see Fig. A7

e) approximate values: 70·5, 42, 4·5, 9·5

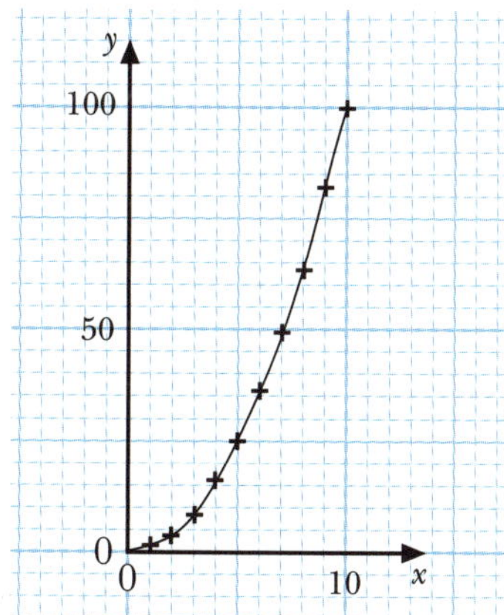

Fig. A7

Chapter 13

Exercise 13a (page 99)

1 $x = 6$ 2 $x = 6$ 3 $x = \frac{1}{2}$
4 $x = 2$ 5 $x = 3$ 6 $x = 1$
7 $a = 3$ 8 $z = 5$ 9 $n = 6$
10 $y = 3{\cdot}4$ 11 $r = 3\frac{1}{2}$ 12 $d = 3\frac{1}{3}$

Exercise 13b (page 99)

1 **a)** $2x$ **b)** $8n$ **c)** $6m + 4$
d) $2y - 5$ **e)** $a - 3$ **f)** $5d$
g) $3h$ leones **h)** $3t - 7$ **i)** $2k - 9$ leones
j) $2g + 23$ goals

2 **a)** $4x$ cm **b)** $3a + 4$ metres
c) $6c$ cm **d)** $8b$ metres
e) $2h + 20$ metres **f)** $5t$ cm
g) $6b$ metres **h)** $5k$ cm
i) $4(y - 2)$ metres **j)** $14x$ cm

Exercise 13c (page 100)

1 29 2 13 3 5
4 40 5 19 6 6
7 Le7 8 5 9 Le19, Le10
10 56, 79 goals 11 8 m 12 3 m, 6 m
13 15 cm 14 15 m, 5 m 15 3 m
16 3 cm 17 6 cm 18 17 mm
19 3 m 20 1·5 cm

Exercise 13d (page 101)

1 $a = 2$ 2 $a = -3$ 3 $b = -6$
4 $x = 1\frac{2}{3}$ 5 $a = -1$ 6 $y = \frac{3}{4}$
7 $n = -\frac{3}{4}$ 8 $m = \frac{2}{3}$ 9 $a = 5$
10 $t = 4$ 11 $n = 2$ 12 $c = 1$
13 $q = -1$ 14 $x = 3$ 15 $m = -4$
16 $x = -\frac{1}{2}$ 17 $h = 3$ 18 $a = 4\frac{2}{3}$
19 $f = 2$ 20 $e = 6$ 21 $x = 3\frac{1}{8}$
22 $x = 1$ 23 $x = -12$ 24 $n = \frac{2}{3}$

Exercise 13e (page 101)

1 $x = 4$ 2 $x = 8$ 3 $a = 6$
4 $y = 2$ 5 $x = -10$ 6 $x = 3$
7 $s = 6$ 8 $b = -9$ 9 $f = -1$
10 $x = -3$ 11 $a = -14$ 12 $b = 2$
13 $e = 3$ 14 $d = \frac{3}{4}$ 15 $x = \frac{3}{4}$
16 $x = -2$ 17 $y = 5$ 18 $y = -6$
19 $x = 24$ 20 $x = -5$ 21 $z = 3$
22 $y = 2$ 23 $v = -3$ 24 $n = 2\frac{1}{2}$

Exercise 13f (page 102)

1 9 2 15 3 6
4 7, 8 5 13, 15 6 $16\frac{1}{2}$ m
7 72 kg 8 17 9 8
10 Le700 11 31 12 Le115

Exercise 13g (page 103)

1 $x = 15$ 2 $x = 2\frac{1}{2}$ 3 $a = 36$
4 $a = 6$ 5 $z = 10$ 6 $x = 2$
7 $x = 14$ 8 $a = 19$ 9 $a = -3$
10 $y = 19$ 11 $n = 5$ 12 $a = 3$
13 $x = 2$ 14 $x = -3$ 15 $x = 8$
16 $x = 2$ 17 $z = \frac{1}{2}$ 18 $x = -14$
19 $x = 12$ 20 $x = 4$ 21 $m = 6$
22 $x = 1\frac{2}{5}$ 23 $x = 7$ 24 $t = 3$

25 $e = 2$ **26** $d = \frac{3}{4}$ **27** $m = 1$
28 $a = 5\frac{1}{8}$ **29** $a = 5$ **30** $x = 4$

Exercise 13h (page 104)

1 15 **2** 32 **3** 7
4 5 **5** 40, 42
6 a) $x + 24$ **b)** 12
7 Le800, Le1 000
8 a) $\frac{1}{2}x$ **b)** $\frac{1}{3}x$ **c)** \$96
9 a) $\frac{4d}{5}$ **b)** $\frac{3d}{4}$ **c)** $d = 30$
10 a) $y - 3$ years **b)** $y + 4$ years **c)** 17 years
11 18 **12** Le12 **13** Le600 000
14 37 **15** 50 **16** 64

Chapter 14

Exercise 14a (page 107)

1 a) Le300, Le175, Le450, Le410, Le130, Le355
b) 7 m, 8 m, 4·2 m, 1·8 m, 2·5 m, 9·3 m
2 b) i) 37·5 km/h, ii) 5·3 s
3 a)

time (min)	0	1	2	3	4	5	6
distance (m)	0	100	200	300	400	500	600

c) i) 570 m, ii) 3·35 min
4 a)

length (m)	1	2	3	4	5	6
cost (Le)	6000	12 000	18 000	24 000	30 000	36 000

c) i) Le22 800, ii) 2·3 m
5 a)

petrol (litres)	0	10	20	30	40	50
distance (km)	0	70	140	210	280	350

c) i) approx 155 km, ii) approx 33 litres
6 a)

fuel (gallons)	0	1	2	3	4	5	6
cost (Le)	0	8000	16 000	24 000	32 000	40 000	48 000

c) i) Le36 000, ii) 7·5 gallons

7 a)

sugar (kg)	1	2	3	4	5	6
cost (Le)	2 000	4 000	6 000	8 000	10 000	12 000

c) i) Le5 000, ii) 3·75 kg
8 a)

time (h)	0	1	2	3	4	5
distance (m)	0	−7·5	−15	−22·5	−30	−37·5

c) i) 3·3 h, ii) −11·25 m
9 a)

distance (km)	3	6	9	12	15
time (min)	2	4	6	8	10

c) i) 5·2 km, ii) 6·7 min
10 a)

time (h)	$\frac{1}{2}$	1	$1\frac{1}{2}$	2	$2\frac{1}{2}$	3
distance (km)	9	18	27	36	45	54

c) i) 29 km, ii) 2·2 h

Exercise 14b (page 109)

1 a)

tickets	0	1	2	3	4	5
cost (Le)	0	2 000	4 000	6 000	8 000	10 000

2 a)

pills	10	20	30	40	50	60
cost (Le)	800	1 600	2 400	3 200	4 000	4 800

d) Le1 360
3 a)

sides	3	4	5	6	7
angle sum	180	360	540	720	900

4 a)

tyres	1	2	3	4	5
cost (Le)	48 000	96 000	144 000	192 000	240 000

Exercise 14c (page 112)

1 b) i) 1·8°C, ii) 43 min
2 b) i) 182 mm, ii) 720 g
3 a)

week	0	1	2	3	4	5	6
mass (kg)	3·4	3·7	4·0	4·3	4·6	4·9	5·2

c) 37 days (5·3 weeks)
4 a)

petrol (kl)	1	2	3	4	5
delivery (Le)	2 000	2 000	2 000	2 000	2 000
basic (Le)	16 000	32 000	48 000	64 000	80 000
total (Le)	18 000	34 000	50 000	66 000	82 000

c) i) Le74 000, ii) 5·5 kl
5 a)

area (m^2)	$\frac{1}{2}$	1	$1\frac{1}{2}$	2	$2\frac{1}{2}$
handling (Le)	100	100	100	100	100
basic (Le)	200	400	600	800	1 000
total (Le)	300	500	700	900	1 100

c) i) $1\frac{1}{8}$ m², ii) Le550

Exercise 14d (page 114)

1 a) ₵125 b) ₵287.50 c) ₵187.50
d) ₵87.50 e) ₵200
2 a) ₦10 b) ₦5.60 (say ₦5.50)
c) ₦2.40 (say ₦2.50) d) ₦3.80 (say ₦3.75)
e) ₦13
3 a) 4 min b) 500 m
c) i) 1 250 m, ii) 1 750 m
d) 2 100 m e) $14\frac{1}{2}$ min
4 a) Le120 b) Le60 c) Le138
d) Le30 e) Le156 f) Le105
5 a) ₦3.25 b) ₦6.75 c) ₦4
d) ₦7 e) ₦6.50 f) ₦1.50
6 a) 50% b) 40% c) 90% d) 60%
e) 33% f) 67% g) 17% h) 83%
i) 13% j) 43% k) 53% l) 97%
m) 25% n) 75% o) 38% p) 82%
7 a) 24 b) 6 c) 9 d) 21
e) 16 f) 14 g) 19 h) 4
8 a) $2\frac{1}{2}$ h b) 3·2 h c) 80 km/h, 62·5 km/h
d) $\frac{185 - 60}{3 - 1} = \frac{125}{2} = 62{\cdot}5$ km/h
9 a) 45 km b) A, 120 km; B, 137·5 km
c) 35 km (approx.) d) A, 0·6 h; B, 0·8 h
10 a) 11.00 hours b) 12.30 hours
c) $\frac{1}{4}$ hour d) 2 km, $\frac{1}{2}$ hour
e) 4 km, $\frac{3}{4}$ hour f) 5 km
g) 12.00 hours h) 12.30 hours
i) 2·7 km j) 1·7 km
11 a) 4 km/h b) $5\frac{1}{3}$ km/h
c) 4 km/h d) 12 km/h
12 a) 75% b) 60% c) 40% d) 90%
e) 45% f) 55% g) 25% h) 65%
i) 68% j) 13% k) 78% l) 33%
13 b) i) 10°C, ii) 66°C, iii) 45°C, iv) 85°C,
v) 37°C, vi) 93°C, vii) −18°C,
viii) −10°C
14 b) i) D49.50, ii) D84, iii) D41.50, iv) D90
c) i) $7.70, ii) $3.25, iii) $7.00, iv) $6.00

Chapter 15

Exercise 15a (page 119)

1 Different calculators may give different results for many of these key sequences. The important thing is to get to know how *your* calculator operates.
2 For non-scientific calculators with an eight-digit display:
a) 99 999 999 b) 0·000 000 1
3 Looks like SHELL
4 Looks like SOIL
5 a)
7^1 7
7^2 49
7^3 343
7^4 2 401
7^5 16 807
7^6 117 649
7^7 823 543
7^8 5 764 801
b) Final digits comprise the repeating sequence 7, 9, 3, 1
c) Final two digits comprise the repeating sequence
07, 49, 43, 01

Exercise 15b (page 121)

1 Final answers:

a) 9 b) 4 c) 28 d) 86
e) 30 f) 97 g) 36 h) 27
i) 24·3 j) 15·5

2 a) i), ii), iv), v), vii) and viii) are incorrect

b) Corrections:

i) 13 ii) 67 iv) 908
v) 915 vii) 28 viii) 84

3 The outcomes are all negative:

a) −5 b) −10 c) −33 d) −37
e) −67 f) −216 g) −655 h) −56

4 The bill is correct

5 Le4 979

Exercise 15c (page 123)

1 a) 5 896 b) 73 c) 27 d) 2 116
e) 42 679 f) 7 g) 136 h) 615

2 a) i) 61·199 2 ii) 61·20
b) i) 1 282·386 7 ii) 1 282·39
c) i) 333·423 52 ii) 333·42
d) i) 1·850 898 2 ii) 1·85
e) i) 8* ii) 8
f) i) 28* ii) 28
g) i) 983·952 99 ii) 983·95
h) i) 63·625 5 ii) 63·63

*Some calculators may give rounding errors in these cases.

3 a) i), iii), iv), v), vi) and viii) are incorrect

b) Corrections:

i) 45 iii) 5 628
iv) 46 v) 33·333 333
vi) 3·315 viii) 5·065 110 6

4 1.5 09 or 1.5 000 000 depending on calculator

5 a) 11 111 111 (calculator display)
b) 12345679 (calculator display)

6 31 536 000

7 b) age × 365 c) age × 365 × 24
d) age × 365 × 24 × 60
e) most calculators will not cope with this if your age is above 3

8 a) Le14 435 per month
b) Le475 per day (365-day year)

9 Le262 500

10 a) 9·17 km b) 9 166·67 m c) 152·78 m

Exercise 15d (page 124)

1 b) 68 ÷ 17 + 45 c) 42 ÷ 3 + 22
d) 18 × 5 + 63 e) (171 − 15) × 18
g) (6 + 3) × 487 h) (31 − 14) × 100

2 a) 229 b) 560 c) 70 d) 21
e) 784 f) 7 g) 22·361 077 h) 23·32

3 a) 26 b) 12 c) 12
d) 435 e) 3·994 867 4 f) 282·76

Exercise 15e (page 126)

1 a) 1·96 b) 5·29 c) 46·24
d) 51·84 e) 24·01 f) 72·25
g) 31·36 h) 96·04 i) 9·61
j) 3·24 k) 32·49 l) 18·49

2 a) 324 b) 961 c) 1 024
d) 225 e) 841 f) 1 936
g) 4 900 h) 400 i) 3 844
j) 3 481 k) 6 561 l) 9 801

3 a) 2·89 b) 8·41 c) 6 241
d) 2 704 e) 92·16 f) 25
g) 4 096 h) 6 561 i) 1 296

4 a) 16 900 b) 168 100 c) 756 900
d) 250 000 e) 7 290 000 f) 68 890 000

5 For any number in the form N·5,
$N{\cdot}5^2 = N \times (N + 1) + 0{\cdot}25$

6 a) 144 and 441 b) 169 and 961
the digits are in reverse order

7 a) 18·49 cm^2 b) 0·001 849 m^2

8 a) 57 600 m^2 b) 5·76 hectares

9 a) 7·5 cm b) 56·25 cm^2

10 a), b), d) and f) are true

11 a) 0·16 b) 0·49 c) 0·25
d) 0·012 1 e) 0·230 4 f) 0·096 1
g) 0·422 5 h) 0·688 9 i) 0·072 9
j) 0·036 1 k) 0·336 4 l) 0·592 9

Exercise 15f (page 128)

1 a) 2 and 3 b) 3 and 4 c) 4 and 5
d) 5 and 6 e) 5 and 6 f) 5 and 6
g) 6 and 7 h) 7 and 8 i) 8 and 9
j) 8 and 9 k) 7 and 8 l) 9 and 10

2 a) 3 b) 9·49 c) 1·67
d) 5·29 e) 2·17 f) 6·86
g) 6 h) 1·90 i) 5
j) 1·58 k) 2·51 l) 7·94

3 a) 2·65 b) 8·37 c) 26·5
d) 83·7 e) 1·70 f) 5·39
g) 17·0 h) 53·9 i) 170
j) 15·8 k) 50 l) 6·16
m) 19·5 n) 61·6 o) 195
p) 3·16 q) 10 r) 31·6
s) 1·41 t) 20·7 u) 22·4
v) 268 w) 91·7 x) 31·0

4 a) 3·05 b) 8·83 c) 21·4

d) 2·92 e) 7·81 f) 24·7
g) 7·68 h) 2·43 i) 2·24
j) 22·4 k) 80 l) 44·7

5 to 3 s.f. $\sqrt{10} = 3{\cdot}16$ and $\pi = 3{\cdot}14$, a difference of 0·02; $\sqrt{10}$ is quite a good approximation for π

6 side ≃ 6·71 cm; perimeter = 27 cm to nearest cm

7 a) $m = 6{\cdot}40$ b) $m^2 = 40{\cdot}96$
c) $m^2 < 41$; this is because the tables contain rounded numbers and are not fully accurate

8 a) 0·458 b) 0·583 c) 0·656
d) 0·787 e) 0·742 f) 0·854
g) 0·927 h) 0·959 i) 0·831
j) 0·883 k) 0·768 l) 0·990

Chapter 16

Exercise 16a (page 131)

1 a) 1 : 3 b) 1 : 2 c) 3 : 5

2 a) 9 cm b) 4 cm c) 4 cm
d) 7·3 cm e) 13 cm f) 15 cm
g) 4·5 cm h) 7·5 cm i) 15·3 cm
j) 14·3 cm k) 11·9 cm

3 a) 60 m b) 55 m c) 10 m
d) 75 m e) 820 m f) 18·6 m
g) 430 km h) 7·4 km i) 2·26 m
j) 6·3 m

Exercise 16b (page 133)

1 15 m 2 68 m 5 210 m

6 AC = 12·2 m, XK = 10·8 m, PH = 8·5 m, QY = 7·8 m

7 64 m 8 $121\frac{1}{2}°$ 9 8·9 m

10 PC ≃ 37 m 11 AD ≃ 124 m

12 approximately 47 m

Exercise 16c (page 135)

1 a) 120 km b) 540 km
c) 200 km d) 420 km
e) 220 km f) 530 km
g) 1 300 km h) 970 km
i) 1 020 km j) 760 km
k) 740 km l) 420 km

2 a) Freetown Road, Sefadu Road
b) A1 trunk road, Airport Road
c) Kabala Road, Kenema Crescent, A6 trunk road
d) Kabala Road, Kenema Crescent
e) Sefadu Road, Kenema Crescent
f) Kenema Crescent, Sefadu Road
g) Freetown Road, Bo Avenue, A1, Airport Road
h) Kenema Crescent then as (g)
i) Sefadu Road then as (g)
j) Freetown Road, Kenema Crescent

3 a) 1 500 m b) 2 400 m c) 2 750 m
d) 750 m e) 1 000 m f) 1 750 m
g) 2 600 m h) 100 m i) 150 m
j) 2 100 m

4 a) i) 1 900 m ii) 2 750 m
b) i) 3 250 m ii) 7 500 m
c) i) 1 400 m ii) 2 000 m
d) i) 1 650 m ii) 2 750 m
e) i) 3 500 m ii) 4 250 m

Exercise 16d (page 136)

1 a) 3 b) brown
c) yellow and green
d) blue e) live (L)
f) 2 g) 5·1 cm

2 a) 6 b) living room
c) kitchen d) 3
e) living room f) 11
g) bedroom 3 h) living room, kitchen
i) cupboards j) 8 m × 4 m
k) 5·5 m × 3 m l) 134 m^2

Revision exercises 4–7

Revision exercise 4 (page 138)

1 12 litres 2 300

3 a) $37\frac{1}{2}$% b) 96 c) 20%

4 $37\frac{1}{2}$ refrigerators/hour

5 6%

6 a) Le6 916 000 b) Le8 736 000 c) Le1 820 000

7 a) 263 b) Le415 725

8 Le219 000; Le72 000 9 Le1 200 000, Le2 340 000

10 Le1 924.80

Revision exercise 5 (page 139)

1 HCF = $3a^2m$, LCM = $6a^3m^2$

2 a) $5(2 + 3b)$ b) $x(x - a)$
c) $2a(2b - a)$ d) $9xy(3x - 4y)$

3 a) xm **b)** $2ef$ **c)** $8abx$ **d)** $4pr^2$

4 a) $\frac{4x}{m}$ **b)** $\frac{10x}{9}$ **c)** $\frac{23}{3a}$ **d)** $\frac{q-p}{pq}$

5 a) $\frac{11a+7}{6}$ **b)** $\frac{2b+3}{12}$ **c)** $\frac{3a+2}{6}$

6 a) $a = 2$ **b)** $t = 6\frac{1}{2}$
c) $h = 7$ **d)** $x = 3$

7 Le4 400, Le6 100

8 a) $x = 9$ **b)** $a = 4\frac{1}{2}$ **c)** $m = 3\frac{2}{3}$

9 14, 16

10 a) $r = 25$ **b)** $x = 2\frac{2}{5}$
c) $m = 5$ **d)** $x = 2\frac{1}{2}$

Revision exercise 6 *(page 140)*

1

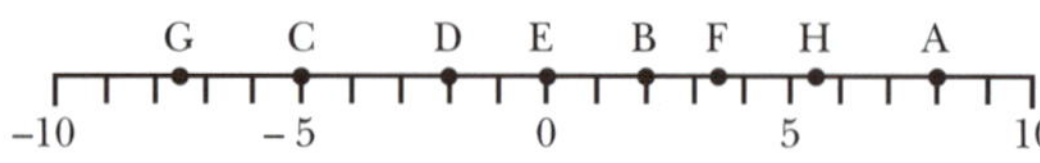

Fig. A8

2 P(3, 4), Q(0, 3), R(1, 2), S(3, 0), T(2, −1), U(0, −2), V(−2, −4), W(−4, −1), X(−3, 1), Y(−2, 3), Z(−4, 4)

3 E, F, C, B, G, A, H, D

4 b) parallelogram **c)** $(0, \frac{1}{2})$

5 c) CUP

6 a) Le1 270 **b)** Le380 000 **c)** Le620

7 a) 11·9 cm **b)** 4·17 h **c)** approx. 12·5 h

8 a) 50 km **b)** 40 min
c) i) 75 km/h, ii) 100 km/h

9 a)

x	0	45	90	135	180
y	180	135	90	45	0

c) i) $y = 140$, ii) $x = 52$

10 a) 2.66 fr CFA **b)** Le36·00

Revision exercise 7 *(page 143)*

1 a) 12 cm **b)** 6·6 cm
c) 7·9 cm

2 a) 43·2 km **b)** 36 km
c) 7·4 m

3 Le272 500, Le247 975

4 62·8 litres

5 a) 39·69 **b)** 23·04 **c)** 2 304
d) 115 600

6 a) 2·83 **b)** 8·94 **c)** 6·48
d) 20·5 **e)** 92·2 **f)** 94·9

7 a) 30 **b)** 840 **c)** 2·1
d) 25

8 7·9 cm **9** 2 : 5 **10** XR ≈ 35 m

Chapter 17

Exercise 17a *(page 147)*

1 5 cm

2 a) 25 unit^2 **b)** 9 + 16 = 25 unit^2
c) the area of the square on the hypotenuse is equal to the sum of the areas of the squares on the other two sides

3 a) 169 unit^2 **b)** 25 + 144 = 169 unit^2
c) See 2(c)

4 b) 10 cm **d)** 100 cm^2
e) 64 cm^2 and 36 cm^2
f) 64 cm^2 + 36 cm^2 = 100 cm^2

5 b) 17 cm **d)** 289 cm^2
e) 64 cm^2 and 225 cm^2
f) 64 cm^2 + 225 cm^2 = 289 cm^2

Exercise 17b *(page 149)*

1 a) AC = 10 m **b)** AC = 15 cm
c) AC = 13 m **d)** AC = 17 cm
e) AB = 7 m **f)** AB = 15 cm
g) BC = 60 m **h)** BC = 10 cm
i) AB = 9 mm **j)** AB = 20 m

2 a) 13 **b)** 3 **c)** 17 **d)** 2
e) 12 **f)** 9 **g)** 8

Exercise 17c *(page 150)*

1 a) (6, 8, 10), (9, 12, 15), (12, 16, 20), (15, 20, 25)
b) (10, 24, 26), (15, 36, 39), (20, 48, 52), (25, 60, 65)
c) (14, 48, 50), (21, 72, 75), (28, 96, 100), (70, 240, 250)
d) (16, 30, 34), (24, 45, 51), (32, 60, 68), (40, 75, 85)

2 a), c), d), e), g), h), j)

3 (9, 40, 41) → $9^2 = 40 + 41$
(11, 60, 61) → $11^2 = 60 + 61$

4 (12, 35, 37) → $\frac{1}{2}$ of $12^2 = 35 + 37$
(14, 48, 50) → $\frac{1}{2}$ of $14^2 = 48 + 50$

5 (13, 84, 85) (16, 63, 65)
(15, 112, 113) (18, 80, 82)
(17, 144, 145) (20, 99, 101)
(19, 180, 181) (22, 120, 122)
(21, 220, 221) (24, 143, 145)

Exercise 17d (page 151)

1 16·1 cm
2 7·3 m
3 2 060 m
4 2·5 m
5 574 km
6 10·8 m each
7 6·7 m
8 10 m approx
9 18 m
10 12·7 m
11 14·7 m
12 4·4 m

Chapter 18

Exercise 18a (page 154)

1 **a)** 0 mm **b)** 81 mm **c)** 203 mm
d) 89 mm **e)** 660 mm **f)** 249 mm
g) 160 mm **h)** 41 mm **i)** 0 mm
j) 3 mm **k)** 46 mm **l)** 516 mm

2 Kabala: August Yele: July
Bo: June Port Loko: June

3 Kabala: January, February, March, December
Yele: January, February, November, December
Bo: January, December
Port Loko: January

4 For Kabala and Yele the rainfall decreases from August to September. For Bo and Port Loko the rainfall increases from August to September

5 The rainfall increases

Exercise 18b (page 155)

1 departs, arrives
2 **a)** 6.00 pm **b)** 11.45 pm
3 5 h 45 min
4 10 min
5 **a)** 6.00 am **b)** 11.30 am
6 5 h 30 min
7 10 min
8 **a)** 2 h 3 min **b)** 1 h 48 min **c)** 15 min

Exercise 18c (page 156)

1 Cotonou, Lomé
2 Monrovia
3 Accra, Lomé, Cotonou, Lagos
4 Freetown, Monrovia
5 Douala
6 Lagos, Kano, Jeddah
7 Kano, Cairo
8 Port Harcourt, Lagos, Kano
9 Kano
10 Monrovia, Accra, Lomé, Cotonou, Lagos

Exercise 18d (page 156)

1 **a)** 14 00 hours **b)** 20 30 hours
c) 09 00 hours **d)** 15 00 hours
e) 13 30 hours **f)** 05 45 hours
g) 04 15 hours **h)** 23 55 hours
i) 20 55 hours **j)** 06 10 hours
k) 12 00 hours **l)** 00 03 hours

2 **a)** 5 am **b)** 11 pm **c)** 10 am
d) 3 pm **e)** 5.30 pm **f)** 2.15 am
g) 9.45 pm **h)** 2.15 pm **i)** 9.25 am
j) 6.19 pm **k)** 7.40 am **l)** 11.57 pm

3 **a)** WT 753 **b)** 45 min **c)** 19 10 hours
d) 1 h 45 min

4 **a)** WT 754 **b)** 45 min **c)** 21 10 hours

Exercise 18e (page 157)

1 **a)** i) 238 km ii) 277 km iii) 217 km
iv) 381 km v) 77 km vi) 282 km
vii) 397 km viii) 64 km ix) 141 km
x) 331 km
b) Falaba and Panguma (397 km)
c) Bo and Bumpe (27 km)
d) i) 251 km ii) 333 km iii) 378 km
e) 465 km

2 **a)** 8
b) 40 min
c) morning: 1 h, afternoon: 20 min
d)

subject	**periods**
Language	5
Literature	5
Mathematics	5
Science	5
Economics	5
Commerce	4
Geography	4
History	4
Religious Knowledge	3

3 **a)** 11
b) 0
c) May
d) i) March
ii) March is the warmest time of the year

e) August
f) record players, radios, refrigerators
g) i) it gives an accurate record of the value of stock on hand,
ii) it helps in planning when to buy items

4 a) 8
b) 7
c) i) Aliyageen; ii) 3;
iii) John, Musa, Ojo; iv) 71
d) 66 for, 52 against

Chapter 19

Exercise 19a *(page 160)*

1 a) 44 cm, 154 cm^2
b) 132 m, 1 386 m^2
c) 220 mm, 3 850 mm^2
d) 11 m, $9\frac{5}{8}$ m^2
e) 176 mm, 2 464 mm^2
f) 440 cm, 15 400 cm^2
g) 22 m, 38·5 m^2
h) 264 mm, 5 544 mm^2
i) 484 cm, 18 634 cm^2
j) 88 cm, 616 cm^2

2 a) 125·6 cm, 1 256 cm^2
b) 62·8 m, 314 m^2
c) 37·68 mm, 113 mm^2
d) 251·2 cm, 5 024 cm^2
e) 314 cm, 7 850 cm^2
f) 50·24 mm, 200·96 mm^2
g) 31·4 cm, 78·5 cm^2
h) 87·92 cm, 615·4 cm^2
i) 53·38 mm, 226·87 mm^2
j) 376·8 cm, 1 130 cm^2

Exercise 19b *(page 160)*

1 c) 5 cm d) 22 cm
e) 110 cm^2 f) no
g) 7 cm; 22 cm; both answers should be the same

2 a) 10 cm b) 7 cm
c) 22 cm d) 22 cm

Exercise 19c *(page 161)*

1 a) 6 800 cm^2 b) 19 000 cm^2
c) 470 cm^2 d) 110 cm^2
e) 570 cm^2 f) 16 000 cm^2

2 180 mm

3 30 cm

4 a) 1 200 cm^2 b) 750 cm^2
c) 1 300 cm^2 d) 25 cm^2

5 a) 630 cm^2 b) Le945

6 a) 310 cm^2 b) 100 cm^2
c) 410 cm^2

Exercise 19d *(page 163)*

1 77 cm^3 2 22 m^3, 22 kl 3 44 kl
4 35 cm 5 3·85
6 a) $5\,028\frac{4}{7}$ cm^3 b) 3 520 g
7 a) 3 080 cm^3 b) 24·64 kg
8 a) $\frac{22}{7}$ m^3 b) 6·6 t
9 9·8 cm 10 7·7 hours

Chapter 20

Exercise 20a *(page 165)*

1 a) horizontal b) vertical
c) vertical d) horizontal
e) neither f) vertical
g) horizontal h) vertical
i) neither j) horizontal

2 a) seat of chair, shelves, book on table, top and bottom edges of door, top of door frame, set-square on table
b) light cord, flagpole, table legs, drawer fronts, left- and right-hand edges of notice board
c) door handle, light switch, support bracket for shelves, chair legs, broom handle

Exercise 20b *(page 166)*

1 a) 30° b) 40° c) 25° d) 25°
2 a) 10° b) 10°
3 a) 15° b) 15°
4 a) 45° b) 28°
5 52°

Exercise 20d *(page 170)*

1 $8\frac{1}{2}$ m 2 28 m 3 7·5 m
4 6 m 5 9 m 6 80 m
7 $30\frac{1}{2}$ m 8 35 m 9 12 m
10 350 cm 11 95 m 12 2 400 m

Chapter 21

Exercise 21a *(page 173)*

1 Since the woman's family history shows an even chance of males and females, it is equally likely that either a boy or a girl will be born next

2 The 'rainmaker' may be able to say that rain is coming, but it is likely that his prediction is based on past experience; throwing the kola nuts may help him to concentrate; rainfall records are fairly useful, but they cannot always predict the future accurately

Exercise 21b *(page 173)*

3 b) probability $\simeq \frac{1}{2}$

5 probability $\simeq \frac{1}{4}$

9 probability $\simeq 0{\cdot}26$

10 probability $\simeq \frac{1}{6}$

Exercise 21c *(page 175)*

1 a) 0·2 **b)** 0·4 **c)** 0·9

2 a) $\frac{1}{6}$ **b)** 0 **c)** $\frac{5}{6}$ **d)** 1

3 a) $\frac{3}{5}$ **b)** $\frac{2}{5}$ **c)** 1 **d)** 0

4 a) $\frac{2}{5}$ **b)** $\frac{3}{5}$ **c)** 1 **d)** 0

5 a) $\frac{7}{10}$ **b)** $\frac{3}{10}$ **c)** 0 **d)** 1

6 a) $\frac{1}{2}$ **b)** 1 **c)** 0

7 $\frac{24}{25}$ **8** $\frac{9}{10}$

9 a) 0 **b)** 0 **c)** $\frac{3}{7}$ **d)** $\frac{4}{7}$

10 a) 40 **b)** $\frac{5}{8}$

11 $\frac{3}{5}$ **12** 35 people

13 a) $\frac{1}{5}$ **b)** $\frac{1}{20}$ **c)** $\frac{3}{4}$ **d)** 4 **e)** 1

14 $\frac{39}{40}$ **15** $\frac{9}{10}$

16 $\frac{1}{4}$ (however, this may not be reliable; it could be that Ebenezer has improved since the earlier games)

17 a) $\frac{5}{8}$ **b)** $\frac{3}{8}$ **c)** 1 **d)** 0

18 $\frac{9}{20}$

19 a) 48% **b)** $\frac{12}{25}$ (approx $\frac{1}{2}$)

20 a) 150 **b)** 50% **c)** 26% **d)** $\frac{1}{2}$ **e)** about 5

Chapter 22

Exercise 22a *(page 178)*

1 a) $6 < 11$ **b)** $-1 > -5$
c) $0 > -2{\cdot}4$ **d)** $-3 < +3$
e) $x > 12$ **f)** $y < -2$
g) $4 > a$ **h)** $a < 4$
i) $15 < b$ **j)** $b > 15$

2 a) true **b)** true
c) false **d)** false
e) false **f)** true
g) false **h)** true

3 a) $>$ **b)** $<$ **c)** $<$ **d)** $>$
e) $<$ **f)** $>$ **g)** $<$ **h)** $>$

Exercise 22b *(page 179)*

1 a) $h < 5$ **b)** $m < 50$
c) $x > 5$ **d)** $t < 5$
e) $n < 24$ **f)** $m < 20$
g) $s < 25$ **h)** $t > 120$

2 a) $h < 1{\cdot}5$ **b)** $c < 800$
c) $b > 1\,200$ **d)** $g > 60$
e) $p > 28$ **f)** $m < 55$
g) $t > 6$

3 $m > 28$

4 $y > 700$

5 $x > 15$

6 $x < 60$

7 a) length > 6 cm **b)** perimeter > 24 cm

8 a) length < 7 cm **c)** area < 49 cm^2

Exercise 22c *(page 179)*

1 a) $a \leqslant 12$ **b)** $n \geqslant 5$
c) $t \leqslant 38$ **d)** $s \geqslant 2\,400$
e) $n < 36$ **f)** $v \leqslant 120$

2 a) $l \leqslant 7$ **b)** $s \leqslant 140$
c) $h \geqslant 160$ **d)** $p \leqslant 5$
e) $d \geqslant 6$ **f)** $g \geqslant 100$

3 $x < 27$, $y \geqslant 27$

4 $a < 12$, $b \geqslant 12$, $a < b$

5 a) circumference $\leqslant 6\pi$ **b)** area $\leqslant 9\pi$

Exercise 22d *(page 180)*

1 a) $x < 3$ **b)** $x > 2$
c) $x \geqslant -2$ **d)** $x \leqslant 5$
e) $x > -4$ **f)** $x \leqslant -4$
g) $x > -2$ **h)** $x \geqslant 2\frac{1}{2}$
i) $x \geqslant -1$ **j)** $x < 2$

2

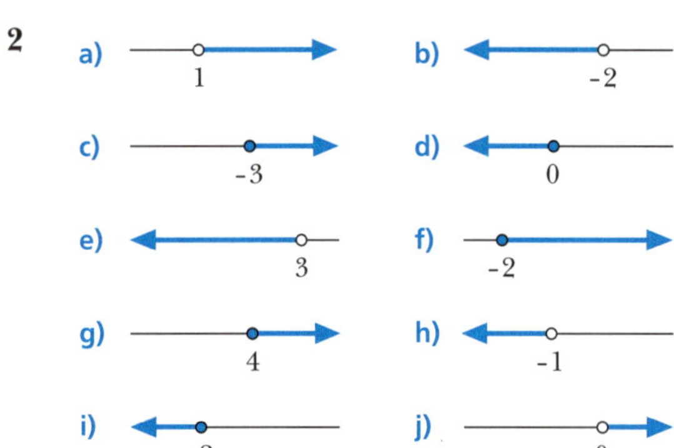

Fig. A9

Exercise 22e (page 181)

1 $x < 5$
2 $x \geqslant 3$
3 $a > 2$
4 $y \leqslant 8$
5 $x < 6$
6 $x > 5$
7 $x \leqslant -6$
8 $x < -5$
9 $x < 3$
10 $x \geqslant 9$
11 $x \leqslant 4$
12 $x > -2$
13 $x \geqslant -2\frac{1}{4}$
14 $x \geqslant 2\frac{2}{3}$
15 $x < 4$
16 $x \geqslant 2$
17 $x < -5$
18 $x \geqslant -7$
19 $x > 5\frac{1}{4}$
20 $x \geqslant -\frac{2}{3}$

Exercise 22f (page 181)

1 $x = 0, -1, -2, \ldots$
2 $x = 6, 7, 8, 9, \ldots$
3 $x = 5, 6, 7, \ldots$
4 $x = 2, 1, 0, \ldots$
5 $x = -3, -4, -5, \ldots$
6 $x = -3, -2, -1, \ldots$
7 $x = 0, -1, -2, \ldots$
8 $x = -2, -1, 0, \ldots$
9 $x = 5, 4, 3, \ldots$
10 $x = 4, 5, 6, \ldots$
11 $x = -4, -3, -2, \ldots$
12 $x = -4, -5, -6, \ldots$
13 $x = 1, 0, -1, \ldots$
14 $x = -5, -4, -3, \ldots$
15 $x = -1, -2, -3, \ldots$
16 $x = 4, 5, 6, \ldots$
17 $x = 2, 1, 0, \ldots$
18 $x = -4, -3, -2, \ldots$
19 $x = -2, -3, -4, \ldots$
20 $x = 3, 2, 1, \ldots$

Exercise 22g (page 182)

1 $x > -4$
2 $a > 2$
3 $m \geqslant -3$
4 $d \leqslant -8$
5 $m \leqslant -7$
6 $x < -7$
7 $y \geqslant -14$
8 $a \geqslant -\frac{1}{24}$
9 $t \geqslant -\frac{4}{3}$
10 $n > 4$
11 $y \geqslant -4$
12 $y \leqslant 4$
13 $a > 2$
14 $n \geqslant -1$
15 $x < -16$
16 $x \leqslant -1$
17 $x \geqslant 7$
18 $x \leqslant -3$
19 $r \leqslant -2$
20 $t \leqslant -1\frac{1}{2}$

Exercise 22h (page 183)

1 $x > 8$
2 $y < 10{\cdot}7$
3 $n \leqslant 18$
4 5, 6, 7
5 1, 0, −1, −2
6 $x < 2800$
7 19
8 $x \geqslant 12$
9 $h < 4$
10 x has a value between 3 and 6
11 b has a value from 1 to 17
12 4
13 a) 5 **b)** 7
14 over 2 h
15 over 21 km/h

Chapter 23

Exercise 23a (page 186)

1 a) West **b)** South-east **c)** South **d)** North
2 a) 180° **b)** 180° **c)** 45° **d)** 90° **e)** 135° **f)** 45° **g)** 45° **h)** 180°

Exercise 23b (page 186)

1 a) N **b)** S
2 a) E **b)** W
3 a) SW **b)** NE
4 a) SE **b)** NW
5 a) NE **b)** SW
6 a) W **b)** E
7 a) NW **b)** SE
8 a) S **b)** N

Exercise 23c (page 187)

1 N58°E **2** S40°E **3** N18°W **4** S60°W
5 S20°E **6** N70°W **7** S75°W **8** S40°E

Exercise 23e (page 189)

1 a) 056° **b)** 240° **c)** 120° **d)** 270° **e)** 327° **f)** 090° **g)** 133° **h)** 180°
2 040°, 120°, 230°, 290°
3 045°, 128°, 200°, 249°, 303°
4

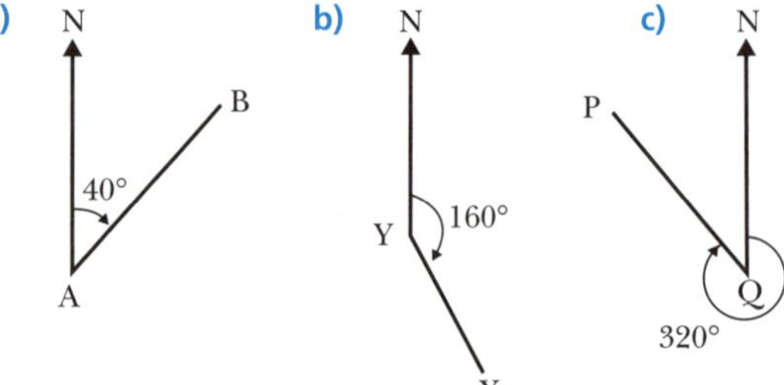

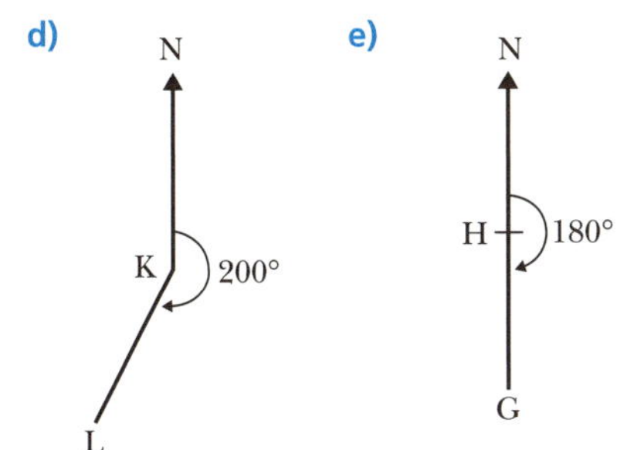

Fig. A10

5 a) i) 250°, ii) 070°
b) i) 150°, ii) 330°
c) i) 057°, ii) 237°
d) i) 000°, ii) 180°
e) i) 270°, ii) 090°
f) i) 319°, ii) 139°
g) i) 015°, ii) 195°

Exercise 23f (page 191)

1 a) 20 m b) 20·5 m
2 $075\frac{1}{2}°$, 60 m
3 36 m
4 358°, 052°
5 061°, 40 m (30 m is an acceptable answer from a good drawing)

Exercise 23g (page 193)

1 5 km, 037°
2 3·6 km, 236°
3 410 km, 284°
4 22 km, 109°
5 3 760 m, 020°
6 450 km, 640 km
7 a) 93 km b) 154 km
8 a) 2·4 km b) 336°
9 a) 310°, 310 km
b) 200 km north, 240 km west

Chapter 24

Exercise 24a (page 194)

c) a circle f) they are equal

Exercise 24b (page 196)

1 a) 5 cm b) 10 cm c) 13 cm d) 17 cm
2 a) 6 cm b) 4 cm c) 5 cm d) 2 cm
3 a) 20π cm^2 b) 60π cm^2
c) 65π cm^2 d) 136π cm^2
4 a) 108π cm^2 b) 56π cm^2
c) 55π cm^2 d) 20π cm^2
5 235·5 cm^2 6 704 cm^2
7 a) 301 cm^2 b) 452 cm^2
c) 283 cm^2 d) 703 cm^2

Exercise 24c (page 196)

4 3 full cones should fill the cylinder
5 a) $\frac{1}{3}$ b) 3

Exercise 24d (page 197)

1 a) 308 cm^3 b) 0·924 cm^3
c) $1\frac{4}{7}$ m^3 d) 550 cm^3
2 18 000 cm^3
3 9 cm
4 234 cm^3
5 35·2 m^3
6 13·2 cm^3

Exercise 24e (page 198)

1 a) 20 m^2 b) 60 m^3
2 a) 20 m b) 30 m^2
3 a) 4·3 m b) between 50 and 60
4 a) 90 cm b) 2 m^2 c) 15 m
5 4 000
6 400 ml
7 430 cm^3
8 a) d = 22 cm b) 9 litres
9 15 litres
10 from 100 to 110 litres

Revision exercises 8–10

Revision exercise 8 (page 201)

1 17 cm
2 21 cm
3 a) and d)
4 a) 12 cm b) 14 cm
5 3·3 m
6 1 628 cm^2
7 496 cm^3
8 92π cm^2
9 528 cm^3
10 30 (approximately)

Revision exercise 9 *(page 202)*

1 a) 06 25 hours **b)** 18 45 hours
c) 19 55 hours **d)** 23 50 hours
2 325 km
3 a) $\frac{9}{10}$ **b)** 27
4 276
5 $800x + 1\,100y < 3\,000$
6 a) $x < 5$ **b)** $x < -3$
c) $x < 2$ **d)** $x \leq 3$
7

Fig. A11

8 a) $\frac{3}{5}$ **b)** $\frac{2}{5}$ **c)** 1
9 a) Plane 1 **b)** 09 50 hours **c)** 55 min
10 a) 6 h 20 min **b)** i) 6 h ii) 8 h 25 min

Revision exercise 10 *(page 203)*

1 a) AB, BC, AC, DE, EF or FD
b) AE, BF or CD
2 a) 90° **b)** 225° **c)** 135° **d)** 270°
3 061°, 103°, 188°, 260°, 336°
5 6 m
6 5·8 m
7 $22\frac{1}{2}$ m
8 9·8 km, 233°
9 a) 4·1 km **b)** 1·7 km
10 180 cm

Index

Numbers in italics indicate where subject is referred to in chapter summaries.

abbreviations 154
acute-angle bearing 187, *193*
addition: algebraic fractions 87–88, *89*; directed numbers 36; with calculators 121–122
additive inverse 41, *45*, 98
airline charts and timetables 155–156
algebra 85–89, *89*
algebraic expressions 53–57, *57*
algebraic fractions 87–89, *89*
algebraic processes 3–5
algebraic terms 53–54, *57*, 85–86, *89*
angles: between lines 46–47; corresponding 46; in a polygon 46–52, *52*; in a quadrilateral 48–49; in a triangle 47–48
interior 50–51; of elevation/ depression 165–171, *171*; vertically opposite 46; *see also* acute-angle bearing, right-angled triangle
answers 213–240
approximation 58–60
area 207; circle 160; cone 194–196; cylinder 160–161; *see also* surface area
arithmetic 58–62, *62*, 76–84, *84*, 118–129, *129*, 154–159, *159*
axes *see* axis
axis 91; horizontal 17; vertical 17; *see also* *x*-axis, *y*-axis

balance method 98–99, *105*, *184*
bearings 185–193, *193*
body measures 61, *62*
brackets 54–56, *57*, 88–89, *89*, 101–102, *105*; 123–124

calculator 118–119, *129*
calculator skills 118–124
calendar 208
capacity 208
Cartesian graph 96, *97*
Cartesian plane 90–96, *97*
centigramme 207
centimetre 207
Chinese proof 148
choosing scales 109–111, *117*
circle 209; area 160
circumference 160
clinometer 168, *171*
commission 83, *84*
common fractions 69
compass 185; bearings 186, *193*
cone 194–200, *200*, 209; *see also* curved surface area
continuous graphs 106–107, *117*
continuous line 106
conversion graphs 112–113, *117*
coordinates 91–96, *97*; *see also* *x*-coordinate, *y*-coordinate
cross-reference 154, *159*
cube 209
cubic centimetre 208
cubic metre 208
cubic millimetre 208
cuboid 209
currencies 208
curved surface area 195, *200*
cylinder 160–164, *164*, 209

data 154, *159*
decagon 50
decagramme 207
decametre 207
decigramme 207
decimal: fractions 22, 25, *28*, 69; places 27, *28*
decimetre 207
deficit 59
depression 166–169, *171*
Descartes 91
digits 21–22, *28*, 209
directed algebraic terms 53–54, *57*
directed numbers 36–40, *40*, 100–101
directions 185–193, *193*
direct proportion 70, *75*
discontinuous graphs 108–109, *117*
discount 78
distance chart 158
distances 190–193, *193*
distance/time graphs 113–114, *117*
divisibility 13–15; tests 209
division: algebraic fractions 87; by negative numbers 182; directed numbers 39–40; with calculators 122–123

electricity bills 80, *84*
elevation 165–171, *171*
equations 98–105, *105*
equivalent fractions 87
estimation 60–62, *62*, 125, 127–128, *129*, 198, *200*
expansion 53–57, *57*
experimental probability

172–173, *177*
factorisation 85–86, *89*
factors 12; of algebraic terms 85–86, *89*
false accuracy 59
Fibonacci sequence 17
fractions 69, 103–104, *105*; *see also* algebraic fractions, common fractions, decimal fractions, equivalent fractions, probability as a fraction

geometry 5–9
gramme 207; *see also* centigramme, decagramme, decigramme, hectogramme, kilogramme, milligramme
graphs 16–18, *19*, 90, *117*; information from 112–114; of inequalities 180; *see also* continuous graphs, conversion graphs, discontinuous graphs, distance/time graphs, straight line graphs
greater than 178–179, 209
grouping digits 21–22, *28*

hand span 61
HCF *see* highest common factor
hectare 207
hectogramme 207
hectometre 207
heptagon 50, 51
hexagon 50, 51
highest common factor 13, 85–86, *89*
hire purchase 79
horizontal 165, *171*
horizontal axis 17
hour 207
hypotenuse 147, *153*
identity 41–43, *45*
income tax 77–78, *84*
indices 23
inequalities 178–183, *184*
inequality symbols 178, 179, *184*
instalment 79
interest 76, *84*; *see also* interest rate, simple interest
interest rate 74
intermediate sides of a triangle 149
inverse 41–45, *45*; operations 43–44; proportion 70, *75*; *see also* additive inverse, multiplicative inverse

kilogramme 207
kilolitre 208
kilometre 207
kite 31–32, 33

large numbers 20–22, 27–28, *28*
laws of indices 23, *28*
LCM *see* lowest common multiple
length 207
less than 178–179, 209
lines of symmetry 31–32
litre 208
lowest common multiple 13, 86, *89*, 103, *105*

magnetic compass 185, *193*
maps 134–135
mass 207
measurement *see* angles, area, body measures, capacity, circumference, length, mass, SI units, surveying, tables, unit, volume
measures 61–62, *62*, 207–208
mensuration: 5–9, 198, *200*; formulae 209
metre 207
milligramme 207
millilitre 208
millimetre 207
million 20
minute 207
mixed operations 123–124
money 208
multiplication: algebraic fractions 87; directed numbers 36–39; table 208; with calculators 122–123
multiplicative inverse 42, *45*
negative multipliers 37–38, 182
negative numbers 182
net: cone 194; cylinder 160
nonagon 50–51
not greater than 179, 209
not less than 179, 209
number 1–3; line 90, *97*; patterns 15–19, *19*
numbers: directed 36–40, *40*; estimating 60; large 20–22, 27–28, *28*; negative 182; ordered pair of 92; prime 12; properties of 12–15, *19*; rounding off 26, 58, *62*; small 22–23, 27–28, *28*; square 17, 18–19, *19*, 124–125; triangle 17
numeration 1–3

octagon 50
operations *see* inverse operations, mixed operations
ordered pair 92, *97*
origin 91, *97*, *117*

pace 61
parallel lines 29
parallelogram 29–30, 32–33, 209
patterns 15–19, *19*, 34–35, 35
pentagon 50, 51
percentages 69, 73–74, *75*
perfect square 18–19, *19*, 125
pi (π) 160–163, *164*, 195–198, *200*
plane shapes 29–35, *35*
plane surface 90–91
plotting 95–96, *97*
points 90–96, *97*; of the compass 185–186
polygon 46–52, *52*
position of a point 90–96, *97*
positive multipliers 36–37
Post Office charges 80–81, *84*
prime factors 12
prime number 12
prism 162–163, *164*; *see also* right-triangular prism

probability 172–177, *177*; as a fraction 174–175
profit and loss 82, *84*
properties of numbers 12–15, *19*
proportion 69–71, *75*; *see also* direct proportion, inverse proportion
Pythagoras 148–149
Pythagoras' rule 147–149, *153*, 209
pythagorean triple 150, *153*

quadrilaterals 29–33, *35*, 48–49, 50, 51

railway timetables 155
rate 74, *75*
ratio 71–73, *75*
reciprocal 42, *45*
rectangle 33, 209
regular polygon 50, *52*
removing brackets 54–56, *57*
required outcome 174–175, *177*
review of Book 1 1–11
revision 1–11, 12–13, 36, 46–48, 58, 63–68, 69, 98–99, 138–146, 160, 201–206
rhombus 30–31, 32–33
right-angled triangle 147–149, *153*
right-triangular prism 209
rounding off 26, 58, *62*

scale drawing 130–137, *137*, 190–192
scales 109–111, *117*, 130–131, *137*
second 207
sequence 15–18, *19*; *see also* Fibonacci sequence
s.f. *see* significant figures
sharing 72–73
sieve of Eratosthenes 12
significant figures 26, *28*, 58, 198, *200*
signs 39–40, *40*
simple interest 74
SI units 207–208
slant height 195
small numbers 22–23, 27–28, *28*
solving equations 98–105, *105*
solving inequalities 181
solving triangles 147–153, *153*
square 33, 209
square centimetre 207
square kilometre 207
square metre 207
square millimetre 207
square numbers 17, 18–19, *19*, 124–125, 210; *see also* perfect square, table of squares
square root 18–19, *19*; tables 125–128, 211–212
standard form 22, 25, *28*
statistics 9–11
straight line graphs 106–117
substitution 54
subtraction: algebraic fractions 87–88, *89*; with calculators 121–122
surface area: cone 194–196, *200*; cylinder 161, *164*
surveying 190–191, *193*
symbols 178, 179, *184*, 209
symmetry *see* lines of symmetry

table of squares 124–126, 210
table of values 106–107
tables 124–128, *129*, 207–212
tabulated data 154, *159*
tax *see* income tax, Value Added Tax
taxable income 77–78
technical drawings 134, 136
term 15–17, 101–104; *see also* algebraic terms
three-figure bearing 187–189, *193*
time 207
timetables 155–156
tonne 207
transversal 46
trapezium 32
travel graphs 113–114, *117*
triangle 47–48, 50, 147–153, *153*, 209; *see also* intermediate sides, right-angled triangle, right-triangular prism, solving triangles
triangle numbers 17

unit 70; *see also* area, capacity, length, mass, SI units, volume
unitary method 69–70, *75*
unknown 98, *105*

Value Added Tax 79–80, *84*
VAT *see* Value Added Tax
vertical 165, *171*
vertical axis 17
volume 208; cone 196–197; cylinder 162–163, *164*; prism 162–163, *164*
word problems 99, 102, 104, *105*, 183
x-axis 91, *97*
x-coordinate 92, *97*

y-axis 91, *97*
y-coordinate 92, *97*